THE PREDECESSORS OF SHAKESPEARE

Advisory Editor: Alfred Harbage

The Predecessors of Shakespeare

A Survey and Bibliography of Recent Studies in English
Renaissance Drama

Edited by

Terence P. Logan and Denzell S. Smith

UNIVERSITY OF NEBRASKA PRESS · LINCOLN

Publishers on the Plains

CONTENTS

Preface	vii
List of Abbreviations	xi
CHRISTOPHER MARLOWE Robert Kimbrough	3
ROBERT GREENE William Nestrick	56
THOMAS KYD Dickie A. Spurgeon	93
THOMAS NASHE Robert J. Fehrenbach	107
JOHN LYLY Joseph W. Houppert	125
GEORGE PEELE Charles W. Daves	143
THOMAS LODGE Joseph W. Houppert	153
ANONYMOUS PLAYS Anne Lancashire and Jill Levenson	161
The Rare Triumphs of Love and Fortune	161
The Famous Victories of Henry V	165
I & II The Troublesome Reign of King John	176
The Wars of Cyrus	189
The Taming of a Shrew	194
Edward III	206
Fair Em	215
King Leir	219
Mucedorus	226
Soliman and Perseda	230
Arden of Feversham	240
The Life and Death of Jack Straw	252
Locrine	258
The True Tragedy of Richard III	272
A Knack to Know a Knave	280
I Richard II, or Thomas of Woodstock	288
I Selimus	301
The Tragical History of Guy Earl of Warwick	310
OTHER DRAMATISTS Terence P. Logan and Denzell S. Smith	312
List of Contributors	323
Index	325

PREFACE

This volume is part of a larger project, Recent Studies in English Renaissance Drama, which in additional volumes will survey scholarship and criticism exclusive of Shakespeare. The publication dates of E. K. Chambers's *The Elizabethan Stage,* 4 vols. (1923), and of the initial volumes of G. E. Bentley's *The Jacobean and Caroline Stage,* 7 vols. (1941-68), indicated the appropriate starting points. The analytical and descriptive account of scholarship found in the surveys of other periods and genres has here been combined with a reasonably complete enumerative bibliography. The sources for this series are the author entries in thirteen bibliographies and lists: *Essay and General Literature Index, International Index* (since 1965, *Social Sciences and Humanities Index*), *Journal of English and Germanic Philology, MLA International Bibliography, Modern Humanities Research Association Annual Bibliography of English Language and Literature, Readers' Guide to Periodical Literature, Research Opportunities in Renaissance Drama, Shakespeare Quarterly, Shakespeare Survey, Studies in Bibliography, Studies in Philology, Yearbook of Comparative and General Literature,* and *The Year's Work in English Studies.* These entries were supplemented by selected general studies of Elizabethan drama drawn from the bibliographies and analyzed according to the playwrights discussed, and by the additional research of individual contributors. Though the sources checked for this volume date from 1923 through 1968, contributors were encouraged to include especially significant material published both before and after these limits. Entries were restricted to published material, except for the anonymous plays where edition theses are included.

Each essay begins with a general section, including, when relevant, biographical material, general studies of the plays, and general studies of the works at large. The second section treats criticism of individual plays, arranged according to the approximate critical importance of the play, and concludes with a brief statement of the current state of criticism. The third section is on canon (including apocrypha), dates, and the state of the standard and other editions of the plays and nondramatic works. The arrangement of this section is generally chronological and follows the preferred dates given in the *Annals of English Drama*, by Alfred Harbage, revised by Samuel Schoenbaum (1964), and the *Supplements to the Revised Edition* (1966, 1970). At the discretion of the individual contributors items were discussed either in the commentary or listed in the appropriate See Also section. These general guidelines were adapted to suit the specific material published on a given author. The material on the anonymous plays was organized independently to conform to the significantly different nature of studies in this area; the sequence of titles in this section follows the chronology of the *Annals*. Finally, a simple annotated bibliography format, arranged according to the chronology of the criticism, was used for minor named dramatists, who have been included only when there is some recent scholarship on their plays; dramatic criticism only is listed. A logic of primary subject interest was followed in determining the position of material which covers two or more topics. In selected cases cross-references are made in subsequent sections; however, it is assumed that later sections, especially those on individual plays, will be used in conjunction with the earlier discussions of more inclusive general studies. When a book is part of a series, the series title is noted only when it is necessary as a finding tool or when it indicates the nature of the work.

Many obligations have been incurred in preparing this volume. The contributors and editors have made heavy demands on the library staffs and general resources of their home institutions. Reference and research librarians in over a dozen university libraries have contributed to the task of assembling and verifying what, at times, seemed to be an unending quantity of material. This assistance is gratefully acknowledged. Special library assistance was given by the staffs of the Folger Shakespeare Library, Widener Library of Harvard University, and the Library of Congress. Individual essays were read and criticized by several specialists; we are especially grateful to Arthur Freeman, Anne Lancashire, and Merritt E. Lawlis for providing independent readings of essays in this volume. For more general advice, including assistance in planning the format and encouragement at various stages, we are grateful to Charles Forker, William L. Godshalk, Robert Hapgood, Anne Lancashire, and Martin Wine. Professors Alfred Harbage and Samuel Schoenbaum gave permission to use information from the revised *Annals of English Drama* and to use the *Annals* as a principle of organization. Permission to use the Master List and Table of Abbreviations of the *MLA International Bibliography* was granted by the

Bibliographer of the Association, Harrison T. Meserole. Our list of journal and series abbreviations conforms to the MLA list except that we include several older titles not in the current MLA tables.

Professor Alfred Harbage has been generous of his time and special knowledge from the outset. This volume and the entire project has greatly profited from his advice, learning, and insights into both scholarship and humanity.

Terence P. Logan
Denzell S. Smith

LIST OF ABBREVIATIONS

AION-SG	*Annali Istituto Universitario Orientale, Napoli, Sezione Germanica*
AN&Q	*American Notes and Queries*
Archiv	*Archiv für das Studium der Neueren Sprachen und Literaturen*
ASNSP	*Annali della Scuola Normale Superiore de Pisa*
AUMLA	*Journal of the Australasian Universities Language and Literature Association*
AUR	*Aberdeen University Review*
BBr	*Books at Brown*
BFLS	*Bulletin de la Faculté des Lettres de Strasbourg*
BHR	*Bibliothéque d'Humanisme et Renaissance*
BJRL	*Bulletin of the John Rylands Library*
BLM	*Bonniers Litterära Magasin*
BNYPL	*Bulletin of the New York Public Library*
Boek	*Het Boek*
BRMMLA	*Bulletin of the Rocky Mountain Modern Language Association*
BUSE	*Boston University Studies in English*
CE	*College English*
CJ	*Classical Journal*
CL	*Comparative Literature*
CLAJ	*College Language Association Journal*
ClareQ	*Claremont Quarterly*
ColQ	*Colorado Quarterly*
CompD	*Comparative Drama*
CritQ	*Critical Quarterly*
CS	*Cahiers du Sud*
DA	*Dissertation Abstracts*
Drama	*Drama: The Quarterly Theatre Review*
DramS	*Drama Survey*
DUJ	*Durham University Journal*
EA	*Etudes Anglaises*
EDH	Essays by Divers Hands
EJ	*English Journal*

ELH	*Journal of English Literary History*
ELN	*English Language Notes*
EM	*English Miscellany*
E&S	*Essays and Studies by Members of the English Association*
ES	*English Studies*
ESA	*English Studies in Africa*
ESQ	*Emerson Society Quarterly*
ESRS	*Emporia State Research Studies*
ETJ	*Educational Theatre Journal*
Expl	*Explicator*
FK	*Filológiai Közlöny*
FurmS	*Furman Studies*
HAB	*Humanities Association Bulletin*
Hispano	*Hispanófila*
HLQ	*Huntington Library Quarterly*
HTR	*Harvard Theological Review*
IER	*Irish Ecclesiastical Record*
JEGP	*Journal of English and Germanic Philology*
JHI	*Journal of the History of Ideas*
JQ	*Journalism Quarterly*
JWCI	*Journal of the Warburg and Courtauld Institute*
KR	*Kenyon Review*
L&P	*Literature and Psychology*
LCrit	*Literary Criterion*
LHR	*Lock Haven Review*
Library	*The Library*
McNR	*McNeese Review*
MLN	*Modern Language Notes*
MLQ	*Modern Language Quarterly*
MLR	*Modern Language Review*
Month	*The Month*
MP	*Modern Philology*
MSpr	*Moderna Språk*
MuK	*Maske und Kothurn*
N&Q	*Notes and Queries*
Neophil	*Neophilologus*
NM	*Neuphilologische Mitteilungen*
NS	*Die Neueren Sprachen*
NSE	Norwegian Studies in English
NTg	*De Nieuwe Taalgids*

PBA	Proceedings of the British Academy
PBSA	Papers of the Bibliographical Society of America
PLPLS-LHS	Proceedings of the Leeds Philosophic and Literary Society, Literary and Historical Section
PMLA	Publications of the Modern Language Association of America
PP	Philologica Pragensia
PQ	Philological Quarterly
PTRSC	Proceedings and Transactions of the Royal Society of Canada
QQ	Queen's Quarterly
QR	Quarterly Review
QRL	Quarterly Review of Literature
RAA	Revue Anglo-Américaine
RBPH	Revue Belge de Philologie et d'Histoire
REL	Review of English Literature
RenD	Renaissance Drama
RenP	Renaissance Papers
RES	Review of English Studies
RIP	Rice Institute Pamphlets
RLC	Revue de Littérature Comparée
RLMC	Rivista di Letterature Moderne e Comparate
RLV	Revue des Langues Vivantes
RMS	Renaissance and Modern Studies
RN	Renaissance News
RORD	Research Opportunities in Renaissance Drama
RRDS	Regents Renaissance Drama Series
RS	Research Studies
SAB	South Atlantic Bulletin
SAQ	South Atlantic Quarterly
SB	Studies in Bibliography: Papers of the Bibliographical Society of the University of Virginia
ScS	Scottish Studies
SEL	Studies in English Literature, 1500-1900
SELit	Studies in English Literature (English Literary Society of Japan)
SFQ	Southern Folklore Quarterly
ShAB	Shakespeare Association Bulletin
ShakS	Shakespeare Studies
ShN	Shakespeare Newsletter

ShS	*Shakespeare Survey*
SJ	*Shakespeare-Jahrbuch*
SJH	*Shakespeare-Jahrbuch* (Heidelberg)
SJW	*Shakespeare-Jahrbuch* (Weimar)
SOF	*Sudöst-Forschungen*
SP	*Studies in Philology*
SQ	*Shakespeare Quarterly*
SR	*Sewanee Review*
SRen	*Studies in the Renaissance*
SSF	*Studies in Short Fiction*
SuAS	Stratford-upon-Avon Studies, ed. John Russell Brown and Bernard Harris
SzEP	Studien zur Englischen Philologie
TDR	*Tulane Drama Review* (since 1968, *The Drama Review*)
TEAS	Twayne's English Author Series
TFSB	*Tennessee Folklore Society Bulletin*
TLS	[London] *Times Literary Supplement*
TSE	*Tulane Studies in English*
TSL	*Tennessee Studies in Literature*
TSLL	*Texas Studies in Literature and Language*
UDR	*University of Dayton Review*
UFMH	University of Florida Monographs, Humanities Series
UMSE	*University of Mississippi Studies in English*
UTQ	*University of Toronto Quarterly*
VUSH	Vanderbilt University Studies in the Humanities
WF	*Western Folklore*
WSt	*Word Study*
WTW	Writers and Their Work
YWES	*Year's Work in English Studies*
ZAA	*Zeitschrift für Anglistik und Amerikanistik*

THE PREDECESSORS OF SHAKESPEARE

CHRISTOPHER MARLOWE

Robert Kimbrough

The standard editions are the one-volume, old-spelling *The Works of Christopher Marlowe* (1910), ed. C. F. Tucker Brooke, and the six-volume, modernized-spelling *The Works and Life of Christopher Marlowe* (1930–33), gen. ed. R. H. Case. There is a concordance by Charles Crawford: *The Marlowe Concordance*, in *Materialien zur Kunde des älteren englischen Dramas*, Series I, vol. 34 (1911); Series II, vols. 2 (1928), 3 (1929), 6 (1931), 7 (1932).

I. GENERAL

A. BIOGRAPHICAL

The best life of Marlowe is that by C. F. Tucker Brooke, which appeared, along with his edition of *Dido, Queen of Carthage,* in the R. H. Case edition of the works of Marlowe. Writing in 1930, Brooke had the advantage of being able to incorporate the discovery by J. Leslie Hotson of the coroner's report of the death of Marlowe, which Hotson presented in *The Death of Christopher Marlowe* (1925). Because of the exciting nature of Hotson's discovery, and because of the vagueness of "coroner's quest law" itself, much speculation has been stimulated by the controversial details surrounding the death of Marlowe; see, for example, Samuel A. Tannenbaum, *The Assassination of Christopher Marlowe: A New View* (1928). But Brooke presented the facts only as Hotson had gathered them, and included the relevant documents among the eighteen appendices to his biography. (An earlier important work by Brooke, because it collects all allusions to Marlowe, is "The Reputation of Christopher Marlowe," *Transactions of the Connecticut Academy of Arts and Sciences* 25 [1922] : 347-408.)

Further important discoveries were made by Mark Eccles in the early thirties and reported in his *Christopher Marlowe in London* (1934). Eccles made the already provocative portrait of Marlowe more so by adding accounts of two separate altercations with the authorities in and around the city of London.

The encyclopedic account of Marlowe's life, as well as of his works, is in two volumes by John Bakeless, *The Tragicall History of Christopher Marlowe* (1942, an outgrowth of his earlier *Christopher Marlow: The Man in His Time* [1937]). Bakeless fully recapitulates the work of Brooke, Hotson, and Eccles, and contributes a fuller account of Marlowe's Cambridge years than was previously available. Although Bakeless speculates rather freely, his observations are sufficiently conservative not to obscure his vast accumulation of sound facts and opinions.

Paul H. Kocher, *Christopher Marlowe: A Study of His Thought, Learning, and Character* (1946), after studying all the available facts and documents, including the plays and poems, concludes that Marlowe was a revolutionary atheist. His main piece of evidence is the so-called "Baines document," a report of the alleged remarks of Marlowe concerning established religion and other institutions. Although Kocher believes that this is the hearsay "atheist lecture" which Marlowe allegedly read to Sir Walter Raleigh and some of his friends, the actual revelation of Kocher's study is how harmless, old-hat, and jejune are these gibes at aspects of the Elizabethan establishment.

A more "objective" study of Marlowe's thought was presented earlier in the first part of *Marlowe's "Tamburlaine": A Study in Renaissance Moral Philosophy,* by Roy W. Battenhouse (1941). Although Battenhouse is interested primarily in the *Tamburlaine* plays, his approach to them is through what he feels to be the traditional nature of Marlowe's thought. A more sophisticated reinvestigation of the background of Marlowe's thought than either of these studies appears in the introductory chapters, and reappears as a recurring theme, in Douglas Cole's *Suffering and Evil in the Plays of Christopher Marlowe* (1962). While Cole's central concern is with the thematic objectivity of Marlowe's plays (see below, I,B and II,B), his presentation of the traditional learning which he feels shaped Marlowe's art is itself valuable. Other important studies concerning the background of Marlowe's learning are: Ethel Seaton, "Marlowe's Light Reading," in *Elizabethan and Jacobean Studies Presented to Frank Percy Wilson in Honour of His Seventieth Birthday,* ed. Herbert Davis and Helen Gardner (1959), pp. 17–35; Mario Praz, "Machiavelli and the Elizabethans," *PBA* 14 (1928): 49-97; W. M. Merchant, "Marlowe and Machiavelli," *Comparative Literature Studies* 13 (1944): 1-7.

The overlapping of biography and criticism in studies of Marlowe is aptly indicated by the title of Harry Levin's *The Overreacher* (1952), which points both to a biographical characteristic and an artistic theme. Levin's book will be discussed later; however, his conclusion that Marlowe was a frustrated visionary should be indicated here, along with the roughly similar conclusions of J. B. Steane, *Christopher Marlowe: A Critical Study* (1964), and Una Ellis-Fermor, *Christopher Marlowe* (1927). Less significant works which attempt to balance biography and criticism are: Frederick S. Boas, *Christopher Marlowe: A Biographical and Critical Study* (1940), which is a later version of *Marlowe and His Circle* (1931); Philip Henderson, *And Morning in His Eyes: A Book about Christopher Marlowe* (1937) (Henderson has also written *Christopher Marlowe*, Men and Books Series [1952], and *Christopher Marlowe*, WTW [1956; rev. ed. 1962]); Charles Norman, *The Muses' Darling: The Life of Christopher Marlowe* (1946); Michel Poirier, *Christopher Marlowe* (1951); and Robert E. Knoll, *Christopher Marlowe*, TEAS (1969).

Three other works ought to be mentioned. First, A. L. Rowse, *Christopher Marlowe: A Biography* (1964). The critical controversy which Rowse's biography set off, while not so great as that which followed his study of Shakespeare in 1963, demonstrated the severe limitations of reading works of literature as historical documents. More controversial because of its sensational thesis was Calvin Hoffman's *The Murder of the Man Who Was Shakespeare* (1955). Hoffman asserted that Marlowe did not die on 30 May 1593, but lived on in overseas secrecy to write the plays which we have come to know as Shakespeare's. The inadequacies of this book are demonstrated in Alfred Harbage's review in the *New York Times Book Review*, 12 June 1955, pp. 1, 10-11. Other works which discuss the question of Marlovian authorship of Shakespeare are H. N. Gibson, *The Shakespeare Claimants: A Critical Survey of the Four Principal Theories Concerning the Authorship of the Shakespearean Plays* (1962); George McMichael and Edgar M. Glenn, eds., *Shakespeare and His Rivals: A Casebook on the Authorship Controversy* (1962); R. C. Churchill, *Shakespeare and His Betters: A History and a Criticism of the Attempts which Have Been Made to Prove that Shakespeare's Works Were Written by Others* (1958); and William and Elizabeth Friedman, *The Shakespearean Ciphers Examined: An Analysis of Cryptographic Systems*

Used as Evidence that Some Other Than William Shakespeare Wrote the Plays Commonly Attributed to Him (1957). Finally, although it does not add essentially to what we know about Marlowe, and although its thesis is simply that Marlowe was, after all, just another Elizabethan, still of value is A. D. Wraight and Virginia F. Stern, *In Search of Christopher Marlowe: A Pictorial Biography* (1965), which is encyclopedic and contains valuable illustrations.

Here are the essential, established facts of the life of Christopher Marlowe in summary:

The son of a shoemaker, Marlowe was baptized in Canterbury 26 February 1564. In 1579 he entered the King's School at the cathedral at Canterbury. There is evidence that he was at Cambridge in December 1580 (see Bakeless), and on 17 March 1581 he registered in Christ College as a pensioner. Marlowe took his B.A. at the end of the Lent term 1584 and completed work for an M.A. at the end of Lent term 1587. The records of the Privy Council for 29 July 1587 show that a letter was written to University officers urging that Marlowe be given his degree at the end of the Vacation semester at the request of the Queen and it was granted at the July commencement.

From Eccles we know that in 1589 and in 1592 Marlowe was living in the theater area, Shoreditch, and that Kyd claimed that for some time up to 1591 they shared a room in that section. On 12 May 1593 Kyd was arrested and three pages of "vile heretical concepts" were found among his papers. The papers themselves are unimportant, being part of a manuscript copy of a book printed forty years earlier containing Arian theology, but Kyd claimed they belonged to Marlowe who had left them behind. The charge was stated after Marlowe's death in two letters to the Lord Keeper of the Seal, Sir John Puckering, so we do not know whether a claim by Kyd led to the issue by the Privy Council of a warrant for Marlowe's arrest on 18 May 1593. The warrant directed the arresting officer "to repair to the house of Master Thomas Walsingham in Kent, or any other place where he shall understand Christopher Marlow to be remaining," and on 20 May Marlowe presented himself for "daily attendance on their lordships" until he was actually to be called before them. Free, and checking in daily, Marlowe had lunch at Madame Bull's tavern at Deptford on 30 May 1593 with Ingram Frizar, Robert Poley, and Nicholas Scheres, all of whom were connected with Sir Francis Walsingham in her majesty's secret service. During an argument over the bill Marlowe was killed by Frizar.

B. GENERAL STUDIES OF THE PLAYS

Most of the books mentioned above also contain general studies of the plays; for the most part, they will not be reintroduced here. This section is divided into three parts: book-length studies; articles, essays, and introductions; and studies of the relationship of Marlowe and Shakespeare.

Book-Length Studies

Of all the books on Marlowe, only seven seem indispensable to a sound study of the playwright: Harry Levin, *The Overreacher: A Study of Christopher Marlowe* (1952); Una Ellis-Fermor, *Christopher Marlowe* (1927); John Bakeless, *The Tragicall History of Christopher Marlowe*, 2 vols. (1942); Paul H. Kocher, *Christopher Marlowe: A Study of His Thought, Learning, and Character* (1946); Douglas Cole, *Suffering and Evil in the Plays of Christopher Marlowe* (1962); David Bevington, *From "Mankind" to Marlowe: Growth of Structure in the Popular Drama of Tudor England* (1962); and J. B. Steane, *Marlowe: A Critical Study* (1964). The central thesis of each of these books will be discussed here, and they also will be referred to in the discussion of individual plays, Section II,A, below.

In *The Overreacher*, Harry Levin characterizes Marlowe as possessing an Icarian conflict and points out that an Icarian view is necessarily a tragic view. Marlowe realizes that "every man is limited by conditions, as if—like Faustus—he had signed a contract; but his recognition of those realities which frame his life is, in its way, a victory over them; and the incongruity between them and his ideals of perfection is the wisdom of Mephistophilis—irony."

Earlier critical stimulus was provided by Ellis-Fermor's *Christopher Marlowe*, which supplies fine critical insights and adheres to a rigid autobiographical point of view within the study of the plays. Even though Ellis-Fermor agrees that drama is for the most part an objective genre, she feels that the essential Marlowe, a frustrated idealist and revolutionary iconoclast, appears in all of his works.

Bakeless exhaustively recapitulates all the possible biographical influences and primary sources which might in any degree lie behind the shaping of Marlowe's various works. Kocher made a pioneering effort to isolate Marlowe's essential ideas and feelings and to delineate central themes. Douglas Cole takes a wider, albeit similar approach, attempting to eschew biography entirely by pointing out the orthodox and narrowly theological orientation of Marlowe's education, and demonstrating how this pedagogical influence permeates all of the plays. But Cole does allow a biographical bias to influence his readings of the plays, feeling that Marlowe was dominated by particularly strong desires to exploit human suffering and to be overwhelmed by a fascination for evil.

In contrast to Cole's thematic approach, Bevington's is structural. The popular drama of the sixteenth century was written for traveling troupes of actors often numbering no more than "four men and a boy," who were limited in personnel, staging facilities, and finances. Yet these players inherited a view of dramatic art which had a predilection for inclusiveness of characterization, elaborate mechanical and visual contrivance, and sumptuous production; thus their problem was how to achieve a maximum of scope with a minimum of means. Analysis of the plays used by the players reveals that dramatists constructed plays to achieve such effects through the technique of doubling roles for actors. The structural and thematic effects of doubling are suppression of one character so another can appear; a linear and episodic plot organized by theme and variation into a progressive sequence that justifies the suppression of a character for a new one; symmetry of form; the constant use of soliloquy for costume change and commentary on the action; and compression of characterization. Bevington shows that doubling continued in the London public theaters, and that plays written for it, including Marlowe's, retain these structural and thematic effects.

Although J. B. Steane announces at the outset of his book that he is one of the growing number who feel that Marlowe studies should move away from concern with the man and his thought in order to focus more directly on the work, his predilections with regard to the man, his thought, and the nature of Renaissance art result in yet another spiritual biography of a disturbed young man who was not really, in the full sense, a dramatist—a practitioner within a craft. Steane treats drama as if it were but another form of poetry, not poetry in the Renaissance sense of an objective discipline to be mastered through the exercise of rhetorical imitation, but poetry as written by the Romantics. As a result, he believes that Marlowe's plays (taken in Steane's sense of their sequence) merely reveal a mind which is narrowing in on itself in total disillusion with the world.

Studies in other languages are: Nicola D'Agostino, *Christopher Marlowe* (1950, an outgrowth of his essay, "Ideologia del Marlowe." *RLMC* 2 [1947] : 249-66), which, like Levin's book, is one of the first in the last two decades to see a close relationship between the spirit of Marlowe and the spirit of present anguished generations; and Dennis Marlon, *Christopher Marlowe, dramaturge* (1955).

Articles, Essays, and Introductions

Several paperback books collect essays on Marlowe: Ralph J. Kaufmann, ed., *Elizabethan Drama: Modern Essays in Criticism* (1961); Max Bluestone and Norman Rabkin, eds., *Modern Studies in English Renaissance Drama: Shakespeare's Contemporaries* (1961; 2nd ed. 1970); Irving Ribner, guest ed., *Tulane Drama Review,* vol. 8, no. 4 (1964); and Clifford Leech, ed., *Marlowe: A Collection of Critical Essays* (1964). Because each of the essays collected in the various volumes is important in itself, each appears elsewhere in this survey, with its original source and its reprinted availability mentioned.

Kaufmann reprints M. M. Mahood's "Marlowe's Heroes" from her *Poetry and Humanism* (1950). Miss Mahood feels that Marlowe captures the essence of Renaissance humanism in the two parts of *Tamburlaine, Faustus,* the *Jew,* and *Edward II,* in each of which the tragic hero embodies some aspect of the spiritual adventures of Marlowe's generation. Her thesis is that Marlowe was sufficiently removed from his age to be able to see some of the potential impoverishment in a humanist emphasis, and that this is reflected in his plays as his heroes shrink in stature from the titanic to the puny. Her analysis of the ironies in the presentation of Faustus is particularly valuable. This part of Miss Mahood's chapter is also reprinted by Bluestone and Rabkin (1st ed.) under the title "Tragedy of Renaissance Humanism."

Some of the thirteen articles in the Marlowe issue of *TDR* are discussed elsewhere; of special relevance here are those by Harry Morris, John Russell Brown, and Jocelyn Powell. Morris, in "Marlowe's Poetry," treats Marlowe's achievement as a poet, tracing the development of poetic technique through the plays, but characterizing the unique poetic style of each. John Russell Brown, in "Marlowe and the Actors," focuses on three aspects of Marlowe's drama—rhetorical structure, visual elements, and the fact that the hero is always viewed ironically—in order to determine the overall style within which a play should be acted. And Jocelyn Powell, in "Marlowe's Spectacle," discusses Marlowe's plays as an attempt to "fuse the timeless soul-searching of the morality with the relentless progress of the chronicle"; in short, to fuse fable and narrative. The fable is largely created by traditional dramatic emblems, by sophisticated visual imagery, and by speeches which do not further the action or deepen our understanding of the speaker's psychology, but rather focus attention upon the moral significance of the actions.

Clifford Leech begins his collection with an essay by T. S. Eliot from *Elizabethan Essays* (1934) on the impact of Marlowe's style on his age, and with Harry Levin's final chapter from *The Overreacher*, "The Dead Shepherd," in which Levin brings together conclusions on Marlowe and his place in literary history. Leech concludes his volume with his own essay "Marlowe's Humor," reprinted from *Essays on Shakespeare and Elizabethan Drama in Honor of Hardin Craig*, ed. Richard Hosley (1962). Although seemingly narrow in scope, Leech's essay effectively attacks the widely held assumption that Marlowe had no sense of humor, and points out the broad range of that humor, from the savage to the gentle. (An essay which anticipated Leech is that by William Peery, "Marlowe's Irreverent Humor: Some Open Questions," *TSE* 6 [1956] : 15–29.)

The introductions to the four collections mentioned above are valuable, as are those by Irving Ribner, *The Complete Plays of Christopher Marlowe* (1963), and Leo Kirschbaum, *The Plays of Christopher Marlowe* (1962). Ribner's introduction is an expansion of his essay "Marlowe's 'Tragicke Glasse,' " in *Essays on Shakespeare and Elizabethan Drama*, ed. Hosley (1962).

Finally, Marlowe's anniversary year, 1964, saw many general reassessments, three of which are especially noteworthy: Rudolf Böhm, "Die Marlowe—Forschung der letzten beiden Jahrzehnte," *Anglia* 73 (1965): 324–43, 454–70; Hermann Peschmann, "Christopher Marlowe, 1564–1593: 'Infinite Riches in a Little Room,' " *English* 15 (1964): 85–89; and Eugene M. Waith, "Marlowe and the Jades of Asia," *SEL* 5 (1965): 229–45 (rpt. in the 2nd ed. of Bluestone and Rabkin).

Studies of the Relationship of Marlowe and Shakespeare

The traditionally held view that Shakespeare was a follower of Marlowe theatrically and aesthetically is challenged by F. P. Wilson in *Marlowe and the Early Shakespeare* (1953). Wilson argues that Marlowe was indebted to Shakespeare for innovations in Elizabethan drama. A variation on the older point of view is expressed by Nicholas Brooke in "Marlowe as Provocative Agent in Shakespeare's Early Plays," *ShS* 14 (1961): 34–44; Shakespeare, in trying to imitate Marlowe, was stimulated to overtake him, since he could not assimilate the Marlovian vein. But Hereward T. Price, "Shakespeare and His Young Contemporaries," *PQ* 41 (1962): 37–57, asserts that Marlowe and the rest merely wrote plays, while Shakespeare independently created drama. In "Marlowe and Shakespeare," *SQ* 15 (1964): 41–53, Irving Ribner concludes: "Though Shakespeare learned something from Marlowe, the debt is not as fundamental as sometimes claimed." (*SQ* 15 is printed in book form as *Shakespeare 400*, ed. James G. McManaway [1964].) Stanley Wells, "Shakespeare's Life, Times, and Stage," *ShS* 19 (1966): 143–54, points out that the dramatists' differences are greater than their resemblances. In a more imaginative study than these, Hendrick Röhrman, *Marlowe and Shakespeare: A Thematic Exposition of Some of Their Plays* (1952), finds the source of much modern fragmentation in Renaissance searches for power and self-assertion.

C. STUDIES OF THE POETRY

Because of Marlowe's blank-verse "mighty line," and especially because of the impact on the stage of the hyperbole of *Tamburlaine,* almost every general study of the plays discusses Marlowe's poetic achievements. A pioneering work in this area is C. F. Tucker Brooke, "Marlowe's Versification and Style," *SP* 19 (1922): 186–205. And see T. S. Eliot, "Christopher Marlowe," in his *Elizabethan Essays* (1934); Howard Baker, *Induction to Tragedy: A Study in a Development of Form in "Gorboduc," "The Spanish Tragedy," and "Titus Andronicus"* (1939); Harry Morris, "Marlowe's Poetry" (above, I,B); and more recently, Robert Speaight, "Marlowe: The Forerunner," *REL* 7 (1966): 25–41, which concludes that Marlowe was a master of narrative verse, not dramatic, and was the forerunner of Milton and Pope, not Shakespeare.

General studies of the poems as poetry are too few in number. The encyclopedic account of Marlowe's poetry is by L. C. Martin in his introduction to the *Poems* in the R. H. Case edition (1932). Full critical discussions of the poems are given by Levin and Steane in the works already discussed. Brief mention of Marlowe the poet is made by J. B. Broadbent, *Poetic Love* (1964), pp. 64–65.

The poem on which most concern has focused is, of course, *Hero and Leander.* The seminal study is that by Douglas Bush, *Mythology and the Renaissance Tradition in English Poetry* (1932; rev. ed. 1963). Bush was the first to call *Hero and Leander* an epyllion, a term also used by Hallett Smith in his discussion of the poem in *Elizabethan Poetry*

(1952). Paul W. Miller, "The Elizabethan Minor Epic," *SP* 55 (1958): 31–38, picks up the term and attempts to define a specific Renaissance genre called the epyllion; however, Walter Allen, Jr., "The Non-Existent Classical Epyllion," *SP* 55 (1958): 515–18, questions Miller and rejects the category.

The most rewarding approach to the poem is through the Ovidian influence. Bush investigates the sources and concludes that "all the best qualities of the Italianate Ovidian tradition are embodied and transcended" in the poem. Russell A. Fraser, "The Art of *Hero and Leander*," *JEGP* 57 (1958): 743–54, and Paul M. Cubeta, "Marlowe's Poet in *Hero and Leander*," *CE* 26 (1965): 500–505, stress the Ovidian aspects; they ignore Marlowe the man and concentrate on Marlowe the poet, showing him to be a careful craftsman: delightfully objective, urbane, and capable of satire and parody. Both applaud the humor of the poem. More restricted articles which pick up the Ovidian tradition are by Frederick Candelaria, "Ovid and the Indifferent Lovers," *RN* 13 (1960): 294–97, which discusses the influence of *Amores,* II.iv, and Eugene B. Cantelupe, "*Hero and Leander,* Marlowe's Tragi-Comedy of Love," *CE* 24 (1963): 295–98. Other important works are the introduction by J. B. Fort in his translation and edition, "*Héro et Léandre*" . . . *étude critique* (1950); and Jay L. Halio, "Perfection and Elizabethan Ideas of Conception," *ELN* 1 (1964): 179–82.

The fullest discussion of Chapman's continuation of Marlowe's poem is by Bush. C. S. Lewis, "*Hero and Leander,*" *PBA* 38 (1952): 23–38 (rpt. in Paul J. Alpers, ed., *Elizabethan Poetry: Modern Essays in Criticism* [1967]), feels the two parts can best be understood in conjunction, with Marlowe's part thought of as a song of innocence, and Chapman's as a song of experience. However, Veselin Kostič, "Marlowe's *Hero and Leander* and Chapman's Continuation," in *Renaissance and Modern Essays Presented to Vivian de Sola Pinto in Celebration of His Seventieth Birthday,* ed. G. R. Hibbard, with G. A. Panichas and Allan Rodway (1966), pp. 25–34, argues that the collaboration was *not* a fortunate accident because Chapman's intentions completely contradicted Marlowe's. An approach similar to Lewis's is used by Mike Long, "An Elizabethan 'Structure of Feeling,' " *Cambridge Review* 89 (1966): 58–61. While Kostič feels that Marlowe's superhuman, universal orientation is completely contradictory to Chapman's earthly orientation, Long suggests that Marlowe is this-worldly, and Chapman is sacramental and transcendental. But he sees no essential contradiction between these worlds of Marlowe and Chapman; rather they are complementary.

Venus and Adonis is also best understood within the Ovidian tradition, and many comparisons have been made between Marlowe's poem and Shakespeare's. Only one need be singled out: Clifford Leech, "Venus and Her Nun: Portraits of Women in Love by Shakespeare and Marlowe," *SEL* 5 (1965): 248–68.

Although Steane (I,B) discusses Marlowe's *Elegies* at some length, there is only one scholarly and critical study of Marlowe's Ovid: Eric Jacobsen, *Translation: A Traditional Craft. An Introductory Sketch with a Study of Marlowe's "Elegies"* (1958). Marlowe's translation from the first book of Lucan's *Pharsalia* deserves more critical attention; only two short notes stand out: L. C. Martin, "Lucan-Marlowe-?Chapman," *RES* 24 (1948): 317–21, and William Blisset, "Caesar and Satan," *JHI* 18 (1957): 221–32. Marlowe's "The Passionate Shepherd," if it is his, is usually printed in conjunction with Raleigh's reply. Two recent articles provide discussions: S. K. Heninger, Jr., "The Passionate Shepherd and the Philosophical Nymph," *RenP*, 1962, pp. 63–70; and Louis H. Leiter, "Deification through Love: Marlowe's 'Passionate Shepherd to his Love,' " *CE* 27 (1966): 444–49. While Heninger believes that Marlowe's use of the traditions of the pastoral is muted in order to protect his shepherd, Leiter feels that the mythology is highly emotionalized, vivified, and almost deified. An essay which studies two early editions of the poem is by Curt F. Bühler, "Four Elizabethan Poems," in *John Quincy Adams Memorial Studies,* ed. James G. McManaway, Giles E. Dawson, and Edwin E. Willoughby (1948), pp. 695–706. Musical aspects of the poem are treated by Frederick W. Sternfeld, " 'Come Live with Me and Be My Love,' " in *The Hidden Harmony: Essays in Honor of Philip Wheelwright* (1966), pp. 173–92.

For bibliographical information see: E. K. Chambers, *The Elizabethan Stage,* 4 vols. (1923); Samuel A. Tannenbaum, *Christopher Marlowe: A Concise Bibliography* (1937; *Supplement,* 1947), both reprinted in *Elizabethan Bibliographies,* vol. 5 (1967); Irving Ribner, *Tudor and Stuart Drama,* Goldentree Bibliographies (1966); and Robert C. Johnson, *Elizabethan Bibliographies Supplements VI, Christopher Marlowe: 1946–1965* (1967).

II. CRITICISM OF INDIVIDUAL PLAYS AND STATE OF SCHOLARSHIP

A. INDIVIDUAL PLAYS

Doctor Faustus

No Elizabethan play outside the Shakespeare canon has raised more controversy than *Doctor Faustus*. There is no agreement concerning the nature of the text and the date of composition (see below, III,A); and the centrality of the Faust legend in the history of the western world precludes any definitive agreement on the interpretation of the play, the doctor being the product of revolution, both of the Renaissance and the Reformation. A typical point of view is that of Una Ellis-Fermor in *Christopher Marlowe* (1927), and in *The Frontiers of Drama* (1945, partly rpt. by Leech), who says that Marlowe celebrates in the play a world which is strictly satanic and evil. This is also essentially Levin's position, but Leo Kirschbaum, in *"Faustus:* A Reconsideration," *RES* 19 (1943): 225–41, believes that the logic of the play, stated simplistically, is that if you are good you go to heaven, and if you are bad you go to hell, and that Faustus was bad.

Elaborating upon Kirschbaum, Nicolas Brooke, "The Moral Tragedy of Doctor Faustus," *Cambridge Journal* 5 (1952): 662–87, feels that Marlowe has simply taken his source, the Faust book, and treated it in the morality tradition. Clifford Davidson, "Doctor Faustus of Wittenberg," *SP* 59 (1962): 514–23, believes that Marlowe has taken a generally orthodox Protestant position and treated the idea of salvation from a negative point of view; while Joseph Westlund, "The Orthodox Christian Framework of Marlowe's *Faustus,*" *SEL* 3 (1963): 191–205, believes that this theme received positive illustration through Faustus' fate. Ariel Sachs, "The Religious Despair of Doctor Faustus," *JEGP* 63 (1964): 625–47, goes so far as to contend that the play is written in absolute accord with a rigorous Calvinist doctrine of predestination.

Two other critics put Marlowe in the camp of orthodoxy: George I. Duthie, "Some Observations on Marlowe's *Doctor Faustus,*" *Archiv* 203 (1966): 81–96, states that Faustus is damned from the beginning, and that we should interpret the most beautiful poetry, which occurs at the end of the play, as an indication of Marlowe's "orthodox Christian scheme of values"; and T. McAlindon, "Classical Mythology and Christian Tradition in Marlowe's *Doctor Faustus,*" *PMLA* 81 (1966): 214–23, sees the themes of the play as Christian, and holds that the interwoven classical mythology supports this orthodoxy. But Susan

Snyder, "Marlowe's *Doctor Faustus* as an Inverted Saint's Life," *SP* 63 (1966): 565-77, returns essentially to the view that orthodoxy is parodied in the play.

Many critics take a middle ground between these two extremes. Arthur Mizener, "The Tragedy of Marlowe's *Doctor Faustus,*" *CE* 5 (1943): 70-75 (rpt. in the 1st ed. of Bluestone and Rabkin), believes that Faustus is caught in an ironic dilemma between Renaissance experimental thought and medieval Christianity. Robert B. Heilman, "The Tragedy of Knowledge: Marlowe's Treatment of Faustus," *QRL* 2 (1946): 316-32, through an analysis of imagery and structure, comes to the conclusion that Marlowe presents Faustus as a tragic figure, both in terms of an Everyman guilty of pride and as an intellectual who through *hubris* destroys his understanding of nature, refusing to accept limitations; the play, however, goes further and reaffirms man's ability to search transcendentally despite any attendant disillusion about superhuman power. Helen Gardner, "Milton's 'Satan' and the Theme of Damnation in Elizabethan Tragedy," *ES* 1 (1948): 46-66 (rpt. by Kaufmann), believes that Faustus is a prototype for Milton's Satan; both are men who have sold their souls to evil and are incapable of repentance. Richard B. Sewall, *The Vision of Tragedy* (1959), maintains that *Doctor Faustus* is the first play which presents Renaissance compulsions within Hebraic-Christian traditions; moreover, the play is fully modern in that it shows man's desires for mastery over nature and for freedom from traditional limitations. In the end, Faustus transcends his dilemma in a "classical apotheosis" and reveals a capacity for both good and evil. A similar lead is followed by J. P. Brockbank, *Marlowe: "Doctor Faustus"* (1962, partially rpt. by Leech), who stresses the last act of *Doctor Faustus* in terms of the tension between morality tradition and heroic tragedy, each of which "in its own way triumphs over the other," with the result that the play "adheres to the rich and searching morality of Augustinian thought; but does not allow us to come comfortably to rest in it."

Two of the more provocative recent essays on *Faustus* are by C. L. Barber and Robert Ornstein, both of whom are as much interested in Marlowe as in his titular hero. Barber, in "The Form of Faustus' Fortunes Good or Bad," *TDR* 8, no. 4 (1964): 92-119 (rpt. in the 2nd ed. of Bluestone and Rabkin), treats the play as Marlowe's dramatization of "blasphemy as heroic endeavor." The tension between the action and the poetic incantation of the verse expresses a "struggle for omnipotence and transcendent incarnation," but ultimately the play shows both a tragic and a comic failure—unconsciously Faustus makes a ritualistic substitution of gluttony for the ritual of communion. However, through this substitution, Marlowe was able to sublimate his own frustration regarding the cultural demands of orthodoxy on the individual. (Barber's essay is part of an ongoing Freudian study of Marlowe.) Ornstein, in "Marlowe and God: The Tragic Theology of *Dr. Faustus,*" *PMLA* 83 (1968): 1378–85, differing both from those who hold Marlowe a precursor of modern thought and feeling and from those who judge Faustus's fate from some orthodox point of view, asserts that the bent of Marlowe's "mind is more medieval than modern, and his response to experience is more antihumanistic than humanistic"; *Doctor Faustus* is Marlowe's "testament of despair" in which we see "a perfect correspondence between the nihilism of Marlowe's art and of his life. For it is the horror of the void—of loss and impotence—humanly experienced which is conveyed by Faustus' last soliloquy."

While Barber and Ornstein go beyond the play to consider Faustus as Marlowe's alter-ego, others are content to stay within the dramatic limits of the play in their search for the cause of Faustus' fall: Lily B. Campbell, "*Doctor Faustus*: A Case of Conscience," *PMLA* 67 (1952): 219–39, shows that Faustus falls irrecoverably into despair; Roland M. Frye, "Marlowe's *Doctor Faustus:* The Repudiation of Humanity," *SAQ* 55 (1956): 322–28, believes that Faustus' rejection of humanity gives the play unity and constitutes the reason for Faustus' failure; Joseph T. McCullen, "Doctor Faustus and Renaissance Learning," *MLR* 51 (1956): 6–16, taking a strongly anti-subjective stand, analyzes the hero to show that his fall is due mainly to the sin of sloth, that he "brings tragedy upon himself because of his limited and defective knowledge"; and Cyrus Hoy, " 'Ignorance in Knowledge': Marlowe's Faustus and Ford's Giovanni," *MP* 57 (1960): 145–54, feels that Faustus' basic sensuality overcomes any potential for intelligence, but that his sin finally is to accept ignorance as the highest good.

In a general study of the play which emphasizes the textual problems related to the Quartos of 1604 and 1616, Percy Simpson, "Marlowe's *Tragical History of Doctor Faustus,*" *E&S* 14 (1929): 20–34 (rpt. in his *Studies in Elizabethan Drama* [1955]), raises a question which has been of some concern of late: whether or not Marlowe wrote the comic parts of the play. Whereas Simpson believes that he did not, Robert Ornstein, "The Comic Synthesis in *Doctor Faustus,*" *ELH* 22 (1955): 165–72, supported by Levin, shows the tragic and comic parts approaching each other until "the difference between hero and clown is one of degree, not kind." The pertinence of the comic parts is further pursued by John H. Crabtree, Jr., "The Comedy in Marlowe's *Dr. Faustus,*" *FurmS* 9 (1961): 1–9. Muriel C. Bradbrook, "Marlowe's *Doctor Faustus* and the Eldritch Tradition," in *Essays on Shakespeare and Elizabethan Drama,* ed. Hosley (1962), pp. 83–90, not only supports the relevance of the comic scenes, but further justifies their presence: "Set against these tragic issues, much of the conjuring which fills the middle of the play may seem now irrelevant and tasteless. Perhaps it would become more explicable, if not more acceptable, were it seen as a development of what I shall call the Eldritch tradition. Eldritch diabolism, while both comic and horrific, is amoral and does not involve personal choice or the notion of personal responsibility." Warren D. Smith, "The Nature of Evil in *Doctor Faustus,*" *MLR* 60 (1965): 171–75, defends the often criticized middle parts of the play, showing that "the shallow frivolity is a fitting dramatic contrast to the titanic desires of the protagonist of the first part of the play and the profound despair at the end."

Sherman Hawkins, "The Education of Faustus," *SEL* 6 (1966): 193–209, argues that the middle scenes provide a "symbolic pattern which integrates the middle of the play and relates it to the beginning and end." The most ambitious claim for a formal unity in the play is by G. K. Hunter, "Five-Act Structure in *Doctor Faustus,*" *TDR* 8, no. 4 (1964): 77–91, who sees it essentially planned in five clear stages following the Renaissance idea of the five-act structure. He makes no claim for priority between the two main extant texts; rather, he shows how they both provide evidence that the "original" text had formal overall structure. In a contrasting and somewhat negative approach, Kenneth Muir, "Marlowe's *Doctor Faustus,*" *PP* 9 (1966): 395–408, believes that the play in either extant version does not exhibit much sense of structure on Marlowe's part.

Many other studies are more limited in scope. W. W. Greg, "The Damnation of Faustus," *MLR* 41 (1946): 97–107 (rpt. both by Leech and by Bluestone and Rabkin, 1st ed.), was the first to suggest that, once Faustus made his pact with the devil, he took on an infernal nature and was incapable of salvation; furthermore, when he kisses Helen, a spirit from hell, he "commits the sin of demoniality," thus damning himself irrevocably. Gerald Morgan, "Harlequin Faustus: Marlowe's Comedy of Hell," *HAB* 18 (1967): 22–34, suggests that the play should not be approached so much from the tragic point of view as from a comic. Martin Versefield, "Some Remarks on Marlowe's *Faustus*," *ESA* 1 (1958): 134–43, shows that patristic and scholastic theology and metaphysics play a part in the thematic framework. Philip J. Traci, "Marlowe's Faustus as Artist: A Suggestion About a Theme in the Play," *RenP*, 1966, pp. 3–9, suggests that the play is neither a morality nor a tragedy of search for knowledge; it may best be understood with Faustus playing the role of an artist who, as seen by his enrapturement by the beauty of Helen, sacrifices his soul to art in his attempt to reach full expression. Finally, two essays treat the play from the comparatist approach: Douglas Cole, "Faust and Anti-Faust in Modern Drama," *DramS* 5 (1966): 39–52, finds that the Faust of twentieth-century drama is no longer searching for absolute truth, but for his own identity; and Erich Kahler, "Doctor Faustus from Adam to Sartre," *CompD* 1 (1967): 75–92, traces the Faust motif in the manner his title suggests.

Two works intended for students offer introductions to the play. J. P. Brockbank, *Marlowe: "Doctor Faustus"* (1962) is an extended treatment of backgrounds and critical approaches. Irving Ribner, ed., *Marlowe's "Doctor Faustus": Text and Major Criticism* (1966) is a casebook which reprints the studies of the play by Ellis-Fermor, Kirschbaum, Mahood, Levin, Ornstein (on the comic parts), Sewall, and Barber, discussed above. Each has a selected bibliography.

I Tamburlaine

Because Marlowe's first two plays, *I* and *II Tamburlaine*, appeared together in print under the general title *Tamburlaine the Great*, much attention has been paid to whether we are dealing with two separate plays, or one single play in two parts. The classic study of *Tamburlaine* as a ten-act drama is by Roy W. Battenhouse, *Marlowe's "Tamburlaine": A Study in Renaissance Moral Philosophy* (1941). Battenhouse believes that the first part cannot stand alone but must be complemented by the second, the two halves together constituting a typical sixteenth-century morality drama of the fall from Fortune's wheel of a man of pride.

A corrective to the single-play reading is provided by Clifford Leech, "The Structure of *Tamburlaine*," *TDR* 8, no. 4 (1964): 32–46, who discusses the two parts of *Tamburlaine* as separately conceived works. He believes that Part I was written in a five-act structure, built upon a series of contrasts between Tamburlaine and each of his successively more worthy adversaries, whereas Part II possesses a looser, almost haphazard structure, which reflects the protagonist's loss of control over his situation. Leech's discussion is an outgrowth of his earlier article "The Two-Part Play: Marlowe and the Early Shakespeare," *SJ* 94 (1958): 90-106, where he first suggested that *II Tamburlaine* was written because of the success of the earlier play, much as the success of Part I of *Henry VI* led to sequels. (Earlier, this question of sequel-plays was raised by G. K. Hunter, *"Henry IV* and the Elizabethan Two-Part Play," *RES* 5 (1954): 239-48; Hunter concludes that each part of a two-part play is related to the other primarily on the basis of parallel presentation of incidents and only secondarily on preservation of similar traits of character and strands of plot.)

The unity of the two plays is, however, still defended in various ways: Peter V. LePage, "The Search for Godhead in Marlowe's *Tamburlaine,"* *CE* 26 (1965): 604-9, defends *Tamburlaine* as a psychological and aesthetic unity in the full Aristotelian sense; and Mary E. Rickey, "Astronomical Imagery in *Tamburlaine,"* *RenP*, 1954, pp. 63-70, traces a unity through imagery—for example, the sun rises in Part I and sets in Part II. John Le Gay Brereton, "Marlowe's Dramatic Art Studied in his *Tamburlaine,"* in *Writings on Elizabethan Drama,* ed. R. G. Howarth (1948, first pub. 1925), pp. 65-80, studied the two parts together as a two-fold tragedy "of a vast scheme of epic proportions"; but he treats each separately and is particularly relevant in his dramatic criticism of Part I. His essay also pleads that Marlowe be studied as a dramatic artist, not as an autobiographical projector. The best structural analysis of each of the plays is by George I. Duthie, "The Dramatic Structure of Marlowe's *Tamburlaine the Great, Parts I and II,"* *E&S* 1 (1948): 101-26 (rpt. in the 1st ed. of Bluestone and Rabkin).

There have been several recent studies of *I Tamburlaine* by itself. Robert Kimbrough, *"1 Tamburlaine:* A Speaking Picture in a Tragic Glass," *RenD* 7 (1964): 20-34, emphasizes both the conceptual originality of Marlowe and the dramatic subtlety and irony which the play affords when it is studied not as a biographical document but as an objective artifact. Two earlier articles charted out this objective approach: Leslie Spence, "The Influence of Marlowe's Sources on *Tamburlaine I,"* *MP* 24 (1926): 181-99, and "Tamburlaine and Marlowe," *PMLA* 42 (1927): 604-22; both point to the well-known sources, Marlowe's dramatic use of them, and his additions, especially the character of Zenocrate.

A subtle awareness of the irony of the action is displayed by Katherine Lever, "The Image of Man in *Tamburlaine, Part I,*" *PQ* 35 (1956): 421-27, when she traces conflicts between the visual image of a man's descent into brutality and the auditory image of his quest for divinity. This is also the general thesis of a monograph by Frank B. Fieler, *"Tamburlaine, Part I" and Its Audience,* UFMH, no. 8 (1961) who believes that Marlowe consciously tries at first to create a favorable impression of Tamburlaine on his audience and then gradually reverses the nature of that impression. On the other hand, Eugene M. Waith, *The Herculean Hero in Marlowe, Chapman, Shakespeare, and Dryden* (1962), believes that the audience would not adversely judge Tamburlaine because they would see him as a variation on the figure of Hercules, a positive force in the mythic tradition of the western world. Another study concerned with the artistic presentation of materials is by Siegfried Syler, "Marlowe's Technique of Communicating with His Audience, as Seen in His *Tamburlaine, Part I,*" *ES* 48 (1967): 306-16.

The "high astounding terms" of *I Tamburlaine* naturally have invited studies of the language of the play. In addition to Brooke's early discussion of Marlowe's versification and style, and Howard Baker's in his *Induction to Tragedy* (both mentioned above in I,C), Moody E. Prior, *The Language of Tragedy* (1947), shows how the language, in spite of its rhetorical nature, is related thematically to the dramatic form of the whole; Prior does not find the structure of the play to be either sound or successful. The best stylistic study of the play is Donald Peet's "The Rhetoric of *Tamburlaine,*" *ELH* 26 (1959): 137-55, which makes a full-dress rhetorical analysis of its language, drawing from the textbooks of the day.

Other studies have been devoted to the impact of Marlowe's play on its age and on other playwrights. Three stand out: William A. Armstrong, *"Tamburlaine* and *The Wounds of Civil War,*" *N&Q* 5 (1958): 381-83; Irving Ribner, "Greene's Attack on Marlowe: Some Light on *Alphonsus* and *Selimus,*" *SP* 52 (1955): 162-71; and Irving Ribner, *"Tamburlaine* and *The Wars of Cyrus,*" *JEGP* 52 (1954): 569-73.

II Tamburlaine

Because it is clearly a sequel, *The Return of Tamburlaine* has often been ignored or considered inferior. One of the first, and still important essays, is by Helen Gardner, "The Second Part of *Tamburlaine the Great,*" *MLR* 37 (1942): 18-24 (rpt. in the 1st ed. of Bluestone and

Rabkin). She demonstrates that the theme of the play is that the fulfillment of man's desires and aspirations is "limited by forces outside the control of his will." Because this is *not* the theme of Part I, her study shows how many scenes of the second play which have often been considered irrelevant actually fit in.

The remarks of Theodore Spencer in *Death and Elizabethan Tragedy: A Study of Convention and Opinion in the Elizabethan Drama* (1936) show how Marlowe's sophisticated, in-depth handling of the subject of death in a totally human way was an innovation and achievement valuable in itself. This same topic has been elaborated by Susan Richards, "Marlowe's *Tamburlaine II:* A Drama of Death," *MLQ* 26 (1965): 375-87, who shows how the idea of death unifies the action and imagery of the play, and affords an insight into the character of Tamburlaine, for as his power to give death grows, he loses the power to withstand it.

C. L. Barber's second essay on Marlowe written from a Freudian point of view is "The Death of Zenocrate: 'Conceiving and Subduing Both' in Marlowe's *Tamburlaine*," *L&P* 16 (1966): 15-24 (see also the response of Norman N. Holland, "Comment on 'The Death of Zenocrate,'" *L & P* 16 [1966]: 25-26). Frankly exploratory, Barber is concerned with the questions of why Marlowe created a Tamburlaine and his own relationship to his character. Although Barber's means of exploration is through the figure of Zenocrate in both of the plays, he acknowledges the separation of the parts; in fact, he believes that Marlowe took a step forward in dramatic writing in the second part when he was able to separate the attitude toward death which Zenocrate shows from that which Tamburlaine shows. In the first play Marlowe had so sublimated himself as hero that he was not able to present any points of view fully other than those professed by Tamburlaine.

The Jew of Malta

Until recent years little was written on *The Jew of Malta*. On the one hand, scholars tended to dismiss the text of 1633 as so completely degenerated from what the original must have been like that serious critical interpretation was not even attempted (see below, III,A). On the other hand, critics tended to focus only on Barabas as Jew (see below, IV,B). The catalyst for much modern criticism was the remark by T. S. Eliot that the play was a farce, "with serious, even savage, comic humour" (*Elizabethan Essays,* 1934). Critics have tended to respond in one of two ways: if this is so, why; if not, why not?

Although more concerned with Barabas than with the total play, Bernard Spivack, *Shakespeare and the Allegory of Evil* (1958), helpfully provides the scholarly basis for critics who wish to proceed in either of these two ways. Barabas is alienated by his faith and by his own character as Mammon; yet he is also related to the traditional vice-figure with all of its traditional theatrical evocations. A study by Harold Fisch, *The Dual Image* (1959), shows that Marlowe was in close touch with the medieval Judas-Devil image and the ritual murder theme of medieval anti-Semitism. However, Fisch goes on to say that although Marlowe played on this folk tradition for the creation of shocking hyperbole, his real interest in Barabas was to depict the influence of the diabolic Machiavelli and the energy which such a man could tap. Another study that explores both the anti-Semitism and the anti-Machiavellianism in the play is the introduction by Richard W. Van Fossen for his edition of *The Jew of Malta* (1964); this is also a useful guide to the background, sources, and critical opinions of the play.

In an article equally concerned with Marlowe criticism as it is with the play, Alfred Harbage, "Innocent Barabas," *TDR* 8, no. 4 (1964): 47–58, questions the idea that Marlowe was an iconoclast by suggesting that *The Jew of Malta* is more concerned with the evil Barabas himself as a comic, popular, anti-Semitic figure than as a character who subtly comments upon and undercuts his fellow-men. Barabas is innocent in the sense that he is "innocent-minded."

Three other recent articles also focus on Barabas while making detailed studies of the structure and themes of the play; at the same time, each contains special emphasis on some relevant scholarly background. G. K. Hunter, "The Theology of Marlowe's *The Jew of Malta,*" *JWCI* 27 (1964): 211–40, details how Marlowe, through ironic presentation, is able to present a man who by definition is evil, yet is able to excite some degree of sympathy, thereby forcing us to raise questions about the values which the Elizabethan audience was assumed to have held. More sympathetic is Allan Warren Friedman, "The Shackling of Accidents in Marlowe's *Jew of Malta,*" *TSLL* 8 (1966): 155–67, who feels that the play might better be entitled simply "Barabas" because it is held together by Barabas's "decreasing ability to circumscribe events" and concludes that Barabas is a thoroughly human being, not a mere stereotype. On the contrary, Eric Rothstein, "Structure as Meaning in *The Jew of Malta,*" *JEGP* 65 (1966): 260–73 (rpt. in the 2nd ed. of Bluestone and Rabkin), sees Barabas as a complete stereotype and suggests we should look beyond him to evaluate the corrupt world from which he has to take his identity and in which he is forced to live.

Edward II

While *The Jew of Malta* is now more popular with scholars and critics than it formerly was, the opposite is the case with *Edward II*. Once received as Marlowe's "best made" play, today latent ambiguities and contradictions seem more apparent. W. D. Briggs, in the introduction to his edition of the play (1914), established the critical opinion that the play represented Marlowe at his dramatic finest, an opinion echoed by Robert Fricker, "The Dramatic Structure of *Edward II*," *ES* 34 (1953): 204-17.

With regard to the question of the play's relationship to chronicle history, one should consult both Irving Ribner, *The English History Play in the Age of Shakespeare* (1957; rev. ed. 1965), and F. P. Wilson, *Marlowe and the Early Shakespeare* (1953). Ribner places the play strongly within the chronicle history tradition; Wilson also discusses its place in that tradition but feels that the main interest of the play lies in its depiction of character rather than of political events. (Ribner's chapter on Marlowe derives from an essay in *ELH* 22 [1955] : 243-53, reprinted in both editions of Bluestone and Rabkin; Wilson's chapter is reprinted by Leech.) A position similar to Wilson's is taken by Clifford Leech, "Marlowe's *Edward II:* Power and Suffering," *CritQ* 1 (1959): 181-96, who feels that power and suffering are the subjects of the play rather than the presentation of ideas; the play is full of contradictions and multiplicity and thereby is a reflection of the human pageant of life.

Wolfgang Clemen, *English Tragedy before Shakespeare: The Development of Dramatic Speech* (trans. T. S. Dorsch, 1961; German ed. 1955; excerpts rpt. by Leech), takes a simpler and more formal approach: as seen in the first part of the play, a gradual sacrifice of emotional significance and poetry is intentional in order to emphasize in the second part of the drama, in which Edward passes from active to passive, a reintroduction of intensity to convey the anguish and martyrdom of Edward. On the other hand, Eugene M. Waith, "*Edward II:* The Shadow of Action*,*" *TDR* 8, no. 4 (1964): 59-76, believes that *Edward II* reveals the constrained, frustrating emotions of life, the pathos and horrors of man's fate: the play is "a play of blocking—the characters crossing each other and reacting to the frustration of being crossed." And the most powerful emotions of the play arise from the desire of characters to escape this predicament.

Finally, Marion Perret, "Edward II: Marlowe's Dramatic Technique," *REL* 7, no. 4 (1966): 87–91, discusses the minor role of the prince as "an artistic tool to reveal others." He, along with his uncle Kent, functions as a chorus character pointing out to the audience "where power parts company with moral right."

The Massacre at Paris

Because of the unanimous belief that the extant text of the *Massacre* represents a drastically fragmented version of what the original must have been, full critical analysis appears only in the book-length studies. David Galloway, "The Ramus Scene in Marlowe's *The Massacre at Paris*," *N&Q* 198 (1953): 146–47, suggests that the confrontation of the Duke and Ramus is not extraneous or distracting; rather, it provides the pause in the rapid action of the play which allows dramatic tension to heighten and affords the opportunity for a conventional speech before death.

Dido, Queen of Carthage

As is the case with the *Massacre,* there are not many separate studies of *Dido.* Don Cameron Allen, "Marlowe's *Dido* and the Tradition," in *Essays on Shakespeare,* ed. Hosley (1962), pp. 55–68, provides a detailed history of the Dido tradition, followed by a short discussion of Marlowe's play; Thomas P. Harrison, Jr., "Shakespeare and Marlowe's *Dido, Queen of Carthage,*" *Studies in English* (Univ. of Texas), 35 (1956): 57–63, anticipates Steane in suggesting that the management of non-classical situations involving the protagonist provided precedents for and influence on Shakespeare, especially in *Antony and Cleopatra* when Antony tries to break away from Cleopatra; and John P. Cutts, "*Dido, Queen of Carthage,*" *N&Q* 5 (1958): 371–74, sees a serious, albeit ironic, theme of "rule of love" running throughout the play as a unifying device. The most fruitful way to understand *Dido,* however, is to see it as an outgrowth of typical academic, rhetorical exercises, for the play is a fun-filled imitation of the most famous episode in the most important work of literature studied by students in the Renaissance, and, having been written for the boys, is best received in a spirit of lightness.

B. OVER-ALL STATE OF CRITICISM

Because 1964 was an anniversary year, several complete critical reassessments were made. Five, in order of approximate importance, are: Harry Levin, "Marlowe Today," *TDR* 8, no. 4 (1964): 22–31; Douglas Cole, "Christopher Marlowe, 1564–1964, A Survey," *ShN* 14 (1964): 44; Irving Ribner, "Marlowe and the Critics," *TDR* 8, no. 4 (1964): 211–25; J. Michael Miller, "Marlowe, 1964," *ClareQ* 9 (1964): 15–32; and Raymond Mortimer, "Marlowe: English Genius of the Renaissance," *TLS*, 2 Feb. 1964, p. 35. Nicholas Brooke, "Marlowe the Dramatist," in *Elizabethan Theatre*, SuAS, vol. 9 (1966), pp. 87–105, points out that the recent trend in Marlowe criticism has been to see him as a dramatist concerned with form and dramatic technique.

III. CANON

A. CHRONOLOGY AND TEXT

While there is little doubt concerning the Marlowe canon, there is no certainty concerning the order in which his plays were written. As a glance at Chambers, *The Elizabethan Stage* (1923), vol. 3 shows, most of the dates were set early, but, for the most part, on arbitrary grounds. A re-examination of the whole question of chronology would be beneficial.

The standard and still reliable discussion is by C. F. Tucker Brooke, "The Marlowe Canon," *PMLA* 37 (1922): 367–417. A later discussion is by Kenneth Muir, "The Chronology of Marlowe's Plays," *PLPLS-LHS* 5 (1938–39): 345–56; and the latest is that by Alfred Harbage, as revised by Samuel Schoenbaum, *Annals of English Drama, 975–1700* (1964). Although the present writer has some reservations about the conclusions of Harbage and Schoenbaum, their dates of performance (in italics) and first edition are given after each title and have been followed for the chronological arrangement of the section.

Dido, Queen of Carthage, classical legend (*1587–93;* 1594)

Dido was first published in 1594, the year following Marlowe's death, with the title page stating in part, "Played by the Children of Her Majesty's Chapel. Written by Christopher Marlowe, and Thomas Nashe." The role of Nashe has long been disputed and is currently felt not to have been great. In all probability he functioned as some sort of editor for this publication. Because the children of the Chapel Royal were active as players during the early 1580s until their commercial playing was terminated by the Queen at the end of 1584; because they performed early in 1587 at Ipswich and Norwich; and because it is probable that they acted before the Queen in 1591, each of these times provides a possible date for the play. However, given the scanty evidence with regard to the various playing companies, private and public, until after the theaters opened following the plague of 1592–94, other dates are also possible.

Based mainly upon evidence of what he feels is an increased familiarity with stage technique and a style influenced by Kyd, T. M. Pearce, "Evidence for Dating Marlowe's *Tragedy of Dido*," in *Studies in the English Renaissance Drama in Memory of Karl Julius Holzknecht,* ed. Josephine W. Bennett, Oscar Cargill, and Vernon Hall, Jr. (1959), pp. 231–47, dates the play early in 1591. Others who feel that the play is immature date it back into Marlowe's Cambridge career.

Regardless of when it was written, the play is best understood within the context of academic drama because it is of a kind different from Marlowe's other plays, each written for the public theater. The number of parts, the presence of song, the emphasis on verbal cleverness over physical activity are some of the indications of academic or private auspices. Surely the play is written in the vein to which Marlowe had been exposed at King's School in Canterbury, as well as at college in Cambridge. As a result, there is no reason why it could not have been written for, and performed by, the children in 1584 when they were under the directorship of John Lyly, nor is there compelling reason not to feel that Marlowe could have written the play for presentation by the boys early in 1587.

I and *II Tamburlaine,* heroical romance (*1587–88;* 1590)

The two *Tamburlaine* plays were the only ones by Marlowe published during his lifetime, when, in 1590, they appeared together with the following title page (modernized): "*Tamburlaine the Great.* Who, from a Scythian Shepherd, by his rare and wonderful Conquests, became a most puissant and mighty Monarch. And (for his tyranny, and terror in War) was termed, The Scourge of God. Divided into two Tragical Discourses, as they were sundry times showed upon Stages in the City of London. By the Right Honourable the Lord Admiral, his servants. Now first and newly published . . . ."

I Tamburlaine, as the work by Ethel Seaton (see I,A, and IV,B) and others would indicate, was written while Marlowe was still at Cambridge and had access to various books at the library there. In two essential ways the play is revolutionary: it is the first play written by a university-trained man to be sold to the public players, a fact which immediately drew other university-trained people to the theaters, thus elevating the whole level of writing for the players; and, of course, the play, by its style and the nature of its action, made such an impact upon the Elizabethan audience that other playwrights were encouraged to imitate Marlowe's mighty line and some of his extravagant action. Because Marlowe finished work for his M.A. degree in the spring of 1587 and because a letter dated 16 November 1587 indicates that *II Tamburlaine* was in repertory, the dating of these two plays affords no great problem: both were presented in the fall theatrical season of 1587.

The Jew of Malta, tragedy (ca. *1589–90;* 1633)

Until the 1940s, the scholarly consensus was that *Doctor Faustus* followed hard upon *I* and *II Tamburlaine* because of a general likeness of style in parts of those three plays; the question of early versus late date will be discussed below. Similarly, *The Jew of Malta* is given an early date, usually around 1589, because of the received opinion that its style is like that of *I* and *II Tamburlaine,* and because it too has a central hero. An allusion in the Prologue to the death of the Duke of Guise suggests a date of performance later than 23 December 1588, or at least proves that the composition of the prologue came after that date.

Even though Marlowe's name appears on the title page, the matter of composition is complicated by the fact that the first edition of the play did not appear until 1633, with a dedicatory epistle, two prologues, and two epilogues written by Thomas Heywood, who seems to have been closely connected with the publication. The late date and the appearance of Heywood have given rise to two questions: how "good" a text is *The Jew of Malta*; and does Heywood's hand appear to any extent in the version that we have?

For a long time the opinion was held, as typified by M. C. Bradbrook, that the first two acts pretty well represent what Marlowe originally wrote, but that the last three acts reveal a gradual degeneration within the text of the play, that oft-repeated performance had slowly turned what originally had been intended as a tragedy into something much more like farce. Recent criticism (see above, II,A) has reversed this tendency, finding in the text an artistic integrity. Bibliographical evaluation of the text has also taken a turn in the opposite direction, starting with Leo Kirschbaum, "Some Light on *The Jew of Malta,*" *MLQ* 7 (1946): 53–56, who asserts that the play has textual integrity. This point of view is taken up in two articles by J. C. Maxwell, "The Assignment of Speeches in *The Jew of Malta,*" *MLR* 43 (1948): 510–12, and, "How Bad is the Text of *The Jew of Malta?*" *MLR* 48 (1953): 435–38. Although Maxwell, from the critical point of view, does agree thàt the play changes after Act II, he feels that this was an intentional change on Marlowe's part and not the result of an over-exposure of the stereotyped Jew in the theater. The presence of Heywood is decided as that of advisory editor by Robert Ford Welsh, "Evidence of Heywood Spellings in *The Jew of Malta,*" *RenP,* 1963, pp. 3–9; and a description of the first edition of the *Jew* is given by F. S. Hook, "Marlowe, Massinger, and Webster Quartos," *N&Q* 4 (1957): 64–65.

Doctor Faustus, tragedy (*1588–92;* 1604)

The questions of the date and text of *Doctor Faustus* have never been answered satisfactorily, nor are they likely to be, in spite of the fact that much complicated, closely reasoned argumentation has been presented for and against: (1) an "early" date of 1588–89, (2) a "late date" of mid- or late 1592, (3) the essential integrity of the 1604 text, and (4) the actual "priority" of the 1616 text.

One clarifying yet complicating fact affecting both date and text is the consensus that both texts incorporate materials which are extant in *The History of the Damnable Life and the Deserved Death of Doctor John Faustus* (1592), a translation from German by one "P. F. Gent." of the *Historia von D. Johan Fausten* (1587). This fact is clear because the translation, while faithful in detail, is unique in phrasing and additions which are picked up in the play; it is complicated, however, by the ambiguous statement on the title page (modernized): "Newly imprinted, and in convenient places imperfect matter amended." Simply put, some parts of the 1604 text and more parts of the 1616 text derive from an English text like this *Faust Book,* but is this a "first edition" of a translation of the *Faustbuch,* or a "second edition" of an earlier translation? Major advocates of the "first edition" are C. F. Tucker Brooke, "The Marlowe Canon," *PMLA* 37 (1922): 367–417; Frederick S. Boas, ed., *Doctor Faustus* [1616 text] (1932); and W. W. Greg, *"Doctor Faustus": 1604–1616; Parallel Texts* (1950). Those on the side of a "second edition" are Chambers, and Paul H. Kocher in three articles, "The English *Faust Book* and the Date of Marlowe's *Faustus,*"

MLN 55 (1940): 95–101; "Some Nashe Marginalia Concerning Marlowe," *MLN* 57 (1942): 45–49; and "The Early Date for Marlowe's *Faustus,*" *MLN* 58 (1943): 539–42.

Earlier arguments for the early date were based on the assumptions that, because the play has a central hero and exuberant blank verse, it must fall after the Tamburlaine plays; that a Faust ballad of February 1589 was written to capitalize on the success of the play; and that Greene's *Friar Bacon and Friar Bungay* (1589–90) could only have been written in imitation of Marlowe.

Although they offer no fixed conclusions, four studies suggest looking beyond a specific relationship between the *Faustbuch* of 1587 and the *Faust Book* of 1592 when considering the questions of source and date: Raymond A. Houk, *"Doctor Faustus* and *A Shrew,"* PMLA 62 (1947): 950–57, who suggests that there were common sources in earlier versions of each play; Harold Jantz, "An Elizabethan Statement on the Origin of the German Faust Book: With a Note on Marlowe's Sources," *JEGP* 51 (1952): 137–53, who posits an intermediate Latin translation between the German and English texts of the Faust material, a translation available to Marlowe; Barbara Cooper, "An Ur-*Faustus?*" *N&Q* 6 (1959): 66–68; and Curt A. Zimansky, "Marlowe's *Faustus:* The Date Again," *PQ* 41 (1962): 181–87, who brings in counter-evidence to Greg's bibliographical insistence on 1592.

The 1604 text was for a long time believed to have been closer to Marlowe's manuscript than the 1616, which represented a version with the additions by Birde and Rowley for which Henslowe paid £4 in 1602. This position was selectively questioned by Percy Simpson, "The 1604 Text of Marlowe's *Doctor Faustus,*" *E&S* 7 (1921): 143–55, the textual analysis which led to the editions of Boas (1932) and Greg (1950); and in two speculative essays by Leo Kirschbaum (who anticipated Greg's conclusions), "An Hypothesis Concerning the Origin of the 'Bad Quartos,' " *PMLA* 60 (1945): 697–715, and "The Good and Bad Quartos of *Doctor Faustus,*" *Library* 26 (1946): 272–94. The current theory is that the 1604 text (or A-text, to use Greg's term) represents a debased acting version of the play dating back to the mid-1590s, which was based on a memorial reconstruction of a lost promptbook made around 1592 for provincial performance during the plague, the original promptbook having been prepared from Marlowe's manuscript; this same manuscript survived to serve as a direct source for the 1616 text (or B-text), but with two essential qualifications: Marlowe changed his manuscript *after* the original, soon-to-be-lost promptbook was prepared, and the manuscript was so badly damaged that the editor of the B-text was forced to depend upon the A-text for many readings.

Because Greg's argument is so hypothetical and deductive, one should read the review article by Fredson Bowers, "The Text of Marlowe's *Faustus*," *MP* 49 (1952): 195–204, who gives praise where it is due, but points out the weaknesses of most of Greg's deduced models.

Although no text of the play since 1950 has departed much from Greg, the bibliographical question is far from answered. What must be recognized is that we have two texts of the play, each bibliographically different from the other, and each critically different from the other.

Between the two texts, then, certain differences must concern both scholars and critics. The A-text follows the English *Faust Book* more closely in "serious" passages than does the B-text; yet the A-text does not use the *Faust Book* in any "comic" passages except for the "Horse-courser" episode toward the end, while the "comic" passages in the B-text which are not in the A-text all come from the *Faust Book*. Lucifer has a larger and more controlling role in the B-text than in the A-text, while the Old Man has a larger part and more compelling presence in the A-text. Finally, and most important, the two endings are completely different: in the A-text there is no plotting among devils prior to the last hour, Faustus is on-stage alone until his last three lines (at which point a stage direction indicates an entrance of devils), and all of his agonies are internal; in the B-text the whole question of a choice still open to Faustus is removed by the presence of Lucifer and devils on-stage before Faustus's entrance and during his last hour, and any ambiguity concerning Faustus's fate is removed by the addition of a scene in which the scholars view and examine the havoc wrought by the devils on Faustus's body.

Edward II, history (*1591–93;* 1594)

Although the play was entered in the Stationers' Register in 1593 and there is strong feeling that it was published in that year, the first extant version is that of 1594 with the following title page (modernized): "*The Troublesome Reign and Lamentable Death of Edward the Second, King of England: With the Tragical Fall of Proud Mortimer.* As it was sundry times publicly acted in the honourable city of London, by the Right Honourable, the Earl of Pembroke, His Servants.

Written by Chri. Marlowe, Gent. . . ." Although the history of Pembroke's Men is quite obscure, they do not seem to have come into organization until about 1591–92, making *Edward* one of Marlowe's last plays. But a late date for *Edward II* has traditionally been assigned because of the scholarly belief that the play is Marlowe's best constructed, and that he learned play construction when he roomed with Kyd for a period around 1591. Robert Ford Welsh, "The Printer of the 1594 Octavo of Marlowe's *Edward II*," *SB* 17 (1964): 197–98, has established that the printer for William Jones was not Richard Brabcock, but Robert Robinson.

The Massacre at Paris, foreign history (*30* [*26*] *Jan. 1593;* [*1594?*] & MS)

The *Massacre* is usually dated 1593, for a "tragedey of the gvyes" was marked as a new play for Strange's Men by Henslowe on 26 January 1593, but the title page of the first edition, which carries no date, states the following (modernized): "*The Massacre at Paris:* With the Death of the Duke of Guise. As it was played by the Right Honourable, the Lord High Admiral, his servants. Written by Christopher Marlow . . . ." As Chambers points out *(Elizabethan Stage,* vol. 3), some time in 1590 or 1591 the Admiral's Men merged with Strange's Men, and the Admiral's Men did not reappear as a separate company until after the plague of 1592–94. The play could have been written, then, any time between the death of the Duke of Guise in December 1588, and the fall of 1592, which logically is the last date for any active dramatic writing until the theaters opened again in 1594.

The major questions surrounding this play are the state of the text and the nature of the so-called "Collier Leaf." Rejected as spurious by C. F. Tucker Brooke (in his 1910 edition of the *Works*) and Chambers, later scholars (see IV,C) now consider the manuscript genuine; the argument is summarized by J. M. Nosworthy, "The Marlowe Manuscript," *Library* 26 (1945): 158–71, and Ribner has incorporated the manuscript readings into his recent edition of the play (1963). Because the extant text is short and incoherent, according to Leo Kirschbaum in "A Census of Bad Quartos," *RES* 14 (1938): 20–43, it is a bad quarto, one which represents a memorial reconstruction made by someone specifically paid by a publisher. On the other hand, Dora Jean Ashe, "The Non-Shakespearean Bad Quartos as Provincial Acting Versions," *RenP,* 1954, pp. 57–62, believes that the text represents a purposefully cut-down play-script for a traveling group of players.

B. UNCERTAIN ASCRIPTIONS; BORROWINGS; INFLUENCE; APOCRYPHA

The only disputed play openly ascribed to Marlowe is *"Lust's Dominion; or the Lascivious Queen,* a tragedy written by Christopher Marlowe, Gent. . . . 1657."* Even before Chambers, this claim of authorship never was taken seriously. For the latest scholarship on the question, see the two articles by Gustav K. Cross, "The Vocabulary of *Lust's Dominion,"* *NM* 59 (1958): 41–48, and "The Authorship of *Lust's Dominion,"* *SP* 55 (1958): 39–61; and the older but still pertinent works by S. R. Golding, "The Authorship of *Lust's Dominion,"* *N&Q* 155 (1928): 399–402, and John Le Gay Brereton, ed., *Lust's Dominion* (1931).

John P. Cutts, "The Marlowe Canon," *N&Q* 6 (1959): 71–74, believes, as many have suggested, that the opening lines of the Prologue to *Doctor Faustus* indicate the existence of a now-lost play on the Hannibal and Scipio story. In the past, Marlowe's hand has been found in many other plays, especially the early works of Shakespeare, but these claims are no longer taken as seriously as they once were; they are listed in IV,D (below).

With the use of computers in the field of literary analysis, the question of attribution and influence will be opened again. Two articles laying out areas of future work are by C. B. Williams, "Literature and Statistics," *Listener,* 11 June 1964, pp. 960–61, and Ephim G. Fogel, "Electronic Computers and Elizabethan Texts," *SB* 15 (1962): 23–26.

C. CRITIQUE OF THE STANDARD EDITIONS

The best one-volume edition of the works is still that by C. F. Tucker Brooke, *The Works of Christopher Marlowe* (1910). Brooke's edition is valuable because it retains old spellings and carries full critical apparatus, as well as such useful items as Chapman's continuation of *Hero and Leander,* a transcription of the "Collier Leaf" appended to the *Massacre,* and all of the scenes of the 1616 text of *Faustus* which do not occur in the 1604 text.

The most complete edition of Marlowe is the six-volume, modern-spelling edition prepared under the guidance of R. H. Case. Each volume contains a full accounting of the sources, the text, the date, and critical appraisals of each of the works, and has full annotations. Although they first appeared in 1930–33, each has been reissued and several have been revised. They are: Volume 1, C. F. Tucker Brooke, ed., *The Life of Marlowe and the Tragedy of Dido, Queen of Carthage*

(1930); Volume 2, Una M. Ellis-Fermor, ed., *Tamburlaine the Great: In Two Parts* (1930; rev. ed. 1950); Volume 3, H. S. Bennett, ed., *The Jew of Malta* and *The Massacre at Paris* (1931); Volume 4, L. C. Martin, ed., *Poems* (1931); Volume 5, Frederick S. Boas, ed., *The Tragical History of Doctor Faustus* (1932; the first modern edition based on the 1616 text); and Volume 6, H. B. Charlton and R. D. Waller, eds., *Edward II* (1933; rev. ed. 1955 by F. N. Lees).

Two recent modern-spelling editions of the plays are those by Irving Ribner, *Complete Plays of Christopher Marlowe* (1963), and Leo Kirschbaum, *The Plays of Christopher Marlowe* (1962). Kirschbaum does not believe that *Dido* and the *Massacre* have been proved conclusively to be the work of Marlowe and does not include them. A work long awaited is the critical, old-spelling edition currently being prepared by Fredson Bowers for the Cambridge University Press.

D. SINGLE-WORK EDITIONS

Two general editions of Elizabethan dramatists eventually will have the complete plays of Marlowe in their series: the Revels Plays and the New Mermaid Series. The Regents Renaissance Drama Series will have most of the plays. In the Revels, John D. Jump has edited *Doctor Faustus* (1962), using the 1616 text with no major departures from Greg, and H. J. Oliver has edited in one volume *Dido, Queen of Carthage,* and *The Massacre of Paris* (1963). Both are modern-spelling editions with full introductions. For the New Mermaid, Roma Gill has edited *Doctor Faustus* (1965); W. Moelwyn Merchant, *Edward the Second* (1965); and Thomas W. Craik, *The Jew of Malta* (1966). In the Regents series, Richard Van Fossen has edited *The Jew of Malta* (1964), and John D. Jump, *Tamburlaine the Great, Parts I and II* (1967).

The indispensable edition of *Faustus* is *"Doctor Faustus": 1604–1616; Parallel Texts,* by W. W. Greg (1950). Also of interest is his *"The Tragical History of the Life and Death of Doctor Faustus": A Conjectural Reconstruction* (1950). A useful edition is that by Paul H. Kocher, *The Tragical History of Doctor Faustus* (1950), which retains the 1604 text as the copy-text, as does the edition by Louis B. Wright and Virginia A. La Mar, *The Tragedy of Doctor Faustus* (1959). For the comparatist, there is the edition and translation by Sir John Anster, *"The Tragical History of Doctor Faustus" and Goethe's "Faust, Part 1"* (1956). Also useful are the edition of the *Faust Book* by William Rose,

"The History of the Damnable Life and Deserved Death of Doctor John Faustus," 1592, together with *"The Second Report of Faustus, Containing His Appearances and the Deeds of Wagner,"* 1594 (1925), and the edition by Basil Ashmore, *The Tragical History of Doctor Faustus* (1949), which includes the 1592 edition of *The History of the Damnable Life and Deserved Death of Doctor John Faustus*.

A useful school text of *Tamburlaine* is edited by Tatiana A. Wolff, *Tamburlaine the Great, Parts I and II* (1964).

Greg edited *Edward II* for the Malone Society (1925). The first scholarly edition of *Edward II* was by W. D. Briggs (1914), an edition useful not only for its text, but for its introduction and annotations. Other useful editions of *Edward II* are by Osborne William Tancock (1952), E. E. Reynolds (1955), and Roma Gill (1967).

W. W. Greg edited *The Massacre at Paris* for the Malone Society (1928).

E. EDITIONS OF THE POETRY

The most significant recent edition of *Hero and Leander* is by Elizabeth Story Donno, *Elizabethan Minor Epics* (1963), which has a full introduction and includes Chapman's completion of Marlowe's work. The edition, with a French translation, by J. B. Fort (1950; above, I,C) includes a comprehensive introduction and notes and prints the continuation.

IV. SEE ALSO

A. GENERAL

Biographical

Alexander, Peter. "Shakespeare, Marlowe's Tutor." *TLS*, 2 April 1964, p. 280 (see T. W. Baldwin, *TLS*, 23 April 1964, p. 343).

Allen, Don Cameron. "Meres and the Death of Marlowe." *TLS*, 4 Feb. 1932, p. 76.

Ashton, J. W. "The Fall of Icarus." *PQ* 20 (1941): 345-51.

Atkinson, A. D. "Marlowe and the Voyagers." *N&Q* 194 (1949): 247-50, 273-75.

———. "A Possible Schoolfellow of Marlowe." *N&Q* 194 (1949): 379.

Bakeless, John Edwin. "Marlowe and His Father." *TLS*, 2 Jan. 1937, p. 12.

Baldwin, T. W. "A Line in Gabriel Harvey." *TLS*, 18 Jan. 1941, p. 31.

Barrington, Michael. "Marlowe's Alleged Atheism." *N&Q* 195 (1950): 260-61 (and see letter by Lynette and Eveline Feasey, *N&Q* 195 [1950] : 392-93).

Blunden, E. "Shakespeare Oddities." *N&Q* 7 (1960): 334-35.

Boas, Frederick S. "Greene, Marlowe, and Machiavelli." *TLS*, 3 Aug. 1940, p. 375.

———. "Informer Against Marlowe." *TLS*, 16 Sept. 1949, p. 608.

Bowen, Gwynneth. "Shakespeare and His Contemporaries." *Shakespearean Authorship Review*, no. 7 (1962), pp. 1-6.

Bradbrook, M. C. *The School of Night: A Study in the Literary Relationship of Sir Walter Raleigh.* 1936.

Brereton, John Le Gay. "The Case of Francis Ingram." In *Writings on Elizabethan Drama*, ed. R. G. Homarelt (1948), pp. 14-20.

Bridges-Adams, William. *The Irresistible Theatre.* 1957.

Briggs, W. D. "A Document Concerning Christopher Marlowe." *SP* 20 (1923): 153-59.

Brooke, C. F. Tucker. *Essays on Shakespeare and Other Elizabethans.* 1948.

Brooks, E. St. John. "Marlowe in 1589-1592." *TLS*, 27 Feb. 1937, p. 151 (see F. S. Boas, *TLS*, 6 Mar. 1937, p. 171).

Brown, I. "How Bright a Boy?" *Drama*, no. 75 (Winter, 1964), pp. 27-29.

Buckley, George T. *Atheism in the English Renaissance.* 1932.

———. "Who was the 'late Arrian?' " *MLN* 49 (1934): 500-503.

Camden, Carroll, Jr. "Marlowe and Elizabethan Psychology." *PQ* 8 (1929): 69-78.

Carpenter, Nan C. "A Reference to Marlowe in Charles Butler's *Principles of Musik* (1636)." *N&Q* 198 (1953): 16-18.

Chambers, E. K., ed. *The Shakespeare Allusion-Book.* 1932.

Churchill, R. C. "Keats and Marlowe." *Contemporary Review* 167 (1945): 173-79.

Cox, C. B. "Brutalities of Power." *Spectator*, 4 Sept. 1964, pp. 313-14.

Danchin, F. C. "La mort de Christopher Marlowe." *RAA* 3 (1925): 48-53.

Darby, Robert H. "Christopher Marlowe's Second Death." *West Virginia Univ. Bulletin, Philological Studies* 4 (1943-44): 81-85.

de Kalb, E. "R. Poley: An Associate of Marlowe." *Nineteenth Century* 104 (1928): 715-16.

———. "R. Poley's Movements as a Messenger of the Court, 1588 to 1601." *RES* 9 (1933): 13-18.

Denonain, J. J. "Un nommé Christopher Marlowe, Gentleman." *Caliban* 1 (1964): 51-74.

Disher, M. Willson. "The Trend of Shakespeare's Thought." *TLS*, 20 Oct. 1950, p. 668; 27 Oct., p. 684; 3 Nov., p. 700 (see also 17 Nov., p. 727; 1 Dec., p. 767; 8 Dec., p. 785).

Djivelegov, A. "The Influence of Italian Culture on Marlowe's and Shakespeare's Way of Thinking." *Transactions of the Lunacharsky State Institute of Theatrical Art* [USSR], 1940, pp. 143-60.

Douglas, A. "John Marlowe and William Hughes." *TLS*, 28 May 1938, p. 370.

Durrell, Lawrence. "The Rival Poet." *TLS*, 5 Jan. 1951, p. 7.

Dyde, S. G. "One Point of Contact Between Marlowe and Shakespeare." *QQ* 34 (1927): 320-25.

Eagle, Roderick L. "The Mystery of Marlowe's Death." *N&Q* 197 (1952): 399-402.

Eccles, Mark. "Christopher Marlowe in Newgate." *TLS*, 6 Sept. 1934, p. 604.

———. "Christopher Marlowe in Kentish Tradition." *N&Q* 169 (1935): 20-23, 39-41, 58-61, 134-35.

Feasey, Lynette. "A Note on William Rankins." *N&Q* 195 (1950): 20.

Feasey, Lynette and Eveline. "The Validity of the Baines Document." *N&Q* 194 (1949): 514-17.

Feldman, Abraham B. "Playwrights and Pike Trailers in the Low Countries." *N&Q* 198 (1953): 184-87.

George, J. "An Allusion to Marlowe." *N&Q* 195 (1950): 138-39.

Gray, A. K. "Some Observations on Christopher Marlowe, Government Agent." *PMLA* 43 (1928): 682-700.

Gyller, Harold. "Shakespeare och Marlowe." *BLM* 25 (1956): 138-40.

Harrison, G. B. *Elizabethan Plays and Players.* 1940.

Hart, Alfred. *Shakespeare and the Homilies.* 1934.

Haydn, Hiram. *The Counter-Renaissance.* 1950.

Henderson, Philip. "Marlowe as Messenger." *TLS*, 12 June 1953, p. 381.

Herrington, H. W. "Christopher Marlowe, Rationalist." In *Essays in Memory of Barrett Wendell* (1926), pp. 121-52.

Hotson, J. Leslie. "Tracking Down a Murderer." *Atlantic*, June 1925, pp. 733-41.

——. "Christopher Marlowe among the Churchwardens." *Atlantic*, July 1926, pp. 37-44.

——. "More Light on Shakespeare's Sonnets." *SQ* 2 (1951): 111-18.

Howarth, R. G. "Notes on Chapman." *N&Q* 192 (1947): 70-72.

Hughes, Pennethorne. "The Vogue for Marlowe." *Month* 8 (1952): 141-51.

Ireland, G. "Ingram Frizer Laid More Low than Christopher Marlowe." *ShAB* 5 (1930): 192-94.

Johnson, Francis R. "Marlowe's Astronomy and Renaissance Sceptics." *ELH* 13 (1946): 241-54.

Klein, John W. "Was Mercutio Christopher Marlowe?" *Drama*, no. 60 (Spring, 1961), pp. 36-39.

——. "Christopher Marlowe." *TLS*, 8 Oct. 1964, p. 924 (see Edward Fisher, *TLS*, 15 Oct. 1964, p. 939, and John W. Klein, *TLS*, 22 Oct. 1964, p. 959).

Knights, L. C. *Further Explorations: Essays in Criticism.* 1965.

Kocher, Paul H. "The Development of Marlowe's Character." *PQ* 17 (1938): 331-50.

——. "Marlowe's Atheist Lecture." *JEGP* 39 (1940): 98-106 (rpt. in *Marlowe: A Collection of Critical Essays,* ed. Clifford Leech [1964], pp. 159-66).

——. "Backgrounds of Marlowe's Atheist Lecture." *PQ* 20 (1941): 304-24.

——. "Some Nashe Marginalia concerning Marlowe." *MLN* 57 (1942): 45-50.

——. "Christopher Marlowe, Individualist." *UTQ* 17 (1947): 111-20.

Lawrence, C. E. "Christopher Marlowe, the Man." *QR* 255 (1930): 231-46.

Leech, Clifford. *When Writing Becomes Absurd: The Acting of Shakespeare and Marlowe, Two Addresses.* 1964 (rpt. from *ColQ* 13 [1964]: 6-24).

McNeir, Waldo F. "Greene's Tomliuclin: Tamburlaine or Tom a Lincoln?" *MLN* 58 (1943): 380-82.

"Marlowe and the Absolute." *TLS*, 24 Feb. 1956, p. 116 (see Curt A. Zimansky, *TLS*, 6 April 1956, p. 207).

Maugeri, Aldo. *Greene, Marlowe, e Shakespeare: Tre studi biografici.* 1952.

Meyerstein, E. H. W. "The Forged Letter from Peele to Marlowe." *TLS*, 29 June 1940, p. 315 (see reply from St. John Brooks, 20 July 1940, p. 351).

Moore, Hale. "Gabriel Harvey's References to Marlowe." *SP* 23 (1926): 337-57.
Morozov, M. M. *Kristofer Marlo.* 1954.
Mundy, P. D. "The Ancestry of Christopher Marlowe." *N&Q* 1 (1954): 328-31.
Ornstein, Robert. *"The Atheist's Tragedy." N&Q* 2 (1955): 284-85.
Ostrovsky, A. N. *Kristofer Marlo: Izbyanye Statyi i peryevodi, Vstupityelnaya statya R. M. Samarina.* 1954.
Parfenov, A. *Kristofer Marlow (1564-1593).* 1964.
Parr, Johnstone. *Tamburlaine's Malady and Other Essays on Astrology in Elizabethan Drama.* 1953.
Pearce, T. M. *Christopher Marlowe, Figure of the Renaissance.* 1934.
Powell, E. D. B. "Marlowe and Keats." *TLS,* 5 April 1947, p. 157.
Powys, Llewelyn. *Thirteen Worthies.* 1923.
Robertson, J. M. *Marlowe: A Conspectus.* 1931.
Rowse, A. L., and G. B. Harrison. *Queen Elizabeth and Her Subjects.* 1935.
Schick, J. "Christopher Marlowe: seine Personlichkeit und sein Schaffen." *SJ* 64 (1928): 159-79.
Schneider, Reinhold. "Christopher Marlowe der Dichter der Macht." *Die Literatur* 38 (1936): 215-18.
Seaton, Ethel. "Marlowe, R. Poley, and the Tippings." *RES* 5 (1929): 273-81.
———. "R. Poley's Ciphers." *RES* 7 (1931): 137-50.
———. "Marlowe and His Father." *TLS,* 5 June 1937, p. 428.
Shield, H. A. "The Death of Marlowe." *N&Q* 4 (1957): 101-3.
———. "Charles Sledd, Spymaster." *N&Q* 7 (1960): 47-48.
Smith, Winifred. "Anti-Catholic Propaganda in Elizabethan England." *MP* 28 (1930): 208-12.
Southern, A. C. "Richard Baines." *TLS,* 21 Oct. 1949, p. 681.
Stalker, A. *Shakespeare, Marlowe, and Nashe.* 1936.
Stern, Alfred. "Shakespeare und Marlowe." *Archiv* 156 (1929): 195-202.
Symons, Arthur. "A Note on the Genius of Marlowe." *English Review* 36 (1923): 306-16.
Tarnawski, Władysław. *Krysztof Marlowe.* 1922.
Thaler, Alwin. "Churchyard and Marlowe." *MLN* 38 (1923): 89-92.
Thurston, Gavin. "Christopher Marlowe's Death." *Contemporary Review* 205 (1964): 156-59, 193-200.
Urry, William. "Marlowe and Canterbury." *TLS,* 13 Feb. 1964, p. 136.
Vannovsky, Alexander A. *The Path of Jesus from Judaism to Christianity as Conceived by Shakespeare.* 1962. [Disclosure of a hidden Jewish plot in Shakespeare's *Hamlet.*]
Ward, Bernard M. "Alphonso Ferraboeco." *RES* 8 (1932): 201-2.
Wham, Benjamin. " 'Marlowe's Mighty Love': Was Marlowe Murdered at Twenty-Nine?" *American Bar Association Journal* 46 (1960): 509-13.
Williams, David Rhys. *Shakespeare Thy Name is Marlowe.* 1966.
Williams, F. B. "New Data on I. Frizer." *TLS,* 15 Aug. 1935, p. 513.
Wolff, Max J. "Die soziale Stellung der englischen Renaissancedramatiker." *Englische Studien* 71 (1936-37): 171-90.
Zanco, Aurelio. *Christopher Marlowe, saggio critico.* 1937.

General Studies of the Plays

Albright, Evelyn May. *Dramatic Publication in England, 1580–1640: A Study of Conditions Affecting Content and Form of Drama.* 1927.

Anichkov, E. V. "Christopher Marlowe." *Zapadnye Literatury i Slavyanstvo* 2 (1926): 88–94.

Archer, William. *The Old Drama and the New.* 1924.

Armstrong, W. A. "The Elizabethan Conception of the Tyrant." *RES* 22 (1946): 161–81.

———. "The Influence of Seneca and Machiavelli on the Elizabethan Tyrant." *RES* 24 (1948): 19–35.

Aronstein, Philipp. *Das englische Renaissancedrama.* 1929.

Artz, Frederick. *From the Renaissance to Romanticism: Trends in Style in Art, Literature, and Music, 1300–1830.* 1963.

Biesterfeldt, Peter Wilhelm. "Die Oberbühne bei Marlowe." *Archiv* 160 (1931): 51–60.

Boas, Frederick S. *An Introduction to Tudor Drama.* 1933.

———. *An Introduction to Stuart Drama.* 1946.

Bradbrook, M. C. *Themes and Conventions of Elizabethan Tragedy.* 1935.

———. *English Dramatic Form: A History of Its Development.* 1965.

Brawley, Benjamin G. *A Short History of the English Drama.* 1921.

Brie, Friedrich. "Deismus und Atheismus in der englische Renaissance." *Anglia,* 48 (1924): 54–98, 105–68.

Brooke, C. F. Tucker. *The Tudor Drama.* 1911.

Burchardt, Carl. "Christopher Marlowe." *Edda* 18 (1922): 120–33.

Cawley, Robert R. *The Voyagers and Elizabethan Drama.* 1938.

Chang, Joseph S. " 'Of Mighty Opposites': Stoicism and Machiavellianism." *RenD* 9 (1966): 37–57.

Clark, Eleanor G. *Elizabethan Fustian: A Study of the Social and Political Backgrounds of the Drama, with Particular Reference to Christopher Marlowe.* 1937.

———. *Raleigh and Marlowe: A Study in Elizabethan Fustian.* 1941.

Clarkson, P. S., and C. T. Warren. *The Law of Property in Shakespeare and the Elizabethan Drama.* 1942.

Cookman, A. V. "Shakespeare's Contemporaries on the Modern English Stage." *SJ* 94 (1958): 29–41.

Courthope, W. J. "Shakespeare's Early Tragedies: Influence of Marlowe." In *A History of English Poetry* 4 (1903): 54–69.

Craig, Hardin. *The Enchanted Glass.* 1935.

———. "Morality Plays and Elizabethan Drama." *SQ* 1 (1950): 64–72.

Craik, T. W. "The Tudor Interlude and Later Elizabethan Drama." In *Elizabethan Theatre,* SuAS, vol. 9 (1966), pp. 37–57.

Cruttwell, Patrick. *The Shakespearean Moment and its Place in the Poetry of the Seventeenth Century.* 1954.

Cunliffe, J. W. *The Influence of Seneca on Elizabethan Tragedy.* 1893.

Cunningham, John E. *Elizabethan and Early Stuart Drama.* 1965.

Dilthey, Wilhelm. *Die grosse Phantasiedichtung, und andere Studien zur vergleichenden Literature-geschichte.* 1954.

Doran, Madeleine. *Endeavors of Art: A Study of Form in Elizabethan Drama.* 1954.

Eckhardt, Eduard. *Das englische Drama im Zeitalter der Reformation und der Hochrenaissance.* 1928.

Einstein, Lewis David. *Tudor Ideals.* 1921.

Ergang, Robert. *The Renaissance.* 1968.

Farnham, Willard. "The Lost Innocence of Poetry." In *Essays in Criticism,* Univ. of California Publications in English, Series 1, vol. 1 (1929), pp. 25–47.

———. *The Medieval Heritage of Elizabethan Tragedy.* 1936.

Fenton, Doris. *The Extra-Dramatic Moment in Elizabethan Plays Before 1616.* 1930.

Gabler, Hans Walter. *Zur Function dramatischer und literatischer Parodie im elisabethanischen Drama: Beiträge zur Interpretation ausgewählter Dramen aus dem Werk Lylys Marlowes und Greenes und dem Frühwerk Shakespeares.* 1966.

Gassner, John. *Masters of the Drama.* 1940.

Gassner, John, and Ralph G. Allen, eds. *Theatre and Drama in the Making.* 1964.

Gerrard, Ernest A. *Elizabethan Drama and Dramatists, 1583–1603.* 1928.

Gillespie, Gerald. "The Rebel in Seventeenth-Century Tragedy." *CL* 18 (1966): 324–36.

Greaves, Margaret. *The Blazon of Honor: Studies in Medieval and Renaissance Magnanimity.* 1964.

Gregor, J. *Shakespeare.* 1935.

Grosse, F. *Das englische Renaissancedrama im Spiegel zeitgenössischer Staatstheorien.* 1935.

Harbage, Alfred. *Shakespeare and the Rival Traditions.* 1952.

———. "Intrigue in Elizabethan Tragedy." In *Essays on Shakespeare and Elizabethan Drama in Honor of Hardin Craig,* ed. Richard Hosley (1962), pp. 37–44.

Hart, Alfred. "Vocabularies of Shakespeare's Plays." *RES* 19 (1943): 128–40.

Heninger, S. K., Jr. *A Handbook on Renaissance Meteorology.* 1960.

Hillier, Richard I. "The Imagery of Color, Light, and Darkness in the Poetry of Christopher Marlowe." In *Elizabethan Studies and Other Essays in Honor of George F. Reynolds,* Univ. of Colorado Studies, Ser. B, Studies in the Humanities, vol. 2, no. 4 (1945), pp. 101–25.

Holzknecht, Karl J. *Outlines of Tudor and Stuart Plays, 1497–1642.* 1947. [*Tamburlaine, Doctor Faustus, Jew of Malta, Edward II.*]

Hosking, G. L. *The Life and Times of Edward Alleyn.* 1952.

Hotson, J. Leslie. *The Commonwealth and Restoration Stage.* 1928.

Howarth, R. G. *Literature of the Theatre: Marlowe to Shirley.* 1952.

Jewkes, Wilfred T. *Act Division in Elizabethan and Jacobean Plays, 1583–1616.* 1958.

Kitagawa, Teiji. *A Study of Christopher Marlowe.* 1964.

Klein, David. *The Elizabethan Dramatists as Critics.* 1963.

Knight, G. Wilson. *The Golden Labyrinth: A Study of the British Drama.* 1962.

Koskenniemi, Inna. *Studies in the Vocabulary of English Drama, 1550–1600, Excluding Shakespeare and Ben Jonson.* 1962.

Lambin, Georges. "Destin de Christopher Marlowe." *CS* 10 (1933): 166–69; rpt. in *Le Théâtre Élizabéthain* (1940), pp. 214–19.

——. "Marlowe et la France." *EA* 19 (1966): 55–59.

Lawrence, William J. *Pre-Restoration Stage Studies.* 1927.

Leech, Clifford. "Shakespeare, Elizabethan and Jacobean." *QQ* 72 (1965): 5–25.

——. "The Dramatists' Independence." *RORD* 10 (1967): 17–23.

Lewis, C. S. *The Discarded Image: An Introduction to Medieval and Renaissance Literature.* 1964.

Lievsay, John L. "Continental Antecedents of Elizabethan Drama." *TSL* 7 (1962): 87–97.

Lindabury, R. V. *A Study of Patriotism in the Elizabethan Drama.* 1931.

Lucas, F. L. *Seneca and Elizabethan Tragedy.* 1922.

McCann, Franklin T. *English Discovery of America to 1585.* 1952.

Macdonald, J. F. "The Use of Prose in English Drama before Shakespeare." *UTQ* 2 (1934): 465–81.

Margeson, J. M. R. *The Origins of English Tragedy.* 1967.

Maxwell, J. C. "The Plays of Christopher Marlowe." In *The Age of Shakespeare* (vol. 2 of *The Pelican Guide to English Literature,* ed. Boris Ford), (1956), pp. 162–78.

Mehl, Dieter. *The Elizabethan Dumb Show: The History of a Dramatic Convention.* 1966; German ed. 1964.

Mincoff, Marco K. *Christopher Marlowe: A Study of His Development.* 1937.

Nicoll, Allardyce. *An Introduction to Dramatic Theory.* 1923.

——. *British Drama: An Historical Survey from the Beginnings to the Present Time.* 1925; rev. ed. 1963.

Oppel, Horst. *"Titus Andronicus": Studien zur dramengeschichtlichen Stellung von Shakespeares früher Tragödie.* 1961.

Oras, Ants. "Lyrical Instrumentation in Marlowe: A Step toward Shakespeare." In *Studies in Shakespeare,* ed. Arthur D. Matthews and Clark M. Emery (1953), pp. 74–87.

——. *Pause Patterns in Elizabethan and Jacobean Drama: An Experiment in Prosody.* 1960.

Ornstein, Robert. *The Moral Vision of Jacobean Tragedy.* 1960.

Paletta, Gerhard. *Fürstengeschick und innerstaatlicher Machtkampf im englischen Renaissance-Drama.* 1934.

Palmer, D. J. "Elizabethan Tragic Heroes." In *Elizabethan Theatre,* SuAS, vol. 9 (1966), pp. 11–35.

Parkes, H. B. "Nature's Diverse Laws: The Double Vision of the Elizabethans." *SR* 58 (1950): 402–18.

Parrott, Thomas Marc, and Robert Hamilton Ball. *A Short View of Elizabethan Drama.* 1943.

Partridge, A. C. *Orthography in Shakespeare and Elizabethan Drama: A Study of Colloquial Contractions, Elision, Prosody, and Punctuation.* 1964.

Phelps, W. L. *Essays on Books.* 1922.

Poirier, Michel. "Le 'Double Temps' dans *Othello.*" *EA* 5 (1952): 107–16.

Powell, Arnold F. *The Melting Mood: A Study of the Function of Pathos of English Tragedy through Shakespeare.* 1949.

Powys, Llewelyn. "Christopher Marlowe." *Freeman* 6 (1923): 584–85.

Praz, Mario. "Christopher Marlowe." *ES* 13 (1931): 211–23.

Ransom, Harry. "Some Legal Elements in Elizabethan Plays." *Studies in English* (Univ. of Texas), 16 (1938): 53–76.

Rebora, Piero. *L'Italia nel dramma inglese (1558–1642).* 1925.

Reed, Robert R., Jr. *The Occult on the Tudor Stage.* 1966.

Rees, Ennis. "Chapman's *Blind Beggar* and the Marlovian Hero." *JEGP* 57 (1958): 60–63.

Ribner, Irving. "Marlowe and Machiavelli." *CL* 6 (1954): 348–56.

———. "The Tudor History Play: An Essay in Definition." *PMLA* 69 (1954): 591–609.

———. *Jacobean Tragedy: The Quest for Moral Order.* 1962.

Rossiter, A. P. *English Drama from Early Times to the Elizabethans: Its Background, Origins, and Developments.* 1950.

Saleski, R. E. "Supernatural Agents in Christian Imagery: Word Studies in Elizabethan Dramatists." *JEGP* 38 (1939): 431–39.

Sanders, Wilbur. *The Dramatist and the Received Idea: Studies in the Plays of Marlowe and Shakespeare.* 1968.

Sarbu, Aladár. "A moralitáshagyomóny Marlowe, Shakespeare és Ben Jonson müveiben" [The tradition of moralities in Marlowe's, Shakespeare's, and Ben Jonson's works]. In *Shakespearetanulmányok* (1964), pp. 229–46.

Schelling, Felix E. *Foreign Influences in Elizabethan Plays.* 1923.

———. *Elizabethan Playwrights: A Short History of the English Drama from Medieval Times to the Closing of the Theaters in 1642.* 1925.

Schücking, Levin Ludwig. "The Baroque Character of the Elizabethan Tragic Hero." *PBA* 24 (1938): 85–111.

Seaton, Ethel. "Fresh Sources for Marlowe." *RES* 5 (1929): 385–401.

Sheavyn, Phoebe. *The Literary Profession in the Elizabethan Age.* 1964.

Sibly, John. "The Duty of Revenge in Tudor-Stuart Drama." *REL* 8 (1967): 46–54.

Sims, James H. *Dramatic Uses of Biblical Allusions in Marlowe and Shakespeare.* 1966.

Smet, Robert de [Romain Sanvic]. *Le théâtre élizabéthain.* 1955.

Spens, Janet. *Elizabethan Drama.* 1922.

Stanley, Emily B. "The Use of Classical Mythology by the University Wits." *RenP*, 1956, pp. 25–33.

Střibrný, Zdeněk. "Christopher Marlowe (1564–1593)." *Casopis pro Moderni Filoloqii a Literatura* 43 (1961): 1–23 (English summary, pp. 24–25).

Stroup, Thomas B. "The Testing Pattern in Elizabethan Tragedy." *SEL* 3 (1963): 175–90.

———. *Microcosmos: The Shape of the Elizabethan Play.* 1965.

Stuart, Donald C. *The Development of Dramatic Art.* 1928.

Sykes, H. Dugdale. *Sidelights on Elizabethan Drama.* 1924.

Symonds, A. E. *Shakespeare's Predecessors in the English Drama.* 1924.

Talbert, Ernest W. *Elizabethan Drama and Shakespeare's Early Plays: An Essay in Historical Criticism.* 1963.

Taylor, George Coffin. "Marlowe's 'Now.'" In *Elizabethan Studies and Other Essays in Honor of George F. Reynolds,* Univ. of Colorado Studies, Ser. B, Studies in the Humanities, vol. 2, no. 4 (1945), pp. 93–100.

Thompson, E. *Sir Walter Raleigh.* 1936.
Thorp, Willard. *The Triumph of Realism in Elizabethan Drama (1558-1612).* 1928.
Tilley, Morris Palmer, and J. K. Ray. "Proverbs and Proverbial Allusions in Christopher Marlowe." *MLN* 50 (1935): 347-55.
Tomlinson, Thomas B. *A Study of Elizabethan and Jacobean Tragedy.* 1964.
Turner, Robert Y. "Pathos and the *Gorboduc* Tradition, 1560-1590." *HLQ* 25 (1962): 97-120.
———. "Shakespeare and the Public Confrontation Scene in Early History Plays." *MP* 62 (1964): 1-12.
Wallis, N. Hardy. *The Ethics of Criticism and Other Essays.* 1924.
Wells, Henry W. *Elizabethan and Jacobean Playwrights.* 1939.
———. "Senecan Influence on Elizabethan Tragedy: A Re-Estimation." *SAB* 19 (1944): 71-84.
Wickham, Glynne. " 'Exuent to the Cave': Notes on the Staging of Marlowe's Plays." *TDR* 8, no. 4 (1964): 184-94.
Williams, Charles. *The English Poetic Mind.* 1932.
Wilson, F. P. *Elizabethan and Jacobean.* 1945.
Withington, Robert. *Excursions in English Drama.* 1937.
Wynne, Arnold. *The Growth of English Drama.* 1914.

Studies of the Poetry

Anders, H. "*Hero and Leander* und Anacreon." *SJ* 62 (1926): 161.
Andersen, J. C. *The Laws of Verse.* 1928.
Baldwin, T. W. "Marlowe's Musaeus." *JEGP* 54 (1955): 478-85.
Bradbrook, M. C. "*Hero and Leander.*" *Scrutiny* 2 (1933): 59-64.
Bush, Douglas. "The Influence of *Hero and Leander* on Early Mythological Poems." *MLN* 42 (1927): 211-17.
———. "Notes on *Hero and Leander.*" *PMLA* 64 (1929): 760-64.
———. "*Hero and Leander* and *Romeo and Juliet.*" *PQ* 9 (1930): 396-99.
———. *English Literature in the Earlier Seventeenth Century.* 1945; 2nd ed. 1962.
Buxton, John. *Elizabethan Taste.* 1963.
"Christopher Marlowe's Mighty Line." *WSt,* April 1932, p. 1.
Dent, Robert W. "Ovid, Marlowe, and *The Insatiate Countess.*" *N&Q* 10 (1963): 324-25.
Eden, John M. "Hero and Belinda." *N&Q* 4 (1957): 12-13.
Forsythe, Robert S. "The Passionate Shepherd and English Poetry." *PMLA* 40 (1925): 692-742.
Greg, W. W. "The Copyright of *Hero and Leander.*" *Library* 24 (1944): 165-74.
Holmes, Elizabeth. *Aspects of Elizabethan Imagery.* 1929.
Kocher, Paul H. "A Marlowe Sonnet." *PQ* 24 (1945): 39-45.
McNeal, Thomas H. "The Names 'Hero' and 'Don John' in *Much Ado.*" *N&Q* 198 (1953): 382.
Marsh, T. N. "Marlowe's *Hero and Leander,* I, 45-50." *Expl* 21 (1962): item 30.
Maxwell, J. C. "*Hero and Leander* and *Love's Labour's Lost.*" *N&Q* 197 (1952): 334-35.
Miles, Josephine. *Renaissance, Eighteenth-Century, and Modern Language in English Poetry: A Tabular View.* 1960.

Miller, Paul W. "A Function of Myth in Marlowe's *Hero and Leander*." *SP* 50 (1953): 158-67.

——. "The Problem of Justice in Marlowe's *Hero and Leander*." *N&Q* 4 (1957): 163-64.

Nosworthy, J. M. "The Publication of Marlowe's *Elegies* and Davies's *Epigrams*." *RES* 4 (1953): 260-61.

——. "Marlowe's *Ovid* and Davies's *Epigrams*—A Postscript." *RES* 15 (1964): 397-98.

O'Brien, Gordon Worth. *Renaissance Poetics and the Problem of Power*. Institute of Elizabethan Studies [Chicago], no. 2 (1956).

Robertson, J. M. "The Evolution of English Blank Verse." *Criterion* 2 (1924): 171-87.

Rollins, Hyder E., ed. *England's Helicon, 1600-1614.* 2 vols. 1935.

Schaus, Hermann. "The Relationship of *Comus* to *Hero and Leander* and *Venus and Adonis*." *Studies in English* (Univ. of Texas), 25 (1945-46): 129-41.

Segal, Erich. "Hero and Leander: Góngora and Marlowe." *CL* 15 (1963): 338-56.

Shannon, G. P. "Against Marot as a Source of Marlowe's *Hero and Leander*." *MLQ* 9 (1948): 387-88.

Smart, George K. "English Non-Dramatic Blank Verse in the Sixteenth Century." *Anglia* 69 (1937): 370-97.

Smith, E. *The Principles of English Metre.* 1923.

Smith, Hallet. *Elizabethan Poetry: A Study in Conventions, Meaning and Expression.* 1952.

Staton, Walter F., Jr. "The Influence of Thomas Watson on Elizabethan Ovidian Poetry." *SRen* 6 (1959): 243-50.

Stevenson, D. L. *The Love-Game Comedy.* 1946.

Strachey, J. St. L. "*Hero and Leander*." *Spectator*, 4 Oct. 1924, pp. 471-72.

Tannenbaum, Samuel A. "An Unfamiliar Version of 'The Passionate Shepherd to His Love.' " *PMLA* 45 (1930): 814-16.

Ting, N. T. "The Historical Sources of Patrick Hannay's *Sheretine and Mariana*." *JEGP* 43 (1944): 242-47.

Williams, Martin T. "The Temptations in Marlowe's *Hero and Leander*." *MLQ* 16 (1955): 226-31.

Young, G. *An English Prosody on Inductive Lines.* 1928.

Zocca, Louis R. *Elizabethan Narrative Poetry.* 1950.

B. INDIVIDUAL PLAYS

Doctor Faustus

Adolf-Altenberg, G. *La storica figura del Doctor Faust ed il motivo faustiano nella literatura europea.* 1960.

Bachrach, A. G. H. *De warachtighe Historie van Doctor Faustus.* 1960.

Baker, Donald C. "Ovid and Faustus: The *Noctis Equi*." *CJ* 55 (1959): 126-28.

Beall, Charles N. "Definition of Theme by Unconsecutive Event: Structure as Induction in Marlowe's *Doctor Faustus*." *RenP*, 1962, pp. 53-61.

Bøgholm, N. "Marlowe og *Doctor Faustus*." *Tilskueren* 53 (1936): 427-34.

Bradbrook, Frank W. "Marlowe and Keats." *N&Q* 5 (1958): 97-98.

Briggs, K. M. *Pale Hecate's Team: An Examination of the Beliefs in Witchcraft and Magic among Shakespeare's Contemporaries and His Immediate Successors.* 1962.

Briggs, William D. "Marlowe's *Faustus*, 305-18, 548-70." *MLN* 38 (1923): 385-93.

Brooke, C. F. Tucker. "Notes on *Doctor Faustus.*" *PQ* 12 (1933): 17-23.

Brown, Beatrice D. "Christopher Marlowe, Faustus, and Simon Magus." *PMLA* 54 (1939): 82-121.

Brown, P. W. F. "Saint Clement and Doctor Foster." *N&Q* 1 (1954): 140-41.

Butler, E. M. *The Fortunes of Faust.* 1952.

Butrym, Alexander. "A Marlowe Echo in Kyd." *N&Q* 5 (1958): 96-97.

Cain, H. E. "Marlowe's 'French Crowns.'" *MLN* 49 (1934): 380-84.

Cameron, Kenneth W. "Transcendental Hell in Emerson and Marlowe." *ESQ* 6 (1957): 9-10.

Carpenter, Nan C. "Music in *Doctor Faustus:* Two Notes." *N&Q* 195 (1950): 180-81.

——. " 'Miles' versus 'Clericus' in Marlowe's *Faustus.*" *N&Q* 197 (1952): 91-93.

Castle, E. "Das angeblich älteste Lateinische Faust-Drama: eine Mystifikation." *Theater u. Welt* 1 (1937): 51-56.

Cellini, Benvenuto. "Echi di Greene nel *Doctor Faustus* di Marlowe." *RLMC* 3 (1952): 124-29.

Christ, Henry I. "*Macbeth* and the Faust Legend." *EJ* 46 (1957): 212-13.

Chudoba, F. "Goetha a Marlowe." *Goetheiv Sboruik*, 1932, pp. 364-70.

Danchin, F. C. "Du nouveau sur Shakespeare." *RAA* 9 (1932): 224-32.

Dédéyan, Charles. *La thème de Faust dans la littérature européenne.* 1954.

Deyermond, A. D. "Skelton and the Epilogue to Marlowe's *Doctor Faustus.*" *N&Q* 10 (1963): 410-11.

Ellis-Fermor, Una. "*The Devil to Pay* and the Faust Legend." *English* 3 (1939): 383-86.

Elton, William. " 'Shore's Wife' and *Doctor Faustus.*" *N&Q* 195 (1950): 526.

Evans, M. Blakemore. "A Note on *Faust and Faustus.*" *JEGP* 32 (1933): 81-82.

Fabian, Bernhard. "Marlowe's *Doctor Faustus.*" *N&Q* 3 (1956): 56-57.

——. "A Note on Marlowe's *Faustus.*" *ES* 41 (1960): 365-69.

Frey, Leonard H. "Antithetical Balance in the Opening and Close of *Doctor Faustus.*" *MLQ* 24 (1963): 350-53.

Fukuda, Tsutomu. " 'Was This the Face?' " *N&Q* 4 (1957): 407.

Gilbert, Allan H. " 'A Thousand Ships.' " *MLN* 66 (1951): 477-78.

Goldman, Arnold. " 'The Fruitful Plot of Scholarism Graced.' " *N&Q* 11 (1964): 264.

Green, Clarence. "*Doctor Faustus:* The Tragedy of Individualism." *Science and Society* 10 (1946): 275-83.

Grigson, Geoffrey. " 'The Topless Towres.' " *TLS*, 23 Apr. 1964, p. 343.

Grotowski, Jerzy. "*Doctor Faustus* in Poland." *TDR* 8, no. 4 (1964): 120-33.

Hankins, John E. "Biblical Echoes in the Final Scene of *Doctor Faustus.*" In *Studies in English in Honor of Raphael Dorman O'Leary and Selden Lincoln Whitcomb.* Univ. of Kansas Publications, Humanistic Studies, vol. 6, no. 4 (1940), pp. 3-7.

Hart, Jeffrey P. "Prospero and Faustus." *BUSE* 2 (1956): 197–206.
Hecksher, W. S. "The Source of 'Was This the Face?' " *JWCI* 1 (1938): 295–97.
Heller, Erich. "Faust's Damnation: The Morality of Knowledge." *Listener*, 11 Jan. 1962, pp. 60–62.
Heller, Otto. *"Faust" and "Faustus": A Study of Goethe's Relation to Marlowe.* 1931.
Homan, Sidney R., Jr. *"Doctor Faustus,* Dekker's *Old Fortunatus,* and the Morality Plays." *MLQ* 26 (1965): 497–505.
Hooft, Bart Hendrik van't. *Das holländische Volksbuch vom Doktor Faust.* 1926.
Horrell, Joseph. "Peter Fabell and *Doctor Faustus." N&Q* 183 (1942): 35–36.
Hussey, Maurice. "Marlowe's Quotations." *N&Q* 193 (1948): 538–39.
Jarrett, H. S. "Verbal Ambiguities in Marlowe's *Faustus." CE* 5 (1944): 339–40.
Jump, John D. "Spenser and Marlowe." *N&Q* 11 (1964): 261–62.
Kaula, David. "Time and the Timeless in *Everyman* and *Doctor Faustus." CE* 22 (1960): 9–14.
Kirschbaum, Leo. "Mephistophilis and the Lost 'Dragon.' " *RES* 18 (1942): 312–15; 21 (1945): 233–35.
Kleinstück, J. *Untersuchungen zu Marlowes "Faust."* 1947.
Kline, Peter. "The Spiritual Center in Eliot's Plays." *KR* 21 (1959): 457–72.
Kocher, Paul H. "The Witchcraft Basis in Marlowe's *Faustus." MP* 38 (1940): 9–36.
Langston, Beach. "Marlowe's *Faustus* and the *Ars Moriendi* Tradition." In *A Tribute to George Coffin Taylor,* ed. Arnold Williams (1952), pp. 148–67.
Leendertz, P. "Het voelksboek van Faust." *Boek* 17 (1928): 265–72.
McCloskey, J. C. "The Theme of Despair in Marlowe's *Faustus." CE* 4 (1942): 110–13.
Martin, Betty C. " 'Shore's Wife' as Source of the Epilogue to *Doctor Faustus." N&Q* 195 (1950): 182.
Maxwell, J. C. "Two Notes on Marlowe's *Faustus." N&Q* 194 (1949): 334–35.
———. "Notes on *Doctor Faustus." N&Q* 11 (1964): 261–62.
Mayer, H. "Faust, Aufklärung, Sturm und Drang." *SOF* 13 (1944): 101–20.
Means, Michael H. "Literary Genres and Literary Meaning." *UDR* 2 (1965): 37–47.
Meek, Harold G. *Johann Faust: The Man and the Myth.* 1930.
Moulton, R. G. *World Literature.* 1930.
Neubert, F. *Vom "Doctor Faustus" zu Goethes "Faust."* 1932.
Nosworthy, J. M. "Coleridge on a Distant Prospect of Faust." *E&S* 11 (1957): 69–96.
Ostrowski, Witold. "The Interplay of the Subjective and the Objective in Marlowe's *Doctor Faustus."* In *Studies in Language and Literature in Honour of Margaret Schlauch,* ed. M. Brahmer, S. Helsztyński, and J. Krźyzanowski (1966), pp. 293–305.
Palmer, D. J. "Magic and Poetry in *Doctor Faustus." CritQ* 6 (1964): 56–67.
Palmer, P. M., and R. P. More. *The Sources of the Faust Tradition.* 1936.
Patrides, C. A. "Renaissance and Modern Views on Hell." *HTR* 57 (1964): 217–36.
Pearce, T. M. "Jasper Heywood and Marlowe's *Doctor Faustus." N&Q* 197 (1952): 200–201.
Perkinson, R. H. "A Restoration 'Improvement' of *Doctor Faustus." ELH* 1 (1934): 305–24.

Politzer, Heinz. "Of Time and *Doctor Faustus.*" *Monatshefte* 51 (1959): 145-55.
Praz, Mario. "Il dottor Faust' Marlowe e Goethe." *Cultura,* Apr.-June 1932, pp. 238-47.
——. "On *Faustus* and *Faust.*" *ES* 14 (1932): 84-88.
Ransom, Mariann, Roderick Cook, and T. M. Pearce. "German Valdes and Cornelius in Marlowe's *Doctor Faustus.*" *N&Q* 9 (1962): 329-31.
Reed, Robert R., Jr. "Nick Bottom, *Doctor Faustus,* and the Ass's Head." *N&Q* 6 (1959): 252-54.
Rosenberg, W. L. "Marlowe's *Faustus* and Goethe's *Faust.*" *Die Neue Zeit* 7 (1925): 10-11.
Sams, Henry W. "*Faustus* and the Reformation." *Bulletin of the Citadel* 5 (1941): 3-9.
Sanders, Wilbur. "Marlowe's *Doctor Faustus.*" In *Shakespeare's Contemporaries,* ed. Max Bluestone and Norman Rabkin, 2nd ed. (1970), pp. 112-27. (Adapted from *Melbourne Critical Review* 7 [1964]: 78-91, and from *The Dramatist and the Received Idea . . .* [1968].)
Sayers, Dorothy L. "The Faust Legend and the Idea of the Devil." *Publications of the English Goethe Society* 15 (1946): 1-20.
Schelling, Felix E. *Shakespeare Biography and Other Papers Chiefly Elizabethan.* 1937.
Schirmer-Imhoff, Ruth. "Faust in England: Ein Bericht." *Anglia* 70 (1951): 150-85.
Searle, J. "Marlowe and Chrysostom." *TLS,* 15 Feb. 1936, p. 139.
Seiferth, Howard. "The Concept of the Devil and the Myth of the Pact in Literature Prior to Goethe." *Monatshefte* 44 (1952): 271-89.
Sharpe, Robert Boies. *Irony in Drama: An Essay on Impersonation, Shock, and Catharsis.* 1959.
Smith, James. "Marlowe's *Doctor Faustus.*" *Scrutiny* 8 (1939): 36-55.
Steadman, John M. "Faustus and Averroes." *N&Q* 3 (1956): 416.
——. "Averroes and *Doctor Faustus:* Some Additional Parallels." *N&Q* 9 (1962): 327-29.
Steiner, A. "The Faust Legend and the Christian Tradition." *PMLA* 54 (1939): 391-404.
Tachibana, Tadae. "Goethe's Helena and Marlowe's Helen." *Eigo-Kinkyn,* Aug. 1949.
Tapper, Bonno. "Aristotle's 'Sweet Analutikes' in *Doctor Faustus.*" *SP* 27 (1930): 215-19.
Theens, K. *Doktor Johann Faust. Geschichte der Faustgestalt vom 16. Jahrhundert bis zur Gegenwart.* 1948.
Tilley, Morris Palmer. "Two Notes on *Doctor Faustus.*" *MLN* 53 (1938): 199-220.
Ueda, Tamotsu. "Goethe und die englischen Literatur." *Hiyoshi Ronbundshu* 7 (1961): 1-8.
Versfeld, Martin. "Some Remarks on Marlowe's *Faustus.*" *ESA* 1 (1958): 134-43.
Walton, Charles E. "Una M. Ellis-Fermor to W. W. Greg on *The Damnation of Faustus:* An Unpublished Letter." *ESRS* 15 (1966): 5-7.
Walz, John A. "Notes on the Puppet Play of *Doctor Faustus.*" *PQ* 7 (1928): 224-30.

———. "Some New Faustsplitter." *JEGP* 43 (1944): 153–62.

Witte, W. *"Doctor Faustus." AUR* 33 (1950): 113–17.

Wolthuis, G. W. "The Rector in Marlowe's *Doctor Faustus." Neophil* 25 (1939): 49–50.

———. "Marlowe, *Doctor Faustus,* II.ii.172." *ES* 30 (1949): 14–15.

I Tamburlaine

Allen, Don Cameron. "Notes on *Tamburlaine." TLS,* 24 Sept. 1931, p. 730.

———. "Renaissance Remedies for Fortune: Marlowe and the Fortunati." *SP* 38 (1941): 188–97.

Anderson, Ruth L. "Kingship in Renaissance Drama." *SP* 41 (1944): 136–55.

Armstrong, William A. "Ben Jonson and Jacobean Stagecraft." In *Jacobean Theatre* SuAS, vol. 1 (1960), pp. 43–61.

———. *Marlowe's "Tamburlaine": The Image and the Stage.* 1966.

Battenhouse, Roy W. "Tamburlaine, the 'Scourge of God.' " *PMLA* 56 (1941): 377–98.

Blanchart, Paul. "Le théatre contemporain et les Élisabéthains." *EA* 13 (1960): 145–58.

Blau, Herbert. "Language and Structure in Poetic Drama." *MLQ* 18 (1957): 27–34.

Boas, Guy. *"Tamburlaine* and the Horrific." *English* 13 (1951): 275–77.

Brooks, Charles. *"Tamburlaine* and Attitudes Toward Women." *ELH* 24 (1957): 1–11.

Camden, Carroll, Jr. "Tamburlaine, the Choleric Man." *MLN* 44 (1929): 430–35.

Chambers, E. K. "The Date of Marlowe's *Tamburlaine." TLS,* 28 Aug. 1930, p. 684.

Chew, Samuel C. *The Crescent and the Rose: Islam and England during the Renaissance.* 1937.

Clurman, Harold. "Christopher Marlowe." In *Lies Like Truth: Theatre Reviews and Essays* (1958), pp. 146–48.

Cormican, L. A. "(I) Medieval Idiom in Shakespeare, and (II) Shakespeare and the Medieval Ethic." *Scrutiny* 17 (1957): 298–317.

Cunningham, J. V. *Woe or Wonder: The Emotional Effect of Shakespearean Tragedy.* 1951.

Cutts, John. "The Ultimate Source of Tamburlaine's White, Red, Black, and Death?" *N&Q* 5 (1958): 146–47.

———. "Tamburlaine 'As Fierce Achilles Was.' " *CompD* 1 (1967): 105–9.

Dick, Hugh G. *"Tamburlaine* Sources Once More." *SP* 46 (1949): 154–66.

Ellis-Fermor, Una M. *"Tamburlaine the Great." TLS,* 8 June 1933, p. 396.

Feasey, Lynette and Eveline. "Marlowe and the Homilies." *N&Q* 195 (1950): 7–10.

———. "Marlowe and the Commination Service." *N&Q* 195 (1950): 156–60.

———. "Marlowe and the Prophetic Dooms." *N&Q* 195 (1950): 356–59, 404–7, 419–21.

———. "Marlowe and the Christian Humanists." *N&Q* 196 (1951): 266–68.

Flynn, J. G. "The 'Senseless Line' Problem in *I Tamb.* III, iii, 156–158." *TLS,* 18 July 1935, p. 464.

Guthrie, Tyrone. *"Tamburlaine,* and What It Takes." *Theatre Arts* 40 (1956): 21–23, 84–86.

Hookham, Hilda. "Tamburlaine the Great Emir." *History Today* 9 (1959): 151–59.

——. *Tamburlaine the Conqueror.* 1962.

Izard, T. C. "The Principal Source for Marlowe's *Tamburlaine.*" *MLN* 58 (1943): 411–17.

Jacquot, Jean. "La pensée de Marlowe dans *Tamburlaine the Great.*" *EA* 6 (1953): 322–45.

Johnson, Francis R. "Marlowe's 'Imperiall Heaven.' " *ELH* 12 (1945): 35–44.

Kernodle, George. "The Open Stage: Elizabethan or Existentialist?" *ShS* 12 (1959): 1–14.

Langvad, Vibeke. "Stilen i Marlowes *Tamburlaine.*" *Edda* 42 (1942): 122–40.

Liu, J. Y. "The Name of the Arabian King in Marlowe's *Tamburlaine.*" *N&Q* 195 (1950): 10.

——. "The Interpretation of Three Lines in Marlowe's *Tamburlaine*, Part I." *N&Q* 195 (1950): 137–38.

——. "A Marlo-Shakespearean Image Cluster." *N&Q* 196 (1951): 336–37.

McGee, Arthur R. "Macbeth and the Furies." *ShS* 19 (1966): 55–67.

Maxwell, J. C. "Whetstone and Marlowe." *MLN* 63 (1948): 436.

——. "*Tamburlaine, Part I*, IV. iv. 77–79." *N&Q* 197 (1952): 444.

Mezzadri, Piero. "Nota su *Tamburlaine.*" *Letterature Moderne* 6 (1956): 611–21.

Mills, Laurens J. "*Tamburlaine* (I, ii, 242–243)." *MLN* 52 (1937): 101–3.

Morris, Helen. *Elizabethan Literature.* 1952.

Muir, Kenneth. "*Locrine* and *Selimus.*" *TLS*, 12 Aug. 1944, p. 391.

Muller, Herbert Joseph. *The Spirit of Tragedy.* 1956.

Nosworthy, J. M. "The Shakespearean Heroic Vaunt." *RES* 2 (1951): 259–61.

O'Connor, John J. "Another Human Footstool." *N&Q* 2 (1955): 332.

Pearce, T. M. "Marlowe and Castiglione." *MLQ* 12 (1951): 3–12.

Prior, Moody E. "Imagery as a Test for Authorship." *SQ* 6 (1955): 381–86.

Quinn, Michael. "The Freedom of *Tamburlaine.*" *MLQ* 21 (1960): 315–20.

Ribner, Irving. "The Idea of History in Marlowe's *Tamburlaine.*" *ELH* 20 (1953): 251–66.

Schuster, Erika, and Horst Oppel. "Die Bankett-Szene in Marlowes *Tamburlaine.*" *Anglia* 77 (1959): 310–45.

Scudder, H. H. "An Allusion in *Tamburlaine* (1 *Tam*, IV, iv, 77–84)." *TLS*, 2 March 1933, p. 147.

Seaton, Ethel. "Marlowe's Map." *E&S* 10 (1924): 13–35. Rpt. in *Marlowe: A Collection of Critical Essays*, ed. Clifford Leech (1964), pp. 36–56.

Sherbo, Arthur. "Fletcher 'In Flagrante Delicto.' " *N&Q* 194 (1949): 92–93.

Smith, Hallett. "*Tamburlaine* and the Renaissance." In *Elizabethan Studies and Other Essays in Honor of George F. Reynolds*, Univ. of Colorado Studies, Ser. B, Studies in the Humanities, vol. 2, no. 4 (1945), pp. 126–31.

Sternlicht, Sanford. "*Tamburlaine* and the Iterative Sun-Image." *English Record* 16 (1966): 23–29.

——. "The Iterative Sun-Image in Marlowe's Plays: Part II." *English Record* 17 (1967): 28–35.

Taylor, Robert T. "Maximinus and *Tamburlaine.*" *N&Q* 4 (1957): 417–18.

Thomson, J. Oliver. "Marlowe's 'River Araris.' " *MLR* 48 (1953): 323–24.

Thorp, Willard. "The Ethical Problem in Marlowe's *Tamburlaine.*" *JEGP* 29 (1930): 385–89.

Tomlinson, W. E. *Der Herodes-Charakter im englische Drama.* 1934.

van Dam, B. A. P. "Marlowe's *Tamburlaine.*" *ES* 16 (1934): 1-17, 49-58.

Waith, Eugene M. "Marlowe and the Jades of Asia." *SEL* 5 (1965): 229-45. Rpt. in *Shakespeare's Contemporaries,* ed. Max Bluestone and Norman Rabkin (2nd ed., 1970), pp. 75-90.

Wekling, Mary Mellen. "Marlowe's Mnemonic Nominology, with Especial Reference to *Tamburlaine.*" *MLN* 73 (1958): 243-47.

Wild, Friedrich. "Studien zu Marlowes *Tamburlaine.*" In *Studies in English Language and Literature Presented to Professor Dr. Karl Brunner on the Occasion of His Seventieth Birthday,* ed. Siegfried Korninger (1958), pp. 232-51.

Wyler, Siegfried. *Der Begriff der Macht in Christopher Marlowes "Tamburlaine I."* 1965.

II Tamburlaine

Armstrong, William A. "The Enigmatic Elizabethan Stage." *English* 13 (1961): 216-20.

Gilbert, Allan. "*Tamburlaine's* 'Pampered Jades.' " *RLMC* 4 (1953): 208-10.

Kocher, Paul H. "Marlowe's Art of War." *SP* 39 (1942): 207-25.

McCullen, Joseph T., Jr. "The Use of Parlor and Tavern Games in Elizabethan and Early Stuart Drama." *MLQ* 14 (1953): 7-14.

Maxwell, J. C. " 'Crasis' [*II Tamburlaine* V.iii.91-92] ." *TLS,* 4 Jan. 1947, p. 9.

Nathanson, Leonard. "*Tamburlaine's* 'Pampered Jades' and Gascoigne." *N&Q* 5 (1958): 53-54.

Neville, E. H. "*Tamburlaine.*" *TLS,* 12 July 1947, p. 351.

Pearce, T. M. "Tamburlaine's 'Discipline to His Three Sonnes': An Interpretation of *Tamburlaine, Part II.*" *MLQ* 15 (1954): 18-27.

Simpson, Percy. "Pampered Jades [*Tamburlaine,* Act IV, iv] ." *TLS,* 22 Sept. 1945, p. 451.

The Jew of Malta

Babb, Howard S. "Policy in Marlowe's *The Jew of Malta.*" *ELH* 24 (1957): 85-94.

Black, Matthew. "Enter Citizens." In *Studies in the English Renaissance Drama,* ed. Josephine W. Bennett, Oscar Cargill, and Vernon Hall, Jr. (1960), pp. 16-27.

Bowers, Fredson T. "The Audience and the Poisoner of Elizabethan Tragedy." *JEGP* 36 (1937): 491-504.

Cardozo, J. L. *The Contemporary Jew in the Elizabethan Drama.* 1925.

Carpenter, Nan C. "Infinite Riches: A Note on Marlovian Unity." *N&Q* 196 (1951): 50-52.

Clark, A. M. *Thomas Heywood.* 1931.

Cole, Douglas. "The Comic Accomplice in Elizabethan Revenge Tragedy." *RenD* 9 (1966): 125-39.

Coleman, Edward D. *The Jew in English Drama.* 1943.

Dameron, J. Lasley. "Marlowe's 'Ship of War.' " *AN&Q* 2 (1963): 19-20.

D'Andrea, Antonio. "Studies on Machiavelli and His Reputation in the Sixteenth Century: I. Marlowe's Prologue to *The Jew of Malta.*" *Medieval and Renaissance Studies* (Warburg Institute), 5 (1961): 214-48.

Dean, Leonard F., Michael Bristol, and Neil Kleinman. *Marlowe's "The Jew of Malta."* Midwest Monographs, Ser. 1 (Drama), no. 2 (1967). [Program notes on Marlowe's life, the Elizabethan theater, and the play.]

Flosdorf, J. W. "The 'Odi et Amo' Theme in *The Jew of Malta." N&Q* 7 (1960): 10–14.

Freeman, Arthur. "A Source for *The Jew of Malta." N&Q* 9 (1962): 139–41.

Grebanier, Bernard. *The Truth About Shylock.* 1962.

Halio, Jay L. "Perfection and Elizabethan Ideas of Conception." *ELN* 1 (1964): 179–82.

Harrison, Thomas P., Jr. "Further Background for *The Jew of Malta* and *The Massacre at Paris." PQ* 27 (1948): 52–56.

———. "The Literary Background of Renaissance Poisons." *Studies in English* (Univ. of Texas), 27 (1948): 35–67.

Hughes, James Quentin. *The Building of Malta during the Period of the Knights of Saint John of Jerusalem, 1530–1795.* 1966.

Hunt, Leigh. "Bellamira and *The Jew of Malta."* In *Leigh Hunt's Dramatic Criticism,* ed. Lawrence Huston Houtchens and Carolyn Washburn Houtchens (1949), pp. 190–99. [Review of plays produced at Covent Garden in 1818.]

Kocher, Paul H. "English Legal History in Marlowe's *Jew of Malta." HLQ* 26 (1962): 155–63.

Kreisman, Arthur. "The Jews of Marlowe and Shakespeare." *ShN* 8 (1958): 29.

Landa, M. J. *The Jew in Drama.* 1926.

———. *The Shylock Myth.* 1942.

Michelson, H. *The Jew in Early English Literature.* 1926.

Modder, M. F. *The Jew in the Literature of England.* 1939.

Parrott, Thomas Marc, and Robert Hamilton Ball. *A Short View of Elizabethan Tragedy.* 1943.

Pearce, T. M. "Marlowe's *The Jew of Malta,* IV, vi, 7–10." *Expl* 9 (1951), item 40.

Peavy, Charles E. "*The Jew of Malta:* Anti-Semitic or Anti-Catholic?" *McNR* 11 (1959–60): 51–60.

Philipson, D. *The Jew in English Fiction.* 1927.

Purcell, H. D. "Whetstone's *English Myrror* and Marlowe's *Jew of Malta." N&Q* 13 (1966): 288–90.

Ribner, Irving. "The Significance of Gentillet's *Contre-Machiavel." MLQ* 10 (1949): 153–57.

Rusche, H. G. "Two Proverbial Images in Whitney's *A Choice of Emblemes* and Marlowe's *The Jew of Malta." N&Q* 11 (1964): 261.

Speaight, Robert. "Shakespeare in Britain." *SQ* 16 (1965): 313–24.

Spencer, Hazelton. "Marlowe's Rice 'With a Powder.' " *MLN* 47 (1932): 35.

Stephens, Rosemary. " 'In Another Country': Three as Symbol." *UMSE* 7 (1966): 77–83.

Stockley, W. F. P. "The Jews of Christopher Marlowe and of William Shakespeare." *IER* 44 (1934): 67–88.

Wright, Celeste T. "The Usurer's Sin in Elizabethan Literature." *SP* 35 (1938): 178–94.

Zitt, Hersch L. "The Jew in the Elizabethan World Picture." *Historia Judaica* 14 (1952): 53–60.

Edward II

Berdan, John M. "Marlowe's *Edward II.*" *PQ* 3 (1924): 197–207.

Briggs, W. D. "The Meaning of the Word 'Lake' in *Edward II.*" *MLN* 39 (1924): 437–38.

Brodwin, Leonora Leet. "*Edward II:* Marlowe's Culminating Treatment of Love." *ELH* 31 (1964): 139–55.

Crundell, H. W. "The Death of Edward II in Marlowe's Play." *N&Q* 179 (1940): 207.

Ellis-Fermor, Una. "Marlowe and Greene: A Note on Their Relations as Dramatic Artists." In *Studies in Honor of T. W. Baldwin*, ed. Don Cameron Allen (1958), pp. 136–49.

Johnson, Samuel Frederick. "Marlowe's *Edward II.*" *Expl* 10 (1952), item 53.

Laboulle, Louise J. "A Note on Bertold Brecht's Adaptation of Marlowe's *Edward II.*" *MLR* 54 (1959): 214–20.

Maugeri, Aldo. "*Edward II,*" "*Richard III*" e "*Richard II*": *note critiche.* 1952.

Mills, Laurens J. "The Meaning of *Edward II.*" *MP* 33 (1934): 11–32.

Muir, Kenneth, and Sean O'Loughlin. *The Voyage to Illyria: A New Study of Shakespeare.* 1937.

Reynolds, George F. *Staging of Elizabethan Plays at the Red Bull Theatre, 1605–1625.* 1940.

Robertson, Toby. "Directing *Edward II.*" *TDR* 8, no. 4 (1964): 174–83.

Sampley, Arthur M. "A Parallel Between Peele's *Descensus Astraeae* and Marlowe's *Edward II.*" *MLN* 50 (1935): 506.

Smith, G. C. Moore. "'Edwardum Occidere Nolite Timere Bonum Est' (Marlowe's *Edw. II*, V, iv, 8)." *TLS*, 9 Aug. 1928, p. 581 (see H. Johnstone, *TLS*, 16 Aug. 1928, p. 593).

Sunesen, Bent. "Marlowe and the Dumb Show." *ES* 35 (1954): 241–53.

Wada, Yuichi. "Edward II as Tragic Hero." *SELit* 41 (1964): 1–17.

The Massacre at Paris

Allodoli, Ettore. "La morte di Ramus secondo Marlowe." *Rinascita* 6 (1943): 171–76.

Bakeless, John. "Christopher Marlowe and the Newsbooks." *JQ* 14 (1937): 18–22.

Dodds, M. H. "*Julius Caesar* and the Duke of Guise." *N&Q* 180 (1941): 276–79.

Kocher, Paul H. "Francois Hotman and Marlowe's *The Massacre at Paris.*" *PMLA* 56 (1941): 349–68.

——. "Contemporary Pamphlet Backgrounds for Marlowe's *The Massacre at Paris.*" *MLQ* 8 (1947): 151–73, 309–18.

Woelcken, F. "Shakespeare's *Julius Caesar* und Marlowe's *Massacre at Paris.*" *SJ* 63 (1927): 192–94.

Dido, Queen of Carthage

Forbes, C. A. "Tragic Dido." *Classical Bulletin* 29 (1953): 51–53.

Lees, F. N. "*Dido, Queen of Carthage* and *The Tempest.*" *N&Q* 11 (1964): 147–49.

Maxwell, J. C. "Vergilian Half-Lines in Shakespeare's Heroic Narrative." *N&Q* 198 (1953): 100.

Rogers, David M. "Love and Honor in Marlowe's *Dido, Queen of Carthage.*" *Greyfriar; Siena Studies in Literature* 6 (1963): 3–7.
Turner, Robert Y. "The Causal Induction in Some Elizabethan Plays." *SP* 60 (1963): 183–90.

C. CANON, CHRONOLOGY, AND TEXT

Adams, Joseph Quincy. "*The Massacre at Paris* Leaf." *Library* 13 (1934): 447–69.
Baldwin, T. W. *On the Literary Genetics of Shakspere's Plays, 1592–1594.* 1959.
Clark, Eleanor G. *The Pembroke Plays: A Study in the Marlowe Canon.* 1928.
Crundell, H. W. "Nashe and *Doctor Faustus.*" *N&Q* 9 (1962): 327.
Danchin, F.-C. "Trois corrections au texte de Marlowe." *RAA* 10 (1933): 330. [*Jew of Malta.*]
———. "La date du *Faustus.*" *RAA* 10 (1933): 515–16.
Ellis-Fermor, Una. "The '1592' 8vo of *Tamburlaine.*" *TLS*, 2 May 1929, p. 362.
Flasdieck, Hermann M. "Zur Datierung von *Doctor Faust.*" *ES* 64 (1929): 320–51.
Goldstein, Leba M. "An Account of the Faustus Ballad." *Library* 16 (1961): 176–89.
Greg, W. W. "*Faustus* and the Stationers' Register." *Library* 7 (1927): 386.
Hunter, G. K. "*The Wars of Cyrus* and *Tamburlaine.*" *N&Q* 8 (1961): 395–96.
Lees, F. N. "A 'Faustus' Ballad." *N&Q* 194 (1949): 534.
———. "The Faustus Ballad." *Library* 18 (1963): 64.
Moore, Hale. "Gabriel Harvey's References to Marlowe." *SP* 23 (1926): 337–57. [*Faustus.*]
Nosworthy, J. M. "Some Textual Anomalies in the 1604 *Doctor Faustus.*" *MLR* 41 (1946): 1–8.
Oliver, H. J. "Marlowe's *Massacre at Paris.*" *TLS*, 11 Nov. 1965, p. 1003.
Oliver, Leslie Mahin. "Rowley, Fox, and the Additions to *Doctor Faustus.*" *MLN* 60 (1945): 391–94.
Pitcher, Seymour M. "The 1663 Edition of *Faustus.*" *MLN* 56 (1941): 588–94.
Shapiro, I. A. "The Significance of a Date." *ShS* 8 (1955): 100–105. [*Faustus.*]
Sisson, Charles J. *Lost Plays of Shakespeare's Age.* 1936.
Smith, Marion B. *Imagery and the Marlowe Canon.* 1940.
Tannenbaum, Samuel A. *Shakespearean Scraps.* 1933. [*Massacre at Paris.*]
Taylor, Rupert. "Chronology of Marlowe's Plays." *PMLA* 51 (1936): 643–88.
van Dam, B. A. P. "The Collier Leaf." *ES* 16 (1934): 166–73. [*Massacre at Paris.*]
Wells, Henry W. *A Chronological List of Extant Plays, 1581–1642.* 1940.

D. UNCERTAIN ASCRIPTIONS; BORROWINGS; INFLUENCE; APOCRYPHA

Alexander, Peter. "*The Taming of the Shrew.*" *TLS*, 16 Sept. 1926, p. 614.
———. "Christopher Marlowe and *The Taming of the Shrew.*" *TLS*, 7 June 1928, p. 430 (*see TLS*, 21 June 1928, p. 468).
Baldwin, T. W. "The Genesis of Some Passages Which Spenser Borrowed from Marlowe." *ELH* 9 (1942): 157–87; 12 (1945): 165.

Bond, R. W., ed. *The Taming of the Shrew.* 1929.

Brooke, C. F. Tucker. "The Authorship of *II Henry VI.*" Appendix to his edition of *II Henry VI* (1923), pp. 152-56.

Bush, Douglas. "Marlowe Echoes Spenser." *TLS*, 1 Jan. 1938, p. 12.

Crow, John. "Marlowe Yields to Jervis Markham." *TLS*, 4 Jan. 1947, p. 12 (see *TLS*, 11 Jan. 1947, p. 23; 18 Jan. 1947, p. 37; 8 Feb. 1947, p. 79; 21 June 1947, p. 313). [Lyric: "I walked along a stream for pureness rare."]

Crundell, H. W. "Nashe and *Doctor Faustus.*" *N&Q* 9 (1961): 327.

Erdman, David C., and Ephim G. Fogel, eds. *Evidence for Authorship: Essays on Problems of Attribution.* 1966.

Gaw, Allison. *The Origin and Development of "I Henry VI" in Relation to Shakespeare, Marlowe, Peele, and Greene.* Univ. of Southern California Studies, 1st Ser., no. 1, (1926).

Golding, S. R. "The Authorship of *Edward III.*" *N&Q* 154 (1928): 313-14.

Howarth, R. G. "Notes on Chapman." *N&Q* 192 (1947): 70-72.

Keller, W. "*Titus Andronicus* and Christopher Marlowe." *SJ* 74 (1928): 137-62.

Knickerbocker, W. S. "A Shaksperian Alarum." *SR* 45 (1937): 91-105. [*Henry VI.*]

———. "Shaksperian Excursion: Who Wrote *II and III Henry VI?*" *SR* 45 (1937): 328-42.

Kocher, Paul H. "Nashe's Authorship of the Prose Scenes in *Doctor Faustus.*" *MLQ* 3 (1942): 17-40.

Mincoff, Marco. "The Composition of *Henry VI, Part I.*" *SQ* 16 (1965): 279-87.

Muir, Kenneth. *Shakespeare as Collaborator.* 1960.

Oliphant, E. H. C. "Marlowe's Hand in *Arden of Feversham.*" *Criterion* 4 (1926): 76-93.

———. *The Plays of Beaumont and Fletcher.* 1927. [*Julius Caesar.*]

———. "Collaboration in Elizabethan Drama." *PQ* 8 (1929): 1-10.

Parrott, Thomas Marc. "Marlowe, Beaumont, and *Julius Caesar.*" *MLN* 44 (1929): 69-77.

———. "*The Taming of a Shrew.*" In *Elizabethan Studies and Other Essays in Honor of George F. Reynolds,* Univ. of Colorado Studies, Ser. B, Studies in the Humanities, vol. 2, no. 4 (1945), pp. 155-65.

Robertson, J. M. *The Shakespeare Canon.* Parts 1-4. 1922-32. [See index under Marlowe.]

———. *An Introduction to the Study of the Shakespeare Canon.* 1924. [See index under Marlowe.]

———. "A Marlowe Mystification." *TLS*, 11 Dec. 1924, p. 850. (See Arthur Melville Clark, *TLS*, 16 July 1925, p. 480 ["Elegies" translation].)

Rossiter, A. P., ed. *Woodstock, A Moral History.* 1946.

Schaubert, Else V. "Die Stelle vom 'Rauhen Pyrrhus' (*Hamlet,* II.ii.460-551) in ihrem Verhältnis zu Marlowe-Nashes *Dido . . .*" *Anglia* 53 (1929): 374-439.

Walley, Harold R. "Shakespeare's Debt to Marlowe in *Romeo and Juliet.*" *PQ* 21 (1942): 257-67.

Watkins, W. B. C. "The Plagiarist: Spenser or Marlowe?" *ELH* 11 (1944): 249-65.

Wills, M. M. "Marlowe's Role in Borrowed Lines." *PMLA* 52 (1937): 902-5.

Wilson, J. Dover. "Marlowe and *As You Like It.*" *TLS*, 6 Jan. 1927, p. 12.

E. EDITIONS OF PLAYS

Collections

Hampden, J., ed. *Three Plays: "Tamburlaine the Great," "Doctor Faustus," "Edward the Second."* 1940.

Messiaen, Pierre, ed. *Theatre anglais, Moyen-Age et XVIe siecle.* 1948.

Mullary, Peter F., ed. *Christopher Marlowe's "Doctor Faustus," "Tamburlaine I and II," "The Jew of Malta," and "Edward the Second."* 1966.

Neilson, William Allan, ed. *Marlowe's "Tamburlaine the Great" and "Doctor Faustus."* 1923.

Praz, Mario, ed. *Teatro elisabettiano: Kyd, Marlowe, Heywood, Marston, Jonson, Webster, Tourneur, Ford.* 1948. [*Doctor Faustus, The Jew of Malta, Edward II.*]

Ridley, M. R., ed. *Christopher Marlowe, Plays and Poems.* 1955.

Rosati, Salvatore, ed. *Due drami ("Edward II" e "Doctor Faustus").* 1962.

Weimann, Robert, ed. *Dramen der Shakespearezeit.* 1964. [*Doctor Faustus* and *Edward II.*]

Single Plays

Doctor Faustus

Cabral, A. de Oliveira, trans. *O "Fausto" de Marlowe.* 1949.

Danchin, F.-C., trans. *La tragique histoire du Docteur Faust.* 1935.

Guidi, Augusto, ed. *La civiltà elisabelliana.* 1962.

Hampden, John, ed. *Doctor Faustus.* 1929.

Mingazzini, Cura di Rosa Marnoni, ed. *Marlowe, The Tragical History of Doctor Faustus.* 1952.

Ornstein, Robert, and Hazelton Spencer, eds. *Elizabethan and Jacobean Tragedy: An Anthology.* 1964.

Peel, J. D., ed. *The Tragical History of Doctor Faustus.* 1928.

Robbins, R. H., ed. *Tragical History of Doctor Faustus.* 1948.

Seebass, Aldof, trans. *Die tragische Historie vom Doktor Faustus.* 1949.

Sleight, A. H., ed. *The Tragical History of Doctor Faustus.* 1953.

Stauffer, R. M., ed. *The Progress of Drama through the Centuries.* 1927.

Swander, Homer D., ed. *Man and the Gods: Three Tragedies.* 1964.

The Tragical History of Doctor Faustus. Borzoi Dramatist Series, 1928.

The Tragicall History of Doctor Faustus. Golden Hours Press, 1932.

Tamburlaine

Bald, R. C., ed. *Six Elizabethan Plays (1585-1635).* 1963. [Part I.]

Cellini, Benvenuto, ed. *Drammi pre-Shakespeariani.* Collana di Letterature Moderne, vol. 4 (1958). [Part I.]

Guthrie, Tyrone, and Donald Wolfit, eds. *Tamburlaine the Great, An Acting Version.* 1951.

Sheriffs, R. S., illus. *The Life and Death of Tamburlaine the Great.* 1930.

The Jew of Malta

Melchiori, Giorgio, ed. and trans. *Christopher Marlowe: "L'Ebreo di Malta."* 1943.

Edward II

Baldini, Gabrielle, ed. and trans. *Eduardo II.* 1953.
Devroor, J., trans. *Roudom Shakespeare. Christopher Marlowe: "Edward II"; Beaumont and Fletcher: "Philaster." Overgesit uit lict Engelich.* 1926.
Edward the Second. Aquilla Press. 1924.
Pons, C., trans. *Edouard II.* 1964.
Valene, Marie-Claire, trans. *Edouard II.* 1962.

F. EDITIONS OF POETRY

Alexander, Nigel, ed. *Elizabethan Narrative Verse.* Stratford-upon-Avon Library, 1968.
Baldini, Gabriele, ed. *"Hero and Leander" e "Venus and Adonis."* 1952.
———. ed. and trans. *"Venus and Adonis," testo critica, mente riveduto e commentato, saggio di una interpretazione e versione italiana a fronte.* 1952. [Includes *Hero and Leander.*]
Marnau, Fred, ed. *Marlowe, A Selection of Poems.* 1948.
Mattingly, Garrett, ed. *Hero and Leander.* 1927.
Ovid's Elegies. Translated by Christopher Marlowe. Together with the Epigrams of Sir John Davies. London [Etchells and MacDonald], 1925.

ROBERT GREENE

William Nestrick

A. B. Grosart's edition of the *Complete Works,* 15 vols. (1881-86) includes Storozhenko's biography (1878) of Greene. The plays have been edited by J. Churton Collins, 2 vols. (1905) and, for the Mermaid series, by Thomas H. Dickinson (1909). A complete edition, under the general editorship of I. A. Shapiro and Johnstone Parr, is in progress.

I. GENERAL

A. BIOGRAPHICAL

The few facts we possess about Greene's life must be pieced out by reference to his autobiographical works and to general information about his milieu, friends, education, and life in Elizabethan England. Storozhenko's biography, even when first translated, was recognized as inadequate, and in his introduction to the plays, Collins attempts to rectify confusion resulting from indiscriminate use of the semi-autobiographical novels. The biographical chapters in René Pruvost, *Robert Greene et ses romans* (1938), give a detailed account of Greene's surroundings and contemporaries. J. C. Jordan's *Robert Greene* (1915) should be read with the qualifications suggested by the following articles.

Kenneth Mildenberger, "Robert Greene at Cambridge," *MLN* 66 (1951): 546-49, has examined the Cambridge records and discovered that a Robert Greene matriculated at Corpus Christi in 1573; nothing shows that the Corpus Christi Greene ever received a degree. This information supplements the previously established facts that Robert Greene matriculated at St. Johns in 1575, received a B.A. in 1580, and received an M.A. while a member of Clare in 1582-83. Commenting upon the Corpus Christi Greene, Johnstone Parr, in "Robert Greene and His Classmates at Cambridge," *PMLA* 77 (1962): 536-43, notes that although students did change colleges, there was no need to matriculate twice; it was also unusual to move to another college after receiving the B.A. Parr makes inferences about Greene on the basis of the careers of his classmates and connections between these Cantabridgians and Greene's prose works.

Edwin Haviland Miller, in "The Relationship of Robert Greene and Thomas Nashe (1588-1592)," *PQ* 33 (1954): 353-67, finds that from late 1589 to 1592 Nashe disavowed intimacy with Greene, but by 1592 they evidently settled their differences. Miller thinks that Greene censured the Harveys at Nashe's instigation. Greene's most famous animosity is considered by W. Schrickx, "Nashe, Greene, and Shakespeare in 1592," *RLV* 22 (1956): 55-64, who finds reason to suppose that Greene's desertion of the Queen's men for the Admiral's was resented by Shakespeare. Most biographies of Marlowe and Shakespeare make mention of Greene if only to explain his notorious attacks. Marcel Brion's "Vie de Robert Greene," *CS* 20 (1933): 170-74 (rpt. in *Le théâtre élizabéthain* [1940], pp. 220-25), uses the autobiographical writings freely.

B. GENERAL STUDIES OF THE PLAYS

Recent studies of Greene's plays have been confined to articles and to chapters of larger works dealing with Elizabethan drama or with Greene's non-dramatic works. Many of the received opinions about Greene's chief characteristics and excellences, his charm, his humor, his patient, suffering women, his homely "English" touches are found in the general estimates of Collins, Dickinson, and Jordan and in surveys such as Thomas Marc Parrott and Robert Hamilton Ball's *A Short View of Elizabethan Drama* (1943) and C. F. Tucker Brooke's *The Tudor Drama* (1911). In the second volume of *The Development of English Humor* (1952), Louis Cazamian, while praising Greene's humor for "a sympathy with life and a respect for the essential decencies," concludes that Greene's contribution to the growth of English humor was slight. Una Ellis-Fermor, "Marlowe and Greene: A Note on their Relations as Dramatic Artists," in *Studies in Honor of T. W. Baldwin,* ed. Don Cameron Allen (1958), pp. 136-49, traces Greene's development from "imitation in our own popular sense to imitation in Aristotle's and du Bellay's." In *Alphonsus,* she finds Greene picking up Marlowe's worst tricks, although there are touches of "Greene's peculiar gift for sweetness and poignancy in cadence and thought." *Orlando* confronts us with the problem of distinguishing between intentional parody and unintentional imitation. As opposed to Faustus' magic, Friar Bacon's docs not lead to the loss of souls, though it may lead to human disaster. With *James IV*, there is no question of debt to Marlowe—in fact, Marlowe's weak Edward, redeemed by the kingliness and magnanimity of his death, may owe something to the mediation of Greene's genius.

In the 1960s a new sophistication appears in Greene criticism. Norman Sanders takes a genetic approach in "The Comedy of Greene and Shakespeare," in *Early Shakespeare*, SuAS, vol. 3 (1961), pp. 35–53. Sanders centers on "the indeterminate areas of comic vision, in the special quality of their imaginative response to life and art." In the latter part of *Alphonsus*, Greene expands sympathetically in the subplot, which was more congenial to his talents than the main one. Carinus is the only character who suggests humanity, and Greene's natural sympathy helps explain his success with him. *Orlando* may have provided Greene with a growing realization of the comic potential in the romantic situations of lovers meeting at a time when normal expression of their love is impossible and when one of the pair is unrecognized by the other. In *James IV*, Greene surrounds the central amatory couple with less perfect examples of love; he relies chiefly on juxtaposition (e.g., Sacripant shows self-love instead of true love), whereas Shakespeare uses interrelation. Barriers to the expression of love are usually created by the lovers themselves, frequently through delusion or spiritual blindness. Sanders also sees a complicated linking of plots: in *Friar Bacon* the connection is made through an audience awareness of the nature of dramatic illusion itself. The frame story of *James IV*, with Nano stepping back and forth between frame and "reality," creates this same distancing effect.

Wolfgang Clemen, *English Tragedy before Shakespeare* (trans. T. S. Dorsch, 1961; German ed., 1955), sets out to trace the relations of the set speech to other formal elements of drama. Clemen summarizes Greene's development thus: "Greene begins with a technique of cumbersome, high-flown declamation, governed by the conventions of formal rhetoric; he finally achieves a type of speech which approaches the tone of conversation, and is natural and at times realistic, though it is true that we encounter this only in occasional passages in his last two plays." Greene's work exhibits "new potentialities . . . for the mutual interrelationship between the set speech and dramatic technique." After *Alphonsus* and *Orlando,* Greene might have been expected to develop his own style, but he never succeeded. His "originality" is shown in externals—new theatrical effects, new dramatic *genres*—rather than in dramatic realization. Situations and themes determine style and language. The "woodland air" quality is shown to be confined to a handful of scenes and passages. Clemen concludes that Greene fails to prepare for moments of crisis or to unify his play around a central interest.

Kenneth Muir, "Robert Greene as Dramatist," in *Essays on Shakespeare and Elizabethan Drama in Honor of Hardin Craig,* ed. Richard Hosley (1962), pp. 45–54, argues that Greene's best work was nondramatic, and that critics have praised his plays for qualities which they do not possess. With Clemen, he questions the critical admiration of Greene's characterizations of women. Muir recognizes the type of Patient Griselda in both Margaret and Dorothea, but he questions the right of critics to talk about subtle characterization and then fall back on conventions and types when objections are raised on psychological or emotional grounds.

Some of the general considerations of Greene's plays treat the plays generically or thematically. Works on form in Elizabethan drama, like Madeleine Doran's *Endeavors of Art* (1954) offer relevant perceptions about the plays while viewing larger artistic problems. In *The Growth and Structure of Elizabethan Comedy* (1955), M. C. Bradbrook treats the plays generically and sees *Orlando* as a fairy tale; *James IV, Friar Bacon,* and *George a Greene* are grouped as comical histories because they include a king or prince revelling and giving his friendship to a particular craft or a particular town, a love interest and a popular hero, magic and horseplay, and songs and shows. Among Greene's comical histories, *James IV* is ranked as "the most pretentious and least successful" by Bradbrook. It rates higher with Marvin T. Herrick in *Tragicomedy* (1955), who finds in it "virtually every quality needed by Beaumont and Fletcher for the full development of English tragicomedy." Herrick notes the links of the plays, especially *James IV,* to Senecan tragedy and Terentian comedy.

E. C. Pettet's *Shakespeare and the Romance Tradition* (1949) shows how Greene conforms to romance conventions but departs from the norm in his neglect of courtship; this neglect extends to the elaborate descriptions of feminine beauty in Greene's nondramatic poetry. A growing ability to achieve animation in his lovers is revealed. Greene breaks out of romantic conventions in diversifying the social classes through the antics of low-life characters. In Pettet's view he relies less than Lyly upon conventional romantic settings, rarely employs verbal scene-painting, and leaves what settings there are quite vague. A fresh view of Greene's plays as dreams of glory and domestic fantasies for London audiences is offered by David Bevington in *Tudor Drama and Politics: A Critical Approach to Topical Meaning* (1968).

Greene's works offer material for studies of character types. Lawrence Babb finds examples of conventional appearances associated with malcontents in "Sorrow and Love on the Elizabethan Stage," *ShAB* 18 (1943): 137–42. Mary Hallowell Perkins, in *The Servant Problem and the Servant in English Literature* (1928), finds that servants play little part in Greene's plays except in the formal capacity of revealing plans of the master in dialogue with him. The servant-clown is also examined by Olive Mary Busby, *Studies in the Development of the Fool in the Elizabethan Drama* (1923); Slipper represents a subtler and wittier version of Miles.

J. F. Macdonald assesses Greene's contribution to prose convention in "The Use of Prose in English Drama Before Shakespeare," *UTQ* 2 (1933): 465–81. In addition to defining regularities in the dramatic use of prose, Macdonald explains deviations—the use of prose when noblemen are disguised as low-life and the change from prose to verse in cases of religious conversion. Philip W. Timberlake gives a metrical examination in *The Feminine Ending in English Blank Verse* (1931). William J. Lawrence, in *Pre-Restoration Stage Studies* (1927), includes *Friar Bacon, Alphonsus,* and *James IV* in a group of plays he thinks intended for inn-yard performance and examines special effects.

Special studies show Greene's knowledge of law and ignorance of geography. Particular questions (seals and bonds, hanging, forfeiture) are handled by Harry Ransom in "Some Legal Elements in Elizabethan Plays," *Studies in English* (Univ. of Texas) 16 (1936): 53–76 and by P. S. Clarkson and C. T. Warren in *The Law of Property in Shakespeare and the Elizabethan Drama* (1942). Robert Ralston Cawley, both in *The Voyagers and Elizabethan Drama* (1938) and *Unpathed Waters* (1940), decides that in spite of Greene's having been widely travelled, he gives little evidence of it in his work.

C. THE WORKS AT LARGE

The nondramatic side of Greene's output has been more extensively treated by the critics than the dramatic. René Pruvost's *Robert Greene et ses romans* (1938) remains the fullest treatment of the prose. Fernando Ferrara's *L'opera narrativa di Robert Greene* (1957) takes into consideration more recent controversies. Both Pruvost and Ferrara make connections with the dramatic work. Pruvost points out that

Dorothea takes her place beside the other faithful wives badly treated: Barmenissa in *Penelope's Web,* Isabel in *Never too Late,* and Philomela. In her resolution to renounce the world, Margaret is in the line of Mamillia and her cousin, Publia. Angelica, surrounded by pretenders for her hand, resembles Sylvia, whose story is told by Mamillia. As a victim of a false accusation by a rejected suitor, Angelica also resembles Castania in *Gwydonius.* Pruvost notes Greene's interest in proverbial material. For his cony-catching pamphlets and rustic characters, he almost belongs to the line of Chaucer. A criticism of the prose, namely that Greene leaves his characters up in the air and fails to create a time or place for them, supports some of the recent trends in criticizing the English settings of Greene's plays. Pruvost maintains that, despite the fact that Greene was known as a plagiarist, no definite sources have been found for many of the stories.

Ferrara stresses the worth of Greene as a narrator, the first to write prose both artistically and in a native English idiom. The influence of Italian writers on Greene's development is outlined. Giraldi Cinthio helped orient Greene toward certain forms consonant with his attitudes without profoundly modifying his art; Bandello and Boccaccio freed him from the shackles of a too complex and artificial style as well as from a moral didacticism. Of the parts of Cinthio used by Greene, only one was available in translation. Ferrara finds various resemblances between the prose and the drama. *A Looking Glass for London and England* and *Mirrour of Modestie* both show how Greene was able to combine roots in the traditional literature of England (such as medieval religious drama) with popular national spirit and new humanistic learning. Character resemblances include Cratyna in *Penelope's Web* and Margaret: both are faithful, loving, and passionate. Sephestia combines the faithfulness and coquetry one also finds in Margaret, and by these qualities is distinguished both from the Patient Griselda and the wanton Rhodope types. Thematically, *Ciceronis Amor* and *Friar Bacon* both treat the triumph of friendship, though Ferrara admits the conventionality of this theme.

C. S. Lewis, *English Literature in the Sixteenth Century Excluding Drama* (1954), divides the fiction of the period into three classes: the romantic, the realistic, and the rhetorical; although Greene works in all three, he makes a particularly sizeable contribution to the third.

Most chroniclers of English fiction, from Sir Walter Raleigh to Ernest Baker, *The History of the English Novel* (10 vols., 1924–36), have seen in Greene's canon a gradual substitution of the London of his time for a fancied pastoral world. Baker and Edward Wagenknecht, *Cavalcade of the English Novel* (1943), both deplore his weakness in characterization and praise his narrative skill. Margaret Schlauch, in *Antecedents of the English Novel, 1400-1600* (1963), continues this view. She notes Greene's willingness to combine varied materials in constructing his quasi-classical romance plots, and that *Never Too Late* introduces elements related to contemporary real life; and she feels that the pamphlets are superior in dealing with urgent social problems and in offering a style and idiom adaptable for low-life scenes on the stage. Bruce E. Teets, "Two Faces of Style in Renaissance Prose Fiction," in *Sweet Smoke of Rhetoric: A Collection of Renaissance Essays,* ed. Natalie Grimes Lawrence and J. A. Reynolds (1964), pp. 69-81, contrasts the *estilo culto* with a native, realistic prose tradition. "Since the unplanned, cumulative sentence was suitable for describing ordinary life or that of the lower classes, Robert Greene found it advantageous in his popular works, which may be considered an approach to sociological realism."

An unusually rich reading of Greene's fiction is found in Walter R. Davis, *Idea and Act in Elizabethan Fiction* (1969). Romance motifs such as travel and disguise become ways of discussing experience and the self. Davis sees Greene beginning in the Lylyan mode of fiction as the comment of experience on precepts and ending with a total divorce of ideas and action as well as a rejection of the very grounds of fiction itself. In *Mamillia,* Greene is less interested in concepts than is Lyly generally; instead, he emphasizes fortune, fate, and the forces of love. In *Gwydonius,* experience is educative by forcing roles upon the hero, and fortune can bring out good or bad. *Arbasto* reduces experience to the pressures of bad luck on the personality. And in *Philomela,* the world of action grows still darker. In Greene's second period, that of collections of short tales (1585-88), exemplary ideals and the actions of the world start to revolve in separate and distinct spheres, and through them, Greene began his separation from Lyly's view of reality. The pastoral romances continue this separation. Davis sees in *Pandosto* "an almost Calvinistic assumption of the inconsequentiality of human purposes" and in *Menaphon,* stylistically the most sophisticated of the romances, a view of life "much like the modern 'absurd.' " The realistic pamphlets complete the cleavage between precepts associated with the divine and the pointless amorality of human affairs.

James Applegate, in "The Classical Learning of Robert Greene," *BHR* 28 (1966): 354-68, finds that Greene used classical adornments more for romances and repentance pamphlets than for political and sociological treatises. Especially cited are Ovid, Terence, Horace, and Plutarch. Although Greene probably had access to a reference compendium, the utility of the work was limited, since "if he had been able to turn to a topical heading and find a classical example directly to his purpose, we would not find him, as in fact we frequently do, putting a certain figure to inappropriate use when another figure would fit his purpose nicely."

Greene's acquaintance with proverb dictionaries is discussed by Charles Speroni, "Un'ignota fonte Italiana di Robert Greene," *CL* 14 (1962): 366-76. One of the first collections to group proverbs in families was Orazio Rinaldi's *Dottrina delle virtù, et fuga de'vitii* (1585). Greene translated this as *The Royal Exchange* (1590) but claimed that it was a translation of *La Burza Reale*. This assertion Speroni sees as another of Greene's tricks, since Greene does not even name the author. Greene omits some of the maxims, and to maintain the alphabetical order, he gives the key word in Italian with its translation; he also adds commentaries and citations. Speroni has edited the *Dottrina* with the Spanish and English translations: *The Aphorisms of Orazio Rinaldi, Robert Greene, and Lucas Gracian Dantisco,* University of California Publications in Modern Philology, vol. 88 (1968).

The implications in these recent works that Greene wore his learning lightly bear out the earlier conclusions of Don Cameron Allen, "Science and Invention in Greene's Prose," *PMLA* 53 (1938): 1007-18, and John Leon Lievsay, "Greene's Panther," *PQ* 20 (1941): 296-303. Lievsay concludes, in accord with Allen, that Greene's innovations in euphuistic science were not superior to the material that he could have found in the conventional encyclopedias. He neglected typological interpretations because he was interested only in superficial comparisons. "In his faulty presentation of even so congenial a matter as panther-lore, Greene is merely paying once again the inevitable price of his hack work."

Both Pruvost and Ferrara treat the sources and analogues of Greene's fiction. John S. Weld, "Some Problems of Euphuistic Narrative: Robert Greene and Henry Wotton," *SP* 45 (1948): 165-71, identifies Wotton's *Courtlie Controuersie of Cupid's Cautels* (1578) as one of the sources for *Mamillia*. Wotton's work is a translation of Jacque D'Yver's *Le printemps D'Yver* (1572) and, though there is a possibility that Greene used the French original, Weld finds the phrase "as bold as blind

Bayard" in both Wotton and Greene's epistles dedicatory. Greene simply inserts the static medieval debates on love into his own narrative, and where Wotton's phrasing is not sufficiently ornamental, further embroiders it.

An interpretation of *Mamillia* as a debate with Lyly, who represented the detractors of women, is given in Jaroslav Hornát, "*Mamillia:* Robert Greene's Controversy with *Euphues,*" *PP* 5 (1962): 210-25. Greene's women show true heroism: Publia, the stoic resolution of a sufferer, and Mamillia, active self-sacrifice. Mamillia, moreover, has no counterpart in *Euphues.* Hornát sees the story in the appended correspondence of Sylvia choosing the witty Englishman over wealth and beauty as an answer to Fidus' narrative in *Euphues and his England,* where Iffida chooses the rich man. Lyly's "A Cooling Card for Philautus" is based on Ovid, and so Greene, in attacking Ovid at the beginning of his "Anatomie of Lovers Flatteries," called attention to the controversy with Lyly. Hornát's "Two Euphuistic Stories of Robert Greene: *The Carde of Fancie* and *Pandosto,*" *PP* 6 (1963): 21-35, suggests that the title of the first work opposes Lyly's "cooling card" and hence belongs, like *Mamillia,* to the erotomachy between Lyly and Greene. Euphues was cured of folly by woman's infidelity; Gwydonius is ennobled by faithful love. The two stories, Gwydonius-Castania and Thersandro-Lewcippa, have two plans: a broader one about the hostility of two dukedoms (the rulers are naturally the lovers' parents), and a narrower one, based on the love themes. "The whole mechanism of action is built up on the transversal of both plans, which are not only complementary, but also in mutal tension." Hornát considers the first half of *Pandosto* as a novella with a tragic end; the second half as pastoral romance.

Robert W. Dent, "Greene's *Gwydonius:* A Study in Elizabethan Plagiarism," *HLQ* 24 (1961): 151-62, shows how Greene uses both his own earlier *Mamillia* and Pettie's *Petite Pallace;* moreover, Dent can find little artistic reason for changes made in the course of borrowing. For the first prefatory essay in *Planetomachia,* Greene translated almost all of Lucian's *De Astrologia.* Johnstone Parr, in "Sources of the Astrological Prefaces in Robert Greene's *Planetomachia,*" *SP* 46 (1949): 400-410, checks Greene's references from Ptolemy and concludes that he used some school text or compendium of universal knowledge. Stanley Wells shows that for a number of "euphuisms" in *Planetomachia* Greene was indebted to *The Secrets and Wonders of the World* (1565-66), a translation of Pliny in "Greene and Pliny," *N&Q* 8

(1961): 422-24. John Lawlor, in *"Pandosto* and the Nature of Dramatic Romance," *PQ* 41 (1962): 96-113, tests the relationship between *The Winter's Tale* and Greene's romance. He focuses on differences of plot and characterization, particularly the character of Leontes, the omission of crude domestic comedy, alterations of tone away from the labored exchanges of the lovers, and the use of the sheepshearing feast as meeting place of youth and age and occasion for a dialogue on art and nature.

Criticism of Greene's pamphlets has centered on bibliographical or biographical questions. *Groatsworth of Wit* has an allusion to a young Juvenal "that lastlie with mee together writ a Comedie." This has been variously identified as *Summer's Last Will and Testament, A Knack to Know a Knave,* and *George a Greene.* Recently, "a Comedie" has been taken in the broader sense to include nondramatic writing: Edwin Haviland Miller, "Relationship of Greene and Nashe" (I,A), thinks the work referred to is *Defence of Cony-Catching,* and Donald J. McGinn has nominated *A Quip for an Upstart Courtier* ("A Quip from Tom Nashe," in *Studies in the English Renaissance Drama in Memory of Karl Julius Holzknecht,* ed. Josephine W. Bennett, Oscar Cargill, and Vernon Hall, Jr. [1959], pp. 172-88). McGinn argues that *Quip* contains the most extensive verbal similarities to Nashe's *Pierce Pennilesse;* hence R. B. McKerrow's theory (stated in vol. 5 of his edition of Nashe's works) that Nashe inserted the attack against the Harveys under his own name only after Greene withdrew still holds. McGinn also points out that *Quip* is a dialogue and could be considered a comedy in the dramatic sense of the word. He suggests that collaboration was not confined to this single work but occurs in all of Greene's pamphlets that disclose numerous verbal resemblances. In an appendix in *Thomas Nashe: A Critical Introduction* (1962), G. R. Hibbard answers McGinn by referring to *Strange News,* where Nashe states that the anti-Harvey passages in *Quip* were Greene's work, and by showing that the context of "Comedie" demands a dramatic interpretation. Hibbard posits a lost play because *Summer's Last Will* had not yet been publicly performed. In "Was Greene's 'Young Juvenal' Nashe or Lodge?" *SEL* 7 (1967): 55-66, Philip Drew notes that it is now generally taken for granted that "Juvenal" was Nashe when there is still a strong possibility that he was Lodge, with whom Greene had collaborated on *A Looking Glass for London and England,* "technically" a comedy. Although Drew finds the balance in favor of Lodge, the main thrust of his summation of evidence is a warning not to use the passage on young Juvenal as evidence in considering other problems such as collaboration or the dating of *A Looking Glass.*

From "young Juvenal" it is only a few words to Greene's famous attack on Shakespeare as an "upstart crow." Almost any edition of *3 Henry VI* will have some discussion about the "Tiger's Hart wrapt in a Player's hide." Silvano Gerevini, in "Shakespeare 'Corvo Rifatto,' " *Letterature Moderne* 7 (1957): 195-205, warns against interrelating three separate problems: the authenticity of *Henry VI*; the interpretation of Greene's reference as a charge of plagiarism; and the bibliographical status of *The First Part of the Contention and The True Tragedy of Richard Duke of York.* The occasion for Gerevini's essay was J. Dover Wilson's "Malone and the Upstart Crow," *ShS* 4 (1951): 56-68, where the passage is interpreted as an accusation that Shakespeare had stolen and adapted plays upon Henry VI by Greene and his friends.

Aligning himself with those who favor the plagiarist theory, Sidney Thomas, in "The Meaning of Greene's Attack on Shakespeare," *MLN* 66 (1951): 483-84, finds some evidence that Elizabethans associated the concept of borrowed plumage with literary theft. For the evidence on the other side, see René Pruvost, "Robert Greene a-t-il accusé Shakespeare de plagiat?" *EA* 12 (1959): 198-204, where the "upstart crow" is traced back to Horace's Third Epistle and is discovered in several other works by Greene, including an example where it is used to distinguish the actor who can only repeat others' words. Henry Chettle's reply, as others have noted, does not seem to refer to plagiarism. Arthur Freeman offers another Horatian crow to show Elizabethan familiarity with the image: "Notes on the Text of *2 Henry VI* and the 'Upstart Crow,' " *N&Q* 15 (1968): 128-30.

Much of the evidence adduced to support the charge of plagiarism has been shown to be at least equivocal. Sigurd Burckhardt, in *Shakespearean Meanings* (1968), reads Greene's admonition to his fellow playwrights as a warning against any future collaboration with players, more especially with Shakespeare. "Implicit in his words . . . is bitterness that—in some dispute with a player 'conceited' enough to imagine he can write plays by himself—his colleagues did not side with him [Greene], at least as forcefully and unequivocally as they should have." Muriel C. Bradbrook, "Beasts and Gods: Greene's *Groats-worth of Witte* and the Social Purpose of *Venus and Adonis*," *ShS* 15 (1962): 62-72, reads the "upstart crow" passage as a piece of vilification and Shakespeare's poem as a response. In "The Printing of *Greenes*

Groatsworth of Witte and *Kind-Harts Dreame*," *SB* 19 (1966): 196-97, Sidney Thomas, by examining type fonts, running titles, and ornaments, shows that the printers of both works were John Wolfe and John Danter. Louis Marder reports on Warren B. Austin's computer-assisted study of the authorship of the posthumous Greene pamphlets in "Greene's Attack on Shakespeare: A Posthumous Hoax?" *ShN* 16 (1966): 29-30.

Waldo F. McNeir, in "The Date of Greene's 'Vision,' " *N&Q* 195 (1950): 137, agrees with Churton Collins's dating as early in 1590. In addition to the reference to *Mourning Garment* as a forthcoming work (licensed 2 Nov. 1590), McNeir notes an allusion to *The Royal Exchange* (licensed 15 April 1590).

Edwin Haviland Miller, in "Robert Parsons' *Resolution* and *The Repentance of Robert Greene*," *N&Q* 1 (1954), 104-8, demonstrates a debt to Parsons' recital of woes in store for the damned. Miller's *The Professional Writer in Elizabethan England: A Study of Nondramatic Literature* (1959), considers the prodigal-son theme in a larger perspective: though fashionable, the theme may reflect Greene's own religious insecurity and not necessarily his insincerity. The book also describes Greene's exploitation of patrons. In two notes, *N&Q* 196 (1951): 509-12, and 197 (1952): 446-51, Miller treats the bibliographical problems of *The Defence of Cony-Catching*. Terry Pearson, *N&Q* 6 (1959): 150-53, uses the *Defence* to connect Philip Stubbes with Chesire and to prove Stubbes was not a university man. Francis R. Johnson has augmented and corrected the *Short-title Catalogue* account in his "The Editions of Robert Greene's Three Parts of *Conny-Catching;* A Bibliographical Analysis," *Library* 9 (1954): 17-24. Waldo F. McNeir, "Heywood's Sources for the Main Plot of *A Woman Killed with Kindness*," in *Studies in the English Renaissance Drama*, ed. Josephine W. Bennett et al. (1959), pp. 189-211, identifies *The Conversion of an English Courtesan*, appended to *Disputation of a He Cony-catcher and a She Cony-catcher*, as the source for Heywood's play; Greene himself was improving upon a story told by Gascoigne.

Edwin Haviland Miller, "The Editions of Robert Greene's *A Quip for an Upstart Courtier* (1592)," *SB* 6 (1954): 107-16, increases the number of editions in the year of initial publication from two to at least six. Miller suggests that the deletion of the Harvey attack cannot be considered separately, since it is one of six alterations made in the text, in "Deletions in Robert Greene's *A Quip for an Upstart Courtier* (1592)," *HLQ* 15 (1952): 277-82. Miller has also shown that Greene's comments on usurers, brokers, pickpockets, and so on were not the product of experience but of reading, in *N&Q* 198 (1953): 148-52, 187-91. Leonard Nathanson explains an obscure line, "then conscience was not a broome man in Kent Street but a Courtier," on the basis of Lady Conscience in a play by Wilson, in *"A Quip for an Upstart Courtier* and *The Three Ladies of London," N&Q* 3 (1956): 376-77. R. B. Parker has discovered a Dutch edition of *Quip* which shows variants that cannot be traced to any extant English edition and concludes that we must postulate a lost or made-up edition of *Quip* as the immediate source: "A Dutch Edition of Robert Greene's *A Quip for an Upstart Courtier* (1601)" *N&Q* 7 (1960): 130-34. His "Alterations in the First Edition of Greene's *A Quip for an Upstart Courtier," HLQ* 23 (1960): 181-86 and I. A. Shapiro's "The First Edition of Greene's *Quip for an Upstart Courtier," SB* 14 (1961): 212-18, reconsider the accepted order of the two states of sheet F. Parker attributes the emendation of the baker passage to Greene, since the corrected version is longer. He further argues that if Greene made a stop-press emendation to eliminate blasphemy as early as the first printing of *Quip*, he may have had a hand in similar alterations in the second edition and may have canceled his attack on the Harveys for reasons of conscience. Shapiro disagrees on the identification of the reviser. The Huntington text of $F4^v$ is a revision of that found in the Bodleian copy, and the text was changed to remove the blasphemous comparison of the baker's behavior in the pillory to that of Christ on the cross. The publisher was probably responsible.

Anthony Esler, "Robert Greene and the Spanish Armada," *ELH* 32 (1965): 314-32, outlines the "cultural symbolism" in the *Spanish Masquerado*. The bibliographical problems of this work are discussed in Leslie Mahin Oliver, *"The Spanish Masquerado:* A Problem in Double Edition," *Library* 2 (1947): 14-19. Arthur Freeman adds to the Greene canon a translation from a French work for the funeral of Gregory XIII, "An Unacknowledged Work of Robert Greene," *N&Q* 12 (1965): 378-79. It is an example of Elizabethan Catholica ostensibly presented for ridicule, but effectively unaltered from its original intent. Samuel A. Tannenbaum prepared the *Concise Bibliography* (1939), followed by a *Supplement,* with Dorothy R. Tannenbaum (1945). These are reprinted in *Elizabethan Bibliographies,* vol. 3 (1967). Robert C. Johnson, in his volume on the University Wits for *Elizabethan Bibliographies Supplements* (1968), continues these. A selected list appears in Irving Ribner, *Tudor and Stuart Drama* (Goldentree Bibliographies, 1966).

II. CRITICISM OF INDIVIDUAL PLAYS AND STATE OF SCHOLARSHIP

A. INDIVIDUAL PLAYS

Friar Bacon and Friar Bungay

The best general treatments are the introductions by Daniel Seltzer to his edition for the Regents Renaissance Drama Series (1963) and by J. A. Lavin for his New Mermaid edition (1969). Both discuss the dating problem, stage history, and early editions. Seltzer notes the importance of the stage directions as evidence for the study of Elizabethan theatrical performances and suggests that the play was printed from theatrical copy. Lavin thinks it unlikely that the actual promptbook was supplied as printer's copy; instead the printer's copy was a transcript (probably of Greene's fair or foul papers) in which the play had been only partly prepared for acting. In an appendix, Seltzer offers suggestions for the way the scene with the brazen head and the hand "that breaketh down the Head with a hammer" may have been staged. Lavin examines the problems of staging the scenes with the prospective glass as well as that with the brazen head. In view of Greene's revisions of his sources, Seltzer finds the playwright "trying to equate his wizard-hero . . . to that danger which, in most forms of tragicomedy, will threaten and test the felicity of true love." The question of what magic meant to the Elizabethan admits of a wide solution. Seltzer rejects the "white magic" excuse, and allies Greene's presentation with popular lore. Greene avoids his source's "scientific" explanation of the magical glass in order to keep its harmful powers. On the literary side, romances offer examples of magicians supporting the power of lust, as Bacon helps Prince Edward's desires. Margaret herself combines the romantic figures of the lady of nobility who lives in lowly surroundings and the figure of Patient Griselda. This latter conventional type helps account for the lack of psychological motivation: "The testing is . . . a hyperbolic restatement of a character already perceived by the audience." Seltzer seeks a balance between "realistic" and "conventional" approaches to the play. Greene maintains "suspense and a comic decorum simultaneously, by humanizing the traditional emblem behind his heroine and by undercutting Bacon's magic with occasional slapstick humor." The religious, issues of Bacon-as-Faustus are not allowed to darken the play beyond a certain point because

Greene connects the sinfully proud magician with the foolish pride of scholars: "a sorcerer is funny if he is also an over-proud scholar."

David Bevington, in *Tudor Drama and Politics* (1968), points out ways in which Greene suited the play to his audience. Greene emphasizes Margaret's rustic origins and makes only Spanish women her explicit foils; her unwelcome wooers are representatives of the landed gentry and hence anathema to popular taste. "One senses not that Greene was consciously cynical of his popular themes and morality, but that he concocted an unstable vision of goodness he yearned for and then mistrusted because it eluded him. Hence the occasional tendency to lay on with heavy hand, as if laughing at the excesses of his own idealized fancy."

In efforts to demonstrate the play's unity, critics have sought connections among the various episodes. The classic example is William Empson's study of the double plot in *Some Versions of Pastoral* (1935; rpt. in *Shakespeare's Contemporaries,* ed. Max Bluestone and Norman Rabkin, 1961, 2nd ed. 1970). Greene is dramatizing a literary metaphor in the stories about Margaret and Bacon: "the power of beauty is like the power of magic." Both powers "are individualist, dangerous, and outside the social order." Margaret plays earth-goddess to Bacon's earth-magic. The double plot is an "excellent vehicle" for other implications because "it could suggest so powerfully without stating anything open to objection."

Kenneth Muir, "Robert Greene as Dramatist" (I,B), finds magic to be the element common to four plot lines: the making of the brazen head, the rivalry of the Prince and Lacy, the later one of Lambert and Serlsby, and the competition between Bacon and Vandermast. Muir demonstrates that the play falls apart if analyzed through criteria such as realistic motivation and realistic characterization; if "character" and "motivation" and even "craft" do not yield positive results, perhaps attention ought to be directed to "plot conventions" and "rhetoric," since these seem to take precedence in Greene's dramatic decisions. Norman Sanders, "Comedy of Greene and Shakespeare" (I,B), finds a linking mechanism in the audience's awareness of the dramatic illusion, and Alan S. Downer, in *The British Drama* (1950), explains how the joining is facilitated by the nature of the Elizabethan theater: while Bacon and Edward are watching the magic glass in the inner stage, the scene which they observe is enacted on the outer stage.

In his study of construction in Elizabethan drama, "Shakespeare and His Young Contemporaries," *PQ* 41 (1962): 37-57, Hereward T. Price takes a dim view of Greene's "organic" unity. *Friar Bacon* has a double plot, "that is two stories that bump into one another occasionally." He suggests that the theme of forgiveness is common to the two sides of the plot, but still does not think that this thematic continuity leads to "the close integration of drama."

The language of the play has been analyzed by Wolfgang Clemen, *English Tragedy before Shakespeare* (I,B). Greene is unable to maintain a "free and easy style" and usually lapses into style and language dictated by the specific situation and theme instead of the condition of the persons and the style of the play as a whole. Like Muir, Clemen praises the diction of the clowns because it is "robust and realistic." Seltzer, in his edition, answers this type of criticism when he describes Margaret's mixed vocabulary of homely and classical imagery as "explicitly regal" and "explicitly humble." That there may be artistic and formal reasons for having Margaret use classical imagery, that this language does have an effect upon the aura surrounding Margaret, does not contradict the assertion that, again, from a "realistic" viewpoint, in the very kind of appraisal called for by enthusiasts of the country maid, simple problems of verisimilitude arise in a way that they do not for Shakespeare or even Marlowe.

The combination of folk motifs and literary conventions provides ground for source-hunting. Waldo F. McNeir, "Traditional Elements in the Character of Greene's Friar Bacon," *SP* 45 (1948): 172-79, outlines the tradition of magician-heroes: in dignifying Friar Bacon, omitting vulgar japes and humble birth, Greene made his character closer to the tradition of Merlin, Maugis, Virgilius, and other benevolent sorcerers. Eugene Waith, in *The Pattern of Tragicomedy in Beaumont and Fletcher* (1952), shows through a comparison with *Endymion* that Greene's emphasis on action puts him closer to the romance tradition and further from the pastoral than Lyly. A source is indicated by Allan H. MacLaine's title, "Greene's Borrowings from his Own Prose Fiction in *Bacon and Bungay* and *James the Fourth*," *PQ* 30 (1951): 22-29. Significant material is found in the later group of romances: the repetition of incidental allusions, conventional ideas, and stereotyped descriptions; plot ideas; and character types. Romances written a year or two before the plays show heroines, like Fawnia and Sephestia, who approach the color and animation of Margaret, Dorothea, and Ida.

The relation of *Friar Bacon* to *Doctor Faustus* remains uncertain. If *Doctor Faustus* is dated 1592, the debt would be Marlowe's to Greene. With an earlier date of 1588-89, *Friar Bacon* may be an imitation or a parody. Parrott and Ball, in *A Short View of Elizabethan Drama* (I,B), hold that it is neither imitation nor parody. The only recent supporter of the parody thesis is Louis Cazamian, *Development of English Humor* (I,B), who finds the play only "discreetly tinged" with the "spirit of quiet parody." The question is important to Una Ellis-Fermor's argument (in "Marlowe and Greene," I,B), since she sees *Friar Bacon* as a better example of imitation than *Alphonsus* and *Orlando*. Perhaps the best argument for the independence of the two works is her illustration of the differences between the moods, the treatment of magic, and the personalities of the protagonists in the two plays.

It is no longer possible to whitewash *Friar Bacon* with "white magic." Frank Towne, in " 'White Magic' in *Friar Bacon and Friar Bungay?" MLN* 67 (1952): 9-13, contends that there is no sign either in the tradition of Bacon the necromancer as it reached the Renaissance or in Greene's play that Bacon practiced only "white magic." In part, the article is a rebuttal of Robert Hunter West's *The Invisible World: A Study of Pneumatology in Elizabethan Drama* (1939). Towne insists that Bacon is saved from eternal damnation not by the veniality of his sin, but by repentance. In a reply, *MLN* 67 (1952): 499-500, West agrees with Towne but asserts that he did not call Bacon a theurgist. He distinguishes between Bacon's tacit compact with devils and the express compact of Faustus.

The Scottish History of James IV

Although *Friar Bacon* is Greene's most popular play, literary historians and critics tend to hold *James IV* in higher esteem as a piece of dramatic craftsmanship. Despite the general praise, *James IV* has not received a separate, full "reading" in the last twenty years. The best critical comments come from the general studies by Sanders, "Comedy of Greene and Shakespeare"; Clemen, *English Tragedy before Shakespeare;* and Muir, "Robert Greene as Dramatist" (all in I,B). While acknowledging real improvements in exposition and a noteworthy success with some of the chief scenes, these critics also indicate shortcomings. Sanders and Muir agree that the happy ending is dramatically unhappy. The convincing presentation of evil in James and Ateukin makes it difficult for Sanders to accept the comic dénouement of James's repentance. The compelling depiction of James's villainy has the effect of creating justified demands in the audience for equal psychological realism in Dorothea's responses, and as Muir notes, we cannot help feeling that her lack of indignation causes her to shrink into pasteboard. Clemen questions the ultimate conviction of the moral side of the play. The plot is almost entirely lacking in real moral purpose; moralizing gestures substitute for moral action. Where the plot gives rise to situations in which deeply felt emotions must be translated into words, there are only worn-out formulas of rhetorical tragedy.

The frame story has come in for comment, some of it adverse. To Enid Welsford's charge in *The Court Masque* (1927) that the dumb shows were quite irrelevant and simply diverting, Dieter Mehl's *The Elizabethan Dumb Show: The History of a Dramatic Convention* (trans. 1965; German ed. 1964), answers that pantomimes are used to illuminate moral statements; they demonstrate the vanity of earthly glory, and they receive comment from a character in the play. Muir objects to critics (e.g., Collins) who see in Bohan and Oberon prefigurations of Shakespeare's Jaques, Oberon, and Prospero; the participation of frame characters in the play contradicts the temporal relationship established between the frame and the story proper. A defense comes from Sanders, who finds this interplay makes the audience aware of dramatic illusion: the "reality" of Dorothea's suffering is at once shattered and reinforced as the audience is simultaneously distanced from and brought closer to the world of the play. J. A. Lavin, in his introduction to the New Mermaid edition (1967), feels that "the *ubi sunt* and *memento mori* themes of the three dumb-shows presented by Oberon do not correspond to the outcome of the play proper; the lesson they teach about worldly pomp is only relevant in a general way to a tragi-comedy concerning flattery and lust, in which the king survives to live happily, unlike the monarchs of the dumb-shows."

Both Glynne Wickham, in *Early English Stages, 1300–1600*, vol. 2, part 1 (1963), and Ernest William Talbert, in *Elizabethan Drama and Shakespeare's Early Plays: An Essay in Historical Criticism* (1963), link *James IV* with the moralities. The former shows how the ethical debate of a morality play is presented in soliloquy as "contrarious thoughts." The latter sees the struggle between the virtues and vices for control of the central figure: by relating Dorothea to virtue in the commonwealth, "Greene preserves her position in a dramatic movement that affects public as well as private affairs."

Waldo F. McNeir, in "The Original of Ateukin in Greene's *James IV*," *MLN* 62 (1947): 376–81, links Ateukin with the Italian adventurer John Damian, who ingratiated himself with James IV by a pretense of skill as a surgeon, apothecary, alchemist, and astrologer; an account of this imposter is given in John Leslie's *Historie of Scotland*

(1578) and is repeated in the 1587 edition of Holinshed's *Chronicles*. For further evidence see Ruth Hudson, "Greene's *James IV* and Contemporary Allusions to Scotland," *PMLA* 47 (1932): 652-67. Johnstone Parr distinguishes between Ateukin the astrologer and Damian the alchemist and shows a design in Greene's selection of astral configurations: the "particular configurations of Saturn, Sol, and Venus in the king's nativity would . . . endow James with precisely such qualities as he exhibits throughout the play, and would presage for him such fortunes—or misfortunes—as he encounters," in *Tamburlaine's Malady and Other Essays on Astrology in Elizabethan Drama* (1953). The literary tradition for Ateukin is discussed by Marvin T. Herrick in *Tragicomedy* (1955); there is a strong Terentian influence.

Examining Greene's own prose fiction, Allan H. MacLaine, "Greene's Borrowings" (above, *Friar Bacon*), finds the conventional idea that a king can force a woman's love but prefers to win it by entreaty; the use of a chorus framework; and some prefiguration of Dorothea in Barmenissa (*Penelope's Web*), of Ida in Fawnia (*Pandosto*) and Argentina (*Orpharion*), and of James's surrender of Ida (*Penelope's Web, Orpharion*). In general, however, there is far less self-imitation than in *Friar Bacon,* and this comparative purity of style supports the theory that *James IV* should be dated later than *Friar Bacon.* Piero Rébora, in *L'Italia nel dramma inglese, 1558-1642* (1925), treats Greene's in- debtedness to Cinthio. Greene could have found models for the type of noble woman represented by Dorothea and for the romantic aspect of the play in Cinthio. Popular attitudes toward Scotland and their relationship to the play are discussed in Evelyn May Albright's *Dramatic Publication in England, 1580-1640: A Study of Conditions Affecting Content and Form of Drama* (1927), and Richard Vliet Lindabury's *A Study of Patriotism in the Elizabethan Drama* (1931).

The Comical History of Alphonsus King of Aragon

Most interpretations of *Alphonsus* begin by establishing its relation- ship to *Tamburlaine.* Irving Ribner, "Greene's Attack on Marlowe: Some Light on *Alphonsus* and *Selimus,*" *SP* 52 (1955): 162-71, contends that Greene rejects Marlowe's glorification of self-sufficiency as an ideal of kingship. Greene answers Marlowe's humanistic philosophy of history by affirming the will of the gods as the ruling force in human affairs. Whereas Marlowe contended that a man of lowly birth could rise by merit to be king, Greene chooses as his hero the son of a king who has been unjustly deprived of his title. Amurack is Greene's version of Marlowe's ideal: the unchristian tyrant; Alphonsus exemplifies the Christian legitimate king. Ernest William Talbert, *Elizabethan Drama* (above, *James IV*) warns about interpreting Turkish heroic dramas as answers to *Tamburlaine* instead of as examples of its influence.

Una Ellis-Fermor, "Marlowe and Greene" (I,B), indicates kinds of borrowing from Marlowe in the play: images inherited at some removes from Seneca and overused words like "glittering." Greene's own gift for sweetness and poignancy and his sense of homely values find expression in Carinus, especially at the end of the play. Norman Sanders, "Comedy of Greene and Shakespeare" (I,B), also notes Greene's natural sympathy for Carinus as the representative of common sense, tenderness, and homely wisdom. For a stylistic comparison with *Tamburlaine* see Wolfgang Clemen, *English Tragedy before Shakespeare* (above, I,B). Greene has taken over the rant and bombast. In the set speeches, Greene includes much narrative, reporting of action, and then clumsily attempts to change back to dialogue. G. B. Harrison contends that the stage directions of *Alphonsus* suggest that the play was printed from an author's manuscript, and that the author was a literary man visualizing his play rather than a man of the theater (*Elizabethan Plays and Players* [1940]).

John Sibly's "The Duty of Revenge in Tudor and Stuart Drama," *REL* 8 (1967): 46–54, groups *Alphonsus* with plays which, though not histories, "show successful usurpers suffering death or at least dispossession." Sibly finds in the Bond of Association a "real-life exemplar for extra-legal stage revenge," which helps explain why Alphonsus was applauded for turning even a usurper's son off the throne that was his by descent. This interpretation marks a departure from Harry Ransom's claim, in "Some Legal Elements in Elizabethan Plays," *Studies in English* (Univ. of Texas), 16 (1936): 53–76, that the king's attitudes toward legal process are not connected with contemporary law.

A Looking Glass for London and England

As a collaborative effort in which the division of labor between Lodge and Greene is uncertain, *A Looking Glass* is usually given passing mention or neglected entirely in studies of Greene's development. The over-obvious sermons and uneconomical duplication of the prophets, weaknesses perceived by Kenneth Muir, "Robert Greene as Dramatist" (I,B), are not features that encourage separate critical consideration of the play.

Richard Levin, in "The Unity of Elizabethan Multiple-Plot Drama," *ELH* 34 (1967): 425–46, maintains that the authors "intend to equate the vices of Rasni's royal court in the main plot and those of the Usurer in the subplot, so that here a roughly similar differentiation in the tones of the two actions serves to emphasize the warning of the looking glass by universalizing its applicability, the seriousness of the first being appropriate to the higher class and more heinous sins portrayed there, and the realism of the second to its lower level of society and criminality." The play is often viewed in the tradition of moralities. Eberhard Lucius, for example, in *Gerichtsszenen im älteren englischen Drama* (1928), sees Greene going back to the morality style of trial scenes.

Ola Elizabeth Winslow finds Adam's comic relief ill-timed and counter to the moral import of the play as a whole, in *Low Comedy as a Structural Element in English Drama from the Beginnings to 1642* (1926). J. F. Macdonald, "The Use of Prose" (I,B), makes a stylistic point: the usurer's business is conducted in prose, but his conversion rises to poetry. Alice Walker, in her review of Greg's edition, *RES* 10 (1934): 223–25, points out that Adam's line "O Peter, Peter, put up thy sword" (I.2) does not indicate the name of a ruffian but refers to John 18:11.

Sidney R. Homan has seen the influence of the play in Dekker's *If It Be Not a Good Play, the Devil Is in It*, *N&Q* 13 (1966): 301–2; and textual emendations are offered by T. W. Greene, *TLS*, 13 March 1924, p. 160, and by J. C. Maxwell, *N&Q* 192 (1947): 428. Charles Read Baskervill, "A Prompt Copy of *A Looking Glass for London and England*," *MP* 30 (1932): 29–51 examines a copy which served as promptbook for Elizabethan players. Passages are changed for the law, the London audience, and the succession of James to the throne, but not, except for a missing line, to correct textual corruptions. The manuscript markings are appended to Greg's edition (1932).

Orlando Furioso

Kenneth Muir, "Robert Greene as Dramatist" (I,B), presents the case for Greene's incompetence: the characterization is crude, Orlando's madness is unconvincing, and the climax is bungled. Parrott and Ball, *Short View of Elizabethan Drama* (I,B), read the play as a conscious burlesque of *Tamburlaine* and *The Spanish Tragedy*. Una Ellis-Fermor, "Marlowe and Greene" (I,B), argues for a *Tamburlaine* parody with Sacrapant as her chief evidence; Greene fails to present any aesthetic ·

harmony, and so the line between intentional parody and unintentional imitation is doubtful. Wolfgang Clemen, *English Tragedy before Shakespeare* (I,B), finds Greene parodying the outward features of the style and diction of *Tamburlaine:* the string of apostrophes, the protestations and execrations, the hyperbole, the profusion of mythological names are presumably mannerisms Greene would have used in imitating Marlowe. The swaggering bumptiousness of Marlowe's hero is burlesqued by being transferred to courting scenes. The major parallels are listed by Charles W. Lemmi, *"Tamburlaine* and Greene's *Orlando Furioso," MLN* 32 (1917): 434-35. Lemmi argues that the comic use of *Tamburlaine* occurs largely in the mad scenes, where the lunatic hero was a natural subject of laughter to an Elizabethan audience. Norman Sanders, "Comedy of Greene and Shakespeare" (I,B), sees an advance in *Orlando* over *Alphonsus.* Greene may have recognized the comic possibilities of the lovers meeting at a time when normal expression of their love is impossible. An original twist is introduced by having one of the pair unrecognized by the other.

The source for *Orlando* is discussed by Waldo F. McNeir in "Greene's Medievalization of Ariosto," *RLC* 29 (1955): 351-60. Although Greene uses modified forms of Ariosto's characters, the stories in which they figure in the original contribute nothing to the plot. The serious tone brings the play closer to the spirit of medieval romance. Greene lacks Ariosto's skepticism in treating supernatural features and tones down Orlando's behavior during his madness. McNeir also notes changes in the characterization of Angelica. Again, the changes point in the direction of the medieval romance. General discussions of Greene's use of Ariosto are given in Piero Rébora, *L'Italia nel dramma inglese, 1558-1642* (1925) and Charles W. Lemmi, "The Sources of Greene's *Orlando Furioso," MLN* 31 (1916): 440-41. Morris Robert Morrison extends Lemmi's comparison in *MLN* 49 (1934): 449-51.

Norman Gelber sees Greene emphasizing the individuality of women by placing Angelica's ideal moral behavior in a framework of anti-feminist speeches, in "Robert Greene's *Orlando Furioso:* A Study of Thematic Ambiguity," *MLR* 64 (1969): 264-66. Eudo C. Mason finds in Orlando the first sustained piece of insane tragic raving against women in Elizabethan drama, though its pre-Marstonian style makes the satire rather harmless, in "Satire on Woman and Sex Tragedy," *ES* 31 (1950): 1-10.

The conventional aspects of Orlando's frenzy are listed by Edgar Allison Peers in *Elizabethan Drama and Its Mad Folk* (1914). Joseph T.

McCullen, Jr., in "Madness and the Isolation of Characters in Elizabethan and Early Stuart Drama," *SP* 48 (1951): 206–18, finds Orlando comically unconscious of improper conduct despite efforts of friends to aid him. His horseplay belongs to an irresponsible character divorced from mankind. Rolf Soellner, in "The Madness of Hercules and the Elizabethans," *CL* 10 (1958): 309–24, while admitting the proximity of this behavior to the comical, prefers to study Orlando in the tradition of *Hercules furens*, especially for his hyperbolic rhetoric. J. F. Macdonald, "The Use of Prose" (I,B), traces Orlando's changing styles of speech.

George a Greene, the Pinner of Wakefield

Malcolm A. Nelson rejects the idea that the play is based upon *The Famous History of George a Greene*, in "The Sources of *George a Greene, the Pinner of Wakefield*," *PQ* 42 (1963): 159–65. Rather, the play is the source of the romance, which was not written until at least five years after the 1593 performance. Although Nelson does not rule out an earlier lost prose romance, he finds the clearest sources in popular ballads like "The Jolly Pinder of Wakefield" (Child 124) and "A Gest of Robyn Hode" (Child 117). William E. Simeone relates *George a Greene* to the pastoral tradition of Robin Hood: "Renaissance Robin Hood Plays," in *Folklore in Action: Essays for Discussion in Honor of MacEdward Leach*, ed. Horace P. Beck (1962), pp. 184–99. A long analysis is provided in David Bevington's *Tudor Drama and Politics* (I,B). The play exemplifies Greene's "dual longing to glorify the figure of the virile, bluff, typical English yeoman and yet paradoxically to exaggerate that figure to the point where the author is detached, safe from commitment." An historical counterpart to the Earl of Kendal is found in the Earl of Atholl, one of the conspirators who murdered James I of Scotland, by Clarence L. Wentworth, *TLS*, 4 July 1936, p. 564.

John of Bordeaux, or The Second Part of Friar Bacon

W. L. Renwick, who gave the play the title by which it is known, warns that some references to *Friar Bacon* (e.g., in Henslowe) may be to this second part (in the Introduction to his Malone Society edition [1936]). At least three of the main character-names are drawn from Lodge's *Rosalynde*. The plot is similar to that of *A Knack to Know an Honest Man*, but it is not certain which play came first. The author is clearly a university man, and since indebtedness is chiefly to Greene's works, Renwick decides in favor of Greene himself. Harry R. Hoppe claims that "bad" as the text of the MS is, it was actually used as the prompt copy by some Elizabethan acting company: "*John of Bordeaux:* A Bad Quarto That Never Reached Print," in *Studies in Honor of A. H. R. Fairchild,* ed. Charles T. Prouty, University of Missouri Studies, vol. 21 (1946), pp. 121–32. Benvenuto Cellini argues that the three comic scenes with Perce are later insertions by Greene; he also notes stylistic (especially metrical) variations in several scenes, and finds a source for the romantic plot in *Huon of Bordeaux* (see his edition of *Friar Bacon and Friar Bungay* and *John of Bordeaux* [1952]).

Waldo F. McNeir, "Robert Greene and *John of Bordeaux,*" *PMLA* 64 (1949): 781–801, examines the evidence that Greene imitated his own successes and wrote his own sequels. He shows the dependence of *John of Bordeaux* on *Friar Bacon* and the characteristics shared with Greene's other works. There is a change in the characterization of Friar Bacon: instead of being jolly and frolic, Bacon is now old, reverent, and worthy. If the sequel came shortly after *Friar Bacon,* the image of the older Bacon devoting himself to a better life may have had a special appeal to Greene at that time. McNeir also reconstructs the conclusion of John of Bordeaux from the mutilated extant portion and hints found earlier in the play, in "Reconstructing the Conclusion of *John of Bordeaux,*" *PMLA* 66 (1951): 540–43.

III. CANON

A. PLAYS IN CHRONOLOGICAL ORDER

A major obstacle to studies of Greene is uncertainty about the canon and chronology. To accept only the likely possibilities among the unproven ascriptions would double the number of plays certainly attributed to Greene. The current status of the canon discourages genetic and developmental approaches. Additional influence and development studies are suggested in the now dated synthesis provided by Rupert Taylor, "A Tentative Chronology of Marlowe's and Some Other Elizabethan Plays," *PMLA* 51 (1936): 643–88.

The chronology, limits of date (in italics preceding semicolon), first publication dates, and type are from Alfred Harbage, *Annals of English Drama, 975–1700,* rev. Samuel Schoenbaum (1964). W. W. Greg describes the first quartos in *A Bibliography of the English Printed Drama to the Restoration,* 4 vols. (1939–59). E. K. Chambers discusses canon and dating in *The Elizabethan Stage,* vols. 3 and 4 (1923). Attributions and criteria for ascriptions are also given by Schoenbaum in *Internal Evidence and Elizabethan Dramatic Authorship* (1966).

Alphonsus, King of Aragon, heroical romance (*1587-88*; 1599)

An obscure passage in the preface to *Perimedes* (1588) suggests that Greene had attempted a play and failed because he could not dare God "out of heaven with that Atheist *Tamburlan."* On the basis of the relationship between Marlowe's play and *Alphonsus,* W. W. Greg (Malone Society ed., 1926) dates it immediately after *Tamburlaine.* Collins (1905 edition of the plays), arguing from internal evidence, chooses the late date 1591.

Friar Bacon and Friar Bungay, comedy (ca. *1589-92*; 1594)

Seltzer, in the RRDS edition (1963), evaluates the arguments about the play's relationship to *Faustus, Fair Em,* and contemporary events and concludes that 1589-90 is the most plausible date.

A Looking Glass for London and England, biblical moral (*1587-91*; 1594)

Waldo F. McNeir, "The Date of *A Looking Glass for London," N&Q* 2 (1955): 282-83, supports a date late in 1589 or early in 1590. There is a reference to Ninevites in *Vision* (1590) which the play would need to antedate. The theme of repentance cannot, of course, be used to connect the play with Greene's period of repentance. Nor can other references to Nineveh or Jonah in contemporary works (including Greene's) be taken as certain allusions to the play, as Dickinson (Mermaid edition, 1909) warns. Some critics accept an earlier date than the *Annals'* preferred 1590.

Robert Adger Law, "Two Parallels to Greene and Lodge's *Looking Glass," MLN* 26 (1911): 146-48, finds parallels to Doctor Faustus in Adam's final speech in IV.iv and the usurer's repentance (V.ii). An episode in *The Famous Historie of Fryer Bacon* resembles Adam's concealment of food; Law dates Greene's interest in Bacon's history after *Faustus,* and arrives at a date of 1589-91. In a later article, *"A Looking Glass* and the Scriptures," *Studies in English* (Univ. of Texas), 19 (1939): 31-47, he shows the play's use of the Bishop's Bible for its scriptural passages. Greene's other works do not have such prominent verbal repetition in biblical passages, and he attributes to Lodge the usurer scenes and the parts of the play having to do with Jonas and Oseas' speeches. Law gives Greene the Adam story and the plan of the play as a whole since it resembles *Friar Bacon.*

The Scottish History of James IV, history (ca. *1590–91;* 1598)

T. W. Baldwin, *On the Literary Genetics of Shakspere's Plays, 1592–1594* (1959), accepts Fleay's arguments (1891) and arrives at a date not later than 1590. Collins, in his edition, suggests that the motto upon which Fleay bases his dating may have been inserted by the publisher.

Orlando Furioso, romantic comedy (*1588–92;* 1594)

An allusion to the Armada sets 1588 as the earliest date for composition; it is an old play when Henslowe notes a performance in February, 1592. The charge that Greene sold the play to both the Queen's company and the Admiral's men indicates that the play had belonged to the Queen's company until December 26, 1591; hence the latest date for composition. Some critics (e.g., Jordan) favor a date closer to the Spanish defeat for first performance. Harbage and Schoenbaum prefer 1591.

B. UNCERTAIN ASCRIPTIONS; APOCRYPHA

Job, biblical history (*1586–93?;* lost)

John Warburton lists among the plays he owned until "they was unluckely burnd or put under Pye bottoms" a history of Job by "Rob. Green." Greg (cited in Chambers, *Elizabethan Stage,* vol. 3) suggests a confusion with Sir Robert Le Grys.

I & II The Troublesome Reign of King John, history (ca. *1587–91;* 1591)

Fleay has Greene, Peele, and Lodge writing the scenes from a plot by Marlowe. Other discussions are in Geoffrey Bullough's *Narrative and Dramatic Sources of Shakespeare,* vol. 4 (1962) and E. A. J. Honigmann's Arden edition of *King John* (1954). See the section on anonymous plays in this volume.

The Taming of a Shrew, comedy (ca. *1588–93;* 1594)

Echoes of Marlowe have been pointed out by Frederick S. Boas (1908 ed.). Chambers sums up: "For author, Marlowe, Kyd, Greene, and Peele have all been suggested, but, so far as we know, Marlowe did not repeat himself, and the others did not plagiarize him, in this flagrant manner." If certain lines are parodied in *Menaphon,* Greene's authorship would seem all the more doubtful. See Paul V. Rubow, ed.,

Tvold kan tæmmes, The Taming of a Shrew (1957) and the discussion
in the section on anonymous plays in this volume.

Titus Andronicus, tragedy (*1594,* possibly originally written in
1589-90; 1594)

Only surmise connects this play with Greene. See the Peele canon
section.

George a Greene, the Pinner of Wakefield, romantic comedy (*1587-93*;
1599)

Although virtually all Greene editors include this play, they do so
with awareness that the grounds for attribution are inconclusive. The
MS notes on the title page of the 1599 quarto were first discovered by
Collier, so the possibility of forgery must be added to uncertainties
about the notes themselves. Charles A. Pennel, "The Authenticity of
the *George a Greene* Title-Page Inscriptions," *JEGP* 64 (1965): 668-76,
clears this suspicion by examining Collier's treatment of the play over a
period of forty years; in 1863, when his own reputation was under
attack, Collier questioned the inscriptions. Pennel argues for accepting
the second note ("Juby saith that the play was made by Ro. Gree") and
dismissing the "Shakespeare" note. In another article, "Robert Greene
and 'King or Kaiser,'" *ELN* 3 (1965): 24-26, he demonstrates a
similarity between the vocabulary of the play and that of undoubted
works of Greene; the phrase "King or Kaiser" does occur four times in
Greene's other works and not in the works of contemporaries. In this
article he goes back to the work of H. Dugdale Sykes, whose "Robert
Greene and *George a Greene, The Pinner of Wakefield*" is in *RES* 7
(1931): 129-36, and 9 (1933): 189-90. R. C. Bald also discusses the
inscriptions in *Library* 15 (1934): 295-305. A plea for consistency in
attribution of works like *Locrine, Selimus,* and *George a Greene* is
made by Dean B. Lyman, Jr., "Apocryphal Plays of the University
Wits," in *English Studies in Honor of James Southall Wilson,* ed.
Fredson Bowers (1951), pp. 211-21.

Henslowe notes five performances between 29 December 1593, and
22 January 1594, but does not mark it as a new play. The play refers to
Tamburlaine. Jordan, *Robert Greene* (I,A), although admitting that
nothing is known about the date, decides that if the play is by Greene,
it belongs just before or just after *James IV.* Harbage and Schoenbaum
also prefer 1590. Charles A. Pennel, in his critical edition (Ph.D. diss.,
Univ. of Illinois, 1962), dates the play in 1591 through its association

with Sussex's men, that company's amalgamation with the Queen's men
in 1591, and Greene's literary activities in 1591-92.

Edward III, history (ca. *1590-95*; 1596)

C. F. Tucker Brooke, in *The Shakespeare Apocrypha* (1908), rejects
Greene because of the lack of his "mythological jargon" and favors
Peele.

Fair Em, the Miller's Daughter, romantic comedy (ca. *1589-91*; ?1593)

Edward Phillips (1675) assigned the play to Greene, who, however,
mocks it in the preface to *Farewell to Folly*. H. S. D. Mithal, "The
Authorship of *Fair Em* and *Martin Mar-Sixtus*," *N&Q* 7 (1960): 8-10,
notes that the play may have been written earlier in 1587. See the
anonymous play section.

King Leir, legendary history (ca. *1588-94*; 1605)

Fleay and Robertson argue for Greene's hand. See the discussion in
the anonymous play section.

Mucedorus, romantic comedy (*1588-98*; rev. *1610*; 1598)

Malone and Hopkinson (cited in Chambers, *Elizabethan Stage*, vol. 4)
accept Green as the original author. Collins, in his edition, counters:
"No scene or passage in *Mucedorus* has any trace of Greene's hand in
it." See the anonymous play section.

Locrine, pseudo-history (*1591-95*; 1595)

C. F. Tucker Brooke, in *The Shakespeare Apocrypha* (1908) writes,
"The importance, character, and success of the comic element, the
excessive richness of mythological allusion . . . the extreme rarity of
run-on lines, and the general appearance of over-decoration all indicate
that the author of *Locrine* is . . . Robert Greene." Brooke also believes
that the play was written "before Greene fell under the spell of
Tamburlaine." See the discussions of *Selimus* below and of this title in
the anonymous play section.

II Henry VI (*I The Contention betwixt the Two Famous Houses of
York and Lancaster*), history (ca. *1590-92*; 1594)
III Henry VI (*The True Tragedy of Richard Duke of York*), history (ca.
1590-92; 1595)

For Greene's parody of *III Henry VI*, I.iv. 137, see I,C, the discussion of the "upstart crow" reference. Malone's ascription (cited in Chambers) is based on this passage as an attack for plagiarism. There is no evidence that the play owes anything to Greene. Now that *The Contention* and *The True Tragedy* have been seen to be bad quartos or memorial versions of *II* and *III Henry VI*, "the argument for other hands has fallen back on parallels of vocabulary with Greene, Peele, Nashe, or Marlowe," according to Andrew S. Cairncross in the Arden *III Henry VI* (1964). J. Dover Wilson's New Cambridge edition of *I- III Henry VI* (1952), advocates a theory of composite authorship with Greene doing the plotting.

John of Bordeaux, or the Second Part of Friar Bacon, comedy (*1590- 94*; MS)

It is likely that this follows closely upon *Friar Bacon and Friar Bungay*. Renwick, in his edition for the Malone Society (1936), suggests that entries referring to *Friar Bacon* as an old play acted by Strange's men in 1592 may refer to *John of Bordeaux* (with *Friar Bacon* belonging to the Queen's players). Harbage and Schoenbaum think 1592 the most probable choice. Additional scholarship bearing on date and authorship has been discussed above in II,A. For a survey of theories about Chettle's involvement, see Harold Jenkins, *The Life and Works of Henry Chettle* (1934).

A Knack to Know A Knave, comedy (*10 June, 1592*; 1594)

Charles M. Gayley, *Representative English Comedies* (1930), vol. 1, thinks this is the comedy written by Greene and the "young Juvenal." See I,C, and the discussion of authorship in the anonymous play section of this volume.

I Selimus, heroical romance (*1586- 93*; 1594)

Grosart includes the play in his edition of the complete works. Passages from the play are attributed to Greene by Robert Allott in *England's Parnassus* (1600). (Gayley, however, notes that Allott is not very trustworthy in assignments.) The plot comes from Primaudaye, whose work Greene frequently plundered in this period. F. G. Hubbard, "*Locrine* and *Selimus,*" in *Shakespeare Studies by Members of the Department of English in the University of Wisconsin* (1916), pp. 17- 35, decides that *Locrine* precedes *Selimus* and that the latter borrows from *Locrine*. Admitting that *Selimus* borrows Spenser through *Locrine,* Baldwin Maxwell, *Studies in the Shakespeare*

Apocrypha (1956), offers another hypothesis: "The author of *Selimus*, possibly while writing that play and certainly after reading the story of Selimus and Corcut, set about a revision of *Locrine*. From the historical account of the wanderings of Corcut he constructed the wholly unauthorized wanderings of Humber. In *Locrine* he found or introduced many lines from Spenser, some of which, along with lines of his own, he used again in the play temporarily laid aside to permit this revision. He may but need not have been the author of an earlier form of *Locrine*." Maxwell concludes, "If the author of *Selimus* was Robert Greene, Greene must also have been the reviser of *Locrine*; but if *Selimus* was written by an imitator of Greene, that imitator must also have revised *Locrine*." Maxwell also calls attention to similarities between *Locrine* and *Alphonsus*. Brooke, *Shakespeare Apocrypha* (1908), summarizes the internal evidence: "In the variety and amount of mythological reference, in general dramatic structure, in the number and kind of borrowings from Spenser, Marlowe, and Greene himself, there is little doubt that *Selimus* bears more likeness to *Orlando Furioso* and *Alphonsus, King of Arragon* than to any work of any contemporary writer." He would, however, place *Selimus* before *Alphonsus* instead of after. See the anonymous play section in this volume.

The Thracian Wonder, comedy (*1590-* ca. *1600*; 1661)

John Le Gay Brereton, in "The Relation of *The Thracian Wonder* to Greene's *Menaphon*," *MLR* 2 (1906): 34–38, argues that the author treats his material "much as we might expect Greene to do if he were dramatising one of his own novels shortly after the date of its composition."

Thomas Lord Cromwell, history (ca. *1599-1602*; 1602)

A. F. Hopkinson, in his edition (1891) and in *Essays on Shakespeare's Doubtful Plays* (1900), thinks Shakespeare revised an original play by Greene. The claim has received no subsequent support.

C. CRITIQUE OF THE STANDARD EDITION

A. B. Grosart's achievement falls short of his aspiration in his edition of the *Complete Works* (1881–86). Even the nondramatic prose texts are flawed. For example, Grosart reprints *Planetomachia* from a defective copy and omits one of the three "Tragical Histories." (Pruvost reprints the missing section as an appendix to *Robert Greene et ses romans.*) J. Churton Collins' edition of the plays (1905) attempts to correct the deficiencies for the dramatic texts. It has become the standard edition *faute de mieux*. In a hostile review, *MLR* 1 (1905): 238–51, Greg says of Collins' text: "It is impossible to pretend that it is even moderately satisfactory." He finds that Collins prints from transcripts of the original quartos with no consistent attempt to read the proofs with the originals; further, he charges that there is no evidence that Collins has himself consulted a single one of the original editions. The forthcoming edition under the general editorship of I. A. Shapiro and Johnstone Parr will replace Grosart and Collins.

D. SINGLE-WORK EDITIONS

In the absence of a sound complete edition, it is fortunate that there exist good editions of single plays. The Malone Society editions supplement Collins's edition. Several recent editions notably increase textual precision. Daniel Seltzer, in his edition of *Friar Bacon and Friar Bungay*, RRDS (1963), uses the Corpus Christi College copy of the 1594 quarto (discovered in 1936) as control text and records all important corrections. J. A. Lavin's New Mermaid edition of the play (1969) is based on the Huntington Library copy and also records corrections and emendations. Lavin's edition of *James IV* (1967, New Mermaid) collates the four extant copies of the quarto. The Revels series will include a *James IV*, edited by Norman Sanders. The Malone Society has published editions of *Orlando Furioso* (1907), *Alphonsus, King of Aragon* (1926), *Friar Bacon and Friar Bungay* (1926), and *A Looking Glass for London and England* (1932), by W. W. Greg; *James IV* (1921), by A. E. H. Swaen with W. W. Greg; a diplomatic edition of *John of Bordeaux* (1936), by W. L. Renwick with W. W. Greg; and *George a Greene* (1911), by F. W. Clarke (this last play also available in Farmer's Tudor Facsimile Texts [1913]). Benvenuto Cellini's edition of *Friar Bacon and Friar Bungay* and *John of Bordeaux* (1952) gives a reconstructed text of the second play.

W. W. Greg has edited the player's part of *Orlando* for the Malone Society in *Two Elizabethan Stage Abridgements: "The Battle of Alcazar" & "Orlando Furioso": An Essay in Critical Bibliography* (1923). Greg's conjectures about the part and the 1594 Quarto are attacked by B. A. P. van Dam in *ES* 11 (1929): 182–203, 209–20, who denies that the corrections in the transcript imply a careful collation with the original and thinks the Quarto is a stenographer's report. Sujit Kumar Mukherjee summarizes the bibliographical arguments in "The

Text of Greene's *Orlando Furioso,*" *Indian Journal of English Studies* (Calcutta), 6 (1965): 102–7.

E. NONDRAMATIC WORKS

Many single-work critical editions of the prose have been prepared as doctoral theses. A facsimile reproduction of *Ciceronis Amor* and *A Quip for an Upstart Courtier* has been printed with an introduction by Edwin Haviland Miller (1954). *The Third Part of Cony-Catching* is included in *Three Elizabethan Pamphlets,* ed. G. R. Hibbard (1952). A. V. Judges collects the rogue literature in *The Elizabethan Underworld* (1930). F. Ferrara has edited *Gwydonius* and *The Mourning Garment* for Collana di Letteratura Moderna (1960). *The Carde of Fancie* is available in the Everyman volume of *Shorter Novels: Elizabethan and Jacobean* (1929), edited and with an introduction by George Saintsbury and notes by Philip Henderson. *Pandosto* is reprinted in James Winny's *The Descent of Euphues* (1957) and Merritt Lawlis, *Elizabethan Prose Fiction* (1967). G. B. Harrison edited *A Notable Discovery of Coosnage* and *The Second and Last Part of Conny-Catching,* Bodley Head Quartos, vol. 1 (1923); *The Thirde & Last Part of Conny-catching* and *A Disputation between a Hee Conny-catcher and a Shee Conny-catcher,* Bodley Head Quartos, vol. 3 (1923); *Greenes Groatsworth of Witte* and *The Repentance of Robert Greene,* Bodley Head Quartos, vol. 6 (1923); and *The Blacke Bookes Messenger* and *The Defence of Conny-catching,* Bodley Head Quartos, vol. 10 (1924).

IV. SEE ALSO

A. BIOGRAPHICAL

Most biographical studies of Shakespeare and Marlowe mention Greene. The list below is selective.

Bakeless, John. *The Tragicall History of Christopher Marlowe.* 2 vols. 1942.

Bing, Just. "Shakespeare's Debut." *Edda* 40 (1940): 1–30.

Boas, Frederick S. *Christopher Marlowe: A Biographical and Critical Study.* 1940; rev. ed. 1953.

Brion, Marcel. "Robert Greene." *Correspondant* 282 (1930): 734–45.

Eccles, Mark. *Christopher Marlowe in London.* 1934.

Harrison, G. B. *Shakespeare's Fellows: Being a Brief Chronicle of the Shakespearean Age.* 1923.

Henderson, Philip. *And Morning in His Eyes: A Book about Christopher Marlowe.* 1937.

Holland, H. H. *Shakespeare, Oxford, and Elizabethan Times.* 1933.
Jones, Gwyn. *Garland of Bays.* 1938. [Fictional biography.]
Kettner, Eugene J. "*Love's Labour's Lost* and the Harvey-Nashe-Greene Quarrel." *ESRS* 10 (1962): 29–39.
McNeal, Thomas H. "Studies in the Greene-Shakespeare Relationship." *SAB* 15 (1940): 210–18.
McNeir, Waldo F. "Spenser's 'Pleasing Alcon.' " *EA* 9 (1956): 136–40.
Maugeri, Aldo. *Greene, Marlowe e Shakespeare, tre studi biografici.* 1952.
Shield, H. A. "Links with Shakespeare." *N&Q* 195 (1950): 205–6. [Greene as rival poet.]

B. GENERAL

Aronstein, Philipp. *Das englische Renaissancedrama.* 1929.
Ascoli, G. *La Grande-Bretagne devant l'opinion française.* 1930.
Baker, G. P. "The Plays of the University Wits." In *The Cambridge History of English Literature,* ed. A. W. Ward and A. R. Waller, 5 (1910): 136–59.
Bartley, J. O. "The Development of the Stage Scotchman and Welshman." *MLR* 38 (1943): 279–88.
Dunn, Esther Cloudman. *The Literature of Shakespeare's England.* 1936.
Eckhardt, Eduard. *Das englische Drama im Zeitalter der Reformation und der Hochrenaissance. Vorstufen, Shakespeare und seine Zeit.* 1928.
Gassner, John. *Masters of the Drama.* 1940; 3rd ed. 1954.
Gerrard, Ernest A. *Elizabethan Drama and Dramatists, 1583–1603.* 1928.
Harrison, G. B. *Elizabethan Plays and Players.* 1940.
Jewkes, Wilfred T. *Act-Division in Elizabethan and Jacobean Plays, 1583–1616.* 1958.
Moore, John Robert. "The Songs of the Public Theaters in the Time of Shakespeare." *JEGP* 28 (1929): 166–202.
O'Conner, W. V. *The New Woman of the Renaissance.* 1942.
Parrott, Thomas Marc. *William Shakespeare.* 1934.
Pearson, Lu Emily. *Elizabethan Love Conventions.* 1933.
Pinto, Vivian de Sola. *The English Renaissance.* 1938; rev. ed. 1966.
Reed, Robert Rentoul, Jr. *The Occult on the Tudor and Stuart Stage.* 1965.
Schelling, Felix E. *Elizabethan Playwrights: A Short History of the English Drama from Medieval Times to the Closing of the Theatres in 1642.* 1925.
Sharpe, Robert Boies. *The Real War of the Theaters.* 1935.
Smet, Robert de [Romain Sanvic]. *Le théâtre élisabéthain.* 1955.
Thorndike, A. H. *English Comedy.* 1929.
Thorp, Willard. *The Triumph of Realism in Elizabethan Drama.* 1928.
Wells, Henry W. *Poetic Imagery.* 1924.
Wilson, Edward M. "Family Honour in the Plays of Shakespeare's Predecessors and Contemporaries." *E&S* 6 (1953): 19–40.
Winslow, Ola Elizabeth. *Low Comedy as a Structural Element in English Drama from the Beginnings to 1642.* 1926.
Wright, Louis B. "Stage Duelling in the Elizabethan Theatre." *MLR* 22 (1927): 265–75.

C. WORKS AT LARGE

Allen, Don Cameron. *The Star-Crossed Renaissance*. 1941.

Arms, George, and Louis G. Locke. "Greene's 'Sweet Are the Thoughts.' " *Expl* 3 (1945), item 27.

Arnold, Paul. "Esoterisme du Conte d'Hiver." *Mercure de France* 318 (1953): 494–512. [*Pandosto.*]

Bloor, R. H. U. *The English Novel from Chaucer to Galsworthy*. 1935.

Buckley, George T. *Atheism in the English Renaissance*. 1932.

Bush, Douglas. *Mythology and the Renaissance Tradition in English Poetry*. 1932; rev. ed. 1963.

Camden, Carroll, Jr. "Chaucer and Greene." *RES* 6 (1930): 73–74.

Camp, Charles W. *The Artisan in Elizabethan Literature*. 1923.

Crane, William G. *Wit and Rhetoric in the Renaissance*. 1937.

Crawford, Jack R. *What to Read in English Literature*. 1928.

Dean, James S., Jr. "Antedating from Robert Greene." *N&Q* 10 (1963): 296–98.

Drinkwater, John. *English Poetry*. 1938.

Fisher, Margery. "Notes on the Sources of Some Incidents in Middleton's London Plays." *RES* 15 (1939): 283–93.

Forsythe, Robert S. "Notes on *The Spanish Tragedy*." *PQ* 5 (1926): 78–84. [Use of *Planetomachia*.]

Gagen, Jean Elisabeth. *The New Woman: Her Emergence in English Drama: 1600–1730*. 1954.

Genouy, Hector. *L'elément pastoral dans la poésie narrative et le drame en Angleterre, de 1579 à 1640*. 1928.

Goree, Roselle Gould. "Concerning Repetitions in Greene's Romances." *PQ* 3 (1924): 69–75.

——. "Further Repetitions in the Works of Robert Greene." *PQ* 18 (1939): 73–77.

Harman, E. G. *Gabriel Harvey and Thomas Nashe*. 1923.

Harris, Lynn H. "Greene's 'Sephestia's Song to Her Child.' " *Expl* 5 (1946), item 12.

Harrison, G. B. "Books and Readers, 1591–94." *Library* 8 (1927): 273–302.

Honigmann, E. A. J. "Shakespeare's 'Lost Source-Plays.' " *MLR* 49 (1954): 293–97.

Jenkins, Harold. "On the Authenticity of *Greene's Groatsworth of Wit* and *The Repentance of Robert Greene*." *RES* 11 (1935): 28–41.

Johnson, Francis R. "The First Edition of Gabriel Harvey's *Foure Letters*." *Library* 15 (1935): 212–23.

Jusserand, J. J. *The School for Ambassadors and Other Essays*. 1924.

Kabell, Aage. *Metrische Studien II: Antiker Form sich nähernd*. 1960.

Kennard, J. S. *The Friar in Fiction*. 1923.

Klein, David. *The Elizabethan Dramatists as Critics*. 1963.

Knapp, M. "A Note on Nashe's Preface to Greene's *Menaphon*." *N&Q* 164 (1933): 98.

Lavin, J. A. "Two Notes on *The Cobler's Prophecy*." *N&Q* 9 (1962): 137–39.

Lievsay, John Leon. "Robert Greene, Master of Arts, and 'Mayster Steeven Guazzo.' " *SP* 36 (1939): 577–96.

McNeal, Thomas H. " 'The Clerk's Tale' as a Possible Source for *Pandosto*." *PMLA* 47 (1932): 453–60.

McNeir, Waldo F. "Greene's 'Tomliuclin': *Tamburlaine* or *Tom a Lincoln?" MLN* 58 (1943): 380-82.
———. "A Proverb of Greene's Emended." *N&Q* 197 (1952): 117.
Miller, Edwin Haviland. "Another Source for Anthony Nixon's *The Scourge of Corruption* (1615)." *HLQ* 17 (1954): 173-76.
———. "Samuel Rid's Borrowings from Robert Greene." *N&Q* 199 (1954): 236-38.
———. "A Bestseller Brought up to Date: Later Printings of Robert Greene's *A Disputation Between a He Conny-Catcher and a She Conny-Catcher (1592)." PBSA* 52 (1958): 126-31.
Mills, Laurens J. *One Soul in Bodies Twain.* 1937.
Morris, Harry. "Richard Barnfield: 'The Affectionate Shepherd.' " *TSE* 10 (1960): 13-38.
Muir, Kenneth. "Greene and *Troilus and Cressida." N&Q* 2 (1955): 141-42.
Parrott, Thomas Marc. "Marlowe, Beaumont, and *Julius Caesar." MLN* 44 (1929): 69-77.
Pruvost, René. *Matteo Bandello and Elizabethan Fiction.* 1937.
Quaintance, Richard E., Jr. "The French Source of Greene's 'What Thing is Love.' " *N&Q* 10 (1963): 295-96. [Mellin de Saint Gelais.]
Robin, P. Ansell. *Animal Lore in English Literature.* 1932.
Rollins, Hyder Edward, ed. *The Phoenix Nest.* 1931.
———, ed. *England's Helicon.* 2 vols. 1935.
Sanders, Chauncey Elwood. "Robert Greene and His Editors." *PMLA* 48 (1933): 392-417.
Sanders, Chauncey Elwood, and William A. Jackson. "A Note on Robert Greene's *Planetomachia* (1585)." *Library* 16 (1936): 444-47.
Sanders, Norman. "Greene's 'Tomliuolin.' " *N&Q* 9 (1962): 229-30.
Smith, Charles G. "Sententious Theory in Spenser's Legend of Friendship." *ELH* 2 (1935): 165-91.
Smith, Hallett. *Elizabethan Poetry.* 1952.
South, Helen Pennock. "The Upstart Crow." *MLN* 25 (1927): 83-86.
Staton, Walter F., Jr. "The Characters of Style in Elizabethan Prose." *JEGP* 57 (1958): 197-207.
Sutherland, James. *On English Prose.* 1958.
Ungerer, Gustav. *Anglo-Spanish Relations in Tudor Literature.* 1956. [*Spanish Masquerado.*]
Vincent, Charles Jackson. "Natural History in the Works of Robert Greene." *Harvard University Summaries of Theses, 1938.* 1940.
———. "Pettie and Greene." *MLN* 54 (1939): 105-11.
Wagenknecht, Edward. *Cavalcade of the English Novel.* 1943; rev. ed. 1954.
Walker, Hugh. *English Satire and Satirists.* 1925.
Watson, Harold Francis. *The Sailor in English Fiction and Drama, 1550-1800.* 1931.
Weaver, Charles P. *The Hermit in English Literature from the Beginnings to 1660.* 1924.
Weld, John S. "W. Bettie's *Titania and Theseus." PQ* 26 (1947): 36-44.
Wells, Stanley W. "Impartial." *N&Q* 6 (1959): 353-54. [*Perimedes.*]
———. "Some Words in 1588." *N&Q* 9 (1962): 205-7.

White, Harold O. *Plagiarism and Imitation during the English Renaissance: A Study in Critical Distinctions.* 1935.
Wright, Louis B. *Middle-Class Culture in Elizabethan England.* 1935.

D. INDIVIDUAL PLAYS

Friar Bacon and Friar Bungay

Cellini, Benvenuto. "Echi di Greene nel *Doctor Faustus* di Marlowe." *RLMC* 3 (1952): 124-29.
Chambers, E. K. "Elizabethan Stage Gleanings." *RES* 1 (1925): 182-86.
McCallum, J. D. "Greene's *Friar Bacon and Friar Bungay.*" *MLN* 35 (1920): 212-17.
Round, P. Z. "Greene's Materials for *Friar Bacon and Friar Bungay.*" *MLR* 21 (1926): 19-23.
Schelling, Felix E. *Shakespeare Biography and Other Papers Chiefly Elizabethan.* 1937.
Simpson, Evelyn. "A Greene Quarto." *TLS*, 21 Nov. 1936, p. 980.
Stanley, Emily B. "The Use of Classical Mythology by the University Wits." *RenP*, 1956, pp. 25-33.
Wells, Henry W. *Elizabethan and Jacobean Playwrights.* 1939.

James IV

Kennedy, Milton Boone. *The Oration in Shakespeare.* 1942.
Kernodle, George R. *From Art to Theatre: Form and Convention in the Renaissance.* 1944.
Laserstein, Käte. *Der Griseldisstoff in der Weltliteratur.* 1926.
Maxwell, J. C. "Greene's 'Ridstall Man.' " *MLR* 44 (1949): 88-89.
Ploch, Georg. "Über den Dialog in den Dramen Shakespeares und seiner Vorläufer." *Giessener Beiträge zur Erforschung der Sprache und Kultur Englands und Nordamerikas* 2 (1925): 129-92.
Wright, Herbert G. "Greene's 'Ridstall Man.' " *MLR* 30 (1935): 347.

Alphonsus King of Aragon

Chew, Samuel C. *The Crescent and the Rose: Islam and England during the Renaissance.* 1937.
Turner, Robert Y. "The Causal Induction in Some Elizabethan Plays." *SP* 60 (1963): 183-90.
Van Dam, B. A. P. "R. Greene's *Alphonsus.*" *ES* 13 (1931): 129-42.

A Looking Glass for London and England

Lawrence, William J. *Pre-Restoration Stage Studies.* 1927.
Paradise, N. Burton. *Thomas Lodge.* 1931.
Roston, Murray. *Biblical Drama in England.* 1968.
Stroup, Thomas B. "The Testing Pattern in Elizabethan Tragedy." *SEL* 3 (1963): 175-90.
Sturman, Berta. "A Date and a Printer for *A Looking Glass for London and England,* Q4." *SB* 21 (1968): 248-53. [1603-5; Ralph Blower.]

Orlando Furioso

Herpich, Charles A. "Greene-Marlowe Parallel." *N&Q* 6 (1906): 185.

Houk, Raymond A. "Shakespeare's *Shrew* and Greene's *Orlando.*" *PMLA* 42 (1947): 657–71.

Joseph, Bertram. "Theefe of Thessaly." *TLS*, 22 March 1947, p. 127 (and responses by H. K. Barton, 5 April, p. 157; Ethel Seaton, 19 April, p. 183; and Bertram Joseph, 21 June, p. 309).

Shackford, Martha Hale. "Shakespeare and Greene's *Orlando Furioso.*" *MLN* 39 (1924): 54–56.

Sykes, H. Dugdale. *Sidelights on Elizabethan Drama.* 1924.

George a Greene

Kirschbaum, Leo. "A Census of Bad Quartos." *RES* 14 (1938): 20–43.

THOMAS KYD

Dickie Spurgeon

The standard edition of Kyd's complete works is Frederick S. Boas's *The Works of Thomas Kyd* (1901; re-issued with corrections 1955). Charles Crawford's *A Concordance to the Works of Thomas Kyd* was published in 1906–10 as vol. 15 of *Materialien zur Kunde des älteren englischen Dramas.*

I. GENERAL

A. BIOGRAPHICAL

Arthur Freeman covers the life in *Thomas Kyd: Facts and Problems* (1967). There are biographies in Joseph de Smet, *Thomas Kyd, l'homme, l'œuvre, le milieu, suivi de "La Tragédie Espagnole," version complète, comprenant les scènes ajoutées en 1602* (1925); Félix Carrère, *Le théâtre de Thomas Kyd* (1951); and (more briefly) Philip Edwards, *Thomas Kyd and Early Elizabethan Tragedy*, WTW (1966).

B. GENERAL STUDIES OF THE PLAYS

Critics of Kyd have focused almost exclusively on *The Spanish Tragedy*. General criticism is included below under the entry for that play. Samuel Tannenbaum published *Thomas Kyd: A Concise Bibliography* in 1941 (rpt. in vol. 4 of *Elizabethan Bibliographies* [1967]). More recently, there is a selective Kyd bibliography in Irving Ribner's *Tudor and Stuart Drama* (1966) for the Goldentree series and a continuation of Tannenbaum in Robert C. Johnson's *Minor Elizabethans* (1968), vol. 9 of *Elizabethan Bibliographies Supplements.*

II. CRITICISM OF INDIVIDUAL PLAYS AND STATE OF SCHOLARSHIP

A. INDIVIDUAL PLAYS

The Spanish Tragedy

Moody E. Prior, *The Language of Tragedy* (1947), suggests that the play "occupies an intermediate position between the academic experiments of the middle years of the sixteenth century and the fully developed Elizabethan tragedy." Kyd makes use of a flexible blank verse nearer the rhythm of normal speech than was earlier dramatic blank verse. He retains much of the formal, patterned rhetoric of earlier tragedy, but he makes the rhetorical devices dramatically functional in a way in which they formerly were not by bringing the rhetoric and especially the imagery into a closer relation with the main patterns of action and emotion. Wolfgang Clemen's study of the evolution of the dramatic set speech, *English Tragedy before Shakespeare* (trans. T. S. Dorsch, 1961; German ed. 1955), assigns Kyd a central role in the conversion of the set speech to "a theatrical medium of outstanding effectiveness." Hieronimo's soliloquies in II.v and III.xii; the Viceroy's lament in I.iii; and Hieronimo's lament in III.ii are closely integrated with plot and character. Kyd limits the functions of the set speeches, placing them carefully in the play relative to emotional changes in the speaker and linking them organically with stage business and properties. Kyd advanced dramatic writing significantly by creating a character whose gradual isolation, secrecy, and increasing involvement in intrigue require soliloquy to be his characteristic utterance. (Parts of Clemen's study are reprinted in the 1st [1961] and 2nd [1970] eds. of *Shakespeare's Contemporaries,* ed. Max Bluestone and Norman Rabkin.)

Howard Baker, *Induction to Tragedy: A Study in a Development of Form in "Gorboduc," "The Spanish Tragedy," and "Titus Andronicus"* (1939), gives Kyd an important place in the development of dramatic blank verse. He suggests that Kyd found in the epic and semi-dramatic blank verse of Douglas, Surrey, Grimald, and Sackville a model which he drew upon directly for *The Spanish Tragedy,* adapting the language and traditional epic images for the expression of personal emotion on the stage. An analysis of Kyd's use of the figures of nondramatic verse is given by Jonas A. Barish, *"The Spanish Tragedy,* or The Pleasures and Perils of Rhetoric," in *Elizabethan Theatre,* SuAS, vol. 9 (1966), pp.

59–85. Barish finds Kyd the first dramatist able to use the schemes and tropes of the poetical miscellanies in a truly functional way by linking the intricate patterns of language in the figures to character and action. Freeman, *Thomas Kyd: Facts and Problems* (1967), follows Prior, Clemen, and Barish in emphasizing the importance of Kyd's adaptation of formal rhetoric to popular drama. However, Kyd was unable to create a language appropriate to moments of highest emotion and his best quality remains a kind of "pleasing directness" growing out of a diction and imagery more conservative than Marlowe's.

   Though not directly concerned with Kyd, two articles provide background for understanding Seneca's influence on Kyd. Hardin Craig, "The Shackling of Accidents: A Study of Elizabethan Tragedy," *PQ* 19 (1940): 1–19 (rpt. in *Elizabethan Drama: Modern Essays in Criticism,* ed. Ralph J. Kaufmann [1961], pp. 22–40), discusses the distinctions between Senecan tragedy and other forms dominant in the period. Henry W. Wells, "Senecan Influence on Elizabethan Tragedy: A Re-estimation," *ShAB* 19 (1944): 71–84, deemphasizes the borrowing of rhetorical style, aphorisms, ghosts, and other relatively superficial elements and argues for a more organic influence. T. S. Eliot, *Selected Essays* (1932), found Kyd's borrowing of the form of the tragedy of blood and rhetoric from Senecan drama much less important than his addition of intrigue and sensationalism from Italian drama. B. L. Joseph, *"The Spanish Tragedy* and *Hamlet*: Two Exercises in English Seneca," in *Classical Drama and Its Influence: Essays Presented to H. D. F. Kitto,* ed. M. J. Anderson (1965), pp. 121–34, discusses parallels between the two plays, mostly for the purpose of showing the limitations of Kyd's use of Seneca and Shakespeare's transcendence of those limitations. Howard Baker, Willard Farnham, and Fredson Bowers have questioned the extent of Seneca's influence on Kyd, Baker in "Ghosts and Guides: Kyd's *Spanish Tragedy* and the Medieval Tragedy," *MP* 33 (1935): 27–35, and *Induction to Tragedy* (1939); Farnham in *The Medieval Heritage of Elizabethan Tragedy* (1936); and Bowers in *Elizabethan Revenge Tragedy* (1940). Baker comments on the differences between Kyd and Seneca. Farnham sees Kyd as introducing into English drama "a new kind of tragedy presenting involved romantic intrigue instead of simple rise and fall." Bowers agrees that Kyd used Seneca importantly, but emphasizes his borrowings from the Italian *novelle* and other sources. Alfred Harbage, "Intrigue in Elizabethan Tragedy," in *Essays on Shakespeare and Elizabethan Drama in Honor of Hardin Craig,* ed. Richard Hosley

(1962), pp. 37-44, regards Kyd as the first to raise to prominence in Elizabethan tragedy the intrigue of New Comedy and such native tricksters as Merrygreek and Diccon. Kyd's use of "comic methods with tragic materials" created "a new and oddly mixed response—of amusement and horror, revulsion and admiration" and influenced Marlowe, Middleton and Rowley, Webster, Shakespeare, and Heywood in similar efforts.

The Elizabethan attitude toward revenge is treated by Lily B. Campbell, "Theories of Revenge in Renaissance England," *MP* 28 (1931): 281-96, and by Fredson Bowers, "The Audience and the Revenger of Elizabethan Tragedy," *SP* 31 (1934): 160-77. Percy Simpson provides a general discussion, "The Theme of Revenge in Elizabethan Tragedy," *PBA* 21 (1935): 101-36, rpt. in *Studies in Elizabethan Drama* (1955). The most extensive study of the theme of revenge in *The Spanish Tragedy* and the drama of the period is in Fredson Bowers's *Elizabethan Revenge Tragedy,* which identifies the characteristics of revenge tragedy and traces the type up to about 1607. Kyd's play established the pattern of revenge as the central action, revenge against a Machiavellian opponent watched over by a ghost and delayed by doubt, weakness, and madness of the revenger, whose eventual success depends upon intrigue. Bowers sees little relevance in the Ghost and Revenge, but finds Kyd's use of Hieronimo's suspicion of a trap in the note from Bel-Imperia and madness in Hieronimo a brilliant solution to the problem of delay. He believes that Hieronimo has the sympathy of the audience at first but loses it in the *Vindicta mihi* speech (III.xiii.1-45), which establishes him as an "Italianate villain." Hieronimo's killing of Castile further alienates the audience. Eleanor Prosser, *Hamlet and Revenge* (1967), examines the moral response of the Elizabethan audience to revenge on the stage: since the audience did not look on revenge as a sacred duty, the *Vindicta mihi* speech probably automatically excluded Hieronimo from sympathy, as Bowers argues.

A number of essays take up the question of the unity of the play. S. F. Johnson, *"The Spanish Tragedy,* or Babylon Revisited," in *Essays on Shakespeare,* ed. Hosley, pp. 23-36, defends the unity of the play in a discussion of the play within the play, Hieronimo's silence, and the anti-Spanish bias of the work. Johnson suggests that the play within the play was probably staged in "sundry languages" and links those languages and other events to the biblical story of the Tower of Babel in an analysis of the biblical background of the play. Hieronimo's silence is defended by emphasizing his stoic philosophy and the seriousness with which oath-breaking was taken in Elizabethan times. The killing of Castile is required to complete Andrea's revenge, and the assignment of souls at the end conforms to God's law. William Empson, *"The Spanish Tragedy," Nimbus* 3 (1956): 16-29 (rpt. in *Elizabethan Drama,* ed. Kaufmann, pp. 60-80), sees the play as "an attempt to apply the technique and atmosphere of the *ur-Hamlet* to the highly topical theme of the royal marriages of Spain." He suggests that the Ghost of Andrea learns in the course of the play that he has been murdered by Bel-imperia's father and brother, who plan to marry her to Balthazar. Although he devotes considerable space to showing how Hieronimo becomes increasingly more deluded and finally mad, Empson leaves Hieronimo's moral status ambiguous. Herbert R. Coursen, Jr., "The Unity of *The Spanish Tragedy," SP* 65 (1968): 768-82, supports Empson, arguing that the unity of the play is apparent if one recognizes that "the motivating force of the play—the plot in the sense Aristotle uses the term—is the dynastic ambition of the House of Castile." The relation of the Alexandro-Villuppo episode to the main action of the play is discussed by William H. Wiatt, "The Dramatic Function of the Alexandro-Villuppo Episode in *The Spanish Tragedy," N&Q* 5 (1958): 327-29 (rpt. in *Shakespeare's Contemporaries,* ed. Bluestone and Rabkin, 2nd ed. [1970], pp. 57-60).

The argument that the *Vindicta mihi* speech establishes Hieronimo as a villain is challenged by John D. Ratliff, "Hieronimo Explains Himself," *SP* 54 (1957): 112-18, and by David Laird, "Hieronimo's Dilemma," *SP* 62 (1965): 137-46. Ratliff argues that the speech is meant to persuade the audience that Hieronimo must act against his son's murderers as a matter of self-preservation, since he has no recourse through legal means and is in danger of becoming their next victim. Laird finds the speech a rational consideration of the issues raised by revenge which draws the audience into sympathy with Hieronimo but settles nothing as far as the ethical problem is concerned. Kyd is simply exploiting the dramatic situation. Philip Edwards, *Thomas Kyd and Early Elizabethan Tragedy,* WTW (1966), develops a similar view, suggesting that our dominant impression as the play ends is not of justice, but a vision of painful struggle "in a world too complex for any individual to begin to control or even to understand." Ejner J. Jensen, "Kyd's *Spanish Tragedy:* The Play Explains Itself," *JEGP* 64 (1965): 7-16, regards the Ghost and Revenge as an essential part of the play and asserts Hieronimo's retention of the audience's sympathy. He questions whether the play is based on Christian morality and contends that the dialogue and action establish that Hieronimo has a divinely justified right to revenge. The theme of justice is the focus of an article by G. K. Hunter, "Ironies of Justice in *The Spanish Tragedy*," *RenD* 8 (1967): 89–104 (rpt. in *Shakespeare's Contemporaries*, ed. Bluestone and Rabkin, 2nd ed. [1970], pp. 61–73). Hunter discusses contrasts between divine and human justice. Hieronimo is the instrument of divine justice, forced to be unjust in doing justice.

The major characters are examined by Michael H. Levin, " 'Vindicta mihi!': Meaning, Morality, and Motivation in *The Spanish Tragedy*," *SEL* 4 (1964): 307–24. The characterizations of Hieronimo and Bel-Imperia create a powerful sympathy which prevents an unfavorable judgment and makes the play "a dramatic exposition of vengeance, not an explanation." D. J. Palmer, "Elizabethan Tragic Heroes," in *Elizabethan Theatre* SuAS, vol. 9 (1966), pp. 11–35, discusses Hieronimo's character. Kyd, along with Marlowe, created a new integration of character and dramatic situation by making the tragic hero more self-aware than he had been in earlier plays. The relation of the structure of the play to the development of Hieronimo's character is commented on by Ernest W. Talbert in *Elizabethan Drama and Shakespeare's Early Plays* (1963). The serious theme of the play, the problem of a just revenge, is subordinate to melodrama. There are comments on Lorenzo in Philip Edwards, *Thomas Kyd,* and Fredson Bowers, *Elizabethan Revenge Tragedy* (both above).

Kyd's use of the dumb show and play within a play is discussed by Anne Righter, *Shakespeare and the Idea of the Play* (1962), and by Dieter Mehl, *The Elizabethan Dumb Show: The History of a Dramatic Convention* (1965; German ed. 1964). Righter points out that Kyd's use of the Ghost and Revenge to create a closer bond between the audience and the play marks the beginning of a more naturalistic theater. Mehl credits Kyd with striking originality as the first Elizabethan dramatist to integrate fully the dumb show into the play, the first to introduce a presenter to direct the dumb show at the stage audience rather than at the audience proper, and the first to use the play within a play.

Charles K. Cannon, "The Relation of the Additions of *The Spanish Tragedy* to the Original Play," *SEL* 2 (1962): 229–39, provides a summary of earlier criticism of the additions and argues for their close relation to the theme of revenge. They clear up the original play's confused development of the revenge theme, expand the themes of night and madness, and raise Hieronimo's experience to the plane of universal human tragic experience. Levin L. Schücking, *Die Zusätze zur "Spanish Tragedy"* (1938), and *"The Spanish Tragedy* Additions: Acting and Reading Versions," *TLS*, 12 June 1937, p. 442, argues that the play is too long for acting and that material in the original is awkwardly repeated if the additions are considered part of the regular text. Frederick S. Boas disputes this view in *"The Spanish Tragedy* Additions," *TLS*, 26 June 1937, p. 480. In the introduction to the Revels edition (1959), Philip Edwards questions the integration of the additions and prints them at the end of the regular text, though he finds the third and the fifth fairly harmonious with the main text.

No direct source has been discovered for the main story of *The Spanish Tragedy*. Fredson Bowers, "Kyd's Pedringano: Sources and Parallels," *Harvard Studies and Notes in Philology and Literature* 13 (1931): 241–49, concludes that the execution of Pedringano was probably understood by the original audience as an allusion to a similar execution reported of the Earl of Leicester. Arthur Freeman, *Thomas Kyd*, discusses other possible sources for the play.

Peter W. Biesterfeldt, *Die dramatische Technik Thomas Kyds* (1936), discusses staging and Kyd's effort to combine the structural elements of classical and native tragedy. Peter B. Murray, *Thomas Kyd*, TEAS (1969), incorporates the main conclusions of Kyd criticism in a scene by scene analysis of the play.

Cornelia

Félix Carrère, *Le théâtre de Thomas Kyd* (1951), and Alexander M. Witherspoon, *The Influence of Robert Garnier on Elizabethan Drama* (1924), discuss the accuracy of Kyd's translation of Robert Garnier's *Cornélie*.

B. OVER-ALL STATE OF CRITICISM

Most of the substantial criticism of Kyd has dealt with his place in the development of English drama. His pioneering role has been adequately investigated, perhaps even somewhat exaggerated. There has been relatively little emphasis on the aesthetic value of his work.

III. CANON

A. PLAYS IN CHRONOLOGICAL ORDER

The following list adopts the chronology used by Alfred Harbage, *Annals of English Drama, 975-1700* (1940; rev. Samuel Schoenbaum, 1964). The dates in parentheses following the title of each entry are those of first performance (in italics) and first edition. The early editions of the plays are described in W. W. Greg, *Bibliography of the English Printed Drama to the Restoration,* 4 vols. (1939-59). Carl J. Stratman, *Bibliography of English Printed Tragedy, 1565-1900* (1966), lists editions (except of *Cornelia*) up to 1966, including anthologies and collections, and gives library locations. E. K. Chambers, *The Elizabethan Stage* (1923), vol. 5, discusses the canon.

The Spanish Tragedy, tragedy (*1582-92*; ca. 1592)

Authorship, text, sources, printing history, and date are treated in Arthur Freeman, *Thomas Kyd* (above); in Philip Edwards's introduction to the Revels edition (1959, partly rpt. in *Shakespeare's Contemporaries,* ed. Bluestone and Rabkin [1961]); and in the introductions to the Malone Society Reprints of the 1602 edition (1925), edited by W. W. Greg and Frederick S. Boas, and the 1592? edition (1948), edited by W. W. Greg and D. Nichol Smith. The introductions to the Malone Society Reprints expand conclusions about the complicated printing history of the early texts first advanced by Greg in *"The Spanish Tragedy*—A Leading Case?" *Library* 6 (1925): 47-56, and disputed by Leo Kirschbaum, "Is *The Spanish Tragedy* a Leading Case? Did a Bad Quarto of *Love's Labour's Lost* Ever Exist?" *JEGP* 37 (1938): 501-12. The evidence for Kyd's authorship of the play is generally considered conclusive. However, Levin L. Schücking, *Zur Verfasserschaft der "Spanish Tragedy"* (1963), suggests that Kyd may have shared authorship with another writer, possibly Thomas Watson. Philip Edwards, *Thomas Kyd* (above), dismisses Schücking's suggestion.

The outside limits of the play are 1582-92. T. W. Baldwin, "On the Chronology of Thomas Kyd's Plays," *MLN* 40 (1925): 343-49, and *On the Literary Genetics of Shakspere's Plays, 1592-1594* (1959), argues for 1582-85, favoring a date nearer 1582 than to 1585. Most recent investigations date the play nearer the upper limits. In his edition for the Regents Renaissance Drama Series (1967), Andrew S. Cairncross dates the play "about 1585-1587." Freeman prefers 1585-87, Carrère the first half of 1588, and Philip Edwards, *Thomas Kyd,* the late 1580s, around 1587, a shift from his earlier preference for about 1590 in the introduction to the Revels edition.

Cornelia, tragedy (*1594;* 1594)

Félix Carrère, *Le théâtre de Thomas Kyd* (1951), and Arthur Freeman, *Thomas Kyd: Facts and Problems* (1967), discuss the text and its canonicity.

B. UNCERTAIN ASCRIPTIONS; APOCRYPHA

Freeman and Carrère provide full comment on the many plays that have been attributed to Kyd at one time or another. One of the broadest extensions of the canon is in Arthur Acheson, *Shakespeare, Chapman, and "Sir Thomas More"* (1931).

Hamlet, tragedy (ca. *1587- 90;* lost)

There has long been a controversy over possible allusions to *The Spanish Tragedy* and to Kyd as the author of a lost *Hamlet* in Thomas Nashe's preface to Greene's *Menaphon* (1589). There are those who doubt that the passage alludes to an *ur-Hamlet* or to Kyd as its author, but many have accepted V. Østerberg's argument, in *Studier over Hamlet-Teksterne,* vol. 1 (1920), paraphrased in English by J. Dover Wilson, *RES* 18 (1942): 385- 94, that the passage alludes to a *Hamlet* by Kyd. Freeman provides brief summaries of the various interpretations of Nashe and concludes that *The Spanish Tragedy* is probably alluded to, but dismisses the problem of the *ur-Hamlet* as a Shakespearean concern. George I. Duthie's view, in *The "Bad" Quarto of Hamlet* (1941), that the *ur-Hamlet* had only an "infinitesimal" textual influence on the First Quarto, is now generally accepted. Henry D. Gray, "Thomas Kyd and the First Quarto of *Hamlet,*" *PMLA* 42 (1927): 721- 35, argues that the verse attributed to Kyd in the First Quarto is not at all like the verse of *The Spanish Tragedy.* There are attempted reconstructions of the lost *Hamlet* in another article by Gray, "Reconstruction of a Lost Play," *PQ* 7 (1928): 254- 74; Fredson Bowers, *Elizabethan Revenge Tragedy* (II,A, above); William W. Lawrence, "Ophelia's Heritage," *MLR* 42 (1947): 409- 16; and Brian T. Cleeve, "The Lost *Hamlet,*" *Studies. An Irish Quarterly Review* 46 (1957): 447- 56. Robert Adger Law, "Belleforest, Shakespeare, and Kyd," in *Joseph Quincy Adams Memorial Studies,* ed. James G. McManaway, Giles E. Dawson, and Edwin E. Willoughby (1948), pp.

279–94, argues that the differences between *Hamlet* and the story in Belleforest are explainable in terms of the usual changes Shakespeare made in adapting a story and need not be attributed to an *ur-Hamlet.*

Soliman and Perseda, tragedy (ca. *1589–92*; ca. 1592)

Arthur Freeman summarizes the earlier arguments for Kyd's authorship in *Thomas Kyd: Facts and Problems* (1967). He finds the evidence convincing and adds new arguments. Attribution is based chiefly on similarities of language and plot construction. Félix Carrère, *Le théâtre de Thomas Kyd* (1951), holds that differences in the handling of the comic episodes in *The Spanish Tragedy* and *Soliman and Perseda* suggest that *Soliman and Perseda* is the work of another author, probably an imitator of Kyd.

T. W. Baldwin, "On the Chronology of Thomas Kyd's Plays," *MLN* 40 (1925): 343–49, and *On the Literary Genetics of Shakspere's Plays, 1592-1594* (1959), dates the play 1585–86 on several grounds, among them possible allusions to the Babington conspiracies of 1584. Freeman prefers 1588–92, noting that those were the years in which the Turkish play was popular and that a later dating helps explain verbal parallels between *Soliman and Perseda* and *Edward II* (ca. 1592). Arthur Acheson, *Shakespeare, Chapman, and "Sir Thomas More"* (1931), attempts to establish 1578 as the date of the play. And see the discussion in the anonymous-play section of this volume.

Arden of Feversham, realistic tragedy (*1585–92*; 1592)

Arden of Feversham is attributed to Kyd by Félix Carrère, who has edited the play in Aubier's *Collection bilingue* (1950). Arthur Freeman, *Thomas Kyd,* rejects Kyd's authorship. See the anonymous-play section in this volume.

Portia, tragedy (*1594*; lost)

Arthur Freeman, *Thomas Kyd,* discusses this translation, planned in 1594 but evidently never completed.

The First Part of Hieronimo, pseudo-history (*1600–1605*; 1605)

Andrew S. Cairncross maintains, in his combined edition of this play and *The Spanish Tragedy,* RRDS (1967), that the surviving text of *The First Part of Hieronimo* is a memorial version of an original play written by Kyd as the first part of a two-part series of which *The Spanish Tragedy* is the second part.

C. CRITIQUE OF THE STANDARD EDITION

The standard edition is Frederick S. Boas, *The Works of Thomas Kyd* (1901; re-issued with corrections 1955). The introduction and texts are unsatisfactory. There are extensive reviews by A. H. Thorndike, *MLN* 17 (1902): 283–94, and by W. W. Greg, *MLQ* 4 (1901): 185–90. Boas used a late edition (1615?) of *The Spanish Tragedy* as copy-text and collated it inaccurately against the 1592? edition. He admitted readings to his text of *Soliman and Perseda* from Smeeton's nineteenth-century reprint of the 1599 edition, which he mistook for an early text, and he removed passages that he considered offensive from Richard Baines's note. Charles Crawford's *Concordance* (1906–10) is largely based on the Boas edition and shares its limitations. A new Oxford English Text of the *Works* is in preparation.

D. TEXTUAL STUDIES

The introductions to Greg's editions of the 1592? and 1602 texts of *The Spanish Tragedy* for the Malone Society (1948 and 1925, respectively) contain accounts of the printing history of the early texts.

The five additions (totaling 320 lines) to *The Spanish Tragedy* have been variously assigned to Shakespeare, Dekker, and others, but most often to Ben Jonson. Edwards notes, in the introduction to the Revels edition (1959), that it is now general opinion that the additions were done in 1597 by an unknown writer, not in 1602 by Jonson, as was formerly thought. But in the introduction to the Malone Society Reprint (1948) of the 1592? edition, Greg and Smith speculate that there may have been two sets of additions by Jonson and present the hypothesis (not original with them) that the surviving additions may be memorial reconstructions of the earlier. Andrew S. Cairncross, in his combined edition, RRDS (1967), of *The First Part of Hieronimo* and *The Spanish Tragedy,* argues that the additions may be memorially reconstructed versions of passages written earlier by Kyd himself.

Edwards's introduction contains a study of the copy behind the 1592? text, which he believes was based on a "neat" authorial manuscript up to III.xv, where the text becomes corrupt, perhaps as a result of revision aimed at shortening the play, or perhaps from the use of inferior copy.

A. T. Hazen, "Type-Facsimiles," *MP* 44 (1947): 209–17, discusses the difficulties created when Smeeton's reprint (1810?) of the 1599 edition of *Soliman and Perseda* has been taken for an original.

E. SINGLE-WORK EDITIONS

Philip Edwards's edition of *The Spanish Tragedy* in the Revels Series (1959) is a useful text. Andrew S. Cairncross has edited *The First Part of Hieronimo* and *The Spanish Tragedy* in a single volume in the Regents Renaissance Drama Series (1967). The play has been edited for Crofts Classics (1951) by Charles T. Prouty; the New Mermaid Series (1964) by B. L. Joseph; and Fountainwell Drama Texts (1968) by Thomas W. Ross. Reprints of the early texts are available in the Malone Society Reprints of the 1602 edition (1925), edited by W. W. Greg and Frederick S. Boas, and the 1592? edition (1948), edited by W. W. Greg and D. Nichol Smith. There is a facsimile of the 1592? edition by Scolar Press (1966).

IV. SEE ALSO

A. GENERAL

Baldwin, T. W. "Thomas Kyd's Early Company Connections." *PQ* 6 (1927): 311-13.

Boas, Frederick S. "Elizabethan Drama." *YWES* 6 (1925): 155-56. [Exceptions to T. W. Baldwin's chronology.]

Buckley, George T. "Who Was 'The Late Arrian'?" *MLN* 49 (1934): 500-503.

Freeman, Arthur. "New Records of Thomas Kyd and His Family," *N&Q* 12 (1965): 328-29.

B. INDIVIDUAL PLAYS

The Spanish Tragedy

Boas, Frederick S. *An Introduction to Tudor Drama.* 1933.

Carrère, Félix. "*La Tragédie Espagnole* de Thomas Kyd et *Le Coeur Brisé* de John Ford." *EA* 8 (1955): 1-10.

Chickera, Ernst de. "Divine Justice and Private Revenge in *The Spanish Tragedy.*" *MLR* 57 (1962): 228-32.

Cole, Douglas. "The Comic Accomplice in Elizabethan Revenge Tragedy." *RenD* 9 (1966): 125-39.

Fuzier, Jean. "Thomas Kyd et l'ethique du spectacle populaire." *Les Langues Modernes* 59 (1965): 451-58.

Gerrard, Ernest A. *Elizabethan Drama and Dramatists, 1583-1603.* 1928.

Goodstein, Peter. "Hieronimo's Destruction of Babylon." *ELN* 3 (1966): 172-73.

Habicht, Werner. "Sénèque et le théâtre populaire pré-Shakespearien." In *Les tragédies de Sénèque et le théâtre de la Renaissance*, ed. Jean Jacquot (1964), pp. 175-87.

Harrison, G. B. *Elizabethan Plays and Players*, 1940.

Honigmann, E. A. J. "Shakespeare's 'Lost Source-Plays.'" *MLR* 49 (1954): 293-307.

Hunter, G. K. "The Spoken Dirge in Kyd, Marston and Shakespeare: A Background to *Cymbeline.*" *N&Q* 11 (1964): 146-47.

McDiarmid, Matthew P. "The Influence of Robert Garnier on Some Elizabethan Tragedies." *EA* 11 (1958): 289-302.

Mehl, Dieter. "Forms and Functions of the Play within a Play." *RenD* 8 (1965): 41-61.

Mendell, Clarence W. *Our Seneca.* 1941.

Parrott, Thomas Marc, and Robert Hamilton Ball. *A Short View of Elizabethan Drama.* 1943.

Pearce, T. M. "Evidence for Dating Marlowe's *Tragedy of Dido.*" In *Studies in the English Renaissance Drama*, ed. Josephine W. Bennett, Oscar Cargill, and Vernon Hall, Jr. (1959), pp. 231-47.

Price, Hereward T. "Shakespeare and His Young Contemporaries." *PQ* 41 (1962): 37-57.

Rubow, Paul V. *Shakespeare og hans samtidige: En raekke kritiske studier* [Shakespeare and his contemporaries: a group of critical studies]. 1948.

Schaar, Claes. " 'They Hang Him in the Arbor.' " *ES* 47 (1966): 27-28.

Schelling, Felix E. *Elizabethan Playwrights: A Short History of the English Drama from Mediaeval Times to the Closing of the Theaters in 1642.* 1925.

Smith, James L. " 'They Hang Him in the Arbour': A Defence of the Accepted Text." *ES* 47 (1966): 372-73.

Smith, John H., Lois D. Pizer, and Edward K. Kaufman. "*Hamlet, Antonio's Revenge* and the *Ur-Hamlet.*" *SQ* 9 (1958): 493-98.

Stoll, Elmer E. "*Hamlet* and *The Spanish Tragedy*, Quartos I and II: A Protest." *MP* 35 (1937-38): 31-46.

———. "*Hamlet* and *The Spanish Tragedy* Again." *MP* 37 (1939): 173-86.

Stuart, Donald C. *The Development of Dramatic Art.* 1928.

Tomlinson, Thomas B. *A Study of Elizabethan and Jacobean Tragedy.* 1964.

Turner, Robert Y. "Pathos and the *Gorboduc* Tradition, 1560-1590." *HLQ* 25 (1962): 97-120.

Ure, Peter. "On Some Differences between Senecan and Elizabethan Tragedy." *DUJ* 10 (1948): 17-23.

Wittig, Kurt. "Gedanken zu Kyds *Spanish Tragedie.*" In *Strena Anglica: Festschrift für Otto Ritter*, ed. Gerhard Dietrich and F. W. Schulze (1956), pp. 133-77.

Cornelia

Rees, Joan. "*Julius Caesar*—An Earlier Play, and an Interpretation." *MLR* 50 (1955): 135-141.

C. TEXTUAL STUDIES

The Spanish Tragedy

Butrym, Alexander. "A Marlowe Echo in Kyd." *N&Q* 5 (1958): 96-97.

Crundell, H. W. "The 1602 Additions to *The Spanish Tragedy.*" *N&Q* 164 (1933): 147-49.

———. "The 1602 Additions to *The Spanish Tragedy.*" *N&Q* 167 (1934): 88.

———. "The Authorship of *The Spanish Tragedy* Additions." *N&Q* 180 (1941): 8-9.

Empson, William. "Hamlet When New." *SR* 61 (1953): 15-42, 185-205.

Forsythe, Robert S. "Notes on *The Spanish Tragedy.*" *PQ* 5 (1926): 78-84.

Hapgood, Robert. "The Judge in the Firie Tower: Another Virgilian Passage in *The Spanish Tragedy.*" *N&Q* 13 (1966): 287-88.

Howarth, R. G. "The 1602 Additions to *The Spanish Tragedy.*" *N&Q* 166 (1934): 246.

———. "George Herbert." *N&Q* 187 (1944): 122.

Jewkes, Wilfred T. *Act Division in Elizabethan and Jacobean Plays, 1583-1616.* 1958.

Levin, Harry. "An Echo from *The Spanish Tragedy.*" *MLN* 64 (1949): 297-302.

Maxwell, J. C. "Kyd's *Spanish Tragedy,* III, xiv, 168-9." *PQ* 30 (1951): 86.

Mustard, Wilfred P. "Notes on Thomas Kyd's Works." *PQ* 5 (1926): 85-86.

Price, Hereward T. "*Titus Andronicus* and the Additions to *The Spanish Tragedy.*" *N&Q* 9 (1962): 331.

Priess, Max. "Thomas Kyds *Spanish Tragedy* und die Zusätz in der Ausgabe von 1602." *Englische Studien* 74 (1941): 329-41.

Reiman, Donald H. "Marston, Jonson, and *The Spanish Tragedy* Additions." *N&Q* 7 (1960): 336-37.

Robertson, John M. *Literary Detection: A Symposium on Macbeth.* 1931.

Ross, Thomas W. "Kyd's *The Spanish Tragedy:* A Bibliographical Hypothesis." *BRMMLA* 22 (1968): 13-21.

Schücking, Levin L. "*The Spanish Tragedy* Addition." *TLS,* 19 June 1937, p. 464.

———. "*The Spanish Tragedy* Additions." *TLS,* 17 July 1937, p. 528.

Tannenbaum, Samuel A. *The Booke of Sir Thomas Moore.* 1927.

Wells, William. "Thomas Kyd and the Chronicle-History." *N&Q* 178 (1940): 218-24, 238-43.

Cornelia

McDiarmid, Matthew P. "A Reconsidered Parallel between Shakespeare's *King John* and Kyd's *Cornelia.*" *N&Q* 3 (1956): 507-8.

THOMAS NASHE

Robert J. Fehrenbach

The standard edition is *The Works of Thomas Nashe,* 5 vols., ed. Ronald B. McKerrow (1904– 10), reprinted with additional notes by F. P. Wilson (1958).

I. GENERAL

A. BIOGRAPHICAL

In reviewing Nashe's works in chronological order, G. R. Hibbard, in *Thomas Nashe: A Critical Introduction* (1962), deals with events and relationships in the author's life. Though the emphasis of the book is on the literature, not biography, Hibbard gives the best biographical summary of Nashe since McKerrow's edition. In "Thomas Nashe, Robert Cotton the Antiquary, and *The Terrors of the Night,"* *RES* 12 (1961): 7– 23, and "Nashe's Visit to the Isle of Wight and His Publications of 1592–4," *RES* 14 (1963): 225– 42, C. G. Harlow claims that Nashe did not visit the Isle of Wight in February, 1593, as both McKerrow and Hibbard believe, but that he was there from December, 1593, to February, 1594; in February, 1593, the writer was a guest of Robert Cotton at Conington where he composed the first draft of *The Terrors of the Night.* This chronology clears up some bibliographical confusion surrounding *The Terrors.*

E. D. Mackerness in "Thomas Nashe and William Cotton," *RES* 25 (1949): 342– 46, examines Nashe's autumn, 1596, correspondence with a servant of Sir George Carey. Mackerness argues that by requesting patronage from such a socially insignificant figure, Nashe reveals that he had fallen on bad times. C. G. Harlow in "Thomas Nashe and William Cotton, M.P.," *N&Q* 8 (1961): 424– 25, disagrees with Mackerness' judgment of Cotton's social standing and, therefore, with his conclusions about Nashe's plight.

B. GENERAL STUDIES OF THE PLAYS

Hibbard, in the only full-length study of Nashe, touches upon the two lost plays in which Nashe is believed to have had a hand, *Terminus et Non Terminus* and *The Isle of Dogs*, and some of the Nashe apocrypha, but he understandably focuses his dramatic criticism on the one extant play that is totally and undeniably Nashe's: *Summer's Last Will and Testament* (see II,A).

C. THE WORKS AT LARGE

In the standard criticism of Nashe, Hibbard's 1962 study (above), Nashe is seen as a virtuoso, a jester, a professional fool. It is impossible to find his real personality in his works; as a writer he played roles. Chameleon-like though he was, two major and definite interests pervade his work: his opposition to Puritanism, and his devotion to literature and the humane studies. Nevertheless, there is usually very little substance in his works. He was more concerned about playing with words than about what he was saying. Hibbard concludes: "Nashe is and will remain a minor author of genius, but still a minor writer." C. S. Lewis, in his brief comments in *English Literature in the Sixteenth Century Excluding Drama* (1954), praises Nashe's gusto and exuberant style. He believes him to be the "greatest of the Elizabethan pamphleteers," and "one of our most original writers." Nashe's subjects are not important; and in that sense, Nashe becomes a writer of " 'pure' literature," a literature in which the images, not the thoughts, are important.

Nashe's most widely read work, *The Unfortunate Traveller, or The Life of Jack Wilton,* understandably has received the greatest attention in recent scholarship. Most of the major studies are attempts to define in terms of established critical theory this peculiar but always appealing piece of prose fiction. The critical discussions usually touch upon whether the work should be called a novel, whether it is in the picaresque tradition, and whether it owes anything to the Spanish picaresque novel, *Lazarillo de Tormes.* Over fifty years ago McKerrow, in the standard edition, said there was no "direct evidence" connecting Nashe's work with the Spanish tale, and to date no one has discovered any.

Fredson T. Bowers argues in "Thomas Nashe and the Picaresque Novel" in *Humanistic Studies in Honor of John Calvin Metcalf* (1941), pp. 12–27, that *The Unfortunate Traveller* is the "first English picaresque novel." It is not, however, a novel "consistent in its parts," but the sixteenth-century English understood the Spanish picaresque novel to be nothing "more than a collection of knavish jests." Lionel Stevenson in *The English Novel: A Panorama* (1960) says that *The Unfortunate Traveller* is written "in the vein of the picaresque novel," and C. S. Lewis, in *English Literature in the Sixteenth Century* (above), believes that the work is more a "medley with picaresque elements than a fully fledged picaresque novel." In *An Introduction to the English Novel*, 2 vols. (1951), Arnold Kettle sees the work as a special kind of picaresque novel. Jack Wilton as a rogue is an outcast not "morally bound" to society's standards. The novel is an attack on the feudal society by one of the exploited. It is not a clear, well-organized attack, for Nashe was "not yet fully conscious of what it meant to be bourgeois," but he sensed the possibilities of the "new world" and his prose fiction reflects that sensibility.

Though most scholars call the work a novel for the purposes of convenience, not all agree that it is indeed a novel. Lionel Stevenson says that perhaps it is "the first historical novel." H. F. B. Brett-Smith, in the introduction to his edition of *The Unfortunate Traveller* (1920), is more definite: Nashe "certainly founded our historical novel." Walter Allen, however, in *The English Novel* (1954), says that the work is "not in any modern sense a novel," and John Berryman in his edition (1960) states simply, "It is not a novel." Stanley Wells, in his edition of some of Nashe's works (III,C), holds that *The Unfortunate Traveller* "has no organizing principle; it is not a unified work of art," but quickly adds that these were not Nashe's intentions; the tale is brilliantly episodic.

E. A. Baker in his *History of the English Novel*, 10 vols. (1924–36), discusses Nashe as an early contributor to realistic fiction. Nashe's realism, however, in its exaggeration is a bit romantic itself. His work is "definitely down to earth," and he deals with "real life," but his intention is to "present the romance of actuality." Richard A. Lanham in "Tom Nashe and Jack Wilton: Personality as Structure in *The Unfortunate Traveller*," *SSF* 4 (1967): 201–16, argues that the problems created by any attempt to classify this multi-faceted work in conventional critical terms are solved if Jack Wilton's personality is seen as the "central form of the novel." The form and style of the work are as varied as its hero's neurotically wrathful, violent, anti-authoritarian, and anti-establishment personality.

Accepting the variety of the piece, Agnes M. C. Latham in "Satire on Literary Themes and Modes in Nashe's *Unfortunate Traveller*," *E&S* 1 (1948): 85–100, maintains that "whatever Nashe may have intended when he began the book, before he had finished it it had turned into a spirited parody of popular literary themes and styles of the day." These include revenge stories, sonneteering, Ciceronianism, and learned orations. Hibbard, too, accepts the diversity of *The Unfortunate Traveller* and sees Nashe as an improviser creating a work as various in form and meaning as the "contemporary literary scene with its jestbooks, its chronicles, its anti-Puritan pamphlets, its Petrarchan love poetry, its pastorals depicting an ideal world, its attacks on Italian luxury and loose living, its elegiacal histories and, above all, its revenge plays." For Hibbard, *The Unfortunate Traveller* is not a novel, it is not in the picaresque tradition, and it is not realistic. There is no unity to the work; it is "held together by the personality of the author," the virtuoso who must exhibit his virtuosity at the expense of unity.

Besides the Spanish picaresque tradition, other possible influences on *The Unfortunate Traveller* have been discussed. Of interest are: Katherine Duncan-Jones, "Nashe and Sidney: The Tournament in *The Unfortunate Traveller*," *MLR* 63 (1968): 3–6; N. W. Bawcutt's two notes: "Possible Sources for *The Unfortunate Traveller*," *N&Q* 7 (1960): 49–50, and "Nashe and Bodin," *N&Q* 14 (1967): 91; Philip Drew, "Edward Daunce and *The Unfortunate Traveller*," *RES* 11 (1960): 410–12; and Ernest C. York, "Nashe and Mandeville," *N&Q* 4 (1957): 159–60.

In recent years considerable attention has been given to the relationship of Nashe's writings to various contemporary dramatists. V. Østerberg in "Nashe's 'Kid in Aesop': A Danish Interpretation by V. Østerberg," translated and paraphrased by John Dover Wilson in *RES* 18 (1942): 385–94, claims that the "Kid in Aesop" mentioned by Nashe in his Preface to Greene's *Menaphon* is Thomas Kyd, author of the old *Hamlet*. E. A. J. Honigmann argues against this interpretation in "Shakespeare's 'Lost Source-Plays,' " *MLR* 49 (1954): 293–307, and William Montgomerie in "Sporting Kid (The Solution of the 'Kidde in Aesop' Problem)," *Life and Letters To-day* 36 (Jan., 1943): 18–24, also examines the reference in the Preface.

Sidney Thomas sees parallels between the *Duchess of Malfi* and *Christ's Tears over Jerusalem* in "Webster and Nashe," *N&Q* 3 (1956): 13; and James Savage finds "literary antecedents" of Jonson's *Bartholomew Fair* in Nashe's *Lenten Stuffe* in "Some Antecedents of the Puppet Play in *Bartholomew Fair*," *UMSE* 7 (1966): 43–64.

The use Shakespeare made of the Nashe-Harvey quarrel in *Love's Labor's Lost* is discussed by: W. Schrickx, *Shakespeare's Early Con-*

temporaries: The Background of the Harvey-Nashe Polemic and "Love's Labour's Lost," (1956); Richard David, editor of the New Arden *Love's Labour's Lost* (1951); Ray B. Browne, "The Satiric Use of 'Popular' Music in *Love's Labour's Lost,*" *SFQ* 23 (1959): 137–49; Eugene J. Kettner, *"Love's Labour's Lost,* and the Harvey-Nashe-Greene Quarrel," *ESRS* 10, no. 4 (1962): 29–39; Rupert Taylor, *The Date of "Love's Labour's Lost"* (1932); Frances A. Yates, *A Study of "Love's Labour's Lost"* (1936); M. C. Bradbrook, *The School of Night: A Study in the Literary Relationship of Sir Walter Raleigh* (1936); and Alfred Harbage, *"Love's Labor's Lost* and the Early Shakespeare," *PQ* 41 (1962): 18–36.

Other articles concerned with the relationship between Shakespeare's works and those of Nashe are: Frank W. Bradbrook, "Thomas Nashe and Shakespeare," *N&Q* 1 (1954): 470; D. R. Godfrey, "The Player's Speech in *Hamlet:* A New Approach," *Neophil* 34 (1950): 162–69; G. Blakemore Evans, "Thomas Nashe and the 'Dram of Eale,' " *N&Q* 198 (1953): 377–78 [*Hamlet*]; Joseph W. DeMent, "A Possible 1594 Reference to *Hamlet,*" *SQ* 15 (1964): 446–47; George R. Coffman, "A Note on Shakespeare and Nashe," *MLN* 42 (1927): 317–19 [*I Henry IV*]; C. G. Harlow, "Shakespeare, Nashe, and the Ostrich Crux in *I Henry IV,*" *SQ* 17 (1966): 171–74; G. Blakemore Evans, "Shakespeare's *I Henry IV* and Nashe," *N&Q* 6 (1959): 250; E. M. M. Taylor, "Lear's Philosopher," *SQ* 6 (1955): 364–65; A. Davenport, "Shakespeare and Nashe's *Pierce Penilesse,*" *N&Q* 198 (1953): 371–74 [*Macbeth*]; M. A. Shaaber, "Shylock's Name," *N&Q* 195 (1950): 236; John Dale Ebbs, "A Note on Nashe and Shakespeare," *MLN* 66 (1951): 480–81 [*Titus Andronicus*]; Ernest C. York, "Shakespeare and Nashe," *N&Q* 198 (1953): 370–71 [*Titus Andronicus*]; and W. Schrickx, *"Titus Andronicus* and Thomas Nashe," *ES* 50 (1969): 82–84.

The Nashe-Harvey quarrel, its motivations, issues and results, both stylistic and personal, is covered in several articles and books. Its influence on Shakespeare in *Love's Labor's Lost* is among the more popular approaches to the polemic. (See IV,A, for other discussions of the quarrel.) The fascination with Nashe's prose is reflected in the many articles on his style (see especially Donald J. McGinn's *PMLA* article below and items in IV,A which refer to style in their titles). Nashe as a critic is examined by several scholars. (See Michael R. Best's article discussed in II,A, below, and items in IV,A, annotated "Nashe as a critic," as well as those titles which bear on literary criticism or refer to Nashe's Preface to Greene's *Menaphon.*)

Authorship of certain nondramatic works has interested recent scholars. Though McKerrow included *An Almond for a Parrat* in his edition of Nashe, he had strong reservations about Nashe's authorship. Using mainly stylistic evidence, Donald J. McGinn argues in "Nashe's Share in the Marprelate Controversy," *PMLA* 59 (1944): 952- 84, that *An Almond for a Parrat* is Nashe's. Philip Drew, in "Nashe's Authorship of *An Almond for a Parrat,*" *N&Q* 7 (1960): 216- 17, and in "Thomas Nashe, Sebastian Münster and *An Almond for a Parrat,*" *N&Q* 7 (1960): 378- 80, agrees.

The possibility that Nashe collaborated with Greene on several pamphlets that have been considered wholly Greene's is discussed by Edwin Haviland Miller in "Further Notes on the Authorship of *The Defence of Cony-Catching* (1592)," *N&Q* 197 (1952): 446- 51, and "The Relationship of Robert Greene and Thomas Nashe (1588- 1592)," *PQ* 33 (1954): 353- 67, and by Donald J. McGinn in "A Quip from Tom Nashe," in *Studies in the English Renaissance Drama in Memory of Karl Julius Holzknecht,* ed. Josephine W. Bennett, Oscar Cargill, and Vernon Hall, Jr. (1959), pp. 172- 88. Hibbard rebuts McGinn in an appendix to his book on Nashe.

A list of Nashe's works and scholarship can be found in Samuel A. Tannenbaum's *Thomas Nashe: A Concise Bibliography* (1941) rpt. 1967 in vol. 6, *Elizabethan Bibliographies,* by Samuel A. and Dorothy R. Tannenbaum; and in Robert C. Johnson, *Elizabethan Bibliographies Supplements V* (1968). A selected list appears in Irving Ribner, *Tudor and Stuart Drama,* Goldentree Bibliographies (1966).

II. CRITICISM OF INDIVIDUAL PLAYS AND STATE OF SCHOLARSHIP

A. INDIVIDUAL PLAYS

Summer's Last Will and Testament

Hibbard, in *Thomas Nashe: A Critical Introduction,* describes the play as an occasional play, written at Archbishop Whitgift's country palace in Croyden, for presentation there in early autumn, 1592. The country and the court, simplicity and sophistication, especially in the character of Will Summers, Henry VIII's jester, exist side by side in the play. Nashe celebrates the old and the traditional, and attacks modernity. He "is on the side of folly, wit and excess, not on that of moderation." Hibbard concludes that it is a minor piece of Elizabethan drama, "outside the main stream of development," but "it is a work of distinction." "No earlier English comedy has anything like the intellectual content or the social relevance that it has."

Hibbard agrees with C. L. Barber's judgment in *Shakespeare's Festive Comedy: A Study of Dramatic Form and Its Relation to Social Custom* (1959) that *Summer's Last Will and Testament* is a holiday play, a play that has roots in the folk festivals of the countryside. The drama, written for and performed in the autumn, deals with the death of summer and the cycle of the seasons and, according to Barber, has a "thematic coherence" similar to that found in various Elizabethan season festivals and holidays.

According to Michael R. Best, in "Nashe, Lyly, and *Summers Last Will and Testament*," *PQ* 48 (1969): 1-11, Nashe wrote the one extant play now positively attributed to him "by greatly expanding a short entertainment written by Lyly for the Queen on progress" in August, 1591. This theory "explains many of the peculiarities of the play" including conflicting evidence about its premiere performance date and its audience at Croydon. Both Nashe's critical interest and satirical talents are demonstrated in the play through Best's reading many of Will Summers' (Nashe's addition) remarks as critical of Lyly's reputation and his euphuistic style.

A prosodic examination of the play is offered by J. E. Bernard, Jr., in *The Prosody of the Tudor Interlude* (1939). This "last of the interludes," almost totally written in prose and blank verse, is "free from the artlessness that characterizes the folk drama." Douglas Hewitt in "The Very Pompes of the Divell—Popular and Folk Elements in Elizabethan and Jacobean Drama," *RES* 25 (1949): 10-23, briefly refers to the use of "folk ceremonies" in this play. Alice S. Venezky in *Pageantry on the Shakespearean Stage* (1951) and M. C. Bradbrook in *The Growth and Structure of Elizabethan Comedy* (1955) treat the play as a pageant.

J. V. Cunningham turns his attention to the famous poem found in *Summer's Last Will and Testament:* "Adieu, farewell, earth's bliss." In *Tradition and Poetic Structure: Essays in Literary History and Criticism* (1960), he argues that the structure of the poem is a "practical syllogism explicitly propounded." (Cunningham's essay is reprinted under its chapter title, "Logic and Lyric: Marvell, Dunbar, Nashe" in *Discussions of Poetry: Form and Structure,* ed. Francis Murphy [1964].) In "The Practice of Historical Interpretation and Nashe's 'Brightnesse Falls from the Ayre,'" *JEGP* 66 (1967): 501-18, Wesley Trimpi observes that readers often assume that *ayre* is a misprint for *hayre* in the line "Brightnesse falls from the ayre." He argues that "Brightnesse" refers to lightning, metaphorically "unexpected disaster," and therefore *ayre* is no misprint. Other references to this poem are found in Percy Walker's "Metaphor as Mistake," *SR* 66 (1958): 79–99, and in Harry Morris's "Nashe's 'Brightnesse Falls from the Ayre,' " *RN* 12 (1959): 167–69.

B. OVER-ALL STATE OF CRITICISM

The criticism of Nashe's drama is similar to Nashe's drama: respectable but small in quantity. In almost a half century there have been only three major examinations of *Summer's Last Will and Testament*, and two of these are parts of larger studies. Of the three, Hibbard's study has the greater breadth; he discusses the play's date, the occasion and nature of its first performance, its thematic variety, and its place in the contemporary drama. Barber develops an important but more narrow interest: the influences of the folk festival tradition on the play. Best is only slightly less interested in detecting Lyly's hand in the drama than in commenting on Nashe's role as literary critic and satirist.

III. CANON

A. PLAYS IN CHRONOLOGICAL ORDER

The order of the plays is based on the original performance date (in italics preceding the semicolon) which, along with the date of the first edition and the type of play, is taken from *Annals of English Drama, 975–1700*, by Alfred Harbage, rev. Samuel Schoenbaum (1964) and Schoenbaum's *Supplement to the Revised Edition* (1966). And see E. K. Chambers, *The Elizabethan Stage* (1923), vol. 3.

Summer's Last Will and Testament, comedy (*1592*; 1600)

Hibbard believes the first performance occurred between mid-September and mid-October in Croydon, at the country palace of Archbishop Whitgift, where it was composed shortly before its presentation. Best, "Nashe, Lyly" (II,A), theorizes that the original form of the play was a sketch written by Lyly in August, 1591.

B. UNCERTAIN ASCRIPTIONS; APOCRYPHA

Terminus et Non Terminus, satirical show (*1586–88*; lost)

The play perhaps was written by Nashe in collaboration with "another" while at Cambridge, and performed at St. John's College. (See Hibbard.)

Dido, Queen of Carthage, classical legend, tragedy (ca. *1587–93*; 1594)

Many consider this a collaboration of Marlowe and Nashe. On the title page of the 1594 edition appears: "Written by Christopher Marlowe, and *Thomas Nashe. Gent.*" Hibbard concisely states the majority view, however, when he says that Nashe's share in the play "can have amounted to little or nothing." H. J. Oliver, who edited the play for the Revels Plays, *"Dido Queen of Carthage" and "The Massacre at Paris"* (1968), is not so sure. Certain observations of Oliver's, especially bibliographical, make him reluctant to dismiss the possibility that Nashe had a hand in the composition of the play. Brief references to this question of authorship are found in John P. Cutts, "Dido, Queen of Carthage," *N&Q* 5 (1958): 371–74, and in J. C. Maxwell, "Virgilian Half-Lines in Shakespeare's 'Heroic Narrative,' " *N&Q* 198 (1953): 100.

A Knack to Know a Knave, comedy (*1592*; 1594)

Harbage and Schoenbaum list the playwright as anonymous, with possible attribution to Kempe, Peele, or Wilson. Richard Simpson in *The School of Shakespeare* (1878) was the first to suggest Nashe as the author. C. M. Gayley, in *Representative English Comedies* (1907), agreed that Nashe's authorship was a possibility. Hibbard, however, "can see no grounds for it," and G. R. Proudfoot, the editor of the Malone Society edition (1963), gives no argument for Nashe. Arthur Freeman in "Two Notes on *A Knack to Know a Knave,*" *N&Q* 9 (1962): 326–27, briefly comments on the possibility of Nashe's authorship. See the discussion in the anonymous-play section of this volume.

Doctor Faustus, tragedy (*1588–92*; 1604)

This has been attributed in part to Nashe. Though he does not believe that Nashe collaborated with Marlowe on the original composition of *Doctor Faustus,* Paul H. Kocher in "Nashe's Authorship of the Prose Scenes in *Faustus,*" *MLQ* 3 (1942): 17–40, argues that Nashe "wrote substantially all of the prose scenes" in the play that appear in the 1604 quarto, and that he wrote them for an autumn, 1594, revival of the play. H. W. Crundell in "Nashe and *Dr. Faustus," N&Q* 9 (1962): 327, gives minor but additional support to Kocher's contention.

I Henry VI, history (*3 March 1592*; 1623)
II Henry VI, history (ca. *1590-92*; 1594)

In 1952, J. Dover Wilson revived the authorship controversy elaborately discussed by Allison Gaws in *The Origin and Development of "Henry VI" in Relationship to Shakespeare, Marlowe, Peele, and Greene* (1926). Gaws argued that several playwrights, including Nashe, had a hand in writing *Henry VI, Part I.* Most critics thought the issue had been laid to rest by Peter Alexander in *Shakespeare's "Henry VI" and "Richard III"* (1929) and later in *Shakespeare's Life and Art* (1939) where Alexander argued that *Henry VI* is entirely Shakespeare's. Wilson, in the introduction to his three-volume edition of *Henry VI* (1952), contends that sections of the three-part history are by others and that specifically III.iii and iv, IV.vii, and V.iii of *Part I* are by Nashe as well as sections of *Part II,* especially the scenes with Jack Cade. Wilson's claim is based upon internal evidence and parallels to Nashe's known works. He receives some support from P. G. Nilsson in "The Upstart Crow and *Henry VI," MSpr* 58 (1964): 292-303, and from G. Blakemore Evans's review of Wilson's edition in *SQ* 4 (1953): 84-92. But the weight of scholarship is clearly against Wilson. Andrew S. Cairncross in his New Arden edition of the first two parts of *Henry VI* (*Part I,* 1962 and *Part II,* 1957) insists that Shakespeare wrote the entire *Henry VI* and that Nashe had no hand in the composition. C. G. Harlow attacks Wilson's method when he argues, in "A Source for Nashe's *Terrors of the Night,* and the Authorship of *I Henry VI," SEL* 5 (1965): 31-47, and 269-81, that Shakespeare and Nashe used the same source for these two works and that, therefore, there is no necessity or justification for ascribing parts of *Henry VI* to Nashe's known works. In 1946, prior to Wilson's edition of *Henry VI,* E. M. W. Tillyard reviewed the controversy in *Shakespeare's History Plays* and agreed with Alexander's ascription of the plays solely to Shakespeare. Since the publication of Wilson's edition of *Henry VI,* those who have expressed opposition to his argument are: Leo Kirschbaum, "The Authorship of *I Henry VI," PMLA* 27 (1952): 809-22; Warren B. Austin, "A Supposed Contemporary Allusion to Shakespeare as a Plagiarist," *SQ* 6 (1955): 373-80; E. A. J. Honigmann, "Shakespeare's 'Lost Source-Plays,' " *MLR* 49 (1954): 293-307; Irving Ribner, *The*

English History Play in the Age of Shakespeare (1957; rev. ed. 1965); Geoffrey Bullough, *Narrative and Dramatic Sources of Shakespeare,* vol. 3 (1960); Peter Alexander, *Shakespeare* (1964); and Samuel Schoenbaum, *Internal Evidence and Elizabethan Dramatic Authorship* (1966). Nonetheless, Guy Lambrechts in "La composition de la première partie de *Henri VI*," *BFLS* 46 (1967): 325–54, insists that the play we have is a revision by Shakespeare of a collaboration of Nashe and Greene.

The Isle of Dogs, satirical comedy (*July, 1597;* lost)

This apparently scurrilous play was probably completed by Ben Jonson. It offended the Privy Council which closed the theaters on 28 July 1597 and ordered the arrest of some of those connected with the drama. In "Nashe, Jonson, and the Oldcastle Problem," *MP* 65 (1968): 307–24, Alice Lyle Scoufos argues that Nashe in *Lenten Stuffe* and Jonson in *Every Man in His Humor* satirize the Cobham family. She conjectures that these attacks on the family derived from the playwrights' troubles over *The Isle of Dogs* for which they blamed the influence of the Cobhams in the Privy Council. Perhaps, she says, the family was "touched" by the satirical play.

C. CRITIQUE OF THE STANDARD EDITION

The 1904–10 edition of Nashe's works by Ronald B. McKerrow is a superlative scholarly product. Not only did McKerrow provide a model for future editors of Elizabethan literature, but he also provided an edition of Nashe's works that, some sixty years later, has made a new edition unnecessary. Because McKerrow's edition was limited to seven hundred and fifty copies, however, there was a need for a reprint; this F. P. Wilson supplied in 1958 with a lithographic reproduction, described as "Reprinted from the original edition with corrections and supplementary notes." The additional notes are from McKerrow's marginalia in his own copy, from scholarship published since 1910, and from some contributions made especially for the reprint. Almost all of McKerrow's errata are incorporated in the text.

A more recent edition of Nashe appeared in 1964 as the first volume of the Stratford-upon-Avon-Library, titled *Thomas Nashe: Selected Writings,* edited by Stanley Wells. Wells admits his indebtedness to McKerrow and Hibbard, but the texts are based on a fresh collation of early editions. Unlike the conservative McKerrow edition, the text is modernized in form and spelling. The volume contains a glossary as well as an appendix noting variant readings. The brief introduction emphasizes Nashe as a literary artist. *Summer's Last Will and Testament* is included.

D. TEXTUAL STUDIES

There have been no comments on the text of *Summer's Last Will and Testament* except those by McKerrow and Wells in their editions (see III,C). D. F. Foxon in *Thomas J. Wise and the Pre-Restoration Drama* (1959) discusses and describes the made-up copies of *Summer's Last Will and Testament* in Wise's Ashley Library in the British Museum and those in the John H. Wrenn Collection in the University of Texas Library.

E. NONDRAMATIC WORKS

The several single editions of nondramatic works since McKerrow (below, IV,C) have added little to his textual work. Though occasionally an editor relies on a text other than McKerrow for a few words, all express their indebtedness to the definitive text. John Berryman's 1960 edition of *The Unfortunate Traveller,* with its long introduction and Michael Ayrton's illustrations, is a good popular edition.

IV. SEE ALSO

A. GENERAL

Acheson, Arthur. *Shakespeare, Chapman, and "Sir Thomas More."* 1931.

Albright, Evelyn May. *Dramatic Publication in England, 1580–1640: A Study of Conditions Affecting Content and Form of Drama.* 1927.

Allen, Don Cameron. *Frances Meres's Treatise "Poetrie": A Critical Edition.* 1933. [Nashe as a critic.]

———. "*The Anatomie of Absurditie:* A Study in Literary Apprenticeship." *SP* 32 (1935): 170–76.

———. "A Text from Nashe on the Latin Literature of the Sixteenth Century." *RS* 5 (1937): 205–18.

Anikst, Alexander. "Shakespeare as Seen by His Contemporaries." In *Foreign Classical Art,* ed. B. Wipper, et al. (1966), pp. 7–30.

Aronstein, Philipp. *Das englische Renaissancedrama.* 1929.

Ashley, Robert, and Edwin M. Moseley, eds. *Elizabethan Fiction.* 1953. [Includes *The Unfortunate Traveller.*]

Atkins, J. W. H. *English Literary Criticism: The Renascence.* 1947; 2nd ed. 1951.

Austin, Warren B. "Concerning a Woodcut." *SQ* 8 (1957): 245. [Mentions Nashe-Harvey quarrel.]

———. "Thomas Nashe's Authorship of a Sonnet Attributed to Shakespeare." In *Shakespeare in the Southwest: Some New Directions,* ed. T. J. Stafford (1969), pp. 94–105. ["Phaeton to His Friend."]

Ayrton, Michael. "The Deadly Stockado." *London Magazine* 4, no. 7 (1957): 40–45.

Baker, Howard. *Induction to Tragedy: A Study in a Development of Form in "Gorboduc," "The Spanish Tragedy," and "Titus Andronicus."* 1939. [Nashe as a critic.]

Baker, Oliver. *In Shakespeare's Warwickshire and the Unknown Years.* 1937.

Baldwin, T. W. "A Line in Gabriel Harvey." *TLS*, 18 Jan. 1941, p. 31. [Quarrel with Nashe.]

———. *On the Literary Genetics of Shakspere's Plays, 1592–1594.* 1959.

———. *"Errors* and Marprelate." In *Studies in Honor of DeWitt T. Starnes,* ed. Thomas P. Harrison (1967), pp. 9–23.

Barber, C. L. *The Idea of Honour in the English Drama, 1591–1700.* 1957.

Baskervill, Charles Read. *The Elizabethan Jig and Related Song Drama.* 1929.

Boas, Frederick S. *An Introduction to Tudor Drama.* 1933.

Brown, Huntington. *Rabelais in English Literature.* 1933.

Buckley, George T. *Atheism in the English Renaissance.* 1932.

Bühler, Curt F. "Honorificicabilitudinitatibus." *AN&Q* 3 (1965): 131.

Busby, Olive M. *Studies in the Development of the Fool in the Elizabethan Drama.* 1923.

Bush, Douglas. *Mythology and the Renaissance Tradition in English Poetry.* 1932; rev. ed. 1963.

Butler, Pierce. *Materials for the Life of Shakespeare.* 1930.

Cairncross, Andrew S. *The Problem of "Hamlet": A Solution.* 1936.

Campbell, Lily B. *Shakespeare's "Histories": Mirrors of Elizabethan Policy.* 1947.

Cawley, Robert R. *The Voyagers and Elizabethan Drama.* 1938.

Cazamian, Louis. *The Development of English Humor.* 1952.

Chew, Samuel C. *The Crescent and the Rose: Islam and England during the Renaissance.* 1937.

Churchill, R. C. *Shakespeare and His Betters: A History and a Criticism of the Attempts Which Have Been Made to Prove That Shakespeare's Works Were Written by Others.* 1958.

Clark, Eleanor G. *Elizabethan Fustian: A Study in the Social and Political Backgrounds of the Drama, with Particular Reference to Christopher Marlowe.* 1937.

Clark, Eva Turner. *Shakespeare's Plays in the Order of Their Writing.* 1930.

Clemen, Wolfgang. *English Tragedy before Shakespeare: The Development of Dramatic Speech.* Trans. T. S. Dorsch, 1961; German ed. 1955. [Nashe as a critic.]

Crane, William G. *Wit and Rhetoric in the Renaissance: The Formal Basis of Elizabethan Prose Style.* 1937.

Croston, A. K. "The Use of Imagery in Nashe's *The Unfortunate Traveller." RES* 24 (1948): 90–101.

Davenport, A. "An Elizabethan Controversy: Harvey and Nashe." *N&Q* 182 (1942): 116–19.

Davis, Walter R. *Idea and Act in Elizabethan Fiction.* 1969.

De Beer, E. S. "Thomas Nashe: The Notices of Rome in *The Unfortunate Traveller." N&Q* 175 (1943): 67–70.

Doran, Madeleine. *Endeavors of Art: A Study of Form in Elizabethan Drama.* 1954.

Drew, Philip. "Was Greene's 'Young Juvenal' Nashe or Lodge?" *SEL* 7 (1967): 55–66.

Duhamel, P. Albert. "The Ciceronianism of Gabriel Harvey." *SP* 49 (1952): 155–70. [Mentions quarrel with Nashe.]

Eckhardt, Eduard. *Das englische Drama im Zeitalter der Reformation und der Hochrenaissance vorstufen Shakespeare und seine Zeit.* 1928.

Feasey, Eveline and Lynette. "Nashe's *The Unfortunate Traveller:* Some Marlovian Echoes." *English* 7 (1948): 125–29.

Feasey, Lynette. "The Unfortunate Traveller." *TLS,* 2 Oct. 1948, p. 555.

French, A. L. "Hamlet's Nunnery." *ES* 48 (1967): 141–45.

Geraldine, Sister M. "Erasmus and the Tradition of Paradox." *SP* 61 (1964): 41–63.

Gerrard, Ernest A. *Elizabethan Drama and Dramatists, 1583–1603.* 1928.

Gibbons, Sister Marina. "Polemic, the Rhetorical Tradition, and *The Unfortunate Traveller.*" *JEGP* 63 (1964): 408–21.

Grebanier, Bernard. *The Truth About Shylock.* 1962.

Greg, W. W., ed. *English Literary Autographs, 1550–1650.* 3 vols. 1925–32.

Gurr, Andrew. "Elizabethan Action." *SP* 63 (1966): 144–56.

Hall, Vernon, Jr. *Renaissance Literary Criticism: A Study of Its Social Content.* 1945.

Harbage, Alfred. *Shakespeare and the Rival Traditions.* 1952.

Harder, Kelsie B. "Nashe's Rebuke of Spenser." *N&Q* 198 (1953): 145–46.

———. "Nashe and Spenser." In *Essays in Honor of Walter Clyde Curry,* ed. Richmond C. Beatty and Edgar H. Duncan (1954), pp. 123–32.

Harlow, C. G. "Thomas Nashe and the Council-Table Ass." *N&Q* 10 (1963): 411–12.

Harman, Edward George. *Gabriel Harvey and Thomas Nashe.* 1923.

Harris, Bernard. "Dissent and Satire." *ShS* 17 (1964): 120–37.

Harrison, G. B. *Shakespeare's Fellows: Being a Brief Chronicle of the Shakespearean Age.* 1923.

———. *Elizabethan Plays and Players.* 1940.

Hibbard, G. R., ed. *Three Elizabethan Pamphlets.* 1951. [Includes *Pierce Penilesse his Supplication to the Devil.*]

Holmes, Elizabeth. *Aspects of Elizabethan Imagery.* 1929.

Howarth, R. G. *Two Elizabethan Writers of Fiction: Thomas Nashe and Thomas Deloney.* 1956.

Hunter, J. B. "*The Unfortunate Traveller* of Thomas Nashe as a Sidelight on Elizabethan Security." *N&Q* 196 (1951): 75–76.

Johnson, Francis R. "The First Edition of Gabriel Harvey's *Four Letters.*" *Library* 15 (1934): 212–223. [Mentions quarrel with Nashe.]

Kaiser, Walter. *Praisers of Folly.* 1963.

Kane, Robert J. "Anthony Chute, Thomas Nashe, and the First English Work on Tobacco." *RES* 7 (1931): 151–59.

Kaula, David. "The Low Style in Nashe's *The Unfortunate Traveller.*" *SEL* 6 (1966): 43–57.

Kernan, Alvin. *The Cankered Muse: Satire of the English Renaissance.* 1959.

Kirkman, A. J. "Word Coinage." *TLS,* 4 May 1962, p. 325.

Klein, David. *The Elizabethan Dramatists as Critics.* 1963.

Knapp, Mary. "A Note on Nashe's Preface to Greene's *Menaphon.*" *N&Q* 164 (1933): 98.

Knights, L. C. "Elizabethan Prose." *Scrutiny* 2 (1934): 427-38 (rpt. in Knights's *Drama and Society in the Age of Jonson* [1937]).

Koskenniemi, Inna. *Studies in the Vocabulary of English Drama, 1550-1600, Excluding Shakespeare and Ben Jonson.* 1962.

Kuhl, Ernest. "Chaucer and Thomas Nashe." *TLS,* 5 Nov. 1925, p. 739.

Lawlis, Merritt E., ed. *The Novels of Thomas Deloney.* 1961.

Lawrence, William J. *Pre-Restoration Stage Studies.* 1927.

Liedstrand, Frithjof. *Metapher und Vergleich in "The Unfortunate Traveller" von Thomas Nashe und bei seinen Vorbildern Francois Rabelais und Pietro Aretino.* 1929.

Lievsay, John L. *The Elizabethan Image of Italy.* 1964.

McGinn, Donald J. "The Real Martin Marprelate." *PMLA* 58 (1943): 84-107.

———. "The Allegory of the 'Beare' and the 'Foxe' in Nashe's *Pierce Penilesse.*" *PMLA* 61 (1946): 431-53.

———. *John Penry and the Marprelate Controversy.* 1966.

Mackerness, E. D. "A Note on Thomas Nashe and 'Style.' " *English* 6 (1947): 198-200.

———. "*Christs Teares* and the Literature of Warning." *ES* 33 (1952): 251-54.

McPherson, David C. "Aretino and the Harvey-Nashe Quarrel." *PMLA* 84 (1969): 1551-58.

Marcus, Hans. "Thomas Nashe über Deutschland." *Archiv* 192 (1955): 113-33.

Marsh, T. N. "Humor and Invective in Early Tudor Polemic Prose." *Rice Institute Pamphlet* 44, no. 1 (1957): 79-89.

Miller, Edwin Haviland. "Deletions in Robert Greene's *A Quip for an Upstart Courtier* (1592)." *HLQ* 15 (1952): 277-82.

———. *The Professional Writer in Elizabethan England: A Study of Nondramatic Literature.* 1959.

Morris, Helen. *Elizabethan Literature.* 1958.

Mustard, Wilfred P. "Notes on Thomas Nashe's Works." *MLN* 40 (1925): 469-76.

Ong, Walter J. "Oral Residue in Tudor Prose Style." *PMLA* 80 (1965): 145-54.

Parks, George B. "The First Italianate Englishmen." *SRen* 7 (1961): 197-216.

Parrott, Thomas Marc, and Robert Hamilton Ball. *A Short View of Elizabethan Drama.* 1943.

Peñuelos, Marcellino C. "Algo más sobre las picaresca: Lázaro y Jack Wilton." *Hispano* 37 (1954): 443-45.

Perkins, David. "Issue and Motivations in the Nashe-Harvey Quarrel." *PQ* 29 (1960): 224-33.

Peter, John. *Complaint and Satire in Early English Literature.* 1956.

Petti, Anthony G. "Political Satire in *Pierce Peñilesse His Svplication to the Divill.*" *Neophil* 45 (1961): 139-50.

———. "Beasts and Politics in Elizabethan Literature." *E&S* 16 (1963): 68-90.

Pratt, S. M. "Antwerp and the Elizabethan Mind." *MLQ* 24 (1963): 53-60.

Praz, Mario. *Studi sul concettismo.* 1946.

Q., D. "Bacon, Nashe and Dante." *N&Q* 190 (1946): 78.

Raab, Felix. *The English Face of Machiavelli: A Changing Interpretation, 1500–1700.* 1964.

Re, Arundell del. *The Secret of the Renaissance and Other Essays and Studies.* 1930.

Robin, P. Ansell. *Animal Lore in English Literature.* 1932.

Rosenberg, Eleanor. *Leicester: Patron of Letters.* 1955. [Nashe-Harvey quarrel.]

Rossiter, A. P. *English Drama from Early Times to the Elizabethans: Its Background, Origins, and Development.* 1950.

Sackton, Alexander H. "Thomas Nashe as an Elizabethan Critic." *Studies in English* (Univ. of Texas), 26 (1947): 18–25.

Saintsbury, George, ed. *Shorter Novels, Elizabethan and Jacobean.* Notes by Philip Henderson. 1929. [Contains *The Unfortunate Traveller.*]

Salyer, Sandford M. "Hall's Satires and the Harvey-Nashe Controversy." *SP* 25 (1928): 149–70.

Schaubert, E. von. "Die Stelle vom 'Rauhen Pyrrhus' (*Hamlet II*, 2, 460–551) in ihrem Verhältnis zu Marlowe-Nashes *Dido,* zu Seneca und dem *Urhamlet* und damit ihrer Bedeutung für Datierungsfragen, Quartoproblem und Nashes Angriff auf Thomas Kyd." *Anglia* 53 (1929): 374–439.

Schelling, F. E. *Foreign Influences in Elizabethan Plays.* 1923.

———. *Elizabethan Playwrights: A Short History of the English Drama from Mediaeval Times to the Closing of the Theaters in 1642.* 1925.

Schlauch, Margaret. *Antecedents of the English Novel, 1400–1600.* 1963.

Schrickx, W. "Nashe, Greene and Shakespeare in 1592." *RLV* 22 (1956): 55–64.

———. "Onion, a Sobriquet Relevant to Thomas Nashe?" *RLV* 27 (1961): 322–28.

Sibley, G. M. *The Lost Plays and Masques, 1500–1642.* 1933.

Snortum, Niel K. "The Title of Nashe's *Pierce Penniless.*" *MLN* 72 (1957): 170–73.

Spencer, Theodore. *Death and Elizabethan Tragedy: A Study of Convention and Opinion in the Elizabethan Drama.* 1936.

Sprott, S. E. "Raleigh's 'Sceptic' and the Elizabethan Translation of Sextus Empiricus." *PQ* 42 (1963): 166–75.

Stafford, John. "The Social Status of Renaissance Literary Critics." *Studies in English* (Univ. of Texas), 25 (1945–46): 72–97.

Stamm, Fanny. *"Der Unfortunate Traveller" des Thomas Nashe: eine Studie über das Verhältnis der englisches zur italienisches Renaissance.* 1930.

Staton, Walter F., Jr. "The Characters of Style in Elizabethan Prose." *JEGP* 57 (1958): 197–207.

Sternfeld, Frederick W. "Lasso's Music for Shakespeare's 'Samigo.' " *SQ* 9 (1958): 105–16.

Stevens, F. G. "Parolles and Jack Wilton's Captain." *Shakespeare Review* 1 (1928): 190–96.

Strathmann, E. A. *Sir Walter Raleigh: A Study in Elizabethan Skepticism.* 1951.

Stürzl, Erwin. *Der Zeitbegriff in der elisabethanischen Literatur: The Lackey of Eternity.* 1965.

Summersgill, Travis L. "The Influence of the Marprelate Controversy upon the Style of Thomas Nashe." *SP* 48 (1951): 145-60.
——. "Harvey, Nashe, and the Three Parnassus Plays." *PQ* 31 (1952): 94-95.
Sutherland, James. *On English Prose.* 1957.
——. *English Satire.* 1958.
Talbert, Ernest William. *Elizabethan Drama and Shakespeare's Early Plays: An Essay in Historical Criticism.* 1963.
Teets, Bruce E. "Two Faces of Style in Renaissance Prose Fiction." In *Sweet Smoke of Rhetoric: A Collection of Renaissance Essays,* ed. Natalie Grimes Lawrence and J. A. Reynolds (1964), pp. 69-81.
Thomas, Sidney. "New Light on the Nashe-Harvey Quarrel." *MLN* 63 (1948): 481-83.
Treneer, Anne. *The Sea in English Literature from Beowulf to Donne.* 1926.
Vines, Sherard. *The Course of English Classicism.* 1930. [Nashe as a critic.]
Wagenknecht, Edward. *Cavalcade of the English Novel.* 1943.
Walker, Hugh. *English Satire and Satirists.* 1925.
Weimann, Robert. "Thomas Nashe és az Érzsebetkori humanismus" [Thomas Nashe and Elizabethan Humanism] . *FK* 7 (1961): 285-99.
Wells, Henry W. *Elizabethan and Jacobean Playwrights.* 1939.
Welsford, Enid. *The Fool: His Social and Literary History.* 1935.
White, Harold Ogden. *Plagiarism and Imitation During the English Renaissance.* 1935. [Nashe as a critic.]
Wilson, F. P. "Another Allusion to Thomas Nashe." *N&Q* 7 (1960): 51.
Wilson, H. S. "The Cambridge Comedy *Pendantius* and Gabriel Harvey's *Ciceronianus.*" *SP* 45 (1948): 578-91. [Quarrel with Nashe.]
Wilson, J. Dover. "Malone and the Upstart Crow." *ShS* 4 (1951): 56-68.
Wood, James O. " 'Feare No Colours.' " *N&Q* 13 (1966): 54-55.
——. " 'Dexterious.' " *N&Q* 13 (1966): 253-54.
Wright, Celeste Turner. "Mundy and Chettle in Grub Street." *BUSE* 5 (1961): 129-38.
Wright, Herbert G. "Some Sixteenth and Seventeenth Century Writers on the Plague." *E&S* 6 (1953): 41-55.
Zbierski, Henryk. *Shakespeare and the "War of the Theatres."* 1957.

B. TEXTUAL STUDIES

Greg, W. W. "Was the First Edition of *Pierce Penniless* a Piracy?" *Library* 7 (1952): 122-24.
Kinsman, Robert S. "Priscilla's 'Grote'; An Emendation in Nashe's *Unfortunate Traveller.*" *N&Q* 7 (1960): 50-51.
Kocher, Paul H. "Some Nashe Marginalia Concerning Marlowe." *MLN* 57 (1942): 45-49.
Miller, William E. "*The Hospitall of Incurable Fooles.*" *SB* 16 (1963): 204-7.
Sanderson, James L. "An Unnoted Text of Nashe's 'The Choise of Valentines.' " *ELN* 1 (1964): 252-53.
Wilson, J. Dover. "The Origins and Development of Shakespeare's *Henry IV.*" *Library* 26 (1945): 2-16.

C. EDITIONS

Ayrton, Michael, illus. and introd. *The Unfortunate Traveller.* 1948.

Chassé, Charles, trans. *Thomas Nashe. "Le voyageur malchanceux ou la vie de Jack Wilton."* 1954.

Chew, Samuel C., ed. *The Unfortunate Traveler; or, The Life of Jack Wilton.* 1926.

Harrison, G. B., ed. *Thomas Nashe, "Pierce Penilesse, His Svpplication to the Divell" (1592).* 1924.

Henderson, Philip, ed. *The Unfortunate Traveller.* Illus. Haydn Mackey. 1930.

JOHN LYLY

Joseph W. Houppert

The standard edition is R. W. Bond, *The Complete Works of John Lyly*, 3 vols. (1902). A forthcoming edition by G. K. Hunter will presumably replace Bond.

I. GENERAL

A. BIOGRAPHICAL

G. K. Hunter's *John Lyly: The Humanist as Courtier* (1962) is the first full-length study since Albert Feuillerat's *John Lyly: Contribution à l'histoire de la Renaissance en Angleterre* (1910). Hunter examines Lyly's career in the light of Renaissance humanism. In his first chapter, "Humanism and Courtship," he argues that Lyly's reputation has suffered because of the dual role he was forced to play as humanist and courtier. By Lyly's day the court of Elizabeth had established a mode of life which was able to use the humanistic training without depending upon it, but the humanists' and courtiers' interests pointed in different directions. The humanist admired peace, orderly government, and study; the courtier admired war and honor. Against this background of opposed tendencies, Hunter concludes that Lyly's wit is not simply a superficial show of rhetorical brilliance but a device which keeps the author detached from the courtly passions of his creations. Mark Eccles's review of Hunter's book, in *JEGP* 63 (1963): 160, questions whether John Lyly was a humanist as defined by Hunter and suggests that the chapter seems more relevant to William Lily than to his grandson.

Warren B. Austin, "John Lyly and Queen Elizabeth," *N&Q* 176 (1939): 146–47, quotes a letter dated 9 February 1604, from Tobie Duresme to Sir Julius Caesar to show that Lyly was still seeking a royal pension after Elizabeth's death. In "William Withie's Notebook:

Lampoons on John Lyly and Gabriel Harvey," *RES* 23 (1947): 297–309, Austin adds a note on Lyly's differences with Harvey, who satirized Lyly's patron, the Earl of Oxford. In coming to Oxford's defense, Lyly popularized the incident. Deborah Jones, "John Lyly at St. Bartholomew's," in *Thomas Lodge and Other Elizabethans,* ed. Charles J. Sisson (1933), pp. 363–408, contributes original information about neighborhood difficulties experienced by Lyly's family.

A number of appreciative biographical sketches have appeared: K. N. Colville, *Fame's Twilight: Studies of Nine Men of Letters* (1923); Samuel L. Wolff, "The Humanist as Man of Letters: John Lyly," *SR* 31 (1923): 8–35; the Earl of Crawford and Balcarres, "John Lyly," *BJRL* 8 (1924): 312–44; H. J. Massingham, "John Lyly," in *The Great Tudors,* ed. Katharine Garvin (1935), pp. 565–80; and Rose Macaulay, "Lyly and Sidney," in *English Novelists,* ed. Derek Verschoyle (1936), pp. 33–50.

Reginald Charles Churchill's *Shakespeare and His Betters* (1958) treats the attempts to prove that Shakespeare's works were written by others, among them John Lyly. And see Percy Allen's *The Case for Edward de Vere 17th Earl of Oxford as "Shakespeare"* (1930).

B. GENERAL STUDIES OF THE PLAYS

G. K. Hunter's *John Lyly: The Humanist as Courtier* (I,A) is the most comprehensive study. Lyly's methods as a dramatist are analyzed and each play separately criticized. Lyly's success lies in his ability to organize his materials by two means: his patterned style and his mode of construction. Three unifying techniques are examined: unification around debate (*Campaspe, Sapho and Phao, Endymion, Midas*); harmonious variety *(Gallathea, Love's Metamorphosis, The Woman in the Moon);* and subplot intrigue (*Mother Bombie*). Hunter also takes up the concept of appearance and reality. He suggests that Lyly was aware that his plays were "unreal," but that for Lyly the courtly audience was the reality and the fount of truth. His plays could approach truth only by mirroring the court's virtues, and be but a shadow of that true perfection.

Hunter's arrangement of the plays around unifying techniques breaks with the older tradition represented by T. W. Baldwin, *Shakspere's Five-Act Structure* (1947), who analyzes the comedies in terms of protasis, epitasis, and catastrophe. Hunter's reluctance to adopt the classical formula is shared by Michael R. Best, "Lyly's Static Drama," *RenD,* 1 (1968): 75–86, who argues that in Lyly's plays there is almost no action at all. The soul of Lyly's comedies is in theme and character.

Hereward T. Price, "Shakespeare and His Young Contemporaries," *PQ* 41 (1962): 37-57, admits that Lyly was innovative in his use of courtship and love as subjects, but argues that the plays lack construction and that Lyly does not know what drama is. Ifor Evans, *A Short History of English Drama* (1948; rev. ed. 1965), cites Lyly's virtues but includes him among a group of dramatists whose light and color have now disappeared. Thomas Marc Parrott and Robert Hamilton Ball, *A Short View of Elizabethan Drama* (1943), contend that the action in Lyly's plays is anything but exciting, that the plots are slight, and that the plays are often a curious blend of the classical, the romantic, and the realistic. Robert A. Law, "The 'Pre-conceived Pattern' of *A Midsummer Night's Dream*," *Studies in English* (Univ. of Texas), 23 (1943): 5-14, argues that Shakespeare's play lacks structure because it follows a pre-conceived pattern established partly by Lyly.

In *The Growth and Structure of Elizabethan Comedy* (1955), Muriel C. Bradbrook emphasizes that Lyly gave order and grace to Elizabethan comedy. His plays provided a model of elegant speech, and a mirror of manners. The form which Lyly evolved was verbal, exquisitely phrased for youthful speakers, but not fully dramatic. J. W. H. Atkins, *English Literary Criticism: The Renascence* (1947; 2nd ed. 1951), says that although indebted to Roman comedy, Lyly proposes a dramatic form of a different kind, and emphasizes the need for a refinement of comedy. Lyly rejects the rigidity of classical drama and relies instead on the domestic tradition of mingled elements. In refusing to classify his plays as comedies or tragedies, Lyly denies that the boundaries of dramatic form have been permanently fixed. Madeleine Doran, *Endeavors of Art: A Study of Form in Elizabethan Drama* (1954), adds that Lyly's departures were only apparent, and cites a late fourteenth-century authority. Doran sees the unity in his plays arising from feeling or tone rather than from careful plot construction.

David Lloyd Stevenson, in *The Love-Game Comedy* (1946), argues that Lyly was the first Elizabethan dramatist to perceive that the opposed attitudes in the quarrel over the definition of romance could be used for stage purposes. Lyly's lovers, however, never come completely to life; they simply voice current attitudes toward love. Lyly was able to present in dramatic form the complex love dilemma which attracted the attention of courtly gentlemen and ladies. Robert Y. Turner, "Some Dialogues of Love in Lyly's Comedies," *ELH* 29

(1962): 276–88, also focuses on Lyly's conversations used to dramatize love. Since the circumstances are unfavorable to the lovers' disclosure of true sentiments, they are forced to speak enigmatically (partly from fear and partly from sensitivity to the delicate nature of love). The resulting tension creates dialogue in which each assertion is tentative, and this dialogue, by not mentioning love directly, gives an unmistakable sense of what it is like to be in love. Marco Mincoff, "Shakespeare and Lyly," *ShS* 14 (1961): 15–24, suggests that in *Sapho and Phao* and *Gallathea* Lyly had developed high love comedy of a delicate and subtle nature as far as he was able, and that it was left to Shakespeare to take it further. Shakespeare derived at least one aspect of the appearance-and-reality complex from Lyly.

Bernard Huppé, "Allegory of Love in Lyly's Court Comedies," *ELH* 14 (1947): 93–113, identifies Lyly's own conception of love with Euphues's declaration that true or virtuous love must be grounded upon time, reason, favor, and virtue. This conception informs the allegory in *Sapho and Phao, Endymion, Love's Metamorphosis,* and *The Woman in the Moon.* The amoral and the moral, passion and chastity, are in conflict, and chastity is fortified by the example of the Virgin Queen. Paul A. Olson, "*A Midsummer Night's Dream* and the Meaning of Court Marriage," *ELH* 24 (1957): 95–119, relates Shakespeare's play to Lyly's court comedies. Lyly's plays require an audience sensitive to emblematic meanings. His plays grew out of a court consistently interested in art which builds meanings from the materials of traditional emblems and allegories. Jocelyn Powell, "John Lyly and the Language of Play," in *Elizabethan Theatre,* SuAS, vol. 9 (1966), pp. 147–67, claims that throughout Lyly's works the emphasis is on figures of thought, on definition and exploration, thinking not feeling. The emotions are exercised not by plot or character but by mood. The involvement in different modes of being provides the emotional experience of the work. The plays are a game for the mind. Alfred Harbage, "*Love's Labor's Lost* and the Early Shakespeare," *PQ* 41 (1962): 18–36, relates Shakespeare's play to Lyly's court comedies. In *Campaspe* there is an incipient philosophical "academy" and a conflict between love and kingly resolves. In *Gallathea* Diana's nymphs confess their broken vows and agree to succumb to passion. In *Endymion* the Tophas-Epiton-Bagoa triad resembles the Armado-Moth-Jacquenetta triad.

G. Wilson Knight, *The Golden Labyrinth: A Study of the British Drama* (1962), sees Lyly as the founder of a religion of love. The plays, he argues, are rich in psychological subtlety and honor love in all of its variations; they are moralities with Cupid as God. Lyly's esoteric sexology anticipates the recurring emphasis on bisexual, boy-girl figures in subsequent comedy. And see Knight's "Lyly," *RES* 15 (1939): 146–63, rpt. in *Shakespeare's Contemporaries,* ed. Max Bluestone and Norman Rabkin (1961), pp. 12–20; 2nd ed. (1970), pp. 12–21.

Lyly's most recent critic, Peter Saccio, *The Court Comedies of John Lyly: A Study in Allegorical Dramaturgy* (1969), like Hunter, denies the validity of Baldwin's "five-act" approach. Saccio favors an allegorical approach, but quite different from that advanced by Huppé. "The situationalism of Lyly's comedies frees the audience for allegorical perception because of the peculiar kind of absorption it invites." Lyly's comedies are not built on a principle of suspense; therefore, the audience is interested in what is happening now, not in what will happen next. The audience, then, "can attend to the gradual expansion of the central images of *Gallathea* or the elaborate pattern built up by the anecdotes of *Campaspe*. On a stage ever the same because of the fixed houses, the seen actors and properties move back and forth creating an unseen reality." The result of Lyly's allegorical technique is a play with a "central reality slowly turning like a prism for us to inspect its various facets."

The songs in the plays have received attention since W. W. Greg, "The Authorship of the Songs in Lyly's Plays," *MLR* 1 (1905): 43–52, challenged Lyly's authorship. W. J. Lawrence, "The Problem of Lyly's Songs," *TLS,* 20 Dec. 1923, p. 894; and R. W. Bond, "Lyly's Songs," *RES* 6 (1930): 295–99, and "Addendum on Lyly's Songs," *RES* 7 (1931): 442–47, disagree with Greg. John R. Moore, "The Songs in Lyly's Plays," *PMLA* 42 (1927): 623–40, agrees with Greg. M. Hope Dodds, "Songs in Lyly's Plays," *TLS,* 28 June 1941, p. 311, takes exception to an earlier anonymous note, "Thomas Dekker and the Underdog: The Compassionate Realist," *TLS,* 31 May 1941, pp. 262, 264, which suggested that the songs in the 1632 edition might have been added by Thomas Dekker. Michael R. Best, "A Note on the Songs in Lyly's Plays," *N&Q* 12 (1965): 93–94, agrees with Hunter, *John Lyly,* that Blount obtained the songs which appear for the first time in his edition of 1632 from the music library of the Paul's choir. Arguing for Lyly's authorship of the songs, also, is Anne B. Lancashire, ed., *"Gallathea" and "Midas,"* RRDS (1969), pp. 162–63.

Geoffrey Tillotson, "The Prose of Lyly's Comedies," in *Essays in Criticism and Research* (1942), points out that Lyly complicates his inherently simple ends by fusing stylistic means with thematic purpose. Lyly's developed sense of English was based on the rhythm of words in combination, and of associations of words combined in small or large groups. Zdeněk Stříbrný, "John Lyly a Dvorské Drama," *PP* 6 (1963): 100–112, traces the development of euphuism in Lyly's dramas. Although Lyly's style in *Euphues* was not suitable to the stage, he did not abandon it. Lyly's carefully balanced plays and his antithetical groups of characters merely adapt the principles of euphuism from the realm of style to the structure of the drama as a whole.

C. THE WORKS AT LARGE

There is no full-length study of the nondramatic works. Hunter's *John Lyly* (I,A) shows that the structure of *Euphues* approximates that of the dramas. It can be divided into five sections, or acts, each distinct in time and place, and representing a stage in the development of the theme. Like *Euphues, Euphues and His England* is a moral story illustrating a young man's education through experience. Jaroslav Hornát, "Lyly's *Anatomy of Wit* and Ascham's *Scholemaster,*" Acta Universitatis Carolinae (1961), emphasizes Lyly's dependence on humanistic works devoted to pedagogy and courtly conduct, and, particularly, on Ascham's *Scholemaster.* Euphues himself is envisaged as Ascham's "quick wit," and this was Lyly's source for the portrait of the hero. George B. Parks, "Before *Euphues,*" in *Joseph Quincy Adams Memorial Studies,* ed. James G. McManaway, Giles E. Dawson, and Edwin E. Willoughby (1948), pp. 475–93, using a stylistic examination of such writers as Belleforest, Fenton, and Pettie, concludes that *Euphues* is a psychological novel that is not an innovation but near the end of a tradition of prose fiction.

The origin of euphuism has occasioned extensive examination. William Ringler, "The Immediate Source of Euphuism," *PMLA* 53 (1938): 678–86, finds the source in the academic lectures of John Rainolds. Walter J. Ong, "Oral Residue in Tudor Prose Style," *PMLA* 80 (1965): 145–54, agrees: Lyly's style connects directly with oral performance, deriving from figured oratorical style generally and particularly from Rainolds. Lyly's use of epithets also has direct sanction in the Tudor collections of epithets, perhaps particularly the *Epitheta* of Joannes Ravisius Textor. J. Swart, "Lyly and Pettie," *ES* 23 (1941): 10–18, sees Pettie as a link between the Middle Ages and Lyly. Ludwig Borinski, "The Origin of the Euphuistic Novel and Its Significance for Shakespeare," in *Studies in Honor of T. W. Baldwin,* ed. Don Cameron Allen (1958), pp. 38–52, traces the origin of the euphuistic tradition to Pettie, and demonstrates Pettie's debt to Belleforest and Aeneas Sylvius Piccolomini. Bruce E. Teets, "Two Faces of Style in Renaissance Prose Fiction," in *Sweet Smoke of Rhetoric: A Collection of Renaissance Essays,* ed. Natalie G. Lawrence and J. A. Reynolds (1964), pp. 69–81, sets up a dichotomy between the native, realistic tradition represented by Deloney and Nashe, and the *estilo culto,* or artificial mode of expression represented by Lyly and Sidney. Teets suggests that Lyly's style can be traced back to Gorgias.

P. Albert Duhamel, "Sidney's *Arcadia* and Elizabethan Rhetoric," *SP* 45 (1948): 134–50, provides a rhetorical analysis of Euphues' speech on women to argue that while Elizabethan writers had been schooled in the use of classical topics, many of them, including Lyly, drew upon the topics to amplify their matter. Walter N. King, "John Lyly and Elizabethan Rhetoric," *SP* 52 (1955): 149–61, takes issue with Duhamel. The context of *Euphues* demands deliberately feeble logic. King warns that passages of Elizabethan rhetoric should not be analyzed out of context. Jonas A. Barish, "The Prose Style of John Lyly," *ELH* 23 (1956): 14–35, correlates certain categories of Lyly's style with categories of meaning, and stresses the similarity of the style of *Euphues* and that of the plays. Barish suggests that a passion for logic ultimately led to a rigid style, too removed from common speech.

Relying on Barish and Hunter for details on style and background, Walter R. Davis, *Idea and Act in Elizabethan Fiction* (1969), contributes the idea that Lyly "stresses not only the painfulness of experience along with the necessity of undergoing it, but also the residue of bitter memory, the scars, along with the wisdom it produces." The value of *The Anatomy of Wit* is that it "refreshes the reader's sense of the wisdom of conventional wisdom." *Euphues and His England,* on the contrary, "implies that the conventional theoretical wisdom must be overridden if it is to live and grow." *Euphues* is included in *Elizabethan Prose Fiction,* ed. Merritt Lawlis (1967), and prefaced by a perceptive analysis of Lyly's style.

The *Concise Bibliography* by Samuel A. Tannenbaum was published in 1940 and reprinted in vol. 5 of *Elizabethan Bibliographies,* by Samuel A. and Dorothy R. Tannenbaum (1967). *Elizabethan Bibliographies Supplements V: Robert Greene 1945–1965, Thomas Lodge 1939–1965, John Lyly 1939–1965, Thomas Nashe 1941–1965, George Peele 1939–1965,* by Robert C. Johnson, was published in 1968. Irving Ribner, *Tudor and Stuart Drama,* Goldentree Bibliographies (1966), offers selected titles.

II. CRITICISM OF INDIVIDUAL PLAYS AND STATE OF SCHOLARSHIP

A. INDIVIDUAL PLAYS

Endymion

Joseph A. Bryant, Jr., "The Nature of the Allegory in Lyly's *Endymion*," *RenP*, 1956, pp. 4–11, offers a Christian interpretation. Elizabeth stood at the top of a hierarchy which had to be preserved intact. Endymion could love Cynthia but not possess her. The three debating ladies in Endymion's dream (Act V) function as the Daughters of God: Mercy, Justice, and Peace or Truth. Their presence at the end of the play anticipates the solution. When Cynthia, as Christian mercy, stoops to kiss Endymion, it is a gift, not something merited. Hunter, *John Lyly* (I,A), treats *Endymion* as a play, not as historical or philosophical allegory. The focus is on Lyly's technique as a dramatist, on his ability to handle parallel instances, as in the parallel yet contrasting loves of Endymion, Eumenides, Corsites, and Sir Tophas.

David Lloyd Stevenson, in *The Love-Game Comedy* (I,B), uses *Endymion* to show that Lyly was the first comic dramatist to bring to the stage the complexities of Elizabethan views of love. Endymion is the romantic lover incarnate. Eumenides, on the other hand, is a matter-of-fact lover who is content to have his fortunes creep on the surface of the earth. Daniel C. Boughner, "The Background of Lyly's Tophas," *PMLA* 54 (1939): 967–73, instances Italian and Latin parallels. Josephine W. Bennett, "Oxford and *Endimion*," *PMLA* 57 (1942): 354–69, sees Endymion as Lord Oxford, Corsites as Henry Lee, and the play as generally concerned with Oxford's troubles with Anne Vavasour. *Endymion* is included in Karl J. Holzknecht's *Outlines of Tudor and Stuart Plays, 1497–1642* (1947).

Saccio's allegorical approach (*Court Comedies,* I,B) leads him to conclude that Cynthia is not to be understood, but to be contemplated. "One might call the play, with its radiating central image, its mathematical elaboration, its receding depths, its near motionless and queer timelessness, more a contemplation than a comedy."

Love's Metamorphosis

Paul E. Parnell, "Moral Allegory in Lyly's *Loves Metamorphosis*," *SP* 52 (1955): 1–16, suggests that the allegory is playful. It is not a morality play, and the allegory does not sustain formal analysis. The characters are presented sometimes symbolically, at other times realistically. The direction of the moral allegory is generally clear. But since the allegory is embedded in real people, this final moral must be qualified by the consciousness of human imperfection.

Hunter, *John Lyly* (I,A), sees the play as a dramatic version of the Petrarchan situations as they appeared in English sonnet-sequences. It is an anatomy of love, in which the three foresters and the three nymphs represent various aspects of the Petrarchan conventions. The identification of Ceres with Queen Elizabeth is questioned. Saccio, *Court Comedies* (I,B), agrees with Hunter about the Petrarchan function of the foresters and nymphs, but claims that it is the incompleteness of such love that Cupid corrects. "Cupid comes to represent love in the Neoplatonic sense initially doubted by the foresters: love as that which orders and preserves the world, whose power is absolute and whose realm is everywhere."

Campaspe

Hunter, *John Lyly,* demonstrates that Lyly arranges his episodes, scenes, and shows as illustrations round a central debate-theme: does true kingliness consist in the power to control others or in the power to command ourselves? The plot is centered on the magnanimity of Alexander and the climax is in his perception that he should not stoop to compete in love any more than in philosophy or painting. Self-knowledge is the key to Alexander's royal superiority.

According to Saccio, *Court Comedies* (I,B), the characters in *Campaspe* are "mobilized in incidents selected to present a general idea of propriety, of the duties of men and of their places among one another." *Campaspe* is not a love story primarily, although the love-affair is the chief episode. "The individual characters and the particular ideas that appear in *Campaspe* are like nodes or cruces. The anecdotes and their juxtaposition weave lines of relationship among these nodes; they create an elaborately reticulated pattern. Each line of reticulation involves a particular kind of propriety, the kind that governs that particular situation. As a whole the reticulation creates the idea of propriety as a universal, illuminating the total spectacle presented to us."

Ernest G. Mathews, "Gil Polo, Desportes, and Lyly's 'Cupid and My Campaspe,' " *MLN* 56 (1941): 606– 7, adds a note on Lyly's Italian sources. And see David Bevington, "John Lyly and Queen Elizabeth: Royal Flattery in *Campaspe* and *Sapho and Phao,*" *RenP,* 1966, pp.

57-67. Holzknecht's *Outlines of Tudor and Stuart Plays* (above, *"Endymion"*) includes *Campaspe*.

Sapho and Phao

According to Hunter, *John Lyly*, the advance from the earlier *Campaspe* lies less in the direction of artistry and more in Lyly's ability to extract from a given situation the maximum compliment to a queen. Whereas in *Campaspe* Alexander's power could express itself in war, in *Sapho and Phao* the sovereign lady must express herself in love. The plot here conducts us on a tour of the landscape of love.

Saccio, *Court Comedies* (I,B), finds *Sapho and Phao* unsatisfactory. It lacks the complex structure of *Campaspe*, the pace of *Gallathea*, and although the function of the Sybil is clear—she dispenses Ovidian advice—the play lacks economy.

Gallathea

Hunter, *John Lyly*, sees harmonious variety in the interrelation of gods and men, and the interaction between man and nature. These interrelated forces find their thematic relevance in the statement of Gallathea to her father: "Destiny may be deferred, not prevented." The ending of the play, especially the metamorphosis, has occasioned some criticism. Madeleine Doran, *Endeavors of Art* (I,B), regards the play as simply "a pretty myth of love." Hunter argues that the structure of the play demands such an ending. The play lacks a controlling royal figure who can reject error and reestablish right. The characters in *Gallathea* are kept in a continual state of unbalance, which moves the action of the play.

Saccio's analysis (*Court Comedies*, I,B) reveals a far better play than that envisaged by either Hunter or Doran. "The juxtaposed scenes create a series of internal echoes, parallels, and balanced contrasts that dance forward with expanded meaning and rhythm. The central movement forward is the exfoliation of the central figures of the gods." The symbolic energy of the gods is used by Lyly to create meaning, as the traditional wealth of Cupid, Neptune, Venus, and Diana flows into the action of the play. "In short, allegorical dramaturgy has in *Campaspe* the multilinear power of a child's connect-the-dots design: given the dots, dramatic action reveals the proper structure that intricately ties them into a firm whole. Allegorical dramaturgy has in *Gallathea* a more organic power, the expanding power of opening blossoms: given the buds, dramatic action reveals the depths that lie within."

Midas

The debate in *Midas,* Hunter claims, takes place between War (Martius), Wealth (Mellacrites), and Love (Eristus), the counsellors of Midas. Each, however, proposes improper ends. It remains for the King's daughter, Sophronia (Wisdom), to denounce the advice of these three false counsellors. The equation of Midas with Philip II is reasonable but incidental.

Michael R. Best, "A Theory of the Literary Genesis of Lyly's *Midas,*" *RES* 17 (1966): 133–40, attempts to justify Lyly's craftsmanship by positing the existence of earlier Midas plays. The "Gallimaufrey" which Lyly speaks of in the Prologue to *Midas* is, perhaps, an allusion to an *urMidas I* and *urMidas II.* In bringing the two separate plays together, Lyly sacrificed unity.

Anne B. Lancashire, ed., *"Gallathea" and "Midas"* (1969), sees both plays illustrating a single thesis: "knowledge versus folly (or wilful blindness) as the central problem of human existence." *Gallathea,* she argues, is a more sophisticated play than *Midas,* which is more explicitly concerned with moral and political ends.

Mother Bombie

Although *Mother Bombie* reflects Lyly's basic method, repetition and balance, Hunter maintains that it differs from the other comedies in subject-matter and form. This is Lyly's single exploration into the Terentian mode of comedy. Lyly places his witty pages at the center of the action of *Mother Bombie.* Since the pages outwit everyone else, wit becomes the motive of the plot. Lyly adopts the Terentian manner, but does not create a comedy of situation.

The Woman in the Moon

Hunter says this presents a series of symmetrically arranged episodes which show the various phases of Lyly's imaginary world. *The Woman in the Moon* is not a satire on women. Johnstone Parr, "Astrology Motivates a Comedy," in *Tamburlaine's Malady and Other Essays on Astrology in Elizabethan Drama* (1953), pp. 38–49, treats Lyly's use of astrology to motivate the comedy. Lyly capitalized on the aristocratic interest in horoscope-casting.

B. OVER-ALL STATE OF CRITICISM

In his *JEGP* review (I,A) of Hunter's *John Lyly*, Mark Eccles observes that "both *Euphues* and the plays call for closer study, but he [Hunter] has mapped out the territory and suggested directions for future criticism." Saccio's *Court Comedies* (I,B) is the first book to explore the territory, at least as far as the plays are concerned. A recent combined edition of *Midas* and *Gallathea* by Anne B. Lancashire, RRDS (1969), suggests that other single editions of the works, with introductions and notes, may be forthcoming.

Lyly's debt to Continental influences requires further study. Violet M. Jeffrey's *John Lyly and the Italian Renaissance* (1928) is incomplete and frequently inaccurate as Hunter and John L. Lievsay, *Stefano Guazzo and the English Renaissance, 1575-1675* (1961), suggest. Opposed to Jeffrey is Laura Torretta, "L'Italofobia di John Lyly e i rapporti dell *Euphues* col Rinascimento italiano," *Giornale Storico della Letteratura Italiana* 103 (1934): 205-53.

Most recent interpretative criticism has focused on either Lyly's use of allegory or rhetoric. Much remains to be done in other areas. Hunter makes a start with his remarks on Lyly's handling of the theme of appearance and reality, a point also noted by Marco Mincoff, "Shakespeare and Lyly" (I,B). Other thematic interpretations may supplement the structural analyses.

III. CANON

A. PLAYS IN CHRONOLOGICAL ORDER

This list follows the dating in Alfred Harbage, *Annals of English Drama, 975-1700,* rev. Samuel Schoenbaum (1964), which is also the source for the type of play, the acting date (in italics preceding semicolon), and the original date of publication. For descriptions of the original quartos see W. W. Greg, *A Bibliography of the English Printed Drama to the Restoration,* 4 vols. (1939-59), and see the discussions of canon in E. K. Chambers, *The Elizabethan Stage* (1923), vol. 3.

Campaspe, classical legend—comedy (*1580-84*; 1584)

Sapho and Phao, classical legend—comedy (*1582-84*; 1584)

Gallathea, classical legend—comedy (*1584-88*; 1592)

John Russell Brown and Margaret Cottier, "A Note on the Date of Lyly's *Gallathea*," *MLR* 51 (1956): 220-21, argue, unconvincingly, that a version of the play may have been written by Lyly as early as

1583. Anne B. Lancashire, ed., *"Gallathea" and "Midas,"* argues for a date of composition between 1583 and 1585.

Mother Bombie, comedy (*1587–90*; 1594)

Endymion, classical legend—comedy (*Feb. 2* [?], *1588*; 1591)

Love's Metamorphosis, pastoral (ca. *1588–90*; 1601)

Midas, comedy (*1589–90*; 1592)

The Woman in the Moon, comedy (*1590–95*; 1597)

The Entertainment at Chiswick, royal entertainment (*July 28–29, 1602*)

B. UNCERTAIN ASCRIPTIONS; APOCRYPHA

The Entertainment at Cowdray, royal entertainment (*August 14, 1591*; 1591)

The Entertainment at Elvetham, royal entertainment (*September 20–23, 1591*; 1591)

The Queen's Welcome at Theobalds, royal entertainment (*May 10–20, 1591*; MSS)

The Entertainment at Bisham, royal entertainment (*August 21, 1592*; 1592)

The Entertainment at Rycote, royal entertainment (*September 10, 11, 1592*; 1592)

The Entertainment at Sudeley, royal entertainment (*September 28, October 1, 2, 1592*; 1592)

The Entertainment at Mitcham, royal entertainment (*September 13, 1598*; MS)

J. Leslie Hotson, ed., *Queen Elizabeth's Entertainment at Mitcham* (1953), attempts to establish Lyly's authorship through a stylistic comparison with Lyly's other works. Chiyuki Yamamoto, "Notes on the Language of Adespotum *Entertainment at Mitcham*," in *Studies in English Grammar and Linguistics: A Miscellany in Honor of Takanobu Otsuka,* ed. Kazuo Araki et al. (1958), pp. 221–39, examines *The Entertainment at Mitcham* from a linguistic point of view, and tentatively supports Hotson's attribution. Other critics remain unconvinced. Kenneth Muir, in a review of Hotson's edition, *RES* 5 (1954): 407–9, says the case for Lyly's authorship is not greatly helped by Hotson's arguments. Supporting Muir is D. J. Gordon in a review in *MLR* 50 (1955): 195–96.

The Maid's Metamorphosis, comedy (*1599–1600;* 1600)

Samuel Schoenbaum, *Internal Evidence and Elizabethan Dramatic Authorship* (1966), points out that the attribution to Lyly is now generally rejected. Hunter does not include it.

The Entertainment at Harefield, royal entertainment (*July 31–August 2, 1602;* MSS [fragments])

C. CRITIQUE OF THE STANDARD EDITION

Since Bond's 1902 edition there has been little recent textual criticism; most of it takes the form of corrections or additions to Bond's explanatory notes. The most frequent contributor has been Wilfred P. Mustard. "Hippocrates' Twins," *MLN* 38 (1923): 313, suggests that the source for Hippocrates' twins (Bond, 2: 77) may be Saint Augustine's *City of God,* V, 2; "Notes on Lyly's *Euphues,*" *MLN* 40 (1925): 120–21, cites a parallel missed by Bond; "Notes on John Lyly's Plays," *SP* 22 (1925): 267–71, identifies further parallels in Lyly's court comedies; "Note on John Lyly's *Midas,*" *MLN* 41 (1926): 193, suggests that a line in *Midas* (Bond, IV.iv.48) is adapted from Virgil's Epigram of Wine and Women, an elegiac couplet in the *Anthologia Latina;* " 'Agrippa's Shadows,' " *MLN* 43 (1928): 325, argues that the reference to Agrippa's shadows in the second Prologue to *Campaspe* must refer to the shades of the dead which Agrippa was said to command; "Note on Lyly's *Euphues,*" *MLN* 43 (1928): 537, traces to Plutarch an instance of the severity of Cato.

In *"Much Ado About Nothing* (V.i.178)," *MLN* 40 (1925): 186–88, Morris Palmer Tilley finds a proverbial source in P. Syrus common to Lyly and Shakespeare, and in *"Euphues* and Ovid's *Heroical Epistles,"* *MLN* 45 (1930): 301–8, Tilley claims that the first half of Luculla's reply to Euphues' proposal of marriage (Bond, 1: 220–22) is based on Helen's Epistle to Paris (Epistle 17) in Ovid's *Heroical Epistles.* Allen R. Benham, "A Note on Lyly's *Euphues,*" *PQ* 7 (1928): 201–2, finds in *A Newe Ballade of the Marigolde,* by William Forrest, a source for a line in *Euphues* (Bond, 2: 215).

Don Cameron Allen, "A Note on Lyly's *Midas,* II," *MLN* 61 (1946): 503–4, corrects an error in an earlier article, "A Note on Lyly's *Midas,*" *MLN* 60 (1945): 326–27, in which he claimed that the originator of the metaphor of the cosmic egg (Bond, 3: 127) was Rabbi Saadia ben Gaon. The metaphor is, rather, of classical origin, and can be found in many writers, among them Eusebius and Plutarch. In "Neptune's 'Agar' in Lyly's *Gallathea*," *MLN* 49 (1934): 451–52, Allen argues that Lyly's monster derives from Natales Comes. A. Davenport, "Notes on Lyly's 'Campaspe' and Shakespeare," *N&Q* 1 (1954): 19–20, finds an additional source parallel in Diogenes Laertius. J. Krzyzanowski, "Some Conjectural Remarks on Elizabethan Dramatists," *N&Q* 193 (1948): 233–34, corrects an error in Bond (2: 515), who confuses the King of Epyrus with the philosopher Pyrrho. The fact that G. K. Hunter is currently engaged in a new edition of Lyly's complete works suggests that Bond's edition is no longer considered adequate.

D. TEXTUAL STUDIES

No important textual studies have appeared since the edition of *Euphues, the Anatomy of Wit* and *Euphues and His England* by Morris W. Croll and Harry Clemons (1916). Of slight interest is Wilfred T. Jewkes, *Act Division in Elizabethan and Jacobean Plays, 1583–1616* (1958), who argues that Lyly's plays were probably printed from his original manuscripts. In support he instances the careful printing of the quartos, the relative absence of stage directions, and the clear act and scene divisions (except in *The Woman in the Moon,* where only act divisions can be found).

E. SINGLE-WORK EDITIONS OF THE PLAYS

W. W. Greg has edited a reprint of *Alexander and Campaspe* (1934) and Kathleen M. Lea, of *Mother Bombie* (1948), for the Malone Society. Anne Lancashire has edited *Midas* and *Gallathea* for the Regents Renaissance Drama Series (1969). R. W. Ingram, "Editions of English Renaissance Drama in Progress and Planned: A Rough Checklist," *RenD* 7 Supplement (1964): 13–49, indicates that another edition of *Mother Bombie* is in progress. Of all the plays, only *Endymion* and *Campaspe* are regularly included in anthologies.

F. NONDRAMATIC WORKS IN SINGLE-WORK EDITIONS

Euphues is frequently reprinted and the edition by Merritt Lawlis in *Elizabethan Prose Fiction* (1967) departs from Bond's preference for the first edition and uses the second as copy-text; Lawlis's text is based on a careful collation and he gives detailed notes.

IV. SEE ALSO

A. GENERAL

Ackerman, Catherine A. "John Lyly and Fashionable Platonism in Caroline Poetry." *LHR* 1 no. 3 (1961): 19–23.

Albright, Evelyn May. *Dramatic Publication in England, 1580–1640: A Study of Conditions Affecting Content and Form of Drama.* 1927.

Aronstein, Phillip. *Das englische Renaissancedrama.* 1929.

Babb, Lawrence. *The Elizabethan Malady: A Study of Melancholia in English Literature from 1580 to 1642.* 1951.

Boas, Frederick S. *An Introduction to Tudor Drama.* 1933.

Bowen, Gwynneth. "Shakespeare and His Contemporaries." *Shakespearean Authorship Review,* no. 7 (1962): 1–6.

Bradbrook, M. C. *English Dramatic Form: A History of Its Development.* 1965.

Briggs, K. M. *The Anatomy of Puck.* 1959.

———. *Pale Hecate's Team.* 1962.

Bush, Douglas. *Mythology and the Renaissance Tradition in English Poetry.* 1932; rev. ed. 1963.

Catel, Jean. "John Lyly, immoraliste." *CS* 20 (1933): 145–53; rpt. in *Le théâtre élizabéthain* (1940), pp. 185–96.

Cazamian, Louis. *The Development of English Humor.* 1952.

Childs, Ralph. "The Birthplace of John Lyly." *N&Q* 160 (1931): 297.

Craik, T. W. "The Tudor Interlude and Later Elizabethan Drama." In *Elizabethan Theatre,* SuAS, vol. 9 (1966), pp. 37–57.

Crane, William G. *Wit and Rhetoric in the Renaissance.* 1937.

Croce, Benedetto. "Il Lyly e l'Italinesimo in Inghilterra." *Conversazioni Critiche,* ser. 3, 2nd ed. (1951), pp. 295–96.

Dannenberg, Friedrich. *Das erbe Platons in England bis zur Bildung Lylys.* 1932.

Espiner-Scott, Janet. "Sénèque dans la prose anglaise de More à Lyly (1500–1580)." *RLC* 34 (1960): 177–95.

Evans, Robert O. "Aphorism—An Aspect of Euphuism." *N&Q* 3 (1956): 278–79.

Gerrard, Ernest A. *Elizabethan Drama and Dramatists, 1583–1603.* 1928.

Gosse, Edmund. *Silhouettes.* 1925.

Greg, W. W. *English Literary Autographs, 1550–1650.* 1925.

Harbage, Alfred. *Shakespeare and the Rival Traditions.* 1952.

Harris, Bernard. "Later Elizabethan and Early Stuart Drama." *YWES* 46 (1965): 161–72.

Hillebrand, Harold N. *The Child Actors.* 1926.

Hornát, Jaroslav. "*Mamillia*: Robert Greene's Controversy with *Euphues*." *PP* 5 (1962): 210–18.

Hoskins, Frank L. "Shakespeare and the Prodigious Page Tradition." *RenP,* 1957, pp. 106–110.

Hunter, G. K. *Lyly and Peele.* 1968.

Jewkes, Wilfred T. "The Literature of Travel and the Mode of Romance in the Renaissance." *BNYPL* 67 (1963): 219–36.

Jones, Marion. "The Court and the Dramatists." In *Elizabethan Theatre,* SuAS, vol. 9 (1966), pp. 169–95.

Jorgensen, Paul A. "The Courtship Scene in *Henry V.*" *MLQ* 11 (1950): 180–88.

Kahin, Helen A. "Jane Anger and John Lyly." *MLQ* 8 (1947): 31-35.

Klein, David. *The Elizabethan Dramatists as Critics.* 1963.

Koskenniemi, Inna. *Studies in the Vocabulary of English Drama, 1550-1600, Excluding Shakespeare and Ben Jonson.* 1962.

Lancashire, Anne B. "Lyly and Shakespeare on the Ropes." *JEGP* 68 (1969): 237-44.

Latham, Minor W. *The Elizabethan Fairies.* 1930.

Le Comte, Edward S. *Endymion in England: The Literary History of a Greek Myth.* 1944.

Lewis, C. S. *English Literature in the Sixteenth Century Excluding Drama.* 1954.

Lyman, Dean B., Jr., "Apocryphal Plays of the University Wits." In *English Studies in Honor of James Southall Wilson,* ed. Fredson Bowers (1951), pp. 211-21.

Mills, Laurens J. *One Soul in Bodies Twain.* 1937.

Mincoff, Marco. "Plot Construction in Shakespeare." *Godišnik na Sofiiskiya Universitet, Itoriko-filolo-gičeski Fakulet* (Annuaire de l'Université de Sofia, Faculté Historico-philologique) 37 (1941): 1-51.

Moore, John B. *The Comic and the Realistic in English Drama.* 1925.

Morris, Helen. *Elizabethan Literature.* 1958.

Muir, Kenneth. "Shakespeare among the Commonplaces." *RES* 10 (1959): 283-89.

Murphy, D. "Shakespeare's Debt to John Lyly." *Irish Monthly Magazine* 42 (1934): 553-55.

Pruvost, René. *Matteo Bandello and Elizabethan Fiction.* 1937.

Reed, Robert R., Jr. *The Occult on the Tudor Stage.* 1966.

Ringler, William. *Stephen Gosson.* 1942.

Sarlos, Robert K. "Development and Operation of the First Blackfriars Theatre." In *Studies in the Elizabethan Theatre,* ed. Charles T. Prouty (1961): 137-78.

Schelling, Felix E. *Elizabethan Playwrights.* 1925.

Schirmer, Walter F. *Antike, Renaissance, und Puritanismus.* 1933.

Schlauch, Margaret. *Antecedents of the English Novel, 1400-1600.* 1963.

Smet, Robert de [Romain Sanvic]. *Le théâtre élisabéthain.* 1955.

Smith, Constance. "Some Ideas on Education before Locke." *JHI* 23 (1962): 403-6.

Soellner, Rolf. "Shakespeare and the 'Consolatio.' " *N&Q* 1 (1954): 108-9.

Stanley, Emily B. "The Use of Classical Mythology by the University Wits." *RenP,* 1956, pp. 25-33.

Starnes, D. T. "Chaucer, John Lyly, and *Sphaera Civitatis* (1588)." *N&Q* 171 (1936): 95.

Stenberg, Theodore. "Elizabeth as Euphuist before *Euphues.*" *Studies in English* (Univ. of Texas), 7 (1928): 65-78.

———. "More about Queen Elizabeth's Euphuism." *Studies in English* (Univ. of Texas), 13 (1933): 64-77.

Thieme, Heinz. *Zur Verfasserfrage des dekkerschen Stückes "The Pleasant Comedy of Old Fortunatus."* 1934.

Tilley, Morris Palmer. "A Parody of *Euphues* in *Romeo and Juliet.*" *MLN* 41 (1926): 1-8.

———. *Elizabethan Proverb Lore in Lyly's "Euphues" and in Pettie's "Petite Pallace,"* with Parallels from Shakespeare. 1926.

Tucker, T. G. *The Sonnets of Shakespeare.* 1924.

Vančura, Zdeněk. "Euphuism and Baroque Prose." *Časopis pro moderní filologii* 18 (1932): 291–96.
Vesci, Ornella. "Imagini della regina." *AION-SG* 11: 145–70.
Wagner, Bernard M. "Elizabethan Dramatists." *TLS*, 28 Sept. 1933, p. 65.
Wakameda, Takeji. "John Lyly." *SELit* 8 (1928): 567–83.
Ward, Bernard M. "John Lyly and the Office of the Revels." *RES* 5 (1929): 57–59.
Willcox, Alice. "Medical References in the Dramas of John Lyly." *Annals of Medical History* 10 (1938): 117–26.
Williamson, George. *The Senecan Amble.* 1951.
Wilson, Elkin C. *England's Eliza.* 1939.
Zandvoort, R. W. "What is Euphuism?" In *Mélanges de linguistique et de philologie, Fernand Mossé in memoriam* (1962), pp. 508–17.

B. INDIVIDUAL PLAYS

Howarth, R. G. "Dipsas in Lyly and Marston." *N&Q* 175 (1938): 24–25.
Lievsay, John L. "Some Renaissance Views of Diogenes the Cynic." In *Joseph Quincy Adams Memorial Studies,* ed. James G. McManaway, Giles E. Dawson, and Edwin E. Willoughby (1948), pp. 447–55.
Whiting, George W. "Canary Wine and *Campaspe*." *MLN* 45 (1930): 148–51.

GEORGE PEELE

Charles W. Daves

The standard edition is the Yale *Life and Work of George Peele,* gen. ed. Charles T. Prouty, 3 vols. (1952, 1961, 1970).

I. GENERAL

A. BIOGRAPHICAL

The most complete biography is David H. Horne's *The Life and Minor Works of George Peele* (1952), vol. 1 of the Yale edition, which examines the documentary records and corrects the legends of a rakish, dissolute youth. Also of interest is Thorleif Larsen's "The Early Years of George Peele, Dramatist, 1558-1588," *PTRSC* 22 (1928), sec. ii: 271-318, which tentatively reconstructs the life from the writings. Forthcoming in TEAS is *George Peele* by Leonard R. N. Ashley.

B. GENERAL STUDIES OF THE PLAYS

Thomas Marc Parrott and Robert Hamilton Ball, in *A Short View of Elizabethan Drama* (1943), emphasize the "extraordinary variety" in Peele's work. They see Peele's greatest contribution as his part in transforming the native drama, especially by giving it a sense of beauty; he is more a lyric than a dramatic poet. Wolfgang Clemen's *English Tragedy before Shakespeare: The Development of Dramatic Speech,* trans. T. S. Dorsch (1961; German ed. 1955), concentrates on Peele's gifts for expressive language and effective presentation of individual episodes and situations. Clemen echoes other critics in noting Peele's lack of dramatic structure. Madeleine Doran, *Endeavors of Art: A Study of Form in Elizabethan Drama* (1954), relates the "shapeless unselectivity of incident" characteristic of Peele's plays in part to an uncritical following of diffuse sources.

In "Il linguaggio drammatico di George Peele," *EM* 15 (1964): 61-87,

Clotilde De Stasio argues against the view that Peele is more a lyric than a dramatic poet by pointing out examples of language appropriate to particular scenes. G. Wilson Knight in *The Golden Labyrinth: A Study of the British Drama* (1962) describes the "truly Elizabethan" Peele, a patriot and deviser of public pageants, and especially praises *David and Bethsabe.*

C. THE WORKS AT LARGE

P. H. Cheffaud's *George Peele (1558-1596?)* (1913) deals with the plays, the poems, and text and chronology. This work must be supplemented by later criticism and scholarship. C. F. Tucker Brooke's "A Latin Poem by George Peele (?)," *HLQ* 3 (1939-40): 47-67, offers comment on the poem and its authorship and prints the poem itself, *Pareus.* The *Concise Bibliography* by Samuel A. Tannenbaum was published in 1940, and reprinted in *Elizabethan Bibliographies,* by Samuel A. and Dorothy R. Tannenbaum, vol. 6 (1967). A continuation compiled by Robert C. Johnson, *Elizabethan Bibliographies Supplements V,* appeared in 1968. A selected list appears in Irving Ribner, *Tudor and Stuart Drama,* Goldentree Bibliographies (1966).

II. CRITICISM OF INDIVIDUAL PLAYS AND STATE OF SCHOLARSHIP

A. INDIVIDUAL PLAYS

The Old Wives' Tale

In vol. 3 of the Yale edition, Frank S. Hook discusses staging, folk tale sources by topic, the identification of Huanebango with Gabriel Harvey, and summarizes criticism. He suggests that the play "is essentially naive: it presents an amalgam of folktales and motifs cleverly joined together." While the "resulting story has no hidden meaning . . . the manner of presentation is highly artful."

M. C. Bradbrook, "Peele's *Old Wives' Tale:* A Play of Enchantment," *ES* 43 (1962): 323-30 (rpt. in *Shakespeare's Contemporaries,* ed. Max Bluestone and Norman Rabkin, 2nd ed. [1970], pp. 23-30), explains the nature of the play in "a theatre of representation and statement" and accounts for its lack of explicit structural connections. Herbert Goldstone, "Interplay in Peele's *The Old Wives' Tale,*" *BUSE* 4 (1960): 202-13 (rpt. in *Shakespeare's Contempories,* 2nd ed. pp. 31-41), outlines the means used to transform the contrasting elements into a unity; he discredits possible satirical or burlesque aspects of the play. Thorleif Larsen concurs, in *"The Old Wives' Tale* by George Peele," *PTRSC* 29 (1935), sec. ii: 157–70; far from being a satire or burlesque of a romance, the play is a charming, simple expression of romanticism.

The use of folk tales and folk motifs for plot and dramatic parody is discussed by Charles S. Adams in "The Tales in Peele's *Old Wives' Tales*," *Midwest Folklore* 13 (1963): 13–20. Sarah L. C. Clapp, "Peele's Use of Folk-lore in *The Old Wives' Tale*," *Studies in English* (Univ. of Texas), 6 (1926), 146–56, discusses the weaving of motifs into a coherent design.

The Arraignment of Paris

R. Mark Benbow, in vol. 3 of the Yale edition, describes the play's sources in classical and medieval mythology and pastoral; its achievement lies in its synthesis and development of the dramatic traditions of the private and court theaters. He gives a full account of the dramatic tradition.

Andrew Von Hendy's "The Triumph of Chastity: Form and Meaning in *The Arraignment of Paris*," *RenD* 1 (1968): 87–101, contends that the play is "significant and well-designed" if the strong influence of masques and entertainment is taken into account. The compliment to Queen Elizabeth brings to focus all aspects of the work; Chastity wins over "moral and political subversion" and is the symbol of the queen's majesty and political stability. In "The Structural Significance of Myth and Flattery in Peele's *Arraignment of Paris*," *SP* 65 (1968): 163–70, Henry G. Lesnick argues for the "structural integrity" of the *Arraignment* in a unity of action on the "historico-mythical" level and for a resolution of conflict in the concluding idyllic atmosphere.

Inga-Stina Ekeblad, in "On the Background of Peele's *Araygnment of Paris*," *N&Q* 3 (1956): 246–49, outlines the tradition of the "judgment" motif especially as applied to Elizabeth. John D. Reeves' "The Judgment of Paris as a Device of Tudor Flattery," *N&Q* 1 (1954): 7–11, lists chronologically uses of the myth of Paris for contemporary praise.

The Battle of Alcazar

The most comprehensive account of the play is by John Yoklavich in the second volume of the Yale edition. Warner G. Rice, "A Principal Source of *The Battle of Alcazar*," *MLN* 58 (1943): 428–31, traces the influence of Freigius's *Historia de bello africano*. And see Thorleif

Larsen, "The Historical and Legendary Background of Peele's *Battle of Alcazar,*" *PTRSC* 33 (1939) sec. ii: 185-97. The play's interest as the first full dramatic treatment of a black Moor on the English stage is discussed by Eldred Jones in *Othello's Countrymen: The African in English Renaissance Drama* (1965).

Edward I

The fullest account is the introduction in the second volume of the Yale edition, by Frank S. Hook, which judges it to have an "anomalous position" in the Peele canon and in the development of English drama. Irving Ribner, to the contrary, in *The English History Play in the Age of Shakespeare* (1957; rev. ed. 1965), emphasizes the significance of *Edward I* in helping to shape the genre of the English history play that Shakespeare made into popular art.

Holger Nørgaard argues that one ballad was a source and the other written after the play in "Peele's *Edward I* and Two Queen Elinor Ballads," in *English Studies Presented to R. W. Zandvoort,* Supplement to *ES* 45 (1964): 165-68. Frank S. Hook's "The Ballad Sources of Peele's *Edward I,*" *N&Q* 3 (1955): 3-5, proposes that the play is based on one ballad and incorporates material from the other.

The Love of King David and Fair Bethsabe

Elmer Blistein, in vol. 3 of the Yale edition, discusses sources, critical history, and the use of David in the drama before 1600. He chooses a middle ground between the extremes of censure and praise that criticism of the play has elicited.

Inga-Stina [Ekeblad] Ewbank, in "The House of David in Renaissance Drama: A Comparative Study," *RenD* 8 (1965): 3-40, discredits the "shapelessness" often seen in the play. There is, rather, a purposeful design and a unity of theme in an "elastic" form free of imposed "well-made" structure, which she stresses by examination of other treatments of the David story. The civil and moral disorder in the House of David is paralleled in the seemingly episodic structure, and the many thematic interests are brought into unity as aspects of David's guilt. In an earlier article, she concentrates on the fusion of biblical materials and the Ovidian mythological tradition in "*The Love of King David and Fair Bethsabe:* A Note on George Peele's Biblical Drama," *ES* 39 (1958): 57-62. Lily B. Campbell, in *Divine Poetry and Drama in Sixteenth-Century England* (1959), considers the work as "a divine play in the tradition of divine poetry" under the influence of Du Bartas.

B. OVER-ALL STATE OF CRITICISM

Most study has been directed to the canon, dating, and sources of the plays. With all three volumes of the Yale edition now in print, an edition which gives reliable texts and sums up the scholarship, the way is clear for further critical appraisal.

The Old Wives' Tale has elicited most criticism. Hopeful signs of interest in other plays appear in such works as that of Andrew Von Hendy on *The Arraignment of Paris* (II,A) and recent studies of *David and Bethsabe.*

III. CANON

A. PLAYS IN CHRONOLOGICAL ORDER

Plays are listed by first performance dates (given in italics) in Alfred Harbage, *Annals of English Drama, 975-1700,* rev. Samuel Schoenbaum (1964), which is also the source for dates of first editions and for dramatic type. W. W. Greg, in *A Bibliography of the English Printed Drama to the Restoration,* 4 vols. (1939-59), describes the first quartos. The problem of scholars attributing to Peele "nearly every masterless play of his epoch" is briefly considered by E. K. Chambers in *The Elizabethan Stage,* 4 vols. (1923), and in Samuel Schoenbaum's *Internal Evidence and Elizabethan Dramatic Authorship* (1966).

The articles by Thorleif Larsen are indispensable. "The Canon of Peele's Works," *MP* 26 (1928-29): 191-99, reviews earlier scholarship and makes convincing conjectures. In "The Growth of the Peele Canon," *Library* 11 (1930): 300-311, Larsen outlines the ascriptions to Peele and notes where the evidence is cited. Also helpful is Harold M. Dowling's "The Date and Order of Peele's Plays," *N&Q* 164 (1933): 164-68, 183-85, which discerns a gradual deterioration in matter and method from Peele's early lyrical-pastoral period. This is supplemented by R. G. Howarth's "Peele's Plays," *N&Q* 167 (1934): 33. A full listing of works with commentary is found in Larsen's "A Bibliography of the Writings of George Peele," *MP* 32 (1934-35): 143-56. *Authorship and Evidence* (1968), by Leonard R. N. Ashley, provides a useful summary of scholarship on plays dubiously ascribed to Peele.

The Arraignment of Paris, classical legend—pastoral (ca. *1581-84*; 1584)

Benbow, vol. 3, Yale edition, summarizes the arguments for authorship and date.

The Hunting of Cupid, pastoral (play?) (*1581-91*; lost ed., ca. 1591)

John P. Cutts, in "Peele's *Hunting of Cupid,*" *SRen* 5 (1958): 121-32, speculates that *The Hunting of Cupid* may have been a pastoral poem, not a play as many scholars have assumed.

The Love of King David and Fair Bethsabe, biblical history (ca. *1581-94;* 1599)

Elmer Blistein, vol. 3, Yale edition, concludes that the play was written during the winter and spring of 1593/4. He finds no evidence that it was ever performed. Arthur M. Sampley, in "The Text of Peele's *David and Bethsabe,*" *PMLA* 46 (1931): 659-71, contends that the play underwent revision in two stages: a severe abridgment of the original text, and a reworking with additions by a later hand.

The Pageant before Woolstone Dixie, civic pageant (*29 Oct. 1585*; 1585)

The Battle of Alcazar, foreign history (*1588-89*; 1594)

W. W. Greg's *Two Elizabethan Stage Abridgements: "The Battle of Alcazar" and "Orlando Furioso"* (1923), deals with questions of attribution, textual history, the theatrical "plot," the quarto, and the relation of the plot to the quarto, and prints Greg's reconstructed transcript of the "plot."

The Old Wives' Tale, romance (ca. *1588-94*; 1595)

Hook, vol. 3, Yale edition, offers internal evidence to support Peele's authorship and examines arguments for dating, concluding that the evidence merely permits the limits of 1588 to 1595. He treats at length the printer's copy.

Thorleif Larsen in "The Date of Peele's *Old Wives' Tale,*" *MP* 30 (1932-33): 23-28, maintains that the play probably was written between January, 1593, and May, 1594. S. Musgrove's "Peele's *Old Wives' Tale:* An Afterpiece?" *AUMLA* 23 (1965): 86-95, proposes that it was a brief extravaganza designed to follow a comedy. He takes exception to Harold Jenkins' discussion of textual problems in "Peele's *Old Wives' Tale,*" *MLR* 34 (1939): 177-85 (rpt. in *Shakespeare's Contemporaries,* ed. Bluestone and Rabkin (1961), pp. 22-30), which views the extant version of the play as a "playhouse revision," cut and adapted for a touring company.

Edward I, history (*1590-93*; 1593)

In "The Two Compositors in the First Quarto of Peele's *Edward I,*" *SB* 7 (1955): 170-77, Frank S. Hook shows that two compositors set the play, dividing it not quite evenly. Dora Jean Ashe's "The Text of Peele's *Edward I,*" *SB* 7 (1955): 153-70, argues that the first published quarto is "a radical and unskillful stage revision of a Peele manuscript."

Descensus Astraea, civic pageant (*29 Oct. 1591*; 1591)
Anglorum Feriae, tilt (*17 Nov. 1595*; MS)

B. UNCERTAIN ASCRIPTIONS; APOCRYPHA

Iphigenia (trans. of Euripides), Latin(?) tragedy (*1576-80*; lost)
The Turkish Mahomet and Hiren the Fair Greek, heroical romance (*1581-94*; lost)
I & II The Troublesome Reign of King John, history (ca. *1587-91*; 1591)
The authorship is discussed in the section on anonymous plays in this volume.

The Pageant for Martin Calthrop, civic pageant (*29 Oct. 1588*; lost)
The Life and Death of Jack Straw, history (*1590-93*; 1593)
The edition of Kenneth Muir and F. P. Wilson (1957) challenges the canonicity. See the discussion in the anonymous plays section.

Polyhymnia, with Lee, tilt (*17 Nov. 1590*; 1590)
Locrine, pseudo-history (*1591-95*; 1595)
The authorship is discussed in the section on anonymous plays in this volume.

The Queen's Welcome at Theobalds, royal entertainment (*10-20 May 1592;* MSS)
A Knack to Know a Knave, comedy (*10 June 1592*; 1594)
The authorship is discussed in the section on anonymous plays in this volume.

Titus Andronicus, tragedy (*1594*; 1594)
In his edition (1948), Dover Wilson suggests that Peele wrote the play in 1593, revised it, and later Shakespeare revised it in 1594. J. C.

Maxwell, in "Peele and Shakespeare: A Stylometric Test," *JEGP* 49 (1950): 557- 61, develops a more convincing argument that the first act is by Peele and the rest of the play largely by Shakespeare. In the Arden Edition (1953), Maxwell again presents his case for Peele's authorship of Act I and sums up the arguments of others for Peele's part in the composition.

The Wisdom of Doctor Dodypoll, comedy (*1599- 1600*; 1600)

M. H. Matson's edition (1965) discounts Peele's authorship and accepts Chambers' listing in *The Elizabethan Stage* as anonymous.

Alphonsus, Emperor of Germany, tragedy (before *1604*(?); 1654)

C. CRITIQUE OF THE STANDARD EDITION

The volumes in the *Life and Work of George Peele*, gen. ed. Charles T. Prouty, are as follows. Volume 1, David H. Horne's *The Life and Minor Works of George Peele* (1952), has introductions. Volume 2 (1961) contains *Edward I*, ed. Frank S. Hook, who discusses editorial problems and relates the play to English drama of the time; and *The Battle of Alcazar,* ed. John Yoklavich, who deals with the sources and theatrical "plot." Volume 3 (1970), which has *The Araygnement of Paris,* ed. R. Mark Benbow, *David and Bethsabe,* ed. Elmer M. Blistein, and *The Old Wives' Tale,* ed. Frank S. Hook, completes the Yale edition. These volumes are comprehensive and meticulously edited.

IV. SEE ALSO

A. GENERAL

Bush, Douglas. *Mythology and the Renaissance Tradition in English Poetry.* 1932; rev. ed. 1963.

Dowling, Harold M. "A Few Points concerning Peele." *N&Q* 164 (1933): 96- 97.

———. "Miscellaneous Notes on Peele." *N&Q* 165 (1933): 272- 74.

Keeler, Clinton. "*A Farewell to Arms:* Hemingway and Peele." *MLN* 76 (1961): 622- 25.

Larsen, Thorleif. "The Father of George Peele." *MP* 26 (1928- 29): 69- 71.

———. "George Peele in the Chancellor's Court." *MP* 28 (1930- 31): 204- 7.

Mazzaro, Jerome L. "George Peele and *A Farewell to Arms:* A Thematic Tie?" *MLN* 75 (1960): 118- 19.

Smart, George K. "English Non-Dramatic Blank Verse in the Sixteenth Century." *Anglia* 61 (1937): 370- 97.

Stanley, Emily B. "The Use of Classical Mythology by the University Wits." *RenP,* 1956, pp. 25- 33.

B. INDIVIDUAL PLAYS

The Old Wives' Tale

Cazamian, Louis. *The Development of English Humor.* 1952.

Hall, Edgar A. *"Comus, Old Wives' Tale,* and Drury's *Alvredus."* In *Manly Anniversary Studies in Language and Literature* (1923), pp. 140–44.

Jones, Gwenan. "The Intention of Peele's *Old Wives' Tale." Aberystwyth Studies* 7 (1925): 79–93.

Lyons-Render, Sylvia. "Folk Motifs in George Peele's *The Old Wives' Tale." TFSB* 26 (1960): 62–71.

Ross, Anne. "Severed Heads in Wells: An Aspect of the Well Cult." *ScS* 6 (1962): 31–48.

Wilson, Robert H. "Reed and Warton on the *Old Wives' Tale." PMLA* 55 (1940): 605–8.

The Arraignment of Paris

Ekeblad, Inga-Stina. *"The Araygnement of Paris* Once More." *N&Q* 3 (1956): 548.

Gilbert, Allan H. "The Source of Peele's *Arraignment of Paris." MLN* 41 (1926): 36–40.

Jeffrey, V. M. "Italian and English Pastoral Drama of the Renaissance, II: The Source of Peele's *Arraignment of Paris." MLR* 19 (1924): 175–87.

Reeves, J. D. "The Cause of the Trojan War According to Peele." *N&Q* 2 (1955): 333.

———. "Peele's *Arraignment* Again." *N&Q* 3 (1956): 456.

Simpson, Percy. "The Rhyming of Stressed with Unstressed Syllables in Elizabethan Verse." *MLR* 38 (1943): 127–29.

The Battle of Alcazar

Farnham, Willard. *The Medieval Heritage of Elizabethan Tragedy.* 1936.

Greg, W. W. *Dramatic Documents from the Elizabethan Playhouses.* 1931.

Edward I

Burckhardt, Sigurd. *Shakespearean Meanings.* 1968.

Reeves, John D. "Persius and the Flying Horse in Peele and Heywood." *RES* 6 (1955): 397–99.

———. "Two Perplexities in Peele's *Edward the First." N&Q* 3 (1956): 328–29.

Reeves, John D., and Hølger Norgaard. "A Supposed Indebtedness of Shakespeare to Peele." *N&Q* 197 (1952): 441–43.

Ribner, Irving. "Shakespeare and Peele: The Death of Cleopatra." *N&Q* 197 (1952): 244–46.

The Love of King David and Fair Bethsabe

Blair, Carolyn. "On the Question of Unity in Peele's *David and Bethsabe.*" In *Studies in Honor of John C. Hodges and Alwin Thaler,* ed. Richard B. Davis and John L. Lievsay (1961), pp. 35–41.

Donnarel, A. "Sur un passage du *David et Bethsabee* de G. Peele." *RAA* 2 (1924–25): 433–34.

Lambin, G. "De Peele à Sidney, à propos d'une coquille." *RAA* 2 (1924–25): 242–43.

——. "Du Bartas et le style de Peele." *RAA* 3 (1925–26): 54–56.

Sampley, Arthur M. "The Version of the Bible Used by Peele in the Composition of *David and Bethsabe*." *Studies in English* (Univ. of Texas), 8 (1928): 79–87.

Sykes, H. Dugdale. "Peele's Borrowings from Du Bartas." *N&Q* 147 (1924): 349–51, 368–69.

Turner, Robert Y. "Pathos and the *Gorboduc* Tradition, 1560–1590." *HLQ* 25 (1961–62): 97–120.

C. TEXTUAL STUDIES

Dowling, Harold M. "Peele and Some Doubtful Plays." *N&Q* 164 (1933): 366–70.

Parks, George B. "George Peele and His Friends as 'Ghost'-Poets." *JEGP* 41 (1942): 527–36; rpt. in *ShAB* 22 (1947): 105–14.

Sampley, Arthur M. " 'Verbal Tests' for Peele's Plays." *SP* 30 (1933): 473–96.

——. "Plot Structure of Peele's Plays as a Test of Authorship." *PMLA* 51 (1936): 689–701.

A Knack to Know a Knave

Sykes, H. Dugdale. "The Authorship of *A Knack to Know a Knave*." *N&Q* 146 (1924): 389–91, 410–12.

I Henry VI

Gaw, Allison. *The Origin and Development of "I Henry VI" in Relation to Shakespeare, Marlowe, Peele, and Greene*. 1926.

II Henry VI

Cairncross, Andrew S., ed. *The Second Part of King Henry VI*. 1957.

THOMAS LODGE

Joseph W. Houppert

The only complete edition is Edmund Gosse's *The Complete Works of Thomas Lodge*, 4 vols. (1883), the Hunterian Club edition.

I. GENERAL

A. BIOGRAPHICAL

The facts of Lodge's life are given in Nathaniel B. Paradise, *Thomas Lodge: The History of an Elizabethan* (1931), and "Thomas Lodge, Doctor of Physick," *Yale Journal of Biology* 7 (1935): 449-513; Charles J. Sisson, "Thomas Lodge and His Family," in *Thomas Lodge and Other Elizabethans*, ed. Sisson (1933); Alice E. Walker, "The Life of Thomas Lodge," *RES* 9 (1933): 410-32, and 10 (1934): 46-54; and Edward A. Tenney, *Thomas Lodge* (1935). The most recent biography is Pat M. Ryan's *Thomas Lodge, Gentleman* (1958). Though neither scholarly nor original, the book is helpful in bringing together the combined researches of the above scholars to form a reasonably clear picture of Lodge; it also provides a limited bibliography.

In 1936 the second volume of a *Calendar of the Marquess of Downshire's Manuscripts* was published by the Historical Manuscripts Commission. This contains eight hitherto uncited letters from Lodge to William Trumbull, secretary to Sir Thomas Edmondes. Joseph W. Houppert, "Thomas Lodge's Letters to William Trumbull," *RN* 18 (1965): 117-23, combines these with a document from the manuscript collection of the Folger Library to explain Lodge's activities during his second exile on the continent. James George, "Additional Materials on the Life of Thomas Lodge between 1604 and 1613," in *Papers, Mainly Shakespearian*, collected by George I. Duthie (1964), pp. 90-105, adds to these letters documents from the Hertfordshire Archives and the Royal Archives in Brussels to account for Lodge's activities during his second exile as well as to clarify obscure points about his family, especially his wife. Both George and Houppert challenge Sisson's view that Lodge was "an incurably assertive individualist." They see Lodge as a dedicated physician, using his ingenuity to control the frustration which plagued a Roman Catholic living in England.

Wesley D. Rae, *Thomas Lodge* (1967), examines Lodge's works and life, but adds little to the biography. Rae is principally concerned with Lodge's lyrical poems and romances; on the plays he is neither perceptive nor accurate. Of *The Wounds of Civil War,* he writes that it contains dumb shows; a reading of the text fails to support the claim. He maintains that the fight between Marius and Sulla "is finally resolved when Scilla conquers Rome and Marius commits suicide"; in the play Marius does not kill himself (see IV.ii), and it is only *after* Marius's death that Sulla enters Rome.

B. GENERAL STUDIES OF THE PLAYS

No full-length study of the plays exists. The best introductions are the studies by Nathaniel B. Paradise and Edward A. Tenney (I,A).

C. THE WORKS AT LARGE

Alice Walker, "The Reading of an Elizabethan," *RES* 8 (1932): 264–81, assesses the extent of Lodge's borrowings from French and Italian sources. John J. McAleer, "Thomas Lodge's Verse Interludes," *CLAJ* 6 (1962): 83–89, argues that Lodge's originality was stifled until he was exposed to Sidney's *Arcadia*; Sidney provided a model which allowed Lodge to add a lyric note to his euphuistic style. Walter R. Davis, "Masking in Arden: The Histrionics of Lodge's *Rosalynde*," *SEL* 5 (1965): 151–63, also discusses Lodge and Sidney. In his view, both attempt to explore and extend the possibilities of human existence by placing their characters in an Arcadian setting. Lodge thought that the world as we know it is only the apparent world; the real world, which is never seen, is an ideal of humility and love. As each character enters Arden under a conscious mask, he finds his true self by acting it out dramatically. Thus Rosalynde finds the true role of the lover in frank and direct giving. Davis restates this thesis in his *Idea and Act in Elizabethan Fiction* (1969).

Marco Mincoff, "What Shakespeare Did to *Rosalynde*," *SJ* 96 (1960): 78–89, argues that Shakespeare owed very little to Lodge; he rejected Lodge's pastoral lyricism, choosing rather to focus on two comic themes inherent in *Rosalynde:* love's foolishness, and the clash between appearance and reality. And see Edna D. Romig's *"As You Like It;* Shakespeare's Use of His Source, Lodge's *Rosalynde," Univ. of Colorado Studies* 16 (1929): 300- 322.

Rosalynde is included in *Elizabethan Prose Fiction,* ed. Merritt Lawlis (1967), and prefaced by a short but incisive analysis of Lodge's style.

Knud Sørensen, *Thomas Lodge's Translation of Seneca's "De Beneficiis" Compared with Arthur Golding's Version* (1960), selects Lodge and Golding as typical Elizabethans, and examines their translations from a linguistic point of view. In "Thomas Lodge's 'Seneca,' " *Archiv* 199 (1963): 313- 24, Sørensen adds the information that Lodge used not only Latin but also the French versions of Goulart and Chalvet.

Sam H. Henderson, "Neo-Stoic Influence on Elizabethan Formal Verse Satire," in *Studies in English Renaissance Literature,* ed. Waldo F. McNeir (1962), pp. 56- 86, demonstrates that Lodge, in *A Fig for Momus,* understood the subtleties of the classical satirists and played with the paradoxes of Stoicism. Jaroslav Hornát, "An Old Bohemian Legend in Elizabethan Literature," *PP* 7 (1964): 345- 52, treats the story of Valasca in Lodge's *The Life and Death of William Longbeard* and defines its relation to its source in Aeneas Sylvius' *Historia Bohemica.*

The *Concise Bibliography* by Samuel A. Tannenbaum was published in 1940, and reprinted in *Elizabethan Bibliographies,* vol. 3 (1967). *Elizabethan Bibliographies Supplements V: Robert Greene 1945- 1965, Thomas Lodge 1939- 1965, John Lyly 1939- 1965, Thomas Nashe 1941- 1965, George Peele 1939- 1965,* by Robert C. Johnson, was published in 1968. Selected titles are listed in Irving Ribner, *Tudor and Stuart Drama,* Goldentree Bibliographies (1966).

II. CRITICISM OF INDIVIDUAL PLAYS AND STATE OF SCHOLARSHIP

A. INDIVIDUAL PLAYS

The Wounds of Civil War

Felix Schelling, *Elizabethan Playwrights: A Short History of the English Drama from Mediaeval Times to the Closing of the Theatres in 1642* (1925), outlines the influence of Marlowe's *Tamburlaine,* and William A. Armstrong, *"Tamburlaine* and *The Wounds of Civil War,"*

N&Q 5 (1958): 381–83, suggests that Lodge found a model for his play in Marlowe. He cites the chariot scene common to both plays, and Sulla's description of himself as one who "fettered fortune in the chains of power" as an imitation of Tamburlaine's boast that he holds the "Fates bound fast in iron chains." Wolfgang Clemen, *English Tragedy before Shakespeare: The Development of Dramatic Speech* (trans. T. S. Dorsch, 1961; German ed. 1955) analyzes *The Wounds of Civil War* in terms of set-speech types in pre-Shakespearean drama. Joseph W. Houppert, ed., *The Wounds of Civil War*, RRDS (1969), provides the most recent critical commentary.

A Looking Glass, for London and England

Lily B. Campbell, *Divine Poetry and Drama in Sixteenth-Century England* (1959), agrees with Robert A. Law, *"A Looking Glasse* and the Scriptures," *Studies in English* (Univ. of Texas), 19 (1939): 31–47, that the source is the Bishop's Bible, but adds that the play is not simply a dramatization of the book in Scripture. She disagrees with Law's identification of the play as a miracle; it should be related, not to medieval genres, but to the "divine" or Biblical drama. For additional material on *A Looking Glass,* see the discussion of Robert Greene.

B. OVER-ALL STATE OF CRITICISM

Lodge's dramatic contribution was small but not as negligible as the limited critical corpus would suggest. *The Wounds of Civil War* may be the oldest extant English drama based on classical history. It offers an excellent example of how Elizabethan dramatists of the second rank handled source material; see Appendix A in *The Wounds of Civil War,* ed. Joseph W. Houppert (1969). *A Looking Glass for London and England* has generally received praise in passing comments by critics of Elizabethan comedy, yet no full-length study of it has been made.

What is true of the plays is almost equally true of the nondramatic works. *Rosalynde,* of course, has attracted considerable attention, but the other euphuistic works, *A Margarite of America* and *Euphues Shadow,* have been neglected. Lodge's poetic works, *Phillis* and *Scillaes Metamorphosis,* have also received little study. As a satirist and moralist, Lodge is worth examining for ideas and attitudes current in his time, but *A Fig for Momus, Wits Miserie, An Alarum Against Usurers, The Divel Conjured,* and *Catharos* have been passed over. Announced titles of dissertations suggest that new editions may be forthcoming which will help provide the foundation for a re-evaluation.

III. CANON

A. PLAYS IN CHRONOLOGICAL ORDER

The information on dating is from Alfred Harbage, *Annals of English Drama, 975-1700,* rev. Samuel Schoenbaum (1964), which is also the source for the type of play, the acting date (in italics preceding semicolon), the original date of publication, and for lost plays by or attributed to Lodge. For descriptions of the original quartos see W. W. Greg, *A Bibliography of the English Printed Drama to the Restoration,* 4 vols. (1939-59), and see the discussions of canon in E. K. Chambers, *The Elizabethan Stage* (1923), vol. 3.

A Looking Glass, for London and England, with Robert Greene, biblical moral (*1587-91*; 1594)

Waldo F. McNeir, "The Date of *A Looking Glass for London," N&Q* 2 (1955): 282-83, dates the play in the latter part of 1589 or the early part of 1590. Charles Read Baskervill, "A Prompt-copy of *A Looking-Glass for London," MP* 30 (1932): 29-51, shows that it was still being performed in the early seventeenth century.

The Wounds of Civil War, classical history (*1587-92*; 1594)

B. UNCERTAIN ASCRIPTION

The Play of Plays and Pastimes, moral (*1580-82*; lost)

C. CRITIQUE OF THE STANDARD EDITION

That Gosse's 1883 edition of Lodge's *Works* remains the only complete edition suggests the direction that Lodge scholarship ought to take; substantial interpretative criticism must be based on sound texts. A new complete edition is needed.

D. SINGLE-WORK EDITIONS

A Looking Glasse, for London and Englande was edited by W. W. Greg in 1932 for the Malone Society. *The Wounds of Civil War,* ed. Joseph W. Houppert, RRDS (1969), contains a critical introduction and an appendix which examines the tragedy in light of its sources.

E. EDITIONS OF NONDRAMATIC WORKS

Recent editions of Lodge's nondramatic works are: *"Menaphon" by Robert Greene and "A Margarite of America" by Thomas Lodge,* ed. G. B.

Harrison (1927); *Lodge's "Rosalynde," Being the Original of Shake-speare's "As You Like It,"* ed. W. W. Greg (1907; 2nd ed. 1931); and *Rosalind,* in *Elizabethan Prose Fiction,* ed. Merritt Lawlis (1967). *Scillaes Metamorphosis* is included in Elizabeth S. Donno's *Elizabethan Minor Epics* (1963) and Nigel Alexander's *Elizabethan Narrative Verse,* Stratford-Upon-Avon Library, vol. 3 (1968).

IV. SEE ALSO

A. GENERAL

Acheson, Arthur. *Shakespeare, Chapman, and "Sir Thomas More."* 1931.

Atkins, J. W. H. *English Literary Criticism: The Renascence.* 1947; 2nd ed. 1951.

Atkins, Sidney H. "George Stoddard." *TLS,* 1 June 1933, p. 380.

——. "George Stoddard." *TLS,* 18 Jan. 1934, p. 44.

——. "Lodge's *Fig for Momus.*" *TLS,* 16 Aug. 1934, p. 565.

——. "*A Fig for Momus.*" *TLS,* 7 Feb. 1935, p. 76.

——. "Dyer at Woodstock." *TLS,* 3 Feb. 1945, p. 55.

Beaty, Frederick L. "Lodge's *Forbonius and Prisceria* and Sidney's *Arcadia.*" *ES* 49 (1968): 38–45.

Bush, Douglas. *Mythology and the Renaissance Tradition in English Poetry.* 1932; rev. ed. 1963.

——. *English Literature in the Earlier Seventeenth Century.* 1945; rev. ed. 1961.

Byrne, Muriel St. Clare. "An Early Translation of Seneca." *Library* 4 (1924): 277–85.

Caulfield, Ernest. "*The Countesse of Lincolnes Nurserie* with a Forward by Thomas Lodge; Oxford, 1622." *Amer. Jour. of Diseases of Children* 42 (1932): 155–57.

Clemen, Wolfgang. "Donne and the Elizabethans." In *Art, Science, and History in the Renaissance,* ed. Charles S. Singleton (1967). [Lodge's poem "Phillis," pp. 423–26.]

Colby, E. *English Catholic Poets.* 1936.

Condee, Ralph W. "Lodge and a Lucan Passage from Mirandula." *MLN* 63 (1948): 254–56.

Davenport, Arnold. "Samuel Rowlands and Thomas Lodge." *N&Q* 184 (1943): 13–16.

Davis, Harold H. "An Unknown and Early Translation of Seneca's *De beneficiis.*" *HLQ* 24 (1961): 137–44.

Drew, Philip. "Was Greene's 'Young Juvenal' Nashe or Lodge?" *SEL* 7 (1967): 55–66.

Duncan, Edgar H. "Thomas Lodge's Use of Agrippa's Chapter on Alchemy." *VUSH,* vol. 1 (1951), pp. 96–105.

Fox, Charles A. O. "Thomas Lodge and Shakespeare." *N&Q* 3 (1956): 190.

Genouy, H. *L'élément pastorale dans la poésie ... en Angleterre, 1579–1640.* 1928.

Grubb, Marion. "Lodge's Borrowing from Ronsard." *MLN* 45 (1930): 357–60.

Harbage, Alfred. *Shakespeare and the Rival Traditions.* 1952.

Harman, E. G. *The Countesse of Pembroke's "Arcadia."* 1924.

Hasselkuss, H. K. *Der Petrarkismus in die Sprache der englische Sonett-dichter.* 1927.

Herrick, Marvin T. *Comic Theory in the Sixteenth Century.* 1950.

Himelick, Raymond. *"A Fig for Momus* and Daniel's *Musophilus."* *MLQ* 18 (1957): 247-50.

Hiraoka, Tomokazu. "From *Rosalynde* to *As You Like It.*" *Toyama Diagaku Bungaku.* 1956.

Hornát, Jaroslav. "Spisovatelské počátky Thomase Lodge" [The literary beginnings of Thomas Lodge]. *Časopis pro moderní filologii* 43 (1961): 193-206. [English summary, pp. 206-7.]

Jenkins, Harold. *"As You Like It."* *ShS* 8 (1955): 40-51.

Jewkes, Wilfred T. "The Literature of Travel and the Mode of Romance in the Renaissance." *BNYPL* 67 (1963): 219-36.

John, Lisle C. *The Elizabethan Sonnet Sequences.* 1938.

Kaul, R. K. "Lodge, Shakespeare and the Olde Daunce." *LCrit* 6 (1964): 19-28.

Klein, David. *The Elizabethan Dramatists as Critics.* 1963.

Lathrop, Henry B. *Translations from the Classics into English from Caxton to Chapman, 1477-1620.* 1933.

Lewis, C. S. *English Literature in the Sixteenth Century, Excluding Drama.* 1954.

Miller, Edwin Haviland. "The Sources of Robert Greene's *A Quip for an Upstart Courtier* (1592)." *N&Q* 198 (1953): 148-52, 187-91.

Milligan, Burton A. "Some Sixteenth and Seventeenth Century Satire Against Money Lenders." *ShAB* 22 (1947): 36-46.

Mills, Laurens J. *One Soul in Bodies Twain.* 1937.

Mithal, H. S. D. " 'Short and Sweet.' " *N&Q* 5 (1958): 521-22.

Morris, Helen. *Elizabethan Literature.* 1958.

Pearson, Lu Emily. *Elizabethan Love Conventions.* 1933.

Ringler, William. "The Source of Lodge's *Reply to Gosson."* *RES* 15 (1939): 164-71.

———. "The First Phase of the Elizabethan Attack on the Stage, 1558-1579." *HLQ* 5 (1942): 391-418.

Schlauch, Margaret. *Antecedents of the English Novel, 1400-1600.* 1963.

Scott, Janet G. "Parallels to Three Elizabethan Sonnets." *MLR* 21 (1926): 190-92.

———. *Les sonnets élisabéthains.* 1929.

Seronsy, Cecil C. "The Seven Ages of Man Again." *SQ* 4 (1953): 364-65.

Smith, G. C. Moore. "Lodge and Desportes." *MLR* 18 (1923): 504.

Staton, Walter F., Jr. "The Influence of Thomas Watson on Elizabethan Ovidian Poetry." *SRen* 6 (1959): 243-50.

———. "A Lodge Borrowing from Watson." *RN* 14 (1961): 3-6.

Tolman, A. H. *Falstaff and Other Shakespearean Topics.* 1925.

Walker, Alice. "Italian Sources of Lyrics of Thomas Lodge." *MLR* 22 (1927): 75-79.

Wells, William. "The Authorship of *King Leir."* *N&Q* 177 (1939): 434-38.

Williams, Arnold. "The Two Matters: Classical and Christian in the Renaissance." *SP* 38 (1941): 158-64.

Wilson, F. P. *The Plague in Shakespeare's London.* 1927.
——. "Some English Mock-Prognostications." *Library* 19 (1938): 6-43.
Wright, Herbert G. "Some Sixteenth and Seventeenth Century Writers on the Plague." *E&S* 6 (1953): 41-55.
Zocca, Louis R. *Elizabethan Narrative Poetry.* 1950.

B. INDIVIDUAL PLAYS

Baker, Howard. *Induction to Tragedy: A Study in a Development of Form in "Gorboduc," "The Spanish Tragedy," and "Titus Andronicus."* 1939. [*The Wounds of Civil War.*]
Farnham, Willard. *The Medieval Heritage of Elizabethan Tragedy.* 1936. [*The Wounds of Civil War.*]
Knight, G. Wilson. *The Golden Labyrinth: A Study of the British Drama.* 1962. [*A Looking Glass.*]
Sturman, Berta. "A Date and a Printer for *A Looking Glasse for London and England,* Q4." *SB* 21 (1968): 248-53.
Swaen, A. E. H. "*A Looking-Glass for London and England,* 'Nutmegs and Ginger.'" *MLR* 33 (1938): 404-5.

ANONYMOUS PLAYS

Anne Lancashire   Jill Levenson

Books and articles consulted date from the publication of E. K. Chambers, The Elizabethan Stage, *4 vols.* (*1923*), *to the end of 1967; works published 1920–23 and not cited in Chambers are included, as are some post-1967 works. For additional information, see: G. E. Bentley,* The Jacobean and Caroline Stage, *7 vols.* (*1941–68*); *W. W. Greg,* A Bibliography of the English Printed Drama to the Restoration, *4 vols.* (*1939–59*); *Alfred Harbage,* Annals of English Drama, *975– 1700, rev. Samuel Schoenbaum* (*1964*), *and the* Supplement *by Schoenbaum* (*1966*). *A list of works dealing generally with a large number of anonymous plays will appear in the last volume of this series. The dates following play titles indicate the preferred date of first performance* (*in italics*) *and the date of the first edition, from the* Annals *and the* Supplement; *type classifications are from the* Annals. *Full bibliographical citation is given only for the first reference to a work in each essay; short titles are used for subsequent references. In longer essays, the title of the section in which the work is first cited* (*"Edition," "Text," etc.*) *is usually given in parentheses following the short title.*

The Rare Triumphs of Love and Fortune, mythological moral (*1582;* 1589)

Editions

Since the two nineteenth-century editions by J. P. Collier (1851) and W. C. Hazlitt (in Robert Dodsley's *Select Collection of Old English Plays,* vol. 6 [1874]), the play has been edited only by W. W. Greg in the Malone Society series (1931, for 1930) and by John Isaac Owen in a 1952 University of Illinois Ph.D. dissertation (*DA* 13 [1953] : 99).

The only overall studies of the play are in the introductions to these two editions. Greg deals very briefly with the ambiguity in the title (should it be *The Rare Triumphs of Love and Fortune* or the rare triumphs of *Love and Fortune*: i.e., are the words "the rare triumphs of" part of the title or does "triumphs" here mean simply "shows" or "devices"), the earliest known edition (1589), and the possible identification of the play with a "Historie of Loue and ffortune" played before the Queen at Windsor on 30 December 1582 by the Earl of Derby's servants. He also argues that the printer's copy-text was probably the playhouse manuscript.

Owen's introduction contains sections on text, date, authorship, sources, structure, staging, and the play's place in literature. He suggests a date in the early 1580s or even earlier, rejects previous authorship attributions to Kyd and to Robert Wilson, leaving the author as unknown, and states that the complex structure of the play makes a single source improbable; the germ of the debate between Venus and Fortune may have come from a poem by Turberville, "A Controuersie of a Conquest twixt Fortune and Venus." (He also suggests, with some distortion of the plot, that "one episode of the romance—the curing of the exiled nobleman's son by a sham physician—has several remote parallels and analogues in medieval and Renaissance literature.") Further, he states that the use of a débat as a framework for a romance may be original to this play, and that the play itself is transitional, standing between the old morality drama and the late sixteenth-century fully-developed romantic comedy.

Influences

J. M. Nosworthy, in the introduction to his Arden edition (1955) of Shakespeare's *Cymbeline,* accepts the suggestion made in 1887 by R. W. Boodle that *Cymbeline* is indebted to *Love and Fortune* for the plot strand concerning Belarius and the princes. Nosworthy suggests that Shakespeare read *Love and Fortune* in the course of considering old romantic comedies that the King's Men might revive, in the early Jacobean period, and remembered it when writing *Cymbeline.* (He also believes that Shakespeare took the name Hermione, in *The Winter's Tale,* from *Love and Fortune.*) He cites resemblances, both general and detailed, between the two plays, and also argues that Shakespeare's central concern in *Cymbeline* is with romance, and that *Love and Fortune,* of all his probable sources, is the one that is most fully a romance. With *Love and Fortune* plus Holinshed, Boccaccio, and the prose tale *Frederyke of Jennen,* Shakespeare's sources are, he believes, entirely accounted for; no other "lost" old play need be posited as a possible source. And Shakespeare may even have remembered *Love and Fortune* from having acted in it or from having seen it performed.

Love and Fortune as a *Cymbeline* source is also accepted by Kenneth Muir, *Shakespeare's Sources,* vol. 1 (1957), Irving Ribner, *The English History Play in the Age of Shakespeare* (1957; rev. ed. 1965), and J. A. Bryant, Jr., *Hippolyta's View* (1961).

Arthur Freeman, in "Shakespeare and *Solyman and Perseda,*" *MLR* 58 (1963): 481–87, and in *Thomas Kyd: Facts and Problems* (1967), states that *Love and Fortune* might have suggested the frame story of *Soliman and Perseda.* R. Warwick Bond, ed., *The Complete Works of John Lyly* (1902), vols. 2 and 3, mentions *Love and Fortune* as a possible source for the competition of the planets for influence in Lyly's *Woman in the Moon*; the suggestion is rejected by Johnstone Parr in *Tamburlaine's Malady and Other Essays on Astrology in Elizabethan Drama* (1953). Walther Fischer, "Shakespeares *Sturm* und *The Rare Triumphs of Love and Fortune,*" in *Festschrift zum 75. Geburtstag von Theodor Spira,* ed. H. Viebrock and W. Erzgräber (1961), pp. 144–51, discusses the possible influence of the play on Shakespeare's *Tempest.*

Other Studies

Arthur Acheson, *Shakespeare, Chapman, and "Sir Thomas More"* (1931), calls *Love and Fortune* a very early and largely unaltered play of Kyd's performed at court by Derby's company in December 1582; he compares the play with *Soliman and Perseda.* Dieter Mehl, *The Elizabethan Dumb Show* (1965; German ed. 1964), points out that the play is a courtly drama; Arthur Freeman, "Shakespeare and *Solyman and Perseda,*" says that it would require "a very elaborate presentation, perhaps unavailable outside the court." Félix Carrère, *Le théâtre de Thomas Kyd* (1951), rejects Fleay's Kyd attribution; Benvenuto Cellini, ed., *Drammi Pre-Shakespeariani,* Collana di Letterature Moderne, no. 4 (1958), states that the play's author could be Greene; Muriel St. Clare Byrne, "Anthony Munday's Spelling as a Literary Clue," *Library* 4 (1923–24): 9–23, suggests that the evidence of spelling tests points to Munday as a possible author.

Robert Grams Hunter, in *Shakespeare and the Comedy of Forgiveness* (1965), sees *Love and Fortune* as presenting the basic pattern of dramatic romance, and accepts Shakespeare's probable knowledge of it; the Earl of Derby's Men, to whose repertory it belonged, played in Stratford-on-Avon in 1581. He takes issue with Nosworthy on one point, and discusses the play in the context of his general theme of the comedy of forgiveness: comedy centering on a sinning man-type who is brought in the end to repentance and forgiveness. *Love and Fortune,* he believes, is a not-fully-developed romantic comedy of forgiveness, for the finally-forgiven sinner is not the romantic hero. Forces external to the human characters—the goddesses Love and Fortune—control the action.

Other scholars deal with the play from other points of view. Anne Righter, *Shakespeare and the Idea of the Play* (1962), Robert Y. Turner, "The Causal Induction in Some Elizabethan Plays," *SP* 60 (1963): 183-90, and Dieter Mehl, "Forms and Functions of the Play within a Play," *RenD* 8 (1965): 41-61, and *The Elizabethan Dumb Show* (above), all discuss its frame, Mehl seeing the frame as making of the play within it a dramatic moral exemplum. Ola Elizabeth Winslow, *Low Comedy as a Structural Element in English Drama from the Beginnings to 1642* (1926), comments that Penulo is a modified vice figure; Hardin Craig, "Morality Plays and Elizabethan Drama," *SQ* 1 (1950): 64-72, also connects the play with the moralities. Rolf Soellner, "The Madness of Hercules and the Elizabethans," *CL* 10 (1958): 309-24, links Bomelio with the *Hercules furens* tradition; J. F. Macdonald, "The Use of Prose in English Drama Before Shakespeare," *UTQ* 2 (1932-33): 465-81, cites the play as containing prose dialogue used to indicate insanity or temporary distraction. Bomelio's soliloquies are discussed as non-dramatic formal speeches by Jonas A. Barish, "*The Spanish Tragedy,* or The Pleasures and Perils of Rhetoric," in *Elizabethan Theatre,* SuAS, vol. 9 (1966), pp. 59-85. David Bevington, *Tudor Drama and Politics* (1968), sees, in the play's ending, Queen Elizabeth as explicitly a corrective to the violence and ingratitude of the action of the drama.

Wilfred T. Jewkes, *Act Division in Elizabethan and Jacobean Plays, 1583-1616* (1958), assuming that *Love and Fortune* was the play performed at Windsor on 30 December 1582, states that the 1589 text was printed from playhouse manuscript, "probably the author's copy prepared for the one recorded performance at court."

See Also

Baldwin, T. W. *Shakspere's Five-Act Structure.* 1947.
Chew, Samuel C. "Time and Fortune." *ELH* 6 (1939): 83-113.
Nicoll, Allardyce. *British Drama.* 1962 (5th ed.).
Rottenberg, Annette. "The Early Love Drama." *CE* 23 (1961-62): 579-83.
Russell, Patricia. "Romantic Narrative Plays: 1570-1590." In *Elizabethan Theatre,* SuAS, vol. 9 (1966), pp. 107-29.
Utz, Hans. *Das Bedeutungsfeld "Leid" in der englischen Tragödie vor Shakespeare.* Schweizer Anglistische Arbeiten, vol. 54 (1963).

A. L.

The Famous Victories of Henry V, history (*1586;* 1598)

Editions

The Famous Victories of Henry V (*FV*) recently has been edited by: Joseph Quincy Adams, *Chief Pre-Shakespearean Dramas* (1924); William Smith Wells, "*The Famous Victories of Henry the Fifth*: A Critical Edition," a Ph.D. dissertation *(Abstracts of Dissertations* [Stanford Univ.] 10 [1934–35]: 46–48); Seymour M. Pitcher, *The Case for Shakespeare's Authorship of "The Famous Victories"* (1961); Geoffrey Bullough, *Narrative and Dramatic Sources of Shakespeare,* vol. 4 (1962); Maynard Mack, *I Henry IV* (1965; Signet ed.); Alice Griffin, *The Sources of Ten Shakespearean Plays* (1966); Joseph Satin, *Shakespeare and His Sources* (1966). Several modern editions of Shakespeare's *I* and *II Henry IV* and *Henry V* include extracts from *FV*: e.g., Samuel B. Hemingway, *I Henry IV* (1936; New Variorum), Matthias A. Shaaber, *II Henry IV* (1940; New Variorum), A. R. Humphreys, *I Henry IV* (1960; Arden) and *II Henry IV* (1966; Arden), and J. H. Walter, *Henry V* (1954; Arden).

Adams follows tradition in dating the play before 1588 and calls it our earliest extant chronicle play and the inspirer of Shakespeare's *I* and *II Henry IV* and *Henry V*; Tarlton played the role of Dericke. The extant text seems to have been "cut down and otherwise mangled for traveling purposes; but this has not seriously affected its power to entertain." Bullough also treats *FV* as an old play and as, in its original form, one of Shakespeare's sources, but condemns the extant version as "crude, episodic," and a "decrepit pot-boiler," with a "debased" text "vilely corrupt, and probably much cut"; perhaps it was originally a two-part drama. Alice Griffin describes the play as a "workmanlike compilation from Holinshed and perhaps other chronicles," theatrically good, but without Shakespeare's characterization, poetry, ideas, and selectivity. History, she suggests, seems merely a framework on which to hang the comic scenes; Dericke was played by Tarlton; and the 1598 edition was probably published to capitalize on the current popularity on the stage of Shakespeare's *I* and *II Henry IV*. Satin prints the play as a source for *I* and *II Henry IV* and *Henry V*.

The only extended treatment of the play is in Wells's edition. Wells finds Hall's *Chronicle* of 1548 to be the play's principal source, with John Stow's *Annales of England* (1580) and possibly Holinshed as other sources; the extant quarto text suggests revision and memorial transmission and, as A. E. Morgan suggests (see below, "Text"), a verse or part-verse original; possibly *FV* was revised and revived ca. 1591, and first printed in 1594 in an edition not now extant. Other possible Henry V plays are discussed, and the theory of *FV* as having been taken by the Admiral's Men before publication, and revised as their 1595 Henry V play, is rejected. Wells dismisses Bernard M. Ward's attribution of the play to the Earl of Oxford (see below), examines Sykes's attribution to Samuel Rowley, and concludes that Rowley was possibly responsible for the final revision of *FV*: i.e., for the text from which the extant quarto was printed; Shakespeare may have had a hand in revising the play at one stage.

Text*

Establishing the nature of the existing text has been a primary concern of modern scholarship on *FV*. W. W. Greg, in *Two Elizabethan Stage Abridgments* (1923; Malone Society), suggests that *FV* is an old Queen's Men play in which Tarlton acted Dericke, but that the extant text is not that of the full, original play: "it has been most drastically abridged, possibly from an earlier version in two parts." Probably, he states, it represents the play as performed by the Queen's Men in the provinces, 1592–93; it is not the Henry V play performed in the 1590s by the Admiral's Men, unless that play was a revised version of it. Perhaps there was an earlier edition of the play, which is not now extant; or perhaps publication was intentionally delayed until 1598. Greg argues against the view, expressed to him in a private letter by J. Dover Wilson, that *FV* is a text memorially reconstructed by the Queen's Men from an original play which they had sold; the bareness of the text is fully accounted for by drastic compression. A. E. Morgan, *Some Problems of Shakespeare's "Henry the Fourth"* (Shakespeare Association Papers, no. 11 [1924]), believes *FV* to be a "ruthlessly cut down version" of an early (by 1588) Henry V play or plays, wholly or partly in verse, belonging to the Queen's Men and in which Tarlton played Dericke, and leans toward Dover Wilson's theory (privately communicated to him) of the text as a Queen's Men memorial reconstruction. He theorizes that the original play may have been sold to Creede, who entered it in the Stationers' Register but then, instead of publishing it, resold it to the Admiral's Men, who revised and performed it. (Morgan rejects the possibility of *FV* being the text of this Admiral's Men revision.) Or the Queen's Men may have sold their original play to the Admiral's Men and their cut-text *FV* to Creede,

* Unless otherwise noted, short-title references in subsequent sections are to works first cited in this section.

who published the cut text in a now non-extant 1594 edition and again in 1598 (our *FV*). The original Queen's Men Henry V play or the Admiral's Men Henry V play, he believes, eventually passed to the Chamberlain's Men and was rehandled by Shakespeare.

E. K. Chambers, *William Shakespeare* (1930), vol. 1, concurs with Greg in suggesting that the extant *FV* text is an old Queen's Men play probably abridged from a two-part original; he is against Morgan's theory of a verse original which passed to the Admiral's Men and then, revised, to the Chamberlain's Men to become Shakespeare's source. Robert Boies Sharpe, "We Band of Brothers," *SP* 26 (1929): 166–76, compares the accounts in Holinshed, Shakespeare's *Henry V,* and *FV* of those present at the Battle of Agincourt, to show that Shakespeare and the anonymous *FV* author selected, omitted, and added different names to the roll; he suggests that this was because of Elizabethan political partisanship. *FV*, in its battle list, seems to be connected politically with the Admiral's Men, and may in fact be a revision by them of an original Queen's Men play, "with partisan modifications in favor of the Cecil-Howard faction." *FV* ownership, he states, may have been in dispute among the Queen's, Admiral's, and Chamberlain's Men. In 1935, in *The Real War of the Theaters,* Sharpe cites his *SP* article (while acknowledging that it contains errors and omissions), and declares that our *FV* text may be identical with the Admiral's Men Henry V play of 1595, the Admiral's Men having illegally appropriated a Queen's Men play.

R. Crompton Rhodes, "Dramatic Piracy in Practice," *TLS*, 26 June 1930, p. 534, believes *FV* to be "a kind of penny gaff version of a lost play, and not a text used by the Queen's Majestie's Players. But, as a general principle, I believe that these semi-illiterate texts, and other spurious versions, were the legacies of unauthorized productions by strolling players or provincial companies." Arthur Acheson, *Shakespeare, Chapman, and "Sir Thomas More"* (1931), puts forward some elaborate and unproved theories about complications of *FV* revision and ownership: an original Queen's Men play became in 1591 a Pembroke's play, which next went to the publisher Creede in 1594; Creede sold the stage reversion of it, fraudulently, to some Henslowe writers; Chapman, Peele, and possibly others revised it into the recorded Admiral's Men Henry V play; the Chamberlain's Men prevented publication of the Pembroke's Men version until 1598/99, after they had regained the stage rights to the work.

In 1936 A. S. Cairncross, *The Problem of "Hamlet": A Solution,* gives the debate a new twist. He cites Peter Alexander's work (*TLS*, 16 Sept. 1926, p. 614) on *The Taming of a Shrew* as a bad quarto of *The Taming of the Shrew*, and states that *FV*, like *A Shrew*, is not an old play at all, but a loose piracy of Shakespeare's *Henry IV* and *Henry V* plays, which draws also on *II Henry VI* and *King John*, and perhaps on some chronicles other than Holinshed's or, more probably, on some other play based on such chronicles. E. M. W. Tillyard, *Shakespeare's History Plays* (1944), briefly suggests that *FV* is an abridgement of now-lost earlier plays by Shakespeare on Henry IV and Henry V. A. R. Humphreys, ed., *I Henry IV* ("Editions") calls this "quite unproved speculation."

Leo Kirschbaum, "A Census of Bad Quartos," *RES* 14 (1938): 20–43, accepts *FV* as a bad quarto of a lost original, citing Greg, *Stage Abridgements*, Dover Wilson (as presented by Greg), and Wells, "A Critical Edition" ("Editions"), and suggesting that in his Malone Society Reprint (1928) of *The Massacre at Paris* Greg has swung as well to the bad quarto theory. In "An Hypothesis Concerning the Origin of the Bad Quartos," *PMLA* 60 (1945): 697–715, he argues for memorial reconstruction (and no deliberate abridgement) as the origin of all bad quartos. J. I. M. Stewart, "King Cambyses's Vein," *TLS*, 26 May 1945, p. 247, believes *FV* to have been "fudged up" by actors with faulty memories from a fuller Queen's Men play, "perhaps for provincial performance." In *Library* 26 (1945–46): 2–16, John Dover Wilson, "The Origins and Development of Shakespeare's *Henry VI*," restates and briefly elaborates on the theory first advanced by himself and A. W. Pollard in *TLS*, 9 Jan. and 13 March 1919, pp. 18 and 134, and communicated by him since to both Greg, *Stage Abridgements*, and Morgan, *Shakespeare's "Henry the Fourth"*: *FV* is a memorial revonstruction by Queen's Men actors, for provincial touring, of two plays belonging originally to the Queen's Men and sold by them in 1592–94, probably to Lord Strange's Men. The old play on Henry IV doubtless existed before Tarlton's death in 1588, and the Henry V play by at least 1592. He believes that Nashe may have had a hand in revising the Henry IV play for performance in 1592 by Lord Strange's Men. J. H. Walter, ed., *Henry V* ("Editions"), accepts *FV* as clearly a bad quarto of a lost original (in which Tarlton played before his death) so bad it may perhaps have been reconstructed from an author's plot. Perhaps, he suggests, the boy who played Katherine helped in the reconstruction.

Thomas Marc Parrott, *Shakespearean Comedy* (1949), calls *FV* a "crude old play," extant in a "badly mangled text" which is possibly a second edition brought out "to compete with the sale of Shakespeare's play" [*I Henry IV*]. (He sees the Admiral's Men Henry V play as a different drama.)

In *RenP*, 1954, pp. 57–62, Dora Jean Ashe, "The Non-Shakespearean Bad Quartos as Provincial Acting Versions," supports the view of the *FV* text as a memorial reconstruction for provincial acting, pointing out that general characteristics of such texts are economy of casting and staging requirements, brevity, plague-period dating, and prominent comedy; in her 1953 Ph.D. dissertation for the University of Virginia, "A Survey of Non-Shakespearean Bad Quartos" (*DA* 14 [1954] : 1070–71), she further suggests that the *FV* reporter was probably the actor of the doubled roles of Henry IV and the French King.

C. A. Greer, in "A Lost Play the Source of Shakespeare's *Henry IV* and *Henry V*," *N&Q* 1 (1954): 53–55, stands against the critical consensus in finding *FV* to read, not like an abridgement, but smoothly and logically; he does, however, posit the existence of an earlier, original Henry V play or plays, a source for both *FV* and Shakespeare. He cites Morgan and argues against some of his points. (See below, "Shakespeare Connections.") Irving Ribner, *The English History Play in the Age of Shakespeare* (1957; rev. ed. 1965) finds *FV* to be "a version [of a lost original] almost certainly cut for road presentation," and "full of printer's errors, with much of the prose printed as verse"; Ribner suggests that many corruptions may have been made by actors in the more than ten years of performance between the composition and the printing of the play. Tarlton played Dericke. A. R. Humphreys, ed., *I Henry IV* ("Editions"), states that the *FV* text is "chaotic" and "virtually unplayable" and is apparently a memorially-reconstructed abridgement of a long Henry V play or, more probably, of a two-part play, one part on Hal's pranks and one on Henry's French wars; it was probably acted in the provinces, 1592–94.

See also Shapiro, "Shakespeare and Mundy," below.

Shakespeare Connections

The major scholarly problem posed by *FV* is the question of its relationship to Shakespeare's *I* and *II Henry IV* and *Henry V*. This problem is inextricably interwoven with the problem of the nature of the extant *FV* text; see the previous section for relevant works not mentioned again here. Scholars' theories vary from the conservative extreme of seeing *FV* as Shakespeare's direct and only source to the radical extreme of viewing Shakespeare as *FV*'s source.

Morgan, *Shakespeare's "Henry the Fourth,"* posits as Shakespeare's (ultimate) source a now-lost Queen's Men original (or originals) of the cut-text *FV*, and discusses Shakespeare's alterations of his source. (He also believes *I* and *II Henry IV* to be revisions of earlier versions, from the Queen's Men original, by Shakespeare.) In 1928 Bernard M. Ward, *"The Famous Victories of Henry V*: Its Place in Elizabethan Dramatic Literature,"* RES* 4 (1928): 270–94, argues for *FV* itself as Shakespeare's source—and the source not merely for a few details, as suggested by previous critics, but for the entire design of his trilogy. E. K. Chambers, *William Shakespeare,* posits a now-lost edition of *FV*, ca. 1594, as a source for both Shakespeare and another dramatist doing a separate Henry V play for the Admiral's Men. Acheson, *Shakespeare, Chapman,* sees *I Henry IV* as built on *FV*, and *II Henry IV* and *Henry V* (and *Merry Wives of Windsor*) on a dramatic and historical expansion of *FV*. Robert Adger Law, "Holinshed as Source for *Henry V* and *King Lear,"* Studies in English* (Univ. of Texas) 14 (1934): 38–44, cites similarities to prove that "for the layout of the entire drama, the content of the serious scenes as well as the comic, Shakespeare was . . . indebted directly to *The Famous Victories,* or else to some other play now lost, on which *The Famous Victories* is based practically scene for scene." Alfred Hart, *Stolne and Surreptitious Copies* (1942), finds *FV*, which (he believes) probably predates *Tamburlaine* and is a corrupt text, to be a Shakespeare source, as does Parrott, *Shakespearean Comedy.*

With Cairncross, *Problem of "Hamlet,"* we move to Shakespeare as the *FV* source, with Tarlton having played, before his 1588 death, in an incident in Shakespeare's *I Henry IV* not included in the present text. Tillyard, *Shakespeare's History Plays,* sees *FV* as an abridgement of earlier Shakespearean plays on Henry IV and Henry V. Stewart, "King Cambyses's Vein," however, compares *I Henry IV* and *FV* to arrive at his proposal of the existence of a Henry V play earlier than *FV* or *Henry IV* and *Henry V*; he suggests that Shakespeare, in Falstaff's speech on how he will impersonate Hal's father, is parodying an older play in which Henry IV wept a great deal and which contained much euphuism, traces of both of which he finds in *FV* (which he takes to be descended from this fuller play). Against his arguments, see J. C. Maxwell's Appendix V to Humphreys' *I Henry IV* edition. Walter ("Editions") accepts Morgan's theory of the similarities between

Shakespeare's *I* and *II Henry IV* and *Henry V* and *FV* as being caused by all four plays borrowing from an earlier, now-lost play. C. A. Greer, "A Lost Play," accepts Morgan's theory of a lost source (or sources) for both *FV* and Shakespeare, though rejecting Morgan's description of *FV* as a cut text; in, however, "Shakespeare's Use of *The Famous Victories of Henry the Fifth*," *N&Q* 1 (1954): 238–41, he picks up Ward's argument and elaborates on it, declaring that Shakespeare depended heavily on *FV* as a source, and only in his concluding sentence mentioning the possibility of a lost common source for Shakespeare and *FV* (and Holinshed). Humphreys ("Editions") believes that Shakespeare drew, not on *FV* or (as he posits) its two-part original, but possibly on a later version of each original part; in the later first part, Oldcastle must have been such a prominent figure that Shakespeare in his *Henry IV* could take for granted the audience's familiarity with the character; and probably the later second part was the Admiral's Men *Henry V* play.

Robert Adger Law, "The Composition of Shakespeare's Lancastrian Trilogy," *TSLL* 3 (1961–62): 321–27, sees *FV* or its now-lost predecessor as a Shakespearean source, used less than Holinshed in *I* and *II Henry IV* and less than *I Henry IV* in *II Henry IV*, but used equally with Holinshed in *Henry V*. M. M. Reese, *The Cease of Majesty* (1961), in a footnote calls *FV* an incomplete version of a play Shakespeare must have known in its original form. Ribner, *English History Play*, sees the play as an important Shakespeare source. I. A. Shapiro, "Shakespeare and Mundy," *ShS* 14 (1961): 25–33, suggests the existence of a common "scenario" (and possibly previous versions of it) behind *FV* and Shakespeare's work, which, along with *FV*, influenced Shakespeare.

Involved in the relationship issue are three articles on Shakespeare's source for Falstaff. James Monaghan, "Falstaff and His Forebears," *SP* 18 (1921): 353–61, argues, through various kinds of parallels, that Falstaff is drawn both from the written part of Dericke in *FV* and from Tarlton's improvisations in his acting of the Dericke role, grafted onto the character of Sir John Oldcastle; he sees *FV* as Shakespeare's source especially for *I* and *II Henry IV*. Rudolph Fiehler, "How Oldcastle Became Falstaff," *MLQ* 16 (1955): 16–28, cites Monaghan's article on Falstaff as originating in Sir John Oldcastle and Dericke and suggests that in *FV* one actor may have doubled the roles and thus have made Oldcastle a comic figure, a "caricature of Puritanism." He posits popular legends about Oldcastle and about the wild Prince Hal as the sources of *FV*'s unhistorical depiction of Oldcastle as a highwayman. D. B. Landt, "The Ancestry of Sir John Falstaff," *SQ* 17 (1966): 69–76, sees Falstaff as drawn directly from *FV*, "a product of Shakespeare's transformative powers working upon actual literary materials." He points out, against Monaghan and Fiehler, that there are major differences in role between Falstaff and Oldcastle-and-Dericke. "Shakespeare was dealing with his material as a text, and perhaps a more complete text than is now extant. . . . Falstaff is a carefully developed literary creation, conceived and recreated from several characters, incidents, and bits of dialogue in the earlier play."

Leslie Mahin Oliver, "Sir John Oldcastle: Legend or Literature?" *Library* 1 (1946–47): 179–83, deals not with Falstaff but with the historical Oldcastle and how he became the Oldcastle of *FV*. He believes that no popular Oldcastle legend existed, and that the suggestion of Oldcastle as an outlaw probably came from the Latin chronicles of Thomas Walsingham, or from the "Walsingham-Bale-Foxe" report of Oldcastle's public confession during his examination, and from one paragraph in Fabyan's *Chronicle*. The Oldcastle of *FV*, he states, is not a very important or clearly drawn character.

Leo Kirschbaum, having long believed *FV* to be a bad quarto (see above, "Text"), in *Shakespeare and the Stationers* (1955) discusses the copyright relationship between *FV* and Shakespeare's *Henry V*, and denies that there was a *FV* edition prior to 1598.

Date and Authorship

Date and authorship of *FV* are two questions integrally involved in the tangle of theories about the play's textual origin and its relationship to Shakespeare's works; see previous sections as well as the works listed below. Favorite attributions have been to Tarlton, Samuel Rowley, and Shakespeare.

J. M. Robertson, *The Shakespeare Canon*, pt. 1 (1922), takes the traditional *FV* date of before 1588 and says that the play could be by Tarlton but is probably, as H. Dugdale Sykes had previously argued (1920), by Samuel Rowley. (He posits the existence of a separate Admiral's Men Henry V play, in the 1590s, based on *FV* and written by Marlowe, Peele, and Greene.) Greg, *Stage Abridgements*, accepts, with reservations, the possibility suggested previously by Fleay and Ward that Tarlton wrote the part he played, and argues against Sykes's attribution of the play to Rowley. Sykes, in *Sidelights on Elizabethan*

Drama (1924), reiterates his belief in Rowley's authorship of *FV* in its entirety. (The chapter concerned is a reprint of his earlier work.) E. H. C. Oliphant, "How Not to Play the Game of Parallels," *JEGP* 28 (1929): 1-15, in a general attack on authorship attributions through the citing of parallels, calls Sykes's attribution a strange mixture of the convincing and the unconvincing; in "Bibliographical Clues in Collaborate Plays," *Library* 13 (1932-33): 21-48, Muriel St. Clare Byrne is entirely opposed to Sykes's attribution methods.

Marlowe is named as a collaborator (in *FV* as a Queen's Men play) by Philip Henderson, *And Morning in His Eyes: A Book about Christopher Marlowe* (1937). Irving Ribner, *English History Play*, summarily dismisses previous attributions to Tarlton, Samuel Rowley, and Shakespeare; I. A. Shapiro, "Shakespeare and Mundy" ("Shakespeare Connections"), takes an original slant in briefly suggesting that *FV* might be the result of dialogue written by a succession of other authors, expanding and patching, for a scenario supplied originally by Munday, Greene, or some other dramatist. Seymour M. Pitcher, *Shakespeare's Authorship* ("Editions"), devotes an entire book to an unconvincing attempt to demonstrate Shakespeare's authorship of the anonymous play; the attribution is briefly rejected by David Bevington, *Tudor Drama and Politics* (1968).

Parrott, *Shakespearean Comedy*, accepts the play as written before Tarlton's death in 1588, as do Wilfred T. Jewkes, *Act Division in Elizabethan and Jacobean Plays, 1583-1616* (1958), and T. W. Baldwin, *On the Literary Genetics of Shakspere's Plays, 1592-1594* (1959). Baldwin believes that *FV* may indeed have been produced shortly after the formation of the Queen's Men in 1583.

Two unusual authorship theories are advanced by Bernard M. Ward, *"Famous Victories"* ("Shakespeare Connections"), and Dorothy and Charlton Ogburn, *This Star of England* (1952). Ward, finding *FV* to depend for its historical material on Hall rather than on Holinshed, dates the play before the publication of Holinshed's *Chronicles* (in 1578), ca. 1574, and gives it, in its original form as a "Court masque," to the Earl of Oxford. (David Bevington, *Tudor Drama*, rejects Ward's examination of the play as reflecting Oxford's escapades ca. 1573.) The Ogburns maintain that *FV* "bears the unmistakable stamp of the young Earl of Oxford" (to them, Shakespeare), and was performed at court, Christmas 1574; they present some highly fanciful evidence for their case, and, like Ward, see the play as dependent not on Holinshed but on Hall.

The Play

Irving Ribner, *English History Play,* David Bevington, *Tudor Drama* ("Date and Authorship"), and Bernard M. Ward, "Shakespeare and the Anglo-Spanish War, 1585–1604," *RAA* 6 (1928–29): 297–311, examine *FV* as a history play. Ribner calls it "formless and incoherent and, in general, worthless." Although its hero is historical, the play is not a genuine historical drama, but is in the tradition of the heroic romance: a "non-didactic heroic folk play"; the only historical purpose it serves is the stimulation of patriotism, and its only real importance is in its considerable influence on Shakespeare. See also Ribner's "The Tudor History Play: An Essay in Definition," *PMLA* 69 (1954): 591–609. Bevington, taking the play to be of pre-Armada date and probably the first extant English history play, sees it as a war drama centering on French-English antagonism and the glorification of the unity of English royalty and commoners against foreigners. Hal is a type of Robin Hood folk hero. Ward regards the play as war propaganda.

John B. Moore, *The Comic and the Realistic in English Drama* (1925), points out the comic emphasis of the play and suggests that it was probably the first chronicle play to show to an English audience a king appealing strongly to the audience's affection—"a king who without losing his royal spirit could yet mix in comradeship with low or at least ordinary fellows." Charles J. Sisson, *Le goût public et le théâtre élisabéthain* (1922), and Ola Elizabeth Winslow, *Low Comedy as a Structural Element in English Drama from the Beginnings to 1642* (1926), both deal briefly with the comic scenes, comparing them unfavorably to the comedy in *I Henry IV.* Parrott, *Shakespearean Comedy,* declares that the comic matter "quite overshadows the serious action." C. L. Barber, "The Saturnalian Pattern in Shakespeare's Comedy," *SR* 59 (1951): 593–611, points out that in *FV* "the prince was cast in the traditional role of the prodigal son, while his disreputable companions functioned as tempters in the same general fashion as the Vice of the morality plays."

Style is the concern of Wolfgang Clemen, *English Tragedy Before Shakespeare* (trans. T. S. Dorsch, 1961; German ed. 1955), and Jonas A. Barish, *Ben Jonson and the Language of Prose Comedy* (1967). Clemen states that the prose of the chronicle-history *FV* is unusual, for its period, in being vigorous, natural, and unpretentious; it has not been influenced by the language of other contemporary dramatic genres. At times the dialogue is charged with real human emotion. Barish finds two prose modes in the play: boisterous, lower-class speech and courtly dialogue. Both, he states, are syntactically and rhetorically primitive, but the comic scenes are at least important in representing an early attempt to create a colloquial stage prose.

Other Studies

Composition of *FV* for innyard performance, and at least innyard acting of the play, is posited by William J. Lawrence in *Pre-Restoration Stage Studies* (1927). M. M. Reese, *Shakespeare: His World and His Work* (1953), takes *FV* to be an Admiral's Men play starring Alleyn; in *The Cease of Majesty* ("Shakespeare Connections") he calls it an "immensely popular play [which] paid no heed to fact or motive or historical progression." M. C. Bradbrook, *Shakespeare and Elizabethan Poetry* (1951), states that the importance of *FV* is that, with *Sir John Oldcastle,* it provides us with "a check upon what constituted the popular requisites for a play on Henry V before, and after, the subject had been treated by Shakespeare." "[*FV*] intends to give a 'scenic representation of history,' " claims Alan S. Downer, in *The British Drama* (1950); the play follows Holinshed, without attention to form.

W. L. Halstead, "New Source Influence on *The Shoemaker's Holiday*," *MLN* 56 (1941): 127–29, points out parallels of situation, action, and character between the impressment scene in *FV* and that in Dekker's play. Jewkes, *Act Division* ("Date and Authorship"), suggests that the extant text was printed from a theatrical promptbook discarded after a revision or a revival, or from an author's manuscript which had been prepared for the stage.

See Also

Albright, Evelyn May. *Dramatic Publication in England, 1580–1640.* 1927.

Armstrong, William A. "Actors and Theatres." *ShS* 17 (1964): 191–204.

Baker, Arthur E. *A Shakespeare Commentary.* 1938.

Black, Matthew. "Enter Citizens." In *Studies in the English Renaissance Drama in Memory of Karl Julius Holzknecht,* ed. Josephine W. Bennett, Oscar Cargill, and Vernon Hall, Jr. (1959), pp. 16–27.

Bowling, William G. "The Wild Prince Hal in Legend and Literature." *Washington Univ. Studies* [St. Louis, Mo.], Humanistic Series, 13 (1925–26): 305–34.

Clark, Eleanor Grace. *The Pembroke Plays.* 1928.

Clough, Wilson O. "The Broken English of Foreign Characters of the Elizabethan Stage." *PQ* 12 (1933): 255–68.

Evans, G. Blakemore, ed. "Supplement to *Henry IV, Part 1:* A New Variorum Edition of Shakespeare." *SQ* 7, no. 3 (1956): i–iv, 1–121.

Everitt, E. B. *The Young Shakespeare: Studies in Documentary Evidence.* Anglistica, vol. 2 (1954).

Gerrard, Ernest A. *Elizabethan Drama and Dramatists, 1583-1603.* 1928.

Gray, Henry David. "The Rôles of William Kemp." *MLR* 25 (1930): 261-73.

Hapgood, Robert. "Falstaff's Vocation." *SQ* 16 (1965): 91-98.

Harbage, Alfred. *As They Liked It.* 1947.

Henneke, Agnes. "Shakespeares englische Könige." *SJ* 66 (1930): 79-144.

Humphreys, A. R., ed. *II Henry IV.* 1966; Arden edition.

Keller, Wolfgang. "Shakespeares Königsdramen." *SJ* 63 (1927): 35-53.

Langsam, G. Geoffrey. *Martial Books and Tudor Verse.* 1951.

Leech, Clifford. "The Two-Part Play: Marlowe and the Early Shakespeare." *SJ* 94 (1958): 90-106.

Rhodes, R. Crompton. *Shakespeare's First Folio.* 1923.

Schirmer, Walter F. "Über das Historiendrama in der englischen Renaissance." *Archiv* 179 (1941): 1-7.

———. *Glück und Ende der Könige in Shakespeares Historien.* Arbeitsgemeinschaft für Forschung des Landes nordrhein-westfalen, Geisteswissenschaften, no. 22 (1953).

Turner, Robert Y. "Shakespeare and the Public Confrontation Scene in Early History Plays." *MP* 62 (1964-65): 1-12.

Wells, Henry W. "A Mirror of National Integration." *SAB* 18 (1943): 30-40.

Many modern editions of *I* and *II Henry IV* and *Henry V*, besides those cited here, comment briefly on *FV*, as do other critical works on the same three plays and on Shakespeare in general.

A. L.

I & II The Troublesome Reign of King John, history (*1588;* 1591)

Editions

The *Troublesome Reign of King John* (*TR*) is found in two modern editions: in vol. 4 (1962) of Geoffrey Bullough's *Narrative and Dramatic Sources of Shakespeare*, and in E. B. Everitt and R. L. Armstrong's *Six Early Plays Related to the Shakespeare Canon*, Anglistica, vol. 14 (1965). In an introduction to his section on the sources of Shakespeare's *King John* (*KJ*), Bullough states briefly the various critical views on the relationship between *TR* and *KJ*, and supports the traditional belief that *TR*, which he dates 1590-91, served Shakespeare as a source for *KJ*. He also deals with the possible sources of *TR* (mainly Holinshed and Foxe's *Acts and Monuments*, and perhaps also Matthew Paris's *Chronica Majora*, Polydore Vergil's *Anglica Historia*, Hall, and Bale's *Kynge Johan*), discusses the play at some length, and compares it with *KJ*. Though printed in two parts, *TR* is clearly written as one piece. Everitt dates *TR* in 1588, and discusses the play as a deliberate counterpart thesis to *Edward III*, the latter play showing warrior honor, and *TR,* dishonor. Shakespeare's *KJ* is merely a later version of *TR,* rephrased in characters, thought, and dramatic construction. The assumption underlying the Everitt-Armstrong collection is that all six plays in the volume are early Shakespearean work.

An extract from *TR,* called "The Excommunication of King John," is printed, with a brief introduction, in Allardyce Nicoll, ed., *Readings from British Drama* (1928).

The Troublesome Reign and *King John**

The relationship between *TR* and *KJ* has been a principal concern of modern scholarship on both plays. *TR* traditionally has been held, as in E. K. Chambers, *William Shakespeare* (1930), vol. 1, to be Shakespeare's source (Chambers stating that Shakespeare wrote *KJ* with the book of *TR* in front of him); but in 1936 A. S. Cairncross, *The Problem of "Hamlet": A Solution,* suggested the opposite relationship. In 1926 Peter Alexander, *TLS,* 16 Sept. 1926, p. 614, had argued that the traditionally designated "source" of Shakespeare's *Taming of the Shrew,* the anonymous *Taming of a Shrew,* is in reality a bad quarto (or version) of Shakespeare's play; and, following Alexander's lead, Cairncross argued that *TR* is a similar "loose piracy," postdating and imitating *KJ* (and other plays). See also Alexander's *Shakespeare* (1964) and *Introductions to Shakespeare* (1964). The bad quarto theory has been accepted by E. A. J. Honigmann, ed., *King John* (1954; Arden), who maintains that *TR* was written from *KJ* for performance by the Queen's Men, both plays being composed within a few months of each other in 1590–91. He goes into detail on correspondences between *TR* and other old plays, and on characteristics of *TR* which lead him to place it after *KJ*: "bad quarto" features, dramatic company, use of historical details, structural inconsistencies which can be explained as thoughtless echoing of *KJ*. See also Honigmann's "Shakespeare's 'Lost Source-Plays,' " *MLR* 49 (1954): 293–307. Thomas Marc Parrott, in a review of the edition in *JEGP* 55 (1956): 297–305, calls Honigmann's work "interesting, ingenious, and eccentric," and convincingly attacks his arguments. The bad quarto theory is also accepted, however, by William H. Matchett, ed., *King John* (1966; Signet ed.).

Other scholars are virtually unanimous in placing *TR* before *KJ,* though their views of the actual relationship between the two plays,

* Unless otherwise noted, short-title references in subsequent sections are to works first cited in this section.

and their treatments of it, vary. In his Cambridge edition (1936) of *KJ*, J. Dover Wilson sets forth in detail reasons for the priority of *TR* (e.g., situations clearer in *TR* than in *KJ*, no significant verbal parallels between *TR* and any of Shakespeare's real poetry in *KJ*, *KJ* not printed until 1623), dates it ca. 1588–89, and believes it to be Shakespeare's only source. Shakespeare may, however, Dover Wilson states, have worked upon, not the printed text of *TR*, but the prompt copy of the play, and may even once have acted in *TR* (with the Queen's Men), or have brought the play with him to the Chamberlain's company. Dover Wilson devotes considerable space to showing how Shakespeare reworked *TR* and improved on it. A. P. Rossiter, "Prognosis on a Shakespeare Problem," *DUJ* 33 (1940–41): 126–39, deals, in a general article on Shakespeare's historical sources, with *TR-KJ* relationship possibilities in connection with Alan Keen's discovery of a copy of Hall supposedly annotated by Shakespeare; *TR* is definitely a Shakespeare source, and a comparison of *TR* with *KJ* supports the view that Shakespeare was not a careful historian and worked largely from old plays. (Cf. both books by Alexander, above.) See also Alan Keen and Roger Lubbock, *The Annotator* (1954). E. M. W. Tillyard, *Shakespeare's History Plays* (1944), rejects the Alexander-Cairncross theory and accepts Dover Wilson's arguments, but suggests his own variation on the bad quarto idea: that *TR* may be a bad quarto, not of *KJ* as we know it, but of an early Shakespearean two-part play on John which was later revised by Shakespeare into *KJ*. F. P. Wilson, *Marlowe and the Early Shakespeare* (1953), believes that the evidence is inconclusive as to which play precedes the other, but seems to prefer the traditional view of *TR* as source; if *TR* is the later play, concocted for a rival company or for the reading public, why does it not contain more of Shakespeare's language? Like Tillyard, he suggests that *TR* and *KJ* may both depend on an earlier, now-lost play (perhaps by Shakespeare). Frank O'Connor, *The Road to Stratford* (1948; published 1960 in the U.S. in a slightly different form, under the title *Shakespeare's Progress*), believes *KJ* was written to replace *TR*, and rejects Dover Wilson's view that Shakespeare worked from prompt copy or even that Shakespeare was with the Queen's Men when they had *TR*, because of his own theory that Shakespeare in his treatment of Lady Faulconbridge was confused by *TR*.

Robert Adger Law, "On the Date of *King John*," *SP* 54 (1957): 119–27, disagrees with Honigmann and advances evidence for his own belief in the precedence of *TR* which includes characteristics of style, characterization, structure, and attitude, problems of chronology, and a bibliographical point. He suggests that *KJ* is structurally unlike Shakespeare's other plays because Shakespeare is following *TR*. In *SJ* 96 (1960): 47-63, Kenneth Muir, "Source Problems in the Histories," argues against *TR* as a bad quarto of *KJ*; there are few verbal parallels between the two plays, and *TR* is longer than *KJ* and contains some incidents more clearly motivated than in Shakespeare's play. Muir, like Tillyard and F. P. Wilson, suggests a lost common source, by Shakespeare or, more probably, by another dramatist. I. A. Shapiro, "Shakespeare and Mundy," *ShS* 14 (1961): 25-33, suggests the possibility of a common, basic "scenario" underlying both *TR* and *KJ*, though with Shakespeare definitely indebted to *TR*. In *The Cease of Majesty* (1961), M. M. Reese states that Dover Wilson refuted Honigmann's theory in anticipation, and that *TR*, unlike a derivative play, is longer than *KJ* and has almost double the number of speaking parts. He gives comparative examples of *TR* and *KJ* to show how Shakespeare changed and improved on his source. Arthur Freeman, "Shakespeare and *Solyman and Perseda*," *MLR* 58 (1963): 481-87, argues for a reference in *KJ* to *Soliman and Perseda,* which he dates after 1591, thus making it impossible for *TR* (published 1591) to be a bad quarto of *KJ*.

Less important treatments of the problem are numerous. Ruth Wallerstein, *King John in Fact and Fiction* (ca. 1921), accepting *TR* (written 1589-90) as a *KJ* source, briefly compares the two plays. Hardin Craig, "Shakespeare's Revisions," *Johns Hopkins Alumni Magazine* 19 (1930-31): 331-48, suggests that Shakespeare originally used in *KJ* even more of *TR* than is at present in his play, but cut some (the conspiracy against John's life, and the poisoning), perhaps because of official censorship. Alfred Hart, "Acting Versions of Elizabethan Plays," *RES* 10 (1934): 1-28, states that Shakespeare in *KJ* so completely reworked *TR* that *KJ* has almost none of the thought, metaphors, and distinctive vocabulary of *TR*; he uses the *TR-KJ* relationship as an example of how the young Shakespeare rewrote old plays. In his *Stolne and Surreptitious Copies* (1942), he provides vocabulary tests to establish *TR* as a *KJ* source. Charles Petit-Dutaillis, in *Le Roi Jean et Shakespeare* (1944), argues that Shakespeare wrote *KJ* with *TR* before him, and dates *TR* ca. 1591.

John Elson, "Studies in the King John Plays," in *Joseph Quincy Adams Memorial Studies,* ed. James G. McManaway, Giles E. Dawson, and Edwin E. Willoughby (1948), pp. 183-97, declares that Shakespeare used *TR* as a pattern for *KJ*, and summarizes the two plays simultaneously. See also Thomas Marc Parrott, *Shakespearean Comedy* (1949); Parrott also dates the play as probably several years before 1591. In the annual British Academy Shakespeare Lecture for 1953, J. Isaacs, "Shakespeare's Earliest Years in the Theatre," *PBA* 39 (1953): 119–38, argues for the view that *TR* is the exclusive source of *KJ*, Shakespeare writing his play with *TR* before him and using nothing else but his own knowledge and memory. He rejects all forms of the bad quarto theory. See also, for a very brief comparison of the two plays, his "Sources of Shakespeare's Plays," *Listener*, 4 Aug. 1949, pp. 183–84. Leonard R. N. Ashley, *Authorship and Evidence* (1968), also rejects the bad quarto theory. Matthew P. McDiarmid, "Concerning *The Troublesome Reign of King John*," *N&Q* 4 (1957): 435–38, believes that the motivation in part of *TR* is more logical than in the corresponding part of *KJ*, and that Shakespeare's "inferiority" is because *KJ* came second and Shakespeare could not adapt the older *TR* material to his scheme without distortion. Clara Longworth de Chambrun, *Shakespeare: A Portrait Restored* (1957), calls *TR* a "vulgar entertainment" by Henslowe's company to which *KJ* was Shakespeare's reply. See also Wilfred T. Jewkes, *Act Division in Elizabethan and Jacobean Plays, 1583–1616* (1958), and W. W. Greg, *The Shakespeare First Folio* (1955).

Authorship

The authorship of *TR* remains unknown, in spite of many attempts to attribute the play to various dramatists of the late 1580s and early 1590s. The possibility of Shakespearean authorship has been almost unanimously rejected.

Peele

H. Dugdale Sykes, *Sidelights on Elizabethan Drama* (1924), cites his own earlier *Sidelights on Shakespeare* (1919) for evidence of Peele's authorship of *TR* and attempts to prove through *TR–Alphonsus Emperor of Germany* parallels that Peele wrote the latter play as well. (The chapter concerned is a reprint of a 1916 *N&Q* article.) William J. Lawrence, *Pre-Restoration Stage Studies* (1927), also believes *TR* to have been written by Peele; and E. K. Chambers, *William Shakespeare*, leans towards Sykes's arguments for Peele, as does Peter Alexander in *Shakespeare's "Henry VI" and "Richard III"* (1929). Arthur M.

Sampley, however, in " 'Verbal Tests' for Peele's Plays," *SP* 30 (1933): 473-96, demolishes the methods used by Sykes and by J. M. Robertson (see below, "Others") in reaching their authorship conclusions, and Muriel St. Clare Byrne, "Bibliographical Clues in Collaborate Plays," *Library* 13 (1932-33): 21-48, also attacks Sykes's methods. Thomas Marc Parrott, *Shakespearean Comedy,* states that the play is probably at least in part by Peele; so, because of a dubious grammatical test, does J. C. Maxwell, "Peele and Shakespeare: A Stylometric Test," *JEGP,* 49 (1950): 557-61. The Peele attribution is rejected, however, by Hazelton Spencer, *The Art and Life of William Shakespeare* (1940), Leonard R. N. Ashley, *Authorship and Evidence,* A. P. Rossiter, "Prognosis on a Shakespeare Problem," and William Wells (see below, "Others"). Irving Ribner, *The English History Play in the Age of Shakespeare* (1957; rev. ed. 1965), doubts Peele's authorship.

Marlowe

C. F. Tucker Brooke, "The Marlowe Canon," *PMLA* 37 (1922): 367-417, rejects *TR* as Marlowe's, as does H. W. Herrington, "Christopher Marlowe—Rationalist," in *Essays in Memory of Barrett Wendell* (1926), pp. 119-52, who declares that the "strong speech" of *TR* concerning the occult is not found in any of Marlowe's accepted plays, and that Marlowe's habit of thought and diction would not have changed so radically in one play. Philip Henderson, *And Morning in His Eyes: A Book about Christopher Marlowe* (1937), believes that Marlowe had a hand in one version of the play; but Marion Bodwell Smith, *Marlowe's Imagery and the Marlowe Canon* (1940), concludes from imagery tests that Marlowe had no part in *TR.* The attribution is also rejected by John Bakeless, *The Tragicall History of Christopher Marlowe* (1942), vol. 2, who gives the play to an imitator of Shakespeare when Shakespeare was still strongly influenced by Marlowe. (See also Bakeless, *Christopher Marlowe: The Man in His Time* [1937].)

Munday

Ernest A. Gerrard, *Elizabethan Drama and Dramatists, 1583-1603* (1928), mentions briefly, without giving evidence, that *TR* is chiefly by Anthony Munday. E. A. J. Honigmann, ed., *King John,* suggests that Munday may have been a collaborator in the play. I. A. Shapiro, "Shakespeare and Mundy," puts forward the possibility that Munday wrote the "plot" and others the dialogue of *TR.*

Shakespeare

E. B. Everitt, *The Young Shakespeare: Studies in Documentary Evidence*, Anglistica, vol. 2 (1954), gives the play to Shakespeare. (His book is, sensibly, totally rejected by Robert Adger Law, "Guessing About the Youthful Shakespeare," *Studies in English* (Univ. of Texas), 34 [1955] : 43–50.) So does A. W. Titherley, *Shakespeare's Identity* (1952)—but, for Titherley, "Shakespeare" is William Stanley, sixth Earl of Derby. Titherley believes that the play is one of Shakespeare's apprentice works, is like *I Henry VI*, and was written in part ca. 1582 and was revised and added to in 1588 (hence its patchiness). He suggests a performance at Knowsley by the Queen's company in September 1589. Among others, Wallerstein, *King John in Fact and Fiction*, Rossiter, "Prognosis on a Shakespeare Problem," and Ashley, *Authorship and Evidence*, reject Shakespearean authorship; Law, "On the Date of *King John*," states that "[no] competent scholar today accepts" the Shakespeare attribution.

See also scholarship on the *TR-KJ* relationship.

Others

Wallerstein, *King John in Fact and Fiction*, believes Greene, Lodge, and Peele are all probable as authors. J. M. Robertson, *An Introduction to the Study of the Shakespeare Canon* (1924), argues through weak parallels for *TR* as a collaborate work by Marlowe, Peele, and Lodge and/or Greene, with Drayton perhaps having a hand in the play as well; in *Marlowe: A Conspectus* (1931), he suggests that Marlowe et al. were reworking, in *TR*, an old "actors' play" brought to them to be put into verse. (See Sampley, "Verbal Tests" ["Authorship—Peele"].) Arthur Acheson, *Shakespeare, Chapman, and "Sir Thomas More"* (1931), says that the play was written ca. 1588 mainly by Lodge, with some help from Greene. William Wells, "Thomas Kyd and the Chronicle-History," *N&Q* 178 (1940): 218–24, 238–43, rejects the possibility of Greene or Peele as author, pointing out that in his known works neither one, unlike the *TR* author, pays serious attention to historical facts, and that *TR* is better constructed than are Peele's known plays. He argues against Sykes's Peele parallels (above); and then uses similar parallels himself to give *TR* (along with at least parts of *II* and *III Henry VI* and *Richard III*) to Kyd; genuine Peele characteristics in the drama may be due to revision. Charles Petit-Dutaillis, *Le Roi Jean*, rejects the Kyd attribution and states that the *TR* author is so anti-Papist that he seems to have been a Puritan. Alden Brooks, *Will Shakspere and the Dyer's*

Hand (1943), states that *TR* is probably by Greene, Lodge, and possibly Peele, and probably was a "Will Shakspere property" ("Shakspere" being Edward Dyer), played by the Queen's Men in 1588. E. A. J. Honigmann, ed., *King John,* suggests Samuel Rowley as at least part author and Chettle as a possible author. See also I. A. Shapiro, "Shakespeare and Mundy," and Leonard R. N. Ashley, *Authorship and Evidence.*

Alfred Hart, "Acting Versions," states that vocabulary clues lead indifferently to Marlowe, Greene, Peele, Kyd, and the young Shakespeare, the language in most pre-1594 plays tending to be the same. Jewkes, *Act Division,* declares that previous attributions to Peele, Marlowe, Greene, and Shakespeare are unconvincing; and Ashley, *Authorship and Evidence,* believes that the play must be left as anonymous.

Sources

Mrs. Martin Le Boutillier, "Bale's *Kynge Johan* and *The Troublesome Raigne,*" *MLN* 36 (1921): 55–57, discusses *TR* sources, arguing that the play is at several points indebted to Bale (two-part division; John as a Protestant hero; motive, treatment, and wording of the poisoning scene). A part of her work is corrected by W. W. Greg, who doubts Bale is a source, in "Bale's *Kynge Johan,*" *MLN* 36 (1921): 505. Ruth Wallerstein, *King John in Fact and Fiction,* states that the chief source is Holinshed, with Bale a strong influence, and that the scene including the discovery of Alice the Nun is not wholly invented, for the chronicles say that John took away priests' wives and mistresses and exacted ransom for them; also, the incoherence of John's character in *TR* is due to the author following the chronicles too closely.

Jesse W. Harris, *John Bale: A Study in the Minor Literature of the Reformation,* Illinois Studies in Language and Literature, vol. 25, no. 4 (1940), suggests that Bale's influence on *TR* (and *KJ*) was indirect only, as a part of "the trend of the times" towards a favorable view of John; "such reflections of Bale as are visible in these plays are reflections of a movement in the beginning of which he played an influential role." Thora Balslev Blatt, *The Plays of John Bale* (1968), also denies any influence of Bale's play on *TR*. See also Honor McCusker, *John Bale, Dramatist and Antiquary* (1942), and Barry B. Adams' edition (1969) of *King Johan*; Adams argues especially against Elson's view (below) that Bale is a *TR* source.

Petit-Dutaillis, *Le Roi Jean,* points out that the *TR* author read his chronicles (Holinshed, Fabyan, Hall, and Foxe's *Acts and Monuments*) conscientiously; the dramatist does not seem to have known Matthew Paris's work. A. P. Rossiter, "Prognosis on a Shakespeare Problem," declares that the author apparently read the chronicles of Hall, Holinshed, and Matthew Paris. Matthew P. McDiarmid, "Concerning *The Troublesome Reign*," also deals with sources: Holinshed is a source for the *TR* lines quoted by J. C. Maxwell in his edition (1953) of *Titus Andronicus* as taken by the *TR* author from *Titus*; *TR* draws on Matthew Paris's *Chronica Majora*—though Honigmann says that *KJ* does and *TR* does not. Elson, "King John Plays," argues that the probable sources are Holinshed, Bale, Polydore Vergil's *Anglica Historia,* and Foxe's *Acts and Monuments;* the author showed skill as a plotter in simplifying and ordering the material, and in building up the Bastard from slight hints in Polydore Vergil and Foxe. See also Irving Ribner, *English History Play* ("Authorship—Peele"), and I. A. Shapiro, "Shakespeare and Mundy."

The Play

A considerable amount of criticism of *TR* as dramatic literature has been done in comparisons of the play with *KJ*. Dover Wilson, ed., *King John,* states, for example, that *TR* is in some ways better constructed than *KJ* and that the John of *TR* is a hero but Shakespeare's John is not. Petit-Dutaillis, *Le Roi Jean,* summarizes the two plays simultaneously, comparing them and showing how they both use historical parallels to reflect contemporary political issues. Thomas Marc Parrott, *Shakespearean Comedy,* also compares the plays, and comments that *TR* combines serious history with horseplay. In *Shakespeare's "Histories": Mirrors of Elizabethan Policy* (1947), Lily B. Campbell maintains that Shakespeare, in deriving *KJ* scene by scene from *TR*, did not fundamentally change either the plot or the political significance of the older play; both plays show the conflict between England and the Roman Catholic Church. In her discussion she treats the two plays virtually as one. Adrien Bonjour, however, in "Le problème du héros et la structure du *Roi Jean,* de Shakespeare," *Etudes de Lettres* 23, no. 1 (1950): 3-15, and "The Road to Swinstead Abbey: A Study of the Sense and Structure of *King John,*" *ELH* 18 (1951): 253-74, cites differences between *TR* and *KJ* in treatment of both John and the Bastard; Shakespeare changes the *TR* John from hero to guilty, weak usurper, and enhances the character of the Bastard. Virgil K. Whitaker, *Shakespeare's Use of Learning* (1953), compares *KJ* and its source play to show that Shakespeare, unlike the *TR* author, was interested in character and dramatic effect but was indifferent to historical fact and historical motivation; he also maintains that Shakespeare's Bastard comes intact from *TR*. In *Shakespeare's Historical Plays* (1964), S. C. Sen Gupta also compares *TR* and *KJ*; *TR* "lacks dramatic concentration and unity of spirit." John R. Elliot, "Shakespeare and the Double Image of King John," *ShakS* 1 (1965): 64–84, compares *TR* (Shakespeare's model) and *KJ* to show Shakespeare's "sensitivity to and knowledge of the ambiguities and complexities of sixteenth-century interpretations of King John."

A number of scholars have examined *TR* as a history play. Bernard M. Ward, "Shakespeare and the Anglo-Spanish War, 1585–1604," *RAA* 6 (1928–29): 297–311, sees *TR* as a war-propaganda drama. Irving Ribner, *English History Play* ("Authorship—Peele"), calls *TR* the most important play of the Armada period, and the most advanced in dramatic technique and in the execution of serious historical purpose. He dates it 1588–89, after *Tamburlaine,* and states that a primary purpose of the play is to advocate royal supremacy (against Catholic claims) and English unity (against foreigners). The case of Arthur, he believes, is also a deliberate parallel to that of Mary Stuart. He theorizes that the two-part division of the play may be because of the influence of *Tamburlaine,* though Bale's *Kynge Johan* is also in two parts; but the *TR* John is not a conqueror, but a kind of tragic hero. M. M. Reese, *The Cease of Majesty,* deals also with the play as a thoughtful assertion of royal supremacy (against the counter-claim of the subject's right to depose the king) and of the safety of England through internal unity; historical facts are altered by the author to strengthen contemporary parallels. Reese shows, as well, comparative examples of *TR* and *KJ,* to illustrate how Shakespeare improved upon *TR* and especially how he changed John and the Bastard. David Bevington, *Tudor Drama and Politics* (1968), emphasizes the anti-Catholic sentiments of *TR*: the play "dwells on the unspeakable crime of Catholic-engineered deposition for its lesson of present danger to the English throne." Faulconbridge, Bevington states, is supposedly modeled on Sir John Perrot, illegitimate son of Henry VIII (see Acheson, *Shakespeare's Lost Years,* below), and is the play's folk hero resisting Catholicism; through him—common man and true-born nobleman, patriot and Protestant—the play glorifies the aspirations of its London audience and attacks foreigners and the native aristocracy. Michael Manheim, "The Weak King History Play of the Early 1590's," *RenD* 2 (1969): 71–80, groups

TR with other plays of the period which he believes are concerned with the problem of the weak king. He finds in *TR* "a clear conflict between the king as absolute authority and the king's inadequacies in dealing with the central problems of his reign."

Other Studies

Willard Farnham, *The Medieval Heritage of Elizabethan Tragedy* (1936), believes *TR* foreshadows *Edward II* and is a remarkable play for its early date; the structure is that of a *de casibus* tragedy, but the development of the catastrophe "is in large part psychological," and John is a precursor of Macbeth. The style of the play is examined by Wolfgang Clemen, *English Tragedy before Shakespeare* (trans. T. S. Dorsch, 1961; German ed. 1955), who points out that *TR* shows a "gradual convergence of the emotional and the informative speech" taking place in English history plays; the story is more important than in earlier tragedies, and the set speech is decreasing in length and is becoming more natural, sometimes with a psychological basis.

The comic aspects of *TR* have elicited the attention of John B. Moore, *The Comic and the Realistic in English Drama* (1925), Thomas Marc Parrott, *Shakespearean Comedy,* and A. P. Rossiter, *English Drama from Early Times to the Elizabethans* (1950). Moore comments that the scene with Alice the Nun "is clearly intended to augment the illusion of actuality as well as to afford comic relief"; Parrott, who believes *TR* to have been written in 1587 to take advantage of the success of *Tamburlaine,* admires the comic vigor of two scenes involving friars; and Rossiter comments that "some steps have certainly been made in the direction of capitalizing the necessity of comical side-plot or secondary character and turning them into an implied commentary on the rest."

Arthur Acheson, *Shakespeare's Lost Years in London* (1920), believes that *TR* was written for the Queen's Men ca. 1588 (and acquired by Pembroke's Men in 1591), and that in Faulconbridge the author was portraying Sir John Perrot, natural son of Henry VIII, who was recalled from Ireland in 1588, accused of treason, and arrested in 1591. The author, he suggests, distorted historical facts in Perrot's interest; and the play was published, and rewritten (as *KJ*), further to stir up sympathy for Perrot. In 1931, in *Shakespeare, Chapman, and "Sir Thomas More,"* Acheson cites his 1920 work and repeats his views. E. B. Everitt, *The Young Shakespeare* ("Authorship—Shakespeare"), believes that the role of the Bastard was created specifically for Alleyn, and dates the play in 1588. T. W. Baldwin, *On the Literary Genetics of Shakspere's Plays, 1592–1594* (1959), declares that *TR* was written in pre-Armada years, 1585–88, and uses it in forming a casting pattern for the Queen's Men. William J. Lawrence, *Pre-Restoration Stage Studies* ("Authorship"), suggests that the play was written for innyard performance, and that the vision of five moons in Part 1 must have been achieved through "some sort of mechanical illuminant"; in *From Art to Theatre* (1944), George R. Kernodle declares that the display of moons was done by a machine. See also, for other comments on the play: Dover Wilson, ed., *King John*; Ribner, *English History Play* ("Authorship–Peele"); O'Connor, *The Road to Stratford*; and Peter Alexander, *Introductions to Shakespeare*.

George R. Price, "Compositors' Methods With Two Quartos Reprinted by Augustine Mathewes," *PBSA* 44 (1950): 269–74, discusses the bibliography of the 1622 quarto, using evidence of differing typefaces and of running-title analysis to argue for type-setting by two compositors, one assisting the other. Other bibliographical comments are included in Chambers, *William Shakespeare*, and Ribner, *English History Play*; Chambers believes that *TR* and *KJ* were regarded commercially as identical (see also Greg, "Bale's *Kynge Johan*" ["Sources"]), while Ribner states that this is not necessarily so. Leo Kirschbaum, *Shakespeare and the Stationers* (1955), speculates that the 1622 *TR* edition was brought out to take advantage of the publicity Jaggard was then giving his forthcoming Shakespeare Folio, and in footnotes discusses copyright problems of the 1622 text. Dover Wilson, ed., *King John*, believes that the two-part division of *TR* was simply to allow the publisher to make a profit on two books instead of one, and that, because the two verse prefaces to the readers are similar in style to the play itself, the author must have helped in this scheme. Wilfred T. Jewkes, *Act Division*, suggests that the two prefaces were originally spoken prologues—"It may possibly have been the printer who addressed them to the readers"—and that the printer's copy seems to have been authorial manuscript. Clifford Leech, "The Two-Part Play: Marlowe and the Early Shakespeare," *SJ* 94 (1958): 90–106, accepting Dover Wilson's arguments, comments on the two-part division of the play in relation to *Tamburlaine*; see also Greg, "Bale's *Kynge Johan*" ("Sources").

There is, besides that already cited in other connections, some scholarship on parallels between *TR* and other plays of its period. Dover Wilson, ed., *King John*, sees some connection (probably borrowings from *TR*) between *TR* and *II* and *III Henry VI*, the *Contention*, and the *True Tragedy*. Rupert Taylor, "A Tentative Chronology of Marlowe's and Some Other Elizabethan Plays," *PMLA* 51 (1936): 643–88, links *TR*, through unconvincing parallels, with Marlowe's *Edward II*, *Dido*, *Jew of Malta*, and *Massacre at Paris*, Peele's *Edward I*, Greene's *Friar Bacon and Friar Bungay* and *James IV*, *Arden of Feversham*, *Soliman and Perseda*, and the *Contention* and *True Tragedy*; *TR*, he believes, was produced in late 1590 or early 1591. Hart, *Stolne and Surreptitious Copies*, finds lines in *Edward II* and *Richard II* similar to lines in *TR*. T. W. Baldwin, *Shakspere's Five-Act Structure* (1947), cites Taylor as listing parallels between *Edward II* and *TR* and assuming that *TR* came second; Baldwin believes that Marlowe borrowed from *TR*. If Marlowe used the printed version of *TR*, Baldwin states, *Edward II* could date from the fall of 1591. G. Blakemore Evans, in a review of Dover Wilson's Cambridge editions of *I*, *II*, and *III Henry VI* (*SQ* 4 [1953]: 84–92), points out that *TR* shows a pervasive influence of *I Henry VI*. J. C. Maxwell, ed., *Titus Andronicus* (1953; Arden), sees a parallel between *TR* and *Titus*, with the *Titus* lines being original; cf. McDiarmid, "Concerning *The Troublesome Reign*." Virgil Whitaker, *Shakespeare's Use of Learning* ("The Play"), suggests a *TR* influence on *Richard II*; McDiarmid finds an *Edward II* scene to be modeled on *TR*; Law, "On the Date of *King John*," links *TR* with *Leir*, as does Acheson, *Shakespeare, Chapman* ("Authorship"). A. S. Cairncross. in his Arden edition (1964) of *III Henry VI*, points out parallels between *TR* and *II* and *III Henry VI*, *Richard III*, and Peele's *Arraignment of Paris* and *Battle of Alcazar*, and believes the *TR* author to be the borrower. See also: Cairncross, Arden editions (1962 and 1957) of *I* and *II Henry VI*; Dover Wilson, Cambridge edition (1952) of *II Henry VI*; Freeman, "Shakespeare and *Solyman and Perseda*"; Peter Alexander, *Shakespeare's "Henry VI" and "Richard III"* (1929); E. B. Everitt, *The Young Shakespeare* ("Authorship–Shakespeare").

See Also

Alexander, Peter. *Shakespeare's Life and Art*. 1939.

———. *A Shakespeare Primer*. 1951.

Baker, Arthur E. *A Shakespeare Commentary*. 1938.

Barke, Herbert. *Bales "Kynge Johan" und sein Verhältnis zur zeitgenössischen Geschichtsschreibung*. 1937.

Black, Matthew. "Enter Citizens." In *Studies in the English Renaissance Drama in Memory of Karl Julius Holzknecht*, ed. Josephine W. Bennett, Oscar Cargill, and Vernon Hall, Jr. (1959), pp. 16–27.

Böhm, Rudolf. *Wesen und Funktion der Sterberede im elisabethanischen Drama.* Britannica et Americana, vol. 13 (1964).

Bradbrook, M. C. *Themes and Conventions of Elizabethan Tragedy.* 1935.

Chambers, E. K. *Shakespeare: A Survey.* 1925.

de Nagy, N. Christoph. "Die Funktionen der Gerichtsszene bei Shakespeare und der Tradition des älteren englischen Dramas." *SJH*, 1967, pp. 199–220.

Glunz, H. H. *Shakespeare und Morus.* 1938.

Greenewald, Gerard M. *Shakespeare's Attitude towards the Catholic Church in "King John."* 1938.

Grosse, Franz. *Das englische Renaissancedrama im Spiegel zeitgenössischer Staatstheorien.* Sprache und Kultur der germanischen und romanischen Volker, A. Anglistische Reihe, vol. 18 (1935).

Henneke, Agnes. "Shakespeares englische Könige." *SJ* 66 (1930): 79–144.

Keller, Wolfgang. "Shakespeares Königsdramen." *SJ* 63 (1927): 35–53.

Knights, L. C. *William Shakespeare: The Histories.* WTW, 1962.

Liebermann, F. "Shakespeare als Bearbeiter des *King John.*" *Archiv* 142 (1921): 177–202; 143 (1922): 17–46, 190–203 [not seen].

Reese, Gertrude Catherine. "The Question of the Succession in Elizabethan Drama." *Studies in English* (Univ. of Texas), 22 (1942): 59–85.

Rhodes, R. Crompton. *Shakespeare's First Folio.* 1923.

Rubow, Paul V. *King John.* Historisk-filosofiske Meddelelser, vol. 37, no. 9 (1960). [In Danish.]

Schanzer, Ernest. "*King John*, V.ii.103–4." *N&Q* 2 (1955): 474–75.

Schirmer, Walter F. *Glück und Ende der Könige in Shakespeares Historien.* Arbeitsgemeinschaft für Forschung des Landes nordrhein-westfalen, Geisteswissenschaften, no. 22 (1953).

Sharpe, Robert Boies. *The Real War of the Theaters.* 1935.

Stevick, Robert D. " 'Repentant Ashes': The Matrix of 'Shakespearian' Poetic Language." *SQ* 13 (1962): 366–70.

Weinstock, Horst. *Die Funktion elisabethanischer Sprichwörter und Pseudosprichwörter bei Shakespeare.* 1966.

Williams, Stanley T., ed. *King John.* 1927; Yale.

Many works on and editions of *KJ* comment at least briefly on *TR*: its relationship to *KJ*, its authorship, its dramatic value. Much of the scholarship on *TR* sources, purpose, and connection with *KJ* also deals briefly with the date of *TR*. H. H. Furness's Variorum edition (1919) of *KJ* contains the complete text of *TR* and is not cited in E. K. Chambers, *Elizabethan Stage.*

A. L.

The Wars of Cyrus, classical history (*1588;* 1594)

Editions

Since 1920 the play has been edited only by James Paul Brawner, in Illinois Studies in Language and Literature, vol. 28, nos. 3–4 (1942); the edition includes a complete study of the play. Brawner follows W.

J. Lawrence (see below) in dating *The Wars of Cyrus* in the late 1570s, adds new evidence for the early date, and suggests a first performance in 1576–77; before Lawrence, the play had been thought to imitate and therefore to follow Marlowe's *Tamburlaine*. Brawner denies that *The Wars of Cyrus* significantly resembles *Tamburlaine*: the source of *Cyrus* is Xenophon's *Cyropaedia* and the episodic materials added to the play are not Marlovian; *Cyrus* is not a conqueror play but a romantic tragedy centering on Panthea; Cyrus himself is neither the protagonist nor a Tamburlaine figure; the styles of the two plays are not similar. He accepts as probable Lawrence's attribution of the play to Richard Farrant, and devotes one section of his introduction to Farrant, and one to placing *Cyrus* in the perspective of the court drama of its period. The play is the only extant drama from the early period at the first Blackfriars Theatre. He discusses the *Cyropaedia* as the chief source, and points out that its first six books appeared in an English translation in 1560, and the full eight books in 1567; he cites parallels between *Cyrus* and the *Cyropaedia,* and discusses the dramatist's alterations of and considerable additions to the source material. (See also F. P. Wilson, *The English Drama, 1485–1585,* ed. G. K. Hunter [1969].) Staging is dealt with in terms of the first Blackfriars Theatre.

The text of *Cyrus* is examined in detail. Brawner describes the quarto of 1594, and states that the text as we have it seems to have been revised for printing some time after its original composition. The play was originally written in a regular five-act structure (probably with scene-divisions as well), the acts being of roughly equal length, with music and singing choruses in the act-intervals, and songs throughout. A principle of construction was mechanical, narrative, and ethical balance. For the 1594 printing, the original act-divisions were altered and the choruses and songs removed, the latter probably to make the play seem less old-fashioned, the former possibly "to effect a shift of emphasis from the dominant Panthea story to that of the 'warres' of Cyrus," to capitalize on the popularity of the conqueror play *Tamburlaine.* (Brawner's edited text is divided according to what he believes to be the original act and scene divisions.) Brawner also discusses the typography and printing of the 1594 quarto, and draws attention to (and theorizes about) the fact that Sheet F of the Dyce copy is in a different type face from the rest of the quarto. W. W. Greg, however, in a letter to *TLS,* 14 April 1945, p. 175, states that Sheet F is a modern reprint "of no bibliographical or critical interest."

Useful reviews of Brawner's edition are by Madeleine Doran in *JEGP*

42 (1943): 424–29, and by F. S. Boas in *TLS*, 31 March 1945, p. 156. Boas gives a summary of *Cyrus* scholarship prior to Brawner's work. W. W. Greg, in *TLS*, 14 April 1945, p. 175, corrects two points in Boas' review.

Date and Authorship

William J. Lawrence, in "The Earliest Private-Theatre Play," *TLS*, 11 August 1921, p. 514, is the first to date *The Wars of Cyrus* before Marlowe's *Tamburlaine.* Working from two articles by G. E. P. Arkwright, one in *N&Q*, vol. 5 (1906), and one in *Proceedings of the Musical Association,* 1913–14, Lawrence notes that a manuscript set of part books dated 1581 contains a song attributed to Richard Farrant (died 1580) and evidently belonging to Act V of *Cyrus;* hence the play must date from the Farrant period at the first Blackfriars Theatre. By this dating (ca. 1578), Lawrence points out, *Cyrus* becomes the oldest extant blank-verse theater play, the first known modern five-act play to be performed in an English theater before a public audience, and the first theater play known to have been performed with musical intervals. Lawrence calls *Cyrus* "an incipient chronicle history," and believes that, given the resemblances between *Cyrus* and *Tamburlaine,* Marlowe must have developed the latter play from an early school of private theater dramaturgy, the plays of which included *Cyrus;* Farrant himself is *Cyrus*'s author. Lawrence's views are rejected by John Bakeless, *The Tragicall History of Christopher Marlowe* (1942), vol. 1, who believes that *Cyrus* was written under the influence of *Tamburlaine,* several years before 1594; the anonymous author tries, in Cyrus himself, to turn the Marlovian type of hero into a Christian gentleman.

T. W. Baldwin, *Shakspere's Five-Act Structure* (1947), supports Lawrence's early date for *Cyrus,* and dates the prologue 1576–77. He accounts for *Cyrus*'s early date yet apparent connection with *Tamburlaine* by following Brawner (who in fact draws on and cites Baldwin's work, which was not yet published in 1942) in positing a later structural revision caused by *Tamburlaine,* perhaps with a view to acting but probably simply for the 1594 printing. The 1594 text, he states, has thus been influenced in form—but only in form—by *Tamburlaine.*

Albert C. Baugh's *A Literary History of England* (1948) holds to the old view of *Cyrus* as an imitation of *Tamburlaine.* Irving Ribner, however, in "*Tamburlaine* and *The Wars of Cyrus,*" *JEGP* 53 (1954): 569–73, accepts as probable the new Lawrence-Brawner dating and the

Farrant attribution. (See also his *The English History Play in the Age of Shakespeare* [1957; rev. ed. 1965].) Moreover, he finds a new relationship between *Cyrus* and *Tamburlaine* in the printing of the 1594 quarto. Brawner, he believes, overstates his case for the romantic element in *Cyrus*; the play is a history play as well as a romance, using past events to teach political doctrine of contemporary significance, and "was probably printed at the height of *Tamburlaine*'s popularity as an antidote to dangerous political heresy." *Tamburlaine* presents history as created not by providence but by fortune and human will, and kings as taking their authority not from God but from their own merit and power; the publication of *Cyrus*, in which the king is the morally virtuous agent of God, is the answer of political orthodoxy to the unorthodox *Tamburlaine*. *Cyrus* is, however, not entirely orthodox, in that it presents rebellion against a tyrant as not unlawful. The play, concludes Ribner, is thus an early history play, and Cyrus is one of the earliest in a line of soldier-kings in Elizabethan historical drama, with attributes that become the stock ones of the type: e.g., ferocity in battle and mercy after conquest, and scorn of love (a motif found also in plays such as *Edward III*, *Campaspe*, and *Henry V*, but not in *Tamburlaine*).

G. K. Hunter, "*The Wars of Cyrus* and *Tamburlaine*," *N&Q* 8 (1961): 395–96, is uneasy with the Lawrence-Brawner date, stating that *Tamburlaine* and *Cyrus* are more closely linked than Brawner believes. He offers a list of parallels in phrasing between the two plays, sees a "definite connexion between *The Wars of Cyrus* and the school of Marlowe," and is unwilling to see *Tamburlaine* as deriving from *Cyrus*. He concludes with questions rather than answers: "Was the original play rewritten in the period after *Tamburlaine*? Has the text been handled by a pirate with his head full of Marlovian phrases?"

Other scholars have accepted the earlier dating for *Cyrus*. Robert K. Sarlos, "Development and Operation of the First Blackfriars Theatre," in *Studies in the Elizabethan Theatre*, ed. Charles T. Prouty (1961), calls it a good play for 1576–77, and accepts the Farrant attribution. Benvenuto Cellini, ed., *Drammi Pre-Shakespeariani*, Collana di Letterature Moderne, no. 4 (1958), accepts a date of ca. 1578. Most recently, F. P. Wilson, *English Drama*, discussing the problem of the *Cyrus-Tamburlaine* relationship, leans to the earlier dating.

Text

The 1594 quarto text is generally agreed to be in some way corrupt. Lawrence, "The Earliest Private-Theatre Play," suggests that the quarto "would seem to have been printed from a defaced manuscript in loose sheets"; there are lines missing, scenes wrongly transposed, act-divisions imperfectly marked, and textual indications of songs but no songs included. Brawner, in his edition, accounts for the state of the text by positing a revision of the original prior to the printing of the 1594 edition (see above). T. W. Baldwin, *Shakespere's Five-Act Structure,* discusses at some length the problem of *Cyrus*'s act-divisions and missing choruses, agreeing with Brawner that a structural revision took place, though disagreeing in a few details with the "original" divisions as set down by Brawner. Irving Ribner, *English History Play,* also seemingly accepts a structural revision prior to the 1594 printing.

Wilfred T. Jewkes, *Act Division in Elizabethan and Jacobean Plays, 1583– 1616* (1958), states that the 1594 edition was apparently printed from authorial (or reviser's?) manuscript, or from a non-theatrical transcript, and comments on the apparent reorganization of the text. F. P. Wilson, *The English Drama,* concurs in calling *Cyrus* "a poor text."

The Play

Originally regarded, as in Baugh's *Literary History,* as a "feeble imitation" of *Tamburlaine, The Wars of Cyrus* is now agreed to be a different kind of play from Marlowe's. Lawrence sees it as "an incipient chronicle history," with romantic elements; but Brawner finds it to be an "idea play," a tragic love story on the theme of the captive woman and on related ideas concerning love, honor, and war. Baldwin also calls it an idea play, "using the incidents of the struggle between Cyrus and Antiochus as illustrative material." It presents "two patterns of perfection, Cyrus the perfect warrior, and Panthea the perfect queen." Ribner, *"Tamburlaine* and *The Wars,"* sees the play as both a romance and a history play, with one important theme being the difference between a king and a tyrant. Sarlos, "First Blackfriars Theatre," agrees with Brawner that the play is not a conqueror play and that Panthea is the central character. Cellini, *Drammi Pre-Shakespeariani,* suggests that the play has a moral aim, in presenting the triumph of virtue over vice; F. P. Wilson, *English Drama,* calls it a tragedy of fortune about star-crossed lovers.

Staging and Stage History

Lawrence believes *Cyrus* to be the unnamed play mentioned in the Revels Accounts as performed before the queen at Richmond on 27 December 1578; Sarlos states that *Cyrus* was probably never performed at court. Brawner believes that simultaneous staging was used in producing *Cyrus,* and goes into some detail on probable arrangements; Sarlos agrees on simultaneous staging; but Irwin Smith, *Shakespeare's Blackfriars Playhouse* (1964), states that the play does not necessarily involve the principle of polyscenic setting.

Brawner also deals with the play as designed for boy actors.

A. L.

The Taming of a Shrew, comedy (1589; 1594)

Editions

The text of *The Taming of a Shrew* appears in Geoffrey Bullough's *Narrative and Dramatic Sources of Shakespeare,* vol. 1 (1957), and in Alice Griffin's *The Sources of Ten Shakespearean Plays* (1966), with an introduction in both cases. (See below, passim, for details of the introductions.)

A Shrew and *The Shrew**

Recent critical work on *A Shrew* (*AS*) almost invariably has been concerned with the relationship between it and Shakespeare's *The Taming of the Shrew* (*TS*). Scholars fall, with variations, into three basic groups: (1) those holding the traditional view that *AS* is a source of *TS*; (2) those accepting that *AS* not only postdates *TS* (a theory first put forward in the mid-nineteenth century) but is in fact merely a "bad" version of Shakespeare's play; (3) those believing that the two plays come independently from a common, lost source play.

Peter Alexander, in *"The Taming of a Shrew," TLS,* 16 Sept. 1926, p. 614, contends that *AS* is not a separate play from *TS* but simply a bad quarto of *TS*. He argues that *TS*'s subplot is closer to Ariosto's *I Suppositi* than *AS*'s, and that *AS* contains situations which seem to be bungled versions (caused by faulty memory) of situations in *TS*; *AS* is a memorial reconstruction, for acting by Pembroke's Men, of *TS*, which Pembroke's company originally owned but sold in 1593. He entirely

---

* Unless otherwise noted, short-title references in subsequent sections are to works first cited in this section.

rejects theory (3). In the Cambridge edition (1928) of *TS*, John Dover Wilson (but not his co-editor, Arthur Quiller-Couch) accepts Alexander's case as proved. He adds the suggestion that the name "Sander" in *AS* is a form of the name of the Pembroke's Men actor who played this part, whom he identifies as Alexander Cooke. (See also: Thomas Whitfield Baldwin, *The Organization and Personnel of the Shakespearean Company* [1927]; E. K. Chambers, *William Shakespeare* [1930], vol. 1; William J. Lawrence, *Pre-Restoration Stage Studies* [1927].) In a review of the Cambridge edition, however, in *JEGP* 31 (1932): 152-56, T. W. Baldwin argues, against Wilson, that *AS* and *TS* are so different in plot and cast as to be necessarily two different plays, and the differences are deliberate; *AS* is a *TS* source.

B. A. P. van Dam, in *"The Taming of a Shrew," ES* 10 (1928): 97-106, varies Alexander's theory, suggesting that *AS* is a bad quarto, not of *TS*, but of a separate play based on it, improvised by Pembroke's Men from their memory of *TS*, with some deliberate alterations of *TS* material, after their sale of the latter play. He also argues that the bad quarto is a product of shorthand piracy, possibly with the help of some memorial reconstruction as well. (In "Shakespeare Problems nearing Solution. *Henry VI* and *Richard III*," *ES* 12 [1930]: 81-97, he repeats that *AS* must have been acted from notes only, by players improvising as they went.) John Semple Smart, *Shakespeare: Truth and Tradition* (1928), argues for the pre-Alexander view of *AS* as an imitation of *TS*, by a different dramatist (who also borrowed from parts of Marlowe's plays); the title difference may not even be intentional.

Henry David Gray, *"The Taming of a Shrew," PQ* 20 (1941): 325-33, returns, however, to a variation of Alexander's bad quarto theory, which also becomes a variation of theory (3): that *AS* is a bad quarto of *TS* as the latter play was before Shakespeare revised it into the text we have today (*AS* as a stolen version of an earlier *TS* being a theory going back to the nineteenth century), and that it is a memorial reconstruction by an actor who had roles in the Induction and taming scenes but not in the Bianca scenes, and who was influenced by Marlowe. Sidney Thomas, "A Note on *The Taming of the Shrew*," *MLN* 64 (1949): 94-96, also accepts the bad quarto theory, but, like Gray, believes that *AS* cannot be a bad quarto of *TS*: a comparison of the "principal clowns" in the two plays, Sander (*AS*) and Grumio (*TS*), indicates that Sander is an adult of normal or above-average height, since *AS* contains some traditional comic situations involving a full-grown adult (Sander) and a diminutive page, while Grumio in *TS* is apparently unusually short. This difference, Thomas believes, could not be a result of faulty memory of *TS*, and therefore supports the theory of *AS* as a bad quarto of an earlier version of *TS*. Leo Kirschbaum, however, does not believe that *AS* is in any way a bad quarto ("A Census of Bad Quartos," *RES* 14 [1938] : 20-43).

In *Elizabethan Drama and Dramatists, 1583-1603* (1928), Ernest A. Gerrard opts for a form of theory (3): *AS* is a garbled version of its original (which was later rewritten, and then compiled into *TS*). Raymond A. Houk, a principal modern defender of theory (3), in "The Evolution of *The Taming of the Shrew*," *PMLA* 57 (1942): 1009-38, sums up previous scholarship on the *AS-TS* relationship, gives detailed reasons (involving time schemes and scene placements) for his faith in (3), and tries to reconstruct the form and content of the lost original play. He states that the author of the original was not the author of *AS*; and the latter dramatist is responsible for the lines in *AS* from Marlowe's plays. Two other articles by Houk contain material relevant to his arguments: "Strata in *The Taming of the Shrew*," *SP* 39 (1942): 291-302; and "The Integrity of Shakespeare's *The Taming of the Shrew*," *JEGP* 39 (1940): 222-29. G. I. Duthie also holds a version of view (3), which is also a variation of (2); in *"The Taming of a Shrew* and *The Taming of the Shrew*," *RES* 19 (1943): 337-56, he suggests that *AS* is a memorial reconstruction of a Shakespearean "first sketch" for *TS*, in which the main plot was at the *TS* stage but the subplot was not (and was not necessarily by Shakespeare). (See also the New Penguin edition, 1968, of *TS*, by G. R. Hibbard.) Hardin Craig, *"The Shrew* and *A Shrew*: Possible Settlement of an Old Debate," in *Elizabethan Studies and Other Essays in Honor of George F. Reynolds,* Univ. of Colorado Studies, Ser. B, Studies in the Humanities, vol. 2, no. 4 (1945), pp. 150-54, accepts a form of (3) plus (2) as well: *AS* is a bad quarto of an original Shrew play, written ca. 1589 and perhaps containing imitations of Marlowe, which was rewritten by Shakespeare, with the addition of material from *The Supposes,* into *TS*. Duthie's main thesis, without the bad quarto element, is also found in a 1947 article by Houk, "Shakespeare's *Shrew* and Greene's *Orlando*," *PMLA* 62 (1947): 657-71; parallels between *AS* and *TS* and Greene's *Orlando Furioso* now suggest to him that both *AS* and *TS* were written (the former not by Shakespeare) from some preliminary sketches by Shakespeare, 1592-93, which were probably never acted. I. A. Shapiro, "Shakespeare and Mundy," *ShS* 14 (1961): 25-33, suggests that *AS* and *TS* may have in common a basic "scenario," which was expanded and patched by a number of writers and actors for various companies; he does not, however, reject *AS* as a *TS* source.

The 1921 Yale edition of *TS*, by Henry Ten Eyck Perry, takes the traditional view (1), that *AS* is the direct source of *TS*. (The revised edition of 1954, by Thomas G. Bergin, merely states the three main theories.) The second edition (1929) of the Arden *TS*, by R. Warwick Bond, also accepts (1); it contains a note reviewing Alexander's 1926 *TLS* article and John Dover Wilson's acceptance of it in the Cambridge *TS*, and emphasizing the almost complete difference between the two plays in the actual words of the dialogue. In *Two Elizabethan Stage Abridgements* (1923; Malone Society), W. W. Greg, also apparently assuming view (1), concludes that *AS* as we have it is an old Pembroke's Men play which the company sold possibly to both Shakespeare's company and the printer—in which case there were two manuscripts in existence, and our printed text may therefore not be identical with the text used by the Chamberlain's Men. See also Evelyn May Albright, *Dramatic Publication in England, 1580–1640* (1927). In *The Editorial Problem in Shakespeare* (1942; rev. ed. 1951, 1954), however, Greg states that *AS* is a "derivative" version of *TS*, put together by its author from a fairly full synopsis of *TS*, and with thefts from Marlowe; and in *The Shakespeare First Folio* (1955), he sums up previous *AS* scholarship and accepts view (3) plus (2): that *AS* is a bad quarto of an earlier Shrew play from which *TS* is also derived.

Felix E. Schelling, *Foreign Influences in Elizabethan Plays* (1923), refers in passing to *TS* as a Shakespearean revision of *AS*, and E. K. Chambers in *William Shakespeare*, vol. 1, also accepts view (1), and explicitly rejects Alexander's theory. Alfred Hart, *Stolne and Surreptitious Copies* (1942), through vocabulary tests finds *AS* to be a *TS* source, and notes that the *AS* text has been abridged, probably by actors.

Also in *Elizabethan Studies and Other Essays in Honor of George F. Reynolds,* Thomas Marc Parrott ("*The Taming of a Shrew*—A New Study of an Old Play," pp. 155–65) sums up scholarship to 1945 on the *AS-TS* relationship, and argues that "every effort to derive *A.S.* from *T.S.* runs up against insuperable obstacles"; *AS* is altogether unlike a bad quarto of *TS*. He holds the traditional theory (1)—that *TS* is Shakespeare's reworking of *AS*. (See also his *Shakespearean Comedy* [1949].) Another recent proponent of theory (1) is Geoffrey Bullough; in *Narrative and Dramatic Sources* ("Editions") he very briefly sums up previous views of the *AS-TS* relationship, and states his own belief that

AS is a badly printed version of the old play which was Shakespeare's principal source. The differences between *AS* and *TS*, he maintains, cannot be explained by any theory of abridgement or piracy. He will admit, however, the possibility of *AS* being not a source play by another author but Shakespeare's own first attempt at the shrew-taming theme. He also discusses the play in general, and its differences from *TS*. Finally, in *"The Taming of a Shrew* and *The Taming of the Shrew:* A Case Reopened," *JEGP* 57 (1958): 424–43, John W. Shroeder argues convincingly against the evidence presented by others, especially Houk, for theory (3), and supports *AS* as an "admittedly imperfect" text of an old play which was one of Shakespeare's *TS* sources. Perhaps, he suggests, *AS* is a cut version of the old play; and Shakespeare wrote *TS* from *AS* or from a longer version of it.

Most recently, the proponents of theory (2) have again come to the fore. In "Shakespeare's 'Lost Source-Plays,' " *MLR* 49 (1954): 293–307, E. A. J. Honigmann argues against points made by Houk, "Evolution of *The Taming*," and Duthie, *"The Taming of a Shrew"*; he sees *AS* as a memorial reconstruction, by the Queen's Men, of *TS*. In his 1960 *Shakespeare and Five Acts,* Henry L. Snuggs briefly refers to *AS* as a bad quarto of *TS*. Richard Hosley, in the Pelican edition (1964) of *TS*, states his belief that *AS* is an imitation of *TS*, with intentional alterations in names and other details; he calls this an unusual type of bad quarto. In "Sources and Analogues of *The Taming of the Shrew,*" *HLQ* 27 (1963–64): 289–308, he goes into other details; he reproves Bullough for accepting theory (1), and states his own reasons for preferring (2) to (3). He sees *TS* as "a synthesis of many sources and traditions," with the basic main-plot situation taken from an anonymous verse tale printed by Hugh Jackson ca. 1550, *Here Begynneth a Merry Jest of a Shrewde and Curste Wyfe, Lapped in Morrelles Skin, for Her Good Behavyour* (previously noted by critics as merely an analogue), and animated by modified humanist tradition; the subplot is basically from *The Supposes.* Peter Alexander briefly reaffirms his 1926 stand in his 1964 *Shakespeare* and 1964 *Introductions to Shakespeare* (*AS* is "the ill-digested fragments" of *TS*, a surreptitious version memorially constructed by someone who saw *TS*); and in "A Case of Three Sisters," *TLS*, 8 July 1965, p. 588, he praises Hosley's *HLQ* article and continues from it; he summarizes its chief points on main plot sources, states that Shakespeare's use of these sources does not, in itself, show that he was not acquainted with *AS*, and goes on (unconvincingly) to cite structural features of *AS* which he believes can only be explained as blunderingly derived from *TS*. Finally, he cites an article by George Coffin Taylor (see below, "Authorship—Greene, Kyd") on *AS* as dependent for one speech on Du Bartas, and argues that the *AS* author must have used Sylvester's translation of Du Bartas, which he believes not to have been written before 1594. S. F. Johnson, responding to Alexander's article in *"The Taming of the Shrew," TLS*, 2 Sept. 1965, p. 761, adds the point that the *AS* author doubtless changed the two sisters of *TS* (his source) into three under the influence of standard folklore pattern.

William H. Moore, "An Allusion in 1593 to *The Taming of the Shrew*?" *SQ* 15 (1964): 55–60, suggests, unpersuasively, that a poem by Antony Chute, published in 1593, *Beawtie Dishonoured written under the title of Shores Wife*, contains a line alluding to Shakespeare's *TS*, and that the resulting early date for *TS* puts *AS* later than Shakespeare's play.

The latest contribution to the problem is Jan Harold Brunvand's "The Folktale Origin of *The Taming of the Shrew*," *SQ* 17 (1966): 345–59, which shows that the basic elements and many of the details of Shakespeare's *TS* are found in one type of tale in the oral folk tradition of shrew-taming, centering in Denmark. Brunvand criticizes John W. Schroeder for ignoring, in an article on *AS* sources (see below, "Other Studies"), the folklore background, and points out that *AS* contains fewer of the traditional traits of the folktale than *TS*, and therefore is derivative, and certainly not Shakespeare's only source, if his source at all.

The bibliographical relationship of *AS* and *TS* is mentioned by Chambers in *William Shakespeare*, vol. 1, and is the subject of an article by K. B. Danks, *"A Shrew* and *The Shrew," N&Q* 2 (1955): 331–32, who argues that the two are "one and the same play" (cf. Chambers), of "the same fundamental authorship," with the one title, *The Taming of A Shrew*, the Folio *TS* title being a printer's blunder. (Cf. John Semple Smart, *Shakespeare*, above.) Fredson Bowers, "Some Relations of Bibliography to Editorial Problems," *SB* 3 (1950–51): 37–62, maintains that "whatever relation existed between *A Shrew* and *The Shrew* antedates their printing, and the manuscripts behind the printed copy of each have no bibliographical relation."

Authorship

The question of the play's authorship is largely involved in the *AS-TS* relationship problem, writers on the relationship having to deal, for example, with the possibility of Shakespearean authorship, especially under theory (3), and always with the matter of the Marlovian lines found in *AS*. Thomas Marc Parrott, "A New Study," for example, in stating that *TS* is Shakespeare's reworking of *AS*, builds up an elaborate theory of *AS* authorship; he constructs an "imaginative" hypothesis, on almost no evidence, of *AS* as a collaborate work, ca. 1589-90, for perhaps the Queen's Men, by Samuel Rowley and a young collegian, who used *The Supposes* and other contemporary plays for some of their material. See also the 1921 Yale *TS*, in which the editor, Ten Eyck Perry, holds that the *AS* author was a good dramatist and an admirer and imitator of *Tamburlaine*. There have also been, however, some treatments of authorship apart from those appearing in relationship studies, and *AS* has been attributed, wholly or in part, to a wide variety of dramatists: Greene, Kyd, Marlowe, Munday, Peele, Samuel Rowley, and Shakespeare.

Rowley

In 1920, in *The Authorship of "The Taming of the Shrew," "The Famous Victories of Henry V" and the Additions to Marlowe's "Faustus,"* Shakespeare Association Papers, no. 4, H. Dugdale Sykes argued for Samuel Rowley's authorship of the *AS* prose scenes (and of the prose scenes in *Wily Beguiled,* the verse scenes of both plays being also by the same hand—that of a collaborator with Rowley); this work is cited in Chambers' *Elizabethan Stage.* Sykes repeats his attribution in *Sidelights on Elizabethan Drama* (1924, one chapter of which is a reprint of his 1920 pamphlet): the prose scenes, taming scenes, and Induction all belong to Rowley, because of similarities between them and *When You See Me You Know Me* and the additions—by Rowley, Sykes believes—to *Doctor Faustus.* For attacks on Sykes's methods, see E. H. C. Oliphant, "How Not to Play the Game of Parallels," *JEGP* 28 (1929): 1-15, and Muriel St. Clare Byrne, "Bibliographical Clues in Collaborate Plays," *Library* 13 (1932-33): 21-48. In his *Two Elizabethan Stage Abridgements,* W. W. Greg discusses Sykes's Rowley attribution; Chambers, in *William Shakespeare,* vol. 1, believes that Sykes's case is good; B. A. P. van Dam, *"The Taming of a Shrew,"* sums up previous attribution scholarship and argues against giving the play to either Rowley or Marlowe.

Marlowe

Marlowe has been a candidate largely because of the definitely Marlovian lines found in *AS*. In "The Marlowe Canon," *PMLA* 37 (1922): 367-417, C. F. Tucker Brooke very briefly rejects *AS* as Marlowe's. J. M. Robertson, however, in *The Shakespeare Canon*, pt. 2 (1923), gives the blank verse portions to Marlowe (who, Robertson says, parodies himself in places, and is "poetising" an actor's play), and finds elsewhere hints of Kyd and Greene. (See also his *An Introduction to the Study of the Shakespeare Canon*, [1924].) In his 1931 *Marlowe: A Conspectus*, he states that *AS* was originally an old "actors' play," brought to Marlowe and probably Kyd and Peele to be "blank-versified"; in his 1932 *The Shakespeare Canon*, pt. 4, ii, he calls *AS* "a depravation of the revision of an old actors' play" in which the poetry is by Marlowe (in revision) and the prose, as Sykes says, by Samuel Rowley. Eleanor Grace Clark, *The Pembroke Plays* (1928), supports Marlowe as definitely having a hand in the play, though in an appendix she argues sensibly against Sykes's case for common Samuel Rowley authorship of the prose scenes in *AS*, similar scenes in *The Famous Victories of Henry V*, the additions to *Doctor Faustus*, and parts of *Wily Beguiled*. (She adds, however, that she does herself find a common hand—but not Rowley's—in *Famous Victories, Wily Beguiled*, and *AS*.)

M. C. Bradbrook, *Themes and Conventions of Elizabethan Tragedy* (1935), states that the *Tamburlaine* passages in *AS* are simply copied out into the *AS* text; John Bakeless, *Christopher Marlowe: The Man in His Time* (1937), and *The Tragicall History of Christopher Marlowe* (1942), vol. 2, states that *AS* borrows from *Tamburlaine* and *Doctor Faustus* (and, in the latter book, rejecting both Shakespeare and Marlowe as possible authors, dates the play ca. 1593). Marion Bodwell Smith, *Marlowe's Imagery and the Marlowe Canon* (1940), rejects Marlowe as author of *AS*; his images are copied so slavishly in the play that his authorship is improbable, and the author was likely an actor familiar with Marlowe's vocabulary and stylistic mannerisms. Imagery study, Smith believes, in fact tends to support the theory of the extant *AS* text as a piracy, with Marlowe material brought in to fill the gaps. T. W. Baldwin, however, in *On the Literary Genetics of Shakspere's Plays, 1592-1594* (1959), maintains that Marlowe wrote *AS*, borrowing in *AS* from *Tamburlaine* and borrowing from *AS* for *Doctor Faustus*, and that Nashe and Greene, in *Menaphon*, both parody *AS*, in attacking Marlowe.

In *Shakespearean Comedy*, Thomas Marc Parrott states that *AS* was apparently written in the early 1590s by an enthusiastic admirer of the University wits, especially of Marlowe, whose *Tamburlaine* and *Doctor Faustus* were "pillaged" for *AS*.

Greene, Kyd, Munday, Peele

H. W. Crundell, "Notes on *The Taming of a Shrew*," *N&Q* 163 (1932): 309–10, argues through parallels and the play's use of Du Bartas for Peele as author or at least reviser of *AS*. In *Shakespeare, Chapman, and "Sir Thomas More"* (1931), Arthur Acheson sees the play as the product of several revisions, though originally by Kyd (in fourteeners); our present text contains work by at least Kyd, Marlowe, Peele, and Munday. Félix Carrère, in *Le théâtre de Thomas Kyd* (1951), rejects the Kyd attribution, saying that there is neither external nor internal evidence for his authorship. George Coffin Taylor, "Two Notes on Shakespeare," *PQ* 20 (1941): 371–76, points out, as did Crundell in 1932, that Kate's big speech at the close of *AS* uses several lines from Du Bartas, and that the *AS* author was therefore a man familiar with Du Bartas' work, in the original or in translation. Peele, he states, knew Du Bartas' work, and possibly Samuel Rowley did too; possibly, also, Du Bartas was fairly well known in England as early as 1589. In the same issue of *PQ*, Henry David Gray, *"The Taming of a Shrew,"* rejects Sykes's Rowley attribution and explores and also rejects the possibility of William Birde as author.

I. A. Shapiro, "Shakespeare and Mundy," speculates that *AS* may be the product of dialogue patched by other authors onto a basic plot supplied originally by a dramatist such as Munday or Greene.

Shakespeare

The possibility of Shakespearean authorship of *AS* is dealt with by many scholars in relationship studies: for example, Houk, "Evolution of *The Taming*," who leaves the door open to a Shakespeare attribution. Ernest A. Gerrard's theory, in *Elizabethan Drama,* of the origin and ownership of *AS* (see above and below) leads him to see the play as Shakespeare's, though the author of his posited original of the extant *AS* he leaves as unknown—possibly Greene. Other kinds of studies, however, can also include work on Shakespeare and *AS*. In "Solar Symbolism and Related Imagery in Shakespeare," *RBPH* 29 (1951): 112–28, W. Schrickx maintains on the basis of imagery study that Shakespeare was the author of at least one *AS* passage. Tommy Ruth Waldo and T. W. Herbert, however, in examining musical terms in *TS*, find that in *AS* "musical allusion . . . as a whole does not go in the Shakespearian manner," though it may in brief passages seem Shakespearean ("Musical Terms in *The Taming of The Shrew:* Evidence of Single Authorship," *SQ* 10 [1959] : 185–99). See also Bakeless, *Tragicall History* ("Authorship–Marlowe").

Other Literary Connections

John Bakeless, *Tragicall History* and *Christopher Marlowe* ("Authorship–Marlowe"), Leo Kirschbaum ("The Good and Bad Quartos of *Doctor Faustus*," *Library* 26 [1945–46] : 272–94), and Raymond A. Houk (*"Doctor Faustus* and *A Shrew*," *PMLA* 62 [1947] : 950–57), in considering the 1604 and 1616 texts of *Doctor Faustus*, all deal with the similar lines in Marlowe's play and *AS*. Bakeless says that *AS* uses *Doctor Faustus* as found in the 1616 text—and that the 1616 version of Marlowe's play must therefore have existed before the *Doctor Faustus* revisions of 1602. Kirschbaum is concerned with proving that the 1604 text of *Doctor Faustus* is a bad quarto and the 1616 text a good quarto, and brings in the *Doctor Faustus–AS* parallels, showing that *AS* is nearer the 1616 text than the 1604 text. Houk cites the parallels and suggests that the *AS* and *Doctor Faustus* texts we know have a common source in an earlier (original) form of *Doctor Faustus*.

Parallels between *AS* and other literary works are also considered in T. W. Baldwin's *On the Literary Genetics* ("Authorship–Marlowe"). Baldwin believes that Greene's *Menaphon* uses *AS*, and that *AS* echoes *Love's Labor's Lost*; he accordingly dates *AS* ca. 1589. See also Hart, *Stolne and Surreptitious Copies*, who finds lines which *AS* (a Pembroke's play, he believes) has in common with *Doctor Faustus*, *Tamburlaine*, *Orlando Furioso*, *Arden of Feversham*, *Alphonsus King of Aragon*, and *II* and *III Henry VI*.

Ownership (see also *"A Shrew* and *The Shrew"*)

In *Two Elizabethan Stage Abridgements*, W. W. Greg suggests that the original *AS* belonged to the Queen's Men, who sold it to Pembroke's company, where it was revised by Samuel Rowley; Pembroke's Men then sold the text (as we know it) possibly to both Shakespeare's company and the printer (see the discussion of Greg's book above). He argues against Dover Wilson's pre-Alexander theory (personal communication to Greg) that our *AS* text is a reworking, by the comic man of the Queen's Men and a poet unfamiliar with the original play, of a memorial reconstruction by the Queen's Men of an original Shrew play they sold to Pembroke's Men. If, he argues, the company was so poor that it had to sell its plays, it could hardly have hired an author to help rewrite them.

The ownership history of *AS* given in E. K. Chambers' *William Shakespeare,* vol. 1 is also accepted by Bullough, *Narrative and Dramatic Sources* ("Editions"): *AS* was an Alleyn company play, given to Pembroke's Men in 1592, recovered in 1593, allocated to the Chamberlain's Men in 1594, and sold for printing after having been revised as *TS.* Eleanor Grace Clark, *The Pembroke Plays* ("Authorship— Marlowe"), suggests that *AS* was a Pembroke's play, in part by Marlowe, fraudulently sold by Marlowe a second time to the "Henslowe-Alleyn combination"; when Pembroke's Men discovered the cheat, they gave their text to the printer, and the play was consequently no longer staged at the Rose. Ernest A. Gerrard, *Elizabethan Drama,* believes that the "original" *AS* belonged first to the Admiral's or Strange's Men, and was stolen by Pembroke's Men before 1594 and put through a revision (our present text). Arthur Acheson, *Shakespeare, Chapman* ("Authorship—Greene, Kyd"), states that *AS* and *TS* (a revision of *AS*) "were continuously Burbage properties from 1589 to 1594," and deals with ownership and authorship together, in a theory positing several revisions of an original *AS* in fourteeners by Kyd: the original was an early Kyd play, ca. 1581; it was revised by Kyd and possible collaborators (in the comic parts), at intervals, until 1587; between 1587 and 1589 it was revised by Marlowe; it then went to the Admiral's Men, where it was revised by Peele and some of his assistants; it became a Pembroke's Men property, and was again revised by Marlowe; still later it became *TS.* Our *AS* text is, he states, the play as it was before Marlowe's second revision.

T. W. Baldwin, *On the Literary Genetics* ("Authorship—Marlowe"), believes that the casting pattern of *AS* fits Strange's company better than the Admiral's Men, but that there is not sufficient evidence for the play to be given definitely to either company. Alice Griffin, *Ten Shakespearean Plays* ("Editions"), speculates that *AS* probably became Chamberlain's Men property, and that the 1596 edition was likely published to cash in on the popularity of *TS* on the stage at that time. See also Parrott, *Shakespearean Comedy.*

Other Studies

Discussions of *AS* as dramatic literature are few, though many scholars, such as H. B. Charlton in his *Shakespearian Comedy* (1938), comment briefly, in surveys of Elizabethan drama or in discussions of

TS, on the merits and defects of the play. (Charlton calls it "the crudest kind of medley.") John W. Draper, in *Stratford to Dogberry* (1961), states that the *AS* story inherently implies a contrast between city life and country life (and shows clearly Shakespeare's use of *AS*). Thelma N. Greenfield, "The Transformation of Christopher Sly," *PQ* 33 (1954): 34–42, includes in her discussion of *TS* some comments on *AS*'s frame: unlike *TS*'s, it emphasizes the play's moral for married men. Alice Griffin, *Ten Shakespearean Plays* ("Editions"), states that the subplot lacks comedy and intrigue.

John W. Shroeder, "A New Analogue and Possible Source for *The Taming of a Shrew*," *SQ* 10 (1959): 251–55, presents a newly discovered analogue to the main plot of *AS*, the tale of Queen Vastis given in Caxton's translation (1484) of the *Book of the Knight of La Tour Landry*, and suggests, implausibly, that it may even be an *AS* source. J. H. Brunvand argues effectively against him in "Folktale Origin."

See Also

Charlton, H. B. "*The Taming of the Shrew*." *BJRL* 16 (1932): 353–75.

Curry, John V. *Deception in Elizabethan Comedy*. 1955.

Gray, Henry David. "The Rôles of William Kemp." *MLR* 25 (1930): 261–73.

———. "Chronology of Shakespeare's Plays." *MLN* 46 (1931): 147–50.

Jewkes, Wilfred T. *Act Division in Elizabethan and Jacobean Plays, 1583–1616.* 1958.

Kuhl, Ernest P. "Shakespeare's Purpose in Dropping Sly." *MLN* 36 (1921): 321–29.

———. "The Authorship of *The Taming of the Shrew*." *PMLA* 40 (1925): 551–618.

Lyman, Dean B., Jr. "Apocryphal Plays of the University Wits." In *English Studies in Honor of James Southall Wilson*, ed. Fredson Bowers (1951), pp. 211–21.

Parker, John W. "Some Comments on the *A Shrew-The Shrew* Controversy." *CLAJ* 2 (1959): 178–82.

Peschmann, Hermann. "Christopher Marlowe, 1564–1593." *English* 15 (1964–65): 85–89.

Pruvost, René. *Robert Greene et ses romans*. 1938.

Rhodes, R. Crompton. *Shakespeare's First Folio*. 1923.

Rubow, Paul V. *Trold Kan Taemmes*. Historisk-filosofiske Meddelelser, vol. 37, no. 1 (1957). [In Danish.]

Saito, Isamu. "*A Shrew* and *The Shrew*." *Shuryu* 25 (1964): 196–210 [not seen].

Weinstock, Horst. *Die Funktion elisabethanischer Sprichwörter und Pseudo-sprichwörter bei Shakespeare*. 1966.

Also useful are various books and articles specifically on *TS*, and editions of *TS* not cited here.

A. L.

Edward III, history (*1590;* 1596)

Editions

There have been five recent editions of *Edward III*: in vol. 3 (1953) of *The New Nonesuch Shakespeare* (original ed. Herbert Farjeon; new introduction by Ivor Brown); by James Winny in *Three Elizabethan Plays* (1959); by William A. Armstrong in *Elizabethan History Plays* (1965); by R. L. Armstrong in his and E. B. Everitt's *Six Early Plays Related to the Shakespeare Canon,* Anglistica, vol. 14 (1965); and by Frederick Robert Lapides, "A Critical Edition of *The Raigne of King Edward the Third,*" Ph.D. dissertation, Rutgers, 1966 (*DA* 27 [1966]: 1788-A). There is an Italian translation by Diego Angeli in vol. 2 of his *Opere attribuite a Shakespeare* (1934); and the Countess of Salisbury scenes have been printed in Danish in V. Østerberg's *Grevinden af Salisbury og Marina* (1926).

Winny, in a general introduction to his volume, dates *Edward III* ca. 1594 and argues unconvincingly for the play as a collaborate work by Shakespeare and one other dramatist, Shakespeare being involved in Acts I and II. He states that the play is typical of the chronicle tradition in having little unity of action, but that it shows a development from the earlier chronicle history play towards Shakespearean depth of characterization and sense of drama. William A. Armstrong briefly deals with the sources (Holinshed and Painter), themes, and style of the play. The basic themes, unifying the work, he believes to be the education of princes (in respect for social covenants, such as marriage) and "the illustration of king-becoming virtues" (justice in war, fortitude, mercy); here the play anticipates Shakespeare's *I* and *II Henry IV* and *Henry V.* There is "rich vocabulary, iterative imagery, and fine eloquence." The Everitt-Armstrong introduction discusses editions, then sources (Froissart, probably in Lord Berners' translation; Painter's *Palace of Pleasure*; Holinshed; another unknown work or works). History, it points out, is freely telescoped and altered; and the play illustrates warrior honor, in contrast to *The Troublesome Reign of John,* in which all motives are sordid and ethics tarnished. Behind the Everitt-Armstrong collection as a whole lies the assumption of Shakespearean authorship. Lapides also argues, through image parallels and clusters and vocabulary tests, for Shakespeare as author. He dates the play 1588–92, gives it to the Admiral's Men, studies the author's use of his sources (Froissart and Painter), and discusses plotting, themes, characterization, style, and the play's relation to the development of English drama. Finally he deals with the text: the anonymous printer of the 1596 quarto was Thomas Scarlet, and the printer's copy was probably authorial foul papers. He includes bibliographical descriptions of the quartos of 1596 and 1599, a printing history of Quarto 1, and a discussion of all editions, ancient and modern. Østerberg, in a brief introduction in Danish, argues, through the use of parallel passages, for Shakespearean authorship of the Countess scenes. *Edward III* will appear in G. R. Proudfoot's forthcoming edition of the *Shakespeare Apocrypha*.

Authorship

The authorship of *Edward III* has been the central issue in modern scholarship on the play, attributions having been made to a number of dramatists as sole or collaborate authors: Drayton, Greene, Kyd, Marlowe, Peele, Robert Wilson, Shakespeare.

Drayton

In *Elizabethan Drama and Dramatists, 1583-1603* (1928), Ernest A. Gerrard gives *Edward III* to Michael Drayton. The attribution is repeated by H. W. Crundell, "Drayton and *Edward III,*" *N&Q* 176 (1939): 258-60, who offers unconvincing parallels in manner and episodes between *Edward III* and Drayton's nondramatic work. Kathleen Tillotson, "Drayton and *Edward III,*" *N&Q* 176 (1939): 318-19, argues against Crundell; Crundell, viewpoint unchanged, replies on pp. 356-57.

Bernard H. Newdigate, *Michael Drayton and His Circle* (1941), does not accept Crundell's attribution. He states that the play dates from 1595 or earlier, and we have no evidence that Drayton had yet then become a playwright; also, in his *Heroical Epistles* Drayton gives a very different version of the wooing of Lady Salisbury from that found in the play.

Robert Wilson

S. R. Golding, "The Authorship of *Edward III,*" *N&Q* 154 (1928): 313-15, offers nonexistent verbal parallels with *A Larum for London* to prove that *Edward III* is by Robert Wilson. E. H. C. Oliphant, "How Not to Play the Game of Parallels," *JEGP* 28 (1929): 1-15, attacks Golding's attribution methods in general, and specifically rejects his attribution to Wilson of *Edward III*.

Combined Authorship

Several scholars have posited authorship theories involving collaborate composition of the play or revisions by one or more other writers of an original by one dramatist. Janet Spens, *Elizabethan Drama* (1922), believes the play to have been originally in two parts, with Greene or Shakespeare probably writing (or revising) the first part, and Marlowe (or possibly Peele) writing the second; Shakespeare, whether or not he had any share in the authorship of the original, revised the play into its present form, influenced by Peele's *David and Bethsabe.* Arthur Acheson, *Shakespeare's Sonnet Story* (1922), and *Shakespeare, Chapman, and "Sir Thomas More"* (1931), states that the play was originally by Marlowe and was revised by Shakespeare in 1593-94. (In the former book he contends that the revision was influenced by Southampton's relations with the "Dark Lady.") J. M. Robertson, in *The Shakespeare Canon,* 4 parts (1922-32), *An Introduction to the Study of the Shakespeare Canon* (1924), and *Marlowe: A Conspectus* (1931), argues that *Edward III* is mainly the work of Marlowe, but with Greene later revising Act II, and Peele and Kyd also lending a hand. V. Østerberg, "The 'Countess Scenes' of *Edward III,*" *SJ* 65 (1929): 49-91, believes that before 1592 there existed a collaborate play on Edward III, probably by Marlowe, Kyd, and Greene, which Shakespeare's company acquired ca. 1594; Shakespeare then added to the original the Countess scenes and some revisionary touches. He is especially concerned with countering Robertson's attribution of the Countess scenes to Greene. (Robertson replies in *The State of Shakespeare Study* [1931].) In *Shakespeare and the Homilies* (1934), Alfred Hart rejects Greene and Peele as possible authors, but Clara Longworth de Chambrun, *Shakespeare: A Portrait Restored* (1957), views the play as containing passages by Marlowe, Shakespeare, and possibly Peele.

See also E. K. Chambers, *William Shakespeare* (1930), vol. 1.

Peele

Evidence for Peele's authorship is rejected by Kenneth Muir, *Shakespeare as Collaborator* (1960), as "very slight." Inna Koskenniemi, "Themes and Imagery in *Edward III,*" *NM* 65 (1964): 446-80, finds the image pattern of *Edward III* to be unlike that of Peele's major plays. See also Irving Ribner, *The English History Play in the Age of Shakespeare* (1957; rev. ed. 1965), Alfred Hart, *Shakespeare and the Homilies* (above), and Leonard R. N. Ashley, *Authorship and Evidence* (1968).

Marlowe

Marlowe authorship is rejected by C. F. Tucker Brooke, "The Marlowe Canon," *PMLA* 37 (1922): 367–417, and by John Bakeless, *Christopher Marlowe: The Man in His Time* (1937), and *The Tragicall History of Christopher Marlowe* (1942), vol. 2. (Bakeless suggests in the 1937 work that the anonymous author was an imitator of Marlowe.) Alfred Hart also rejects the Marlowe attribution. Calvin Hoffman, *The Murder of the Man Who Was "Shakespeare"* (1955), gives *Edward III* to Marlowe—in an attempt to give him all Shakespeare's plays as well.

Kyd

William Wells, "Thomas Kyd and the Chronicle-History," *N&Q* 178 (1940): 218–24, rejects previous attributions to Greene and to Peele, arguing that, unlike the author of *Edward III*, neither Greene nor Peele paid serious attention, in his known works, to historical verities. He then suggests Kyd's authorship, but does not follow up the point, the article being concerned not with *Edward III* but with *The Troublesome Reign of King John*. Félix Carrère, *Le théâtre de Thomas Kyd* (1951), does not absolutely deny Kyd a hand in the play; he believes, however, that Kyd probably merely influenced the unknown author. Recently G. Lambrechts, in *"Edward III, oeuvre de Thomas Kyd," EA* 16 (1963): 160–74, through parallels and stylistic tests gives the play to Kyd and dates it in 1594. The Kyd attribution is rejected by Koskenniemi, "Themes and Imagery" (above, "Peele").

Shakespeare

By far the most popular attribution is to Shakespeare. Some give him the entire play, some, Acts I and II; and even some who give the play to other dramatists feel obliged to posit a later revision by Shakespeare of the original (see Acheson, Østerberg, and Spens, "Combined Authorship," above).

Charles J. Sisson, *Le goût public et le théâtre élisabéthain* (1922), believes the Shakespeare attribution to be perhaps possible. V. Østerberg, "The 'Countess Scenes' " ("Combined Authorship"), finds resemblances between the Countess of Salisbury scenes and early Shakespearean plays and poems, in language, dramatic skill, and emotion, and gives a detailed comparison. E. K. Chambers, *William*

Shakespeare, vol. 1, believes that there are two hands in the play, and favors Shakespearean authorship of the Countess scenes and IV.iv. In "The Shakespeare Canon," *QR* 259 (1932): 32–48, E. H. C. Oliphant finds Shakespeare's hand here and there throughout the play. He also states that Shakespeare in his later work shows an acquaintance with *Edward III* which he does not display with plays in which he had no part as an author, and that the versification of *Edward III* is unlike that of any of Shakespeare's known fellows. Alfred Hart, *Shakespeare and the Homilies* ("Combined Authorship"), on the evidence of detailed vocabulary studies of Shakespeare, Kyd, and Marlowe, gives the entire play to Shakespeare. Frank O'Connor, *The Road to Stratford* (1948; published in slightly different form in the U.S., 1960, under the title *Shakespeare's Progress*), also believes the play to be entirely Shakespeare's, because of similarities between it and Shakespeare's poems and known plays of the period. He dates it shortly after *Richard III* and at about the same time as *The Rape of Lucrece.*

In *Shakespeare's Identity* (1952), A. W. Titherley claims the play, because of its style, vocabulary, imagery, thought, and parallels with other "Shakespearean" plays (both accepted ones and others, such as *Fair Em,* also believed by Titherley to be Shakespearean), as genuine early Shakespeare, written ca. 1587 and a model for the later *Henry V.* He specifically rejects Marlowe as author. The major thesis of his eccentric book is that Shakespeare is in reality William Stanley, sixth Earl of Derby. The Shakespeare attribution is also upheld in an unusual way by Dorothy and Charlton Ogburn in *This Star of England* (1952), in which the play is given to the Earl of Oxford, whom they believe to be the real Shakespeare. (They date the play ca. 1579–80.) E. B. Everitt, *The Young Shakespeare: Studies in Documentary Evidence,* Anglistica, vol. 2 (1954), sees similarities between *Edmond Ironside* and *Edward III,* and believes both to be by Shakespeare. His case is dismissed by Robert Adger Law in "Guessing About the Youthful Shakespeare," *Studies in English* (Univ. of Texas), 34 (1955): 43–50.

M. C. Bradbrook, *Shakespeare and Elizabethan Poetry* (1951), calls *Edward III* pseudo-Shakespearean. Kenneth Muir, "A Reconsideration of *Edward III,*" *ShS* 6 (1953): 39–48, sums up previous attribution scholarship, and adds points of his own, concerning vocabulary and imagery (and especially parallels with *Henry V* and *Measure for Measure*), which suggest to him that the play is at least partly (I.ii, II, IV.iv) Shakespeare's. Shakespeare, he states, if not himself the author, at least was well acquainted with and influenced by *Edward III;* and it is even possible that in *Edward III* we have a hasty revision by Shakespeare of another man's play, with some scenes entirely rewritten and others left almost untouched. Muir develops these ideas further in *Shakespeare as Collaborator* (1960). Irving Ribner, *English History Play* ("Authorship–Peele"), sees *Edward III* as an important influence on Shakespeare's Lancastrian tetralogy, and agrees with Muir in giving the first two acts of the play, and probably more, to Shakespeare; possibly the entire play is an early Shakespearean work. The play, he argues, contains parallels in vocabulary, imagery, and phrases with Shakespeare's known work, and also the thoughtful use of history characteristic of Shakespeare's plays but not of Peele's; and the Countess of Salisbury scenes are an integral part of the play, not unrelated scenes which are evidence of collaborate authorship. *Edward III* is given entirely to Shakespeare by Karl Paul Wentersdorf in a 1960 Univ. of Cincinnati dissertation, "The Authorship of *Edward III*" *(DA* 21 [1960] : 905–6). Wentersdorf relies on stylistic evidence, especially that of imagery.

Inna Koskenniemi, "Themes and Imagery" ("Authorship–Peele"), sums up previous attribution work on the play, states that the unity of the play is now generally accepted, and favors Shakespearean authorship of at least some parts, on the evidence of image groups. She also points out the numerous references in Shakespeare's history plays to Edward III. "Typically Shakespearean" image clusters are also found in the play by C. H. Hobday, "Why The Sweets Melted: A Study In Shakespeare's Imagery," *SQ* 16 (1965): 3–17, in the Countess scenes, which he therefore attributes to Shakespeare.

E. M. W. Tillyard, in *Shakespeare's History Plays* (1944), states that the play is of single, non-Shakespearean authorship, the author probably being a young intellectual deeply influenced by Shakespeare.

Date

The date of *Edward III*, although often mentioned in discussions of the authorship problem, has been the sole topic of only one article: Karl P. Wentersdorf's "The Date of *Edward III*," *SQ* 16 (1965): 227–31. Wentersdorf points out the probable use of details from the 1588 battle between the English navy and the Spanish Armada and thus establishes 1588 as probably the earliest possible year of composition. His discovery also supports a date of composition not long after the Armada, ca. 1589–90, as do other points he mentions, which include the play's strongly nationalistic sentiment, its similarities to *I Henry VI*, the restriction of dramatic output caused by the plague of 1592-94, and the printing date of the first quarto (1596). MacD. P. Jackson deals with dating among other matters in *"Edward III, Shakespeare, and Pembroke's Men," N&Q* 12 (1965): 329-31. Basically accepting the cases of Muir, Wentersdorf and Hart for Shakespearean authorship, he suggests that *Edward III* belonged to Pembroke's Men; he argues that parts of *The Contention* and *The True Tragedy*, bad quartos (he believes) memorially constructed by Pembroke's Men actors, rely upon recollections of passages in *Edward III*. The play must thus be dated no later than 1592 or even 1591. Jackson also believes that the knighting of Copland, in *Edward III*, preceded the parallel knighting of Iden in *II Henry VI*. In 1954 Everitt, *The Young Shakespeare* ("Authorship— Shakespeare"), had already claimed the play for Pembroke's Men, 1589-91.

The Play

General discussions of the play appear in E. M. W. Tillyard's *Shakespeare's History Plays*; Irving Ribner's *English History Play*, Kenneth Muir's *Shakespeare as Collaborator* (both in "Authorship— Peele"); M. M. Reese's *The Cease of Majesty* (1961); and David Bevington's *Tudor Drama and Politics* (1968). Tillyard points out that the play contains a unifying principle, the education of both Edward III and the Black Prince, and that it is an unusually intellectual chronicle play. Ribner sees the play as a unified, highly philosophical work on the education of the perfect king: a kind of play perfected by Shakespeare in his Lancastrian tetralogy. The Countess scenes are an integral part of the play, as through the Countess Edward learns "the rights and duties of kingship, the relation of the king's law to moral law"; only then is he free to conquer France. And in war, as in peace, the king's reason must prevail over passion. A parallel theme, Ribner believes, is the education of the Black Prince; and the play's view of history is providential. Muir deals with plot, style, and the value of the various scenes. Reese treats the play as an examination by its author of the stages by which Edward disciplines himself to the perfection expected, by Renaissance standards, of a king; Edward can then stand as a model for the education of his son. According to Reese, the play thus approaches history on an abstract level, its dominant theme being education in goodness and self-mastery through study of the right examples. Bevington believes the play to be a typically patriotic, pro-English war drama, which is nevertheless untypical in being "deeply concerned with an analysis of ethical responsibility in such a potentially aggressive war." He points out that Edward, as king, must learn self-government, and obey moral law; only thus will he be entitled to victory with God's protection. And he must wage war, not in anger, but to save the French from misgovernment. The French people are shown as good citizens in a moral dilemma, caught between the *de facto* rule of a usurper and the legitimate claims of Edward. Bevington suggests that this emphasis on moral law, mercy, and responsibility in warfare is found in no other war play outside the Shakespeare canon.

Bernard M. Ward, "Shakespeare and the Anglo-Spanish War, 1585–1604," *RAA* 6 (1928–29): 297–311, sees *Edward III* as a war-propaganda play. Frank O'Connor, *The Road to Stratford* ("Authorship—Shakespeare"), remarks on the theatrical effect of the play, and believes Acts III–V to be an anticlimax after Acts I–II. M. C. Bradbrook, *Shakespeare and Elizabethan Poetry*, briefly comments that *Edward III* has unity of theme and is similar in theme to (and may have been a model for) Shakespeare's *Henry V*.

Other Studies

Willis Boring Dobson has done a University of Texas Ph.D. dissertation (1956), "*Edward the Third*: A Study of its Composition in Relation to its Sources" (*ShN*, 1957, p. 19). Possible connections between *Edward III* and other plays of its period are mentioned by: R. P. Cowl, "Echoes of *Henry the Fourth* in Elizabethan Drama," *TLS*, 22 Oct. 1925, p. 697 [*I Henry IV*]; William Empson, *Some Versions of Pastoral* (1935) [*Measure for Measure*]; Wolfgang Clemen, "Anticipation and Foreboding in Shakespeare's Early Histories," *ShS* 6 (1953): 25–35 [*Richard III*]; E. B. Everitt, *The Young Shakespeare* ("Authorship—Shakespeare").

Wilfred T. Jewkes, *Act Division in Elizabethan and Jacobean Plays, 1583–1616* (1958), states that the 1596 text was printed from good copy, probably the author's manuscript, which shows little evidence of having been adapted for playhouse use, though "the copy may have been tentatively prepared for the stage."

Arthur Acheson, *Shakespeare, Chapman* ("Combined Authorship"), speculates that *Edward III* was first a Burbage-Alleyn property, then, as revised by Shakespeare, a Pembroke's Men property 1591–94, and finally an Alleyn-Henslowe play. Alleyn, he believes, played the part of the Black Prince. In *Shakespeare and the Stationers* (1955), Leo Kirschbaum declares that there is no real evidence that *Edward III* belonged to Shakespeare's company. T. W. Baldwin, *On the Literary Genetics of Shakspere's Plays, 1592-1594* (1959), fits *Edward III*, through his analysis of its casting pattern, into the repertory of the Admiral's Men; perhaps the play was connected with a group from the company on tour to the Continent in 1590.

Cyrus Hoy, "Renaissance and Restoration Dramatic Plotting," *RenD* 9 (1966): 247-64, uses the handling of the father-as-pander motif in the play, compared to its treatment in Jacobean drama, to point out differences, in form and spirit, between Renaissance and Baroque dramatic styles; Thomas Donovan, *The True Text of Shakespeare and of His Fellow Playwrights* (1923), alters the placement of one line of the text; William J. Lawrence, *Pre-Restoration Stage Studies* (1927), considers the possibility of a stage effect of fog in IV.v.

In *William Poel and the Elizabethan Revival* (1954), Robert Speaight mentions the performances of the Countess scenes (entitled "The King and the Countess") under Poel's direction in 1890, 1897, 1911, and 1926, and discusses their revival in 1952 at the Poel Centenary Matinée at the Old Vic. "Poel had pointed out the discrepancy between the first and second parts of the play, and it is difficult for the sensitive reader to believe that they are by the same hand"; the Countess scenes "powerfully suggested the flow and idiom of Shakespeare's earlier style."

See Also

Albright, Evelyn May. *Dramatic Publication in England, 1580-1640.* 1927.

Bartley, J. O. "The Development of a Stock Character." *MLR* 38 (1943): 279-88.

———. *Teague, Shenkin and Sawney.* 1954.

Cowl, R. P. *Sources of the Text of "Henry the Fourth."* 1928.

Dent, Robert W. "An Early *Hamlet* Echo?" *SQ* 14 (1963): 87-89.

Fogel, Ephim G. "Electronic Computers and Elizabethan Texts." *SB* 15 (1962): 15-31.

Gwynn, Frederick L. "Sweeney Among the Epigraphs." *MLN* 69 (1954): 572-74 (and correction, *MLN* 70 [1955] : 490-91).

Keller, Wolfgang. "Shakespeares Königsdramen." *SJ* 63 (1927): 35-53.

Langsam, G. Geoffrey. *Martial Books and Tudor Verse.* 1951.

Lyman, Dean B., Jr. "Apocryphal Plays of the University Wits." In *English Studies in Honor of James Southall Wilson,* ed. Fredson Bowers (1951), pp. 211-21.

Mackenzie, Agnes Mure. *The Playgoer's Handbook to the English Renaissance Drama.* 1927.

Maxwell, J. C. "Peele and Shakespeare: A Stylometric Test." *JEGP* 49 (1950): 557-61.

Reese, Gertrude Catherine. "The Question of the Succession in Elizabethan Drama." *Studies in English* (Univ. of Texas) 22 (1942): 59-85.

Marion Perret's "*Edward III*: Marlowe's Dramatic Technique," *REL* 7, no. 4 (1966): 87–91, deals not with *Edward III* but with the young Edward III in Marlowe's *Edward II.*

A. L.

Fair Em, romantic comedy (*1590;* 1593?)

Editions

There have been three recent editions of *Fair Em*: one by W. W. Greg for the Malone Society (1928, for 1927); one by Robert William Barzak in a Ph.D. dissertation for the University of Illinois (*DA* 20 [1959]: 287); and one by Standish Henning as a Harvard University Ph.D. dissertation (1960; not listed in *DA* and nowhere described). The play will be included in G. R. Proudfoot's forthcoming edition of the *Shakespeare Apocrypha.*

The editions by Greg and Barzak both contain introductions. Greg describes the single extant copy of the first (undated) quarto of *Fair Em,* and argues that it was printed by at least 1593. He places the composition of the play between 1589 and 1591, through its connections with two of Robert Greene's works (see below) and through the wording of the quarto title page. He discusses the authorship attribution to Robert Wilson as the only attribution worth considering; he suggests that the play may be the *William the Conqueror* acted by Sussex's Men at the Rose on 4 January 1594. Finally, Greg states that the text is suspect: it has no Stationers' Register entry; and it is possibly connected with the printer Danter, and bears on its title page the initials only of two young and obscure booksellers, as publishers. It seems to have been "abridged almost to the point of obscuring the action"; it is "not all of a piece"; but it does not seem, in the later scenes, some of which read like a prose summary, to have been memorially reconstructed.

Barzak has done a good deal of textual work; and he disposes of a ghost 1619 edition, and concludes that the quarto text is a memorial reconstruction, by the actors who played the parts of William the Conqueror and Em, of an abridged version of the original play, created for provincial touring in 1592 or 1593. He dates the play 1590 (because of its Greene connections), rejects previous authorship attributions to Shakespeare, Greene, and Robert Wilson, and suggests Anthony Munday as author, because of similarities between *Fair Em* and known Munday plays, especially *John a Kent and John a Cumber,* and because of what he believes to be satiric hits at Munday in the preface to Greene's *Farewell to Folly*. The probable sources of the play are, he declares, "The Fourth Historie" from Henry Wotton's *A Courtlie controuersie of Cupids Cautels* (1578), rather than the French original, and a lost ballad.

Text

The text is generally agreed to be a bad quarto. Leo Kirschbaum, in "A Census of Bad Quartos," *RES* 14 (1938): 20–43, calls it "as mangled a bad quarto as can be found in the entire canon of 'maimed and deformed' versions," though his examples of textual corruption are not convincing. In "An Hypothesis Concerning the Origin of the Bad Quartos," *PMLA* 60 (1945): 697–715, he argues for memorial reconstruction as the origin of all bad quartos, and for poor memory as the sole cause of the brevity of such texts, and refers to *Fair Em*. See also his *Shakespeare and the Stationers* (1955).

Dora Jean Ashe, in "The Non-Shakespearean Bad Quartos as Provincial Acting Versions," *RenP*, 1954, pp. 57–62, and in more detail in her Ph.D. dissertation for the University of Virginia, "A Survey of Non-Shakespearean Bad Quartos" (*DA* 14 [1954]: 1070–71), deals with *Fair Em* as a bad quarto produced by memorial reconstruction (perhaps by a group, the *DA* summary adds) and suggests that it, along with all other non-Shakespearean bad quartos, is a provincial acting version of its original. It shows economy in casting and staging requirements, is short, and dates from a plague period, when London theaters were closed. The *DA* summary further notes that three marginal stage directions suggest theatrical editing in the manuscript behind the printed quarto.

Wilfred T. Jewkes, *Act Division in Elizabethan and Jacobean Plays, 1583–1616* (1958), states that the quarto was printed from "bad" copy, probably reconstructed and adapted, in the playhouse, for performance.

Authorship

H. Dugdale Sykes, *Sidelights on Elizabethan Drama* (1924), accepts Fleay's 1891 attribution of *Fair Em* to Robert Wilson, and S. R. Golding, in "Robert Wilson and *Sir Thomas More*," *N&Q* 154 (1928): 237–39, assumes Wilson's authorship of the play. (See E. H. C. Oliphant, "How Not to Play the Game of Parallels," *JEGP* 28 [1929]: 1–15, and Muriel St. Clare Byrne, "Bibliographical Clues in Collaborate

Plays," *Library* 13 [1932-33]: 21-48.) T. W. Baldwin, however, in *Shakspere's Five-Act Structure* (1947), gives the play to Munday, whom he believes Greene is scolding in the preface to *Farewell to Folly* (1591) for imitating *Friar Bacon and Friar Bungay* in *Fair Em*. He repeats his attribution in *On the Literary Genetics of Shakspere's Plays, 1592-1594* (1959), and rejects the possibility of Wilson's authorship. A. W. Titherley, *Shakespeare's Identity* (1952), devotes several pages to *Fair Em*, which he believes to be a juvenile work by "Shakespeare"— i.e., William Stanley, sixth Earl of Derby. Derby wrote the play ca. 1581, probably for private performance, and it was presented by Lord Strange's company in London ca. 1587.

H. S. D. Mithal, in "The Authorship of *Fair Em* and *Martin Mar-Sixtus*," *N&Q* 7 (1960): 8-10, briefly reviews previous authorship attributions and supports Robert Wilson's candidacy. In *"Fair Em* and Robert Wilson: Another View," *N&Q* 7 (1960): 348-49, 360, Standish Henning argues sensibly against Mithal that, especially given the corrupt state of the extant text, *Fair Em* must remain anonymous until better evidence comes to light.

Sources and Influences

That *Fair Em* and Robert Greene's *Friar Bacon and Friar Bungay* are in some way related has long been recognized. René Pruvost, *Robert Greene et ses romans* (1938), mentions the allusions to *Fair Em* in Greene's *Farewell to Folly* preface, points out similarities between *Fair Em* and *Friar Bacon*, and agrees with older criticism that *Fair Em* may in part parody *Friar Bacon*, though it is also possible (as recognized in previous scholarship) that *Fair Em* might have been written before Greene's play. T. W. Baldwin, in *Shakspere's Five-Act Structure* and *On the Literary Genetics*, believes that *Fair Em* is modeled on *Friar Bacon*. E. C. Pettet, *Shakespeare and the Romance Tradition* (1949), states that *Fair Em* probably borrows from *Friar Bacon*, though the opposite relationship is just possible.

Rupert Taylor, in "A Tentative Chronology of Marlowe's and Some Other Elizabethan Plays," *PMLA* 51 (1936): 643-88, finds unconvincing parallels between *Fair Em* and Greene's *Alphonsus King of Aragon* and accordingly favors a 1588 date for *Alphonsus*. He also cites two "parallels" between *Fair Em* and Marlowe's *Edward II*, which he uses to date *Edward II* not later than 1589, on the assumption that *Fair Em* echoes it and was written ca. 1590. See also John Bakeless, *The Tragicall History of Christopher Marlowe* (1942), vol. 2.

Other Studies

Alwin Thaler, in *"Faire Em* (and Shakspere's Company?) in Lanca-shire," *PMLA* 46 (1931): 647–58, suggests that *Fair Em*, a Lord Strange's Men play, was written for performance in Lancashire before the Stanley and Trafford families; the play refers to Sir Edmund Trafford (died 1590). (See also Titherley, *Shakespeare's Identity*.) He indulges, in a footnote, in the speculation that Shakespeare may have acted in the play, in the role of William the Conqueror.

Laurens J. Mills, *One Soul in Bodies Twain* (1937), discusses friendship conventions in the play; René Pruvost, *Robert Greene*, rejects the theory (held by Simpson, Fleay, and Hopkinson) that *Fair Em* is an allegory of the theatrical history of its period. K. M. Lea, *Italian Popular Comedy*, vol. 2 (1934), points out a similarity between *Fair Em* and the Italian *commedia dell'arte*. J. W. Ashton, "Conven-tional Material in Munday's *John a Kent and John a Cumber*," *PMLA* 49 (1934): 752–61, remarks that the wooing of Em by Trotter is similar to the wooing of Bess by Young Strowd in *The Blind Beggar of Bednal Green* and that "the contest centering around Em" is therefore not simply a burlesque of the main-plot wooing of Blanche of Denmark. In *The English History Play in the Age of Shakespeare* (1957; rev. ed. 1965), Irving Ribner classifies the play as a historical romance. T. W. Baldwin, *On the Literary Genetics*, describes its form as two plays "mechanically" intertwined, discusses it in relation to the casting pattern he has established for Strange's company, dates it in 1590, and links it with *The Merry Wives of Windsor*.

See Also

Brooks, Alden. *Will Shakspere and the Dyer's Hand*. 1943.
Hoskins, Frank L. "Misalliance: A Significant Theme in Tudor and Stuart Drama." *RenP*, 1956, pp. 72–81.
Kendall, Lyle H., Jr. "Shakespeare Collections, Quartos, Source and Allusion Books in the W. L. Lewis Collection." In *Shakespeare 1964*, ed. Jim W. Corder (1965), pp. 111–77.
Krzyzanowski, J. "Some Conjectural Remarks on Elizabethan Dramatists." *N&Q* 192 (1947): 276–77.
Meader, William G. *Courtship in Shakespeare*. 1954.

A. L.

***King Leir*, legendary history (*1590*; 1605)**

Editions

King Leir has been edited twice since 1920: by E. B. Everitt and R. L. Armstrong in their *Six Early Plays Related to the Shakespeare Canon*, Anglistica, vol. 14 (1965); and by Joseph Satin, as a source for Shakespeare's *King Lear*, in his *Shakespeare and His Sources* (1966). The Everitt-Armstrong introduction discusses text, sources, and themes and techniques. It states that *Leir* and Shakespeare's *Lear* are two forms of the same play, the *Leir* version dating from ca. 1586–87; Holinshed is the probable source; the *Leir* play is "rudimentary in art," little advanced beyond the morality play. The characters are found to be largely generalizations, with Cordella being grace, in the theological sense of the word. The dialogue is ritualistic. The play is related, through parallel imagery and situations, to the other five plays in the collection: *The Weakest Goeth to the Wall, Edmond Ironside, The Troublesome Reign of John, Edward III, Woodstock.* (Behind the book lies the assumption that all six plays are early works by Shakespeare.)

Authorship*

Leir has been assigned to almost every major dramatist working ca. 1590, though modern scholarship has not dealt to any great extent with authorship attributions but has concentrated on the relationship between *Leir* and Shakespeare's *Lear*. No convincing case has been made for any one dramatist as author.

J. M. Robertson, *An Introduction to the Study of the Shakespeare Canon* (1924), believes *Leir* to be a recasting by Kyd of an early play by Greene, Peele, and perhaps Lodge, and dates it in the early 1590s. Arthur M. Sampley, " 'Verbal Tests' for Peele's Plays," *SP* 30 (1933): 473–96, successfully discredits the attribution methods used by Robertson, and, in "Plot Structure in Peele's Plays as a Test of Authorship," *PMLA* 51 (1936): 689–701, makes his own argument against Peele's authorship: Peele's known plays are not well constructed; *Leir* is; *Leir* therefore cannot be by Peele. Arthur Acheson, *Shakespeare, Chapman, and "Sir Thomas More"* (1931), suggests that *Leir* was Lodge's last play, written before August 1591. H. W. Crundell, "Anthony Munday and *King Leir*," *N&Q* 166 (1934): 310–11, makes a wholly implausible attribution to Munday.

* Unless otherwise noted, short-title references in subsequent sections are to works first cited in this section.

William Wells, "The Authorship of *King Leir*," *N&Q* 177 (1939): 434–38, argues against H. Dugdale Sykes's 1919 case for Peele (see also Sampley, " 'Verbal Tests,' " and Muriel St. Clare Byrne, "Bibliographical Clues in Collaborate Plays," *Library* 13 [1932–33] : 21–48), and uses his own unacceptable parallels to give the play to Kyd. The play, he maintains, has only one author, as the style is uniform throughout; and Greene and Lodge were not involved in its composition. In 1940 R. W. Chambers, *King Lear* (W. P. Ker Memorial Lecture for 1939, Glasgow Univ.), classes *Leir* with the best work of Greene, Peele, or Kyd, but assigns no definite author; in 1951 Félix Carrère, *Le théâtre de Thomas Kyd,* rejects previous Kyd attributions.

E. B. Everitt argues, in *The Young Shakespeare: Studies in Documentary Evidence,* Anglistica, vol. 2 (1954), that the play is an early work (probably written before 1588) by Shakespeare; his argument is rejected by Robert Adger Law in "Guessing About the Youthful Shakespeare," *Studies in English* (Univ. of Texas), 34 (1955): 43–50. Law makes his own tentative attribution to Greene or a Greene imitator in "*King Leir* and *King Lear*: An Examination of the Two Plays," in *Studies in Honor of T. W. Baldwin,* ed. Don Cameron Allen (1958), pp. 112–24, and rejects previous attributions to Peele and to Kyd. In *Shakespeare: A Portrait Restored* (1957), Clara Longworth de Chambrun gives "this childish and pretentious text" simply to some Henslowe dramatist in 1594.

I. A. Shapiro speculates briefly, in "Shakespeare and Mundy," *ShS* 14 (1961): 25–33, that *Leir*, with other similar plays of its period, may be the result of dialogue written by other dramatists for a plot composed by Munday, Greene, or some such author; Peter Alexander, *Shakespeare* (1964), suggests that the play is by an imitator of Shakespeare (see below); Irving Ribner, *The English History Play in the Age of Shakespeare* (1957; rev. ed. 1965), very briefly dismisses the Peele attribution. David Bevington, *Tudor Drama and Politics* (1968), states that Lodge "may have contributed" to *Leir*, and dates the play ca. 1588–94. Leonard R. N. Ashley, *Authorship and Evidence* (1968), calls the play unassigned and perhaps unassignable.

Sources and Influences (excluding *Lear*)

Arthur Acheson, *Shakespeare, Chapman,* finds the *Leir* author to have used Warner's *Albion's England* and Spenser's *Faerie Queene*; Félix Carrère, *Le théâtre de Thomas Kyd,* believes Holinshed to be the play's source. Robert Adger Law, "*King Leir* and *King Lear*," looks in detail at *Leir* and finds that it follows the Lear story outline first presented by Geoffrey of Monmouth and repeated by many of his followers, but with many incidents, some of them romantic and melodramatic, added by the anonymous author. Leonard R. N. Ashley, *Authorship and Evidence*, states that *Leir* is based on *The Mirror for Magistrates* and *Albion's England* and shows some influence of *The Faerie Queene*. See also Shapiro, "Shakespeare and Mundy."

Thomas H. McNeal, in "Margaret of Anjou: Romantic Princess and Troubled Queen," *SQ* 9 (1958): 1-10, sees *Leir* as influencing the Margaret-Suffolk scenes at the end of *I Henry VI*; he believes that these scenes were added to the original, earlier play to link it with *II* and *III Henry VI*, in which the character of Margaret has been influenced by the Ragan and Gonorill of *Leir*. He finds borrowings from *Leir* in Shakespeare, not before *I Henry VI*, but "thick and fast" in subsequent plays down to *Lear*; and in "Shakespeare's Cruel Queens," *HLQ* 22 (1958-59): 41-50, he argues that Margaret of Anjou, Beatrice (*Much Ado About Nothing*), Regan, Goneril, and Lady Macbeth are all derived from *Leir*'s Ragan and Gonorill.

For possible connections between *Leir* and other plays of its period, see: (1) *Cymbeline* (*Leir* as a source)—Robert Adger Law, "An Unnoted Analogue to the Imogen Story," *Studies in English* (Univ. of Texas), 7 (1927): 133-35; (2) *Edmond Ironside* and *Edward III* (common Shakespearean authorship with *Leir*, which was probably written before 1588)—E. B. Everitt, *The Young Shakespeare*; (3) *Hamlet*—A. S. Cairncross, *The Problem of "Hamlet": A Solution* (1936), for *Hamlet* as an influence on *Leir*, and W. W. Greg, "Shakespeare and *King Leir*," *TLS*, 9 March 1940, p. 124, for *Leir* as an influence on *Hamlet*; (4) *King John* (echoes *Leir*)—Robert Adger Law, "*King John* and *King Leir*," *TSLL* 1 (1959-60): 473-76; (5) *Locrine*—J. M. Robertson, *An Introduction*, David Bevington, *Tudor Drama*; (6) *Orlando Furioso*—W. W. Greg, *Two Elizabethan Stage Abridgements* (1923; Malone Society), p. 208, and T. W. Baldwin, *On the Literary Genetics of Shakspere's Plays, 1592-1594* (1959), the latter also mentioning Greene's *Farewell to Folly*; (7) *Richard III* (*Leir* as a source)—Wolfgang Clemen, *Kommentar zu Shakespeares "Richard III"* (1957), John Dover Wilson, "The Composition of the Clarence Scenes in *Richard III*," *MLR* 53 (1958): 211-14, and his Cambridge edition (1954) of *Richard III*, Robert Adger Law, "*King John* and *King Leir*" (above); (8) *Troublesome Reign of John* (common Shakespearean authorship with *Leir*)—E. B. Everitt, *The Young Shakespeare*, and Acheson, *Shakespeare, Chapman*.

Leir and *Lear*

Scholarship on the *Leir-Lear* relationship also often finds connections between *Leir* and other Shakespearean plays; but its chief concern is establishing the origin, date, and nature of *Lear* through study of the lesser play. Most scholars since 1920 have agreed that *Leir* is a *Lear* source, but have disagreed on its importance as source material and on how Shakespeare came to utilize it.

E. K. Chambers, in *William Shakespeare* (1930), vol. 1, advances the view that a recent performance of *Leir* was the inspiration of *Lear*, with Shakespeare relying, in composition, on his memory of the performance. Joseph Quincy Adams, however, in "The Quarto of *King Lear* and Shorthand," *MP* 21 (1933–34): 135–63, views the *Leir* quarto (1605) as an attempt by the publisher to pass off an old play, not recently revived, as the popular new one by Shakespeare which must then have been on the boards; *Leir*, for example, is entered in the Stationers' Register in 1605 as a "tragical history," a description true of *Lear* but not of *Leir*. W. W. Greg, "The Date of *King Lear* and Shakespeare's Use of Earlier Versions of the Story," *Library* 20 (1939–40): 377–400, combines elements of both Chambers' and Adams' views. He sums up the known details of performance and publication of *Leir*, dates *Leir* ca. 1590, and concludes, like Adams, that *Leir* was not revived in the seventeenth century and that the publication of the 1605 quarto was an attempt by the publisher to capitalize on the popularity of the then-new *Lear*. He also, however, cites parallels between *Leir* and *Lear* to show that *Leir* was a *Lear* source and that Shakespeare had not merely seen *Leir* performed (in the 1590s) but had read it carefully not long before he wrote *Lear*. Greg's only solution to the problem in which he thus involves himself is to suggest that Shakespeare read the older play in manuscript. (He also suggests additional sources of *Lear*.) The manuscript theory creates, as he states in "Shakespeare and *King Leir*" ("Sources"), difficulties in the dating of *Lear*. Thomas Marc Parrott, *Shakespearean Comedy* (1949), summarizes the action of *Leir*, sees Shakespeare's immediate debt to it as undeniable, and suggests that *Leir* was seen by Shakespeare in a 1605 revival and was also certainly read by him in the 1605 text; he thus dates *Lear* 1605–6. Fitzroy Pyle, *"Twelfth Night, King Lear, and Arcadia,"* *MLR* 43 (1948): 449–55, believes that Shakespeare was inspired to write *Lear* by the 1605 quarto of *Leir*. Hardin Craig, "Motivation in Shakespeare's Choice of Materials," *ShS* 4 (1951): 26–34, is doubtful that Shakespeare had *Leir* at hand when writing

Lear; but Shakespeare was very familiar with *Leir* and possibly at one time had acted in it.

Kenneth Muir, in his Arden edition (1952; corrected 1963) of *Lear,* accepts *Leir* as a Shakespeare source, performed in 1594, and summarizes the play, pointing out Shakespeare's key deviations from it. (See also his *Shakespeare's Sources,* vol. 1 [1957].) He concurs with Greg in placing the publication of *Leir* after the first performances of *Lear,* but, unlike Greg, believes that the parallels between the two plays can be accounted for simply as the result of Shakespeare's memory of *Leir* as earlier performed; Shakespeare may even have acted previously in *Leir,* possibly as Perillus. Irving Ribner, *English History Play,* accepts the 1605 quarto as an attempt to pass off Shakespeare's chief source as Shakespeare's play. Hardin Craig, *A New Look at Shakespeare's Quartos* (1961), Stanford Studies in Language and Literature, no. 22, repeats his 1951 view, and also states that the publisher of the 1605 quarto may not have been trying to pass off *Leir* as *Lear,* "for the Elizabethans rarely, if ever, discriminated among versions of the same story," and the publisher may simply have remembered that he had a play on Lear, and so have printed it. A common, basic "scenario" underlying both *Leir* and *Lear* is suggested by I. A. Shapiro, "Shakespeare and Mundy," who nevertheless does not deny that *Leir* is a *Lear* source.

Robert Adger Law, "Holinshed as Source for *Henry V* and *King Lear,*" *Studies in English* (Univ. of Texas), 14 (1934): 38–44, believes Shakespeare "is heavily in debt to the old drama for suggestions of phrase, of character, of situation, and of entire scenes . . . ; throughout Act I and part of Act II, he follows closely the order of action employed in the old play." Shakespeare did not read Holinshed on Lear; he probably read only *Leir, Mirror for Magistrates,* and Spenser's *Faerie Queene.* In "*King Leir* and *King Lear,*" Law discusses the changes from *Leir* made in *Lear.* Richard H. Perkinson, "Shakespeare's Revision of the Lear Story and the Structure of *King Lear,*" *PQ* 22 (1943): 315–29, includes a comparison of *Leir* and *Lear* in demonstrating how Shakespeare changed his sources to make *Lear* a tragedy. Curtis Brown Watson, *Shakespeare and the Renaissance Concept of Honor* (1960), points out "the striking contrast" between *Leir* and *Lear:* that "the old play is as deeply saturated in Christian themes as Shakespeare's is lacking in precise religious doctrines." Bernard Beckerman, *Shakespeare at the Globe, 1599–1609* (1962), briefly compares the characters of Leir and Lear, stating that Shakespeare individualizes Lear through the depiction of the passions. Thomas H. McNeal, "Shakespeare's Cruel Queens" ("Sources"), cites some adaptations of *Leir* in *Lear*. See also Ribner, *English History Play*.

Alfred Hart, *Stolne and Surreptitious Copies* (1942), treats *Leir*, through vocabulary tests, as a source of *Lear*. A. S. Cairncross, *Problem of "Hamlet"* ("Sources"), however, argues implausibly that *Leir* is an attempt to reproduce the main plot of *Lear*, and so dates *Lear* before 1594. Peter Alexander, *Shakespeare*, also believes that *Leir* follows *Lear*, and suggests that the Lear play mentioned in Henslowe's *Diary* in the 1590s is an earlier one by Shakespeare. Chambrun, *Shakespeare*, does not believe that *Leir* influenced *Lear*; and R. W. Chambers, *King Lear*, denies *Leir* any overwhelming importance as Shakespeare's source.

Leo Kirschbaum has dealt at length with the problem of copyright of Elizabethan plays, as related to *Leir* and *Lear*. In "How Jane Bell Came to Print the Third Quarto of Shakespeare's *King Lear*," *PQ* 17 (1938): 308–11, he argues that Jane Bell legally owned the copyright to *Lear*, through the spelling change of *"Leir"* to *"Lear"* when the copyright of the old play passed from its various former owners eventually to Richard Oulton in 1640 and then to Jane Bell. Perhaps she did not even know that there were two separate plays on Lear. He repeats his view in "The Copyright of Elizabethan Plays," *Library* 14 (1959): 231–50. See also Acheson, *Shakespeare, Chapman*.

The Play

Irving Ribner and David Bevington (both above, "Authorship,") deny *Leir* any importance as a political play; it is "a sentimental fairy tale with no historical pretensions" (Ribner), "a sentimental romance with surprisingly little awareness of the problems of kingship or political division" (Bevington). Robert Adger Law, *"King Leir* and *King Lear,"* calls it not a history but a romantic comedy, in which the characters follow conventional patterns, the tedious exposition results in a large number of scenes, and the diction is naive.

Wolfgang Clemen, *English Tragedy Before Shakespeare* (trans. T. S. Dorsch, 1961; German ed. 1955), discusses *Leir* as illustrating the trend in drama, at its time, away from set speeches and towards emphasis on plot. Its plot, he argues, is full of incident, is skilfully put together, and is developed logically and comprehensively; and the diction is largely sober and factual, with the function of making the action clear.

Other Studies

Wilfred T. Jewkes, *Act Division in Elizabethan and Jacobean Plays,
1583–1616* (1958), states that for the 1605 quarto the printer's
copy-text seems to have been the author's manuscript or a non-
theatrical transcript. Greg, "The Date of *King Lear*" ("*Leir* and *Lear*"),
suggests that the quarto was printed from the playhouse manuscript.
E. B. Everitt, *The Young Shakespeare*, gives *Leir* to the Queen's Men.
T. W. Baldwin, *On the Literary Genetics* ("Sources and Influences"),
states that the play does not fit the casting pattern he has established
for the Queen's company. Jewkes, however, also believes *Leir* to be
probably a Queen's Men play, as do Muir in his Arden edition of *Lear*,
E. K. Chambers, *Shakespeare*, Hardin Craig, "Motivation in Shakespeare's Choice" and *A New Look at Shakespeare's Quartos* (all in "*Leir*
and *Lear*"), and others. Hardin Craig, "Morality Plays and Elizabethan
Drama," *SQ* 1 (1950): 64–72, also finds morality features in *Leir*.

H. W. Crundell, "Canting Terms in Elizabethan Drama," *N&Q* 169
(1935): 222, suggests Perillus' name is from the phrase "a 'parlous' or
'perillous' man," meaning a notable, shrewd fellow; and three unusual
words in the text are discussed by Robert Adger Law, " 'Genouestan
Gawles' and 'Red-Shanks,' " *Proceedings of Conference of College
Teachers of English of Texas* 18 (1953): 6–9. Alan S. Downer,
"Prolegomenon to a Study of Elizabethan Acting," *MuK* 10 (1964):
625–36, comments on the kneeling scene near the play's end.

See Also

Alden, Raymond M. *A Shakespeare Handbook*. 1925.

Bakeless, John. *The Tragicall History of Christopher Marlowe*. 1942. Vol. 2.

Black, Matthew. "Enter Citizens." In *Studies in the English Renaissance Drama in
Memory of Karl Julius Holzknecht*, ed. Josephine W. Bennett, Oscar Cargill, and
Vernon Hall, Jr. (1959), pp. 16–27.

Doran, Madeleine. "Elements in the Composition of *King Lear*." *SP* 30 (1933):
34–58.

Friedländer, Ernst. *Kontrast und Gleichförmigkeit im älteren englischen Drama*.
1934.

Harbage, Alfred. *As They Liked It*. 1947.

Hart, Alfred. "Acting Versions of Elizabethan Plays." *RES* 10 (1934): 1–28.

Isaacs, J. "Shakespeare's Earliest Years in the Theatre." *PBA* 39 (1953): 119–38.

Knowlton, Edgar C. "Nature and Shakespeare." *PMLA* 51 (1936): 719–44.

Law, Robert Adger. "*Richard The Third*: A Study in Shakespeare's Composition."
PMLA 60 (1945): 689–96.

Maxwell, J. C. "Peele and Shakespeare: A Stylometric Test." *JEGP* 49 (1950): 557–61.

Ploch, Georg. *Über den Dialog in den Dramen Shakespeares und seiner Vorläufer.* Giessener Beiträge zur Erforschung der Sprache und Kultur Englands und Nordamerikas, vol. 2, no. 2 (1925).

Reichert, Günter. *Die Entwicklung und die Funktion der Nebenhandlung in der Tragödie vor Shakespeare.* SzEP, vol. 11 (1966).

Rhodes, R. Crompton. *Shakespeare's First Folio.* 1923.

Rubow, Paul V. *Shakespeare og hans samtidige.* 1948. [In Danish.]

Smith, Albert H. "John Nichols, Printer and Publisher." *Library* 18 (1963): 169–90.

Utz, Hans. *Das Bedeutungsfeld "Leid" in der englischen Tragödie vor Shakespeare.* Schweizer Anglistische Arbeiten, vol. 54 (1963).

Winslow, Ola Elizabeth. *Low Comedy as a Structural Element in English Drama from the Beginnings to 1642.* 1926.

The Malone Society reprint of 1907 was reissued with corrections in 1956.

A. L.

Mucedorus, romantic comedy (*1590;* 1598)

Editions

The play has been printed in two collections since 1920: C. R. Baskervill, V. B. Heltzel, and A. H. Nethercot, eds., *Elizabethan and Stuart Plays* (1934); and James Winny, ed., *Three Elizabethan Plays* (1959). The former contains a brief introduction to *Mucedorus,* summing up what is known of the play's history (its popularity, numerous editions, and provincial acting) and dealing with sources and authorship attributions. The author, it states, as C. F. Tucker Brooke suggested in *The Shakespeare Apocrypha* (1908), was probably an obscure, somewhat talented disciple of the University Wits, and the bare outline of the play is from Sidney's *Arcadia*; pastoral and folktale elements are included, and the clown is apparently present because of popular taste; the Induction and Epilogue show the audience's interest in debates, and emphasize the tragi-comic nature of the play. Winny includes the play as an example of Elizabethan plays of romantic adventures, and suggests that the text was either "carelessly transcribed in the printing-house" or written by two authors, one "imperfectly acquainted with blank verse form." He rejects the authorship attribution to Shakespeare, but says that Shakespeare must have known the play, which is "an amiable and harmless piece of entertainment."

The play will presumably appear in G. R. Proudfoot's forthcoming edition of the *Shakespeare Apocrypha*.

Text

Mucedorus exists in two versions, the second (1610) being the first (1598, 1606) with six additional segments. Leo Kirschbaum, "The Texts of *Mucedorus*," *MLR* 50 (1955): 1–5, argues that the first version (A) is a memorial reconstruction (see also his *Shakespeare and the Stationers* [1955]), and that the new parts of the second version (B) were additions written not before 1603, in the theater, by an author working from a good manuscript of the play. He is reluctant to assign *Mucedorus* to the King's Men, even if only in the play's seventeenth-century revival, on the evidence of the 1610 title page alone. Two other of his points are disputed by W. W. Greg and George F. Reynolds. Greg, in a letter to *MLR* 50 (1955): 322, denies Kirschbaum's claim that the mere publication of *Mucedorus*, without Stationers' Register entry of the play, established copyright for its printer in both the bad quarto of the play and the original text itself. (Kirschbaum, however, maintains his original stand, in "The Copyright of Elizabethan Plays," *Library* 14 (1959): 231–50.) Reynolds, in "*Mucedorus*, Most Popular Elizabethan Play?" in *Studies in the English Renaissance Drama in Memory of Karl Julius Holzknecht*, ed. Josephine W. Bennett, Oscar Cargill, and Vernon Hall, Jr. (1959), pp. 248–68, speaks against Kirschbaum's assertion that the published text tells us nothing about the tastes of the actual theater audience but only about those of the reading public; he believes that the text, once printed, was used by strolling companies of actors.

Wilfred T. Jewkes, *Act Division in Elizabethan and Jacobean Plays, 1583–1616* (1958), concludes that the 1598 text was printed from "bad" copy, probably memorially reconstructed for performance, and that the 1610 quarto is a good text, with evidence of playhouse annotation. A. W. Titherley, in his eccentric *Shakespeare's Identity* (1952), suggests that the A text is from an acting copy of an abridged version of the original, provided for the Lord Strange's Men by the author himself, for performance in London; the original was written for private performance.

Authorship

Mucedorus belongs to the Shakespeare apocrypha but is now hardly ever assigned to Shakespeare. A. W. Titherley, *Shakespeare's Identity*, however, includes the play among early works, ca. 1587, by Shakespeare—whom he identifies as William Stanley, sixth Earl of Derby; he finds that *Mucedorus* is Shakespearean in vocabulary, style, and devices, and contains parallels with plays in the accepted Shakespeare canon. The 1610 additions are, he believes, part of the original play, omitted in the first two quartos, perhaps because the play was acted in its entirety before Queen Elizabeth but cut for public performance. The 1610 Epilogue is, he states, a later addition by another author. The only recent Shakespeare attribution worth attention is that by MacD. P. Jackson, in "Edward Archer's Ascription of *Mucedorus* to Shakespeare," *AUMLA* 22 (1964): 233–48. Jackson suggests that the B-text additions were written by Shakespeare, sometime between 1606 and 1610, for court performance of the play; he points out stylistic and dramatic similarities between Shakespeare's known work and the additions.

Arthur Acheson, *Shakespeare, Chapman, and "Sir Thomas More"* (1931), attributes the play to Greene, 1584–85, and believes that it was revised in 1587 and later. Lodge was involved in the revisions. A Lodge-Greene attribution is made by Alden Brooks, in *Will Shakspere and the Dyer's Hand* (1943), who finds, as well, Shakespeare's (i.e., Edward Dyer's) influence in the play. Benvenuto Cellini, ed., *Drammi Pre-Shakespeariani* Collana di Letterature Moderne, no. 4 (1958), rejects the Greene attribution, stating that *Mucedorus* parodies Greene's romances. Leonard R. N. Ashley, *Authorship and Evidence* (1968), sums up previous attribution work on the play and finds it senseless and capricious.

Staging and Stage History

A point of interest in the staging of *Mucedorus* is the appearance of the bear. George F. Reynolds, "*Mucedorus,* Most Popular Elizabethan Play?" maintains that the popularity of the play in the seventeenth century began only after its revival by the King's Men, and must have been first caused, not by anything in the text itself, but by the use in performance of a real bear rather than of the usual man-playing-a-bear. The play then continued in popularity with less literate readers and spectators only. Janet Spens, *Elizabethan Drama* (1922), also believes that a real bear was used; and she, as well as Richard Proudfoot, "Shakespeare and the New Dramatists of the King's Men, 1606–1613," in *Later Shakespeare,* SuAS, vol. 8 (1966), pp. 235–61, suggests that for the bear in *The Winter's Tale* Shakespeare is indebted to *Mucedorus.*

See also Louis B. Wright, "Animal Actors on the English Stage before 1642," *PMLA* 42 (1927): 656–69.

Ola Elizabeth Winslow, *Low Comedy as a Structural Element in English Drama from the Beginnings to 1642* (1926), states that Mouse is superfluous to the action but that the drama is subordinated to him. (See also Titherley, *Shakespeare's Identity*.) Perhaps the play was intended to feature a popular actor, "who may indeed have extemporized most of this nonsense, which was later incorporated into the printed play." William J. Lawrence, *Speeding Up Shakespeare* (1937), suggests that Mouse was originally played by Tarlton, of the Queen's Men.

Charles J. Sisson, *Le goût public et le théâtre élisabéthain* (1922), states that *Mucedorus* was written for the court and delighted both Queen Elizabeth (in 1598) and James I (in 1610). T. W. Baldwin, *On the Literary Genetics of Shakspere's Plays, 1592–1594* (1959), discusses *Mucedorus* in connection with the Lord Strange's Men. David Bevington, *From "Mankind" to Marlowe* (1962), briefly comments on role distribution, and Reynolds, *"Mucedorus,"* speculates on casting possibilities. Titherley suggests that the play was perhaps first performed at Knowsley, at Christmas 1587, then acted at court by the Queen's company, ca. 1588, and kept by Stanley's brother's company until the performance before James I. See also Sharpe, *The Real War of the Theaters*, below.

Other Studies

Mucedorus has been linked with various types of medieval and Renaissance plays. R. J. E. Tiddy, *The Mummers' Play* (1923), and E. K. Chambers, *The English Folk-Play* (1933), connect *Mucedorus* with mummers' plays; K. M. Lea, *Italian Popular Comedy*, vol. 2 (1934), points out similarities between *Mucedorus* and the Italian *commedia dell'arte*. Hardin Craig, "Morality Plays and Elizabethan Drama," *SQ* 1 (1950): 64–72, finds a morality-play connection; Robert Hillis Goldsmith, "The Wild Man on the English Stage," *MLR* 53 (1958): 481–91, discusses Bremo as an example of the wild-man tradition in English drama (and says that Shakespeare must have known *Mucedorus*). Patricia Russell, "Romantic Narrative Plays: 1570–1590," in *Elizabethan Theatre*, SuAS, vol. 9 (1966), pp. 107–29, includes *Mucedorus* in her discussion of the technique in early romantic narrative plays of including both a serious action and a parody of it.

Karl J. Holzknecht, *Outlines of Tudor and Stuart Plays, 1497–1642*

(1947), calls the play an "absurd mixture of pastoralism, chivalric romance, and horseplay," and gives an outline of it, with a brief, factual introduction.

William J. Lawrence, "The King's Players at Court in 1610," *MLR* 15 (1920): 89–90, suggests that the 1610 Epilogue may allude to an earlier court performance of a King's Men play containing a reference to Arabella Stuart and therefore suppressed. Robert Boies Sharpe, *The Real War of the Theaters* (1935), sees in the 1598 Epilogue, in the yielding of Envy to Queen Elizabeth, "a fairly open reference . . . to the ending in Essex's favor of the controversy over Cadiz," and suggests that the play may have been performed by the Chamberlain's Men at court in the season of 1597–98. He also mentions that the work has some Senecan elements. Kirschbaum, "The Texts of *Mucedorus*," believing *Mucedorus* to draw on Book IV of Spenser's *Faerie Queene,* places the composition of the play not before 1596; T. W. Baldwin, *On the Literary Genetics,* states that the drama possibly borrows from *Doctor Faustus* and *Selimus,* and is to be dated 1590–98.

See Also

Bakeless, John. *The Tragicall History of Christopher Marlowe.* 1942. Vol. 2.

Bradbrook, Muriel C. *The Growth and Structure of Elizabethan Comedy.* 1955.

Bradley, Jesse Franklin, and Joseph Quincy Adams. *The Jonson Allusion-Book.* 1922.

Cowl, R. P. *Sources of the Text of "Henry the Fourth."* 1928.

Graves, Thornton S. "Notes on Puritanism and the Stage." *SP* 18 (1921): 141–69.

Mares, Francis Hugh. "The Origin of the Figure Called 'the Vice' in Tudor Drama." *HLQ* 22 (1958–59): 11–29.

Ramondt, Marie. "Vondel, Mucedorus en Pieter Breughel." *NTg* 43 (1951): 10–12.

Wright, Louis B. "Extraneous Song in Elizabethan Drama after the Advent of Shakespeare." *SP* 24 (1927): 261–74.

———. "Variety-Show Clownery on the Pre-Restoration Stage." *Anglia* 52 (1928): 51–68.

A. L.

Soliman and Perseda, tragedy (*1590;* ca. 1592)

Edition

The single recent edition of *Soliman and Perseda* (*S&P*) is John J. Murray's 1959 New York University Ph.D. dissertation (*DA* 20 [1960] : 3284). Murray describes the nature of his text and the way it differs from the standard one of Frederick S. Boas in his 1901 edition of the works of Kyd. Murray's introduction includes discussions of early texts, stage history, *S&P*'s influence on Shakespeare, and aesthetic merit. In the section on date, the editor disagrees with the theories of T. W. Baldwin, "On the Chronology of Thomas Kyd's Plays," *MLN* 40 (1925): 343–49 (see below, "Date and Sources"), and places the work in 1587. The major source, Henry Wotton's *A Courtlie Controversie of Cupids Cautels* (1578), and its use are summarized, and original material on subsidiary sources is offered. In dealing with attribution, Murray reviews earlier scholarship and argues for Kyd's authorship with the assistance of some new evidence based on language and dramatic techniques.

Date and Sources

The question of date is unsettled. In his 1925 *MLN* article (above), Baldwin placed *S&P* at 1585–86, "almost certainly the autumn 1585," on such grounds as its positive attitude towards Spain; the contemporary allusions in Death's compliment to the Queen; data about court performances in the 1584–85 season and the activities of the Admiral's company in the mid-1580s (he assumed the play probably belonged to them); and precedence of *The Spanish Tragedy* ([*SpT*]; *S&P* varies from its source in order to echo the assigned play). Using the date he has found for *S&P*, he tries to fix *SpT* chronologically. These conclusions are challenged by Murray in his edition, and by Philip Edwards, ed., *The Spanish Tragedy* (1959; Revels ed.), who says "it cannot be proved that *The Spanish Tragedy* did not follow *Soliman and Perseda*." Baldwin adjusts his views somewhat in *On the Literary Genetics of Shakspere's Plays, 1592–1594* (1959), where Garnier's influence on Kyd (see Alexander M. Witherspoon, *The Influence of Robert Garnier on Elizabethan Drama* [1924]) and borrowing from *SpT* support his conclusion that *S&P* was written ca. 1585 for the Queen's Men.

In their edition of *Edward II* (1933; rev. F. N. Lees, 1955), H. B. Charlton and R. D. Waller think the anonymous play followed Marlowe's, which was available in manuscript by the fall of 1591. Arthur Acheson, *Shakespeare, Chapman, and "Sir Thomas More"* (1931), dates *S&P* in its earliest form after 1578 and before 1580 (i.e., before *SpT*) because of the facts surrounding the publication of its source and a reference in *SpT*; Kyd's revision of the play took place before 1587, when he broke with Burbage and Alleyn. John Dover Wilson, ed., *King John* (1936; Cambridge ed.), sceptical that *S&P* was ever owned by the Admiral's Men, speculates that the drama might have belonged to Shakespeare's company; perhaps *S&P, SpT,* and *King John* share correspondences because they were produced for the same group during 1590–91. Attempting to determine the sequence of *II Henry VI, III Henry VI, Arden of Feversham,* and *S&P,* Rupert Taylor, "A Tentative Chronology of Marlowe's and Some Other Elizabethan Plays," *PMLA* 51 (1936): 643–88, points out parallels between *S&P* and other dramas which he thinks indicate a composition date after May 1591. A few tenuous topical references and a possible link with Spenser's *The Tears of the Muses* corroborate his theory.

Both Samuel C. Chew, *The Crescent and the Rose* (1937), and Félix Carrère, *Le théâtre de Thomas Kyd* (1951), appear uncertain on this issue and propose the period between 1589 and 1592 (which Carrère acknowledges as E. K. Chambers's suggestion). In *The Tragicall History of Christopher Marlowe,* vol. 2 (1942), John Bakeless says the play may belong to the time of Marlowe and Kyd's early affiliation (if Kyd wrote *S&P*). G. Lambrechts, *"Edward III,* oeuvre de Thomas Kyd," *EA* 16 (1963): 160–74, does not fix a precise date, but places *S&P* between *SpT* and *Edward III* in a sequence of stylistic developments. Arthur Freeman, "Shakespeare and *Solyman and Perseda,*" *MLR* 58 (1963): 481–87, summarizing views previously put forward, dates *S&P* 1591–92 (probably after *SpT*) because of its various connections with the anonymous *Rare Triumphs of Love and Fortune,* Marlowe's *Tamburlaine,* and the anonymous *Selimus.* He thinks Shakespeare's *King John* and *Romeo and Juliet* borrowed from the anonymous work, provides parallels to support this contention, and considers Wilson's suggestion, in his edition of *King John,* that *S&P* belonged to Shakespeare's company. A more extensive discussion of date appears in Freeman's *Thomas Kyd: Facts and Problems* (1967), which devotes a chapter to *S&P.* This fixes limits at 1578 (publication of the source) and November 1592 (Stationers' Register entry for the play); collects evidence to suggest that the anonymous drama was written after *SpT*; questions Baldwin's arguments about date; gives heed to dramatic trends and some verbal correspondences; and consequently changes his limits to 1588 and 1592. He tends to favor a 1591–92 date because of some contemporary connections the play has, "but this is a fairly casual opinion." Leonard R. N. Ashley, *Authorship and Evidence* (1968), conjectures a date between *SpT,* ca. 1588, and *S&P*'s Stationers' Register entry in 1592.

It is generally agreed that the main source of *S&P* is the first story in Wotton's *Courtlie Controversie,* a translation of Jacques Yver's *Prin-*

temps d'Iver (1572): see, for example, Joseph de Smet, *Thomas Kyd, l'homme, l'oeuvre, le milieu suivi de "La Tragédie Espagnole"* (1925); Acheson, (*Shakespeare, Chapman*); Chew, (*Crescent and the Rose,* who also discusses the nature of the play's historical background); Carrère (*Théâtre de Thomas Kyd,* who speaks only of Yver's work). The source of a single passage in *S&P* is a matter of disagreement between Marion Grubb, "Kyd's Borrowing from Garnier's *Bradamante,*" *MLN* 50 (1935): 169–71, and T. W. Baldwin, "Parallels Between *Soliman and Perseda* and Garnier's *Bradamante,*" *MLN* 51 (1936): 237–41. Garnier's general influence is mentioned by Baldwin in *On the Literary Genetics.* The most recent and complete discussion of sources is Freeman's chapter, which refers to Sarrazin's work on *A Courtlie Controversie,* compares *S&P* with its main source, and evaluates scholarship about subsidiary sources.

Attribution

The only serious candidate for the authorship of *S&P* is Thomas Kyd. Almost every scholar who discusses either the play or the playwright acknowledges the connection that has been made between them. Many simply assume that Kyd wrote *S&P,* while others explain why the attribution seems plausible. C. F. Tucker Brooke, in *A Literary History of England,* ed. Albert C. Baugh (1948), explains briefly how Kyd altered for *S&P* the story he had used as the play within a play in *SpT.* In *Playwriting for Elizabethans, 1600–1605* (1949), Mary Crapo Hyde says the correspondence between the prologues of the anonymous play and the acknowledged one provides convincing evidence for Kyd's authorship. Willard Farnham, *The Medieval Heritage of Elizabethan Tragedy* (1936), finds reasonable previous arguments based on style and compares the two plays. Stylistic similarities also sway Zdeněk Stříbrný, *Shakespearovi předchůdci* [Shakespeare's Predecessors], Acta Universitatis Carolinae: Philologica-Monographia, vol. 7 (1965; English summary, pp. 118–32), who notices structural, stylistic, and linguistic parallels between *S&P* and *SpT;* the nature of the poetry, the prose, and the drama indicates Kyd's growth as an artist. (See also Samuel J. Mitchell, "Rhetoric as a Dramatic Element in the Plays of Thomas Kyd," 1951 Univ. of Texas diss.) Andrew S. Cairncross says briefly in his editions of *The First Part of Hieronimo* and *The Spanish Tragedy,* RRDS (1967), that "various links" with *SpT* make it possible to attribute *S&P* to Kyd. In *Thomas Kyd,* Freeman ("Date and Sources") favors the Kyd attribution: "The case for Kyd is quite strong, perhaps as strong as the attribution of *Tamburlaine* to Marlowe." In his synopsis of the case supporting Kyd, he summarizes and evaluates the important available evidence, from Hawkins's in 1773 to Murray's in 1959 (see above, "Edition"), which is based upon parallels of plot, dramatic technique, style, and versification with *SpT*. Acheson, *Shakespeare, Chapman* ("Date and Sources"), argues for Kyd's association with the play by tracing its origins. An eccentric claim for Kyd's collaboration is J. M. Robertson's in *The Shakespeare Canon*, pt. 3 (1925); he credits Kyd with at least the Basilisco scenes to help explain Ben Jonson's 1623 description of the "sporting Kyd."

A substantial number of writers are to different degrees unwilling to associate Kyd unquestionably with *S&P*. Boas, in his edition of Kyd's works, was inclined to support the attribution, but found it was not possible to prove the case conclusively. Later, in *An Introduction to Tudor Drama* (1933), he maintains that it is more plausible to attribute *S&P* to Kyd than *Don Horatio* or *The Comedy of Jeronimo*, because the first play has structural and stylistic similarities with the dramatist's known work. Both here and in "The Soldier in Elizabethan and Later English Drama," *EDH*, vol. 19 (1942), pp. 121–56 (rpt. in *Queen Elizabeth in Drama and Related Studies* [1950], pp. 163–89), he says *S&P* was written by Kyd or one of his school. Similarly, after eliminating Peele from consideration, Chew, *Crescent and the Rose* ("Date and Sources"), examines arguments for and against the playwright and cautiously judges that the evidence suggests Kyd's authorship or influence. Philip Edwards, *Thomas Kyd and Early Elizabethan Tragedy* (1966), gives data to strengthen his claim that the ascription seems logical: the use of *S&P* in altered form in *SpT* and parallels between the two plays in language, action, and framework. Critics who think the work is possibly or probably by Kyd include Kenneth Muir, "The Chronology of Marlowe's Plays," *PLPLS-LHS* 5 (1938–43): 345–56; Daniel C. Boughner, "Milton's Harapha and Renaissance Comedy," *ELH* 11 (1944): 297–306; Irving Ribner, ed., *The Life and Death of King John* (1962, Pelican ed.); David Bevington, *Tudor Drama and Politics* (1968).

Some doubt is cast upon the ascription by critics who distrust the methods that have been developed to attribute anonymous plays. E. H. C. Oliphant, "Marlowe's Hand in *Arden of Feversham*: A Problem for Critics," *The New Criterion* 4 (1926): 76–93, says the assignment to Kyd, based completely on internal evidence, is questionable. Peter Wilhelm Biesterfeldt, *Die dramatische Technik Thomas Kyds* (1936), eliminates *S&P* from his study for this reason, and Dean B. Lyman, Jr., "Apocryphal Plays of the University Wits," in *English Studies in Honor of James Southall Wilson,* ed. Fredson Bowers (1951), pp. 211–21, says Boas's arguments are convincing, but the same kind of evidence could be used to attribute *Hamlet* to Kyd. R. J. E. Tiddy, *The Mummers' Play* (1923), claims that the ascription cannot be made with surety, and Bakeless, *Tragicall History* ("Date and Sources") is on the whole doubtful. In his edition of *SpT,* Edwards notes that the attribution has been founded on plot and stylistic parallels with *SpT* and "the stylistic resemblances are not overwhelming." R. M. Pal, "Thomas Kyd: The Spanish Tragedy," *Agra University Journal of Research* 11 (1963): 67–84, remarks that the play is "doubtfully attributed to Kyd."

The group of scholars who are extremely dubious about Kyd includes de Smet, *Thomas Kyd* ("Date and Sources"), who finds the play unlike Kyd's work in certain ways and inferior to *SpT.* Unconvinced by the correspondences with *SpT* suggested by Kyd supporters, he points out conjectural and contradictory aspects of arguments he considers fragile. Also unconvinced, Baldwin mentions in *On the Literary Genetics* ("Date and Sources") that the blank verse differs from that in *SpT* and Kyd's translation of Garnier's *Cornélie.* An extensive negative argument is offered by Carrère, *Théâtre de Thomas Kyd* ("Date and Sources"), who reviews criticism and, unpersuaded by parallel phrases and analogous dramatic techniques, looks to themes and ideas in *S&P* for parallels with Kyd's acknowledged work. He finds the quality of these inferior: "Nous ne saurions nous expliquer les éloges les plus flatteurs que notre auteur a reçus de ses contemporains, si la pièce de *Soliman et Perseda* lui était imputable." Perhaps an imitator is responsible. Like Carrère, Douglas Cole, *Suffering and Evil in the Plays of Christopher Marlowe* (1962), finds evidence slight, since poetic style and dramatic technique are unlike that of *SpT.*

Scholars have put forward other playwrights. J. M. Robertson, *An Introduction to the Study of the Shakespeare Canon* (1924), suggests Greene may have had a hand and provides supporting data. On the basis of some stylistic evidence, he also conjectures that Peele might possibly have contributed. Lambrechts, *"Edward III"* ("Date and Sources"), who believes Kyd wrote *S&P* and *Edward III*, cites Robertson's suggestion about Greene and says there are closer parallels between *S&P* and *Edward III* than between *S&P* and Greene's work. Greene is mentioned also by Benvenuto Cellini, ed., *Drammi Pre-Shakespeariani,* Collana di Letterature Moderne, vol. 4 (1958), who says the play somewhat recalls Greene, although there are recognizable traces of Kyd; and Oliphant, "Marlowe's Hand" (above), questions in passing whether Peele's hand is present in *S&P*. Ernest A. Gerrard, *Elizabethan Drama and Dramatists, 1583-1603* (1928), sees no distinctive parallels with Kyd or Peele's work, but emphasizes that the play has much in common with Lyly's.

Literary Connections

S&P has often been associated with Marlowe's plays, especially *Edward II*. In "The Marlowe Canon," *PMLA* 37 (1922): 367-417, C. F. Tucker Brooke points out five borrowings from *Edward II* in the anonymous work. Oliphant, "Marlowe's Hand" ("Attribution"), attempts to disentangle the complex relationship between *S&P*, *Edward II*, and *Arden of Feversham*, concluding that Marlowe's hand does not appear in *S&P*. Charlton and Waller use parallel passages from *S&P* and *Arden of Feversham* to help date *Edward II* in their edition of it ("Date and Sources"). They agree with Brooke that Kyd was the borrower and therefore think the manuscript of Marlowe's play had appeared by autumn 1591. In *Christopher Marlowe: A Biographical and Critical Study* (1940), Boas says *S&P* has a number of parallels with *Edward II* and cites two of the most important. The Stationers' Register entry for the anonymous play suggests that *S&P* was the later work, its author indebted to Marlowe. Bakeless, *Tragicall History* ("Date and Sources"), maintains that traces of Marlowe appear in *S&P*, and offers unconvincing parallels. Baldwin, *On the Literary Genetics* ("Date and Sources"), agrees that there are affinities between *S&P* and *Edward II*, but they are too undefined to be helpful in establishing a date for Marlowe's play. On the other hand, T. M. Pearce, "Evidence for Dating Marlowe's *Tragedy of Dido*," in *Studies in the English Renaissance Drama in Memory of Karl Julius Holzknecht*, ed. Josephine W. Bennett, Oscar Cargill, and Vernon Hall, Jr. (1959), pp. 231-47, emphasizing unpersuasive linguistic evidence and similarities between Iarbas in *The Tragedy of Dido* and Basilisco in *S&P*, uses parallels from the anonymous drama (and *SpT*) to place Marlowe's play in the late spring or early summer of 1591.

There are also some connections with Shakespeare. Possible recollections of *S&P* in the Henry IV plays are noted by E. E. Stoll, *Shakespeare Studies* (1927); R. P. Cowl, *Sources of the Text of "Henry the Fourth"* (1929); Boas, "The Soldier in Elizabethan and Later English Drama" ("Attribution"); A. R. Humphreys, ed., *The First Part of King Henry IV* (1960; Arden). Humphreys points out a parallel with *King John*, which had been remarked first by Theobald and is mentioned by modern editors of Shakespeare's play. E. A. J. Honigmann, ed., *King John* (1954; Arden), notes another parallel. Boas saw a connection with *King John* in *An Introduction to Tudor Drama*, "The Soldier in Elizabethan and Later English Drama" (both "Attribution"), and "Aspects of Shakespeare's Reading," in *Queen Elizabeth in Drama and Related Studies* (1950), pp. 56–71. The influence of the anonymous play's rhetorical style on *III Henry VI* is discussed by Andrew S. Cairncross in his Arden edition (1964); although *S&P* was not yet published, it may have been known to the dramatist as part of his company's repertory. (See also Wilson, ed., *King John* ["Date"], and Cairncross's "Pembroke's Men and Some Shakespearian Piracies," *SQ* 11 [1960]: 335–49, where recollections from *S&P*, among other plays, help show that four early Shakespearean quartos were composed by the same group of actor-reporters.) A reference to *S&P* in *The Merchant of Venice*, noted by Charles Knox Pooler in his 1905 Arden edition of the Shakespearean drama, is remarked also by later scholars such as Brooke in Baugh's *Literary History* (where he also saw the link with *King John*); John Russell Brown, ed., *The Merchant of Venice* (1955; Arden); and Freeman in *Thomas Kyd*. Daniel C. Boughner, "Don Armado and the *Commedia Dell' Arte*," *SP* 37 (1940): 201–24, briefly relates Armado in *Love's Labor's Lost* with Basilisco in *S&P*.

There are some miscellaneous links. Witherspoon, *Influence of Robert Garnier* ("Date and Sources"), makes comparisons between *S&P* and Garnier's work. In *Sidelights on Elizabethan Drama* (1924), H. Dugdale Sykes points out borrowings from *S&P* in the anonymous *Wily Beguiled* and suggests that the verse of the second play has been influenced by that of the first. Edwards, in his edition of *SpT*, suggests *S&P* may be the immediate source of the play within a play in *SpT*.

Miscellaneous

Different aspects of staging *S&P* are mentioned by William J. Lawrence in *Pre-Restoration Stage Studies* (1927), *The Physical Conditions of the Elizabethan Public Playhouse* (1927), and *Those Nut-Cracking Elizabethans* (1935); and by Delmar Solem, "Some Elizabethan Game Scenes," *ETJ* 6 (1954): 15–21. Alfred Hart, *Stolne and Surreptitious Copies* (1942), suggests that *S&P* be added to the repertory of Pembroke's Men, and Baldwin, *On the Literary Genetics* ("Date and Sources"), says the drama is built on almost the same casting pattern as that of *The True Tragedy of Richard III* and provides a tabulation for the casting patterns of both works. William Rendle's view that Ben Jonson acted in the play receives a negative response from Fredson T. Bowers, "Ben Jonson the Actor," *SP* 34 (1937): 392–406, and a dubious one from D. F. Rowan, "The 'Swan' Revisited," *RORD* 10 (1967): 33–48.

The nature and casting of comic roles is variously treated by Tiddy, *Mummers' Play* ("Attribution"), Olive Mary Busby, *Studies in the Development of the Fool in Elizabethan Drama* (1923), William J. Lawrence, *Speeding up Shakespeare* (1937), and G. Geoffrey Langsam, *Martial Books and Tudor Verse* (1951). Theodore Spencer, *Death and Elizabethan Tragedy* (1936), briefly discusses the figure of Death; Laurens Joseph Mills, *One Soul in Bodies Twain* (1937), describes the use of friendship material; and Lawrence Babb, *The Elizabethan Malady* (1951), notes instances of melancholy in the play.

Several critics deal with style, structure, and context. Acheson, *Shakespeare, Chapman* ("Date and Sources"), compares the verse forms in *S&P* with those in the rest of Kyd's work. Traudl Eichhorn, "Prosa und Vers im vorshakespeareschen Drama," *SJ* 84–86 (1948-50): 140–98, in addition to describing the adaptability of the prose in *S&P*, compares the prose and verse with that of *SpT*. Dieter Mehl, "Forms and Functions of the Play within a Play," *RenD* 8 (1965): 41–61, notes that the frame portion of *S&P* resembles that of the anonymous *The Rare Triumphs of Love and Fortune* (1582). A dramatic context is provided for *S&P* by F. L. Lucas, *Seneca and Elizabethan Tragedy* (1922), and Ola Elizabeth Winslow, *Low Comedy as a Structural Element in English Drama from the Beginnings to 1642* (1926), who remark the use of Senecan features.

Textual matters receive attention from Henrietta C. Bartlett, *Mr. William Shakespeare* (1922), W. W. Greg, "From Manuscript to Print," *RES* 13 (1937): 190–205, Wilfred T. Jewkes, *Act Division in Elizabethan and Jacobean Plays, 1583–1616* (1958), and Lambrechts, *"Edward III"* ("Date and Sources"). Ashley, *Authorship and Evidence* ("Date and Sources"), offers an aesthetic appreciation of the play. Both text and artistic value are treated in Freeman's excellent chapter in *Thomas Kyd*. The section on publication also covers stage history and the play's influence, and the portion on literary criticism is substantial, focusing ultimately on Kyd's successful handling of comic and tragic themes in a single work. Levin L. Schücking and Frederick S. Boas debate about a possible allusion by the editor of *SpT* to *S&P* in "The

Spanish Tragedy Additions," *TLS*, 19 June 1937, p. 464; 26 June 1937, p. 480; 17 July 1937, p. 528. In Carrère's book an appendix records bibliographical documents related to *S&P* and verbal parallels between the anonymous play and *SpT*. Boughner relates Milton's Harapha to Basilisco in his 1944 *ELH* article ("Attribution"), and Bevington, *Tudor Drama* ("Attribution"), compares the attitudes reflected in *S&P* and *Romeo and Juliet* towards dueling.

See Also

Atkins, J. W. H. *English Literary Criticism: The Renascence.* 1947.

Baumer, Franklin Le Van. "The Conception of Christendom in Renaissance England." *JHI* 6 (1945): 131–56.

Bowers, Fredson T. *Elizabethan Revenge Tragedy, 1587–1642.* 1940.

Cunningham, J. V. *Woe or Wonder: The Emotional Effect of Shakespearean Tragedy.* 1951.

Dawson, Giles E. "An Early List of Elizabethan Plays." *Library* 15 (1935): 445–56.

Doran, Madeleine. *Endeavors of Art: A Study of Form in Elizabethan Drama.* 1954.

Draper, John W. "Falstaff, 'A Fool and Jester.' " *MLQ* 7 (1946): 453–62 (appears as "Falstaff, a 'Knave-Fool,' " in *Stratford to Dogberry* [1961], pp. 189–99).

Hewett-Thayer, Harvey W. "Tieck and the Elizabethan Drama: His Marginalia." *JEGP* 34 (1935): 377–407.

Linton, Marion. "National Library of Scotland and Edinburgh University Library Copies of Plays in Greg's *Bibliography of the English Printed Drama.*" *SB* 15 (1962): 91–104.

McDiarmid, Matthew P. "The Influence of Robert Garnier on Some Elizabethan Tragedies." *EA* 11 (1958): 289–302.

Mustard, Wilfred P. "Notes on Thomas Kyd's Works." *PQ* 5 (1926): 85–86.

Parrott, Thomas Marc, and Robert Hamilton Ball. *A Short View of Elizabethan Drama.* 1943.

Rausch, Heinrich. *Der "Chorus" im englischen Drama bis 1642.* 1922.

Rubow, Paul V. *Shakespeare og hans samtidige* [*Shakespeare and His Contemporaries*]. 1948. [In Danish.]

Schoenbaum, Samuel. *Internal Evidence and Elizabethan Dramatic Authorship.* 1966.

Sharpe, Robert Boies. *The Real War of the Theaters.* 1935.

Wright, Louis B. "Animal Actors on the English Stage before 1642." *PMLA* 42 (1927): 656–69.

J. L.

Arden of Feversham, realistic tragedy (*1591;* 1592)

General

Editions of *Arden of Feversham* have appeared in English and three foreign languages. Several of the English ones are in anthologies: Felix E. Schelling, ed., *Typical Elizabethan Plays: By Contemporaries and Immediate Successors of Shakespeare* (1926); E. H. C. Oliphant, ed., *Shakespeare and His Fellow Dramatists,* vol. 1 (1929); Oliphant's *Elizabethan Dramatists Other than Shakespeare* (1931); Charles Read Baskervill, Virgil B. Heltzel, and Arthur H. Nethercot, eds., *Elizabethan and Stuart Plays* (1934); A. K. McIlwraith, ed., *Five Elizabethan Tragedies* (1938); John Gassner and William Green, eds., *Elizabethan Drama* (1967); Keith Sturgess, ed., *Three Elizabethan Domestic Tragedies* (1969). *Arden* is found as well in *Minor Elizabethan Drama,* vol. 1, a collection introduced by Ashley Thorndike and reprinted often since 1910 with minor changes. With the assistance of D. Nichol Smith, Hugh Macdonald edited the play for the Malone Society (1947, for 1940). This edition provides a concise history of early editions. The various quartos have been reproduced on microprint and microfilm; see *National Union Catalogue.*

Arden has been translated into French by Pierre Messiaen in *Théâtre anglais: moyen âge et XVI*ᵉ *siècle* (1948); by Félix Carrère (1950); and by Laurette Brunius and Loleh Bellon (1957). A translation of two scenes by André Gide in *Le théâtre élizabéthain* (a special issue of *CS* 10 [1933]: 107-17, reprinted with additions 1940, pp. 137-51), receives the approval of Floris Delattre, "Le théâtre élizabéthain," *RAA* 11 (1934): 385-409. Several French scholars mention H.-R. Lenormand's translation for a performance at the Théâtre Montparnasse in 1938. Other foreign editions are Diego Angeli's in *Opere attribuite a Shakespeare,* vol. 1 (1934); G. Baldini's in *Teatro elisabettiano* (1948; ed. Mario Praz); and G. Somlyó's in *Angol reneszánsz drámák,* vol. 1 (1961; ed. Miklós J. Szenczi).

Carrère's edition, which should be read in conjunction with his *Théâtre de Thomas Kyd* (1951), has an extensive introduction. It provides the background of the Arden of Feversham story, compares the playwright's treatment with Holinshed's, and interprets the changes. A review of early editions precedes the weak argument which dates the play at the end of 1591 or beginning of 1592. After summarizing and evaluating attribution scholarship for Shakespeare and Marlowe, Carrère makes a lengthy case for Kyd's authorship based on biographical evidence, and a comparison of themes and style with those of *The Spanish Tragedy, Cornelia,* and a pamphlet called *The Murder of John Brewen* (which he takes to be Kyd's; see Arthur Freeman, *Thomas Kyd: Facts and Problems* [1967], who holds the pamphlet is not part of the Kyd canon). Brunius and Bellon survey the attribution problem, remark the use of Holinshed, describe the play as "drame bourgeois," discuss characterization and the structure of the action, and mention some French productions.

Lionel Cust's *"Arden of Feversham," Archaeologia Cantiana* 34 (1920): 101-38, was reprinted as a small pamphlet with the same title (1920). It gives an extensive history of the actual Feversham tragedy; compares the dramatist's version with Holinshed's; and concludes on the basis of biographies, some local history, and literary data that Marlowe and Shakespeare wrote *Arden* for performances in Kent in the early 1590s (Shakespeare might even have acted in it).

Attribution*

Although the authorship of *Arden* has received a great deal of attention, it remains undetermined. The major claimants are Kyd, Marlowe, and Shakespeare.

C. F. Tucker Brooke, "The Marlowe Canon," *PMLA* 37 (1922): 367-417, is unpersuaded by E. H. C. Oliphant's arguments (in a letter) that Marlowe and Kyd collaborated; Charles Crawford's earlier claims and other stylistic evidence incline him to think Kyd probably wrote *Arden* imitating Marlowe. Like Brooke, Felix E. Schelling, *Elizabethan Playwrights* (1925), accepts Crawford's assignment; and Ernest A. Gerrard, *Elizabethan Drama and Dramatists, 1583-1603* (1928), finds Kyd's hand or influence in style and content. Referring to the claims of Crawford and Brooke, H. B. Charlton and R. D. Waller, eds., *Edward II* (1933; rev. F. N. Lees, 1955), think Kyd probably borrowed from Marlowe's play in writing *Arden.* After summarizing Crawford's arguments, William Wells, "Thomas Kyd and the Chronicle-History," *N&Q* 178 (1940): 218-24, 238-43, confirms the assignment and accounts for echoes from *Edward II* and *The Massacre at Paris* by finding Kyd's hand in them as well. (See also his "The Authorship of *King Leir," N&Q* 177 [1939] : 434-38.)

In assessing Kyd's contribution to *Romeo and Juliet,* J. M. Robertson, *The Shakespeare Canon,* pt. 3 (1925), assumes his responsi-

* Unless otherwise noted, short-title references in subsequent sections are to works first cited in this section.

bility for the anonymous work. T. S. Eliot, "Seneca in Elizabethan Translation," in *Seneca His Tenne Tragedies* (1927), disagrees with Boas and accepts the claims for Kyd. Sykes's proof and the legal references in *Arden* suggest Kyd to Percy Allen, *Shakespeare, Jonson, and Wilkins as Borrowers* (1928), who believes Shakespeare and Marlowe probably contributed as well. Philip Henderson, *And Morning in His Eyes* (1937), acknowledging Marlowe and Shakespeare attributions, concludes that the style most resembles Kyd's.

Marion Grubb at one point assumes Kyd's authorship ("Kyd's Borrowing from Garnier's *Bradamante*," *MLN* 50 [1935] : 169-71) and at another point is less certain ("A Brace of Villains," *MLN* 50 [1935] : 168-69). Some see Kyd as a possible or probable choice: Kenneth Muir, "The Chronology of Marlowe's Plays," *PLPLS-LHS* 5 (1938-43): 345-56; Alan S. Downer, *The British Drama* (1950); A. P. Rossiter, *English Drama from Early Times to the Elizabethans* (1950); Willard Farnham, *The Medieval Heritage of Elizabethan Tragedy* (1936); W. Bridges-Adams, *The Irresistible Theatre*, vol. 1 (1957); Wilfred T. Jewkes, *Act Division in Elizabethan and Jacobean Plays, 1583-1616* (1958); José Axelrad and Michèle Willems, *Shakespeare et le théâtre élizabéthain* (1964).

Philip Edwards is doubtful about Kyd's authorship in both his Revels edition of *The Spanish Tragedy* (1959) and *Thomas Kyd and Early Elizabethan Tragedy* (1966). The later study recognizes certain affinities with the dramatist's work but misses "the Seneca-Garnier cast of *The Spanish Tragedy*" and realizes that the correspondences may be reminiscences. If Boas's ascription of *The Murder of John Brewen* had been confirmed, the *Arden* assignment would have been less dubious. Negative response comes from F. W. Bateson, in "Correspondence," *Scrutiny* 4 (1935): 181-85 (rpt. as "A Comment" in *The Importance of Scrutiny*, ed. Eric Bentley [1948], pp. 16-20), who objects that the attribution is purely speculative. Zdeněk Stříbrný, *Shakespearovi předchůdci* [Shakespeare's Predecessors], Acta Universitatis Carolinae: Philologica-Monographia, vol. 7 (1965; English summary, pp. 118-32), thinks stylistic differences from Kyd's other works outweigh thematic similarities. Freeman, *Thomas Kyd* ("General"), is unconvinced by Crawford and Carrère; he points out an echo of *The Spanish Tragedy* in *Arden*, but "it requires considerable suspension of intelligence to argue this as evidence for Kyd's authorship . . . ."

Marlowe is generally viewed as a collaborator rather than sole author. J. M. Robertson, *An Introduction to the Study of the Shakespeare*

Canon (1924), persuaded by Crawford and Fleay that Kyd had a major part (see above), finds in addition hints of Greene and whole Marlovian passages. He feels ascription to Shakespeare is hazardous. (See also his *Marlowe: A Conspectus* [1931].) E. H. C. Oliphant, "Marlowe's Hand in *Arden of Feversham*: A Problem for Critics," *New Criterion* 4 (1926): 76–93, is concerned with the play's relation to *Edward II* and Marlowe's other plays, the anonymous *Soliman and Perseda,* and *King Leir*. After reviewing earlier attribution scholarship, he employs parallels between *Arden* and Marlowe's dramas to decide whether the known playwright was borrowing from himself or someone else. It is more likely that *Arden* was in part his, with at least two other writers closely collaborating, possibly Kyd and Rowley.

Frederick S. Boas reviews ascription in *Christopher Marlowe: A Biographical and Critical Study* (1940), where he dispenses with the Shakespeare assignment, views the claim for Kyd as reasonable, and makes a case for Marlowe on the basis of writing habits, correspondences with his plays, and style. Moreover, "if *Arden* is anonymous in all its editions, so is *Tamburlaine*." Since no external evidence corroborates this theory, however, it is still possible an unknown artist was responsible. Oliphant's evidence and various comparisons with Marlowe's work lead John Bakeless, *The Tragicall History of Christopher Marlowe,* vol. 2 (1942), to conclude: "There is something of him [Marlowe] in the play, whether it is stray samples of his handiwork, deliberate thefts, or unconscious echoes." After a brief discussion of previous criticism, Gabriele Baldini, "Un apocrifo shakesperiano: *Arden of Feversham,*" *ASNSP* 18 (1949): 93–107, is doubtful about the Kyd assignment, more positive about Marlowe.

A. W. Titherley, *Shakespeare's Identity* (1952), pairs *Arden* with *Thomas Lord Cromwell* as plays cast aside by Shakespeare (who he thinks is actually William Stanley, sixth Earl of Derby) because they did not warrant rewriting. Clara Longworth, Comptesse de Chambrun, *Shakespeare: A Portrait Restored* (1957; French ed. 1947), unearths two clues "that Shakespeare was no stranger to the play." Shakespeare's connection with *Arden* is disputed by James Agate in a 1925 review reprinted in *Brief Chronicles* (1943), where he calls Swinburne's case for the playwright "uncritical rodomontade," and by Max J. Wolff, "Zu *Arden von Feversham,*" *NS* 35 (1927): 424–27. W. W. Greg, "Shakespeare and *Arden of Feversham,*" *RES* 21 (1945): 134–36, throws new light on this ascription. Though the original Shakespeare assignment is held to be Edward Jacob's (a publisher of the play), actually it dates from a catalogue added in 1656 to an edition of *The Old Law* that Edward Archer printed; *Rich. Bernard* in the catalogue is a compositor's error for Shakespeare. But Archer's attributions are generally untrustworthy and Greg's own view "neither here nor there." (See also Greg's "Authorship Attributions in the Early Play-Lists, 1656–1671," *Edinburgh Bibliographical Society Transactions* 2 [1938–45]: 303–29.) The confusion of the prose and verse prevents Traudl Eichhorn, "Prosa und Vers im vorshakespeareschen Drama," *SJ* 84–86 (1948–50): 140–98, from accepting Ottomar Petersen's opinion that Shakespeare was one of *Arden*'s revisers. Kenneth Muir, *Shakespeare as Collaborator* (1960), finds no correspondences in style or content with Shakespeare's known dramas.

The anonymous "Notes on Sales. *Arden of Feversham*," *TLS*, 2 August 1923, p. 524, remarks the Kyd assignment and discovers a new clue in the sale catalogue (1792) of Dr. John Monro's library which recorded "Cloy's Tragedy of Arden of Feversham, 1633." Why was the play attributed to "Cloy"? It is unlikely that he was the former owner of Monro's copy. (See V. Scholderer, "*Arden of Feversham*," *TLS*, 1 February 1936, p. 96, who thinks "Cloy" was the earlier owner and the name an inaccurate transcription of "Wm. Oldys" [the eighteenth-century antiquary].) William J. Lawrence, "The Authorship of *Arden of Feversham*," *TLS*, 28 June 1934, p. 460, offers evidence that there existed an itinerant entertainer called Bartholomew Cloys in the early Caroline period, but there might have been other Cloys. (This article reminds Charles L. Stainer, "*Arden of Feversham*," *TLS*, 12 July 1934, p. 492, of the John Clay mocked in Jonson's *A Tale of a Tub*.) E. H. C. Oliphant, "*Arden of Feversham*," *TLS*, 18 Jan. 1936, p. 55, believes a Cloy existed who might or might not have contributed to *Arden*.

H. W. Crundell, "*Arden of Feversham*," *N&Q* 166 (1934): 456–58, makes a case for Munday's connection with the play on grounds of style, borrowings, and genre. Dorothy and Charlton Ogburn, *This Star of England* (1952), identify the first version as Lord Oxford's "beyond the possibility of refutation." In a 1954 review of *Arden* reprinted in *Curtains* (1961), Kenneth Tynan rules Shakespeare out, considers Kyd, and leaves the question open with, "All in all, I think George [Wilkins] did it." Others who have taken this sensible position include Peter Alexander, *Shakespeare's "Henry VI" and "Richard III"* (1929), who finds the Kyd ascription doubtful and maintains that a decision about Marlowe's authorship must be made before his hand in *II Henry VI* and *III Henry VI* can be demonstrated. Felix Sper, "The Germ of the Domestic Drama," *Poet Lore* 40 (1929): 544–51, agrees with Oliphant that the play is collaborative but does not assign it to specific dramatists. E. K. Chambers, *William Shakespeare*, vol. 1 (1930), says the issue is unsettled; Frederick S. Boas, *An Introduction to Tudor Drama* (1933), that *Arden* is probably by someone imitating Kyd. In *"Arden de Feversham,"* in *Le théâtre élizabéthain* (special issue of *CS* 10 [1933]: 154–61, rpt. with additions 1940, pp. 197–207, and in a translation by Max Bluestone in *Shakespeare's Contemporaries*, ed. Max Bluestone and Norman Rabkin [1961], pp. 149–56), Louis Gillet thinks an unknown contemporary of Shakespeare's might have been responsible, but Shakespeare himself clearly was not. Rupert Taylor, "A Tentative Chronology of Marlowe's and Some Other Elizabethan Plays," *PMLA* 51 (1936): 643–88, remarks possible identity of authorship with *Soliman and Perseda*. In an analysis of *Arden*'s imagery and the ascription problem, Marion Bodwell Smith, *Marlowe's Imagery and the Marlowe Canon* (1940), finds correspondences of individual images and entire passages stronger with Shakespeare's work than with Marlowe's. She tends to believe a third playwright was influenced by them.

Date and Sources

The date issue has attracted little interest. Wolff, *"Arden von Feversham,"* accepts the suggestion that *Arden* was produced about 1590. Charlton and Waller, *Edward II*, and Henderson, *And Morning in His Eyes*, using *Arden* to help place *Edward II* chronologically, fix the anonymous work after Marlowe's, produced about the autumn of 1591. On the other hand, Muir, "The Chronology of Marlowe's Plays," does not find it possible to locate the anonymous play before *Edward II*. Robert Boies Sharpe, *The Real War of the Theaters* (1935), says before April 3, 1592 (Stationers' Register entry). Various literary correspondences suggest early 1591 to Taylor, "A Tentative Chronology," whereas George Fullmer Reynolds, *The Staging of Elizabethan Plays at the Red Bull Theater, 1605–1625* (1940), is satisfied with a range of 1586–92. Baldini, "Un' apocrifo shakesperiano," sees no reason to doubt the usual dating just before publication; Titherley, *Shakespeare's Identity*, arbitrarily says 1581; T. W. Baldwin, *On the Literary Genetics of Shakspere's Plays, 1592–1594* (1959), is dubious about Fleay's assignment before the anonymous *True Tragedy of Richard III*. Finding a strange parallel between *Arden* and the fifth book of *The Fairie Queene*, Grubb, "A Brace of Villains," thinks the anonymous passage is later.

It is generally agreed that Holinshed is the major source. Useful comparisons of the play with the chronicle appear in Willard Thorp, *The Triumph of Realism in Elizabethan Drama, 1558-1612* (1928), Henry Hitch Adams, *English Domestic or, Homiletic Tragedy, 1575-1642* (1943), Max Bluestone, "The Imagery of Tragic Melodrama in *Arden of Feversham*," *DramS* 5 (1966): 171-81, and items above by Gillet and Baldini.

Literary Connections and Dramatic Context

Many correspondences have been discovered between *Arden* and the plays of Marlowe and Shakespeare. Brooke's 1922 *PMLA* study mentions borrowings from *Edward II* as well as parallels in other Marlowe plays. In his 1926 *New Criterion* article, Oliphant, "Marlowe's Hand," recognizes connections not only with Marlowe's plays but also with Rowley's *When You See Me, You Know Me,* the anonymous *Soliman and Perseda,* and *King Leir.* (See also Wells, "The Authorship of *King Leir,*" who cites parallels between *Arden* and *King Leir* in trying to determine the second play's authorship.) Alexander, *Shakespeare's "Henry VI,"* discussing the ascription of *II Henry VI* and *III Henry VI* to Marlowe, raises questions about the many correspondences between *Arden* and *Edward II.* Parallel passages from both *Arden* and *Soliman and Perseda* are offered as evidence in dating *Edward II* by Charlton and Waller in their edition. Similarly, links with *Arden* lead Henderson, *And Morning in His Eyes,* to place *Edward II* in the autumn, 1591, and Muir in his *PLPLS-LHS* article, with additional evidence from *Soliman and Perseda,* to make the *terminus ad quem* early 1592. Boas, *Christopher Marlowe,* and Bakeless, *Tragicall History,* cite Marlovian correspondences to determine the playwright's connection with *Arden* (see above, "Attribution"). Links between *Arden* and *Edward II, The Massacre at Paris* and *The Spanish Tragedy* support Wells's view in his 1940 *N&Q* article that Kyd had a hand in all four plays. Baldwin, *On the Literary Genetics* ("Date"), uses the relation between *Arden* (among other plays) and *Edward II* to locate the second work chronologically; he thinks Marlowe borrowed from *Arden* in *The Massacre at Paris* and possibly in *Edward II.*

Robertson, *The Shakespeare Canon,* pt. 2 (1923), devises a complex connection between *Arden, The Jew of Malta,* and *The Comedy of Errors* which suggests that Shakespeare's play preceded the unacknowledged one and belonged to Marlowe. (See also his *Marlowe: A Conspectus.*) In *Sources of the Text of "Henry the Fourth"* (1929),

R. P. Cowl points out borrowings from *Arden.* Chambers, *William Shakespeare,* uses a reminiscence of *The Comedy of Errors* in *Arden* to assist in dating the former before 1593 (cf. Robertson, above). Crundell's 1934 *N&Q* note examines the resemblances between *Arden,* III.iii, and *Richard III,* I.iv. Smith, *Marlowe's Imagery,* finds many correspondences with Shakespearean images, whereas Karl P. Wentersdorf, "The 'Fence of Trouble' Crux in *Arden of Faversham,*" *N&Q* 4 (1957): 160-61, focuses on a motif which also appears in Shakespeare's plays.

Parallels with a number of works suggest to both Alfred Hart, *Stolne and Surreptitious Copies* (1942), and A. S. Cairncross, "Pembroke's Men and Some Shakespearian Piracies," *SQ* 11 (1960): 335-49, that *Arden* was part of the Pembroke repertory. (Hart includes a table with a comparison of the vocabularies in *Arden* and *The Spanish Tragedy.*) Grubb's two 1935 *MLN* notices remark possible connections with Garnier's *Cornélie* and Spenser's works, especially *The Fairie Queene.* Freeman, *Thomas Kyd* ("General"), notes an echo of *The Spanish Tragedy* in *Arden.* Wolff, *"Arden von Feversham,"* stresses the influence of Seneca on the anonymous playwright, especially his *Agamemnon,* while Eliot, "Seneca in Elizabethan Translation," thinks *Arden* is barely indebted to the classical dramatist, and Mario Praz, *The Flaming Heart* (1958), finds no foreign or classical influence at all.

Arden has been discussed by various scholars in the context of domestic or bourgeois tragedy: see, for example, Charles J. Sisson, *Le goût public et le théâtre élisabéthain jusqu'à la mort de Shakespeare* (1922), Sper, "Germ of the Domestic Drama," and Frederick T. Wood, "The Beginnings and Significance of Sentimental Comedy," *Anglia* 55 (1931): 368-92. Hugh Sykes Davies, *Realism in the Drama* (1933), compares *Arden* with Heywood's work in the genre. The more extensive treatments of the genre include Wolff's *"Arden von Feversham"* and Adams's *English Domestic or, Homiletic Tragedy* ("Date"), Wolff qualifies the term "bürgerlich Tragödie" by stressing the relation of *Arden* to classical tragedy. Though the characters are not of high rank, their transgressions are great (comparable to those in Seneca's *Agamemnon*), and the ancient concept of fate structures events. Adams groups *Arden* with "sixteenth-century murder plays" strongly reminiscent of the contemporary bloody but moral pamphlets. Similarly, the play combines thrills and didacticism, and reflects popular theology.

Otelia Cromwell, *Thomas Heywood: A Study in the Elizabethan*

Drama of Everyday Life (1928); Praz (above), Eliot, Tynan, Farnham ("Attribution"), and Sharpe ("Date and Sources") are particularly interested in *Arden* as a murder play. (In this connection, Farnham compares this anonymous play with *A Warning for Faire Women* and Kyd's *Spanish Tragedy*.) Bluestone, "The Imagery of Tragic Melodrama" ("Date and Sources"), views *Arden* as a tragic melodrama with conflicts of characters and sensibilities.

Stage History and Text

Whereas Hart and Cairncross assigned *Arden* to Pembroke's company (see above, "Literary Connections"), Baldwin, *On the Literary Genetics* ("Date and Sources"), considers Fleay's claim for the Queen's Men and decides to draw no conclusions about ownership. Sharpe, *The Real War* ("Date and Sources"), thinks there may have been a revival at the very end of the sixteenth century. Late nineteenth- and early twentieth-century performances of the play are mentioned in Harold Child, "Revivals of English Dramatic Works, 1919–1925," *RES* 2 (1926): 177–88, and "Revivals of English Dramatic Works, 1901–1918, 1926," *RES* 3 (1927): 169–85; Agnes Mure Mackenzie, *The Playgoer's Handbook to the English Renaissance Drama* (1927); Robert Speaight, *William Poel and the Elizabethan Revival* (1954); Paul Blanchart, "Le théâtre contemporain et les élisabéthains," *EA* 13 (1960): 145–58; Jerome Hanratty, "School Plays in Production: *Arden of Feversham*," *Use of English* 11 (1960): 176–80 (a description of a boys' school production); and Jean Jacquot, "Théâtre et poésie: Gaston Baty et les élisabéthains," *EA* 13 (1960): 205–15, and in Agate, Allen, Reynolds, and Tynan (all above), and Chapman ("Miscellaneous").

To Hart, *Stolne and Surreptitious Copies* ("Literary Connections"), the poorness of the text suggests a report made by actors. Eichhorn, "Prosa und Vers," is also struck by the obscure arrangement of the copy, and Baldini, "Un apocrifo shakesperiano," thinks the 1592 edition was based on actors' copy. Jewkes, *Act Division,* however, finds no indication that the text was readied for performance, and concludes that authorial copy was probably used.

The circumstances surrounding Abel Jeffes's pirated edition of *Arden* are explored by W. W. Greg in *"The Spanish Tragedy*—A Leading Case?" *Library* 6 (1925): 47–56, and, at greater length, in his edition of *The Spanish Tragedy* for the Malone Society (1949, for 1948), with D. Nichol Smith. The anonymous 1923 *TLS* article discusses in some detail the history of the first three editions. In "The Southouse Text of

Arden of Feversham," *Library* 5 (1950): 113-29, J. M. Nosworthy describes in detail an eighteenth-century manuscript of the play. T. S. R. Boase, "Illustrations of Shakespeare's Plays in the Seventeenth and Eighteenth Centuries," *JWCI* 10 (1947): 83-108, reproduces and describes a woodcut illustrating the 1633 quarto of *Arden*.

Miscellaneous

Many critics have analyzed *Arden* in terms of its themes, characterization, and aesthetic value. Gillet's longer study, *Arden de Feversham*, emphasizes the starkness, realism, and modernity of the play, which deals with human passion accurately and sensitively. This interpretation receives support from a thorough analysis of the three central figures. *Arden*'s "idée tragique" is expressed in both the drama's worldly and spiritual levels. The message of salvation gives direction to the strivings of our souls. Adams's *English Domestic or, Homiletic Tragedy* ("Date and Sources") exegesis, also taking into account the drama's severe realism, focuses upon its moral content. Arden's characterization constantly brings to mind the incessant workings of Providence: "Throughout the action, the fortunes of Arden correspond to his state of grace." Baldini, "Un apocrifo shakesperiano," especially interested in the work as realistic and poetic drama, provides a substantial psychological study of the major characters and a cursory one of the rest. (At points he takes issue with Aurelio Zanco, *Considerazioni sull' "Arden of Feversham"* in *Rivista Italiana del Teatro*, no. 3 [1943]; rpt. in *Shakespeare in Russia* [1945].) Madeleine Doran, *Endeavors of Art: A Study of Form in Elizabethan Drama* (1954), describes the effect of the "moralistic element" on the play's structure and characterization; she is very briefly concerned with the influence of the Renaissance stage.

Impressed with the play's social and economic implications, Raymond Chapman, "*Arden of Faversham*: Its Interest Today," *English* 11 (1956): 15-17, looks closely at Arden, Mosbie, Black Will, and Shakebag as products of Elizabethan preoccupations with social change; he links the play with both the Middle Ages and the present time. Sarah Youngblood, "Theme and Imagery in *Arden of Feversham*," *SEL* 3 (1963): 207-18, explains why *Arden* is tragic not only in a medieval or early Renaissance context, but also in a modern sense. Distorted and perverted images from religion and nature underscore the central theme of moral degeneration, emphasize the almost complete absence of spiritual growth in the play, and indicate that the dramatist was a careful craftsman. With reference to Youngblood's interpretation, Bluestone, "The Imagery of Tragic Melodrama" ("Date and Sources"), also discusses the nature of the play's tragedy and images. *Arden's* strength derives from its characters' inner struggles and from the richness of its language. (See also Hardin Craig, *The Enchanted Glass* [1936].) In *Thomas Kyd,* Edwards reviews the aesthetic achievement of the play.

Mackenzie, *Playgoer's Handbook* ("Stage History"), describes the function of the verse; Gerrard, *Elizabethan Drama,* seems affronted by *Arden's* "oratorical bombast"; Davies, *Realism in the Drama* ("Literary Connections"), is impressed by the nature of the poetry; Eichhorn, "Prosa und Vers," remarks the confusion of verse and prose in the text. Helen Morris, *Elizabethan Literature* (1958), finds bits of real poetry within the generally unexciting blank verse. Bain Tate Stewart, "The Misunderstood Dreams in the Plays of Shakespeare and His Contemporaries," in *Essays in Honor of Walter Clyde Curry,* VUSH, vol. 2 (1954), pp. 197–206, explicates Arden's dream about his own death. Allegorical features are pointed out by Henri Fluchère, *Shakespeare and the Elizabethans* (U.S. ed. 1956; English ed. 1953; French ed. 1948); a jibe at Puritans, by Aaron Michael Myers, *Representation and Misrepresentation of the Puritan in Elizabethan Drama* (1931). Laurens Joseph Mills, *One Soul in Bodies Twain* (1937), describes Francklin against a background of friendship conventions. The function of the backgammon game is mentioned by Joseph T. McCullen, Jr., "The Use of Parlor and Tavern Games in Elizabethan and Early Stuart Drama," *MLQ* 14 (1953): 7–14, and Delmar Solem, "Some Elizabethan Game Scenes," *ETJ* 6 (1954): 15–21. Solem is also concerned briefly with staging, as William J. Lawrence is in *Pre-Restoration Stage Studies* (1927). (See also Doran and Bluestone [both above].) Reynolds, *The Staging of Elizabethan Plays* ("Date and Sources"), to make a point about the use of doors in Red Bull plays, offers a thorough discussion of *Arden's* staging with particular attention to this device.

See Also

Ashley, Leonard R. N. *Authorship and Evidence.* 1968.

Babb, Lawrence. *The Elizabethan Malady.* 1951.

Baker, Howard. *Induction to Tragedy.* 1939.

Bartlett, Henrietta C. *Mr. William Shakespeare.* 1922.

Bevington, David. *Tudor Drama and Politics.* 1968.

Blayney, Glenn H. *"Arden of Feversham—An Early Reference." N&Q* 2 (1955): 336.

Boas, F. *An Introduction to Tudor Drama.* 1933.

Boughner, Daniel C. *The Braggart in Renaissance Comedy.* 1954.

———. "Vice, Braggart, and Falstaff." *Anglia* 72 (1954): 35–61.

Bowers, Fredson. "The Audience and the Poisoners of Elizabethan Tragedy." *JEGP* 36 (1937): 491–504.

Bradbrook, M. C. *The Growth and Structure of Elizabethan Comedy.* 1955.

Brewster, Paul G. "Games and Sports in Sixteenth- and Seventeenth-Century English Literature." *WF* 6 (1947): 143–56.

Cairncross, Andrew S., ed. *The Second Part of King Henry VI.* 1957; Arden.

Catalogue of the Pierpont Morgan Library Exhibition on English Drama from the Mid-Sixteenth to the Later Eighteenth Century. 1946.

Cawley, A. C. *English Domestic Drama: "A Yorkshire Tragedy."* 1966.

Cellini, Benvenuto, ed. *Drammi Pre-Shakespeariani.* Collana di Letterature Moderne, vol. 4 (1958).

Clark, Arthur Melville. *Thomas Heywood: Playwright and Miscellanist.* 1931.

Cornelius, Roberta D. "Mosbie's 'Stary Gaile.'" *PQ* 9 (1930): 70–72; 394–96. [Textual note.]

Cunningham, J. V. *Woe or Wonder: The Emotional Effect of Shakespearean Tragedy.* 1951.

Dawson, Giles E. "An Early List of Elizabethan Plays." *Library* 15 (1935): 445–56.

De Reul, Paul. *Présentation du théâtre jacobéen de Marston à Beaumont et Fletcher (1600–1625).* 1943.

Dickey, Franklin. "The Old Man at Work: Forgeries in the Stationers' Registers." *SQ* 11 (1960): 39–47.

Evans, B. Ifor. *A Short History of English Drama.* 1948.

Flasdieck, Hermann M. "Zur Datierung von Marlowes *Faust* (Schluss)." *Englische Studien* 45 (1930): 1–25.

Foakes, R. A., ed. *The Comedy of Errors.* 1962; Arden.

Fogel, Ephim G. "Electronic Computers and Elizabethan Texts." *SB* 15 (1962): 15–31.

Greg, W. W. "*Arden of Feversham.*" *TLS*, 24 Jan. 1924, p. 53. [Textual note.]

Grivelet, Michel. *Thomas Heywood et le drame domestique élizabéthain.* 1957.

Hastings, William T. "The Richest Shakespeare Collection." *BBr* 19 (1963): 113–42.

Hewett-Thayer, Harvey W. "Tieck and the Elizabethan Drama: His Marginalia." *JEGP* 34 (1935): 377–407.

Hibbard, G. R. "The Tragedies of Thomas Middleton and the Decadence of the Drama." *RMS* 1 (1957): 35–64.

Holzknecht, Karl J. *Outlines of Tudor and Stuart Plays, 1497–1642.* 1947.

Hosley, Richard. "The Discovery-Space in Shakespeare's Globe." *SSh* 12 (1959): 35–46.

Jackson, Macd. P. "An Emendation to *Arden of Feversham.*" *N&Q* 10 (1963): 410.

Kendall, Lyle H., Jr. "Shakespeare Collections, Quartos, Source and Allusion Books in the W. L. Lewis Collection." In *Shakespeare 1964,* ed. Jim W. Corder (1965), pp. 113–77.

Krzyzanowski, J. "Some Conjectural Remarks on Elizabethan Dramatists." *N&Q* 192 (1947): 276–77.

Legouis, Pierre. "The Epistolary Past in English." *N&Q* 198 (1953): 111-12.

Lenormand, H.-R. "Le théâtre d' aujourd'hui et les élizabéthains." In *Le théâtre élizabéthain* (1940), pp. 109-18. [Special issue of *CS* 10 (1933): 82-90.]

Linton, Marion. "National Library of Scotland and Edinburgh University Library Copies of Plays in Greg's *Bibliography of the English Printed Drama.*" *SB* 15 (1962): 91-104.

Lucas, F. L. *Tragedy: Serious Drama in Relation to Aristotle's Poetics.* 1927.

Macdonald, J. F. "The Use of Prose in English Drama before Shakespeare." *UTQ* 2 (1933): 465-81.

McManaway, James G. "A Reading in *King Lear.*" *N&Q* 14 (1967): 139.

Mantaigne, André. "*Arden de Feversham,* adapté par M. H. R. Lenormand." *Le Mois* 11 (1938): 226-28.

Matthews, Honor. *Character and Symbol in Shakespeare's Plays.* 1962.

Nicoll, Allardyce. *British Drama.* 5th ed. 1962.

———. " 'Tragical-Comical-Historical-Pastoral': Elizabethan Dramatic Nomenclature." *BJRL* 43 (1960): 70-87.

Niemeyer, P. *Das bürgerliche Drama in England im Zeitalter Shakespeares.* 1930.

O'Connor, William Van. *Climates of Tragedy.* 1943.

Parks, Edd Winfield. "Simms's Edition of the Shakespeare Apocrypha." In *Studies in Shakespeare,* ed. Arthur D. Matthews and Clark M. Emery (1953), pp. 30-39.

Rubow, Paul V. *Shakespeare og hans samtidige* [Shakespeare and His Contemporaries]. 1948. [In Danish.]

Simpson, F. D. "*Arden of Feversham.*" *TLS,* 17 Jan. 1924, p. 40. [Textual note.]

Tannenbaum, Samuel A. "Mosbie's 'Stary Gaile' Again." *PQ* 9 (1930): 213-15. [Textual note.]

Utz, Hans. *Das Bedeutungsfeld 'Leid' in der englische Tragödie vor Shakespeare.* Schweizer Anglistische Arbeiten, no. 54 (1963).

Wadsworth, Frank Whittemore. "*The White Devil,* An Historical and Critical Study." *DA* 15 (1955): 832-33.

Wilson, Edward M. "Family Honour in the Plays of Shakespeare's Predecessors and Contemporaries." *E&S* 6 (1953): 19-40.

J. L.

The Life and Death of Jack Straw, history (*1591;* 1593)

Edition and Attribution

The only recent edition of *Jack Straw* is by Kenneth Muir and F. P. Wilson for the Malone Society (1957). In their introduction, the editors deal briefly with date, authorship, text, and editions, concluding that nothing is known about the date of composition or authorship, and that the play, though short, was padded by the way it was printed.

Various critics have ascribed *Jack Straw* to Peele, J. M. Robertson, in *The Shakespeare Canon,* pt. 2 (1923), and *An Introduction to the Study of the Shakespeare Canon* (1924), agrees with Fleay that the blank verse portions of the play are definitely Peele's, and in the latter book supports this conclusion with verbal parallels. H. Dugdale Sykes is so convinced that Peele's authorship has been established (by the earlier work of Robertson and H. C. Hart) that he uses parallels with *Jack Straw* to establish Peele's part in *Alphonsus Emperor of Germany* (*Sidelights on Elizabethan Drama* [1924]) and *A Knack to Know a Knave* ("The Authorship of *A Knack to Know a Knave*," *N&Q* 146 [1924] : 389-91). Others are to different degrees sceptical. In an article that questions the general validity of verbal tests as proof of authorship, Arthur M. Sampley, " 'Verbal Tests' for Peele's Plays," *SP* 30 (1933): 473-96, casts doubt upon the Peele attributions of Robertson and Sykes. J. C. Maxwell, "Peele and Shakespeare: A Stylometric Test," *JEGP* 49 (1950): 557-61, offers what he admits is ragged and inconclusive grammatical evidence which seems to suggest Peele did not contribute to the play. Briefly comparing *The Battle of Alcazar* and *Jack Straw*, Willard Farnham, *The Medieval Heritage of Elizabethan Tragedy* (1936), remarks that if the hand of Peele really does appear in the anonymous drama, it deals with historical material in a much less sophisticated way than it had in the acknowledged work. Irving Ribner, *The English History Play in the Age of Shakespeare* (1957; rev. ed. 1965), feels the question of authorship is still open. Similarly, Leonard R. N. Ashley, *Authorship and Evidence* (1968), who briefly summarizes the attribution evidence which gives the drama completely or partly to Peele, concludes: "I cannot think that there will be many who will find the arguments overwhelmingly conclusive." Muir and Wilson, in their edition, unconvinced by the cases made for Peele, find no resemblances between *Jack Straw* and Peele's known works; and Wolfgang Clemen, *English Tragedy before Shakespeare* (trans. T. S. Dorsch, 1961; German ed. 1955), observes that the style of the anonymous drama makes the ascription untenable. Finally, in an article which ignores the Peele attribution, Mary Grace Muse Adkins, "A Variant of a Familiar Elizabethan Image," *N&Q* 192 (1947): 69-70, examines the unusual treatment of a single metaphor in *Jack Straw* and theorizes as a result that the play might have been the early work of a great Elizabethan dramatist.

Political Themes

Most criticism of *Jack Straw*, after noting its morality play qualities, discusses its political implications and contemporary allusions. The majority of scholars find the dramatist's views about rebellion unquestionably orthodox, though Henry Hitch Adams, *English Domestic or, Homiletic Tragedy, 1575–1642* (1943), notes departures from orthodox doctrine. E. M. W. Tillyard, *Shakespeare's History Plays* (1944), says *Jack Straw* is barely concerned with history and solidly conventional about the wickedness of revolt. Alfred Hart, *Shakespeare and the Homilies* (1934), grouping the play with Shakespeare's *Richard II* and the anonymous *Woodstock* as anachronistic treatments of Richard's reign, remarks the emphasis *Jack Straw* places on the high seriousness of disobedience and rebellion. A different grouping is provided by John Earle Uhler, "*Julius Caesar* — a Morality of Respublica," in *Studies in Shakespeare*, ed. Arthur D. Matthews and Clark M. Emery (1953), pp. 96–106, who associates *Jack Straw* with the anonymous *True Tragedy of Richard III* and Heywood's *Edward IV*, historical dramas strongly influenced by the moralities which stress the evils of revolt. Ribner, *English History Play* ("Edition and Attribution"), studies *Jack Straw* as part of the morality play tradition (with special reference to *Gorboduc*). Despite various weaknesses, he explains, the play is historically important: it is one of the earliest English dramas without morality figures which deals with a situation from English history and has aims in common with those of Elizabethan historians. Using the device of the contest between forces of good and evil, it teaches a lesson about the viciousness of rebellion.

In a brief analysis of *Jack Straw*, Ernest W. Talbert, *Elizabethan Drama and Shakespeare's Early Plays* (1963), directs attention to the playwright's dogmatism and supports his impression that the work is simply a "dramatic exercise that . . . commemorate[s] the heinousness of revolt." Franz Grosse, *Das englische Renaissancedrama im Spiegel zeitgenössischer Staatstheorien*, Sprache und Kultur der germanischen und romanischen Völker, series A, vol. 18 (1935), had earlier offered two simple explanations for this inflexibility: the author's patriotism and the primitive dramatic form of the play. Robert Y. Turner, "Shakespeare and the Public Confrontation Scene in Early History Plays," *MP* 62 (1964): 1–12, notices that the confrontation scenes in the play clearly indicate censure for the insurgents and approval for the king's forces.

The most detailed examination of the play's extreme conservatism is given by David Bevington, *Tudor Drama and Politics* (1968), who analyzes the black-and-white portrayals of the rebels and the king. The dramatist, plainly showing his disapproval of the lower classes, has given them no motives for their troublemaking. That his sympathies lie wholly with Richard is evident from the monarch's characterization as totally blameless and clement. Both portraits are obviously myopic: the second particularly demanded departures from the sources; the first, a willingness to ignore the causes of a historical movement. Bevington finds contemporary relevance in this one-sided interpretation of events: a defense of Elizabeth's taxation policies and a celebration of the mercy with which she treated both her Catholic enemies and recusant peasants. He points out that even in the context of Elizabethan history plays, this one is unusually conservative, and yet its viewpoint represents not only that of the administration, but also, to some degree, that of the public. It is a work which ignores the real political problems of its age, and in its limitations suggests what kind of art might have resulted if Elizabethan censors had had greater power.

A few scholars recognize a measure of complexity in *Jack Straw*. Farnham, *Medieval Heritage* ("Edition and Attribution"), for example, finding no unity of conception in the play, proposes that the dramatist had not decided whether his subject was "a notable rebel or . . . a notable rebellion"; though it is obvious that right resides with the monarchy, Straw is treated rather charitably. M. M. Reese, *The Cease of Majesty* (1961), discovers multiple implications in the treatment of the insubordination theme: no man is by nature a rebel; both king and subjects have certain important obligations to one another; and the Tudor government's attitude toward social discontents is justified.

Other critics are interested primarily in the play's contemporary application. Eleanor Grace Clark, *Ralegh and Marlowe: A Study in Elizabethan Fustian* (1941), simply states that both internal and external evidence confirms the timeliness of these "bold scenes." Evelyn May Albright, *Dramatic Publication in England, 1580–1640* (1927), sees in the anonymous work a tax situation analogous to that of Elizabethan England, and consequently a warning that in the past oppressive imposts had driven people to revolt; at the same time, however, the dramatist reprimands the rebels. The most extensive study of the play's contemporary relevance is Mary Grace Muse Adkins's "A Theory About *The Life and Death of Jack Straw*," *Studies in English* (Univ. of Texas) 28 (1949): 57–82. Her consideration of striking historical and dramatic differences among the three plays on Richard's reign leads to an analysis of *Jack Straw*: the events it covers, its relation to its sources, and the nature of its orthodoxy with regard to rebellion and the doctrine of divine right. The analysis gives rise to certain provocative questions. Why is Richard presented, and primarily through the rebellion, in such a positive light? Why did the dramatist nevertheless make the rebels' cause considerably sympathetic? Two explanations based on contemporary application of the play are offered: the Peasants' Revolt of *Jack Straw* reflects the problems and unrest of the Elizabethan poor, and the interpretation of Richard is perhaps a defense of the Queen as a wise and merciful sovereign, a plea for loyalty to the monarch. Detailed evidence is drawn from the play, with passing reference to its relation to its source and special reference to the treatment of Richard, in support of these theories. (Much of the material from this article is repeated by Ribner, *English History Play* ["Edition and Attribution"], in his discussion of *Jack Straw*.)

Jack Straw and Other Plays

In his Arden edition of *The Second Part of King Henry VI* (1957), Andrew S. Cairncross mentions that Shakespeare's play borrows from *Jack Straw*. Both W. Bridges-Adams, *The Irresistible Theatre*, vol. 1 (1957), and Geoffrey Bullough, ed., *Narrative and Dramatic Sources of Shakespeare*, vol. 3 (1960), suggest that Shakespeare may have remembered *Jack Straw* in writing *II Henry VI*; the Jack Cade scenes in the two works have features in common. In comparing these two plays, Bevington, *Tudor Drama and Politics* ("Political Themes"), demonstrates that Shakespeare's treatment of the origins of insurrection are more complex, though the rebellion proper in *II Henry VI* closely resembles that in *Jack Straw*. Brents Stirling, "Shakespeare's Mob Scenes: A Reinterpretation," *HLQ* 8 (1945): 213–40, observes that the Cade rebellion in *II Henry VI* may reflect the influence of *Jack Straw*, then points out certain thematic contrasts between both plays and Samuel Rowlands's *Hell's Broke Loose* (1605). In *William Shakespeare*, vol. 1 (1930), E. K. Chambers states that *Jack Straw* is not a source for Shakespeare's *Richard II*. Ashley, *Authorship and Evidence* ("Edition and Attribution"), remarks that there is a possible reference to the anonymous play in Simon Forman's manuscript *Booke of Plaies*. Robertson, *The Shakespeare Canon* ("Edition and Attribution"), had earlier maintained that the reference to an old play about Richard II in Forman's diary could not mean *Jack Straw*, as Fleay had originally suggested; the play mentioned might have been based on *Jack Straw* and on an intermediate drama to which Peele had also contributed. (The shortness of *Jack Straw* argues that it could readily have been compressed to serve as the opening episode of a chronicle play about Richard II.) I. A. Shapiro, "*Richard II* or *Richard III* or . . . ?" *SQ* 9

(1958): 204–6, notes that a line about Richard in a letter by Sir Edward Hoby might possibly allude to *Jack Straw* (if it alludes to a play at all). And G. R. Proudfoot points out some literary affinities between *Jack Straw* and *A Knack to Know a Knave* in his edition of the latter for the Malone Society (1964, for 1963).

Miscellaneous

William J. Lawrence, *Pre-Restoration Stage Studies* (1927), conjectures that originally *Jack Straw* was an inn-yard play, though the text we have was used by country strollers; and in *Speeding up Shakespeare* (1937), he suggests that the character of Tom Miller seems to have been fashioned for Tarlton. Ashley, *Authorship and Evidence* ("Edition and Attribution"), offers a brief stage history of the work to 1611. The treatment of Flemish tradesmen in *Jack Straw*, less dramatic than it was in Holinshed's account, is considered briefly by A. Bronson Feldman, "The Flemings in Shakespeare's Theatre," *N&Q* 197 (1952): 265–69; because our text of the play is clearly a sketch intended for use "ad Libitum" by the actors, conventional ridicule of Low Countrymen does not appear. Ribner, *English History Play* ("Edition and Attribution"), mentions the use of Grafton, Holinshed, and Stow as sources (his authority being Hugo Schutt's 1901 edition of *Jack Straw*) and the debatable issue of date (providing a short survey of early scholarship on this subject). In *Shakespeare and the Stationers* (1955), Leo Kirschbaum deals briefly with the play's history of publication. Marion Linton locates copies of *Jack Straw* in "The Bute Collection of English Plays," *TLS*, 21 December 1956, p. 772, and "National Library of Scotland and Edinburgh University Library Copies of Plays in Greg's *Bibliography of the English Printed Drama*," *SB* 15 (1962): 91–104.

Stylistic and structural matters receive some attention. William Wells, "Thomas Kyd and the Chronicle-History," *N&Q* 178 (1940): 218–24, notices a strong Kydian influence in the anonymous work. Clemen, *English Tragedy before Shakespeare* ("Edition and Attribution") points out that there is no method in the playwright's distribution of prose and verse, and that the lack of uniformity, dramatic sense, and originality in *Jack Straw* is the result of its heavy borrowing from rhetorical drama and the morality tradition. Clifford Leech, "Shakespeare's Use of a Five-Act Structure," *NS* 6 (1957): 249–63, notes that the four-act structure of two Senecan plays may be the precedent for the act division in *Jack Straw* and Kyd's *Spanish Tragedy;* Wilfred T. Jewkes, *Act Division in Elizabethan and Jacobean Plays, 1583–1616*

(1958), briefly discusses the nature of the copy and act divisions; and Allardyce Nicoll, *British Drama* (1962; 5th ed.), finds the structure of *Jack Straw* hardly more advanced than that of the interludes. John B. Moore, *The Comic and the Realistic in English Drama* (1925), remarks that *Jack Straw* is one of the few chronicle plays having the "comico-realistic infusion"; Ola Elizabeth Winslow, *Low Comedy as a Structural Element in English Drama from the Beginnings to 1642* (1926), and S. L. Bethell, "The Comic Element in Shakespeare's Histories," *Anglia* 71 (1952-53): 82-101, consider the comedy of Tom Miller, Nabs, and the goose irrelevant.

See Also

Cellini, Benvenuto, ed. *Drammi Pre-Shakespeariani.* Collana di Letterature Moderne, vol. 4 (1958).

Koskenniemi, Inna. "On the Use of 'Figurative Negation' in English Renaissance Drama." *NM* 67 (1966): 385-401.

Langenfelt, Gösta. " 'The Noble Savage' until Shakespeare." *ES* 36 (1955): 222-27.

J. L.

Locrine, pseudo-history (*1591;* 1595)

General

There are no recent editions of *Locrine,* except for Diego Angeli's Italian translation and brief introduction in *Opere attribuite a Shakespeare,* vol. 2 (1934).

A key to the growth of *Locrine* scholarship is provided by Baldwin Maxwell's comprehensive analysis of the play in *Studies in the Shakespeare Apocrypha* (1956), which includes many notes and summaries of earlier work. Maxwell deals with the questions surrounding the initials "W.S." which appear on *Locrine* and two other dramas, and offers an interpretation of the statement on the title page which indicates revision (though there need not have been an old play). He presents evidence, especially from the comic scenes, which suggests revision and leads to a discussion of the complex relationship between *Locrine* and *Selimus.* He summarizes and evaluates previous studies, with particular attention to Frank G. Hubbard's 1916 article in *Shakespeare Studies.* Maxwell proposes that the *Selimus* dramatist revised *Locrine,* perhaps simultaneously writing his own play; he might in fact have produced the original version of *Locrine.* (See also John Leo Murphy, "Some Problems in the Anonymous Drama of the Elizabethan Stage" [*DA* 24

(1964): 3754], who conjectures that Greene revised both *Locrine* and *Selimus* at the same time.)

Maxwell's review of source scholarship cites the opinion of Willard Farnham, "John Higgins' *Mirror* and *Locrine*," *MP* 23 (1926): 307- 13, that *The Mirror for Magistrates* influenced *Locrine* (see below, "Date and Sources"). Not finding the earlier argument for Higgins's work substantial enough, Maxwell re-emphasizes the use of *The Mirror,* principally the tragedy of Albanact, and suggests in addition that the anonymous playwright borrowed two scenes from Thomas Lodge's *Complaint of Elstred* (printed 1593. See also T. W. Baldwin, *On the Literary Genetics of Shakspere's Plays, 1592- 1594* [1959], who says there is some connection between the two works.) Source then provides a clue to date: 1593 if the *Locrine* dramatist knew Lodge's poem in print; ca. 1591 at the latest if he was familiar with the manuscript. Maxwell also provides a synopsis of the extensive and only "momentarily convincing" arguments from attribution scholarship: Shakespeare, Marlowe, Kyd, Greene, and Peele have been considered, with Peele taking the lead. Maxwell believes that the author of *Selimus* and the reviser of *Locrine* were the same man, either Greene or an imitator, but he does not argue strongly for Greene (though he finds the claims of Grosart and Brooke persuasive) or any other playwright. Useful reviews of Maxwell's book are G. K. Hunter's in *MLR* 52 (1957): 587- 88, and M. A. Shaaber's in *MLN* 72 (1957): 290- 92.

Attribution*

The authorship of *Locrine* remains undetermined. The most controversial attribution resulted from the claim made by J. P. Collier: a manuscript note on a copy of the 1595 edition in Sir George Buc's hand ascribes the play to Charles Tilney, assigns its dumb shows to Buc, and gives *Estrild* as its original title. As Thornton S. Graves explains in "The Authorship of *Locrine*," *TLS*, 8 January 1925, p. 24, critics debate the ascription on the basis of their faith in Collier or inspection of the provocative quarto. After summarizing earlier views, he considers the problem with special reference to Seymour De Ricci's opinion (see *A Catalogue of the Early English Books in the Library of John L. Clawson, Buffalo* [1924]) that the handwriting very much resembles Sir George's and finds no cause to suspect the genuineness of the note, which he looks upon as potentially "weighty" external evidence.

* Unless otherwise noted, short-title references in subsequent sections are to works first cited in this section.

In *William Shakespeare,* vols. 1 and 2 (1930), E. K. Chambers modifies the sceptical view he had taken of the inscription in *The Elizabethan Stage,* vol. 4 (1923), admitting that the copy Collier cites does exist and the note seems trustworthy. Morcover, under certain conditions, the play might have been produced about the time of Tilney's death in September 1586, and since it was obviously revised before publication, possibly the "W.S." of the title page (Shakespeare or someone else) supervised its printing. A firmer positive stand is taken by W. W. Greg, "Three Manuscript Notes by Sir George Buc," *Library* 12 (1931): 307-21, who carefully examines the inscription and provides samples of Buc's handwriting to show the note was not created by any known literary forger. (He thinks the authenticity of the *Locrine* notice confirms that of the *George a Greene* inscription.)

Samuel A. Tannenbaum, *Shaksperian Scraps and Other Elizabethan Fragments* (1933; see chapter 4 as well as chapter 2), strongly disagrees with Chambers (and Greg, as cited by Chambers). Once he has reviewed attribution scholarship concerning Shakespeare and others, he proceeds to the Tilney case. In *Shakspere Forgeries in the Revels Accounts* (1928), he had called the inscription a "gross and palpable forgery" (see Greg's response in his review of this book, *RES* 5 [1929]: 344-58). Here he presents eight considerations, including a study of the note's "macroscopic and microscopic characteristics," to prove it is definitely a forgery, probably by Collier. R. C. Bald, "The *Locrine* and *George-a-Greene* Title-Page Inscriptions," *Library* 15 (1934): 295-305, challenges Tannenbaum. He uses a manuscript known to be in Buc's hand, *A Commentary upon the New Roulle of Winchester, commonly called Liber Domus Dei* (written 1614-21), pointing out how its structural and linguistic features answer some of Tannenbaum's objections about the *Locrine* notice; the manuscript plates and the two inscriptions are reproduced. Bald concludes that a Collier forgery is very unlikely and the evidence Tannenbaum offered actually argues in a convincing way for genuineness. (Baldwin, *On the Literary Genetics* ["General"], convinced by the data Greg and Bald put forth, says if there is an immediate link with *Estrild,* the present text of *Locrine* must be a fairly complete revision.) In "Chapman's Early Years," *SP* 43 (1946): 176-93, Mark Eccles also rejects Tannenbaum's views and maintains that Buc's note on *Locrine* is typical of his handwriting. (See also Eccles's "Sir George Buc, Master of the Revels," in *Thomas Lodge and Other Elizabethans,* ed. Charles J. Sisson [1933], pp. 409-507.) Kenneth Muir, "Who Wrote *Selimus?*" *PLPLS-LHS* 6 (1948-52):

373-76, joining neither camp, simply states that if Tilney was associated with the play, it was clearly altered after he died. Some scholars propose that Peele and Greene collaborated. J. M. Robertson, *An Introduction to the Study of the Shakespeare Canon* (1924), who finds Moorman's ascription to Kyd untenable and thinks *Locrine* was written for Tilney, believes Peele designed, or revised and partly wrote, the play with Greene. He agrees with Fleay's ultimate decision that the "W.S." of the title page is Shakespeare, who prepared the work for the press when Peele was ill. In a later passage, Robertson makes an attempt to assign Peele and Greene portions of *Titus Andronicus* by collating that play with *Locrine*. He indicates the parts of *Locrine* which he conceives were written by each of the playwrights and concludes that perhaps Greene should have the larger share. Similarly, H. Dugdale Sykes, *Sidelights on Elizabethan Drama* (1924), is persuaded along with some other scholars that Peele ("beyond reasonable doubt") and Greene (the evidence is almost as convincing) together wrote *Locrine*. The conclusions of Robertson and Sykes are questioned by Arthur M. Sampley, " 'Verbal Tests' for Peele's Plays," *SP* 30 (1933): 473-96, who distrusts verbal tests as a means of establishing authorship (and, by the way, reads Sykes inaccurately).

Peele and Greene are favored individually (and variously) by several critics. Alden Brooks, *Will Shakspere and the Dyer's Hand* (1943), fancifully interprets the reference to "W.S." and the marginal note: *Locrine* was an old play rewritten by Peele for Shakespeare, still unknown, who then appropriated it with his initials. Equally imaginative, Harold M. Dowling, "Peele and Some Doubtful Plays," *N&Q* 164 (1933): 366-70, theorizes that Peele can be accepted as author only if one reads *Locrine* as a burlesque in the mode of *The Old Wives Tale*; he points out three indications of satirical intent, remarking also that the anonymous play is not typical of Peele. In any case, it appears that the company was inspired enough by the success of *Tamburlaine* and *The Battle of Alcazar* to have a writer (possibly an actor) familiar with the contemporary theatrical scene compose a derivative drama. Ernest A. Gerrard, *Elizabethan Drama and Dramatists, 1583-1603* (1928), conjectures that Shakespeare (the "W.S." of the title page) revised an old play of Greene's on the following evidence: Shakespeare had before reworked a number of Greene's dramas; the rewritten *Locrine* (the original is not extant) contains passages from Greene's *Selimus*; *Locrine* belonged to the Queen's Men when Shakespeare did. He summarizes the changes made by Shakespeare, describes features characteristic of

Greene, and also suggests that since Lodge had used the Locrine story, he might have contributed to the original play, and if Greene wrote *Locrine*, he was also responsible for *The Battle of Alcazar*. Related to Gerrard's view is Arthur Acheson's, in *Shakespeare, Chapman, and "Sir Thomas More"* (1931), that Greene produced the first version of the work for the Queen's company, and that revision occurred later, apparently more than once.

Among those who are not completely committed to Peele or Greene, either together or singly, are: Felix E. Schelling, *Foreign Influences in Elizabethan Plays* (1923); F. Eisinger, *Das Problem des Selbstmordes in der Literatur der englischen Renaissance* (1926); Elizabeth Holmes, *Aspects of Elizabethan Imagery* (1929); W. Bridges-Adams, *The Irresistible Theatre,* vol. 1 (1957); Irving Ribner, *The English History Play in the Age of Shakespeare* (1957; rev. ed. 1965); Margareta Braun, *Symbolismus und Illusionismus im englischen Drama vor 1620* (1962); Hardin Craig, *The Literature of the English Renaissance, 1485–1660,* in *A History of English Literature,* vol. 2, ed. Hardin Craig (1950); David Bevington, *Tudor Drama and Politics* (1968). Marco Mincoff, "Verbal Repetition in Elizabethan Tragedy," *Godišnik na Sofijskya Universitet, Istoriko-filologičeski Facultet* 41 (1945): 1–128, gives a stylistic analysis of *Locrine* with special attention to types of repetition which eliminates both Peele and Greene from the attribution contest; and J. C. Maxwell, "Peele and Shakespeare: A Stylometric Test," *JEGP* 49 (1950): 557–61, offers grammatical evidence not strongly supporting Peele's case, though it argues against identity of authorship with *Selimus* (perhaps by Greene).

Of the remaining scholarship, one view is decidedly eccentric. Dorothy and Charlton Ogburn, *This Star of England* (1952), call *Locrine* an early, unacknowledged work of Lord Oxford, then suggest that someone may have written it under his direction. The rest is cautiously vague. John Bakeless, *The Tragicall History of Christopher Marlowe,* vols. 1 and 2 (1942), undercuts some early Marlowe attributions, but advances no candidate for authorship. Matthew P. McDiarmid, "The Influence of Robert Garnier on some Elizabethan Tragedies," *EA* 11 (1958): 289–302, says the case for community of authorship with *Selimus* is supported by evidence of similar indebtedness to Garnier. Whereas the *Catalogue of the Pierpont Morgan Library Exhibition on English Drama from the Mid-Sixteenth to the Later Eighteenth Century* (1946) expresses certainty that a University Wit produced the play (whose title page suggests an earlier edition is lost),

Wolfgang Clemen, *English Tragedy before Shakespeare* (trans. T. S. Dorsch, 1961; German ed. 1955), is almost sure. Comprehensive surveys of attribution appear in Dean B. Lyman, Jr.'s "Apocryphal Plays of the University Wits," in *English Studies in Honor of James Southall Wilson,* ed. Fredson Bowers (1951), pp. 211–21, and Leonard R. N. Ashley's *Authorship and Evidence* (1968). Lyman points out serious misstatements, oversights, and limitations in existing studies and proposes a direction for future investigation; Ashley thinks the eclectic nature of *Locrine* and available evidence cannot lead to any convincing conclusion.

Date and Sources

Scholars have reached no agreement about the date of *Locrine*. Robertson, *An Introduction,* sets limits for the writing and revision(s) at 1587 and ca. 1594, and in *The Shakespeare Canon,* pt. 3 (1925), he is sure the play preceded *Selimus.* Alexander M. Witherspoon, *The Influence of Robert Garnier on Elizabethan Drama* (1924), suggests the production of the anonymous play corresponded with those of *The Misfortunes of Arthur, Tamburlaine,* and *The Spanish Tragedy* in 1587. In *Elizabethan Playwrights* (1925), Felix E. Schelling says 1591 would be too late, unless the play were viewed as a Senecan burlesque; later he pairs *Locrine* with *King Leir* as two "mythical histories" performed in the early 1590s. Eisinger, *Das Problem des Selbstmordes,* gives a 1594 date. In a discussion about staging river scenes, William J. Lawrence, *Pre-Restoration Stage Studies* (1927), speculates the play was about four years old when it was published in 1595. Gerrard, *Elizabethan Drama,* places *Locrine* after *Selimus* in his partially reconstructed Chamberlain repertory of 1597–1603 (see also Robert Boies Sharpe, *The Real War of the Theaters* [1935]) and proposes it was written ca. 1588 and revised by Shakespeare before 1594. Chambers, *William Shakespeare,* vol. 1, says it might have been as early as autumn 1586 (see above, "Attribution"), and similarly, Acheson, *Shakespeare, Chapman,* thinks it was written originally for the Queen's company in 1585–86, revised ca. 1588–89 and again in the period 1589–90.

Muir, "Who Wrote *Selimus*?", points out weaknesses in Cunliffe's argument that *Locrine* could not have been produced before 1591 and concludes that a precise date has not been established. Ribner, *English History Play,* looks at earlier scholarship, considers models and sources the playwright might have used, sets an anterior limit no earlier than

1588, and tends to believe the drama was subsequent to *Tamburlaine's* publication in 1590. He finds Chambers's date ca. 1591 "judicious" and is convinced the extant text is a revision of an earlier play. He tentatively agrees with Brooke that *Locrine* preceded *Selimus*. (For other critics who believe *Locrine* was first, see below, "*Locrine* and *Selimus*.") Various literary connections suggest to Baldwin, *On the Literary Genetics* ("General"), 1591 or early 1592 for the original *Locrine*, late 1591 and pre-1594 for revision (with perhaps another revision as the play went to press). One insert may have been added during or after autumn 1593. A brief summary of scholarship on the subject is provided by Clemen, *English Tragedy*, who conjectures that *Locrine* was probably written in the late 1580s or early 1590s. Murphy, "Some Problems" ("General"), speculates early 1580s for the original version, revision ca. 1591-92. Robert Y. Turner, "Shakespeare and the Public Confrontation Scene in Early History Plays," *MP* 62 (1964): 1-12, gives as terminuses 1589-95.

References to *Locrine's* many sources—among them the works of Seneca, the academic tragedians, Greene, Kyd, Lodge, Marlowe, Peele and Spenser—appear in: Schelling, *Elizabethan Playwrights* (above); Eisinger, *Das Problem des Selbstmordes*; Frederick S. Boas, *An Introduction to Tudor Drama* (1933); Fredson T. Bowers, *Elizabethan Revenge Tragedy, 1587-1642* (1940); Bakeless, *Tragicall History*, vols. 1 and 2; Muir, "Who Wrote *Selimus?*" and *"Locrine* and *Selimus,"* TLS, 12 August 1944, p. 391; *Catalogue of the Pierpont Morgan Library*; Ribner, *English History Play*; Baldwin, *On the Literary Genetics* ("General"); Clemen, *English Tragedy*. General background is given by Gaynell Callaway Spivey, "Swinburne's Use of Elizabethan Drama," *SP* 41 (1944): 250-63.

Farnham, "John Higgins' *Mirror*" ("General"), studies the relation between *Locrine* and *The Mirror for Magistrates*. Acknowledging earlier source scholarship (particularly Theodor Erbe's 1904 work), Farnham shows how the anonymous playwright used the first five legends in John Higgins's 1574 extension of the original *Mirror*. Some of his evidence depends upon details, like the correspondence of characters' names and an item of fact. The more significant, however, is based on the particular form and philosophy the two works share: their brief tragic tales and their moralizing, which reflects a bleak world view and stresses poetic justice. Ultimately, Higgins's *Mirror* is considered more an influence than a plot source. (Farnham's theory is summarized in his *Medieval Heritage of Elizabethan Tragedy* [1936].)

Locrine and *Selimus*

Locrine and *Selimus* have often been linked because of the many correspondences between them. Maxwell's discussion of the relation (see above, "General") is one of the most extensive. Baldwin, *On the Literary Genetics* ("General"), who attempts to establish precedence and the nature of the connections with Spenser, collects evidence which suggests identity of authorship for some passages, dependence of *Selimus* on *Locrine,* linguistic and structural correspondences, and ownership of both plays by the Queen's company (he accompanies this argument with descriptions and tabulations of the dramas' parallel casting patterns). In "Some Problems in the Anonymous Drama" ("General"), Murphy examines some of the difficulties associated with the pair to raise questions useful for future research. He speculates that Greene revised both *Selimus* and *Locrine* at the same time for the Queen's company and considers the nature of the copy for each play. Although some argue that *Locrine* echoes *Selimus,* Ashley, *Authorship and Evidence,* thinks *Selimus* may be the debtor, and therefore the two works should be placed chronologically close. Neither must necessarily be assigned to Peele, but his influence is a possibility.

Most writers maintain that *Selimus* borrowed from *Locrine*: see, for example, John B. Moore, *The Comic and the Realistic in English Drama* (1925); Jean Jacquot, "Ralegh's 'Hellish Verses' and the *Tragicall Raigne of Selimus,*" *MLR* 48 (1953): 1-9; Arthur Freeman, "Shakespeare and *Solyman and Perseda,*" *MLR* 58 (1963): 481-87. Consequently, a number of scholars disagree with Crawford's assumptions and place *Selimus* after *Locrine*: C. F. Tucker Brooke, "The Marlowe Canon," *PMLA* 37 (1922): 367-417; Sykes, *Sidelights*; Robertson, *The Shakespeare Canon* ("Date and Sources"); Marion Bodwell Smith, *Marlowe's Imagery and the Marlowe Canon* (1940); and Ribner, *English History Play.* Muir showed in his 1944 *TLS* article that *Selimus* echoed and therefore followed *Locrine.* In *PLPLS-LHS* he reasserts this view, adding that the later play must have been produced after *Tamburlaine's* first performance in 1587 and that correspondences with *The Fairie Queene* and *Astrophel and Stella* do not help determine whether the date is after 1591. Contrary to these opinions, Gerrard's, *Elizabethan Drama,* is that *Selimus* was produced first and Shakespeare incorporated material from it into his revision of *Locrine.* Alfred Hart, *Stolne and Surreptitious Copies* (1942), taking no stand, asks: did *Selimus* borrow, or *Locrine*? or is one redundant dramatist responsible for both?

Some scholars are concerned primarily with authorship. Sykes, *Sidelights,* is unconvinced by critics who suggest that Greene and Peele collaborated on both plays. That the comic scenes are the work of one person is Robertson's conjecture in *An Introduction,* where he adds that the dramatist who contributed to *Locrine* probably did a substantial part of *Selimus.* J. C. Maxwell, "Peele and Shakespeare," provides grammatical evidence which makes a single author seem improbable.

Others concentrate on influences. *Selimus* and *Locrine* are related as Senecan in various ways by Henry W. Wells, "Senecan Influence on Elizabethan Tragedy: A Re-Estimation," *SAB* 19 (1944): 71-84; and by Hardin Craig in "Shakespeare and the History Play," in *Joseph Quincy Adams Memorial Studies,* ed. James G. McManaway, Giles E. Dawson, and Edwin E. Willoughby (1948), pp. 55-64, and in his literary history, where he also points out contrasts between the two works. Craig's "Morality Plays and Elizabethan Drama," *SQ* 1 (1950): 64-72, notes features in both plays that reflect morality drama. Marlowe's effect is pointed out by Bakeless, *Tragicall History,* who stresses the importance of *Tamburlaine* (which has led some to attribute the pair to Marlowe); F. P. Wilson, *Marlowe and the Early Shakespeare* (1953), whose brief reference is *Tamburlaine*; Erika Schuster and Horst Oppel, "Die Bankett-Szene in Marlowes *Tamburlaine,*" *Anglia* 77 (1959): 310-45, viewing the correspondent banquet scenes as derivatives from *Tamburlaine* and *Faustus*; Turner, "Shakespeare and the Public Confrontation Scene" (above), interested in similarities in the confrontation scenes; and D. J. Palmer, "Elizabethan Tragic Heroes," in *Elizabethan Theatre,* SuAS, vol. 9 (1966), pp. 10-35, who laments the disastrous results.

In addition, Edd Winfield Parks, "Simms's Edition of the Shakespeare Apocrypha," in *Studies in Shakespeare,* ed. Arthur D. Matthews and Clark M. Emery (1953), pp. 30-39, says William Gilmore Simms made no effort to associate *Locrine* and *Selimus.* Farnham remarks in his early *MP* article ("General") a "piecemeal relationship" between *Locrine* and *Selimus,* among other works; C. F. Tucker Brooke, in *A Literary History of England,* ed. Albert C. Baugh (1948), mentions close correspondences; and Lyman, "Apocryphal Plays," indicates problems in the scholarship which tries linking the two to solve attribution difficulties.

Other Literary Connections and Dramatic Context

Locrine has been associated with a variety of other literary works. Apparent echoes from it in *Orlando Furioso* are pointed out by W. W. Greg in *Two Elizabethan Stage Abridgements* (1923), and are discussed by Baldwin, *On the Literary Genetics* ("General"). Sykes, *Sidelights on Elizabethan Drama*, suggests ties with *Alphonsus, Emperor of Germany*; Chambers, *William Shakespeare*, vol. 1, questions William J. Lawrence, *Shakespeare's Workshop* (1928), who thought the name Innogen in *Much Ado about Nothing* derived from *Locrine*; Rupert Taylor, "A Tentative Chronology of Marlowe's and Some Other Elizabethan Plays," *PMLA* 51 (1936): 643–88, remarks correspondences between *Locrine* and the anonymous *Soliman and Perseda* in an effort to place the latter play chronologically; Brooks, *Will Shakspere*, indicates a number of parallels with *Cymbeline* as he tries to find the author, date, and company for Shakespeare's play; Lyman, "Apocryphal Plays," sees a "very real connection" with *The Spanish Tragedy*. That the unacknowledged *Selimus* borrowed from Spenser indirectly through *Locrine* is shown by Muir in his *TLS* article and restated in *PLPLS-LHS* ("Date and Sources" and "Attribution"). Arthur Freeman, "Two Notes on *A Knack to Know a Knave*," *N&Q* 9 (1962): 326–27, says *Knack* reflects *Locrine* on signature G2r; Turner, "Shakespeare and the Public Confrontation Scene" ("Date"), concentrating on the derivation of *Locrine*'s confrontation scenes, sees the work as part of a tradition of conqueror plays ushered in by *Tamburlaine*; Bevington, *Tudor Drama and Politics*, thinks there are several correspondences with the unacknowledged *King Leir*. Robertson, *An Introduction*, is more impressed by the differences between these two plays on a similar theme, and also sees connections with *Titus*.

Two scholars believe *Locrine* influenced Milton. Holmes, *Aspects of Elizabethan Imagery*, suggests that the Sabrina story comes from both *The Fairie Queene* and the anonymous play, and compares certain stylistic features of Milton and the unknown dramatist. E. E. Slaughter, "Milton's Demogorgon," *PQ* 10 (1931): 310–12, who discusses the possible source and nature of Demogorgon in *Locrine*, thinks Milton probably knew the play (internal evidence for this suggestion in *Paradise Lost* was pointed out by Steevens), which might have contributed to his Demogorgon. Swinburne's revision of *Locrine* receives attention from Spivey, "Swinburne's Use of Elizabethan Drama" ("Date and Sources"), whose comparison of the two plays focuses on plot and characters in general, the first and last acts in particular. (Most studies of Swinburne mention this connection.) The *Catalogue of the Pierpont Morgan Library* remarks the wide variety of borrowings by *Locrine* and the use of the story from which it derived by Milton in *Comus* and by Swinburne.

Most attempts to place *Locrine* in a dramatic context observe and sometimes discuss its combination of classical and popular elements: see, for example, Ola Elizabeth Winslow, *Low Comedy as a Structural Element in English Drama from the Beginnings to 1642* (1926); Willard Thorp, *The Triumph of Realism in Elizabethan Drama, 1558-1612* (1928); A. P. Rossiter, *English Drama from Early Times to the Elizabethans* (1950); Dieter Mehl, *The Elizabethan Dumb Show* (1965; German ed. 1964); Günter Reichert, *Die Entwicklung und die Funktion der Nebenhandlung in der Tragödie vor Shakespeare,* SzEP, vol. 11 (1966). Showing particular interest in the way language is affected, Wolfgang Clemen refers to the mixed influences in "Tradition and Originality in Shakespeare's *Richard III,*" SQ 5 (1954): 247-57; *English Tragedy before Shakespeare*; and *A Commentary on Shakespeare's "Richard III"* (trans. Jean Bonheim, 1968; German ed. 1957). Witherspoon, *Influence of Robert Garnier* ("Date and Sources"), classifies *Locrine* with the tragedies and tragicomedies of which Sidney and his circle disapproved.

A detailed treatment of the manner in which various traditions combined in *Locrine* appears in Bowers's *Elizabethan Revenge Tragedy* ("Date and Sources"). A chronicle history seasoned by Seneca (via *Gorboduc* and *The Misfortunes of Arthur*), *Tamburlaine,* and a "vaguely Kydian" influence, *Locrine* is eclectic in both its origins and achievement, an academic drama becoming adjusted to popular tastes. It is not a revenge tragedy despite the motif of personal revenge which serves a unifying function in the play. Ribner, *English History Play,* discusses *Locrine* in relation to the development of the history play, the effect of its Senecanism and major motifs on later plays of the genre, and its treatment of political themes and purposes. In judging the play aesthetically, he considers the potpourri of traditions it reflects.

Two other items relate to context: Anne Righter, *Shakespeare and the Idea of the Play* (1962), finds in *Locrine* a medieval Player King image, and Ashley, *Authorship and Evidence,* summarizes the traditions from which the play derives.

Structure, Style, and Text

The success of the comedy in *Locrine* is the source of some disagreement. Among those who question its effect is Winslow, *Low*

Comedy as a Structural Element ("Literary Connections"), who reflects that it may serve humor less than the spanning of time intervals, and finds the attempt to create a unified sequence unequal in execution to Lyly's. Gerrard, *Elizabethan Drama,* feels the humorous portions (perhaps the work of Kempe) weaken the tragic ones, and Louis B. Wright, "Variety-Show Clownery on the Pre-Restoration Stage," *Anglia* 52 (1928): 51-68, complains that the comic scenes, too disconnected to form a subplot, are crude interpolations, ineffectively related to the main plot in content and style. (See also S. L. Bethell, "The Comic Element in Shakespeare's Histories," *Anglia* 71 [1952-53]: 82-101.) On the other hand, the low comedy pleases Moore, *The Comic and the Realistic* ("*Locrine* and *Selimus*"), and Farnham, *Medieval Heritage* ("Date and Sources"). Reichert, *Die Entwicklung und die Funktion der Nebenhandlung* ("Literary Connections"), discusses in some detail its relation to the major action. G. Geoffrey Langsam, *Martial Books and Tudor Verse* (1951), briefly analyzes the comic recruiting scene. The possibility of parody in the humorous passages (which perhaps mocks the conventions in the serious ones) is considered by Olive Mary Busby, *Studies in the Development of the Fool in the Elizabethan Drama* (1923); John W. Draper, "Falstaff, 'A Fool and Jester,' " *MLQ* 7 (1946): 453-62 (appears as "Falstaff, a 'Knave-Fool,' " in his *Stratford to Dogberry* [1961], pp. 189-99); Clemen, *English Tragedy before Shakespeare*; and Braun, *Symbolismus und Illusionismus.*

Strumbo is treated by Busby, who considers him an important figure in the evolution of the non-servant clown because of the deliberate nature of his characterization, his role as focus of the subplot, and the various ways he is a precursor of Armado, Bottom, and Falstaff. Charles Read Baskervill, *The Elizabethan Jig* (1929), briefly mentions Strumbo and similar characters in other works, and K. M. Lea, *Italian Popular Comedy,* vol. 2 (1934), discusses the clown and the *commedia dell'arte.*

The ghost scenes are discussed by Gisela Dahinten, *Die Geisterszene in der Tragödie vor Shakespeare,* Palaestra, vol. 225 (1958); Robert Rentoul Reed, Jr., *The Occult on the Tudor and Stuart Stage* (1965); Siegfried Korninger, "Die Geisterszene im elisabethanischen Drama," *SJH* 102 (1966): 124-45; Clemen, *A Commentary on Shakespeare's "Richard III"* ("Literary Connections"). All remark the introduction for the first time of ghosts into the action in confrontation with ordinary mortals and the effect of this innovation on later drama. In addition, Dahinten explains the functions of the five ghost scenes in the plot, including their choric rôle, and Korninger mentions their tendency to moralize. Clemen contrasts the tone and diction of one ghost scene in *Locrine* with that in *Richard III.*

B. R. Pearn, "Dumb-Show in Elizabethan Drama," *RES* 11 (1935): 385–405, notices the allegorical qualities of the dumb shows and the novel function of Até as presenter; and Mehl, *Elizabethan Dumb Show* ("Literary Connections"), discusses the nature, function, and purpose of these devices as well as their associations with emblems. Mehl also describes the origin and rôle of Até, a figure central to Mary V. Braginton's "Two Notes on Senecan Tragedy," *MLN* 41 (1926): 468–69. Taking issue with F. W. Moorman, "The Pre-Shakespearean Ghost," *MLR* 1 (1906): 85–95, who claims that Até imitates a Senecan model without deviation, Braginton contends that the resemblance to Seneca's Fury in *Thyestes* is only in external features, whereas the nature of her speech is very different and her Latin lines unSenecan; perhaps Moorman confused this Até with the one in Peele's *Arraignment of Paris.* The depiction of the five suicides in *Locrine* is discussed by Eisinger, *Das Problem des Selbstmordes,* who feels the play defends suicide as a result of the influence of Seneca and classical philosophy (not Marlowe).

Language and rhetoric inspire some commentary. T. S. Eliot, "Seneca in Elizabethan Translation," in *Seneca His Tenne Tragedies* (1927), finds the writing generally unsatisfactory, though he is interested in the Senecan "declamatory" quality of the blank verse. (Cf. Spivey, "Swinburne's Use of Elizabethan Drama" ["Date and Sources"], who calls the verse forms "acrobatic stunts.") In *Themes and Conventions of Elizabethan Tragedy* (1935), M. C. Bradbrook says that according to tradition, the patterned speech in *Locrine* begins with the revenge action after Act IV, being negligible elsewhere in the play. Traudl Eichhorn, "Prosa und Vers im vorshakespeareschen Drama," *SJ* 84–86 (1948–50): 140–98, judges the revisions of *Locrine* unsuccessful attempts to reconcile contrasting elements of prose and verse (and suggests by inference that "W.S." was reviser rather than author).

The lamentations and how they relate to conventional concepts of tragedy are the concern of J. V. Cunningham, *Woe or Wonder* (1951). Clemen's 1954 *SQ* article ("Connections") contrasts the "curses and forebodings" in *Locrine* (among other English classical tragedies), mere customary, isolated gestures, with the functional and integrated ones of Shakespeare's *Richard III.* In *English Tragedy before Shakespeare* he studies the set speeches: their insulation, subject matter, language (which is characterized by a new lyricism as well as rigid patterns), narrative function, and disposition of didactic elements. R. F. Hill, "Shakespeare's Early Tragic Mode," *SQ* 9 (1958): 455–69, briefly compares the use of stylized language in *Locrine* with that in Shakespeare's plays. Braun, *Symbolismus und Illusionismus*, provides a detailed differentiation of the monologues in the main and secondary plots, as well as the spectral ones and asides; Rudolf Böhm, *Wesen und Funktion der Sterberede im elisabethanischen Drama*, Britannica et Americana, vol. 13 (1964), analyzes the six death speeches, which he concludes serve no real purpose as ornamental pauses or digressions that do not further the plot; and Gerhard Hoffmann, "Wandlungen des Gebets im elisabethanischen Drama," *SJH* 102 (1966): 173–210, points out that the prayers in *Locrine* are for the first time personal and emotional, though they contribute more to rhetorical effect than character development.

Wilfred T. Jewkes, *Act Division in Elizabethan and Jacobean Plays, 1583–1616* (1958), who remarks "typographical confusion" (cf. Muir, "*Locrine* and *Selimus*" ["Date and Sources"]), thinks the text shows signs that its copy was authorial with revisions or a reviser's copy, whereas Murphy, "Some Problems in the Anonymous Drama" ("General"), inclines more towards a transcript from a reviser's foul papers.

See Also

Adams, Joseph Quincy. "Hill's List of Early Plays in Manuscript." *Library* 20 (1939): 71–99.

Anderson, Ruth L. "The Mirror Concept and its Relation to the Drama of the Renaissance." *Northwest Missouri State Teachers College Studies* 3 (1939): 47–74.

Bartlett, Henrietta C. *Mr. William Shakespeare.* 1922.

Briggs, Katharine M. *The Anatomy of Puck.* 1959.

Craig, Hardin. "Revised Elizabethan Quartos: An Attempt to Form a Class." In *Studies in the English Renaissance Drama in Memory of Karl Julius Holzknecht*, ed. Josephine W. Bennett, Oscar Cargill, and Vernon Hall, Jr. (1959), pp. 43–57.

Dawson, Giles E. "Robert Walker's Editions of Shakespeare." In *Studies in the English Renaissance Drama*, ed. Bennett et al., pp. 58–81.

Doran, Madeleine. *Endeavors of Art: A Study of Form in Elizabethan Drama.* 1954.

Fogel, Ephim G. "Electronic Computers and Elizabethan Texts." *SB* 15 (1962): 15–31.

Gibson, H. N. *The Shakespeare Claimants.* 1962.

Greg, W. W. "Authorship Attributions in the Early Play-lists, 1656–1671." *Edinburgh Bibliographical Society Transactions* 2 (1938–45): 303–29.

Herrick, Marvin T. *Tragicomedy.* 1955.

Hoffman, Calvin. *The Murder of the Man Who Was "Shakespeare."* 1955.

Holloway, John. *The Story of the Night: Studies in Shakespeare's Major Tragedies.* 1961.

Kendall, Lyle H., Jr. "Shakespeare Collections, Quartos, Source and Allusion Books in the W. L. Lewis Collection." In *Shakespeare 1964,* ed. Jim W. Corder (1965), pp. 113–77.

Moore, John Robert. "The Songs of the Public Theaters in the Time of Shakespeare." *JEGP* 28 (1929): 166–202.

Rausch, Heinrich. *Der "Chorus" im englischen Drama bis 1642.* 1922.

Sisson, Charles J. *Le goût public et le théâtre élisabéthain jusqu'à la mort de Shakespeare.* 1922.

Smith, G. "The Tennis-Ball of Fortune." *N&Q* 190 (1946): 202–3.

Stamp, A. E. *The Disputed Revels Accounts.* 1930.

Utz, Hans. *Das Bedeutungsfeld 'Leid' in der englische Tragödie vor Shakespeare.* Schweizer Anglistische Arbeiten, no. 54 (1963).

J. L.

The True Tragedy of Richard III, history (*1591;* 1594)

Edition and Attribution

The only twentieth-century edition of *The True Tragedy of Richard III* is W. W. Greg's for the Malone Society (1929). The introduction, which includes brief discussions of the original and nineteenth-century editions of the play, also describes the text, disorganized probably because it was orally transmitted at some point. Greg mentions the single fact known about the play's history, that it was performed by the Queen's company, and speculates that Shakespeare's *Richard III* or perhaps his *Henry VIII* may have been derived from *True Tragedy*.

The attribution problem has received little consideration. In *The Shakespeare Canon,* pt. 1 (1922) and pt. 5 (1932), J. M. Robertson maintains that *True Tragedy* is not Marlowe's; he thinks the extant text may be the work of actors with additions by Kyd and Peele. Félix Carrère, *Le théâtre de Thomas Kyd* (1951), does not believe that Kyd collaborated at any point. Arthur Acheson, *Shakespeare, Chapman, and "Sir Thomas More"* (1931), recognizes some revisions by Lodge, but claims that *True Tragedy* as a whole is neither Lodge's nor Greene's. To Philip Henderson, *And Morning in His Eyes: A Book about Christopher Marlowe* (1937), the play seems the effort of Greene, Kyd, Peele, and possibly Marlowe, when as a "syndicate" they were writing Machiavellian dramas for the Queen's company. V. Østerberg, whose views have been translated by John Dover Wilson, "Nashe's 'Kid in Aesop': A Danish Interpretation by V. Østerberg," *RES* 18 (1942): 385–94 (an excerpt from Østerberg's *Studier over Hamlet-Teksterne* [1920]), says *True Tragedy* is certainly connected with Kyd, whereas Willard

Farnham, *The Medieval Heritage of Elizabethan Tragedy* (1936), posits a link with either Marlowe or his work, though he finds some significant differences between this play and Marlowe's productions. Irving Ribner, *The English History Play in the Age of Shakespeare* (1957; rev. ed. 1965), maintains that the author is unknown.

Date and Sources

The question of date is confused and unsettled. In "Foreign Politics in an Old Play," *MP* 19 (1921): 65-71, Lewis F. Mott fixes terminuses at late 1588 and late 1591; collects contemporary allusions to England's relations with foreign countries (especially Turkey and France) from the concluding eulogy to Elizabeth; and suggests the evidence points to a date at the close of 1589 (and a playwright well versed in foreign affairs). (Ribner, *English History Play*, cites Mott's article when he proposes a 1588-89 date.) Two scholars draw conclusions about date from the activities of the Queen's Men between 1585 and 1591: E. K. Chambers, *William Shakespeare*, vol. 1 (1930), places *True Tragedy* in the period beginning 1585, when the company was producing a number of dramas similarly out-of-date but popular; Henderson, *And Morning in His Eyes*, remarks only that the anonymous play must have been written before the end of 1591, when the group disbanded. In *The Crescent and the Rose* (1937), Samuel C. Chew calls attention to the date ca. 1592 assigned by some earlier critics to *True Tragedy* and states that the allusion in the eulogy to the renewal of the charter of the Levant Company seems to decide the issue. E. A. J. Honigmann, "Shakespeare's 'Lost Source-Plays,' " *MLR* 49 (1954): 293-307, argues on the basis of style and a literary parallel (see below, "Literary Connections") the plausibility of dating *True Tragedy* in the early 1590s. T. W. Baldwin, *On the Literary Genetics of Shakspere's Plays, 1592-1594* (1959), who discusses earlier scholarship on this subject (particularly George B. Churchill's 1900 study in Palaestra), concludes that allusions in the text indicate a composition date ca. 1586-87. M. M. Reese, *The Cease of Majesty* (1961), thinks *True Tragedy* was probably written ca. 1589-90.

Sources are less of an enigma than attribution and date. To differing degrees, scholars regard Thomas Legge's *Richardus Tertius* (1580) as an influence on *True Tragedy*; see F. L. Lucas, *Seneca and Elizabethan Tragedy* (1922); T. S. Eliot, "Seneca in Elizabethan Translation," in *Seneca His Tenne Tragedies* (1927); Robert J. Lordi, "The Relationship of *Richardus Tertius* to the Main Richard III Plays," *BUSE* 5 (1961):

139-53 (see below, "Literary Connections"). John Dover Wilson, "Shakespeare's *Richard III* and *The True Tragedy of Richard the Third,* 1594," *SQ* 3 (1952): 299-306; Farnham, *Medieval Heritage* ("Edition and Attribution"), and Carlo Capra, "Il *Riccardo III* di Shakespeare e il *Mirror for Magistrates,*" *EM* 13 (1962): 31-58, all describe the use of *A Mirror for Magistrates* as a source. (Wilson also points out, as Churchill had shown, that the play goes back to Hall, and compares the way the anonymous playwright and Shakespeare employ chronicle and literary material.) Mott, "Foreign Politics" (above), says the dramatist was writing with a first edition of Hakluyt's *Voyages* before him; Ribner, *English History Play* ("Edition and Attribution"), referring to Churchill, claims the original source for *True Tragedy* was Sir Thomas More, though other material derived from More may have been used; Geoffrey Bullough, *Narrative and Dramatic Sources of Shakespeare,* vol. 3 (1960), finds confusing the handling of Hall or Grafton's *Continuation* of Hardyng; Joseph Satin, ed., *Shakespeare and His Sources* (1966), states that the anonymous play is largely indebted to Holinshed.

Literary Connections

The relation between *True Tragedy* and Shakespeare's *Richard III* is the object of considerable critical discussion. The most substantial arguments on this issue are put forth by writers familiar with the early, comprehensive study of the problem by Churchill, who used parallels to argue that Shakespeare's play might have been remotely influenced by *True Tragedy.* (Chambers, *William Shakespeare* ["Date"] seems doubtful about Churchill's argument and conclusion.) Wilson, in "Shakespeare's *Richard III*" ("Date and Sources"), and, more briefly, in his Cambridge edition of *Richard III* (1954), takes Churchill's evidence as a starting point for his own theory. Adding parallels to those already noticed, he discovers that despite many discrepancies in the two plays, there are striking correspondences that cannot be accounted for by the use of common sources. Two explanations are possible: either a reporter incorporated reminiscences of *Richard III* into the text of *True Tragedy* (an answer suggested by Chambers, see below, "Miscellaneous"); or Shakespeare was the borrower (Churchill's view). Based on the second theory and the assumption that another Richard III drama preceded *True Tragedy,* Wilson's hypothesis is that Shakespeare used *True Tragedy* or the older play. Wilson favors the latter alternative, pointing out that if Shakespeare used the surviving work, he altered it drastically. Bullough, *Narrative and Dramatic Sources* ("Date and Sources"), supports what he interprets as Churchill and Wilson's opinion that Shakespeare was influenced by *True Tragedy* in writing *Richard III,* but finds the relationship between the two dramas unclear. The printing of the anonymous work may have resulted from the success of Shakespeare's play, which could have been the immediate source of certain expressions in *True Tragedy.* (See also Hazelton Spencer in his Arden edition of *Richard III* [1933], who suggests a composition date not later than 1593 for *Richard III* on the basis of a similar conjecture.) Bullough accounts for some features in *Richard III* by reference to the anonymous play, of which he prints relevant portions.

The majority of scholars treat the matter summarily. Many regard *True Tragedy* as a source and differ about the extent to which Shakespeare employed it. That Shakespeare borrowed significantly from *True Tragedy* is the assumption of both Robertson, *The Shakespeare Canon* ("Edition and Attribution"), and Lucas, *Seneca and Elizabethan Tragedy* ("Date and Sources"), who considers this use of the anonymous play its only distinction. Erich Braun, *Widerstandsrecht: Das Legitimitätsprinzip in Shakespeares Königsdramen,* Schriften zur Rechtslehre und Politik, vol. 26 (1960), finding a number of references and borrowings from *True Tragedy* in *Richard III,* considers the unacknowledged work a source and claims that Shakespeare relied on his audience's knowledge of it to make clear certain features of his own play. (*True Tragedy* performs this kind of expository service for Robert Withington, " 'My Neece Plantagenet': A Note on *Richard III,* IV,i,1-2," *PQ* 11 [1932]: 403-5, who uses a passage in the anonymous play to elucidate *Richard III.*) After reviewing other scholarship on the topic, Capra, "Il *Riccardo III"* ("Date and Sources"), sees basic similarities in the tragic structure of the two works and maintains that Shakespeare certainly knew *True Tragedy* and in fact omitted the Jane Shore story from his play because it had been dealt with in the unacknowledged one.

Some critics find just a few reflections of *True Tragedy* in *Richard III*: see Felix E. Schelling, *Elizabethan Playwrights* (1925); Jack R. Crawford, ed., *The Tragedy of Richard the Third* for the Yale Shakespeare (1927); A. L. Attwater, "Shakespeare's Sources," in *A Companion to Shakespeare Studies,* ed. Harley Granville-Barker and G. B. Harrison (1934), pp. 219-41; G. Blakemore Evans, ed., *The Tragedy of Richard the Third* for the Pelican Shakespeare (1959). Others doubt that there is any connection. In *Shakespeare's "Henry VI" and "Richard III"* (1929), Peter Alexander says the relation needs to be clarified. Lily B. Campbell, *Shakespeare's "Histories": Mirrors of Elizabethan Policy* (1947), views the real significance of *True Tragedy* not as a source but as an apparently earlier play on Richard III which deals very differently with political themes. Philip Williams, "*Richard the Third*: The Battle Orations," in *English Studies in Honor of James Southall Wilson*, ed. Fredson Bowers (1951), pp. 125–30, cautious and mindful of textual problems, does not believe it is necessary to consider the anonymous play a possible source, and W. Bridges-Adams, *The Irresistible Theatre*, vol. 1 (1957), says *True Tragedy* contributes little to *Richard III*. Ribner, *English History Play* ("Edition and Attribution"), doubts that Shakespeare used the work; A. Hamilton Thompson in his Arden edition of *Richard III* (1932; 4th ed.) says "there is no textual connection between the two." Aerol Arnold, "The Recapitulation Dream in *Richard III* and *Macbeth*," *SQ* 6 (1955): 51–62, finds the relation between the dream sequence of Richard III in Shakespeare's play and a similar one in *True Tragedy* unclear.

Some writers suggest that *True Tragedy* may have borrowed from *Richard III*. Spencer, in his edition of *Richard III* (above), thinks that if there is a link, the anonymous playwright (or possibly reviser) used material from Shakespeare's work; it is unlikely that Shakespeare was familiar with the unacknowledged drama when he wrote *Richard III*. In his edition of *Richard III* for the New Penguin Shakespeare (1968), E. A. J. Honigmann, after raising several questions about the relationship, inclines to believe Shakespeare's play preceded the authorized text of *True Tragedy*.

There are two theories that *Richard III* is a revision of *True Tragedy*. The more eccentric is by Acheson, *Shakespeare, Chapman* ("Edition and Attribution"), who traces *True Tragedy* (or a play based on it, probably written by Lodge, or Lodge and Greene) through a rewriting by Marlowe into *Richard III* for Pembroke's company and two revisions by Shakespeare for the Lord Chamberlain's (the second revision being the extant text of *Richard III*). Henderson, *And Morning in His Eyes* ("Edition and Attribution"), thinks the anonymous play, originally a collaborate effort for the Queen's company (see above, "Edition and Attribution"), was revised by Marlowe and Shakespeare, and passed into the Chamberlain's repertory as *Richard III*.

The relation between *True Tragedy* and two other Richard III plays is explored by Lordi, "The Relationship of *Richardus Tertius*" ("Date and Sources"). Using evidence based primarily on textual matters and sources, he reduces Churchill's conclusion that *True Tragedy* was indebted to *Richardus Tertius* from a certainty to a possibility: and he questions the parallels and consequently the resemblance found between the anonymous play and the Dutch drama *Roode en Witte Roos* (published 1651) by Oscar James Campbell in a 1919 study.

There are a number of miscellaneous literary connections. H. H. Glunz, *Shakespeare und Morus* (1938), remarks the influence of *Tamburlaine* on *True Tragedy* in characterization, tragic outlook, and political point of view (a comparison which leads him to point out differences between *Richard III* and *True Tragedy*); and Robert Y. Turner, "Shakespeare and the Public Confrontation Scene in Early History Plays," *MP* 62 (1964): 1-12, includes the anonymous work in a group of plays which approximate *Tamburlaine*'s group scenes. In "New Light on *Hamlet*," *Life and Letters* 8 (1932): 185-87, William J. Lawrence explains the significance of a reminiscence from *True Tragedy* in Shakespeare's play. Various correspondences between *Hamlet* and *True Tragedy* are noticed also by M. C. Bradbrook, *Themes and Conventions of Elizabethan Tragedy* (1935); W. W. Greg, *The Editorial Problem in Shakespeare* (1942); Ribner, *English History Play* ("Edition and Attribution"); Bullough, *Narrative and Dramatic Sources* ("Date and Sources"). Baldwin, *On the Literary Genetics* ("Date and Sources"), theorizes that, if his conclusion about dating is correct, then Fleay's suggestion that a ballad was based on *True Tragedy* may be reasonable; and he refers to a connection previously noted between the anonymous play and Peele's *Battle of Alcazar*. Baldwin also uses borrowings from *True Tragedy* in *A Knack to Know a Knave* to help date the latter play, whereas G. R. Proudfoot, ed., *A Knack to Know a Knave, 1594* (Malone Society; 1964, for 1963), simply notes a number of correspondences between the two anonymous works and finds their relationship generally unclear. In "Shakespeare's 'Lost Source-Plays'" ("Date and Sources"), Honigmann finds parallels between A. C.'s *Beawtie Dishonoured Written under the Title of Shores Wife* (1593) and *True Tragedy* which suggest one was modelled after the other. Bullough compares Richard III in *True Tragedy* with Legge's Richard III, Marlowe's Tamburlaine and Faustus, and Shakespeare's Richard III; and Wolfgang Clemen, *A Commentary on Shakespeare's "Richard III"* (trans. Jean Bonheim, 1968; German ed. 1957), points out corresponding features in *True Tragedy* and *Richard III*, and *True Tragedy* and the anonymous *Woodstock*.

Miscellaneous

Ruth L. Anderson, "The Mirror Concept and its Relation to the Drama of the Renaissance," *Northwest Missouri State Teachers College Studies* 3 (1939): 47–74, notes that *True Tragedy* reflects the Elizabethan view of the "pattern of ambition." (See also her "Kingship in Renaissance Drama," *SP* 41 [1944]: 136–55.) B. Ifor Evans, *A Short History of English Drama* (1948), considers the play a step in the development of the chronicle history into tragedy, and E. M. W. Tillyard, *Shakespeare's History Plays* (1946), remarks *True Tragedy's* orthodox stand on rebellion and the emphasis on historical fact rather than historical process. John Earle Uhler, *"Julius Caesar*—a Morality of Respublica," in *Studies in Shakespeare,* ed. Arthur D. Matthews and Clark M. Emery (1953), pp. 96–106, describes *True Tragedy* as a hybrid "historical morality play" related to the anonymous *Jack Straw* and Heywood's *Edward IV,* which also emphasize the evils of anarchy.

A slightly different view is taken by Ribner, *English History Play* ("Edition and Attribution"), who follows Churchill in seeing *True Tragedy* as a combination of history play and revenge tragedy, and concentrates on its place in the development of the history play. Similarly, Bullough, *Narrative and Dramatic Sources,* and Reese, *The Cease of Majesty* (both in "Date and Sources"), regard the play as an attempt to fuse history and Senecan revenge tragedy, with a derivative and orthodox political approach. (Other critics who notice Senecan or revenge play influences on *True Tragedy*—especially in Richard's speech before Bosworth—are Lucas, *Seneca and Elizabethan Tragedy* ["Date and Sources"]; Percy Simpson, "The Theme of Revenge in Elizabethan Tragedy," *PBA* 21 [1935]: 101–36; Henri Fluchère, *Shakespeare and the Elizabethans* [U.S. ed. 1956; English ed. 1953; French ed. 1948]; and Wolfgang Clemen, *English Tragedy before Shakespeare* [trans. T. S. Dorsch, 1961; German ed. 1955].) Farnham, *Medieval Heritage* ("Edition and Attribution"), groups *True Tragedy* with a line of early psychological tragedies, pointing out that retribution in this play is primarily mental and emotional. Honor Matthews, *Character and Symbol in Shakespeare's Plays* (1962), also notices psychological features of the play, in the way the myth of Lucifer's rebellion is related to Richard's wrongdoing. In *English Domestic or, Homiletic Tragedy, 1575–1642* (1943), Henry Hitch Adams discusses the treatment of the Jane Shore story. Bradbrook, *Themes and Conventions* ("Literary Connections"), explains the functionalism of Richard's soliloquy for the actors; his patterned speech is easy to learn and deliver. Gisela Dahinten, *Die Geisterszene in der Tragödie vor Shakespeare,* Palaestra, vol. 225 (1958), describes the nature and function of the ghost scene. Georg Ploch, *Über den Dialog in den Dramen Shakespeares und seiner Vorläufer,* Giessener Beitrage zur Erforschung der Sprache und Kultur Englands und Nordamerikas, vol. 2 (1928), says the playwright knew little about dialogue techniques and contributed nothing to their development. Ineffectual handling of verse and prose is mentioned by Traudl Eichhorn, "Prosa und Vers im vorshakespeareschen Drama," *SJ* 84–86 (1948–50): 140–98. In *Symbolismus und Illusionismus im englischen Drama vor 1620* (1962), Margareta Braun focuses on the language, tone and purpose of the monologues. Clemen, *English Tragedy before Shakespeare* (above), views *True Tragedy* as a stage in the development of early English drama which ultimately produced less formal and more individualized set speeches. Reese, *The Cease of Majesty* ("Date and Sources"), remarks that the poetry is overtly didactic.

Ernest A. Gerrard, *Elizabethan Drama and Dramatists, 1583–1603* (1928), includes *True Tragedy* in his partial reconstruction of the Chamberlain repertory, 1597–1603. Pointing out the absence of act divisions and references to entering doors in the text, William J. Lawrence, *Pre-Restoration Stage Studies* (1927), suggests the play might have been written for inn-yard performance. Baldwin, *On the Literary Genetics* ("Date and Sources"), discusses the casting pattern of *True Tragedy,* which he compares with that of *Soliman and Perseda.*

Robertson, *The Shakespeare Canon* ("Edition and Attribution"), refers to the text from which *True Tragedy* was probably printed and its relation to *Richard III.* More specifically, Chambers, *William Shakespeare* ("Date and Sources"), speculates that the text seems reported, much of the verse becoming prose, and that, though *True Tragedy* may be earlier than *Richard III,* reminiscences of Shakespeare's play may have been introduced by reporters. Leo Kirschbaum, "A Census of Bad Quartos," *RES* 14 (1938): 20–43, cites the text of *True Tragedy* as a bad quarto. Dora Jean Ashe, "A Survey of Non-Shakespearean Bad Quartos," (*DA* 14 [1954]: 1070–71), includes *True Tragedy* in her study and attempts to identify its reporter. In "The Non-Shakespearean Bad Quartos as Provincial Acting Versions," *RenP,* 1954, pp. 57–62, she calls attention to indications of a cut scene and line-cutting. Both Leo Kirschbaum, *Shakespeare and the Stationers* (1955), and Wilfred T. Jewkes, *Act Division in Elizabethan and*

Jacobean Plays, 1583–1616 (1958), consider the text a bad quarto. Honigmann, *Richard III* ("Literary Connections"), says the corrupt text is a confused combination of the authorized one and *Richard III.*

See Also

Ashley, Leonard R. N. *Authorship and Evidence.* 1968.

Bartlett, Henrietta C. *Mr. William Shakespeare.* 1922.

Brewster, Paul G. "Games and Sports in Sixteenth- and Seventeenth-Century English Literature." *WF* 6 (1947): 143–56.

Craig, Hardin. "Shakespeare and the History Play." In *Joseph Quincy Adams Memorial Studies,* ed. James G. McManaway, Giles E. Dawson, and Edwin E. Willoughby (1948), pp. 55–64.

Doran, Madeleine. *Endeavors of Art: A Study of Form in Elizabethan Drama.* 1954.

Meierl, E. "Shakespeare's *Richard III* und seine Quelle." Dissertation, Univ. of Munich. 1954.

Sharpe, Robert Boies. *The Real War of the Theaters.* 1935.

Sisson, Charles J. *Le goût public et le théâtre élisabéthain jusqu'à la mort de Shakespeare.* 1922.

Stoll, E. E. *Shakespeare Studies.* 1927.   J. L.

A Knack to Know a Knave, comedy (*1592;* 1594)

Editions

Two editions of *A Knack to Know a Knave* (*KnKnKn*) have appeared since the publication of E. K. Chambers's *The Elizabethan Stage,* 4 vols. (1923): Paul E. Bennett's 1952 dissertation (*DA* 13 [1953]: 226–27), and G. R. Proudfoot's edition for the Malone Society (1964, for 1963).

The only general discussions of the play appear in the introductions to these editions. Bennett ascribes the original version of *KnKnKn* provisionally to Greene, although he considers attributions to Peele and Nashe and dates the work's composition shortly before its first performance on 10 June 1592. The Edgar-Alfrida story is traced from William of Malmesbury through various Elizabethan histories and chronicles, but a specific source for the romantic half of the play cannot be located. Evidence indicates that the quarto was memorially reconstructed by actors. Bennett also describes stage history and the four extant copies of the quarto.

Proudfoot deals more briefly with many of the same issues. After summarizing attribution scholarship, he concludes: "Nothing is known for certain about the authorship of the play." The date of composition is also uncertain, and the text is probably reported. He describes the

1594 quarto, notes the derivation of the title from a lost recusant book of the 1570s, and points out a number of parallels between *KnKnKn* and the works of Lyly, Greene, and others.

Attribution, Date, and Source

KnKnKn, in whole or in part, has been attributed to Peele, Greene, Kempe, Nashe, and Wilson. The most enthusiastic spokesman for Peele is H. Dugdale Sykes, *Sidelights on Elizabethan Drama* (1924), and "The Authorship of *A Knack to Know a Knave*," *N&Q* 146 (1924): 389–91, 410–12. In the first part of the article, he cites what he regards as close correspondences between *KnKnKn* and *Jack Straw,* a play he is convinced was written by Peele. The second part counters Fleay's suggestion that Peele had composed only the Edgar-Alfrida scenes, Wilson having written the rest. Sykes argues for continuity of authorship: in its original form, the play was completely Peele's; passages where another hand is evident in the extant text are alterations of the original. Though he finds that the alterations resemble the work of Greene, he does not believe Greene created them. (Sykes's attribution is doubtfully received by Arthur M. Sampley, " 'Verbal Tests' for Peele's Plays," *SP* 30 [1933]: 473–96.) In his Cambridge edition of *Titus Andronicus* (1948), John Dover Wilson hypothesizes that both *Titus Andronicus* and *KnKnKn* were produced by Peele (see below, "Literary Connections").

J. M. Robertson, *The Shakespeare Canon,* pt. 5 (1932), agrees with those who ascribe *KnKnKn* to both Peele and Greene; Johanne M. Stochholm in her edition of Massinger's *Great Duke of Florence* (1933) describes the way the plots in the anonymous work have been distributed to Peele and Wilson; and David Bevington, *Tudor Drama and Politics* (1968), says Peele and Will Kempe may have been the authors. With meager grammatical evidence, J. C. Maxwell, "Peele and Shakespeare: A Stylometric Test," *JEGP* 49 (1950): 557–61, suggests the possibility that Peele did not contribute at all. Arthur Freeman, "Two Notes on *A Knack to Know a Knave*," *N&Q* 9 (1962): 326–27, accepts as plausible Chambers's view that Nashe may have been a collaborator, and is almost certain that Greene wrote part. However, George R. Hibbard, *Thomas Nashe* (1962), refuses to believe that Nashe had a hand in what he judges to be a crude, uninventive drama lacking wit and verbal energy. After reviewing previous attribution scholarship, Leonard R. N. Ashley, *Authorship and Evidence* (1968), expresses no opinion on the issue because there are so few data.

The date of *KnKnKn* is also unestablished. Sykes, *N&Q* 146 (1924):
410–12, is persuaded that the Peele portions at least are much earlier
than 1592, even though Henslowe describes the play as "ne" in that
year. He prefers a date close to that of *Jack Straw,* ca. 1588, and
assumes the 1592 performance was a revival. Evidence is provided by T.
W. Baldwin, *On the Literary Genetics of Shakspere's Plays, 1592–1594*
(1959), that the drama was in some ways new when first acted in June,
1592, but that there had existed an earlier form of it ca. 1586–87.
Freeman (above) maintains that the many contemporary allusions to
and by *KnKnKn* are in their dates "curiously compact," and thinks the
play was probably composed just before its initial performance.

The only scholar besides Bennett ("Editions") to discuss sources
extensively is Stochholm, *Great Duke of Florence* (above), who holds
that *KnKnKn* is clearly based on a chronicle account by either
Holinshed or Stow. She compares the play to Holinshed, points out
changes, and suggests they might have been inspired by Lyly's
Campaspe, Greene's *Friar Bacon and Friar Bungay,* the anonymous
Edward III, or another passage in Holinshed.

Literary Connections

Since Steevens located an allusion to Titus and the Goths in *KnKnKn,*
scholars have debated whether the reference is to *Titus Andronicus*
(TA), Titus and Vespasian, or some other Titus play. A. M. Witherspoon in his edition of *TA* for the Yale Shakespeare (1926) assumes
Shakespeare's play is meant. E. K. Chambers, *William Shakespeare,* vol.
1 (1930), also favors *TA.* Joseph Quincy Adams, ed., *Shakespeare's
"Titus Andronicus": The First Quarto, 1594* (1936), is so certain *TA* is
indicated that he uses the allusion to help date Shakespeare's play
shortly before 1592. Wilson, *Titus Andronicus* ("Attribution"), proposes that the disputed lines refer to *TA,* even though *KnKnKn* was first
acted in 1592 and *TA* appeared (he believes) some time in 1593. He
hypothesizes that the anonymous passage and *TA* were both produced
by Peele, who was familiar with the Titus story and was perhaps
projecting its use in a play when he wrote the passage in *KnKnKn.*
While Peter Alexander, *Introductions to Shakespeare* (1964), disagrees
with Wilson's conjecture about identity of authorship, he finds it
reasonable to suppose here (and in *Shakespeare* [1964]) that the lines
in question refer to Shakespeare's character and, in fact, indicate that
by 10 June 1592 *TA* was already well known.

Paul E. Bennett, "An Apparent Allusion to *Titus Andronicus," N&Q*

2 (1955): 422–24, takes exception to the theory that the passage is connected with *TA*. He maintains that *KnKnKn* is a "bad quarto" memorially reconstructed; the relevant lines are questionable in ways that make an allusion to Shakespeare's play dubious. Moreover, with the emendation of the word "Goths" to "Jews" in those lines, it becomes clear to Bennett that the dramatist means Titus Vespasianus and not Titus Andronicus. (In "The Word 'Goths' in *A Knack to Know a Knave*," *N&Q* 2 [1955]: 462–63, Bennett speculates that the word "Goths," the only allusion to *TA* in the anonymous work, got in by accident, because those of Strange-Derby's Men who reconstructed *KnKnKn* were familiar with Shakespeare's play as part of their repertory.) Alfred Hart, *Stolne and Surreptitious Copies* (1942), finds two possible allusions in *KnKnKn* to *Titus and Vespasian* (Wilson notes these as well), and does not mention a reference to *TA* at all. Baldwin, *On the Literary Genetics* ("Attribution"), says simply that the allusion to a story otherwise unfamiliar is evidence that some form of Titus play was on the stage in 1592, a conclusion reached also by Horst Oppel, *"Titus Andronicus": Studien zur dramengeschichtlichen Stellung von Shakespeares früher Tragödie,* Schriftenreihe der deutschen Shakespeare-Gesellschaft, vol. 9 (1961). J. C. Maxwell, in his Arden edition of *TA* (1961, 3rd ed.), states that the passage, which may refer to a still unknown source of Shakespeare's play, is not conclusive evidence for dating *TA*; and Geoffrey Bullough, *Narrative and Dramatic Sources of Shakespeare,* vol. 6 (1966), remarking that *KnKnKn* offers grounds to assume an early date for a Titus play, questions whether the origin of the allusion might be *TA*. Finally, a note in Ernest W. Talbert's *Elizabethan Drama and Shakespeare's Early Plays* (1963) briefly discusses the possible implications of the Titus reference in *KnKnKn*.

Two attempts to date other plays have relied considerably on *KnKnKn*. In "The Date of *John a Kent and John a Cumber*," *PQ* 8 (1929): 225–32, John William Ashton cites both general and specific parallels between the first Turnop scene in Munday's play and the Mad Men of Goteham interlude in *KnKnKn*. Assuming the priority of the latter scene, he concludes that Munday wrote his drama in the second half of 1594 to compete with the Admiral's *Friar Bacon and Friar Bungay,* and included features from *KnKnKn*, which had earlier proved successful for Strange's Men. Curt A. Zimansky, "Marlowe's *Faustus*: The Date Again," *PQ* 41 (1962): 181–87, invites reconsideration of the 1592–93 date generally assigned Marlowe's play in pointing out that *KnKnKn* imitates verse rhythms, rhetorical patterns, and incidents from

Doctor Faustus. (Cf. John Bakeless, *The Tragicall History of Christopher Marlowe,* vol. 1 [1942], who notices only one obvious reflection of Marlowe's play in the anonymous one.) Since Marlowe could not have been the borrower, his *Doctor Faustus* must have been written before *KnKnKn,* which was first performed 10 June 1592.

The relation between Massinger's *Great Duke of Florence* and *KnKnKn,* considered the chief source for the Edgar-Alfrida plot in the acknowledged play, is treated briefly by Maurice Chelli, *Le drame de Massinger* (1923). Stochholm, *Great Duke of Florence* ("Attribution"), offers a thorough investigation and concludes that there are general similarities in the courses of action and two episodes, but characterization and mood differ significantly; several figures in the later work have no counterparts in the earlier; and there is at the most one verbal parallel. Nevertheless, certain correspondent episodes found nowhere else argue that Massinger knew *KnKnKn* and used it, although it might not have been his only source. T. A. Dunn, referring to Stochholm's analysis in *Philip Massinger* (1957), agrees that *The Great Duke of Florence* has certainly drawn upon the anonymous play.

John B. Wainewright's question concerning a possible connection between *KnKnKn* and John Fisher's *A Knack to Know a Knave* (published ca. 1573) is answered vaguely in "Readers' Queries," *N&Q* 149 (1925): 7–8. Robertson, *The Shakespeare Canon* ("Attribution"), disputes the identification made by Pollard between *KnKnKn* and a comedy Greene referred to in his deathbed pamphlet. In "The Oswald Fragment and *A Knack to Know a Knave,*" *N&Q* 196 (1951): 292–93, Paul E. Bennett, like Stochholm, finds unacceptable Greg's earlier view that the central actions of *KnKnKn* and the fragment B. M. Egerton 2623, fol. 37, are related. (Proudfoot [Malone Society ed.] points out that Greg acknowledged his error in a note in his own copy of *MLQ.*) Allusions linking *KnKnKn* with Nashe's *Strange Newes* (Stationers' Register, 1593) and the anonymous play *Locrine* (Stationers' Register, 1594) are cited by Baldwin, *On the Literary Genetics* ("Attribution"). Paul A. Jorgensen, *Redeeming Shakespeare's Words* (1962), thinks that Shakespeare's use of the honesty-knave motif in *Othello* was probably influenced by other dramatic literature, especially *KnKnKn* (thought by some to belong to his company), and that Samuel Rowlands's tract *Diogenes Lanthorne* (1607) also seems to reflect the anonymous work. A reference to *KnKnKn* by Nashe in a famous passage of *Pierce Penilesse his Supplication to the Divell* (1592) is cited by Freeman, "Two Notes" ("Attribution"), who, along with Hart (above) and

Proudfoot ("Editions"), points out a number of allusions in the play to contemporary literature.

Structure and Satire

KnKnKn's relation to morality plays is central to discussions of its form. Describing its tripartite structure, Louis B. Wright, "Social Aspects of Some Belated Moralities," *Anglia* 54 (1930): 107-48, focuses on the morality portion, its political and social nature, and the choric role of Honesty. Baldwin, *On the Literary Genetics* ("Attribution"), remarks that *KnKnKn,* though it has certain affinities with dramas like *Friar Bacon and Friar Bungay,* is fundamentally a morality defined by its cony-catching motif; and Allardyce Nicoll, *British Drama* (1962; 5th ed.), notes that *KnKnKn* combines the atmosphere of romance with the mood that inspired morality drama. The most extensive treatment of *KnKnKn* as a morality is by Alan C. Dessen, "*The Alchemist*: Jonson's 'Estates' Play," *RenD* 7 (1964): 35-54, and "The 'Estates' Morality Play," *SP* 62 (1965): 121-36, who provides a specific dramatic context: *KnKnKn* belongs to a group of "estates" plays (the term was coined by Bernard Spivack, *Shakespeare and the Allegory of Evil* [1958]), a new type of morality drama that had developed by the 1580s and 1590s, and was concerned more with the morality and salvation of a kingdom than with the progress of an individual soul. Their structure, based on a group of social types rather than an Everyman and his tempters, reflects this concern. In the second article, Dessen analyzes *KnKnKn,* which he considers a significant example of this genre in the 1590s. A transitional work between the earlier "estates" plays and the "literal" drama that would evolve from them, *KnKnKn* combines allegory and realism in a way that suggests two aims: preserving the breadth of vision characteristic of the older drama and introducing, through fidelity to detail, a sense of contemporaneity and specificity. (See also his "Middleton's *The Phoenix* and the Allegorical Tradition," *SEL* 6 [1966]: 291-308.)

Bevington, *Tudor Drama and Politics* ("Attribution"), gives a detailed analysis of the social commentary (which he considers clearly representative of the lower-class point of view), examining some of the familiar villains pursued by Honesty and King Edgar: the landed gentry, the courtier, the priest (who was perhaps the first to be lampooned on the stage as a Puritan, as Willard Thorp had pointed out in *The Triumph of Realism in Elizabethan Drama, 1558-1612* [1928]). He describes Honesty, given tremendous power, representing a democratic, political force; and the King, typically inculpable, a victim of the system. The priest is mentioned for his sophistry by Paul N. Siegel, "Shylock and the Puritan Usurers," in *Studies in Shakespeare*, ed. Arthur D. Matthews and Clark M. Emery (1953), pp. 129-38. Aaron Michael Myers, *Representation and Misrepresentation of the Puritan in Elizabethan Drama* (1931), shows how the priest in *KnKnKn* is the first dramatic portrait of a Puritan as a hypocritical knave, a precursor of the later stage Puritan. The figure of the priest is discussed most comprehensively by Mary Grace Muse Adkins, "The Genesis of Dramatic Satire against the Puritan, as Illustrated in *A Knack to Know a Knave*," *RES* 22 (1946): 81-95. She thinks the Martin Marprelate tracts of 1588 and 1589 inspired the anonymous playwright to create his Puritan satire. The character possibly can be traced to literature of the Middle Ages, where he was already conventionalized in terms of hypocrisy and avarice. She concludes that there is no plausible way to locate sources in contemporary life.

Miscellaneous

The comic interlude in *KnKnKn* has attracted some critical attention. Sykes, "The Authorship of *KnKnKn*" ("Attribution"), suggests it was an addition to the 1592 version. That the scene has no function in the dramatic structure of the play is recognized by both Ola Elizabeth Winslow, *Low Comedy as a Structural Element in English Drama from the Beginnings to 1642* (1926), and Louis B. Wright, "Will Kemp and the *Commedia dell' Arte*," *MLN* 41 (1926): 516-20, and "Madmen as Vaudeville Performers on the Elizabethan Stage," *JEGP* 30 (1931): 48-54. Other issues introduced by Winslow and Wright concerning the nature, length, and performance of these "merymentes" are mentioned also by Henry David Gray, "The Rôles of William Kemp," *MLR* 25 (1930): 261-73; J. F. Macdonald, "The Use of Prose in English Drama before Shakespeare," *UTQ* 2 (1933): 465-81; and Thomas Marc Parrott, *Shakespearean Comedy* (1949). In addition, John William Ashton, "Conventional Material in Munday's *John a Kent and John a Cumber*," *PMLA* 49 (1934): 752-61, briefly discusses the dramatic tradition of this interlude, which William A. Armstrong, "Actors and Theatres," *ShS* 17 (1964): 191-204, considers evidence that the anonymous playwright was trying to limit the clowning in his work and prevent Kempe from commanding the stage.

J. O. Bartley, *Teague, Shenkin and Sawney* (1954), remarks that *KnKnKn* is one of the first two extant English plays to represent a

Welsh character, a point suggested earlier by William J. Lawrence, "The Mystery of Elizabethan Masterpieces," *Spectator*, 21 July 1933, p. 85. Lawrence also dealt with a misleading stage direction (*Pre-Restoration Stage Studies* [1927]) and the use of an upper-stage door at one point (*The Physical Conditions of the Elizabethan Public Playhouse* [1927]). Wilfred T. Jewkes, *Act Division in Elizabethan and Jacobean Plays, 1583–1616* (1958), gives a short description of the nature and origin of the text. Another technical matter, the casting pattern of the play, is discussed by Baldwin, *On the Literary Genetics* ("Attribution"), who explains that the adaptation of *KnKnKn* to the typical five-man pattern indicates what the casting practice of the Strange-Admiral Men was in comedy at this time. Laurens Joseph Mills, *One Soul in Bodies Twain* (1937), notes the lack of classical background in the play, the medieval and feudal nature of relationships in it, and the sparseness of friendship material. Macdonald (above) notices the uninspired prose; J. E. Bernard, Jr., *The Prosody of the Tudor Interlude* (1939), analyzes in some detail the careless prosody. He points out that the playwright is inconsistent in assigning verse and prose according to social station and comments that the blank verse has a heavy tread. Jorgensen, *Redeeming Shakespeare's Words* ("Literary Connections"), explores the treatment of the honesty-knave motif, especially the way the word "honesty" is employed in the play.

See Also

Adams, Joseph Quincy. "Hill's List of Early Plays in Manuscript." *Library* 20 (1939): 71–99.

Albright, Evelyn May. *Dramatic Publication in England, 1580–1640.* 1927.

Cellini, Benvenuto, ed. *Drammi Pre-Shakespeariani.* Collana di Letterature Moderne, vol. 4 (1958).

Craig, Hardin. "Revised Elizabethan Quartos: An Attempt to Form a Class." In *Studies in the English Renaissance Drama in Memory of Karl Julius Holzknecht*, ed. Josephine W. Bennett, Oscar Cargill, and Vernon Hall, Jr. (1959), pp. 43–57.

Cruickshank, A. H. "Welsh Portraiture in Elizabethan Drama." *TLS*, 16 November 1922, p. 747.

Flasdeich, Hermann M. "Zur Datierung von Marlowes *Faust* (Schluss)." *Englische Studien* 45 (1930): 1–15.

Goldsmith, Robert H. "Plain, Blunt Englishman." *RenP*, 1957, pp. 94–99.

Harbage, Alfred. *Shakespeare and the Rival Traditions.* 1952.

Jente, Richard. "The Proverbs of Shakespeare with Early and Contemporary Parallels." *Washington Univ. Studies*, Humanistic Ser. 13 (1926): 391–444.

Sharpe, Robert Boies. *The Real War of the Theaters.* 1935.

Wright, Celeste Turner. "Some Conventions Regarding the Usurer in Elizabethan Literature." *SP* 31 (1934): 176–97.

———. "The Usurer's Sin in Elizabethan Literature." *SP* 35 (1938): 178–94.   J. L.

I Richard II, or Thomas of Woodstock, history (*1592;* MS)

General

Woodstock has been edited by Wilhelmina P. Frijlinck for the Malone
Society (1929; checked by W. W. Greg); A. P. Rossiter as *Woodstock: A
Moral History* (1946); William A. Armstrong in *Elizabethan History
Plays* (1965); and E. B. Everitt in *Six Early Plays Related to the
Shakespeare Canon,* ed. E. B. Everitt and R. L. Armstrong, Anglistica,
vol. 14 (1965).

Questions raised about the play by critics such as Paul Reyher, in
"Notes sur les sources de *Richard II*," *RLV* 41 (1924): 1-13, 54-64,
106-14, 158-68, are dealt with in several extensive discussions, three in
editions. Frijlinck provides a detailed description of the manuscript: its
use as prompt-copy, its transmission by a scribe, the difficulty of its
dating, its handwriting, spelling, and punctuation, the scribal inks and
corrections as well as ten other inks and eight additional hands with
their contributions, and deletions and signs of censorship. After a brief
survey of scholarship about date, she finds evidence which supports the
period 1590-93 in the condition of the manuscript, genre of the play,
and correspondences with Marlowe's work. *Woodstock*'s relation to a
group of history plays including the *Henry VI* dramas and *Edward II*
suggests that the anonymous work might have been part of the
Pembroke repertory, a possibility that would bear out an early date. (H.
B. Charlton and R. D. Waller acknowledge this surmise in their edition
of *Edward II* [1933; rev. F. N. Lees, 1955].) On the other hand,
certain pencil marks on the manuscript resemble others which seem to
be Sir George Buc's; if he censored the play initially, the original
production could not have preceded ca. 1603. The play's relationship
to *Richard II* and the free use of Holinshed's Chronicle (the main and,
in all likelihood, sole source) are discussed. A link with the anonymous
drama *Charlemagne* may indicate that the *Woodstock* manuscript
belonged at some point to the Queen's Revels Children, and certain
marginal entries suggest revivals. The essay concludes with an aesthetic
evaluation and a history of editions.

Rossiter's edition offers the most exhaustive analysis of *Woodstock.*
The influence of medieval thought and drama and Tudor political
doctrine on the play introduces the question of its orthodoxy (to be
debated at length by later critics; see below, "Political Themes"):
although the dramatist works within the traditional framework of
divine right and cosmic order, he presents a revolt against the king

without denouncing it as anarchic. An examination of the use of sources—Holinshed primarily, with details from Stow and probably Grafton—indicates that three sequences of historical events have been arranged selectively and logically. The pattern thus created, outside time, enhanced by visual effect and invention, develops the central theme about corrupt and oppressive authority. Characterization is influenced by the pattern of two groups clearly designated "Right" and "Wrong." In this arrangement, Woodstock is the focal point of both Right and the drama. But Richard has an ambiguous rôle, and he disappears at the end. Again the issue of orthodoxy becomes relevant. Was the king excluded finally to avoid confrontation with the doctrine of divine right? The curious conclusion makes it possible to judge that responsible resistance is not a heinous sin. The playwright emerges a combination of orthodox and independent thinker, "somewhere between the quasi-medieval picture which backgrounds Shakespeare and the new world shaped for us by the later struggles of Parliament and King."

Close attention to the comedy in the play, particularly its relation to the main themes, precedes Rossiter's analysis of the characters which ultimately centers on Richard. Then the editor turns to literary relations. A variety of internal evidence demonstrates that *Richard II* is in certain ways dependent on *Woodstock*. The connection between *Edward II* and *Woodstock* is complicated by inconsistencies and questions of precedence. Sceptical of claims for the latter play's indebtedness, Rossiter finds stylistic grounds to speculate that Marlowe might have been influenced by *II Henry VI* and the anonymous work. That *Woodstock* follows *II Henry VI* is clear from parallels in content and style. Consequently a sequence evolves—*II Henry VI, Woodstock, Edward II*—which places in a new light the rôles of the three dramatists in the development of the history play. Date and attribution remain undetermined. Literary relations, Jonson's allusion in *The Devil Is an Ass,* and another clue suggest limits between ca. 1591-94; however, if *Woodstock* preceded *Edward II,* the span may be reduced. While Rossiter cannot identify the playwright by name, he is able to draw a convincing sketch of the man according to his interests, habits of thought, and capabilities as a dramatist. (Several topics in this preface, such as context, literary relations, and orthodoxy, had been introduced earlier, considerably condensed, in Rossiter's "Prolegomenon to the Anonymous *Woodstock* [alias *I Richard II*]," *DUJ* 37 [1945] : 42-51. Bonamy Dobrée's review of the edition in *Spectator,* 6 December 1946,

p. 618, and Harold Jenkins's in *RES* 24 [1948] : 66–68, are useful, and the *TLS* review, 23 November 1946, p. 578, is a thorough appraisal.)

Armstrong's commentary on *Woodstock* seems to be influenced by Rossiter's. In a short but inclusive discussion, he places the work in a political and dramatic context; dates it between 1591 and 1595; assumes Shakespeare's familiarity with it and considers *Richard II* in some ways a sequel; briefly shows the relation between the play and its sources, Holinshed and Stow; analyzes Richard, touching on the issue of orthodoxy; and evaluates *Woodstock* artistically.

There are, in addition, two other comprehensive studies of the play. In *Shakespeare and the Universities* (1923), Frederick S. Boas devotes a chapter (and several other passages) to *I Richard II*. His description of the manuscript could have served as an outline for Frijlinck's. Like later critics, he is uncertain about date; but he is sure that Holinshed was the main source, Stow a minor, and historical exactness subsidiary to formal balance of plot and character. His analysis covers characterization, comedy, and the function of the masque. In determining the relation between *Woodstock* and *Richard II*, Boas weighs a variety of evidence: a dramatic vogue, verbal correspondences, and the way the anonymous work serves as gloss to Shakespeare's, argue for Shakespeare's dependence. Yet certain marginal entries on the manuscript play, among other data, suggest to Boas that *Richard II* may have been the earlier work.

Fred Benjamin Millett, *The Date and Literary Relations of "Woodstock"* (1934), is concerned primarily with the way political themes have been dramatized and with questions relating to date and genre. He is struck by the dramatist's use of symmetry and humor. A review of *Woodstock* scholarship leads him to summarize the problems associated with the play. He tries to cope with one of them, chronology, through a lengthy examination of earlier arguments for Elizabethan and Jacobean dates. Evidence for a seventeenth-century assignment does not eliminate the early 1590s as a possibility; and testimony from style and literary connections indeed supports such a date. (It is in this section that Millett discusses the relation between *Woodstock* and *Edward II*, the *Henry VI* plays, *Richard III* and *Richard II*.) Millett believes that the anonymous play was originally written before 1595, and perhaps revised to a small extent in the seventeenth century. In a concluding section which defines chronicle drama and divides it into three classifications, he describes *Woodstock* as "historical tragedy" and relates it to other plays of its genre.

Attribution, Sources, and Date

Little has been said about authorship and sources. There are two unconvincing ascriptions. J. M. Robertson, *The Shakespeare Canon*, pt. 2 (1923), argues that if *Woodstock* precedes *Richard II*, then the possibility of Peele's contribution to the anonymous play must be considered. (He finds recollections of Peele's style in the work.) Everitt, *Six Early Plays* ("General"), thinks Shakespeare is responsible: *I Richard II* shows "intermittent flashes of real Shakespearean genius." (See also John James Elson, "The Non-Shakespearian *Richard II* and Shakespeare's *Henry IV, Part I*," *SP* 32 [1935]: 177-88, who points out features unlike Shakespeare's.) But most scholars who treat this subject offer no solutions. Irving Ribner, *The English History Play in the Age of Shakespeare* (1957; rev. ed. 1965), for example, says the issue is unresolved, and A. L. Rowse, *Bosworth Field: From Medieval to Tudor England* (1966; London edition entitled *Bosworth Field and the Wars of the Roses*), merely raises a question about attribution.

Elson (above), E. M. W. Tillyard, *Shakespeare's History Plays* (1944), Ribner (above), and Peter Ure, ed., *King Richard II* (1956, Arden), agree that Holinshed was the main source. Tillyard describes how the playwright used chronicle history in accordance with views expressed by Hall and the *Mirror for Magistrates,* and indicates indebtedness to Marlowe and Shakespeare. Elson and Ribner remark that Stow furnished some details, Ribner also mentioning the use of Grafton and dependence on Shakespeare and possibly Marlowe.

Critics generally place the original *Woodstock* in the first half of the 1590s. Acknowledging scholarship which fixes the play shortly before Shakespeare's *Richard II,* Robertson, *The Shakespeare Canon* (above), finds evidence which suggests a time later than 1593. William J. Lawrence's belief in *Shakespeare's Workshop* (1928) that a stage direction argues a date no earlier than 1619 is contested by John Dover Wilson in his Cambridge edition of *Richard II* (1939); he thinks that *Woodstock* belongs to the early 1590s. Elson "The Non-Shakespearean *Richard II*" (above), concurs with those who think the anonymous work was antecedent with limits between 1591 and 1595. He supports his view with data from *Woodstock's* structure, characterization, borrowing, and comedy. Robert Boies Sharpe, *The Real War of the Theaters* (1935), thinks *Woodstock* was written after Shakespeare's play to profit from its success, and Alan Keen, "Hall and Shakespeare," *TLS*, 26 April 1947, p. 197, dates *Woodstock* ca. 1591-94.

The influence of *Richard III*'s ghost scene on *Woodstock*'s helps Gisela Dahinten, *Die Geisterszene in der Tragödie vor Shakespeare,* Palaestra, vol. 225 (1958), date the anonymous work 1593 or 1594. Joseph Satin, ed., *Shakespeare and His Sources* (1966), says ca. 1591.

Others distinguish between the dates of the original and revised manuscript(s). Bertram Lloyd, "Jonson and *Thomas of Woodstock,*" *TLS,* 17 July 1924, p. 449, considers the point made by Boas about marginal entries on the manuscript which raise doubts about an Elizabethan date (see above, "General"). Lloyd finds an allusion in Jonson's *The Devil is an Ass,* II.i, which points to 1616 or earlier; the extant manuscript may be a revision, but the original could have been coetaneous with the *First Part of the Contention,* with which the dramatic reference pairs it. In *Pre-Restoration Stage Studies* (1927), William J. Lawrence also thinks the Jonson allusion may suggest pre-1616 and offers data which shows the promptbook could not have preceded the early Caroline period. E. K. Chambers, *William Shakespeare,* vol. 1 (1930), proposes sixteenth-century origins for both composition and the manuscript, which was probably used later for revivals. W. W. Greg, *Dramatic Documents from the Elizabethan Playhouses,* vol. 2 (1931), says that while the manuscript probably comes from the initial performances, actors' names and some prompt directions may have been added in the seventeenth century. Literary affiliations suggest terminuses for the manuscript after 1592 and before 1595. (See below, "Literary Connections.") Others who accept similar limits generally on the basis of literary associations include Lily B. Campbell, *Shakespeare's "Histories": Mirrors of Elizabethan Policy* (1947); Ribner, *The English History Play* (above), and Rowse, *Bosworth Field* (above). Ure, *King Richard II* (above), thinks data from the manuscript is unclear about the time of composition and original production, and indicative of revivals. In *Orthography in Shakespeare and Elizabethan Drama* (1964), A. C. Partridge maintains that internal evidence, end-stopped verse, tone, and action show the play was first written in the early 1590s (as Rossiter speculates), but the existing manuscript is a transcript made at least ten years later. He provides further orthographical information to support an early seventeenth-century date for the transcript.

Among those who find the play difficult to date are G. E. Bentley, *The Jacobean and Caroline Stage,* vol. 2 (1941); Kristian Smidt, *Iniurious Imposters and "Richard III,"* NSE, vol. 12 (1964); and W. Moelwyn Merchant, ed., *Edward the Second* (1967; New Mermaid).

Matthew W. Black's New Variorum edition of *Richard II* (1955) contains a brief summary of some early scholarship about dating. For discussions of precedence with regard to *Woodstock* and other plays, see below, "Literary Connections."

Literary Connections

Most attention focuses on the relationship with *Richard II*. An allusion to Woodstock by Jonson persuades Lloyd, "Jonson and *Thomas of Woodstock*" ("Attribution"), that the drama was probably known to the audience of *Richard II*. Reyher, "Notes sur les sources" ("General"), disagreeing with nineteenth-century writers who thought *I Richard II* followed *Richard II*, points out passages that Shakespeare might have drawn upon, thinks the correspondences argue against coincidence, and shows that echoes of *Woodstock* appear primarily in the first two acts of Shakespeare's play, which seems to be a sequel. Wilson, *Richard II* ("Attribution"), concludes that the anonymous work is a source for Shakespeare's, its influence primarily verbal, and that it somehow "links" *Richard II* and *Edward II*. Eleanor Grace Clark, *Ralegh and Marlowe: A Study in Elizabethan Fustian* (1941), briefly describes *Richard II* as a sequel to *Woodstock* with additions, and Keen, "Hall and Shakespeare" ("Attribution"), who suggests an annotator of Hall's Chronicle possibly knew the unacknowledged work, is certain Shakespeare was familiar with it in producing *Richard II*.

The way *I Richard II* influenced Shakespeare is explored by both John Le Gay Brereton, *Writings on Elizabethan Drama* (1948; collected by R. G. Howarth), and Thomas Marc Parrott, *Shakespearean Comedy* (1949), who agree that Shakespeare might have known the play firsthand (Parrott supporting those who think Shakespeare might have acted in it) and assumed his audience's familiarity with it. Brereton recognizes some borrowings in *Richard II*, but does not feel the later play is a sequel; the two dramas deal very differently with historical matter. Parrott regards *Woodstock* as a "starting point" for *Richard II* whose weaknesses Shakespeare avoided; perhaps the crudity of the humor in the earlier play accounts for the absence of comedy in the later one. (Elson, "The Non-Shakespearian *Richard II*" ["Attribution"], finds the lack of comedy in *Richard II* an indication that *Woodstock*'s influence was minimal.) Satin, *Shakespeare and His Sources* ("Attribution"), reprinting *Woodstock*, V.ii–v as a source for *Richard II*, thinks these scenes and certain other features affected

Shakespeare's play, but not as directly as *The True Tragedy of Richard III* influenced *Richard III*.

Two critics suggest that Shakespeare used *Woodstock* among a number of other sources: Matthew W. Black, "The Sources of Shakespeare's *Richard II*," in *Joseph Quincy Adams Memorial Studies*, ed. James G. McManaway, Giles E. Dawson, and Edwin E. Willoughby (1948), pp. 199–216, and *The Tragedy of King Richard the Second* (1957; Pelican), who remarks like Brereton and Parrott that Shakespeare either saw a performance or acted in *Woodstock*, and Kenneth Muir, "Shakespeare among the Commonplaces," *RES* 10 (1959): 283–89, showing how several sources had "coalesced" in Shakespeare's mind.

Some scholars are not completely convinced that Shakespeare knew *Woodstock*. Though certain that the anonymous play echoes *Edward II* and the *Contention*, Robertson, *Shakespeare Canon* ("Attribution"), hesitates to assume *I Richard II* preceded Shakespeare's *Richard II* (despite apparent echoes in the second play; see above, "Attribution"). Chambers, *William Shakespeare* ("Attribution"), aware of certain parallels, conjectures that the anonymous play might have contributed to Shakespeare's. Neither Frederick S. Boas, *An Introduction to Tudor Drama* (1933), nor Sarah Dodson, "Holinshed's Gloucester as a Possible Source for Gaunt in Shakespeare's *Richard II*, II.i," *Studies in English* (Univ. of Texas), 14 (1934): 31–37, is sure about *Woodstock*'s priority and influence. (Boas seems more positive in "Aspects of Shakespeare's Reading," in *Queen Elizabeth in Drama and Related Studies* [1950], pp. 56–71.) In his edition of *Richard II* ("Attribution"), Ure reviews the question of precedence as he tries to determine the source for Shakespeare's Gaunt. Verbal echoes and scholarly arguments thus far advanced are not conclusive proof; there are connections also between the Gaunt in *Richard II* and a counterpart in Berners' translation of Froissart; and it is possible that Shakespeare "invented" this character. Ultimately the case remains unresolved. Geoffrey Bullough, *Narrative and Dramatic Sources of Shakespeare*, vol. 3 (1960), who includes excerpts from *Woodstock* as a source for *Richard II*, finds the relationship "a vexed question." He thinks the influence of the anonymous play is slight (it affects II.i primarily), and that Shakespeare's is not a sequel but an examination of the historical period from a different perspective. Whereas (according to Ure) it helps an audience of *Richard II* to know *Woodstock*, familiarity with the earlier play is not essential.

Taking a more negative view, A. P. Rossiter, "Prognosis on a Shakespeare Problem," *DUJ* 33 (1941): 126–39, does not regard *Woodstock* as a forepiece or gloss to *Richard II* (see above, "General"), and Albert Feuillerat, *The Composition of Shakespeare's Plays: Authorship, Chronology* (1953), finds differences between the two plays more striking than likenesses: "*Thomas of Woodstock* is of no significance for the study of the composition of Shakespeare's *Richard II*."

Various comparisons between *I Richard II* and Shakespeare's play are made without discussion of influence by Alfred Hart, *Shakespeare and the Homilies* (1934); Gustav Kirchner, "Das historische und dicterische Bild Richards II," *ZAA* 1 (1953): 131–70; Christopher Morris, *Political Thought in England: Tyndale to Hooker* (1953); Peter Ure, "Two Passages in Sylvester's Du Bartas and Their Bearing on Shakespeare's *Richard II*," *N&Q* 198 (1953): 374–77; Peter Alexander, *Introductions to Shakespeare* (1964). Black's Variorum *Richard II* ("Attribution") indicates the diversity of critical opinion about the connection between the two plays with excerpts from various scholarly works.

The relation of *Woodstock* to other plays about Richard II's reign receives some attention. Mary Grace Muse Adkins, "A Theory about *The Life and Death of Jack Straw*," *Studies in English* (Univ. of Texas), 28 (1949): 57–82, briefly compares *I Richard II*, Shakespeare's *Richard II*, and the anonymous *Jack Straw*. In his edition of *Woodstock*, Everitt, *Six Early Plays* ("General"), speculates that it is the second division of a tripartite series about the king. (He also sees links with *Edmond Ironside*.) Further, Wolfgang Clemen, *A Commentary on Shakespeare's "Richard III"* (trans. Jean Bonheim, 1968; German ed. 1957), focusing on III.iii and V.i of *Woodstock*, finds correspondences not only with *Richard II* but also with *Richard III*. And Elson, "The Non-Shakespearian *Richard II*" ("Attribution"), who thinks Shakespeare might have seen *Woodstock* performed, doubts he knew the manuscript and finds only a slight influence on *Richard II*. He concentrates on connections with *I Henry IV*, hitherto unrecognized, in the treatment of political issues, corresponding comic elements (he emphasizes the relation between Falstaff and Tresilian, whose office is picked up in *II Henry IV*), and verbal parallels. Elson's theory is summarized in Samuel Burdett Hemingway's New Variorum edition of *I Henry IV* (1936), and variously corroborated by A. R. Humphreys, ed., *The First Part of King Henry IV* (1960; Arden), and Bullough, *Narrative and Dramatic Sources* (above), vol. 4 (1962).

Political Themes

A number of discussions about *Woodstock* center on its political implications and contemporary allusions. Elson, "The Non-Shakespearian *Richard II*" ("Attribution"), views *I Richard II,* despite certain technical weaknesses, as an admirable precursor of Shakespeare's histories. Showing how the work distorts the facts of the chronicles, he concludes it is primarily the artist's creation, "as strong in conception and structure as it is weak in historical veracity." For Sharpe, *Real War* ("Attribution"), *Woodstock* is typical of Elizabethan drama in the 1590s because it reflects contemporary discontents; like *Edward IV,* it is an effort to win support for the Queen's taxation policies. Clark, *Ralegh and Marlowe* ("Literary Connections"), pairs it with *Jack Straw* as a drama whose "bold scenes" must have had contemporary application. Kirchner, "Das historische und dicterische Bild" ("Literary Connections"), links the two as distortions of history popularizing Richard's reign. In *Woodstock,* the target is the court, accountable for the present miseries of the populace. Arleigh D. Richardson, III, "The Early Historical Plays," in *Shakespeare: Of an Age and for All Time,* ed. Charles Tyler Prouty (1954), pp. 79–100, groups the play with a number of contemporary historical dramas concerned with government and unfit kings, and conforming to the moral-history pattern Rossiter had pointed out in his edition.

Considerable debate arises over the play's orthodoxy (see above, "General"). Tillyard, *Shakespeare's History Plays* ("Attribution"), exploring the nature and degree of *Woodstock*'s political persuasions and didacticism, finds the morality pattern closer to Hall's than to that in the *Mirror for Magistrates,* and the attitude towards rebellion and loyalty to the monarch totally in keeping with Tudor doctrine. Ernest W. Talbert, *Elizabethan Drama and Shakespeare's Early Plays* (1963), sees nothing unusual about the play's political stand. Finding no subtlety in the treatment of good versus evil, he thinks the point which is made about authority is straightforward and orthodox, underscored by the comic elements, and paralleled in other Elizabethan plays.

In contrast, Morris, *Political Thought in England* ("Literary Connections"), who considers *I Richard II* a fine chronicle history, remarks that it "allows a rebellion to prosper and to seem justified." Although Ribner, *English History Play* ("Attribution"), appears to accept some of Tillyard's conclusions, on the matter of orthodoxy he inclines towards Rossiter; the play's approval of rebellion strikes him as unusual. In addition, Ribner points out that *Woodstock* distorts historical fact to relay its political message and mirror contemporary problems. Its structure derives from morality drama, from the struggle between good and evil for a wavering soul (in this case, for a king); but the reformation part of the pattern had to be adjusted to accommodate royalty. M. M. Reese, *The Cease of Majesty* (1961), says that *I Richard II* is politically conventional until Gloucester's murder, but afterwards a revolt against Richard himself is created and approved by the playwright: "The orthodox cannot have found *Woodstock* reassuring." A thorough analysis of this topic appears in David Bevington, *Tudor Drama and Politics* (1968). Conservative and radical attitudes mix in a play that approves of rebellion as a last resort for coping with royal abuse and yet takes a traditionally positive view of the nobility. Hence, the title character, epitomizing the moderation he advocates, recognizes the limitations of passive obedience, and the rebels are consistently sympathetic. Bevington finds correspondences to issues and attitudes in the play not only in contemporary problems relating to taxation and free speech, but also in historical events ranging from the Pilgrimage of Grace in 1536 to the Northern Rebellion of 1569. Through these associations, he illustrates the complex nature of a play which recommends temperateness and inclines towards extremes. Alexander, *Introductions to Shakespeare* ("Literary Connections"), compares orthodoxy in *Woodstock* and *Richard II*. The anonymous playwright may take an unusual position, but Shakespeare far surpasses him in his unconventional treatment of current doctrine by giving the king full responsibility and retribution for his misgovernment.

Text, Stage History, and Miscellaneous

Lawrence, *Pre-Restoration Stage Studies,* ("Attribution"), briefly describes the promptbook, which he dates not before the early Caroline period. (For other scholarship which distinguishes between the original and revised manuscript[s] and places the latter in the seventeenth century, see above, "Attribution.") Chambers, *William Shakespeare* ("Attribution"), speculates that a scribe probably wrote most of the manuscript; then a variety of hands at different times contributed emendations and additions. He discovers markings which seem to belong to the Master of the Revels, conjectures that the missing last leaf may have had an allowance, and explains that the text is part of a collection probably made by the younger William Cartwright. Greg, *Dramatic Documents* ("Attribution"), describes the prompt copy in detail: its handwriting (like Chambers, he believes a scribe is responsible); alterations (made by a censor or someone he influenced); involvement with Buc; worn condition; signs of revisions; and stage directions. A portion of the manuscript is reproduced with a transcription in the first volume of this study. In *The Editorial Problem in Shakespeare* (1942), Greg again refers to indications of censorship in *Woodstock* and tells how act and scene divisions were acquired. Ludwig Borinski, "Vers und Text in den Dramenmanuskripten der Shakespearezeit," *Anglia* 75 (1957): 391–410, discusses textual corruptions in the *Woodstock* manuscript, and Ribner, *English History Play* ("Attribution"), offers a brief review of textual scholarship. That the manuscript is prompt copy is the opinion of Partridge, *Orthography* ("Attribution"), who feels the variable and archaic spellings resulted from the piece that was transcribed, and that the extant text exemplifies "stratification." Smidt, *Iniurious Imposters* ("Attribution"), is interested in the proportion of lines cut from the manuscript. Everitt's edition ("General") includes a textual description: an experienced but careless copyist prepared the drama for the theater, and some corrections, names, and changes towards performance were added. Bentley, *Jacobean and Caroline Stage* ("Attribution"), with reference to Greg, disagrees with the identification of *George* on the manuscript made by Boas and Nungezer, and suggests "*G*[]*ad*" may indicate Christopher Goad, or Henry or Richard Gradwell. Tillyard, *Shakespeare's History Plays* ("Attribution"), provides a short history of editions.

Stage history is largely undetermined. Chambers, *William Shakespeare* ("Attribution"), pairs *Woodstock* with *Jack Straw* as two plays that cannot conclusively be associated with any company with which Shakespeare was involved; Greg, *Dramatic Documents* ("Attribution"), says the companies which originated and revived the play are unknown; and Bentley, *Jacobean and Caroline Stage* ("Attribution"), remarks that the company is uncertain. Elson, "The Non-Shakespearian *Richard II*" ("Attribution"), referring to the theories of Frijlinck, Boas, and Chambers, states: "Certainly the available evidence does not forbid us to think that the play may have belonged to Shakespeare's company," and yet he hesitates to make the association. Sharpe, *Real War* ("Attribution"), thinks *I Richard II* may have belonged to the Chamberlain's Men. Similarities with *Richard II* (see above, "Literary Connections") cause Parrott, *Shakespearean Comedy* ("Literary Connections"), to think ownership by Shakespeare's company "not only possible, but highly probable."

The masque in *Woodstock* receives some consideration. Frederick S. Boas, "The Play Within the Play," in *A Series of Papers on Shakespeare and the Theatre* by Members of the Shakespeare Association (1925–26; pub. 1927), pp. 134–56, briefly describes its preparation, performance and function. Dieter Mehl, "Forms and Functions of the Play within a Play," *RenD* 8 (1965): 41–61, thinks it serves purposes of contrast. In " 'These pretty devices': A Study of Masques in Plays," in *A Book of Masques: In Honour of Allardyce Nicoll*, ed. T. J. B. Spencer, Stanley W. Wells, et al. (1967), pp. 405–48, Inga-Stina Ewbank thinks there might have been historical precedent for the masque used to murder in *Woodstock*, the first play to make notable use of the device. It is dramatically effective and a significant development in the use of the technique. Bain Tate Stewart, "The Misunderstood Dreams in the Plays of Shakespeare and His Contemporaries," in *Essays in Honor of Walter Clyde Curry*, VUSH, vol. 2 (1954), pp. 197–206, remarks on the prophetic dream of Woodstock's duchess. The ghost scene is treated by both Dahinten, *Die Geisterszene* ("Attribution"), and Siegfried Korninger, "Die Geisterszene im elisabethanischen Drama," *SJH* 102 (1966): 124–45, who point out the untraditional aspects of the scene. Dahinten also describes its thematic functions.

S. L. Bethell, "The Comic Element in Shakespeare's Histories," *Anglia* 71 (1952–53): 82–101, mentions the comedy in *Woodstock* and its affinity with Shakespeare's. The importance of Nimble's part is recognized by Olive Mary Busby, *Studies in the Development of the Fool in the Elizabethan Drama* (1923), and by Daniel C. Boughner, *The Braggart in Renaissance Comedy* (1954), who first observes parallels with the Vice of morality drama generally and with Subtle Shift in *Clyomon and Clamydes* (ca. 1570) specifically, then analyzes the character's many-faceted rôle. (See also his "Vice, Braggart, and Falstaff," *Anglia* 72 [1954]: 35–61.) Traudl Eichhorn, "Prosa und Vers im vorshakespeareschen Drama, " *SJ* 84–86 (1948–50): 140–98, thinks *Woodstock* makes outstanding use of prose to characterize and make social and moral distinctions. The prose of Gascoigne and Greene had functioned similarly but not as subtly. Ribner, *English History Play* ("Attribution"), finds the poetry on the whole "pedestrian" but not detrimental to the drama. In *English Tragedy before Shakespeare* (trans. T. S. Dorsch, 1961; German ed. 1955), Wolfgang Clemen is impressed by the artistry with which serious and comic elements are mixed, situations dramatized, and characters ironically presented. His focus is the diction, differing from that of earlier plays and anticipating

Shakespeare's in its naturalism and vitality. Also impressed with foreshadowings of Shakespeare and the general quality of *Woodstock*, Margareta Braun, *Symbolismus und Illusionismus im englischen Drama vor 1620* (1962), points out how monologues and asides are more realistic and expressive than formal and isolated. Partridge, *Orthography* ("Attribution"), describes the orthography at length.

See Also

Ashley, Leonard R. N. *Authorship and Evidence.* 1968.

Atkinson, A. D. "Notes on *Richard II.*" *N&Q* 194 (1949): 190–92.

Bakeless, John. *The Tragicall History of Christopher Marlowe.* Vol. 2. 1942.

Bartley, J. O. *Teague, Shenkin and Sawney.* 1954.

Black, Matthew. "Enter Citizens." In *Studies in the English Renaissance Drama in Memory of Karl Julius Holzknecht*, ed. Josephine W. Bennett, Oscar Cargill, and Vernon Hall, Jr. (1959), pp. 16–27.

Clemen, Wolfgang. *Clarences Traum und Ermordung.* Sitzungsberichte d. Bayer. Akademie der Wissenschaften, Phil.-hist. Klasse, vol. 5. 1955.

Craig, Hardin. "Textual Degeneration of Elizabethan and Stuart Plays: An Examination of Plays in Manuscript." *Rice Institute Pamphlets* 46 (1960): 71–84.

Downer, Alan S. "Prolegomenon to a Study of Elizabethan Acting." *MuK* 10 (1964): 625–36.

Grosse, Franz. *Das englische Renaissancedrama im Spiegel zeitgenössischer Staatstheorien.* Sprache und Kultur der germanischen und romanischen Völker. Vol. 18. 1935.

Hart, Alfred. "Acting Versions of Elizabethan Plays." *RES* 10 (1934): 1–28.

———. *Stolne and Surreptitious Copies.* 1942.

Holloway, John. *The Story of the Night: Studies in Shakespeare's Major Tragedies.* 1961.

John, Ivor B., ed. *The Tragedy of King Richard II.* 1925; second Arden.

Kirwood, A. E. M. *King Richard the Second.* 1935; English Association—Adelaide Branch, Pamphet no. 1, Extra Series (1935).

Lambrechts, G. "Sur deux prétendues sources de *Richard II.*" *EA* 20 (1967): 118–39.

Lawrence, William J. *Those Nut-Cracking Elizabethans.* 1935.

Lothian, John M., ed. *Richard II.* 1938; New Clarendon Shakespeare.

Moore, John Robert. "The Songs of the Public Theaters in the Time of Shakespeare." *JEGP* 28 (1929): 166–202.

Nicoll, Allardyce. " 'Passing Over the Stage.' " *ShS* 12 (1959): 47–55.

Petersson, Robert T., ed. *The Tragedy of King Richard the Second.* 1921; rev. ed. 1957; Yale.

Reynolds, George Fullmer. *The Staging of Elizabethan Plays at the Red Bull Theater, 1605–1625.* 1940.

Shapiro, I. A. "*Richard II* or *Richard III* or . . .?" *SQ* 9 (1958): 204–6.

Stoll, E. E. *Shakespeare Studies.* 1927.

Talbert, Ernest. *The Problem of Order.* 1962.

Toliver, Harold E. "Falstaff, the Prince, and the History Play." *SQ* 16 (1965): 63-80.

Turner, Robert Y. "Shakespeare and the Public Confrontation Scene in Early History Plays." *MP* 62 (1964): 1-12.

Wright, Louis B. "Animal Actors on the English Stage before 1642." *PMLA* 42 (1927): 656-69.

J. L.

I Selimus, heroical romance (*1592;* 1594)

Introduction

No one has edited *Selimus* since the second decade of this century. The 1594 quarto has been made available in microprint in Henry W. Wells, ed., *Three Centuries of Drama* (Readex Corp., 1956). Scholarship about *Selimus* consists basically of many short notices which solve few of the problems related to its history.

Attribution*

The question of attribution remains open, with most attention centering on Robert Greene. Many critics merely assume Greene's authorship, while others explain why they favor him. C. F. Tucker Brooke, "The Marlowe Canon," *PMLA* 37 (1922): 367-417, unimpressed by Crawford's claims for Marlowe, thinks the arguments of Grosart with others make a Greene assignment more probable. J. M. Robertson, *Marlowe: A Conspectus* (1931), cites Greene's deathbed confession among other reasons for attributing the play wholly or partly to him. (Robertson's earlier views about this ascription are mixed; see below.) In *Marlowe's Imagery and the Marlowe Canon* (1940), Marion Bodwell Smith briefly summarizes previous scholarship on the subject, including Crawford's, analyzes imagery in *Selimus* to determine whether Marlowe contributed to the play, concludes that he probably did not, and finds evidence in the images, rhetoric, and tone to support Greene's case. The importance of a "feigning motif" in *Selimus* convinces Traudl Eichhorn, "Prosa und Vers im vorshakespeareschen Drama," *SJ* 84-86 (1948-50): 140-98, that Greene is responsible. Wilfred T. Jewkes, *Act Division in Elizabethan and Jacobean Plays, 1583-1616* (1958), ascribes the play to Greene on the

---

* Unless otherwise noted, short-title references in subsequent sections are to works first cited in this section.

bases of correspondences with *Alphonsus of Aragon,* Allott's attribution, and Grosart's arguments.

Other critics think Greene is probably the author. A Greene ascription seems reasonable to W. W. Greg, "Authorship Attributions in the Early Play-Lists, 1656–1671," *Edinburgh Bibliographical Society Transactions* 2 (1938–45): 303–29. John Bakeless, *The Tragicall History of Christopher Marlowe,* vol. 2 (1942), who summarizes scholarship about authorship and questions Crawford's Marlowe attribution, considers Greene a more probable choice than Thomas Goffe. (In vol. 1 he assumed Greene wrote the play, and later says stylistic evidence suggests one of the University Wits.) J. C. Maxwell, "Peele and Shakespeare: A Stylometric Test," *JEGP* 49 (1950): 557–61, says Greene may be the author. Both Inga-Stina Ekeblad, "*King Lear* and *Selimus,*" *N&Q* 4 (1957): 193–94, and Robert Y. Turner, "Shakespeare and the Public Confrontation Scene in Early History Plays," *MP* 62 (1964): 1–12, consider Greene the probable author.

Others doubt the ascription. H. W. Herrington, "Christopher Marlowe—Rationalist," in *Essays in Memory of Barrett Wendell* (1926), pp. 119–52, barely recognizes the voice of Greene's plays and pamphlets in *Selimus* (and considers the possibility that Marlowe contributed). To J. M. Robertson, *The Shakespeare Canon,* pt. 4 (1930), the versification is not like Greene's. C. F. Tucker Brooke, in *The Literary History of England,* ed. Albert C. Baugh (1948), knows there is data which links the play with Greene, "but it is not strong enough to overcome the incredulity produced by the general nature of the work." A. P. Rossiter, *English Drama from Early Times to the Elizabethans* (1950), also finds the assignment tenuous. Kenneth Muir, "Robert Greene as Dramatist," in *Essays on Shakespeare and Elizabethan Drama in Honor of Hardin Craig,* ed. Richard Hosley (1963), pp. 45–54, points out that Robert Allott, editor of *Englands Parnassus* and originator of the attribution, generally made unreliable ascriptions; that "T.G." in the 1638 reissue may have meant Thomas Goffe; and that stylistic evidence is weak. Samuel C. Chew, *The Crescent and the Rose* (1937), gives evidence which undermines the Greene attribution.

Collaboration is one of the suggestions put forth by J. M. Robertson in *An Introduction to the Study of the Shakespeare Canon* (1924), where he agrees that Greene's contribution to *Selimus* has been proved but does not want to claim the entire play for him. He finds some evidence suggesting Peele's hand, and lines in Marlowe's style indicating his intervention or that of an imitator. He also reviews previous scholarship on the subject, refutes Crawford's arguments for Marlowe, supports Greene's case, contends Greene or someone influenced by him often copied Marlowe or collaborated with him, and concludes Greene's was the major portion of the play. Philip Henderson, *And Morning in His Eyes: A Book About Christopher Marlowe* (1937), assumes *Selimus* is Peele's, then suggests Greene may have collaborated. That Greene is connected with at least part of the play is Alden Brooks's view in *Will Shakspere and the Dyer's Hand* (1943). John Leo Murphy, "Some Problems in the Anonymous Drama of the Elizabethan Stage," *DA* 24 (1964): 3754, thinks Greene might have revised an earlier version of *Selimus.*

Of the remaining notices, two associate *Selimus* with Kyd: Gösta Langenfelt, " 'The Noble Savage' until Shakespeare," *ES* 36 (1955): 222–27 (misinterprets a phrase by Boas), and Arthur Freeman, *Thomas Kyd: Facts and Problems* (1967). The rest stress the complexity and inconclusiveness of the problem. Recognizing parallels between *Alphonsus, Emperor of Germany* (which he claims for Peele) and *Selimus,* H. Dugdale Sykes, *Sidelights on Elizabethan Drama* (1924), speculates that Peele had a hand in both, but favors the theory that the anonymous author of the second play is copying Peele. Correspondences in *Selimus* with the works of Greene, Kyd, Marlowe, and Peele occur, but style and language generally do not suggest one of these playwrights. Kenneth Muir, "Who Wrote *Selimus?*" *PLPLS-LHS* 6 (1948–52): 373–76, discusses significant questions concerning the issue: the relation of *Selimus* to *Locrine* (see *Locrine,* "*Locrine* and *Selimus*"); correspondences between *Selimus* and other dramatic and poetic works; and the differences between scenes in rhymed and blank verse. Muir hypothesizes that a complete or incomplete play in stanzaic verse was adapted to the popular stage by an imitator of Marlowe. The original writer may have been associated with those dramatists using Seneca as a model. On this premise, a "tentative" case for Greville's composition of the rhymed scenes is made with some external evidence and some based on style and content; the possibility that Greene contributed is not, however, ruled out. Dean B. Lyman, Jr., "Apocryphal Plays of the University Wits," in *English Studies in Honor of James Southall Wilson,* ed. Fredson Bowers (1951), pp. 211–21, points out inconsistencies in the arguments of those who debate Greene's authorship. In *The Jacobean and Caroline Stage,* vol. 4 (1956), G. E. Bentley explains why attribution to Thomas Goffe is not reasonable and remarks that the Greene ascription has been put forward and rejected. Also uncommitted, Baldwin Maxwell, *Studies in the Shakespeare Apocrypha* (1956), finds the claims of Grosart and Brooke for Greene substantial, offers evidence that supports Greene, and considers whether Raleigh or Robert Wilson might have had a part. Matthew P. McDiarmid, "The Influence of Robert Garnier on Some Elizabethan Tragedies," *EA* 11 (1958): 289–302, is inclined to believe in community of authorship with *Locrine*. Philip Edwards, *Thomas Kyd and Early Elizabethan Tragedy* (1966), thinks authorship is undetermined. Leonard R. N. Ashley, *Authorship and Evidence* (1968), describes the attribution controversy, finding it more interesting than the play, and seems tolerant of those who recognize Peele's influence.

Date and Sources

The date of *Selimus* is also undetermined. A passage copied from Kyd's *Cornelia*, written at the end of 1593, leads Sykes, *Sidelights*, to place the play after that date. (See also McDiarmid, "The Influence of Robert Garnier," who finds several borrowed passages from *Cornelia* and consequently dates *Selimus* around the beginning of 1594.) In *An Introduction to the Study*, Robertson thinks *Selimus* represents Greene's work ca. 1590. Arthur Acheson, *Shakespeare, Chapman, and "Sir Thomas More"* (1931), believes the drama was originally written for the Queen's Men in 1587–88; Brooks, *Will Shakspere*, that it was performed by that company in 1588–89. Bakeless, *Tragicall History*, vol. 1, fixes *Selimus* at 1588, before *The Merchant of Venice* and after *The Jew of Malta* and *Tamburlaine*; Jean Jacquot, "Ralegh's 'Hellish Verses' and the *Tragicall Raigne of Selimus*," *MLR* 48 (1953): 1–9, says the final version could not have existed before 1591; Irving Ribner, "Greene's Attack on Marlowe: Some Light on *Alphonsus* and *Selimus*," *SP* 52 (1955): 162–71, gives a date in 1591 or early 1592 (following Chambers), and his *English History Play in the Age of Shakespeare* (1957; rev. ed. 1965), suggests *Selimus* was probably Greene's last play, produced after 1591. Various literary borrowings suggest to T. W. Baldwin, *On the Literary Genetics of Shakspere's Plays, 1592–1594* (1959), very late 1591 or early 1592 for the writing or rewriting of the extant play. Arthur Freeman's "Shakespeare and *Solyman and Perseda*," *MLR* 58 (1963): 481–87, and *Thomas Kyd* set terminuses no earlier than 1591 and before 1593. (The article also suggests that *Selimus* followed *The Spanish Tragedy*.) Uncertain about the play's chronology, Edwards, *Thomas Kyd*, points out that while *Selimus* appears to be influenced by *Tamburlaine* and *The Spanish Tragedy*, its "primitive" dramatic techniques suggest its precedence. David Bevington, *Tudor Drama and Politics* (1968), offers 1591-1592. For scholarship which places *Selimus* after *Locrine*, see *Locrine*, *"Locrine and Selimus,"* in this volume.

Sources are less chaotic though no more established than date. That the major source is probably some form of Paolo Giovio's *Rerum Turcicarum Commentarius* is the opinion of J. L. Cardozo, *The Contemporary Jew in the Elizabethan Drama* (1925) (he accounts for the origins of Abraham's name in *Selimus*), and Chew, *The Crescent and the Rose*. Ribner's article (above) considers Giovio as a possibility, but favors the fifty-ninth chapter of Pierre de La Primaudaye's *French Academy* (following J. C. Jordon, *Robert Greene* [1915]). Sykes, *Sidelights on Elizabethan Drama*, McDiarmid, "The Influence of Robert Garnier," Baldwin, *On the Literary Genetics* (above), and Freeman, *Thomas Kyd*, discuss possible borrowings from Kyd's *Cornelia*. Baldwin also mentions debts to Spenser, Sidney, and possibly Shakespeare. An earlier source play is unacceptable for M. C. Bradbrook, *Themes and Conventions of Elizabethan Tragedy* (1935), but conceivable for Jacquot, "Ralegh's 'Hellish Verses' " (above), and Baldwin. Two sources for a reference to the Golden Age are suggested by Langenfelt, " 'The Noble Savage.' " Discussions of the use of *Locrine* as a source are cited under *Locrine*, *"Locrine and Selimus,"* in this volume.

In several studies, Jean Jacquot explores in great detail the background of Selimus's famous monologue (ii.305-67). In "Ralegh's 'Hellish Verses' " he investigates the relation of the speech to a poem attributed to Sir Walter Raleigh, "Certaine hellish verses" (1603), which is almost identical. Jacquot is swayed by arguments which suggest *Selimus* provided the model for the poem. A number of available literary models for the theatrical lines are cited to underscore its independence of the poem. In *"The Tragicall Raigne of Selimus* et la conception élisabéthaine de l'athée," *EA* 7 (1954): 199-205, Jacquot returns to literary models for the theatrical lines. His list of possible sources includes Giovio, Ovid, Saint Augustine, and Machiavelli. Response to these theories comes from Ribner, "Greene's Attack on Marlowe" (above), who notes the significance of the dramatic libel and maintains that Jacquot is unaware of some of the play's moral and political ends; Baldwin Maxwell, *Studies in the Shakespeare Apocrypha*, suggesting explanations of the connection with Raleigh that Jacquot did not see; Clifford Leech, "The Two-Part Play. Marlowe and the Early Shakespeare," *SJ* 94 (1958): 90-106, who thinks the direction of the borrowing in the "Hellish Verses"—*Selimus* exchange remains undetermined; and McDiarmid, "The Influence of Robert Garnier," who finds several instances of Garnier's influence on the anonymous drama and believes it more feasible that the speech was a modified version of a passage in Garnier's *Porcie* than the pastiche Jacquot proposes.

In "A propos du *Tragicall Raigne of Selimus*: Le problème des emprunts aux classiques à la Renaissance," *EA* 16 (1963): 345–50, Jacquot compares the myth of the Golden Age as it appears in *The Metamorphoses*, Seneca's *Hippolytus*, Garnier's *Porcie*, and *Selimus*, with these conclusions: it is important to recognize Garnier's influence, as McDiarmid has, but his is not necessarily the only influence; it seems Ovid is the basic text to which each later writer referred in turn; there is apparently a cumulative effect of imitation with Ovid at the base; and the anonymous playwright, if he borrowed from *Porcie*, was reminded by Garnier's work of earlier texts. Jacquot's "Sénèque, la renaissance et nous," in *Les tragédies de Sénèque et le théâtre de la renaissance*, ed. Jean Jacquot with the collaboration of Marcel Oddon (1964), pp. 271–307, with reference once more to McDiarmid's article, briefly examines the nature of Seneca and Garnier's effect on the anonymous author. (Without mentioning Jacquot's view, Muir, "Robert Greene as Dramatist," says the controversial speech was perhaps not meant initially to be performed in public.)

Literary Connections

Selimus is most often associated with Marlowe's plays, especially *Tamburlaine*. Many studies merely mention the connection. Smith, *Marlowe's Imagery*, gives evidence based on imagery of *Tamburlaine*'s influence. Bakeless, *Tragicall History*, vols. 1 and 2, recognizes parallels with Marlowe's acknowledged works (as well as borrowings from Spenser like Marlowe's), thinks that Abraham was the first stage Jew to derive from Barabas and that Selimus was almost equally indebted to both the Jew of Malta and Tamburlaine. Fredson Bowers, *Elizabethan Revenge Tragedy, 1587–1642* (1940), in contrast, considers the tyrant's villainy inspired more by *Soliman and Perseda* than by Marlowe's work. Correspondences in substance and style are noted by Muir, "Who Wrote *Selimus*?" In "Greene's Attack on Marlowe," Ribner ("Date"), deals with the relation of *Selimus* and *Alphonsus of Arragon* to *Tamburlaine*. He shows that Greene has copied the superficies of Marlowe's poetic and dramatic style, but has challenged his philosophy. The two weaker plays were seriously conceived (*Selimus*'s title labels it a tragedy), focus on the horrors of tyranny that Tamburlaine represents, and stress the role of providence. Referring to Ribner's article, Leech, "The Two-Part Play" ("Date and Sources"), offers a related view. He also couples *Alphonsus* and *Selimus* as plays which are structurally derivative from *Tamburlaine* (both critics say that the epilogue of *Selimus* promises a second part, which would probably include the tyrant's downfall), and they are commentaries on Marlowe's play. Yet the nature of the commentaries is vitally different: *Alphonsus* expressing admiration for the Tamburlaine ethos; Selimus surpassing Tamburlaine's villainy, and viewed with a modicum of admiration but much dread. Similarly, Douglas Cole, *Suffering and Evil in the Plays of Christopher Marlowe* (1962), pairs *Selimus* with *Alphonsus* as two kinds of Marlovian imitations and finds the anonymous play magnifies *I Tamburlaine*'s bleaker qualities with obvious moral implications. Bevington, *Tudor Drama and Politics* ("Date and Sources"), very briefly compares *Selimus* and *Alphonsus* as condemnations of *Tamburlaine*.

J. B. Steane, *Marlowe: A Critical Study* (1964), analyzes the relationship of *Selimus* to *Tamburlaine*. Though he finds striking correspondences, he notices differences just as striking and more significant. He concludes that the anonymous work might have been a dramatic editorial on Marlowe's; the objective view of Selimus's undoubted villainy and the substance given his opponents indicate an intention different from the one Roy W. Battenhouse assumed in *Marlowe's "Tamburlaine": A Study in Renaissance Moral Philosophy* (1941). A unique and contrary theory appears in Robertson's book on Marlowe. *Selimus* surpasses the physical and spiritual horrors of *Tamburlaine* with "no trace of . . . moral judgment," whereas Marlowe had no admiration for his hero. The stylistic influence of *Tamburlaine* on *Selimus,* especially in diction, is discussed by Wolfgang Clemen, *English Tragedy before Shakespeare: The Development of Dramatic Speech* (trans. T. S. Dorsch, 1961; German ed. 1955). Turner, "Shakespeare and the Public Confrontation Scene," describes the nature of the confrontation scenes in *Selimus* and compares them with those of *Tamburlaine*.

The second major literary connection is with *Locrine*. See *Locrine,* "*Locrine* and *Selimus*" and *passim,* in this volume.

Rupert Taylor, "A Tentative Chronology of Marlowe's and Some Other Elizabethan Plays," *PMLA* 51 (1936): 643–88, mentions parallels between *Selimus* and the anonymous *Soliman and Perseda* in his efforts to place the latter play chronologically. Also trying to date

Soliman and Perseda, Freeman, "Shakespeare and *Solyman and Perseda*" ("Date and Sources"), locates a significant parallel with *Selimus*: the origin of I.v in the first drama appears to be the story of Corcut and Acomet in the second. Four years later in *Thomas Kyd* he seems less sure; Kyd may have created the passage in his play. Nevertheless, the two works can safely be linked as part of a dramatic vogue. Freeman also explores the three-line "echo" in *Selimus* which seems to Sykes and McDiarmid clearly borrowed from *Cornelia* (see above, "Date and Sources"). Pointing out why Crawford's suggestion about *Selimus's* borrowing is "awkward," he gives five possible explanations for the correspondence; ultimately, however, the issue remains unresolved.

Some miscellaneous links receive attention. Cardozo, *The Contemporary Jew in Elizabethan Drama* ("Date and Sources"), and Chew, *Crescent and the Rose,* see a connection between *Selimus* and Thomas Goffe's *Raging Turke*; J. D. Wilson, ed., *II King Henry VI* (1952, Cambridge), with Shakespeare's play; Langenfelt, " 'The Noble Savage,' " with *The Fairie Queene*; Ekeblad, *"King Lear and Selimus,"* with *King Lear*; Mario Praz, *The Flaming Heart* (1958), with Seneca and Ben Jonson's *Sejanus*; Baldwin, *On the Literary Genetics* ("Date and Sources"), with *Mucedorus*; Clemen (above) and Rossiter, *English Drama,* with Seneca's *Thyestes.* A number of correspondences are pointed out by both Sykes, *Sidelights,* and Muir, "Robert Greene" and "Who Wrote *Selimus?*" as well as *"Locrine and Selimus," TLS,* 12 August 1944, p. 391. Jacquot's *"The Tragicall Raigne"* ("Date and Sources") questions a link with Seneca's *Troas.*

Critics offer several dramatic and philosophical contexts for *Selimus*: Hardin Craig, "Ethics in the Jacobean Drama: The Case of Chapman," in *Essays in Dramatic Literature: The Parrott Presentation Volume,* ed. Hardin Craig (1935), pp. 25–46, notices its association with other early Tudor tragedies; Battenhouse, *Marlowe's "Tamburlaine"* ("Literary Connections"), focuses on Elizabethan plays with "monster-heroes" and morality literature; Willard Farnham, *The Medieval Heritage of Elizabethan Tragedy* (1936), mentions Machiavellian conqueror plays. Both F. P. Wilson, *Marlowe and the Early Shakespeare* (1953), and Edwards, *Thomas Kyd,* point out a number of contemporary tragical conventions. In *The Tragicall Raigne* ("Date and Sources"), Jacquot interprets the famous monologue, which had led him in his earlier "Ralegh's 'Hellish Verses' " ("Date and Sources") to recognize how immediately the theater reflected contemporary thought.

The sequel has received some attention. Acheson, *Shakespeare, Chapman* ("Date and Sources"), who compares the plot of *Selimus* with that of *Tamber Cam* in *Alleyn's Papers*, thinks Greene wrote a second part which, with the extant play, was developed by Peele into the *Two Parts of Tamber Cam*. For Chew, *The Crescent and the Rose*, the epilogue provides clues about what the sequel would have been. Benvenuto Cellini, ed., *John of Bordeaux*, Biblioteca di classici stranieri, Serie Inglese, vol. 1 (1952), says there is no proof that a second part was written. Unlike Farnham (above), Jacquot, *The Tragicall Raigne*, Ribner, "Greene's Attack," and Leech, "The Two-Part Play" (all three in "Date and Sources"), think retribution was planned for the second part.

A few brief notices refer to stylistic matters: J. F. Macdonald, "The Use of Prose in English Drama before Shakespeare," *UTQ* 2 (1933): 465–81, remarks the prose-verse distribution; Bradbrook, *Themes and Conventions* ("Date and Sources"), and Brooke in Baugh's *Literary History* briefly describe the verse; Henderson, *And Morning in His Eyes*, says the play was written in Greene's "Tamburlaine-Pistol manner"; Clemen, *English Tragedy* ("Literary Connections"), analyzes the set speeches.

William J. Lawrence, *Speeding up Shakespeare* (1937), thinks Tarlton was the original Bullithrumble. This comic character is one source for an inventive discussion by Brooks, *Will Shakspere*, who proposes that the clown is a parody of Shakespeare and "offers some indication of Shakspere's facetious grace." Harold R. Walley, "Shakespeare's Portrayal of Shylock," in *Essays in Dramatic Literature: The Parrott Presentation Volume*, ed. Hardin Craig (1935), pp. 213–42, describes briefly the treatment of the Jewish physician Abraham and current events which prompted interest in this type of character. (See also Cardozo [above], who describes the role, and E. E. Stoll, *Shakespeare Studies* [1927].)

Ernest A. Gerrard, *Elizabethan Drama and Dramatists, 1583–1603* (1928), includes *Selimus* in his partially reconstructed Chamberlain repertory of 1597–1603. The corruption of the text is recognized in Muir's *"Locrine and Selimus"* ("Literary Connections") and "Who Wrote *Selimus*?" Jewkes, *Act Division*, says vaguely that the copy cannot be shown conclusively to be a promptbook, but has more signs of such an origin than *Alphonsus of Aragon*; Murphy, "Some Problems in the Anonymous Drama," speculates that the manuscript may have been a prompt copy.

See Also

Camden, Carroll, Jr. "Elizabethan Almanacs and Prognostications." *Library* 12 (1931): 194-207.
Dawson, Giles E. "An Early List of Elizabethan Plays." *Library* 15 (1935): 445-56.
Doran, Madeleine. *Endeavors of Art: A Study of Form in Elizabethan Drama.* 1954.
Elton, William R. *"King Lear" and the Gods.* 1966.
Fogel, Ephim G. "Electronic Computers and Elizabethan Texts." *SB* 15 (1962): 15-31.
Holloway, John. *The Story of the Night: Studies in Shakespeare's Major Tragedies.* 1961.
Kirschbaum, Leo. *Shakespeare and the Stationers.* 1955.
Kocher, Paul H. *Christopher Marlowe: A Study of His Thought, Learning, and Character.* 1946.
Linton, Marion. "The Bute Collection of English Plays." *TLS,* 21 December 1956, p. 772.
————. "National Library of Scotland and Edinburgh University Library Copies of Plays in Greg's *Bibliography of the English Printed Drama.*" *SB* 15 (1962): 91-104.
Modder, Montagu Frank. *The Jew in the Literature of England to the End of the Nineteenth Century.* 1939.
Moore, John Robert. "The Songs of the Public Theaters in the Time of Shakespeare." *JEGP* 28 (1929): 166-202.
Sharpe, Robert Boies. *The Real War of the Theaters.* 1935.
Wilson, F. P. *The English Drama, 1485-1585.* Ed. G. K. Hunter, 1969.
Wright, Herbert G. *Boccaccio in England from Chaucer to Tennyson.* 1957.

J. L.

The Tragical History of Guy Earl of Warwick, heroical romance (*1593;* 1661)

The absence of any modern edition and a paucity of scholarship argue a notable lack of interest in this play. After Ronald S. Crane's "The Vogue of *Guy of Warwick* from the Close of the Middle Ages to the Romantic Revival," *PMLA* 30 (1915): 125-94, the only substantial study of the play has been Alfred Harbage's "A Contemporary Attack upon Shakspere?" *SAB* 16 (1941): 42-49. Harbage covers a wide range of topics. He exposes the false leads on the title page which suggest that the play was written by Ben Jonson, connected with the Restoration, and frequently acted. On the bases of subject matter, source evidence, and style, he postulates that the date of composition (for which there is no record at all) is ca. 1593. And he considers the possibility that Dekker contributed to the play. Organizing the meager data available, he hypothesizes that there were two Guy of Warwick plays: one written by Dekker as a fledgling dramatist (ca. 1593); the second, a new version of the first, by Dekker in collaboration with Day (and entered on the Stationers' Register in 1620). These two plays had independent careers, the earlier making its way into print. Harbage is certain that the extant play dates from the last decade of the sixteenth century, and with that conviction he examines a passage from the fifth act for a possible allusion to Shakespeare.

Harvey W. Hewett-Thayer, "Tieck and the Elizabethan Drama: His Marginalia," *JEGP* 34 (1935): 377–407, notes that Tieck, who copied or had copied part of the printed version of the play, found the suggestion for its plot in *The Magnetick Lady*. Hewett-Thayer adds that, though the 1661 *Guy of Warwick* is probably the work of Day and Dekker, it is nevertheless conceivable that it is a completely new work, the earlier play (*Henslowe's Diary*, 1604; Stationers' Register, 1619 or 1620) having been lost. More recently, G. E. Bentley, *The Jacobean and Caroline Stage*, vols. 3 and 5 (1956), has covered in a short discussion some of the same ground as Harbage. He too thinks it is possible that the Day and Dekker version may be lost, calls attention to the misleading statements on the title page, and believes the play to be a Renaissance production (either Elizabethan or early Jacobean). He suggests also that there might have been two, or even three, different dramatic versions of the story. And in his comments on the spurious 1639 imprimatur which appeared in one copy, he refers briefly to several facts and suggestions Greg has offered about the play in his *Bibliography*. Leonard R. N. Ashley, *Authorship and Evidence* (1968), considers the attributions.

J. L.

OTHER DRAMATISTS

Terence P. Logan   Denzell S. Smith

The figures included here were active in the theater at the same time as the major playwrights treated in this volume; their plays have been the subject of some recent scholarship. For additional information see E. K. Chambers, The Elizabethan Stage, 4 vols. (1923), W. W. Greg, A Bibliography of the English Printed Drama to the Restoration, 4 vols. (1939–59), and F. P. Wilson, The English Drama, 1485–1585, ed. G. K. Hunter (1969). Canon and dates are from Alfred Harbage, Annals of English Drama, 975–1700, rev. Samuel Schoenbaum (1964), and the Supplement by Schoenbaum (1966). Playwrights are discussed in alphabetical order. Entries are listed in chronological order for each playwright and date from the publication of The Elizabethan Stage to the end of 1968; the title of each article is followed by a brief summary of its contents.

NICHOLAS BRETON

Whiting, Mary Bradford. "Nicholas Breton Gentleman: A Tercentenary." *Fortnightly Review* 131 (1929): 618–32. Breton is a writer of great mental power and felicity of diction. A close study of his works reveals his love of humanity in an age when most poets recognized only the love between men and women.

Flournoy, Fitzgerald. "William Breton, Nicholas Breton, and George Gascoigne." *RES* 16 (1940): 262–73. The remarkable family history of Breton's youth—during which Gascoigne wooed William Breton's widow, defeated his rival, ignored the will, had himself appointed an elder brother's guardian, and transferred Nicholas' heritage to himself—tinged with skepticism Breton's statements about money.

RICHARD FARRANT

The attribution of The Wars of Cyrus to Farrant is discussed in the essay on the play in the anonymous-play section of this volume.

Lawrence, William J. "The Earliest Private Theatre Play." *TLS*, 11 August 1921, p. 514. A manuscript song by Farrant argues for his authorship of *The Wars of Cyrus*, "the oldest extant blank verse theatre-play." The song may indicate that *The Wars* was the first private theater play to be acted with musical intervals.

EDWARD FORSETT

Smith G. C. Moore. "The Authorship of *Pedantius*." *N&Q* 198 (1953): 427. A note by Forsett in the Library of St. John's College, Cambridge, supports his claims to authorship.

THOMAS HUGHES

Waller, Evangelia H. "A Possible Interpretation of *The Misfortunes of Arthur*." *JEGP* 24 (1925): 219–45. Political allusions and hidden political allegory, especially parallels between the play and affairs in Scotland in the late 1580s, are to be found in characterization, situation, speeches, and changes in source materials.

Reese, Gertrude. "Political Import of *The Misfortunes of Arthur*." *RES* 21 (1945): 81–91. The play uses "the legendary material of Arthur and Mordred for the purpose of reflecting the situation involved in Mary Stuart's execution."

Maxwell, J. C. "Lucan's First Translator." *N&Q* 192 (1947): 521–22. In *The Misfortunes of Arthur*, III.iii, 114 of 130 lines are dependent on Lucan. Hughes, not Marlowe, was the first to translate a substantial portion of Lucan into English blank verse.

Armstrong, William A. "The Topicality of *The Misfortunes of Arthur*." *N&Q* 2 (1955): 371–73. Armstrong questions Waller's allegorical parallels (above): it may be appropriate to associate Mordred with Mary Queen of Scots (rather than with Bothwell), and Arthur with Elizabeth (rather than with James VI of Scotland). The mythological association of Arthur and Elizabeth could explain Hughes's departure from Senecan convention, and may have been meant to praise Elizabeth's wisdom in sending Mary to the block a year earlier.

———. "Elizabethan Themes in *The Misfortunes of Arthur*." *RES* 7 (1956): 238–49. The play makes a sustained effort to combine Senecan themes and literary conventions with themes of current importance in

Elizabethan moral and political thought; the imperfect fusion accounts for faults in action and characterization.

Maxwell, J. C. "Seneca in *The Misfortunes of* Arthur." *N&Q* 7 (1960): 171. There is a borrowing from Seneca in IV.ii.1-4 not recorded in Cunliffe's edition (1912).

Dilke, O. A. W. "Thomas Hughes, Plagiarist." *N&Q* 10 (1963): 93-94. *The Misfortunes of Arthur* contains lines and whole passages translated more or less literally from Seneca and Lucan; Dilke examines Act IV for translations and reminiscences, noting the order in which Hughes borrowed from the originals.

Ramel, Jacques. "Biographical Notices on the Authors of *The Misfortunes of Arthur* (1588)." *N&Q* 14 (1967): 461-67. Ramel reports on Hughes, John Lancaster, Master Penruddock, Francis Flower, and Nicholas Trotte, but omits William Fulbeck and Christopher Yelverton, who are listed in the *Dictionary of National Biography,* and Francis Bacon.

Logan, George M. "Hughes's Use of Lucan in *The Misfortunes of Arthur.*" *RES* 20 (1969): 22-32. Hughes's "attitudes toward and his treatment of the theme of civil war were derived largely from Lucan"; the play has in it 330 lines from Lucan's *Pharsalia.*

WILLIAM KEMPE

Wright, Louis B. "Will Kemp and the *Commedia Dell'Arte.*" *MLN* 41 (1926): 516-20. Through his travels, Kempe probably came under the influence of *commedia dell'arte* clowns and later introduced some of their techniques into English comedy. There are contemporary allusions which support the conjecture. Kempe's familiarity with these techniques may have influenced Shakespeare in his treatment of roles intended for Kempe.

Gray, Henry David. "The Roles of William Kempe." *MLR* 25 (1930): 261-73. This article supplements T. W. Baldwin's *The Organization and Personnel of the Shakespearean Company* (1927) with conjectures on the roles played by Kempe in Shakespeare's plays. Kempe's departure from the company may have influenced Shakespeare's decision to drop Falstaff in *Henry V* and Kempe may have been involved in the pirated edition of *The Merry Wives.*

Baldwin, T. W. "William Kempe Not Falstaff." *MLR* 26 (1931): 170-72. Takes exception to Gray's attempt to expand *The Organization*; Kempe did not play Falstaff.

Gray, Henry David. "Shakespeare and Will Kempe: A Rejoinder." *MLR* 26 (1931): 172-74. Baldwin misinterprets lines from Jonson's *Poetaster*; they do not refer to actors' roles. It is doubtful that actors' wants and strong points much influenced Shakespeare in writing the plays.

Bald, R. C. "Leicester's Men in the Low Countries." *RES* 19 (1943): 395-97. Halliwell-Philipps's extracts from Leicester's household account books prove that Kempe was in the Low Countries in the Earl's service in 1585 and 1586. Kempe is mentioned in a letter by Sidney [but see Mithal, below].

Feldman, Abraham B. "Playwrights and Pike-Trailers in the Low Countries." *N&Q* 198 (1953): 184-87. Kempe apparently entertained Leicester and his troops in Delft in December, 1585.

Mithal, H. S. D. "Will, My Lord of Leicester's Jesting Player." *N&Q* 5 (1958): 427-29. The reference, in a letter of Sidney's from Utrecht to Wallsingham, is not to Kempe, as Chambers suggested in *The Elizabethan Stage* (1923), but to Robert Wilson. Kempe was at Elsinore at the time.

Bald, R. C. "Will, My Lord of Leicester's Jesting Player." *N&Q* 6 (1959): 112. Mithal's dates are incorrect; the reference in the letter discussed above is to Kempe. Wilson, however, was in the Netherlands in Leicester's service.

Mithal, H. S. D. " 'Mr. Kemp, Called Don Gulielmo.' " *N&Q* 7 (1960): 6-8. A letter by Thomas Doyley to Leicester probably refers to a priest, not the actor, as being in Dunkirk in 1585.

THOMAS LEGGE

Lordi, Robert J. "The Relationship of *Richardus Tertius* to the Main Richard III Plays." *BUSE* 5 (1961): 139-53. The author of the *True Tragedy* probably used *Richardus Tertius* occasionally as a source. Despite the possibility that Shakespeare might have known *RT* and despite the striking similarity of the wooing scenes in the two plays, there is virtually no evidence that he used *RT*. The Dutch *Richard* very likely is an adaptation of *RT*. There is no need to posit a lost Richard play to explain correspondences between the four plays.

HENRY PORTER

Shear, Rosetta E. "New Facts About Henry Porter." *PMLA* 42 (1927): 641–55. Shear identifies him as the Porter who matriculated at Brasenose College in 1589, constructs a life, and claims he wrote for Henslowe 1596–1600.

Oliphant, E. H. C. "Who Was Henry Porter?" *PMLA* 43 (1928): 572–75. 1589 or earlier is the composition date of *The Two Angry Women*. Shear (above) is in error about Porter's identity; he is the Henry Porter who matriculated at Christ's College, Cambridge, in 1584 (1586?).

Hotson, Leslie. "The Adventure of the Single Rapier." *Atlantic*, July 1931, pp. 26–31. Hotson traces the disappearance of Porter in the 1599 records of the Southeastern Circuit of the Southwark Assizes, and finds he was killed by rival playwright John Day with a single rapier. He suggests that Porter lacked Day's skill with the rapier, and seeks evidence in the works of each playwright.

Nosworthy, J. M. "Notes on Henry Porter." *MLR* 35 (1940): 517–21. This article tries to bring order to the confusion about the two 1599 editions of *I The Two Angry Women* and its date of composition (before 1589); about Porter's identity; about entries in Henslowe for *I* and *II The Two Angry Women* and *The Two Merry Women*; and about an early composition date.

Maxwell, Baldwin. "*The Two Angry Women of Abington* and *Wily Beguiled*." *PQ* 20 (1941): 334–39. Similarities in style, situation, phraseology, and technique between the two plays, printed in 1599 and 1606 respectively, merely suggest that the author of *Wily* was "widely acquainted with the drama of his time." That author need be neither Peele nor Rowley.

Nosworthy, J. M. "Henry Porter." *English* 6 (1946): 65–69. Nosworthy briefly treats Porter's life, and discusses *I Two Angry*

Women as "domestic comedy verging on farce," claiming that Porter "achieves perfection and approaches greatness."

Bowers, R. H. "Notes on *The Two Women of Abington." N&Q* 193 (1949): 311-14. Bowers lists the early editions and facsimiles and provides extensive glossarial notes to supplement the available unannotated texts.

Nosworthy, J. M. "The Shakespearean Heroic Vaunt." *RES* 2 (1951): 259-61. There are verbal parallels in *Romeo and Juliet, Merry Wives, King Lear, Othello,* and *Coriolanus* to the vaunt of the *miles gloriosus* in Porter's *I Two Angry Women.*

———. "The Two Angry Families of Verona." *SQ* 3 (1952): 219-26. Porter's *I Two Angry Women* preceded *Romeo and Juliet*; thus the verbal parallels between the two plays represent Shakespeare's borrowing, not Porter's, and Porter's impact is partly responsible for *Romeo and Juliet*'s imperfections as a tragedy.

———. "The Case is Altered." *JEGP* 51 (1952): 61-70. Jonson and Porter may have been "coadjutors" in the play which Jonson "was content to renounce," and they may have had some help from Chettle.

Morris, Alton C. "Proverbial Lore in *The Two Angry Women of Abington." Folklore Studies in Honor of Arthur Palmer Hudson. North Carolina Folklore* 13, nos. i-ii (1965): 25-35. The play contains about 150 proverbs not drawn from written material. They are used to create a character (named Nicholas Proverbs), supplement the rural setting, and provide a code of popular ethics. Their abundance supports the critical commonplace that the sixteenth century was the heyday of the proverb in literature, and perhaps suggests that Porter was satirizing the excessive use of proverbs by his fellow dramatists.

ROBERT WILSON

The subplot involving the efforts of the Jew Gerontus to collect a debt from the Italian Merchant Mercadore in The Three Ladies of London *raises the question of Wilson's possible debt to the lost play* The Jew. *The connection results in Wilson's play being at least generally mentioned in studies of the sources of* The Merchant of Venice. *Such treatments are usually only peripherally concerned with Wilson and, except for a standard example, have not been included.*

Baldwin, T. W. "Nathaniel Field and Robert Wilson." *MLN* 41 (1926): 32-34. There were two Robert Wilsons; the actor probably was dead by 1588.

Gourvitch, I. "Robert Wilson 'The Elder' and 'The Younger.' " *N&Q* 150 (1926): 4-6. There was no "younger" Wilson; the "elder" and Henslowe's man are the same person. Wilson is perhaps responsible for parts of *Sir John Oldcastle*.

Golding, S. R. "Robert Wilson and *Sir Thomas More*." *N&Q* 154 (1928): 237-39. Wilson was probably the author of the three MS pages of *More* (II.iv.1-172) which have been attributed to Shakespeare. The Wilson canon is significantly larger than has been supposed and probably includes *Look About You* and *Larum for London*; probably Wilson is also the author of *Fair Em*.

———. "The Authorship of *Edward III*." *N&Q* 154 (1928): 313-15. Parallels with *Larum for London* demonstrate that *Edward III* is also by Wilson; the parallels further support Wilson's authorship of *Sir Thomas More*.

Addy, S. O. "Robert Wilson and *Sir Thomas More*: Wilson's First Play." *N&Q* 154 (1928): 335-36. Golding is correct in attributing *More* to Wilson. Also, a Latin letter by the comedian Thomas Bayly may have resulted in Wilson's writing *Three Ladies* for the Earl of Shrewsbury's comedians.

Tannenbaum, Samuel A. "Robert Wilson and *Sir Thomas More*." *N&Q* 154 (1928): 465-66. Golding is incorrect. The MS handwriting is Munday's and he is the author of the major portion of the play.

Golding, S. R. "Further Notes on Robert Wilson and *Sir Thomas More*." *N&Q* 155 (1929): 237-40. Tannenbaum is incorrect; the MS handwriting on the disputed three pages is Wilson's. Wilson wrote most of the play, with help from Chettle and Heywood, around 1597; Munday revised.

Oliphant, E. H. C. "How Not to Play the Game of Parallels." *JEGP* 28 (1929): 1-15. Oliphant attacks Golding's attribution methods in general; his attribution of *Edward III* to Wilson (above) is specifically rejected.

Kittredge, George Lyman. "The Date of *The Pedler's Prophecie.*" *Harvard Studies and Notes in Philology and Literature* 16 (1934): 97-118. Fleay is wrong in attributing the play to Wilson; the attribution is "quite out of harmony with the style, the atmosphere, and the contents of the drama and is practically vacated by the establishment of so early a date [1561]."

Mann, Irene Rose. "A Political Cancel in *The Cobler's Prophesie.*" *Library* 23 (1942): 94-100. Typographical peculiarities and the use of a different compositor for the F gathering suggest that the sheet may be a cancellans; the presence of topical allegory in the original may have led to the substitution.

Bald, R. C. "Leicester's Men in the Low Countries." *RES* 19 (1943): 395-97. Halliwell-Phillips's transcripts from Leicester's household account books record a payment to Wilson on 4 March 1586 and prove his service in the Low Countries.

Mann, Irene Rose. "The Copy for the 1592 Quarto of *The Three Ladies of London.*" *PQ* 23 (1944): 86-89. The substantive text for the edition is the 1584 quarto.

———. "A Lost Version of *The Three Ladies of London.*" *PMLA* 59 (1944): 586-89. Gosson's *Plays Confuted in Five Actions* apparently refers to a version of the play substantially different from the extant text. There is also internal evidence which suggests significant excisions.

———. "More Wilson Parallels." *N&Q* 186 (1944): 287-88. Golding's attempt to ascribe *Sir Thomas More* to Wilson and Gourvitch's claim for Wilson's authorship of *Sir John Oldcastle* (both above) are dubious; the arguments based on verbal parallels are not convincing.

———. "Notes on the Malone Society Reprint of *The Cobler's Prophecy.*" *Library* 26 (1945): 181-89. Mann collates five copies in place of the three copies used for the reprint; she finds additional variants and speculates on possible causes for them.

———. "The Dibelius Edition of *The Cobler's Prophesie.*" *N&Q* 189 (1945): 48-50. The 1897 Dibelius printing has frequent variants from the quarto copy-text.

Bowers, Fredson. "Thomas Dekker, Robert Wilson, and *The Shoe-maker's Holiday.*" *MLN* 64 (1949): 517–19. A Houghton Library copy of the 1600 quarto has the names of Dekker and Wilson, in an allegedly contemporaneous hand, following the address to the reader. The notation is perhaps a Collier forgery and Wilson's name should not be associated with the play.

Nathanson, Leonard. "*A Quip for an Upstart Courtier* and *The Three Ladies of London.*" *N&Q* 3 (1956): 376–77. Wilson's play may have influenced Greene.

———. " 'Copertiment' and 'Copurtenaunce.' " *MLN* 71 (1956): 349–50. *Three Lords and Three Ladies* has a unique use of "coperti-ment" which may be related to "copurtenaunce" as used by Richard Harvey.

———. "Three Additions to the *O.E.D.*" *N&Q* 3 (1956): 546. Three Wilson compounds not included in the *O.E.D.* are listed.

Bullough, Geoffrey. *Narrative and Dramatic Sources of Shakespeare.* Vol. 1. 1957. Bullough prints excerpts from *The Three Ladies of London* which may be related to the lost *The Jew*; Wilson's play has value as a source of conjecture about the lost play and its possible influence.

Nathanson, Leonard. "Variants in Robert Wilson's *The Three Lords.*" *Library* 13 (1958): 57–59. The seven extant copies reveal variants attributable to stop-press correction on the inner G forme.

Mithal, H. S. D. "Will, My Lord of Leicester's Jesting Player." *N&Q* 5 (1958): 426–28. The reference, in a letter of Sidney's to Walsingham, is probably not to Kempe. Sidney, writing from Utrecht, may have had Wilson in mind; and this mention of service in the Netherlands would help account for an allusion in *Three Lords and Three Ladies.*

———. "*Short and Sweet.*" *N&Q* 5 (1958): 521–22. Chambers treats it as a play title, revised by Chettle under the title *Catiline's Conspiracy*, and assigns the original to Wilson. The possibility, based on a Lodge allusion to Wilson, is not convincing.

Bald, R. C. "Will, My Lord of Leicester's Jesting Player." *N&Q* 6 (1959): 112. Mithal (above) is in error; Sidney is referring to Kempe.

Baldwin, T. W. *On the Literary Genetics of Shakspere's Plays, 1592-1594.* 1959. Baldwin rejects the possibility of Wilson's authorship of *Fair Em.* [Most recent scholarship agrees; for a detailed discussion see the editions and authorship sections under the play title in this volume.]

Mithal, H. S. D. "The Two Wilsons Controversy." *N&Q* 6 (1959): 106-9. The separation of the actor and the Henslowe collaborator, which began with Fleay, is almost certainly an error. The two men are the same, as a reference in *Paladis Tamia* and other evidence demonstrates.

——. " 'Chipping Norton a Mile from Chapel of the Heath.' " *N&Q* 6 (1959): 193. Simplicity's reference to a ballad title in *Three Lords* may refer to an actual ballad on a Chipping Norton scandal (or mesalliance?).

——. "The Authorship of *Fair Em* and *Martin Mar-Sixtus.*" *N&Q* 7 (1960): 8-10. Resemblances to Wilson's known work support a claim for his authorship of both the pamphlet and the play.

Henning, Standish. "*Fair Em* and Robert Wilson: Another View." *N&Q* 7 (1960): 348-49, 360. This article is a detailed refutation of Mithal's attribution: the play should remain anonymous.

Bradbrook, Muriel C. "Beasts and Gods: Greene's *Groats-Worth of Witte* and the Social Purpose of *Venus and Adonis.*" *ShS* 15 (1962): 62-72. The characters Love and Contempt, in Wilson's plays, may have significantly influenced Shakespeare's conception of both Venus and Adonis, and the plot of his poem.

Lavin, J. A. "Two Notes on *The Cobler's Prophecy.*" *N&Q* 9 (1962): 137-39. Lavin corrects details of possible staging given in E. K. Chambers, *The Elizabethan Stage* (1923), vol. 3, and in T. W. Craik, *The Tudor Interlude* (1958).

Mithal, H. S. D. "The Variants in Robert Wilson's *The Three Lords of London.*" *Library* 18 (1963): 142–44. Nathanson's earlier list of variants (above) is worthless. He misses a number of actual variants and includes several spurious variants because of misreading black-letter type.

Logan, Terence P. "Robert Wilson and the *O.E.D.*" *N&Q* 15 (1968): 248. Logan lists antedatings, additions, and corrections.

Wilson, F. P. *The English Drama, 1485–1585.* 1969. This book briefly considers Robert Wilson in terms of the morality tradition. The bibliography, by G. K. Hunter, includes the important early items and reprints and editions of the plays.

LIST OF CONTRIBUTORS

CHARLES W. DAVES is an Assistant Director of the Test Development Division at Educational Testing Service, Princeton, New Jersey. His edition of Samuel Butler's *Characters* was published in 1970.

ROBERT J. FEHRENBACH is Associate Professor of English at the College of William and Mary.

JOSEPH W. HOUPPERT is Associate Professor of English at the University of Maryland.

ROBERT KIMBROUGH is Professor of English at the University of Wisconsin–Madison.

ANNE LANCASHIRE is Associate Professor of English at University College, University of Toronto, and a specialist in English Renaissance drama.

JILL LEVENSON is Assistant Professor of English at Trinity College, University of Toronto. She is also the director of Trinity's Independent Studies Programme.

TERENCE P. LOGAN is Associate Professor of English at the University of New Hampshire and edits the bibliography sections of two journals.

WILLIAM NESTRICK is Assistant Professor of English at the University of California, Berkeley.

DENZELL S. SMITH is Associate Professor of English at Idaho State University.

DICKIE A. SPURGEON is Associate Professor of English at Southern Illinois University–Edwardsville.

INDEX

PERSONS

A.C., 277
Acheson, Arthur, 101, 102, 118, 158, 163, 167, 170, 182, 185, 186, 188, 202, 204, 208, 209, 213, 219, 220, 221, 224, 228, 231, 233, 234, 238, 262, 263, 272, 276, 304, 309
Ackerman, Catherine A., 140
Adams, Barry B., 183
Adams, Charles S., 145
Adams, Henry Hitch, 246, 247, 249, 254, 278
Adams, Joseph Quincy, 52, 165, 222, 230, 271, 282, 287
Addy, S. O., 318
Adkins, Mary Grace Muse, 253, 255–56, 286, 295
Admiral's Men, 31, 57, 81, 166, 167, 169, 170, 171, 172, 175, 204, 206, 214, 231, 283, 287
Adolf-Altenberg, G., 43
Agate, James, 243, 248
Albright, Evelyn May, 38, 74, 118, 140, 175, 197, 214, 255, 287
Alden, Raymond M., 225
Alexander, Nigel, 55, 158
Alexander, Peter, 34, 52, 116, 117, 168, 177, 178, 180, 187, 188, 194–95, 197, 198–99, 203, 220, 224, 244, 246, 276, 282, 295, 297
Allen, Don Cameron, 24, 34, 47, 63, 89, 118, 138–39
Allen, Percy, 126, 242, 248
Allen, Ralph G., 39
Allen, Walter, Jr., 12, 109
Alleyn, Edward, 39, 175, 186, 204, 213, 231
Allodoli, Ettore, 51
Allott, Robert, 84, 302
Anders, H., 42
Andersen, J. C., 42
Anderson, Ruth L., 47, 271, 278
Angeli, Diego, 206, 240, 258

Anichkov, E. V., 38
Anikst, Alexander, 118
Anster, Sir John, 33
Applegate, James, 62–63
Archer, Edward, 228, 244
Archer, William, 38
Ariosto, Lodovico, 77, 194
Arkwright, G. E. P., 191
Arms, George, 89
Armstrong, R. L., 176, 206, 219, 288
Armstrong, William A., 20, 38, 47, 49, 155–56, 175 206, 286, 288, 290, 313
Arnold, Aerol, 276
Arnold, Paul, 89
Aronstein, Philipp, 38, 88, 118, 140
Artz, Frederick, 38
Ascham, Roger, 130
Ascoli, G., 88
Ashe, Dora Jean, 31, 149, 169, 216, 279
Ashley, Leonard R. N., 143, 147, 180, 181, 182, 183, 209, 220, 221, 228, 232, 238, 250, 253, 256, 257, 263, 265, 268, 280, 281, 300, 304, 311
Ashley, Robert, 118
Ashmore, Basil, 34
Ashton, John William, 34, 218, 283, 286
Atkins, J. W. H., 118, 127, 158, 239
Atkins, Sidney H., 158
Atkinson, A. D., 34, 300
Attwater, A. L., 275
Austin, Warren B., 67, 116, 118, 125–26
Axelrad, José, 242
Ayrton, Michael, 118, 119, 124

Babb, Howard S., 49
Babb, Lawrence, 60, 140, 238, 250
Bachrach, A. G. H., 43
Bacon, Francis, 122, 314

Bakeless, John Edwin, 4, 6, 7, 34, 51, 87, 181, 191, 201, 203, 209, 217, 225, 230, 232, 235, 236, 243, 246, 262, 264, 266, 284, 300, 302, 304, 306
Baker, Arthur E., 175, 188
Baker, Donald C., 43
Baker, Ernest A., 61-62, 109
Baker, G. P., 88
Baker, Howard, 11, 20, 94, 95, 119, 160, 250
Baker, Oliver, 119
Bald, R. C., 54, 82, 260, 315, 319, 321
Baldini, Gabriele, 55, 240, 243, 245, 246, 248, 249
Baldwin, Thomas Whitfield, 34, 42, 52, 81, 100, 102, 104, 119, 126, 129, 164, 173, 187, 188, 191, 193, 195, 201, 203, 204, 214, 217, 218, 221, 225, 229, 230-38 passim, 245, 246, 248, 259, 260, 264, 265, 267, 273, 277, 279, 282, 283, 284, 285, 287, 304, 305, 308, 314, 315, 318, 321
Bale, John, 172, 176, 183, 184, 185, 187, 188
Ball, Robert Hamilton, 40, 50, 57, 72, 76, 105, 121, 127, 143, 239
Barber, C. L., 15-16, 18, 21, 113, 114, 119, 174
Barish, Jonas A., 94-95, 131, 164, 174-75
Barke, Herbert, 188
Barrington, Michael, 34
Bartlett, Henrietta C., 238, 250, 271, 280
Bartley, J. O., 88, 214, 286-87, 300
Barton, H. K., 92
Barzak, Robert William, 215-16
Baskerville, Charles Read, 76, 119, 157, 227, 240, 269
Bateson, F. W., 242
Battenhouse, Roy W., 4, 18, 47, 307, 308
Baumer, Franklin Le Van, 239
Bawcutt, N. W., 110

Beall, Charles N., 43
Beaty, Frederick L., 158
Beaumont, Sir Francis, 53, 55, 59, 71, 90, 251
Beckerman, Bernard, 223-24
Bellon, Loleh, 240, 241
Benbow, R. Mark, 145, 147, 150
Benham, Allen R., 138
Bennett, H. S., 33
Bennett, Josephine W., 132
Bennett, Paul E., 280, 282-83, 284
Bentley, Eric, 242
Bentley, G. E., 161, 292, 298, 303-4, 311
Berdan, John M., 51
Bergin, Thomas G., 197
Bernard, J. E., Jr., 113, 287
Bernard, Rich., 244
Berners, Lord. *See* Bourchier, John
Berryman, John, 109, 118
Best, Michael R., 111, 113, 114, 126-27, 129, 135
Bethell, S. L., 258, 269, 299
Bevington, David, 7, 8, 60, 70, 78, 133-34, 164, 173, 174, 185, 212-13, 220, 221, 224, 229, 234, 239, 250, 254-55, 256, 263, 267, 281, 285-86, 297, 305, 307
Biesterfeldt, Peter Wilhelm, 38, 99, 234-35
Bing, Just, 87
Birde, William, 29, 202
Black, Matthew W., 49, 175, 188, 225, 293, 294, 295, 300
Blair, Carolyn, 151
Blanchart, Paul, 47, 248
Blatt, Thora Balslev, 183
Blau, Herbert, 47
Blayney, Glenn H., 250
Blisset, William, 13
Blistein, Elmer, 146, 148, 150
Bloor, R. H. U., 89
Bluestone, Max, 9, 246, 248
Blunden, E., 34
Boase, T. S. R., 249
Boas, Frederick S., 5, 28, 29, 33, 35, 38, 81, 87, 93, 99, 100, 103, 104,

119, 140, 191, 230, 235-39
passim, 242, 243, 245, 246, 251,
264, 290, 292, 294, 298, 299, 303
Boas, Guy, 47
Bøgholm, N., 43
Böhm, Rudolf, 10, 189, 271
Bond, R. Warwick, 125, 129, 138,
139, 163, 197
Bonheim, Jean, 268, 277, 295
Bonjour, Adrien, 184
Boodle, R. W., 162
Borinski, Ludwig, 130-31, 298
Boughner, Daniel C., 132, 234, 237,
239, 251, 299
Bourchier, John, 206, 294
Bowen, Gwynneth, 35, 140
Bowers, Fredson T., 30, 33, 49, 95,
96, 98, 99, 101, 108-9, 199, 238,
239, 251, 264, 268, 306, 320
Bowers, R. H., 317
Bowling, William G., 175
Bradbrook, Frank W., 43, 111
Bradbrook, Muriel C., 17, 27, 35, 38,
42, 59, 66, 111, 113, 127, 140, 144,
175, 189, 201, 210, 213, 230, 251,
271, 277, 278-79, 305, 309, 321
Bradley, Jesse Franklin, 230
Braginton, Mary V., 270
Braun, Erich, 275
Braun, Margareta, 262, 269, 271, 279,
300
Brawley, Benjamin G., 38
Brawner, James Paul, 189-91, 192,
193, 194
Brereton, John Le Gay, 19, 32, 35, 85,
293, 294
Breton, Nicholas, 312
Brett-Smith, H. F. B., 109
Brewster, Paul G., 251, 280
Bridges-Adams, William, 35, 242, 256,
262, 276
Brie, Friedrich, 38
Briggs, Katharine M., 49, 140, 271
Briggs, William D., 23, 34, 35, 44, 51
Brion, Marcel, 57, 87
Bristol, Michael, 50
Broadbent, J. B., 11

Brockbank, J. P., 15, 18
Brodwin, Leonora Leet, 51
Brooke, C. F. Tucker, 3, 4, 11, 20, 25,
28, 31, 32-33, 35 38, 53, 57, 83,
144, 181, 201, 209, 226, 233, 236,
237, 241, 246, 259, 264, 265, 266,
301, 302, 304, 309
Brooke, Nicholas, 10-11, 14, 25, 44
Brooks, Alden, 182-83, 218, 228,
261, 267, 303, 304, 309
Brooks, Charles, 47
Brooks, E. St. John, 35, 36
Brown, Beatrice D., 44
Brown, Huntington, 119
Brown, Ivor, 35, 206
Brown, John Russell, 9, 136-37, 237
Brown, P. W. F., 44
Browne, Ray B., 111
Brunius, Laurette, 240, 241
Brunvand, Jan Harold, 199, 205
Bryant, Joseph A., 132, 163
Buc, Sir George, 259, 260, 288, 298
Buckley, George T., 35, 89, 104, 119
Bühler, Curt F., 13, 119
Bullough, Geoffrey, 81, 117, 165,
176, 194, 197-98, 204, 256, 274
275, 277, 278, 283, 294, 295, 320
Burbage, Richard, 204, 213, 231
Burchardt, Carl, 38
Burckhardt, Sigurd, 66, 151
Busby, Olive Mary, 60, 119, 238, 269,
299
Bush, Douglas, 11, 12, 42, 53, 89,
119, 140, 150, 158
Butler, E. M., 44
Butler, Pierce, 119
Butrym, Alexander, 44, 105
Buxton, John, 42
Byrne, Muriel St. Clare, 158, 163, 173,
181, 200, 216-17, 220

Cabral, A. de Oliveira, 54
Cain, H. E., 44
Cairncross, Andrew S., 84, 100, 102,
103, 104, 116, 119, 152, 167-78,
170, 177, 178, 188, 221, 224, 233,
237, 247, 248, 251, 256

Camden, Carroll, Jr., 35, 47, 89, 310
Cameron, Kenneth W., 44
Camp, Charles W., 89
Campbell, Lily B., 16, 96, 119, 146, 156, 184, 276, 292
Campbell, Oscar James, 277
Candelaria, Frederick, 12
Cannon, Charles K., 98–99
Cantelupe, Eugene B., 12
Capra, Carlo, 274, 275
Cardozo, J. L., 49, 305, 308, 309
Carpenter, Nan C., 35, 44, 49
Carrère, Félix, 93–104 passim, 163, 202, 209, 220, 232, 233, 235, 239, 240–41, 242, 272
Cartwright, William, 297
Case, R. H., 3, 11, 32
Castle, E., 44
Catel, Jean, 140
Caulfield, Ernest, 158
Cawley, A. C., 251
Cawley, Robert Ralston, 38, 60, 119
Cazamian, Louis, 57, 72, 119, 140, 151
Cellini, Benvenuto, 44, 54, 79, 86, 91, 163, 192, 193, 228, 235–36, 251, 258, 287, 309
Chamberlain's Men, 167, 178, 197, 204, 230, 263, 276, 298
Chambers, E. K., 13, 25, 28–29, 31, 32, 35, 47, 79–80, 81 83, 84, 91, 100, 114, 136, 147, 150, 157, 161, 167, 170, 177, 180, 187, 188, 189, 195, 197, 199, 200, 204, 208, 209–10, 222, 225, 229, 232, 245, 247, 256, 260, 263, 264, 267, 273, 274, 279, 280, 281, 282, 292, 294, 297 298, 304, 313, 315, 320, 321
Chambers, R. W., 220, 224
Chambrun, Clara Longworth de. *See* Longworth, Clara
Chang, Joseph S., 38
Chapman, George, 12–13, 32, 34, 167, 308
Chapman, Raymond, 248, 249
Charlton, H. B., 33, 204–5, 231, 236, 241, 245, 246, 288
Chassé, Charles, 124

Cheffaud, P. H., 144
Chelli, Maurice, 284
Chettle, Henry, 66, 84, 123, 183, 317, 318, 320
Chew, Samuel C., 47, 91, 119, 124, 164, 232, 233, 234, 273, 302, 305, 308, 309
Chickera, Ernst de, 104
Child, Harold, 248
Childs, Ralph, 140
Christ, Henry I., 44
Chudoba, F. 44
Churchill, George B., 273–78 passim
Churchill, Reginald Charles, 5, 35, 119, 126
Clapp, Sarah L. C., 145
Clark, Arthur Melville, 49, 53, 251
Clark, Eleanor Grace, 38, 52, 119, 175, 201, 204, 255, 293, 296
Clark, Eva Turner, 119
Clarke, F. W., 86
Clarkson, P. S., 38, 60
Cleeve, Brian T., 101
Clemen, Wolfgang, 23, 58–59, 70, 72, 73, 75, 77, 93, 95, 119, 143, 156, 158, 174, 186, 213, 221, 224, 253, 257, 263, 264, 268, 269, 270–71, 278, 279, 295, 299–300, 307, 308, 309
Clemons, Harry, 139
Clough, Wilson O., 175
Clurman, Harold, 47
Coffman, George R., 111
Colby, E., 158
Cole, Douglas, 4, 7–8, 18, 25, 49, 104, 235, 307
Coleman, Edward D., 49
Collier, Jeremy P., 31, 32, 52, 82, 161, 259, 260, 320
Collins, J. Churton, 56, 57, 67, 73, 80, 81, 83, 86
Colville, K. N., 126
Condee, Ralph W., 158
Cook, Roderick, 46
Cookman, A. V., 38
Cooper, Barbara, 29
Cormican, L. A., 47
Cornelius, Roberta D., 251

Cottier, Margaret, 136–37
Coursen, Herbert R., Jr., 97
Courthope, W. J., 38
Cowl, R. P., 213, 214, 230, 236, 247
Cox, C. B., 35
Crabtree, John H., Jr., 17
Craig, Hardin, 38, 95, 164, 179, 196, 222–23, 225, 229, 250, 266, 271, 280, 287, 300, 308
Craik, Thomas W., 33, 38, 140, 321
Crane, Ronald S., 310
Crane, William G., 89, 119, 140
Crawford, Charles, 3, 93, 103, 241, 242, 243, 265, 301, 302, 303, 308
Crawford, Jack R., 89, 275
Croce, Benedetto, 140
Croll, Morris W., 139
Cromwell, Otelia, 247
Cross, Gustav K., 32
Croston, A. K., 119
Crow, John, 53
Cruickshank, A. H., 287
Crundell, H. W., 51, 52, 53, 105, 115, 202, 207, 219, 225, 244, 247
Cruttwell, Patrick, 38
Cubeta, Paul M., 12
Cunliffe, J. W., 38, 263, 314
Cunningham, John E., 38
Cunningham, J. V., 47, 113, 239, 251, 270
Curry, John V., 205
Cust, Lionel, 241
Cutts, John P., 24, 32, 47, 115, 148

D'Agostino, Nicola, 8–9
Dahinten, Gisela, 269, 279, 292, 299
Dameron, J. Lasley, 49
Danchin, F. C., 35, 44, 52, 54
D'Andrea, Antonio, 49
Daniel, Samuel, 159
Danks, K. B., 199
Dannenberg, Friedrich, 140
Darby, Robert H., 35
Davenport, Arnold, 111, 119, 139, 158
David, Richard, 111
Davidson, Clifford, 14
Davies, Hugh Sykes, 247, 250

Davies, Sir John, 43, 55
Davis, Harold H., 158
Davis, Walter R., 62, 119, 131, 154
Dawson, Giles E., 239, 251, 271, 310
Day, John, 311, 316
Dean, James S., Jr., 89
Dean, Leonard F., 50
De Beer, E. S., 119
Dédéyan, Charles, 44
de Kalb, E., 35
Dekker, Thomas, 76, 103, 129, 175, 310–11, 320
Delattre, Floris, 240
Deloney, Thomas, 120, 121, 131
De Ment, Joseph W., 111
de Nagy, N. Christoph, 189
Denonain, J. J., 35
Dent, Robert W., 42, 64, 214
Derby's Men, 162, 163, 283
De Reul, Paul, 251
De Ricci, Seymour, 259
Dessen, Alan C., 285
De Stasio, Clotilde, 143–44
De Vere, Edward, Earl of Oxford, 126, 132, 166, 173, 210, 244, 262
Devroor, J., 55
Deyermond, A. D., 44
Dibelius, Wilhelm, 319
Dick, Hugh G., 47
Dickenson, Thomas H., 56, 57, 80
Dickey, Franklin, 251
Dilke, O. A. W., 314
Dilthey, Wilhelm, 38
Disher, M. Willson, 35
Djivelegov, A., 35
Dobrée, Bonamy, 289–90
Dobson, Willis Boring, 213
Dodds, M. Hope, 51, 129
Dodsley, Robert, 161
Dodson, Sarah, 294
Donnarel, A., 151
Donno, Elizabeth Story, 34, 158
Donovan, Thomas, 214
Doran, Madeleine, 39, 59, 120, 127, 134, 143, 190–91, 225, 239, 249, 250, 271, 280, 310
Douglas, A., 35

Douglas, Gavin, 94
Dowling, Harold M., 147, 150, 152, 261
Downer, Alan S., 70, 175, 225, 242, 300
Draper, John W., 205, 239, 269
Drayton, Michael, 182, 207
Drew, Philip, 65, 110, 112, 120, 158
Drinkwater, John, 89
Drury, William, 151
Dryden, John, 20
Duhamel, P. Albert, 120, 131
Dunbar, William, 113
Duncan, Edgar H., 158
Duncan-Jones, Katherine, 110
Dunn, Esther Cloudman, 88
Dunn, T. A., 284
Durrell, Lawrence, 35
Duthie, George I., 14, 19, 101, 153–54, 196, 198
Dyde, S. G., 35

Eagle, Roderick L., 35
Ebbs, John Dale, 111
Eccles, Mark, 3–4, 6, 35, 87, 125, 136, 260
Eckhardt, Eduard, 39, 88, 120
Eden, John M., 42
Edwards, Philip, 93, 97–104 passim, 231, 234, 235, 242, 250, 304–5, 308
Eichhorn, Traudl, 238, 244, 248, 250, 270, 278, 299, 301
Einstein, Lewis David, 39
Eisinger, F., 262, 263, 264, 270
Ekeblad, Inga-Stina. *See* Ewbank, Inga-Stina
Eliot, T. S., 10, 11, 21–22, 95, 242, 247, 270, 273
Elizabeth I, 26, 113, 133, 141, 145, 162, 164, 228, 230, 231, 255–56, 296, 313
Elliot, John R., 185
Ellis-Fermor, Una, 5, 7, 14, 18, 33, 44, 46, 47, 51, 52, 57–58, 72, 75, 76–77

Elson, John James, 179–80, 183, 184, 291, 293, 295, 296, 298
Elton, William R., 44, 310
Empson, William, 70, 97, 106, 213
Erbe, Theodor, 264
Erdman, David C., 53
Ergang, Robert, 39
Esler, Anthony, 68
Espiner-Scott, Janet, 140
Evans, B. Ifor, 127, 251, 278
Evans, G. Blakemore, 111, 116, 175, 188, 275
Evans, M. Blakemore, 44
Evans, Robert O., 140
Everitt, E. B., 175, 176–77, 182, 186–87, 188, 206, 210, 212, 213, 219, 220, 221, 225, 288, 291, 295, 298
Ewbank, Inga-Stina [Ekeblad], 145, 146, 151, 299, 302, 308

Fabian, Bernhard, 44
Farjeon, Herbert, 206
Farnham, Willard, 39, 95, 151, 160, 186, 233, 242, 248, 253, 255, 259, 264, 266, 269, 272–73, 274, 278, 308, 309
Farrant, Richard, 190, 191, 192, 312–13
Feasey, Lynette and Eveline, 34, 36, 47, 120
Feldman, Abraham Bronson, 36, 257, 314
Fenton, Doris, 39
Ferrara, Fernando, 60–61, 63, 87
Feuillerat, Albert, 125, 295
Fiehler, Rudolph, 171–72
Field, Nathaniel, 318
Fieler, Frank B., 20
Fisch, Harold, 22
Fischer, Walther, 163
Fisher, Edward, 36
Fisher, Margery, 89
Flasdieck, Herman M., 52, 251, 287
Fleay, Edmond du, 81, 83, 163, 172, 216, 218, 243, 245, 248, 252, 256, 261, 277, 281, 319, 321
Fletcher, John, 48, 53, 55, 59, 71, 251
Flosdorf, J. W., 50

Flournoy, Fitzgerald, 312
Flower, Francis, 314
Fluchère, Henri, 250, 278
Flynn, J. G., 47
Foakes, R. A., 251
Fogel, Ephim G., 32, 53, 214, 251, 271, 310
Forbes, C. A., 51
Ford, John, 16, 54, 104
Forsett, Edward, 313
Forsythe, Robert S., 42, 89, 106
Fort, J. B., 12, 34
Fox, Charles A. O., 158
Fox, Richard, 52
Foxe, John, 172, 176, 184
Foxon, D. F., 118
Fraser, Russell A., 12
Freeman, Arthur, 50, 66, 68, 93, 95–104 passim, 115, 163, 179, 188, 232, 233–34, 237, 238, 241, 242, 247, 265, 267, 281, 282, 284–85, 303, 304, 305, 308
French, A. L., 120
Frey, Leonard H., 44
Fricker, Robert, 23
Friedländer, Ernst, 225
Friedman, Allan Warren, 22
Friedman, William and Elizabeth, 5–6
Frijlinck, Wilhelmina, 288, 290, 298
Frye, Roland M., 16
Fukuda, Tsutomu, 44
Fulbeck, William, 314
Furness, H. H., 189
Fuzier, Jean, 104

Gabler, Hans Walter, 39
Gagen, Jean Elizabeth, 89
Galloway, David, 24
Gardner, Helen, 15, 20–21
Garnier, Robert, 99, 105, 231, 233, 235, 237, 239, 242, 247, 262, 263, 268, 304, 305, 306
Gascoigne, George, 49, 67, 299, 312
Gassner, John, 39, 88, 240
Gaw, Allison, 53, 116, 152
Gayley, Charles M., 84, 115
Gelber, Norman, 77

Genouy, Hector, 89, 158
George, James, 36, 153, 154
Geraldine, Sister M., 120
Gerevini, Silvano, 66
Gerrard, Ernest A., 39, 88, 104, 120, 140, 176, 181, 196, 202, 204, 207, 236, 241, 250, 261–62, 263, 265, 269, 279, 309
Gibbons, Sister Marina, 120
Gibson, H. N., 5, 271
Gide, André, 240
Gilbert, Allan H., 44, 49, 151
Gill, Roma, 33, 34
Gillespie, Gerald, 39
Gillet, Louis, 245, 246, 249
Glenn, Edgar M., 5
Glunz, H. H., 189, 277
Godfrey, D. R., 111
Goffe, Thomas, 302, 303, 308
Golding, Arthur 155
Golding, S. R., 32, 53, 207, 216, 318, 319
Goldman, Arnold, 44
Goldsmith, Robert Hillis, 229, 287
Goldstein, Leba M., 52
Goldstone, Herbert, 144–45
Goodstein, Peter, 104
Gordon, D. J., 137
Goree, Roselle Gould, 89
Gosse, Edmund, 140, 153, 157
Gosson, Stephen, 141, 159, 319
Gourvitch, I., 318, 319
Graves, Thornton S., 230, 259
Gray, A. K., 36
Gray, Henry David, 101, 176, 195, 202, 205, 286, 314, 315
Greaves, Margaret, 39
Grebanier, Bernard, 50, 120
Green, Clarence, 44
Green, William, 240
Greene, Robert, 29, 56–92, 112, 117, 156, 163, 172, 173, 182, 183, 188, 196, 201, 202, 203, 208, 209, 215–21 passim, 228, 235–36, 243, 259, 261–62, 264, 265, 266, 272, 276, 280, 281, 282, 284, 299, 301–9 passim, 320

Greene, T. W., 76
Greenewald, Gerrard M., 189
Greenfield, Thelma N., 205
Greer, C. A., 169, 171
Greg, W. W., 17, 28, 29-30, 33, 34, 42, 46, 52, 76, 79, 80, 81, 86, 100, 103, 104, 120, 123, 129, 136, 139, 140, 147, 148, 151, 157, 158, 161-62, 166, 167, 168, 172, 180, 183, 187, 190, 191, 197, 200, 203-4, 215, 221, 222, 223, 225, 227, 238, 239, 243-44, 248, 251, 252, 257, 260, 267, 271, 272, 277, 284, 288, 292, 297-98, 302, 310, 311, 312
Gregor, J., 39
Greville, Fulke, Lord Brooke, 303
Griffin, Alice, 165, 194, 204, 205
Grigson, Geoffrey, 44
Grimald, Nicholas, 94
Grivelet, Michel, 251
Grosart, A. B., 56, 84, 85-86, 259, 301, 302, 304
Grosse, Franz, 39, 189, 254, 300
Grotowski, Jerzy, 44
Grubb, Marion, 158, 233, 242, 245, 247
Guidi, Augusto, 54
Gurr, Andrew, 120
Guthrie, Tyrone, 47, 54
Gwynn, Frederick L., 214
Gyller, Harold, 36

Habicht, Werner, 104
Halio, Jay L., 12, 50
Hall, Edgar A., 151
Hall, Vernon, Jr., 120
Halstead, W. L., 175
Hampden, John, 54
Hankins, John E., 44
Hanratty, Jerome, 248
Hapgood, Robert, 106, 176
Harbage, Alfred, 5, 22, 25, 39, 79, 81, 82, 84, 95-96, 100, 111, 114, 115, 120, 128, 136, 140, 147, 157, 158, 161, 176, 225, 287, 310-11, 312
Harder, Kelsie B., 120
Harlow, C. G., 107, 111, 116, 120

Harman, Edward George, 89, 120, 159
Harris, Bernard, 120, 140
Harris, Jesse W., 183
Harris, Lynn H., 89
Harrison, G. B., 36, 37, 75, 87, 88, 89, 104, 120, 124, 157-58
Harrison, Thomas P., Jr., 50
Hart, Alfred, 36, 39, 170, 179, 183, 188, 197, 203, 208-9, 210, 224, 225, 237, 247, 248, 254, 265, 283, 284-85, 295, 300
Hart, H. C., 253
Hart, Jeffrey P., 45
Harvey, Gabriel, 34, 37, 52, 57, 65, 67, 68, 88, 89, 110, 111, 118-23 passim, 126, 144
Hasselkuss, H. K., 159
Hastings, William T., 251
Hawkins, Sherman, 17
Hawkins, Thomas, 234
Haydn, Hiram, 36
Hazen, A. T., 103
Hazlitt, W. C., 161
Hecksher, W. S., 45
Heilman, Robert B., 15
Heller, Erich, 45
Heller, Otto, 45
Heltzel, Virgil B., 226, 240
Hemingway, Samuel Burdett, 165, 295
Henderson, Philip, 5, 36, 87, 122, 124, 173, 181, 242, 245, 246, 272, 273, 276, 303, 309
Henderson, Sam H., 155
Heninger, S. K., Jr., 13, 39
Henneke, Agnes, 176, 189
Henning, Standish, 215, 217, 321
Henslowe, Philip, 29, 31, 78, 81, 82, 167, 180, 204, 213, 220, 224, 282, 311, 316, 319, 321
Herbert, T. W., 202-3
Herpich, Charles A., 92
Herrick, Marvin T., 59, 74, 159, 271
Herrington, H. W., 36, 181, 302
Hewett-Thayer, Harvey W., 239, 251, 311
Hewitt, Douglas, 113
Heywood, Jasper, 45

Heywood, Thomas, 27, 28, 49, 54, 67, 96, 151, 247, 251, 254, 278, 318
Hibbard, G. R., 65, 87, 107-17 passim, 120, 196, 251, 281
Hill, Abraham, 271, 287
Hill, R. F., 271
Hillebrand, Harold N., 140
Hillier, Richard I., 39
Himelick, Raymond, 159
Hiraoka, Tomokazu, 159
Hobday, C. H., 211
Hoffman, Calvin, 5, 209, 271
Hoffmann, Gerhard, 271
Holland, H. H., 81
Holland, Norman N., 21
Holloway, John, 272, 300, 310
Holmes, Elizabeth, 42, 120, 262, 267
Holzknecht, Karl Julius, 39, 132, 134, 229-30, 251
Homan, Sidney R., Jr., 45, 76
Honigmann, E. A. J., 81, 89, 104, 110, 116, 177, 178, 179, 181, 183, 184, 198, 237, 273, 276, 277, 280
Hooft, Bart Hendrick van't, 45
Hook, Frank S., 28, 144, 146, 148, 149, 150
Hookham, Hilda, 48
Hopkinson, A. F., 83, 85, 218
Hoppe, Harry R., 79
Hornát, Jaroslav, 64, 130, 140, 155, 159
Horne, David H., 143, 150
Horrell, Joseph, 45
Hosking, G. L., 39
Hoskins, Frank L., 140, 218
Hosley, Richard, 198, 251
Hotson, J. Leslie, 3, 4, 36, 39, 137, 316
Houk, Raymond A., 29, 92, 196, 198, 202, 203
Houppert, Joseph W., 154, 156, 157
Howarth, R. G., 36, 39, 53, 106, 120, 142, 147
Hoy, Cyrus, 16, 214
Hubbard, Frank G., 84, 258
Hudson, Ruth, 74
Hughes, James Quentin, 50
Hughes, Pennethorne, 36
Hughes, Thomas, 313-14

Hughes, William, 35
Humphreys, A. R., 165-76 passim, 236-37, 295
Hunt, Leigh, 50
Hunter, G. K., 17, 19, 22, 52, 98, 105, 125-40 passim, 190, 192 259, 310, 312, 322
Hunter, J. B., 120
Hunter, Robert Grams, 163-64
Huppé, Bernard, 128, 129
Hussey, Maurice, 45
Hyde, Mary Crapo, 233

Ingram, R. W., 139
Ireland, G., 36
Isaacs, J., 180, 225
Izard, T. C., 48

Jackson, MacD. P., 212, 228, 251
Jackson, William A., 90
Jacobsen, Eric, 13
Jacquot, Jean, 48, 248, 265, 304-9 passim
Jantz, Harold, 29
Jarrett, H. S., 45
Jeffrey, Violet M., 136, 151
Jenkins, Harold, 84, 89, 148, 159, 290
Jensen, Ejner J., 97-98
Jente, Richard, 287
Jewkes, Wilfred T., 39, 88, 106, 139, 140, 159, 164, 173, 175, 180, 183, 187, 193, 205, 213, 216, 224, 227, 238, 242, 248, 257-58, 271, 279-80, 287, 301-2, 309
John, Ivor B., 300
John, Lisle C., 159
Johnson, Francis R., 36, 48, 67, 89, 120
Johnson, Robert C., 13, 68, 93, 112, 131, 144, 155
Johnson, Samuel Frederick, 51, 96-97, 199
Johnstone, H., 51
Jones, Deborah, 126
Jones, Eldred, 146
Jones, Gwenan, 151,
Jones, Gwyn, 88

Jonson, Ben, 39, 41, 47, 54, 103, 106, 110, 117, 121, 141, 174, 230, 234, 238, 242, 244, 285, 289, 292, 293, 308, 310, 315, 317
Jordan, J. C., 56, 57, 81, 82, 305
Jorgensen, Paul A., 140, 284, 287
Joseph, Bertram L., 92, 95, 104
Judges, A. V., 87
Jump, John D., 33, 45
Jusserand, J. J., 89

Kabell, Aage, 89
Kahin, Helen A., 141
Kahler, Erich, 18
Kaiser, Walter, 120
Kane, Robert J., 120
Kaufman, Edward K., 105
Kaufmann, Ralph J., 9,
Kaul, R. K., 159
Kaula, David, 45, 120
Keeler, Clinton, 150
Keen, Alan, 178, 291-92, 293
Keller, Wolfgang, 53, 176, 189, 214
Kempe, William, 115, 176, 205, 269, 281, 286, 314-15, **320, 321**
Kendall, Lyle H., Jr., 218, 251, 272
Kennard, J. S., 89
Kennedy, Milton Boone, 91
Kernan, Alvin, 121
Kernodle, George R., 48, 91, 187
Kettle, Arnold, 109
Kettner, Eugene J., 88, 111
Kimbrough, Robert, 19
King, Walter N., 131
Kinsman, Robert S., 123
Kirchner, Gustav, 295, 296
Kirkman, A. J., 121
Kirschbaum, Leo, 10, 14, 18, 27-28, 29, 31, 33, 45, 92, 100, 116, 168, 172, 187, 196, 203, 213-14, 216, 224, 227, 230, 257, 279-80, 310
Kirwood, A. E. M., 300
Kitagawa, Teiji, 39
Kittredge, George Lyman, 319
Klein, David, 39, 89, 121, 141, 159
Klein, John W., 36
Kleinman, Neil, 50

Kleinstück, J., 45
Kline, Peter, 45
Knapp, Mary, 89, 121
Knickerbocker, W. S., 53
Knight, G. Wilson, 39, 128-29, 144, 160
Knights, L. C., 36, 121, 189
Knoll, Robert E., 5
Knowlton, Edgar C., 225
Kocher, Paul H., 4, 7, 28-29, 33, 36, 42, 45, 49, 50, 51, 53, 115-16, 123, 310
Korninger, Siegfried, 269-70, 299
Koskenniemi, Inna, 39, 121, 141, 208, 209, 211, 258
Kostič, Veselin, 12
Kreisman, Arthur, 50
Krźyzanowski, J., 139, 218, 251
Kuhl, Ernest P., 121, 205
Kyd, Thomas, 6, 26, 31, 81, 93-106, 110, 162, 163, 182, 183, 201, 202, 204, 208, 209, 210, 219, 220, 230-48 passim, 257, 261, 264, 268, 272, 303, 304, 305, 308

Laboulle, Louise J., 51
Laird, David, 97
LaMar, Virginia A., 33
Lambin, Georges, 39, 40, 152
Lambrechts, Guy, 117, 209, 232, 235, 238, 300
Lancashire, Anne B., 129, 135, 136, 137, 139, 141
Lancaster, John, 314
Landa, M. J., 50
Landt, D. B., 172
Langenfelt, Gösta, 258, 303, 305, 308
Langsam, G. Geoffrey, 176, 214, 238, 269
Langston, Beach, 45
Langvad, Vibeke, 48
Lanham, Richard A., 109
Lapides, Frederick Robert, 206-7
Larsen, Thorleif, 143, 145-46, 147, 148, 150
Laserstein, Käte, 91
Latham, Agnes M. C., 109-10

Latham, Minor W., 141
Lathrop, Henry B., 159
Lavin, J. A., 69, 73, 86, 89, 321
Law, Robert Adger, 80, 101-2, 127, 156, 170, 171, 178-79, 182, 188, 210, 220-25 passim
Lawlor, John, 65
Lawrence, C. E., 36
Lawrence, William J., 40, 60, 91, 121, 129, 175, 180, 187, 189-94 passim, 195, 214, 229, 230, 237, 238, 244, 250, 257, 263, 267, 277, 279, 287, 291, 292, 297, 300, 309, 313
Lawrence, William W., 101
Lea, Kathleen M., 139, 218, 229, 269
Le Boutillier, Mrs. Martin, 183
Le Comte, Edward S., 141
Lee, Sir Henry, 132, 149
Leech, Clifford, 9, 10, 13, 18-19, 36, 40, 176, 187, 257, 305-6, 307, 309
Leendertz, P., 45
Lees, F. N., 33, 51, 52, 231, 241, 288
Legge, Thomas, 273, 277, 315-16
Legouis, Pierre, 252
Le Grys, Sir Robert, 81
Leiter, Louis H., 13
Lemmi, Charles W., 77
Lenormand, H. R., 240, 252
Le Page, Peter V., 19
Lesnick, Henry G., 145
Lever, Katherine, 20
Levin, Harry, 5, 7, 8, 10, 11, 14, 16, 18, 25, 106
Levin, Michael H., 98
Levin, Richard, 76
Lewis, C. S., 12, 40, 61, 108, 109, 141, 159
Liebermann, F., 189
Liedstrand, Frithjof, 121
Lievsay, John Leon, 40, 63, 89, 121, 136, 142
Lindabury, Richard Vliet, 40, 74
Linton, Marion, 239, 252, 257, 310
Liu, J. Y., 48
Lloyd, Bertram, 292, 293
Locke, Louis G., 89

Lodge, Thomas, 65, 75, 78, 80, 81, 153-60, 182, 183, 219, 220, 228, 259, 262, 264, 272, 276, 320
Logan, George M., 314
Logan, Terence P., 322
Long, Mike, 12-13
Longworth, Clara, Comptesse de Chambrun, 180, 208, 220, 224, 243
Lordi, Robert J., 273, 276-77, 315-16
Lothian, John M., 300
Lubbock, Roger, 178
Lucas, F. L., 40, 238, 252, 273, 275, 278
Lucius, Eberhard, 76
Lyly, John, 26, 62 64, 71, 113, 114, 125-42, 163, 236, 269, 281
Lyman, Dean B., Jr., 82, 141, 205, 214, 235, 263, 266, 267, 303
Lyons-Render, Sylvia, 151

McAleer, John J., 154
McAlindon, T., 14
Macaulay, Rose, 126
McCallum, J. D., 91
McCann, Franklin T., 40
McCloskey, J. C., 45
McCullen, Joseph T., Jr., 16, 19, 77-78, 250
McCusker, Honor, 183
McDiarmid, Matthew P., 105, 106, 180, 184, 188, 239, 262, 304, 305, 306, 308
Macdonald, Hugh, 55, 240
Macdonald, J. F., 40, 60, 76, 78, 164, 252, 286, 287, 309
McGee, Arthur R., 48
McGinn, Donald J., 65, 111, 112, 121
McIlwraith, A. K., 240
Mack, Maynard, 165
Mackenzie, Agnes Mure, 214, 248, 250
Mackerness, E. D., 107, 121
McKerrow, Ronald B., 65, 107, 108, 112, 117, 118
MacLaine, Allan H., 71, 74
McManaway, James G., 252
McMichael, George, 5

McNeal, Thomas H., 42, 88, 89, 221, 224
McNeir, Waldo F., 36, 67, 71, 73, 77, 79, 80, 88, 90, 155, 157
McPherson, David C., 121
Mahood, M. M., 9, 18
Malone, F. M., 66, 83, 84, 123
Manheim, Michael, 185-86
Mann, Irene Rose, 319
Mantaigne, André, 252
Marcus, Hans, 121
Marder, Louis, 67
Mares, Francis Hugh, 230
Margeson, J. M. R., 40
Marion, Jones, 140
Markham, Jervis, 53
Marlon, Dennis, 9
Marlowe, Christopher, 3-55, 57-92 passim, 96, 155-56, 172-73, 181, 182, 188, 190-97 passim, 201-2, 203, 204, 208, 209, 236, 241-47 passim, 262, 264, 266, 272, 273, 276, 277, 283-84, 288-96 passim, 301-8 passim, 313
Marnau, Fred, 55
Marsh, T. N., 42, 121
Marston, John, 54, 77, 105, 106, 142, 251
Martin, Betty C., 45
Martin, L. C., 11, 13, 33
Mason, Eudo C., 77
Massinger, Philip, 28, 281, 284
Massingham, H. J., 126
Matchett, William H., 177
Mathews, Ernest G., 133
Matson, M. H., 150
Matthews, Honor, 252, 278
Mattingly, Garrett, 55
Maugeri, Aldo, 36, 51, 88
Maxwell, Baldwin, 84-85, 258-59, 265, 304, 305, 316
Maxwell, J. C., 28, 40, 42, 45, 48, 49, 51, 76, 91, 106, 115, 149-50, 170-71, 181, 184, 188, 214, 226, 253, 262, 266, 281 283, 302, 313, 314
Mayer, H., 45

Mazzaro, Jerome L., 150
Meader, William G., 218
Means, Michael H., 45
Meek, Harold, G., 45
Mehl, Dieter, 40, 73, 98, 105, 163, 164, 238, 268, 270, 299
Meierl, E., 280
Melchiori, Giorgio, 55
Mendell, Clarence W., 105
Merchant, W. Moelwyn, 5, 33, 293
Messiaen, Pierre, 54, 240
Meyerstein, E. H. W., 36
Mezzadri, Piero, 48
Michelson, H., 50
Middleton, Thomas, 89, 96, 251, 285
Mildenberger, Kenneth, 56
Miles, Josephine, 42
Miller, Edward Haviland, 57, 65, 67-68, 87, 90, 112, 121, 159
Miller, Michael J., 25
Miller, Paul W., 12, 43
Miller, William E., 123
Millett, Fred Benjamin, 290
Milligan, Burton A., 159
Mills, Laurens Joseph, 48, 51, 90, 141, 159, 218, 238, 250, 287
Milton, John, 11, 15, 234, 239, 267, 268
Mincoff, Marco K., 40, 53, 128, 136, 141, 154-55, 262
Mingazzini, Cura di Rosa Marnoni, 54
Mitchell, Samuel J., 233
Mithal, H. S. D., 83, 159, 217, 315, 320, 321, 322
Mizener, Arthur, 15
Modder, Montagu Frank, 50, 310
Monaghan, James, 171, 172
Montgomerie, William, 110
Moore, Hale, 37, 52
Moore, John B., 141, 174, 186, 258, 265, 269
Moore, John Robert, 88, 129, 272, 300, 310
Moore, William H., 199
Moorman, F. W., 261, 270
More, R. P., 45
More, Sir Thomas, 140, 274

Morgan, A. E., 165-71 passim
Morgan, Gerald, 17-18
Morozov, M. M., 37
Morris, Alton C., 317
Morris, Christopher, 295, 296
Morris, Harry, 9, 11, 90, 114
Morris, Helen, 48, 121, 141, 159, 250
Morrison, Morris Robert, 77
Mortimer, Raymond, 25
Moseley, Edwin M., 118
Mott, Lewis F., 273, 274
Moulton, R. G., 45
Muir, Kenneth, 17, 25, 48, 51, 53, 59,
    70, 71, 72-73, 75, 76, 90, 137,
    141, 149, 163, 179, 208, 210-11,
    212, 223, 225, 234, 242, 245, 246,
    252, 253, 260-71 passim, 294,
    302-9 passim
Mukherjee, Sujit Kumar, 86-87
Mullary, Peter F., 54
Muller, Herbert Joseph, 48
Munday, Anthony, 123, 163, 169, 171,
    173, 179, 181, 183, 184, 196, 200,
    202, 215-21 passim, 223, 244,
    283, 286, 318
Mundy, P. D., 37
Munster, Sebastian, 112
Murphy, D., 141
Murphy, John Leo, 258-59, 264, 265,
    271, 303, 309
Murray, John J., 230-31, 234
Murray, Peter B., 99
Musgrove, S., 148
Mustard, Wilfred P., 106, 121, 138,
    239
Myers, Aaron Michael, 250, 286

Nashe, Thomas, 25, 57, 65, 84, 101,
    107-24, 131, 168, 201, 280, 281,
    284
Nathanson, Leonard, 49, 68, 320, 322
Neilson, William Allan, 54
Nelson, Malcolm A., 78
Nethercot, Arthur H., 226, 240
Neubert, F., 45
Neville, E. H., 49
Newdigate, Bernard H., 207

Nicoll, Allardyce, 40, 164, 177, 252,
    258, 285, 299, 300
Niemeyer, P., 252
Nilsson, P. G., 116
Nørgaard, Holger, 146, 151
Norman, Charles, 5
Nosworthy, J. M., 31, 43, 45, 48, 52,
    162, 163, 248-49, 316, 317
Nungezer, Edwin, 298

O'Brien, Gordon Worth, 43
O'Conner, William Van, 88, 252
O'Connor, Frank, 178, 187, 210, 213
O'Connor, John J., 48
Ogburn, Dorothy and Charlton, 173,
    210, 244, 262
Oliphant, E. H. C., 53, 173, 200, 207,
    210, 216, 234, 236, 240, 241, 243,
    244, 246, 316, 318
Oliver, H. J., 33, 52, 115
Oliver, Leslie Mahin, 52, 68, 172
O'Loughlin, Sean, 51
Olson, Paul A., 128
Ong, Walter J., 121, 130
Oppel, Horst, 40, 48, 266, 283
Oras, Ants, 40
Ornstein, Robert, 15, 16, 17, 18, 37,
    40, 54
Østerberg, V., 101, 110, 206-7, 208,
    209, 272
Ostrovsky, A. N., 37
Ostrowski, Witold, 45
Owen, John Isaac, 161, 162

Pal, R. M., 235
Paletta, Gerhard, 40
Palmer, D. J., 40, 45, 98, 266
Palmer, P. M., 45
Paradise, Nathaniel Burton, 91, 153,
    154
Parfenov, A., 37
Parker, John W., 205
Parker, R. B., 68
Parkes, H. B., 40
Parks, Edd Winfield, 252, 266
Parks, George B., 121, 130, 152

Parnell, Paul E., 132–33
Parr, Johnstone, 37, 56–57, 64, 74, 86, 135, 163
Parrott, Thomas Marc, 40, 50, 53, 57, 72, 76, 88, 90, 105, 121, 127, 143, 168–69, 170, 173, 174, 177, 180, 181, 184, 186, 197, 200, 201–2, 204, 222, 239, 286, 293, 294, 298
Partridge, A. C., 40, 292, 298, 300
Patrides, C. A., 45
Pearce, T. M., 26, 37, 45, 46, 48, 49, 50, 105, 236
Pearn, B. R., 270
Pearson, Lu Emily, 88, 159
Pearson, Terry, 67
Peavy, Charles E., 50
Peel, J. D., 54
Peele, George, 81, 83, 84, 115, 143–52, 167, 172, 180–88 passim, 201, 202, 204, 208–9, 211, 219, 220, 234, 235, 236, 252–53, 256, 261–62, 264, 265, 266, 270, 272, 277, 280, 281, 282, 291, 302, 303, 304, 309, 316
Peers, Edgar Allison, 77
Peery, William, 10
Peet, Donald, 20
Pembroke's Men, 30, 31, 167, 186, 194–95, 197, 203–4, 212, 213, 237, 247, 276, 288
Pennel, Charles A., 82–83
Penruddock, Master, 314
Peñuelos, Marcelino C., 121
Perkins, David, 121
Perkins, Mary Hallowell, 60
Perkinson, Richard H., 45, 223
Perret, Marion, 24, 215
Perry, Henry Ten Eyck, 197, 200
Peschmann, Hermann, 10, 205
Peter, John, 121
Peterson, Ottomar, 244
Petersson, Robert T., 300
Petit-Dutaillis, Charles, 179, 182, 183–84
Pettet, E. C., 59, 217
Petti, Anthony G., 121
Phelps, W. L., 40

Philipson, D., 50
Pinto, Vivian de Sola, 88
Pitcher, Seymour M., 52, 165, 173
Pizer, Lois D., 105
Ploch, Georg, 91, 226, 279
Poel, William, 214
Poirier, Michel, 5, 40
Politzer, Heinz, 46
Pollard, A. W., 168, 284
Pons, C., 55
Pooler, Charles Knox, 237
Porter, Henry, 316–17
Powell, Arnold F., 40
Powell, E. D. B., 37
Powell, Jocelyn, 9–10, 128
Powys, Llewelyn, 37, 40
Pratt, S. M., 121
Praz, Mario, 4–5, 40, 46, 54, 122, 240, 247–48, 308
Price, George R., 187
Price, Hereward T., 11, 70–71, 105, 106, 127
Priess, Max, 106
Prior, Moody E., 20, 48, 94, 95
Prosser, Eleanor, 96
Proudfoot, G. Richard, 115, 207, 215, 227, 228, 257, 277, 280–81, 284, 285
Prouty, Charles T., 104, 143, 150
Pruvost, René, 56, 60–61, 63, 66, 85–86, 90, 141, 205, 217, 218
Purcell, H. D., 50
Pyle, Fitzroy, 222

Q., D., 122
Quaintance, Richard E., Jr., 90
Queen's Men, 57, 81, 83, 84, 166–68, 170, 173, 177–78, 182, 183, 186, 187, 198, 200, 203–4, 225, 229, 231, 261–62, 263, 265, 272, 273, 276, 304
Quiller-Couch, Arthur, 195
Quinn, Michael, 48

Raab, Felix, 122
Rae, Wesley D., 154

Ramel, Jacques, 314
Ramondt, Marie, 230
Rankins, William, 36
Ransom, Harry, 41, 60, 75
Ransom, Mariann, 46
Ratliff, John D., 97
Rausch, Heinrich, 239, 272
Ray, J. K., 42
Re, Arundell del, 122
Rébora, Piero, 41, 74, 77
Reed, Robert Rentoul, Jr., 41, 46, 88, 141, 151, 269
Rees, Ennis, 41
Rees, Joan, 105
Reese, Gertrude Catherine, 189, 214, 313
Reese, M. M., 171, 175, 179, 185, 212, 255, 273, 278, 279, 297
Reeves, John D., 145, 151
Reichert, Günter, 226, 268, 269
Reiman, Donald H., 106
Rendle, William, 238
Renwick, W. L., 78-79, 84, 86
Reyher, Paul, 288, 293
Reynolds, E. E., 34
Reynolds, George Fullmer, 51, 227, 228, 229, 245, 248, 250, 300
Rhodes, R. Crompton, 167, 176, 189, 205, 226
Ribner, Irving, 9, 10, 11, 13, 18, 20, 23, 25, 31, 33, 41, 48, 50, 68, 74-75, 93, 112, 116-17, 131, 144, 146, 151, 155, 163, 169, 171, 173, 174, 181, 184, 185, 187, 191-92, 193, 208, 211, 212, 218, 220, 223, 224, 234, 253, 254, 256, 257, 262, 263-64, 265, 268, 273, 274, 276, 277, 278, 291, 292, 296-97, 298, 299, 304, 305, 306-7, 309
Rice, Warner, G., 145
Richards, Susan, 21
Richardson, Arleigh D., 296
Rickey, Mary E., 19
Ridley, M. R., 54
Righter, Anne, 98, 164, 268
Ringler, William, 130, 141, 159
Robbins, R. H., 54

Robertson, John M., 37, 43, 53, 83, 106, 172, 181, 182, 201, 208, 219, 221, 234, 235, 241-43, 246, 247, 252-53, 256, 261, 263, 265, 266, 267, 272, 275, 279, 281, 284, 291, 294, 301, 302-3, 304, 307
Robertson, Toby, 51
Robin, P. Ansell, 90, 122
Rogers, David M., 52
Röhrman, Hendrick, 11
Rollins, Hyder Edward, 43, 90
Romig, Edna D., 155
Rosati, Salvatore, 54
Rose, William, 33-34
Rosenberg, Eleanor, 122
Rosenberg, W. L., 46
Ross, Anne, 151
Ross, Thomas W., 104, 106
Rossiter, A. P., 41, 53, 122, 178, 181, 182, 184, 186, 242, 268, 288-89, 290, 292, 295, 296, 302, 308
Roston, Murray, 91
Rothstein, Eric, 22-23
Rottenberg, Annette, 164
Round, P. Z., 91
Rowan, D. F., 238
Rowley, Samuel, 29, 52, 96, 166, 172-73, 183, 200, 201, 202, 203, 243, 246, 316
Rowse, A. L., 5, 37, 291, 292
Rubow, Paul V., 81-82, 105, 189, 205, 226, 239, 252
Rusche, H. G., 50
Russell, Patricia, 164, 229
Ryan, Pat M., 153

Saccio, Peter, 129, 132, 133, 134, 136
Sachs, Ariel, 14
Sackton, Alexander H., 122
Sackville, Thomas, 94
Saintsbury, George, 87, 122
Saito, Isamu, 205
Saleski, R. E., 41
Salyer, Sandford M., 122
Sampley, Arthur M., 51, 148, 152, 180-81, 182, 219, 220, 253, 261, 281

Sams, Henry W., 46
Sanders, Chauncey Elwood, 90
Sanders, Norman, 58, 70, 72, 73, 75, 77, 86, 90
Sanders, Wilbur, 41, 46
Sanderson, James L., 123
Sanvic, Romain. *See* Smet, Robert de
Sarbu, Aladár, 41
Sarlos, Robert K., 141, 192, 193, 194
Sarrazin, Gustav, 233
Satin, Joseph, 165, 219, 274, 292, 293
Savage, James, 110
Sayers, Dorothy L., 46
Schaar, Claes, 105
Schanzer, Ernest, 189
Schaubert, Else von, 53, 122
Schaus, Hermann, 43
Schelling, Felix E., 41, 46, 88, 91, 105, 122, 141, 155, 197, 240, 241, 262, 263, 264, 275
Schick, J., 37
Schirmer, Walter F., 141, 176, 189
Schirmer-Imhoff, Ruth, 46
Schlauch, Margaret, 62, 122, 141, 159
Schneider, Reinhold, 37
Schoenbaum, Samuel, 25, 79, 80, 81, 82, 84, 100, 114, 115, 117, 136, 138, 147, 157, 161, 239, 312
Scholderer, V., 244
Schrickx, W., 57, 110-111, 122, 202
Schücking, Levin Ludwig, 41, 99, 100, 106, 238-39
Schuster, Erika, 48, 266
Schutt, Hugo, 257
Scott, Janet G., 159
Scoufos, Alice Lyle, 117
Scudder, H. H., 48
Searle, J., 46
Seaton, Ethel, 4, 26, 37, 41, 48, 92
Seebass, Aldof, 54
Segal, Erich, 43
Seiferth, Howard, 46
Seltzer, Daniel, 69-70, 71, 80, 86
Sen Gupta, S. C., 185
Seronsy, Cecil C., 159
Sewall, Richard B., 15, 18
Shaaber, Matthias A., 111, 165, 259

Shackford, Martha Hale, 92
Shakespeare, William, 5, 10-11, 13, 24, 57, 58, 66-67, 70, 81-85 passim, 103, 110-11, 116-17, 128, 138, 149-50, 154-55, 162-88 passim, 194-229 passim, 232, 236-37, 241-47 passim, 256, 258, 261, 265-84 passim, 289-300 passim, 308, 309, 311, 314, 315, 317, 318, 321
Shannon, G. P., 43
Shapiro, I. A., 52, 56, 68, 86, 169, 171, 173, 179, 181, 183, 184, 196-97, 202, 220, 221, 223, 256-57, 300
Sharpe, Robert Boies, 46, 88, 167, 189, 229, 230, 239, 245, 248, 263, 280, 287, 291, 296, 298, 310
Shear, Rosetta E., 316
Sheavyn, Phoebe, 41
Sherbo, Arthur, 48
Sheriffs, R. S., 54
Shield, H. A., 37, 88
Shirley, James, 39
Shroeder, John W., 198, 199, 205
Sibley, G. M., 122
Sibly, John, 41, 75
Sidney, Sir Philip, 110, 126, 131, 152, 154, 158, 226, 268, 305, 314, 320, 321
Siegel, Paul N., 286
Simeone, William E., 78
Simms, William Gilmore, 252, 266
Simpson, Evelyn, 91
Simpson, F. D., 252
Simpson, Percy, 16, 29, 49, 96, 151, 218, 278
Simpson Richard, 115
Sims, James H., 41
Sisson, Charles J., 52, 153, 154, 174, 209, 229, 247, 260, 272, 280
Skelton, John, 44
Slaughter, E. E., 267
Sleight, A. H., 54
Smart, George K., 43, 150
Smart, John Semple, 195, 199
Smeeton, George, 103

Smet, Joseph de, 93, 233, 235
Smet, Robert de [Romain Sanvic], 41, 88, 141
Smidt, Kristian, 292, 298
Smith, Albert H., 226
Smith, Charles G., 90
Smith, Constance, 141
Smith, D. Nichol, 100, 104, 240, 248
Smith, E., 43
Smith, G. C. Moore, 51, 159, 313
Smith, Grover, 272
Smith, Hallett, 11-12, 43, 48, 90
Smith, Irwin, 194
Smith, James, 46
Smith, James L., 105
Smith, John H., 105
Smith, Marion Bodwell, 52, 181, 201, 245, 247, 265, 301, 306
Smith, Warren D., 17
Smith, Winifred, 37
Snortum, Niel K., 122
Snuggs, Henry L., 198
Snyder, Susan, 14-15
Soellner, Rolf, 78, 141, 164
Solem, Delmar, 237, 250
Somlyó, G., 240
Sørensen, Knud, 155
South, Helen Pennock, 90
Southern, A. C., 37
Speaight, Robert, 11, 50, 214, 248
Spence, Leslie, 19
Spencer, Hazelton, 50, 54, 181, 275, 276
Spencer, Theodore, 21, 122, 238
Spens, Janet, 41, 208, 209, 228
Spenser, Edmund, 45, 52, 53, 84, 85, 88, 90, 120, 220, 223, 230, 232, 247, 264, 265, 267, 305, 306
Sper, Felix, 244-45, 247
Speroni, Charles, 63
Spivack, Bernard, 22, 285
Spivey, Haynell Callaway, 264, 267-68, 270
Sprott, S. E., 122
Stafford, John, 122
Stainer, Charles L., 244
Stalker, A., 37
Stamm, Fanny, 122

Stamp, A. E., 272
Stanley, Emily B., 41, 91, 141, 150
Starnes, DeWitt T., 141
Staton, Walter F., Jr., 43, 90, 122, 159
Stauffer, R. M., 54
Steadman, John M., 46
Steane, John M., 46
Steane, J. B., 5, 7, 8, 11, 13, 24, 307
Steevens, George, 267
Steiner, A., 46
Stemberg, Theodore, 141
Stephens, Rosemary, 50
Stern, Alfred, 37
Stern, Virginia F., 6
Sternfeld, Frederick W., 13, 122
Sternlicht, Sanford, 48
Stevens, F. G., 122
Stevenson, David Lloyd, 43, 127, 132, 282
Stevenson, Lionel, 109
Stevick, Robert D., 189
Stewart, Bain Tate, 250, 299
Stewart, J. I. M., 168, 169
Stirling, Brents, 256
Stockholm, Johanne M., 281, 283, 284
Stockley, W. F. P., 50
Stoll, Elmer E., 105, 236, 280, 300, 309
Storozhenko, N., 56
Strachey, J. St. L., 43
Strange's Men, 31, 84, 168, 204, 217, 218, 227, 229, 283, 287
Strathmann, E. A., 122
Stratman, Carl J., 100
Stříbrný, Zdeněk, 41, 130, 233, 242
Stroup, Thomas B., 41, 91
Stuart, Donald C., 41, 105
Sturgess, Keith, 240
Sturman, Berta, 91, 160
Stürzl, Erwin, 122
Summersgill, Travis L., 123
Sunesen, Bent, 51
Sutherland, James, 90, 123
Swaen, A. E. H., 86, 160
Swander, Homer D., 54
Swart, J., 130
Swinburne, Algernon Charles, 243, 264, 267-68, 270

Sykes, H. Dugdale, 41, 82, 92, 152, 166, 172–73, 180, 181, 182, 200, 201, 202, 216, 220, 237, 242, 253, 261, 265, 266, 267, 281, 282, 286, 303, 304, 305, 308
Syler, Siegfried, 20
Symonds, A. E., 41
Symons, Arthur, 37
Szenczi, Miklós J., 240

Tachibana, Tadae, 46
Talbert, Ernest William, 41, 73, 75, 98, 123, 254, 283, 296, 300
Tancock, Osborne William, 34
Tannenbaum, Dorothy R., 68, 112, 131, 144
Tannenbaum, Samuel A., 3, 13, 43, 52, 68, 93, 106, 112, 131, 144, 155, 252, 260, 318
Tapper, Bonno, 46
Tarlton, Richard, 165–73 passim, 229, 257, 308
Tarnawski, Władysław, 37
Taylor, E. M. M., 111
Taylor, George Coffin, 41, 199, 202
Taylor, Robert T., 48
Taylor, Rupert, 52, 79, 111, 188, 217, 232, 245, 267, 307
Teets, Bruce E., 62, 123, 131
Tenney, Edward A., 153, 154
Thaler, Alwin, 37, 218
Theens, K., 46
Theobald, Lewis, 237
Thieme, Heinz, 141
Thomas, Sidney, 66, 67, 110, 123, 195–96
Thompson, A. Hamilton, 276
Thompson, E., 42
Thomson, J. Oliver, 48
Thorndike, Ashley H., 88, 103, 240
Thorp, Willard, 42, 48, 88, 246, 268, 285
Thurston, Gavin, 37
Tiddy, R. J. E., 229, 235, 238
Tieck, Johann Ludwig, 239, 251, 311
Tilley, Morris Palmer, 42, 46, 138, 141
Tillotson, Geoffrey, 129–30

Tillotson, Kathleen, 207
Tillyard, E. M. W., 116, 168, 170, 178, 179, 211, 212, 254, 278, 291, 296, 298
Tilney, Charles, 259, 260, 261
Timberlake, Philip W., 60
Ting, N. T., 43
Titherley, A. W., 182, 210, 217, 218, 227–28, 229, 243, 245
Toliver, Harold E., 301
Tolman, A. H., 159
Tomlinson, Thomas B., 42, 105
Tomlinson, W. E., 49
Torretta, Laura, 136
Tourneur, Cyril, 54
Towne, Frank, 72
Traci, Philip J., 18
Treneer, Anne, 123
Trimpi, Wesley, 113–14
Trotte, Nicholas, 314
Tucker, T. G., 141
Turner, Robert Y., 42, 52, 91, 105, 127–28, 152, 164, 176, 254, 264, 266, 267, 277, 301, 302, 307
Tynan, Kenneth, 244, 247–48

Ueda, Tamotsu, 46
Uhler, John Earle, 254, 278
Ungerer, Gustav, 90
Ure, Peter, 105, 291, 292, 294, 295
Urry, William, 37
Utz, Hans, 164, 226, 252, 272

Valene, Marie-Claire, 55
Vančura, Zdeněk, 142
van Dam, B. A. P., 49, 52, 86, 91, 195, 200
Van Fossen, Richard W., 22, 33
Vannovsky, Alexander A., 37
Venezky, Alice S., 113
Versefield, Martin, 18, 46
Vesci, Ornella, 142
Vincent, Charles Jackson, 90
Vines, Sherard, 123
Von Hendy, Andrew, 145, 147

Wada, Yuichi, 51
Wadsworth, Frank Whittemore, 252

Wagenknecht, Edward, 62, 90, 123
Wagner, Bernard M., 142
Wainewright, John B., 284
Waith, Eugene M., 10, 20, 23-24, 49, 71
Wakameda, Takeji, 142
Waldo, Tommy Ruth, 202-3
Walker, Alice, 76, 153, 154, 159
Walker, Hugh, 90, 123
Walker, Percy, 114
Waller, Evangelia H., 313
Waller, R. D., 33, 231, 236, 241, 245, 246, 288
Wallerstein, Ruth, 179, 182, 183
Walley, Harold R., 309
Wallis, N. Hardy, 42
Walter, J. H., 168, 170-71
Walton, Charles E., 46
Walz, John A., 46, 47
Ward, Bernard M., 37, 142, 166, 170-74 passim, 185, 213
Warner, William, 220
Warren, C. T., 38, 60
Watkins, W. B. C., 53
Watson, Curtis Brown, 223
Watson, Harold Francis, 90
Watson, Thomas, 43, 100, 159
Weaver, Charles P., 90
Webster, John, 28, 54, 96, 110
Weimann, Robert, 54, 123
Weinstock, Horst, 189, 205
Wekling, Mary Mellen, 49
Weld, John S., 63-64, 90
Wells, Henry W., 42, 52, 88, 91, 95, 123, 176, 266, 301
Wells, Stanley W., 11, 64-65, 90, 109, 117-18
Wells, William Smith, 106, 159, 165-66, 168, 181, 182, 209, 220, 241, 246, 257
Welsford, Enid, 73, 123
Welsh, Robert Ford, 28, 31
Wentersdorf, Karl Paul, 211-12, 247
Wentworth, Clarence L., 78
West, Robert Hunter, 72
Westlund, Joseph, 14
Wham, Benjamin, 37

Whetstone, George, 48, 50
Whitaker, Virgil K., 184-85, 188
White, Harold Ogden, 91, 123
Whiting, George W., 142
Whiting, Mary Bradford, 312
Wiatt, William H., 97
Wickham, Glynne, 42, 73
Wild, Friedrich, 49
Wilkins, George, 242, 244
Willcox, Alice, 142
Willems, Michèle, 242
Williams, Arnold, 159
Williams, C. B., 32
Williams, Charles, 42
Williams, David Rhys, 37
Williams, F. B., 37
Williams, Martin T., 43
Williams, Philip, 276
Williamson, George, 142
Wills, M. M., 53
Wilson, Dover. *See* Wilson, John Dover
Wilson, Edward M., 88, 252
Wilson, Elkin C., 142
Wilson, F. P., 4, 10, 23, 42, 107, 117, 123, 149, 160, 178, 179, 190, 192, 193, 252, 253, 266, 308, 310, 312, 322
Wilson, H. S., 123
Wilson, John Dover, 53, 66, 88, 101, 110, 116, 123, 149, 167, 168, 178, 179, 184, 187-88, 195, 197, 203, 221, 231-32, 237, 272, 274-75, 281, 282, 283, 291, 293, 308
Wilson, Robert, 68, 115, 162, 207, 215, 216, 217, 281, 304, 315, 317-22
Wilson, Robert H., 151
Winny, James, 87, 206, 226
Winslow, Ola Elizabeth, 76, 88, 164, 174, 226, 229, 238, 258, 268-69, 286
Wise, Thomas J., 118
Witherspoon, Alexander M., 99, 231, 237, 263, 268, 282
Withington, Robert, 42, 275
Witte, W., 47
Wittig, Kurt, 105

Woelcken, F., 51
Wolff, Max J., 37, 243, 245, 247
Wolff, Samuel L., 126
Wolff, Tatiana A., 34
Wolfit, Donald, 54
Wolthuis, G. W., 47
Wood, Frederick T., 247
Wood, James O., 123
Wotton, Henry, 63-64, 216, 231, 232-33
Wraight, A. D., 6
Wright, Celeste Turner, 50, 123, 287
Wright, Herbert G., 91, 123, 160, 310
Wright, Louis B., 33, 88, 90, 229, 230, 239, 269, 285, 286, 301, 314

Wyler, Siegfried, 49
Wynne, Arnold, 42

Yamamoto, Chiyuki, 137
Yates, Frances A., 111
Yelverton, Christopher, 314
Yoklavich, John, 145, 150
York, Ernest C., 110, 111
Young, G., 43
Youngblood, Sarah, 249-50

Zanco, Aurelio, 37, 249
Zandvoort, R. W., 142, 146
Zbierski, Henryk, 123
Zimansky, Curt A., 29, 36, 283-84
Zitt, Hersch L., 50
Zocca, Louis R., 43, 160

INDEX

PLAYS

Alphabetization and modernized spelling follow Alfred Harbage, Annals of English Drama, 975-1700 (1940; rev. S. Schoenbaum, 1964).

Agamemnon, 247
Alchemist, The, 285
Alphonsus, Emperor of Germany, 150, 180, 253, 267, 303
Alphonsus, King of Aragon, 20, 57, 58, 60, 72, 74-75, 77, 80, 85, 86, 91, 203, 217, 302, 304, 306-7, 309
Anglorum Feriae, 149
Antonio's Revenge, 105
Antony and Cleopatra, 24
Arden of Feversham, 53, 102, 188, 203, 232, 234, 236, 240-52
Arraignment of Paris, The, 145, 147, 150, 151, 188, 270
As You Like It, 53, 155, 158, 159

Bartholomew Fair, 110
Battle of Alcazar, The, 86, 145-46, 148, 150, 151, 188, 253, 261, 262, 277
Bisham, The Entertainment at, 137
Blind Beggar of Alexandria, The, 41
Blind Beggar of Bednal Green, The, 218
Broken Heart, The, 104

Campaspe, 126, 128, 129, 133-34, 136, 138, 139, 142, 192, 282
Case is Altered, The, 317
Catiline's Conspiracy, 320
Charlemagne, 288
Chiswick, The Entertainment at, 137
Clyomon and Clamydes, 299
Cobbler's Prophecy, The, 319, 321
Comedy of Errors, The, 246, 247, 251
Comus, 151, 268
Contention betwixt the Two Famous Houses of York and Lancaster. See II Henry VI

Coriolanus, 317
Cornelia, 100, 101, 105, 106, 241, 304, 305, 308
Cornélie, 99, 235, 247
Cowdray, The Entertainment at, 137
Cymbeline, 105, 162, 163, 221, 267

Descensus Astraea, 149
Devil Is an Ass, The, 289, 292
Dido, Queen of Carthage, 3, 24, 25, 26, 32-33, 51-52, 53, 105, 115, 122, 188, 236
Doctor Faustus, 9, 14-18, 27, 28-30, 32, 33, 34, 39, 43-47, 52, 53, 54, 71, 80, 91, 115-16, 200, 201, 202, 203, 230, 251, 266, 283-84, 287
Don Horatio, or The Comedy of Jeronimo, 234. See also Hieronimo
Duchess of Malfi, The, 110

Edmond Ironside, 210, 219, 221, 295
Edward I, 146, 149, 150, 151, 188
Edward II, 9, 23-24, 30-31, 33, 34, 39, 51, 54, 55, 102, 186, 188, 215, 217, 231, 236, 241, 243, 245, 246, 288, 289, 290, 293, 294
Edward III, 53, 83, 176, 192, 206-15, 219, 221, 232, 233, 238, 282, 318
Edward IV, 254, 278, 296
Elvetham, The Entertainment at, 137
Endymion, 126, 128, 132, 134, 137, 139
Every Man in His Humor, 117

Fair Em, the Miller's Daughter, 80, 83, 210, 215-18, 318, 321
Famous Victories of Henry V, The. See Henry V, The Famous Victories of

Friar Bacon and Friar Bungay, 29, 58, 59, 60, 61, 69-72, 74, 78, 79, 80, 84, 86, 91, 188, 217, 282, 283, 285
Friar Bacon, The Second Part of. See *John of Bordeaux*

Gallathea, 126, 128, 129, 134-35, 136, 137, 139
George a Greene, the Pinner of Wakefield, 59, 65, 82-83, 86, 92, 260
Gorboduc, 94, 254, 268
Great Duke of Florence, The, 281, 282, 284
Guy Earl of Warwick, The Tragical History of, 310-11

Hamlet (Shakespeare), 53, 95, 101-2, 105, 106, 111, 122, 214, 221, 277
Hamlet (ur-*Hamlet*), 97, 101-2, 105, 110, 235
Harefield, The Entertainment at, 138
I Henry IV, 19, 53, 111, 123, 165, 166, 168, 169-72, 174, 175, 176, 206, 213, 214, 230, 236-37, 246, 291, 295
II Henry IV, 19, 123, 165, 166, 168, 169-72, 176, 206, 236, 295, 308
Henry V (Shakespeare), 140, 165, 166-67, 168, 169-72, 176, 192, 206, 210, 213, 223, 314
Henry V, The Famous Victories of, 165-76, 200, 201
I Henry VI, 19, 53, 116-17, 152, 168, 180, 182, 188, 195, 211, 221, 244, 246, 276, 288, 290
II Henry VI (*I The Contention betwixt the Two Famous Houses of York and Lancaster*), 53, 66, 83-84, 116-17, 152, 168, 182, 188, 203, 212, 221, 232, 244, 246, 251, 256, 288, 289, 290, 292, 294
III Henry VI (*The True Tragedy of Richard Duke of York*), 53, 66, 83-84, 182, 188, 203, 212, 221, 232, 237, 244, 246, 288, 290
Henry VIII, 272
Hercules Furens, 164
Hieronimo, The First Part of, 102, 104

Hippolytus, 306
Hunting of Cupid, The, 148
Huon of Bordeaux, 79

If It Be Not Good, the Devil Is in It, 76
Insatiate Countess, The, 42
Iphigenia, 149
Isle of Dogs, The, 108, 117

Jack Straw, The Life and Death of, 149, 252-58, 278, 281, 282, 295, 296, 298
James IV, The Scottish History of, 58, 59, 60, 71, 72-74, 75, 81, 82, 86, 91, 188
Jew, The, 317, 320
Jew of Malta, The, 9, 21-23, 27-28, 33, 39, 49-50, 54, 55, 188, 246, 304
Job, 81
John, King (Shakespeare), 106, 168, 176-80, 181, 182, 183, 184, 185, 186, 187, 189, 221, 231, 232, 234, 237
I & II John, King (Bale's *Kynge Johan*), 176, 183, 185, 187
I & II John, The Troublesome Reign of King, 81, 149, 176-89, 206, 209, 219, 221
John a Kent and John a Cumber, 215, 218, 283, 286
John of Bordeaux, or The Second Part of Friar Bacon, 78-79, 84, 86, 309
Julius Caesar, 51, 53, 90, 105, 254, 278

King Lear, King Leir. See *Lear, Leir*
Knack to Know a Knave, A, 65, 84, 149, 152, 253, 257, 267, 277, 280, 283
Knack to Know an Honest Man, A, 78, 115
Kynge Johan. See *I & II John, King*

Larum for London, A, 318
Lear, King, 170, 219, 220, 221, 222-24, 225, 252, 302, 308, 310, 317

Leir, King, 83, 159, 188, 219-26, 241, 243, 246, 263, 267

Life and Death of Jack Straw, The. See *Jack Straw*

Locrine, 48, 82, 83, 84, 85, 149, 221, 258-72, 284, 303, 304, 305, 307, 308, 309

Look About You, 318

Looking Glass for London and England, A, 61, 65-66, 75-76, 80, 86, 91, 156, 157, 160

Love and Fortune. See *Rare Triumphs of Love and Fortune, The*

Love of King David and Fair Bethsabe, The, 144, 146, 147, 148, 150, 151-52, 208

Love's Labour's Lost, 42, 100, 110, 111, 128, 203, 237

Love's Metamorphosis, 126, 128, 132-33, 137

Lust's Dominion, or The Lascivious Queen, 32

Macbeth, 44, 106, 111, 276

Magnetic Lady, The, 311

Maid's Metamorphosis, The, 138

Mamillia, 62, 63, 64, 140

Mankind, 7

Martin Calthrop, The Pageant for, 149

Massacre at Paris, The, 24, 31, 32, 33, 34, 50, 51, 52, 115, 168, 188, 241, 246

Measure for Measure, 210, 213

Merchant of Venice, The, 237, 304, 317

Merry Wives of Windsor, The, 170, 218, 314, 317

Midas, 126, 129, 135, 136, 137, 138, 139

Midsummer Night's Dream, A, 127, 128

Misfortunes of Arthur, The, 263, 268, 313, 314

Mitcham, The Entertainment at, 137

Mother Bombie, 126, 135, 137, 139

Mucedorus, 83, 226-30, 308

Much Ado About Nothing, 42, 138, 221, 267

Old Law, The, 244

Old Wives Tale, The, 144-45, 147, 148, 150, 151, 261

Orlando Furioso, 57-58, 59, 72, 76-78, 81, 85, 86, 87, 92, 148, 196, 203, 221, 267

Othello, 40, 284, 317

Pedantius, 313

Pedlar's Prophecy, The, 319

Phoenix, The, 285

Play of Plays and Pastimes, The, 157

Poetaster, 315

Polyhymnia, 149,

Porcie, 306

Portia, 102

Raging Turk, The, 308

Rare Triumphs of Love and Fortune, The, 161-64, 232, 238

Richard II (Shakespeare), 51, 188, 254, 256, 288, 289, 290, 291, 292, 293, 294, 295, 297, 298, 300

I Richard II, or Thomas of Woodstock, 55, 219, 254, 277, 288-300

Richard III (Shakespeare), 51, 116, 180, 182, 188, 195, 210, 213, 221, 225, 244, 247, 256, 268, 269, 270, 272, 274, 275, 276, 277, 279, 280, 290, 292, 294, 295, 300, 315-16

Richard III, The True Tragedy of, 238, 245, 254, 272-80, 294, 315

Richard Duke of York, The True Tragedy of. See *III Henry VI*

Richardus Tertius, 273, 276-77, 315-16

Romeo and Juliet, 42, 141, 232, 239, 241, 317

Roode en Witte Roos, 277

Rycote, The Entertainment at, 137

Sappho and Phao, 126, 128, 133, 134, 136

Sejanus His Fall, 308

I Selimus, 20, 48, 74, 82, 83, 84-85, 230, 232, 258, 259, 260, 261, 262, 263, 264, 265-66, 267, 269, 271, 301-10

Shoemaker's Holiday, The, 175, 320

Short and Sweet, 320

Sir John Oldcastle, 175, 318, 319

Sir Thomas More, 216, 318, 319

Soliman and Perseda, 102, 103, 163, 179, 188, 230-39, 243, 245, 246, 265, 267, 279, 304, 306, 307-8

Spanish Tragedy, The, 76, 89, 93, 94-99, 100-01, 102, 103, 104-6, 164, 231, 232, 233, 234, 235, 236, 237, 238, 239, 241, 242, 246, 247, 248, 257, 263, 267, 304

Sudeley, The Entertainment at, 137

Summer's Last Will and Testament, 65, 108, 112-14, 118

Supposes, The, 200

Suppositi, I, 194

I and II Tamar Cham, 309

Tamburlaine the Great, 39, 52, 54, 74, 75, 76, 77, 80, 83, 90, 155, 170, 185, 186, 187, 190, 191, 192, 193, 200, 201, 202, 203, 232, 234, 243, 261, 263, 264, 265, 266, 267, 268, 277, 304, 306-7, 308. See also *I and II Tamburlaine*

I Tamburlaine the Great, 4, 9, 18-20, 21, 26-27, 29, 33, 34, 47-49, 307

II Tamburlaine the Great, 4, 9, 18, 19, 20-21, 26-27, 29, 33, 34, 49

Taming of a Shrew, The, 29, 81-82, 168, 177, 194-205

Taming of the Shrew, The (Shakespeare), 52, 53, 92, 168, 177, 194-99, 200, 202-3, 204, 205

Tempest, The, 51, 163

Terminus et Non Terminus, 108, 115

Theobalds, The Queen's Welcome at, 137, 149

Thomas Lord Cromwell, 85, 243

Thomas of Woodstock. See *I Richard II*

Thracian Wonder, The, 85

Three Ladies of London, The, 68, 317, 318, 319, 320

Three Lords and Three Ladies of London, The, 320, 321, 322

Thyestes, 270, 308

Titus Andronicus, 40, 53, 82, 106, 111, 149-50, 184, 188, 261, 267, 281, 282-83

Titus and Vespasian, 282, 283

Tragical History of Guy Earl of Warwick, The. See *Guy Earl of Warwick,*

Troas, 308

Troublesome Reign of King John, The. See *I & II John, The Troublesome Reign of*

True Tragedy of Richard III, The. See *Richard III, The True Tragedy of*

Turkish Mahomet and Hiren the Fair Greek, The, 149

Twelfth Night, 222

I and II Two Angry Women of Abington, The, 316-17

Two Merry Women, The, 316

ur-*Hamlet.* See *Hamlet*

Warning for Fair Women, A, 248

Wars of Cyrus, The, 20, 52, 189-94, 312, 313

Weakest Goeth to the Wall, The, 219

When You See Me You Know Me, 200, 246

White Devil, The, 252

William the Conqueror, 215

Wily Beguiled, 200, 201, 237, 316

Winter's Tale, The, 65, 162, 228

Wisdom of Doctor Dodypoll, The, 150

Women in the Moon, The, 126, 128, 135, 137, 139, 163

Woman Killed with Kindness, A, 67

Woodstock. See *I Richard II*

Woolstone Dixie, The Pageant before, 148

Wounds of Civil War, The, 154, 155-56, 157, 160